OXFORD MANAGEMENT READERS

STRATEGIC ALLIANCES

STRATEGIC ALLIANCES

Theory and Evidence

Edited by

Jeffrey J. Reuer

OXFORD
UNIVERSITY PRESS

Great Clarendon Street, Oxford OX2 6DP

Oxford University Press is a department of the University of Oxford.
It furthers the University's objective of excellence in research, scholarship,
and education by publishing worldwide in

Oxford New York

Auckland Bangkok Buenos Aires Cape Town Chennai
Dar es Salaam Delhi Hong Kong Istanbul Karachi Kolkata
Kuala Lumpur Madrid Melbourne Mexico City Mumbai Nairobi
São Paulo Shanghai Taipei Tokyo Toronto

Oxford is a registered trade mark of Oxford University Press
in the UK and in certain other countries

Published in the United States
by Oxford University Press Inc., New York

First published 2004

British Library Cataloguing in Publication Data
Data available

Library of Congress Cataloging in Publication Data
Data available

ISBN 0-19-925654-3 (hbk.)
ISBN 0-19-925655-1 (pbk.)

1 3 5 7 9 10 8 6 4 2

Typeset by Newgen Imaging Systems (P) Ltd., Chennai, India
Printed in Great Britain
on acid-free paper by
Biddles Ltd., King's Lynn, Norfolk

Acknowledgments

Farok J. Contractor and Peter Lorange, "Why Should Firms Cooperate? The Strategy and Economics Basis for Cooperative Ventures." Reprinted from *Cooperative Strategies in International Business* edited by Farok J. Contractor and Peter Lorange (1988, pp. 3–30). Copyright © 1988 Elsevier. Reprinted with permission.

Bruce Kogut, "Joint Ventures: Theoretical and Empirical Perspectives", *Strategic Management Journal*, vol. 9 (1988), 319–32. Copyright © 1988 John Wiley & Sons, Limited. Reprinted with permission.

Arvind Parkhe, "International Joint Ventures." Reprinted from the *Handbook for International Management Research* edited by Betty Jane Punnett and Oded Shenkar (1996, pp. 429–459). Copyright © 1996 Arvind Parkhe. Reprinted with permission.

Jean-Francois Hennart, "A Transaction Cost Theory of Equity Joint Ventures," *Strategic Management Journal*, vol. 9 (1988), 361–74. Copyright © 1988 John Wiley & Sons, Limited. Reprinted with permission.

Srinivasan Balakrishnan and Mitchell P. Koza, "Information Asymmetry, Adverse Selection, and Joint Ventures," *Journal of Economic Behavior and Organization*, vol. 20 (1993), 99–117. Copyright © 1993 Elsevier. Reprinted with permission.

Jean-Francois Hennart and Sabine Reddy, "The Choice Between Mergers / Acquisitions and Joint Ventures: The Case of Japanese Investors in the United States," *Strategic Management Journal*, vol. 18 (1997), 1–12. Copyright © 1997 John Wiley & Sons, Limited. Reprinted with permission.

Jeffrey J. Reuer and Mitchell P. Koza, "Asymmetric Information and Joint Venture Performance: Theory and Evidence for Domestic and International Joint Ventures," *Strategic Management Journal*, vol. 21 (2000), 81–8. Copyright © 2000 John Wiley & Sons, Limited. Reprinted with permission.

Bruce Kogut, "Joint Ventures and the Option to Expand and Acquire," *Management Science*, vol. 37 (1991), 19–33. Copyright © 1991 The Institute of Management Sciences. Reprinted with permission.

Tailan Chi and Donald J. McGuire, "Collaborative Ventures and Value of Learning: Integrating the Transaction Cost and Strategic Option Perspectives on Foreign Market Entry," *Journal of International Business Studies*, vol. 27 (1996), 285–308. Copyright © 1996 The Academy of International Business Studies. Reprinted with permission.

Jeffrey J. Reuer and Michael J. Leiblein, "Downside Risk Implications of Multinationality and International Joint Ventures," *Academy of Management Journal*, vol. 43 (2000), 203–14. Copyright © 2000 Academy of Management. Reprinted with permission.

Acknowledgments

Gary Hamel, "Competition for Competence and Interpartner Learning Within International Strategic Alliances," *Strategic Management Journal*, vol. 12 (1991), 83–103. Copyright © 1991 John Wiley & Sons, Limited. Reprinted with permission.

Tarun Khanna, Ranjay Gulati, and Nitin Nohria, "The Dynamics of Learning Alliances: Competition, Cooperation, and Relative Scope," *Strategic Management Journal*, vol. 19 (1998), 193–210. Copyright © 1998 John Wiley & Sons, Limited. Reprinted with permission.

Harry G. Barkema, Oded Shenkar, Freek Vermeulen, and John H. J. Bell, "Working Abroad, Working with Others: How Firms Learn to Operate International Joint Ventures," *Academy of Management Journal*, vol. 40 (1997), 426–42. Copyright © 1997 Academy of Management. Reprinted with permission.

Jeffrey H. Dyer and Harbir Singh, "The Relational View: Cooperative Strategy and Sources of Interorganizational Competitive Advantage," *Academy of Management Review*, vol. 23 (1998), 660–79. Copyright © 1998 Academy of Management. Reprinted with permission.

Ranjay Gulati, "Alliances and Networks," *Strategic Management Journal*, vol. 19 (1998), 293–317. Copyright © 1998 John Wiley & Sons, Limited. Reprinted with permission.

Gordon Walker, Bruce Kogut, and Wwijian Shan, "Social Capital, Structural Holes, and the Formation of an Industry Network," *Organization Science*, vol. 8 (1997), 109–25. Copyright © 1997 Institute for Operations Research and the Management Sciences. Reprinted with permission.

Contents

List of Contributors

Bharat N. Anand	Graduate School of Business Administration, Harvard University
Srinivasan Balakrishnan	University of Minnesota
Harry G. Barkema	Tilburg University
John H. J. Bell	Tilburg University
Tailan Chi	University of Kansas
Farok J. Contractor	Rutgers University
Jeffrey H. Dyer	Brigham Young University
Ranjay Gulati	J. L. Kellogg Graduate School of Management, Northwestern University
Gary Hamel	London Business School
Jean-François Hennart	Tilburg University
Tarun Khanna	Graduate School of Business Administration, Harvard University, Boston, MA, USA
Bruce Kogut	INSEAD
Mitchell P. Koza	INSEAD
Michael J. Leiblein	Ohio State University
Peter Lorange	IMD
Donald J. McGuire	University of Wisconsin-Milwaukee
Nitin Nohria	Graduate School of Business Administration, Harvard University
Arvind Parkhe	Indiana University
Sabine Reddy	School of Business Administration, Wayne State University
Jeffrey J. Reuer	Kenan–Flager Business School, University of North Carolina
Weijian Shan	J. P. Morgan, Hong Kong
Oded Shenkar	Ohio State University
Harbir Singh	The Wharton School, University of Pennsylvania
Freek Vermeulen	London Business School
Gordon Walker	Cox School of Business, Southern Methodist University, Dallas, TX, USA

Introduction—Strategic Alliance Research: Progress and Prospects

Jeffrey J. Reuer

For many managers and researchers, the observation that strategic alliances have altered the business landscape seems apparent, even if the implications are less clear. Not only has the number of alliances increased dramatically during the past two decades, but the character of interfirm collaboration has also changed in several fundamental ways.

Consider how current alliances differ from conventional alliances. The typical alliance tended to be an equity joint venture used for the purpose of entering a developing country while responding to a government's restrictions on foreign investment. Technology transfer was often unilateral, from a multinational firm to a foreign venture, and the foreign investor primarily sought to access the local market on a stand-alone basis. Collaborations routinely took place in commodity and other, less advanced industries.

Today, however, alliances often crop up between actual or potential competitors as well as between firms from developed countries. There has also been an impressive rise in the complexity of alliance deals, with many alliances involving bilateral knowledge flows as well as multiple partners or projects. Alliance investors are more apt to have global market objectives, and the sectoral diversity of alliances has increased greatly (e.g. Harrigan, 1985; Hagedoorn, 1993; Gomes-Casseres, 1996). In short, the "strategic" adjective for alliances has more substance today than it might have had in years past.

Although the rise in alliances is unmistakable, there are often misunderstandings on what an alliance is. For our purposes, we will avoid narrow definitions that attempt to include or exclude particular forms of exchanges between firms, and "alliance" will be used as an umbrella term, incorporating all hybrid forms of exchange that occur between, but do not include, spot market transactions, on the one hand, and complete ownership (e.g. internal development or acquisition) on the other. Within this spectrum, various forms of exchange such as licensing agreements and joint ventures will be distinguished as needed.

There is also debate on the potential impact of alliances on organizations and society at large. One recalls Adam Smith's familiar admonition in the *Wealth of Nations* that "people of the same trade seldom meet together, even for merriment and diversion, but the conversation ends in a conspiracy against the public." Michael Porter's more recent judgment also voices caution and skepticism: "Alliances as a broad-based strategy will only ensure a company's mediocrity, not its international leadership" (Porter, 1990, p. 91). Set alongside these verdicts is Peter Drucker's observation that "the greatest change in corporate structure—and in the way business is being conducted—may be the accelerating growth of relationships based not on ownership but on partnership... semi-formal alliances of all sorts" and Jack Welch's conclusion that "alliances are a big part of this game [of global competition]... The least attractive way to try to win on a global basis is to think you can take on the world all by yourself."

Just as alliances have come to play more central roles in firms' strategies, they have proven equally difficult to manage, and much of the research on alliances has attempted to understand why this is the case. Various academic studies place alliance failure rates in the 30–70 percent range, which may be viewed as being either high or low depending upon an alliance's intended purposes. These failure rates also need to be put into perspective since those for internal corporate venturing, acquisitions, and other projects are also hardly trivial. When one thinks about firms' challenges implementing alliances, the famous exchange between Winston Churchill and Lady Astor comes to mind: To her challenge "Sir, if you were my husband, I would poison your drink," he replied, "Madam, if you were my wife, I would drink it." Unfortunately, however, shallow references to failure rates and invocations of metaphors involving interpersonal relations are ultimately not of much help to those attempting to understand how interfirm collaboration may advance an organization's cause under particular competitive circumstances and how to manage alliances more effectively.

To begin to answer these questions, academics from a great number of fields have conducted many studies on interfirm collaboration. As one indication of this scholarly activity, special issues devoted to alliances have recently appeared in the *Strategic Management Journal*, the *Academy of Management Journal, Organization Science*, and the *Journal of International Business Studies*. Indeed, alliance research has become a cottage industry of sorts, leading Richard Caves to preface his suggestions for the international business field with the proviso that "research on alliances hardly needs pump-priming" (Caves, 1998, p. 16).

The goal of this volume, therefore, is to highlight, synthesize, and organize literature on the theory of alliances as well as some of the empirical evidence to date. Although many fine studies have been omitted in an attempt to balance conflicting demands for depth and breadth, the objective is to provide readers new to the field with an opportunity to read about the progress that has been made in different areas, the debates that have taken place and are still being heard, and the prospects for future work. Below, I comment on each of the sections of the book, highlight key arguments and findings, and offer perspective on some of the studies' main implications.

The volume begins with an overview of the literature on interfirm collaboration and then presents a series of four sections that offer alternative lenses through which alliances may be understood—economic perspectives, real options perspectives, learning perspectives, and relational perspectives. These sections shed light on several important features of the alliance literature's evolution. Notable examples include the significant strengthening of the field's theoretical grounding, the plurality of theoretical perspectives employed, debate on the relative explanatory power of theories of interfirm collaboration as well as their interplay, an enhanced appreciation of the dynamics of alliances, and progressively rigorous empirical investigations into key alliance phenomena and outcomes.

Contents of the Volume

Overview of Research on Interfirm Collaboration

In the first section, several chapters provide relatively far-reaching analyses of alliances and of the literature on interfirm collaboration as it has developed. The first piece, by Contractor and Lorange (1988), highlights the increasing incidence of cooperative arrangements. Their book, *Cooperative Strategies in International Business*, and the conference that led to this volume, was to mark the rise in research on joint ventures in the international business and strategy fields. They first provide a taxonomy of a wide range of collaborative arrangements between firms, from technical assistance and production agreements to franchising and management service agreements to equity joint ventures. Their chapter then lays out numerous contributions that joint ventures, in particular, can provide to parent firms, and they proceed to catalog the various direct and indirect revenue and cost implications of joint ventures vis-à-vis wholly-owned operations. They also specify the mechanisms by which joint ventures allow firms to reduce risk. For many years, these and other benefits have often been cited by researchers and by practitioners, but relatively little evidence has been forthcoming on whether firms are truly deriving the various benefits alliances are thought to offer.

In Kogut's (1988) chapter, he classifies and compares three motivations for joint ventures. The *transaction cost* explanation considers the relative efficiency of exchanging intermediate products through the market interface or within a firm's hierarchy. Because joint ventures are hybrid structures involving a blending of the features of both markets and hierarchies (Williamson 1991), they can be seen as compromise solutions to the hazards of opportunistic behavior, on the one hand, which hierarchies mitigate due to managerial fiat and more elaborate governance mechanisms, and the administrative costs associated with full ownership on the other hand. The *strategic* explanation argues that a firm engages in a joint venture to enhance one's competitive position. For instance, joint ventures may be used to deter entry into an industry (e.g. Vickers, 1985) or to invest in follow-the-leader actions in loose-knit oligopolies subject to strategic uncertainty (e.g. Vernon 1983). The third explanation for joint ventures relies on an *organizational knowledge and learning* perspective, which views joint ventures as a structure, or conduit, through which the firm can access another firm's knowledge. To the extent that the capital desired is specific to an organization rather than an individual (e.g. Nelson and Winter, 1982), and to the extent that the knowledge required is tacit, the transfer of technology through the market may be difficult just as the transfer of know-how through labor markets may be incomplete.

The final chapter in the introductory portion of the book, by Parkhe (1996), provides a different synthesis of the research on joint ventures. His integrative framework relates more closely to the transaction cost paradigm than other perspectives emphasized in the volume as it emphasizes the core behavioral variables of opportunism, forbearance, trust, and reciprocity (e.g. Buckley and Casson, 1988). It also brings together four variables that have served alternatively as alliance phenomena to be explained or as explanations of alliance outcomes in their own right—partnering motives, stability/performance (e.g. Beamish, 1985; Das and Teng, 2000), control and conflict (e.g. Mjoen and Tallman, 1997), and partner selection (e.g. Hitt et al., 2000). He also highlights the importance of understanding better how alliances evolve over time, and he proposes a classification scheme to guide future research.

Economic Perspectives on Interfirm Collaboration

Paralleling developing streams of research in strategy, international business, and other fields, the alliance literature received significant momentum and generated new insights in the late 1980s by adopting the comparative organization perspective insisted upon by transaction cost economics (TCE). Even when one examines problems other than those dealing with the placement of organizational boundaries, which is the primary focus of TCE applications, the challenge of making comparative assessments can be instructive.

The usefulness of the approach has also been evident in the displacement of some established perspectives on alliances. As one example, resource dependence theory provided an early explanation for alliances (e.g. Pfeffer and Nowak, 1976) that has since declined in influence in the field. One of the shortcomings associated with this perspective and highlighted by TCE is that there are a variety of structural solutions (e.g. acquisitions, minority investments, interlocking directorates, etc.) that allow the firm to secure access to key resources.

Along similar lines, many of the writings on alliance strategy and alliance management today often amount to guidelines for good strategy or good management in general rather than informing unique aspects of alliances *per se*. For instance, when the question is posed to executives, "why are firms entering into alliances?" or "what explains the great rise in the number of collaborative agreements?" a familiar litany of responses follows: globalization, industry convergence, risk reduction, quick entry into foreign markets, innovation, learning, synergy, economies of scale, and so forth. Most of these responses are true, perhaps to varying degrees, and they indeed figure prominently in announcements of alliances. However, it is striking that when a transaction cost version of the question is raised—"why does one use an alliance rather than an acquisition?"—the responses tend to be less compelling (Reuer, 2000).

A simple answer is that an acquisition may not be feasible for legal, regulatory, or political reasons. In the former Soviet Union and Soviet bloc, for instance, firms historically used joint ventures to shield themselves from political risk, and some firms more recently have converted initial market entries to wholly owned subsidiaries as legal systems have become more accommodating. Much of the foreign direct investment into China and other developing countries similarly took the form of joint ventures simply due to restrictions on foreign ownership. It is also noteworthy that the more recent draft antitrust guidelines on alliances prepared by the Federal Trade Commission and the US Department of Justice borrow heavily from pre-existing horizontal merger regulations. These guidelines may legitimate a widespread business practice as well as impose limits on firms using more restrictive forms of alliances.

Even when an acquisition is feasible, an alliance may be more efficient by allowing the firm to avoid post-merger integration costs or valuation problems. The former can arise due to structural or cultural integration challenges, and the latter can arise because the target firm has private information on its resources that it cannot credibly convey at low cost. These perspectives are known as indigestibility and information asymmetry, respectively, and are the focus of this section of the book.

Hennart's (1988) chapter challenges some of the conventional explanations for joint ventures. He also provides descriptions of two types of joint ventures—scale and link ventures—in the aluminum industry, but which can also be found in a variety of sectors. The chapter flags two main features of assets that make them amenable to joint venturing. First, the assets are firm-specific in that they cannot be readily dissociated from the firm. Second, the assets are public goods in that they can be shared at low marginal cost, which makes replication comparatively expensive.

Balakrishnan and Koza's (1993) chapter applies Akerlof's (1970) model of the market for lemons to the context of external corporate development. They assume that assets are completely alienable and focus on the *ex ante* inefficiencies in M&A markets rather than the *ex post* costs of assembling the desired resources. The primary prediction is that valuation problems will be significant, and joint ventures more attractive, when the firm is obtaining resources from a target that operates in a dissimilar industry.

Hennart and Reddy's (1997) chapter offers an empirical test of the indigestibility and information asymmetry views using foreign direct investment data on greenfield expansions by Japanese manufacturing firms. Consistent with the indigestibility perspective, they find that investors prefer joint ventures over acquisitions when the target firm is large and non-divisionalized in structure. They present evidence inconsistent with the information asymmetry prediction, however; if anything, firms exhibit a preference for acquisitions rather than joint ventures in inter-industry transactions.

Finally, Reuer and Koza's (2000) chapter considers the theoretical relationship between the information asymmetry and indigestibility perspectives. They argue that information asymmetry and valuation problems are likely to exist under conditions of indigestibility due to the embeddedness and sharing of resources in the target firm. This suggests that it is not possible to reject the information asymmetry view in favor of the indigestibility perspective or draw conclusions on the relative importance of *ex ante* and *ex post* transaction costs based on prior findings. They use more recent data for samples of domestic as well as international joint ventures, and the evidence from both samples lends support to the information asymmetry perspective of strategic alliances.

It should also be noted that in the last decade there have been many other advances within the alliance field using the transaction cost paradigm. For example, research has identified factors leading firms to choose not only whether or not to use an alliance over an alternative arrangement, but also which form an alliance should take (e.g. Gatignon and Anderson, 1988; Pisano 1989; Osborn and Baughn, 1990; Teece, 1992). Researchers typically distinguish equity from non-equity alliances and proceed to relate these structures to various conditions that are supportive of each, but recent research examining the optimal level of disaggregation of governance structures suggests that finer-grained investigations into alliance structures are needed (Oxley, 1997). Although a frequent criticism of the transaction cost paradigm is that it is static and concerns initial governance decisions, recent analyses have also examined how conditions identified by this perspective have implications for the dynamics of alliances and how alliance termination affects parent firms (Park and Russo, 1996; Reuer, 2001; Reuer and Ariño, 2002).

It is also worth emphasizing that advances in the alliance literature are due to other streams of research in economics besides transaction cost theory, yet it is probably fair to say that the impact of these other perspectives in the strategy and management fields has been less substantial to date. For instance, Parkhe (1993) uses game theory to understand the structure of alliances and the incentives for firms to cooperate over time. Axelrod et al. (1995) consider standard setting coalitions and develop a model to explain membership in coalitions. Lerner and Merges' (1998) work represents a novel application of the property rights approach, which they use to examine the structure and evolution of control rights in biotechnology alliances. They suggest that the initial limited availability of funds for a biotechnology firm can lead to a suboptimal distribution of control rights in the alliance. Changes in the availability of funds can, therefore, lead to reallocations of these rights. Reuer et al. (2002) rely upon transaction cost theory and evolutionary economics to examine the post-formation dynamics of alliances, including changes in contracts and boards. These examples of applications of economic theory to the alliance domain are but a few, and recently researchers have also drawn upon work in financial economics on option pricing to understand alliances better, which is highlighted in a separate section below.

Real Options Perspectives on Interfirm Collaboration

Real options theory has advanced thinking on joint ventures by fundamentally recasting received wisdom on the motives for interfirm collaboration as well as the ways in which firms can derive value from joint ventures. Under the traditional logic noted above, joint ventures were a means by which firms could share risk or gain static efficiencies in the presence of contracting problems. In empirical studies, longevity and stability were often used as indicators of collaborative success. Kogut's (1991) extension of real options theory to the domain of joint ventures, presented as the first contribution in this section of the book, suggests instead that by entering joint ventures, firms can limit their downside risk and at the same time access upside opportunities. Under real options reasoning, firms can embrace, rather than avoid, uncertainties by investing in the options that joint ventures afford. Moreover, parent firms can create value by using short-lived joint ventures as part of a sequential investment strategy (e.g., Mitchell and Singh, 1992).

The basic logic is that the joint venture confers a growth option to the investor, and this option resembles a financial call option. The firm invests a smaller amount by entering into a joint venture rather than by making an acquisition, and to the extent that its initial investment in the joint venture is sunk and it does not bear carrying costs associated with keeping the option alive, the firm's downside risk is limited to the initial equity purchase. Over time, the firm monitors market and other cues to determine if the joint venture's value is such that a partner buyout is warranted. For instance, if a technology proves attractive, the value of the joint venture may rise enough such that the firm may gain by acquiring equity; otherwise, the option to expand is held open. Put algebraically, if V_c is the value the call holder places on the entire venture, α_{c0} is the call holder's initial equity, and P is the price at which the equity purchase occurs, then the firm will gain $(1 - \alpha_{c0})V_c - \mathrm{P}$ by buying out the partner, and it will hold the option open otherwise. Chi and McGuire (1996) extend this work with a stochastic model that combines transaction cost and real options considerations to demonstrate how uncertainty about the market and about a partner can lead to value gains from trading options to acquire or sell a joint venture.

Reuer and Leiblein's (2000) chapter empirically investigates whether firms are deriving benefits from joint ventures as predicted by real options theory. An extensive body of research in the alliance literature examines alliance trends, antecedents of the decision to use an alliance over some other form of governance, and factors influencing alternative ways of designing collaborative arrangements between firms. However, despite the many alliance benefits that researchers routinely cite, very little research has been done to examine whether firms are truly obtaining specific benefits from interfirm collaboration. They find that investments in joint ventures—either domestic or international—lead to higher rather than lower levels of subsequent downside risk for firms. They identify several possible reasons why the reality of firms' experiences with joint ventures falls considerably short of the promise held out by real options theory. This evidence indicates the value of probing further the boundary conditions of the predictions from real options theory, and it also points to the need to begin to close the current gap between theoretical and empirical research on real options to ascertain the descriptive and normative value of this perspective on cooperative strategy. Current research is attempting to sort this out, and this work will determine how firms can capture value from using real options to design their alliances and how real options can inform, or be informed by, other theories of interfirm collaboration.

Learning Perspectives on Interfirm Collaboration

Another stream of research that has advanced in the last few years and is still vibrant concerns learning and alliances. Contributions in this area have tended to proceed down one of two paths, and the book offers two examples of each type of study. First, research examines learning within a particular dyad, focusing on the factors influencing how much a parent firm learns from its partner (e.g. Lyles and Salk 1996; Lane and Lubatkin 1998). Some of this research emphasizes that strategic alliances tend to involve a mixture of cooperation and competition, with the learning process often being contentious as collaborators vie for each others' capabilities. Second, research examines firms' learning about how to manage the process of collaboration, investigating whether or not alliances are subject to learning-by-doing. These latter studies are interested in the broader question of whether or not an alliance capability exists.

As an example of the former research focus, Hamel's (1991) chapter offers an inductive study that unearths several of the determinants of inter-partner learning. The core propositions he develops on learning from partners relate to three fundamental factors: (a) the strength of the firm's internalization intent, or its desire to systematically acquire knowledge from the partner rather than just access a partner's know-how; (b) the transparency of the organizations and skills under consideration; and (c) the presence or absence of so-called preconditions for receptivity. Competitive collaboration, as he envisions it, involves a firm regarding the internalization of a partner's skills as a chief benefit of collaboration. The paper offers a series of propositions on interpartner learning as an alliance outcome. For instance, in contrast to transaction cost treatments of alliances, he suggests that the legal and governance structure of a collaborative agreement may exert only a minor influence over learning in an alliance. Evidence from subsequent studies suggests that this is not the case, however (Mowery et al., 1996; Sampson, 1999).

Khanna et al.'s (1998) chapter uses models from the literature on the economics of technology races to formalize thinking on learning alliances and depict how firms' resource expenditures and the alliance evolve as learning by the two firms proceeds. Their paper also provides examples of several pathologies that might arise in resource allocations to alliances over time. In the first, the so-called "three-legged fallacy," a firm does not recognize that it is in a learning race and fails to adjust its resource expenditures over time. The second example deals with a "reluctant loser." In this case, the leader increases its resource expenditures when it reaches a stage first, but the laggard holds its expenditures constant. The final scenario, then, represents a "hesitant winner": when a firm passes the first stage first, it fails to increase its expenditures as the other firm reduces its expenditures in the alliance. They also review four types of biases presented in the behavioral decision theory literature that may lead managers to make suboptimal resource allocation decisions in alliances.

The learning race view of alliances has contributed to the understanding of many aspects of interfirm collaboration and is intuitively appealing, but it has also been the subject of debate in recent years. Inkpen (2000) argues, for instance, that the Khanna et al. framework does not offer insights into the processes of learning, arguing that alliances tend to be messier than depicted in technology race models. Although many of his critiques appear to be directed at the use of economic theories to develop models, he suggests on the basis of his fieldwork that he has not observed a learning race between alliance partners. Hennart et al. (1999) examine the termination of joint ventures by Japanese firms in the United States to explore whether learning race behavior is in evidence. Based on their findings on the stability of such ventures and the way in which they come to an end, they conclude that learning races are not characteristic of their sample of joint ventures. Dussauge et al. (2000) report that link alliances are more unstable than scale alliances, and they attribute their greater instability to interpartner learning.

The final two papers in this section turn to the question of whether firms can develop an alliance capability through experiential learning. In their chapter, Barkema et al. (1997) find that international joint venture survival is advanced by prior domestic joint venture experience, but not by international joint venture experience. Other research has similarly found an insignificant effect of experience accumulation. For example, Simonin (1997) reports that experience by itself does not influence either tangible or intangible benefits from collaboration. By contrast, using an event study approach, Anand and Khanna's (2000) chapter reports positive experience effects in joint ventures, but not in licensing contracts. For the joint venture sample, learning-by-doing is strongest for research joint ventures and weakest for marketing joint ventures.

The mixed findings for experiential learning in the alliance context can be attributable to several factors (Zollo et al. 2002). Relative to manufacturing and other organizational activities for which experiential learning has been documented, alliances are subject to high levels of heterogeneity, which increases the chances that lessons learned in one collaboration will be inappropriately applied to other alliances that might be superficially similar, yet are inherently quite different. Their lower frequency may also be an impediment to learning-by-doing. It is also clear that the assessment of alliance performance has been a vexing problem for researchers as well as managers (e.g. Anderson, 1990; Geringer and Hebert, 1991). The paucity of well-developed performance metrics poses an obstacle for firms attempting to update and refine their alliance practices. Moreover, the complexity of factors driving alliance performance indicates that alliances are subject to significant causal ambiguity.

All of these considerations indicate that studies on experiential learning in the alliance setting need a more solid theoretical grounding in order to identify the boundary conditions of learning-by-doing in firms' corporate development activities. Recent research that goes beyond pure learning-by-doing to identify other possible mechanisms of capability development such as knowledge articulation and codification (Kale, 1999) also holds out promise for answering the question of whether an alliance capability exists and, if so, what its sources are.

Relational Perspectives on Interfirm Collaboration

The final section of the book considers recent relational perspectives on strategic alliances. The first chapter, by Dyer and Singh (1998), makes the argument that some of a firm's critical resources may reside outside of its boundaries and may be embedded in interfirm routines. Using this perspective, they propose four sources of interorganizational competitive advantage. Firms may create assets that are specialized to an alliance partner and by investing in knowledge-sharing routines. Questions arise concerning how any rents that appear will be captured by each of the partners and whether hold-up problems will mitigate the benefits of specific investment. They go on to suggest that long-lived relationships will deter opportunism and that a greater volume of exchange between the partners will warrant more elaborate governance mechanisms.

Dyer and Singh also argue that firms can generate relational rents by leveraging the complementary resource endowments of an alliance partner. The key to this argument, however, is that there is not a competitive market that serves to elevate the price of the resources to be accessed. Their argument is that the competitiveness of the market for partners is imperfect because firms vary in their ability to identify partners and value their contributions due to differences in alliance experience, differences in search and evaluation capabilities, and differences in information due to network positions. An interesting question is whether the competitiveness of the market for partners suffers from these inefficiencies, and whether the alliance market differs from the M&A market in these respects.

Finally, they argue that effective governance is a source of relational rents. More specifically, they propose that firms that are better able to align transactional attributes with governance structures will garner relational rents. A different way of combining transaction cost theory and a capability perspective relies not on the governance decision *per se*, but the firm's ability to manage transactions using a cheaper form of governance for a given level of contracting hazards. For instance, firms with alliance capabilities might be able to use alliances, rather than some more costly form of governance, in hazardous situations otherwise requiring more extensive governance mechanisms. Others attempting this solution would bear significant misalignment costs. Such capabilities can be thought of as hazard mitigating capabilities and have begun to receive empirical attention (Delios and Henisz, 2000). Dyer and Singh conclude their chapter by discussing the mechanisms that preserve relational rents, and they compare their relational perspective with industry structure and resource-based views of competitive advantage.

Gulati's (1998) chapter examines alliances from a network perspective. He lays out several central research questions in the field and illustrates how network perspectives on alliances differ from traditional ones at the dyad level. The first issue concerns the formation of alliances. Traditional analyses, for example, cover the resource complementarities that induce firms to collaborate, whereas network perspectives highlight social structures that at once create new prospects as well as constrain choice. Second, a dyadic perspective would examine the governance of alliances largely through transaction cost theory, whereas a network perspective points out that the structure of network relations may shape contracting hazards and coordination costs. As a third example, research has examined the evolution of alliances, and a network view of this issue would consider how the network in its entirety evolves as well as how dynamics within groups of firms affect a focal alliance. Regarding the implications of alliances for firms, dyadic analyses would tend to examine characteristics of partners and how the alliance influences these partners, while network perspectives would focus on the firm's position in the network and the impact of co-membership of partners in networks.

The final chapter in this section of the book, by Walker et al. (1997), provides an empirical analysis of the formation of a network of alliances in the biotechnology industry. They suggest that the evolution of this network is guided by two forces that are in opposition to one another. The first concerns the pressure that exists for dense regions of relationships to reproduce, which provides a means of developing norms of behavior and diffusing information. The second concerns the actions of entrepreneurs to bridge these regions in order to take advantage of localized relationships. Their evidence suggests that the first force is dominant, with the firms in the industry recreating a stable network that exhibits significant path dependence. A recent study suggests that the relative importance of these two types of embeddedness—relational and structural, respectively—is contingent upon industry context (Rowley et al. 2000).

Concluding Remarks

Taken together, this set of papers illustrates well the alliance literature's progress as well as its future prospects. Despite numerous important advances in the late 1980s and early 1990s, there have been many recent developments in the field, and research activity on alliances remains vibrant. The papers in this volume demonstrate that the alliance literature has a much more solid theoretical footing than in years past. Just as the theoretical base of the field is stronger, theoretical pluralism rather than a single perspective continues to characterize the literature as well as the research agenda. The recent growth of network and evolutionary perspectives of alliances serve as recent examples of this richness. Maturity in the theory of interfirm collaboration is also in evidence, as witnessed by examinations of how different theories relate to one another and account for firms' alliance behavior and outcomes.

Another characteristic of the field's evolution that is brought out by the papers is the progressively rigorous empirical investigations into key alliance phenomena and outcomes. It is unfortunate, however, that far too many of the practical guidelines that are in currency in writings for practitioners and in executive programs are still based on limited evidence or unscientific studies. With the rise in the amount and quality of alliance research, this can be expected to be less and less the case in coming years.

It is also fair to say that much of current alliance research dovetails with the needs of practice. This is a natural development as research has shifted from explaining the antecedents of alliances to their implications for firms. Work that has begun to examine the question of whether and how an alliance capability develops also holds out potential to make an impact on practice. Even though managers are concerned about what happens after an alliance has been formed but before it comes to an end, comparatively little is known about the dynamics of alliances and networks, but progress is being made on this front as well. Research in these areas may enrich the theory of interfirm collaboration as well as contribute to our understanding of the roles that alliances can play in firms' strategies.

References

Akerlof, G. A. (1970), "The market for 'lemons': Qualitative uncertainty and the market mechanism," *Quarterly Journal of Economics*, 84: 488–500.

Anand, B. N. and Khanna, T. (2000), "Do firms learn to create value? The case of alliances," *Strategic Management Journal*, 21: 295–316.

Anderson, E. (1990), "Two firms, one frontier: On assessing joint venture performance," *Sloan Management Review*, 31: 19–30.

Axelrod, R., Mitchell, W. G., Thomas, R. E., Bennett, D. S., and Bruderer, E. (1995), "Coalition formation in standard-setting alliances," *Management Science*, 41: 1493–508.

Balakrishnan, S. and Koza, M. P. (1993), "Information asymmetry, adverse selection, and joint ventures," *Journal of Economic Behavior and Organization*, 20: 99–117.

Barkema, H. G., Shenkar, O., Vermeulen, F,. and Bell, J. H. J. (1997), "Working abroad, working with others: How firms learn to operate international joint ventures," *Academy of Management Journal*, 40: 426–42.

Beamish, P. W. (1985), "The characteristics of joint ventures in developed and developing countries," *Columbia Journal of World Business*, 20: 13–19.

Buckley, P. J. and Casson, M. (1988), "A theory of cooperation in international business," in F. J. Contractor and P. Lorange (eds), *Cooperative Strategies in International Business*. Lexington, MA: D. C. Heath, pp. 31–53.

Caves, R. E. (1998), "Research on international business: problems and prospects," *Journal of International Business Studies*, 29: 5–19.

Chi, T. and McGuire, D. J. (1996), "Collaborative ventures and value of learning: Integrating the transaction cost and strategic option perspectives on foreign market entry," *Journal of International Business Studies*, 27: 285–308.

Contractor, F. J. and Lorange, P. (1988), "Why should firms cooperate? The strategy and economics basis for cooperative ventures," in F. J. Contractor and P. Lorange (eds), *Cooperative Strategies in International Business*. New York, NY: Lexington Books, pp. 3–30.

Das, T. K. and Teng, B.-S. (2000), "Instabilities of strategic alliances: An internal tensions perspective," *Organization Science*, 11: 77–101.

Delios, A. and Henisz, W. J. (2000), "Japanese firms' investment strategies in emerging economies," *Academy of Management Journal*, 43: 305–23.

Dussauge, P., Garrette, B., and Mitchell, W. (2000), "Learning from competing partners: Outcomes and durations of scale and link alliances in Europe, North America and Asia," *Strategic Management Journal*, 21: 99–126.

Dyer, J. H. and Singh, H. (1998), "The relational view: Cooperative strategy and sources of interorganizational competitive advantage," *Academy of Management Review*, 23: 660–79.

Gatignon, H. and Anderson, E. (1988), "The multinational corporation's degree of control over foreign subsidiaries: An empirical test of a transaction cost explanation," *Journal of Law, Economics, and Organization*, 4: 305–36.

Geringer, J. M. and Hebert, L. (1991), "Measuring performance of international joint ventures," *Journal of International Business Studies*, 22: 249–63.

Gomes-Casseres, B. (1996), *The Alliance Revolution: The New Shape of Business Rivalry*. Cambridge, MA: Harvard University Press.

Gulati, R. (1998), "Alliances and networks," *Strategic Management Journal*, 19: 293–318.

Hagedoorn, J. (1993), "Understanding the rationale of strategic technology partnering," *Strategic Management Journal*, 14: 371–86.

Hamel, G. (1991), "Competition for competence and interpartner learning within international strategic alliances," *Strategic Management Journal*, 12: 83–103.

Harrigan, K. R. (1985), *Strategies for Joint Ventures*. Lexington, MA: Lexington Books.

Hennart, J.-F. (1988), "A transaction cost theory of equity joint ventures," *Strategic Management Journal*, 9: 361–74.

—— and Reddy, S. (1997), "The choice between mergers/acquisitions and joint ventures: The case of Japanese investors in the United States," *Strategic Management Journal*, 18: 1–12.

——, Roehl, T., and Zietlow, D. S. (1999), Trojan horse or workhorse? The evolution of US–Japanese joint ventures in the United States. *Strategic Management Journal*, 20: 15–29.

Hitt, M. A., Dacin, M. T., Levitas, E., Arregle, J.-L., and Borza, A. (2000), "Partner selection in emerging and developed market contexts: Resource-based and organizational learning perspectives," *Academy of Management Journal*, 43: 449–67.

Inkpen, A. C. (2000), "A note on the dynamics of learning alliances: competition, cooperation, and relative scope," *Strategic Management Journal*, 7: 775–9.

Kale, P. (1999), Alliance capability and success: A knowledge-based approach. Unpublished dissertation, University of Pennsylvania.

Khanna, T., Gulati, R., and Nohria, N. (1998), "The dynamics of learning alliances: Competition, cooperation, and relative scope," *Strategic Management Journal*, 19: 193–210.

Kogut, B. (1988), "Joint ventures: Theoretical and empirical perspectives," *Strategic Management Journal*, 9: 319–32.

——(1991), "Joint ventures and the option to acquire," *Management Science*, 37: 19–33.

Lane, P. J. and Lubatkin, M. (1998), "Relative absorptive capacity and interorganizational learning," *Strategic Management Journal*, 19: 461–77.

Lerner, J. and Merges, R. P. (1998), "The control of technology alliances: An empirical analysis of the biotechnology industry," *Journal of Industrial Economics*, 46: 125–56.

Lyles, M. A. and Salk, J. E. (1996), "Knowledge acquisition from foreign parents in international joint ventures: An empirical examination in the Hungarian context," *Journal of International Business Studies*, 27: 877–904.

Mitchell, W. and Singh, K. (1992), "Incumbents' use of pre-entry alliances before expansion into new technical subfields of an industry," *Journal of Economic Behavior and Organization*, 18: 347–72.

Mjoen, H. and Tallman, S. (1997), "Control and performance in international joint ventures," *Organization Science*, 8: 257–74.

Mowery, D. C., Oxley, J. E., and Silverman, B. S. (1996), "Strategic alliances and interfirm knowledge transfer," *Strategic Management Journal*, 17: 77–92.

Nelson, R. and Winter, S. (1982), *An Evolutionary Theory of Economic Change*. Cambridge, MA: Harvard University Press.

Osborn, R. N. and Baughn, C. C. (1990), "Forms of interorganizational governance for multinational alliances," *Academy of Management Journal*, 33: 503–19.

Oxley, J. E. (1997), "Appropriability hazards and governance in strategic alliances: a transaction cost approach," *Journal of Law, Economics, and Organization*, 13: 387–409.

Park, S. H. and Russo M. V. (1996), "When competition eclipses cooperation: an event history analysis of joint venture failure," *Management Science*, 42: 875–90.

Parkhe, A. (1993), "Strategic alliance structuring: A game theoretic and transaction costs examination of interfirm cooperation," *Academy of Management Journal*, 36: 794–829.

——(1996), "International joint ventures," in B. J. Punnett and O. Shenkar (eds), *Handbook for International Management Research*. Cambridge, MA: Blackwell Publishers Inc, pp. 429–59.

Pfeffer, J. and Nowak, P. (1976), "Joint ventures and interorganizational interdependence," *Administrative Science Quarterly*, 21: 398–418.

Pisano, G. P. (1989), "Using equity participation to support exchange: Evidence from the biotechnology industry," *Journal of Law, Economics, and Organization*, 5: 109–26.

Porter, M. E. (1990), "The competitive advantage of nations," *Harvard Business Review*, March–April: 73–91.

Reuer, J. J. (2000), "Collaborative strategy: The logic of alliances," in *Mastering Strategy*. London, UK: FT Prentice Hall.

——(2001), "From hybrids to hierarchies: Shareholder wealth effects of joint venture partner buyouts," *Strategic Management Journal*, 22: 27–44.

Reuer, J. J. and Ariño, A. (2002), "Contractual renegotiations in strategic alliances," *Journal of Management*, 28: 51–74.

——and Koza, M. P. (2000), "Asymmetric information and joint venture performance: Theory and evidence for domestic and international joint ventures," *Strategic Management Journal*, 21: 81–8.

——and Leiblein, M. J. (2000), "Downside risk implications of multinationality and international joint ventures," *Academy of Management Journal*, 43: 203–14.

——, Zollo, M., and Singh, H. (2002), "Post-formation dynamics in strategic alliances," *Strategic Management Journal*, 23: 135–51.

Rowley, T., Behrens, D., and Krackhardt, D. (2000), "Redundant governance structures: An analysis of structural and relational embeddedness in the steel and semiconductor industries," *Strategic Management Journal*, 21: 369–86.

Sampson, R. C. (1999), The cost of inappropriate governance in R&D alliances. Unpublished manuscript, New York University.

Simonin, B. L. (1997), "The importance of collaborative know-how: An empirical test of the learning organization," *Academy of Management Journal*, 40: 1150–74.

Teece, D. J. (1992), "Competition, cooperation, and innovation: Organizational arrangements for regimes of rapid technological progress," *Journal of Economic Behavior and Organization*, 18: 1–25.

Vernon, R. (1983), "Organizational and institutional responses to international risk," in R. Herring (ed.), *Managing International Risk*. New York: Cambridge University Press.

Vickers, J. (1985), "Pre-emptive patenting, joint ventures, and the persistence of oligopoly," *International Journal of Industrial Organization*, 3: 261–73.

Walker, G., Kogut, B., and Shan, W. (1997), "Social capital, structural holds, and the formation of an industry network," *Organization Science*, 8: 109–25.

Williamson, O. E. (1991), "Comparative economic organization: The analysis of discrete structural alternatives," *Administrative Science Quarterly*, 36: 269–96.

Zollo, M., Reuer, J. J., and Singh, H. (2002), "Interorganizational routines and performance in strategic alliances," *Organization Science*, 13: 701–13.

I. OVERVIEW OF RESEARCH ON INTERFIRM COLLABORATION

1 Why Should Firms Cooperate? The Strategy and Economics Basis for Cooperative Ventures

Farok J. Contractor and Peter Lorange

Nature is not always red in fang and claw. Cooperation and competition provide alternative or simultaneous paths to success. In business, as in nature, managers must learn the arts of competing and cooperating as equally valid aspects of corporate strategy. Cooperative aspects of international strategy have been relatively neglected until recently. In the past few years, however, there appears to have been a proliferation of international joint ventures, licensing, coproduction agreements, joint research programs, exploration consortia, and other cooperative relationships between two or more potentially competitive firms (Boston Consulting Group, 1985). The role of these relationships in international strategy is the focus of this chapter.

The traditional preference of international executives has largely been to enter a market or line of business alone. This seems to have been particularly true for the larger multinationals, especially those based in the United States. Among smaller international companies and those based in Japan, Europe, and developing nations, there seems to have been a higher propensity to form cooperative relationships (United Nations, 1978; Stopford and Haberich, 1976). Traditionally, cooperative arrangements were often seen as second-best to the strategic option of going it alone in the larger firms. Licensing, joint ventures, coproduction, and management service agreements have been viewed as options reluctantly undertaken, often under external mandates such as government investment laws or to cross protectionist entry barriers in developing and regulated economies. In several socialist and developing nations, this consideration remains important; association with local partners is more frequently necessary for market access and government permissions of various kinds.

What makes the recent spate of cooperative associations different is that they are typically being formed between firms in industrial free-market economies where there are few external regulatory pressures mandating a linkup. Instead of the traditional pattern of a large "foreign" firm trying to access a market by associating itself with a "local" partner, many of the recent partnerships involve joint activities in many stages of the value-added chain, such as production, sourcing, and R&D. These associations often involve firms of comparable rather than unequal size, both may be international in scope, and each may make similar rather than complementary contributions. Further, the territorial scope of some of these new cooperative ventures is global, rather than restricted to a single-country market as in the traditional pattern of joint ventures and contractual agreements. These new forms of cooperative ventures will be the focus of our discussion in this chapter.

1. The Incidence of Cooperative Arrangements in International Business

How important are cooperative arrangements such as joint ventures and licensing, compared with fully owned foreign subsidiaries? For U.S.-based companies, arrangements involving overseas partners, licensees, or local shareholders outnumber fully owned subsidiaries by a ratio of 4 to 1. Compared with the approximately 10,000 fully owned foreign affiliates, there are 14 to 15,000 affiliates in which the U.S. parent's share is less than 100 percent. Of the latter, in about 12,000 affiliates, the U.S. parent has a 10 to 50 percent equity position (minority affiliates roughly equal majority and fully owned affiliates put together).[1] In addition, there are some 30,000 overseas licensees in which U.S. firms or their affiliates have negligible or no equity stake (U.S. Department of Commerce, 1981).

The fact remains that many of the cooperative ventures, particularly those in which the U.S. company has a minority stake, are very small affairs. Hence, the preceding picture can be misleading. By indexes such as assets or number of employees, the fully owned foreign subsidiaries of U.S.-based multinationals continue to account for over two-thirds of the *value* of U.S. foreign investment, even if these subsidiaries are vastly outnumbered by the cooperative arrangements. Companies based in Europe and Japan are said to have a higher propensity than U.S. firms to enter joint ventures and licensing agreements. But the data remain fragmentary and incomplete, making it hard to verify these overall patterns of cooperative activities.

2. An Alternative Paradigm for Multinational Operations

Cooperative arrangements are numerous enough to suggest that our stereotype of the multinational corporation may need to be changed. Traditionally, it has been seen as a monolithic entity, controlling or owning its inputs and outputs, and expanding alone into foreign markets, based on its technological, managerial, and marketing dominance (see Caves, 1971). It could be seen as a transnational chain of control, "internalized" within the firm (Buckley and Casson, 1976). In this view, the corporation reserves for itself the gains from global vertical and/or horizontal integration.

Today, we are in a more negotiated, circumscribed, competitive world, at least as far as several industries are concerned. In many situations, the international firm is better seen as a coalition of interlocked, quasi-arms-length relationships. Its strategic degrees of freedom are at once increased by the globalization of markets (Levitt, 1983) and decreased by the need to negotiate cooperative arrangements with other firms and governments. In linking up with another firm, one or both partners may enjoy options otherwise unavailable to them, such as better access to markets, pooling or swapping of technologies, enjoying larger economies of scale, and benefitting from economies of scope. These benefits are detailed later. As a corollary, each partner is less free to make its own optimizing decisions on issues such as product development, transfer prices, territorial scope, and retention of earnings versus dividend payout.

The rest of this chapter falls into three broad areas. First, we shall discuss various types of cooperative arrangements, with particular emphasis on reviewing the broader strategic implications of the choice of various types of cooperative efforts. Next, we discuss in some detail various rationales for cooperation, identifying seven broad benefits from various types of cooperative efforts. Finally, we suggest a more formalized cost/benefit analysis for deciding to enter into a cooperative arrangement versus choosing the option to go it alone in a fully owned subsidiary.

The fundamental approach of this chapter is to focus on the predecision phase, the time before a commitment has been made to go for a joint venture or to expand strategically in a wholly owned mode. The emphasis is, thus, on planning, analysis, and design before one enters into such an arrangement.

3. Types of Cooperative Arrangements

Between the two extremes of spot transactions undertaken by two firms, on the one end, and their complete merger, on the other hand, lie several types of cooperative arrangements. These arrangements differ in the formula used to compensate each partner (the legal form of the agreement) as well as in the strategic impact on the global operations of each partner. Table 1 ranks these arrangements in order of increasing interorganizational dependence which is generally, but not necessarily, correlated with strategic impact (Pfeffer and Nowak, 1976). This ranking is at present only in the form of a hypothesis, since no empirical work exists comparing the various types of cooperative agreements on the extent of interorganizational dependence they create.

For instance, technical training and start-up assistance agreements are usually of short duration. The company supplying the technology and training is typically

Table 1. Types of Cooperative Arrangements

	Typical compensation method	Extent of interorganizational dependence
Technical training/start-up assistance agreements	L	Negligible
Production/assembly/buyback agreements	m	↓
Patent licensing	r	Low
Franchising	r;m	
Know-how licensing	L;r	
Management/marketing service agreement	L;r	↓
Nonequity cooperative agreements in		Moderate
Exploration	$\pi_i = f(C_V, R_V)$	
Research partnership	$\pi_i = f(C_V, R_i)$	
Development/coproduction	$\pi_i = f(C_i, R_j)$	↓
Equity joint venture	α	High

α = fraction of shares/dividends.
r = royalty as a percentage of turnover.
L = lump-sum fee.
m = markup on components sold or finished output brought back.
π_i = profit of firm i in nonequity joint venture.
C_V, R_V = costs and revenues of the venture.
C_i, R_i = costs and revenues of the firm i.
R_j = revenues of the dominant partner.

compensated with a lump-sum amount and will thereafter have minimal links with the start-up company, unless, of course, there is an additional licensing agreement. Similarly, patent licensing involves a one-time transfer of the patent right. Compensation, however, is often in the form of a running royalty, expressed as a fraction of sales value. In component supply, contract assembly, buyback, and franchising agreements, the principal form of compensation for both partners is the markup on the goods supplied, although there could be a royalty arrangement as well, as typically is the case in franchising. The interdependence between the partners is thus somewhat greater because of delivery, quality control, and transfer-pricing issues associated with the supply of materials, as well as due to the global brand recognition in franchising.

Know-how licensing and management service agreements assume a closer degree of continuing assistance and organizational links. Studies show that most licensing involves the transfer of know-how which is unpatented but proprietary information (Contractor, 1983). It is not simply a matter of transferring a patent right or providing start-up training. It involves extended links between the two firms and ongoing interaction on technical or administrative issues. Payment in these cases will typically be in the form of a lump-sum fee plus running royalties.

The term *joint venture* often implies the creation of a separate corporation, whose stock is shared by two or more partners, each expecting a proportional share of dividends as compensation. But, many cooperative programs between firms involve joint activities without the creation of a new corporate entity. Instead, carefully defined rules and formulas govern the allocation of tasks, costs, and revenues. Table 1 gives three examples. Exploration consortia often involve the sharing of the venture's costs, C_V, and revenue from a successful find, R_V, by formula. By comparison, the costs of a research partnership may be allocated by an agreed-upon formula, but the revenue of each partner depends on what the company independently does with the technology created. In coproduction agreements, such as the Boeing 767 project involving Boeing and Japan Aircraft Development Corporation (itself a consortium of Mitsubishi, Kawasaki, and Fuji), each partner is responsible for manufacturing a particular section of the aircraft. Each partner's costs, C_i, are therefore a function of its own efficiency in producing its part. However, revenue, R_j, is a function of the successful sales of the 767 by the dominant partner, Boeing (Moxon and Geringer, 1984). Each of these examples involves different risk/return trade-offs for the parties. Table 1 lists the major types of cooperative arrangements, indicating how costs and revenues are typically shared, depending on the compensation method. Significantly also, the table indicates how interorganizational dependence increases as one proceeds from simple one-shot cooperative agreements to ongoing formal joint ventures.

4. The Broader Strategic Effects of Forming a Cooperative Venture

So far, we have considered costs and revenues directly associated with the cooperative venture itself. But the legal form that governs the allocation of tasks, compensation, and costs plus the broader strategy consequences are not necessarily that easy to interrelate. Seen in isolation, a cooperative venture may only be a simple startup, technical training agreement, or standard patent license. But if the effect of this cooperative move is to create a long-term customer for a part or active ingredient, the strategic impact goes beyond the arrangement itself. Examples of this kind are frequently found, for instance, in the pharmaceutical industry's licensing practices or in automotive assembly agreements, where the nominal royalty accruing to the headquarters of the technology-licensing group typically will be vastly exceeded by the profit margin earned by the division that supplies the active ingredient for the drug or the automotive parts (Contractor, 1985).

On the other hand, there could be negative strategic impacts external to the venture itself. The worry of creating a future competitor is often overblown, but must be considered when entering into any cooperative venture or transferring technology or know-how to another firm. Let us consider two contrasting examples. A chemical company is helping to set up a PVC plastic plant with a Korean firm. The technology is mature, if not widely known in its most efficient production form. The PVC industry is globally decentralized, and delivery to customers from local sources is a more common pattern than imports. Hence, in this case, there may be little reason to fear that the company receiving the assistance will become a global competitor or otherwise impinge upon the strategy of the firm supplying the technology, except in the one country agreed upon. In this case, the geographic issue is clear.

However, the opposite case of the junior partner turning over time into a global competitor is also well documented. Reich (1984) and Abegglen (1982) relate many examples involving Japanese firms, including the celebrated stories of Western Electric licensing transistor technology to Sony for $25,000 and RCA assisting Japanese companies to make color-television receivers. How significant in cooperative agreements is this problem of being taken over by one's partner will depend on many factors such as the duration of the arrangement, the ability of each partner to go it alone on the partnership's expiration, and their resolve to independently keep up with technical and/or market-related changes in the industry. In this context, it may also be critical to assess the degree to which the relationship leaves the partners mutually interdependent and, thus, potentially vulnerable later on. This question must be assessed differently depending on whether the industry is characterized by global production-interaction efficiencies or by adaptation to the unique country-level circumstances.

In industries "configured" to be country-based (Porter, 1986), are cooperative ventures less dangerous in terms of creating global competition? Yes, but only if the partner is a "local" firm unlikely to make its own direct investments in other countries. Otherwise, even if the industry is territorially fragmented or "multi-domestic," an improved technology can be easily spread by a partner that is already global in scope. Competition from a former joint venture partner or licensee is likely to be felt sooner and in greater intensity in geographically concentrated and global-scope industries.

In general, there are no comprehensive data on this question. Warnings have primarily been voiced vis-à-vis Japanese companies (for example, Reich, 1984; Hamel, Doz, and Prahalad, 1986). Overall, the opinion of the Office of Technology Assessment or of authors such as Contractor (1985) is that U.S. technology transferred to overseas licensees or joint venture partners does not induce a pervasive competitive threat, barring a few notable cases. The technology-receiving oganization is often local in orientation or remains one step behind; the rate of technical change may be rapid enough to diminish the danger from one transfer; or the terms of the agreement itself may limit the other partner via patents or other restrictive clauses. The potential threat can thus often be dealt with through careful creation of a "black-box position" for oneself, emphasizing legal and patent protection; maintaining some control over the venture through staffing; maintaining one's strong independent research momentum; and linking the partner up through a complete system of relationships. It is necessary to see all of these activities together when creating black-box protection (Lorange, 1986).

Overall, the benefits of international cooperative ventures will have to exceed the direct and indirect costs, such as creating competitors. Neither fashion nor phobia accounts for the fact that the number of cooperative arrangements vastly exceeds the number of fully owned subsidiaries as modes of international business organization. There must be de facto strategic rationales or benefits to these arrangements.

5. Rationales for Cooperation

In addressing the conditions necessary for entering into a cooperative relationship, we shall take the viewpoint of any one partner and examine the contribution it makes to a given venture's strategy. It is critical to keep the strategy of one partner in mind. How central is the particular business domain of a joint venture for the partner? What opportunity losses must the partner reckon with as offsetting the benefits from a joint venture, such as limitations on future strategic flexibility and alternative use of management's capacity? We shall examine the overall benefit/cost balance of cooperative relationships in a subsequent section of this chapter. For the moment, let us primarily discuss the benefits—the reasons for *forming* cooperative ventures.

In the broadest terms, joint ventures, licensing, and other types of cooperative arrangements can achieve at least seven more or less overlapping objectives. These are: (1) risk reduction, (2) economies of scale and/or rationalization, (3) technology exchanges, (4) co-opting or blocking competition, (5) overcoming government-mandated trade or investment barriers, (6) facilitating initial international expansion of inexperienced firms, and (7) vertical quasi-integration advantages of linking the complementary contributions of the partners in a "value chain." We have listed the major potential benefits that might be associated with each of these rationales in Table 2. Each of these issues will be discussed in more detail in the following paragraphs.

When considering benefits from cooperative ventures in the broadest sense, they typically create value through either a *vertical* or *horizontal* arrangement. In considering the vertical value-addition process that takes place through a joint venture, it is useful to draw on the value chain approach suggested by Porter (1985, 1986). The *combined* efforts of all partners must add up to a value chain that can produce a more competitive end result. It is important that the partners have complementary strengths, that they together cover all relevant know-how dimensions needed, and that the strategies of the partners are compatible and not in conflict.

Instead of the partners making *complementary* contributions, an alternative model of cooperation is one in which the partners provide *similar* inputs to the venture. The rationales for the latter can be to limit excess capacity, to achieve risk reduction through joint efforts, and to save on costs, as we shall see shortly. Both models exist in international cooperative ventures, but their relative incidence and stability are not definitely known.

Let us now consider in more detail the seven areas for potentially generating benefits outlined in Table 2.

5.1. Risk Reduction

Cooperative ventures can reduce a partner's risk by (1) spreading the risk of a large project over more than one firm, (2) enabling diversification in a product portfolio sense, (3) enabling faster entry and payback, and (4) cost subadditivity (the cost to the partnership is less than the cost of investment undertaken by each firm alone).

Table 2. Strategic Contributions of Joint Ventures

• *Risk Reduction*
Product portfolio diversification
Dispersion and/or reduction of fixed cost
Lower total capital investment
Faster entry and payback
• *Economies of Scale and/or Rationalization*
Lower average cost from larger volume
Lower cost by using comparative advantage of each partner
• *Complementary Technologies and Patents*
Technological synergy
Exchange of patents and territories
• *Co-opting or Blocking Competition*
Defensive joint ventures to reduce competition
Offensive joint ventures to increase costs and/or lower market share for a third company
• *Overcoming Government-mandated Investment or Trade Barrier*
Receiving permit to operate as a "local" entity because of local partner
Satisfying local content requirements
• *Initial International Expansion*
Benefit from local partner's know-how
• *Vertical Quasi Integration*
Access to materials
Access to technology
Access to labor
Access to capital
Regulatory permits
Access to distribution channels
Benefits from brand recognition
Establishing links with major buyers
Drawing on existing fixed marketing establishment

This table is adapted with permission from Farok J. Contractor, "An Alternative View of International Business," *International Marketing Review*, Spring 1986.

Developing, for instance, a new car or airplane is a multibillion dollar undertaking. First, to state the obvious, a joint new undertaking such as the Boeing 767 Project spreads the risk of failure (and the potential gains) over more than one party. This applies also to exploration consortia. But there are other subtler considerations, as can be illustrated by the General Motors–Toyota venture. To the extent that GM did not have to sink $2.5 billion into developing a new small car in the United States, it could invest the capital over a range of larger models (*Business Week*, March 1984). Given the public's fluctuating taste for smaller versus larger automobiles—something Detroit has been largely unsuccessful in predicting over the past two business cycles and oil shocks—a diversification of the product portfolio might insulate auto producers from such variability in demand, at least up to a point. Further, a joint venture can lower the total investment cost of a particular project, or the assets at risk, by combining expertise and slack facilities in the parent firms—the cost subadditivity factor. A good example is utility power pools that enable each regional electric company to make a lower investment than it would operating alone (Herriott, 1986). Finally, the experience of all the partners—their mutual sharing or abdication of markets in favor of the joint venture corporation—make for faster entry with a better design and a quicker payback. Faster entry and certification are also strong factors in pharmaceutical-industry licensing. The industry's complaint is that because certification takes a long time, the monopoly advantage of a patent is eroded and there is not enough time to recoup R&D costs. Clinical testing performed by a licensee often speeds up the certification process.

The risk-sharing function of coalitions may be especially important in research-intensive industries such as computers, where each successive generation of technology tends to cost much more to develop, while at the same time product life cycles might shrink, leaving less time to amortize the development costs. This observation appears to be contradicted by Friedman, Berg, and Duncan (1979), who showed a negative correlation between R&D intensity and the propensity to form joint ventures—as if to suggest that the more valuable a firm's proprietary technology, the more likely it is to go-it-alone. The apparent contradiction is possibly resolved when we consider that (1) Friedman, Berg, and Duncan's data are now a decade old, when the context for developing international strategies was markedly different and (2) industry-level studies typically are difficult to translate to the firm level. A leader such as IBM may well be able to carry on by itself, while the followers such as Siemens, Fujitsu, and Amdahl may have to form joint ventures to share development costs and risks.

Another dimension of risk reduction has to do with containing some of the political risk by linking up with a local partner. Such a partner may have sufficient political clout to steer the joint venture clear of local government action or interference. It may also be that the joint venture has come about as a result of the host government's industrial policy. In such a case, added political-risk reduction can be achieved; the government endorses the joint venture as being beneficial to its economic policy agenda. Government policies favoring joint ventures over fully owned investments are by no means peculiar to less-developed countries (LDCs). Japan has, in fact, been a role model for many developing nations (Contractor, 1983). European policies in this regard are outlined in Gullander (1976) and Mariti and Smiley (1983).

5.2. *Economies of Scale and Production Rationalization*

"I think world trade in built-up vehicles will be largely replaced by trade in vehicle components. . . . The distinction between imports and domestics could very well become meaningless" (Donald Peterson, president of Ford, in the

International Herald Tribune, September 19, 1981). Underlying this remark are two distinct but related concepts. Production rationalization means that certain components or subassemblies are no longer made in two locations with unequal costs. Production of this item is transferred to the lower-cost location which enjoys the highest comparative advantage, thus lowering sourcing cost. But, there is an added advantage. Because volume in the more advantageous location is now higher, *further* reduction in average unit cost is possible due to economies of larger scale. General Motors, for instance, has an extensive global interchange between its affiliates and joint venture partners such as Isuzu and Suzuki (in which it has had an admittedly passive equity stake, so far). Japan serves as a source for transaxles—transmission plus axle subassemblies—for assembly in markets such as Canada, Europe, South Africa, and Australia. Brazil serves as a source of small engines for Ford's U.S. and European markets. Other examples are abundant.

In many situations, too, particularly in more mature businesses, there may be excess capacity and need for industrial restructuring. A joint venture approach may be a practical vehicle for achieving this. Thus, production can be rationalized and output levels reduced within the joint venture context, thereby avoiding a "winner–loser" situation and a protracted stalemate. High exit barriers can thereby be overcome.

Another example is a licensing/franchising operation for the servicing of marine engines and boats in ports all over the world. Ships are drawn to the internationally recognized brand name for the service facility so that they can enjoy identically high standards of service anywhere. Moreover, there are important economies of scale in centralized engine rebuilding, parts inventories, and training—savings passed on to the franchise holder and from there to the customer.

Potential synergistic effects of joint ventures can possibly also be inferred from the findings of McConnell and Nantell (1985), who show that the value of the shares of over two hundred firms listed on the New York and American stock exchanges was increased for those companies that had undertaken joint ventures.

5.3. *Exchanges of Complementary Technologies and Patents*

Joint ventures, production partnerships, and licensing agreements may be formed in order to pool the complementary technologies of the partners. Several alliances in the pharmaceutical and biotechnology fields, for instance, are built on this rationale. Each partner contributes a missing piece. By pooling know-how and patents, a superior product is expected. In general, it is important to consider joint ventures as vehicles to bring together complementary skills and talents which cover different aspects of state-of-the-art know-how needed in high technology industries. Such creations of "electric atmospheres" can bring out significant innovations not likely to be achieved in any one parent organization's "monoculture" context.

Moreover, *faster entry* into a market may be possible if the testing and certification done by one partner are accepted by the authorities in the other partner's territories. Or, one partner may cede the rights to a partially developed process to another firm which refines it further, with the fruits of the development to be shared in a joint venture. This is a typical pattern among smaller and larger firms (Doz, 1986). In this regard, it is useful to remember that a patent is not merely a right to a process or design; it is also a right to a *territory*. Often, the marketing or territorial right is the dominant strategic issue. By pooling or swapping patents, companies also pool or swap territories. Contractor (1985) describes such cross-licensing arrangements. Research partnerships can have a similar intent.

A closely related issue has to do with the pressures faced by a company that has invested heavily in developing a new technological breakthrough. But on its own, it may not have sufficient production or global marketing resources to secure a rapid, global dissemination of the new technology, making it hard to achieve an acceptable payback for its investment. A joint venture approach can be an important vehicle in achieving such dissemination and realistically securing the necessary payback. This may be especially true for smaller firms lacking the internal financial and managerial resources to make their own investments or expand rapidly.

Paradoxically, this may also be true in giant diversified firms. Let us take General Electric (GE) as an example: it has scores of foreign affiliates, as well as several hundred licensing or production contracts plus minority joint ventures. For a company with the number of products GE has, the potential country/product combination of activities must add up to over ten thousand. Not even a giant firm can invest in all of these. Direct investment in fully owned subsidiaries is reserved for the most interesting combinations, while many of the rest are handled by cooperative ventures. Stopford and Wells (1972) confirm in their study that the propensity to form joint ventures is higher when the entry entails product diversification. Berg, Duncan, and Friedman (1982) indicate that large average firm size and rapid growth in an industry correlate positively with joint venture formation.

5.4. Co-opting or Blocking Competition

Potential (or existing) competition can be co-opted by forming a joint venture with the competitor or by entering into a network of cross-licensing agreements (Telesio, 1977). The majority of these are defensive strategic moves. Besides other considerations mentioned earlier, blunting the Japanese auto penetration into the U.S. market is likely to have been one rationale for the GM–Toyota venture.

On the other hand, a joint venture may also be made in a more offensive vein. Caterpillar Tractor is said to have linked up with Mitsubishi in Japan in order to put pressure on the profits and market share that their common competitor Komatsu enjoyed in its important home market, Japan. Japan is said to generate 80 percent of Komatsu's global cash flow (Hout, Porter, and Rudden, 1982). Thus, even though the joint venture may not have great importance in itself for Caterpillar, it may act as a thorn in Komatsu's side and, thus, reduce its competitiveness outside Japan. Vickers (1985) suggests that many R&D partnerships are intended to quickly file patents to stake out the ground against competitors.

Of course, joint ventures are, quite properly, scrutinized by governments for their potential anticompetitive and welfare-limiting effects—but less stringently today, it seems, than a decade ago (Wassink and Carbaugh, 1986).

5.5. Overcoming Government-Mandated Investment and/or Trade Barriers

Here we come to one of the oldest and still common rationales for joint ventures—in many instances, host government policy makes the joint venture form the most convenient way to enter a market. An abundance of examples can be found, particularly in developing countries. Over the past few years, for instance, joint ventures with China have received much attention. We also have frequent examples of joint venture agreements being complemented by barter or countertrade arrangements. General Motors' venture with LZTK in Yugoslavia is an example of this. The joint venture, in fact, produces castings which GM buys for its German assembly lines; in return, GM is able to sell more cars in Yugoslavia by way of countertrade (Barkas and Gale, 1981). These more or less protectionist policies are not exclusive to LDCs or planned economies. Mariti and Smiley (1983) describe how NATO prefers weapons systems developed by multinational consortia, whereby the purchasing countries can participate in parts manufacturing through a cooperative network. Japan is known for its more or less exclusionary policies, and this has been a major contributing factor to the hundreds of U.S. firms using the joint venture route as the most practical way to sell products in the Japanese market (Abegglen, 1982).

5.6. Facilitating Initial International Expansion

For medium- or small-sized companies lacking international experience, initial overseas expansion is often likely to be a joint venture. This may be especially true when the firm is from a socialist or developing country (Lall, 1981). In a cross-sectional study, Dunning and Cantwell (1983) show that the lower the GDP per capita of the host nation originating a multinational firm, the more likely it is to use joint ventures in its initial international expansion. In a typical scenario, such a firm has production capability, but lacks knowledge of foreign markets for which it depends on its partner. Embraer of Brazil, a highly successful aircraft manufacturer, was helped initially by its joint venture with Piper. It makes small commercial jets as well as fighters. Initially aiming for the Brazilian market, Embraer is now a strong exporter, landing orders even in the demanding U.S. market. It gives a good example of a joint venture partner that over time has been turning into a global competitor on its own.

In general, it is an expensive, difficult, and time-consuming business to build up a global organization and a significant international competitive presence. Joint ventures offer significant *time savings* in this respect. Even though one might consider building up one's market position independently, this may simply take too long to be viable. Even though acquisitions abroad might be another alternative for international expansion, it can often be hard to find good acquisition candidates at realistic price levels—many of the "good deals" may be gone. All of these considerations add to the attractiveness of the joint venture approach.

5.7. Vertical Quasi-Integration

Several cooperative ventures involve each partner making essentially *similar* contributions, as described already. However, joint ventures, coproduction, research partnerships, and management or marketing service agreements can also be a form of vertical quasi integration, with each partner contributing one or more *different* elements in the production and distribution chains. The inputs of the partners are, in this case, *complementary*, not similar.

There is usually a strategic optimum, lying *in between* the extremes of complete vertical integration within one organization on the one hand, and completely contractual relationships or out-sourcing on the other hand. Sometimes, a cooperative relationship with another firm is the best way to reach this optimal middle ground. Such ventures can be described as a mode of interfirm cooperation lying between the extremes of complete vertical integration (in one company) of the chain from raw materials to the consumer, to the opposite case where stages of production and distribution are owned by separate companies which contract with each other in conventional market mechanisms (Thorelli, 1986). Empirically, the latter case is observed only rarely. Examples may be found in pockets of the music and publishing industries. One even encounters firms with no assets other than an office that undertake production and sales by contracting out each stage to separate organizations, while they simply "manage" the entire chain (Miles and Snow, 1986). But such one-time contracts mean that none of the parties accept any obligation for future behavior. Strategic direction-setting in any long-term sense may become next to impossible.

A firm may therefore integrate vertically (own more than one stage of the chain), because it may more easily permit longer-run strategic decisions. There is a large literature on vertical integration (Richardson, 1972; and, for the international firm, Buckley and Casson, 1976). Briefly stated, its advantages are these: (1) avoidance of interfirm contracting, transactions, and negotiations costs (Williamson, 1975), (2) reduction in cost or achieving economies of scale from combining common administrative, production, transport, or information processing activities in two or more stages of production or distribution, (3) internalizing technological or administrative abilities and secrets within a single firm, (4) gaining a better understanding of strategy within the industry as a whole (enabling the integrated firm to outperform its more fragmented competitors), and (5) the ability to implement technological changes more quickly and over more stages of the value chain.

On the other hand, there are drawbacks to integration as well. These drawbacks can be overcome to a certain extent by linking up with another firm, where integrating entirely within one firm may be difficult. First, there is the matter of capital investment cost which may become too high for just one company to bear, especially when operating in a risky environment. We see that many joint ventures in uncertain investment fields such as semiconductor R&D or oil exploration are predicated simply on spreading the investment cost and risk.

Second, the vertically integrated firm tends to increase its fixed costs and, thus, its break-even point, thereby potentially increasing its vulnerability to cyclical fluctuation. In the aerospace industry, for instance, the cost of developing new airplanes is very high for even the largest participants, such as Boeing (Moxon and Geringer, 1984). The Boeing 767 is being built in a contracted coproduction cooperative venture with Japan Commercial Aircraft and Aeritalia. Not only are the development risks shared, but fixed costs of Boeing are lowered by contracting major portions of the aircraft to the other partners. There are other strategic advantages as well, such as helping the sales of the aircraft in Japan and Italy.

Third, forward integrating to internalize more elements of marketing channels requires market access, links with major buyers, and brand recognition which can be a critical impediment in international expansion. The history of Japanese firms expanding into the U.S. market shows that in the early stages, they would link up with established U.S. companies. This typically gave them a "beachhead" and a longer learning period before developing channels of their own. Lastly, Porter (1980) indicates some other strategic disadvantages of full integration, such as reduced flexibility to environmental or technological change, dulled incentives for an individual operating unit to remain competitive if internal transfer prices do not reflect their external values, and being deprived of the marketing or technical insights available from outsiders.

A middle position between the two extremes of full integration and purely contractual relationships is often optimal for many companies. Joint ventures, coproduction, management service agreements, and so on provide a means whereby each partner can contribute its distinctive competencies. Many of the specific obligations of each partner may be defined in auxiliary agreements. Because they share in the equity of the venture or share the profits by a formula, the firms typically perceive that they have an overlapping if not identical strategy. The relationship is neither purely contractual nor entirely integrative. We may describe it as a mode of quasi-integration, as Blois (1972) puts it.

There are many typical examples. Take, for instance, the case of a hotel venture located in the Mideast. One partner, an international hotel chain based in the United States, supplies expertise to construct and start the hotel in terms of operating procedures, standards, and building codes. Thereafter, the other partner, a hotel company based in India, staffs and runs the operation under a profit-sharing management service contract, using local and expatriate Indian personnel who are hired at relatively modest salaries. The U.S. partner now provides worldwide brand recognition and a global reservation system.

Let us consider other examples of the contribution made by one of the partners. To carry out the production functions, an important bargaining chip in the so-called planned economies may simply be the permission to produce that one of the partners already has received from the government. In many nations, permission is necessary, even for local firms, before they can begin to produce; in several industrial sectors, foreigners may be excluded altogether. This is a similar but distinct issue from trade barriers, which involve an inability to sell.

In the latter case, what one partner seeks from the other is production destined for *other* markets. Take the case of Marine Resources in Seattle, a joint venture between Bellingham Cold Storage and Sovrybflot. It was perhaps the only joint venture in the United States with Soviet equity participation (Pereyra, 1981). The joint venture was predicated on the United States extending its offshore economic zone to 200 miles in 1976. The Russians being excluded, Americans now catch the fish. But the species available include many plebeian varieties such as pollock and whiting which have to be caught and processed quickly, in huge quantities, to make even a modest profit in international markets. U.S. fleets had neither the huge processing capacity of the Soviet motherships nor the expertise for international trade in such species. The factory ships are based in the Soviet Far East and have considerable excess capacity. At an early stage in the development of fisheries in the U.S. Northwest (with inexperience, slim profit margins, and a seasonal catch), investment in a factory ship was out of the question. Marine Resources contracted with American fishermen for supply of such species, with delivery to be made directly to affiliated Soviet factory ships in midocean; the processed catch was to be sold directly to other countries such as Japan and Korea. The joint venture had staff in Seattle, on-board representatives on the Soviet processing ships, and personnel in Nakhodka, Soviet Union.

Another variation on this theme of government production permission as a strategic contribution made by a partner can be exemplified by Kennecott's seabed mining consortium. To extract nodules from a depth of 3 miles is a speculative and costly venture; Killing (1983) reports that a full-scale test alone costs $150–200 million. Moreover, a large number of technical disciplines are needed, requiring expertise from several companies. For this reason, and in order to spread the risk of exploration, Kennecott formed a joint venture with companies from four industrial nations. But another crucial reason was political: to get the support of several governments at a time when negotiations on the law of the sea in the United Nations may have gone adversely against the mining companies. A similar consideration exists in the Airbus joint venture, except that, in this case, it is not a matter of production permission, but a question of improving the ability to sell the airplane to the national carriers of countries included in the joint venture.

Potential strategic advantages under the distribution-type joint venture category include rapid access to an existing marketing establishment, links with key buyers, knowledge of the local market and culture, and benefits from a recognizable brand name—in total, better market access. Let us now illustrate this with the following example. Tata is a large conglomerate based in India with extensive international contacts. India has potentially a fifth of the world's leather raw material base, but much is wasted. It seemed natural to invest in a leather-finishing operation to add value to the product in India before exporting it. Having tentatively decided to get into the high-quality end of the business, Tata faced the problem of not knowing anything about the international fashion leather market, notwithstanding its expertise in other industries. Instead of merely selling the leather as a commodity to independent European importers, a marketing joint venture was to be set up with TFR in France, a significant leather finisher and marketer in Europe. This would provide inputs to the factory in India regarding the exact color, texture, and other requirements of large European buyers. By making the leather to order instead of selling it to agents as a commodity, the operation earns higher margins. The French partner would make available an existing marketing establishment, links to key buyers, its name and reputation, and knowledge of the ever-shifting sands of fashion.

Being a natural substance, leather has inherent variability. Add to that the myriad of treatment methods, colors, and finishes, and one ends up with thousands of manufacturing combinations. To produce to a standard fit for the fashion market is, therefore, as much an art as a production science. In total, a successful operation requires close integration of the factory personnel with the marketing and manufacturing staff in Europe.

Let us give a few other brief examples to illustrate the span of variety in the forms of these distribution-type joint ventures. One New York-based partner in the restaurant business contributes marketing expertise in the case of a New York Chinese restaurant. The Sichuan Province of the People's Republic of China was to provide the Chinese chefs with local investors providing financing. The TRW–Fujitsu venture for the U.S. market was based on the idea of combining Fujitsu's hardware with TRW's existing distribution network. Fujitsu had no experience in selling in the United States, nor did it have much interest in making the potentially enormous expenditure of establishing its own sales organization from scratch. It wished to conserve resources for achieving greater strength in production.

Conversely, in the Fuji–Xerox venture in Japan, Fuji provided Xerox an entry into the Japanese market as well as links with key buyers (*Electronic Business* March 1984). The latter is an important consideration in Japan because of the strong business conglomeration within Japan's commercial industry sectors (Burton and Saelens, 1982). Personal contacts and referrals within the group are necessary for sales success.

5.8. Two Basic Patterns for Joint Venture Formation

We have discussed seven strategic rationales for forming cooperative relationships. In the broadest terms, they involve risk reduction, cost reduction, and an ability to enter markets or enhance revenues in a manner not possible for each firm alone.

A distinction was drawn between ventures in which the partners make similar inputs ("horizontal" ventures) versus ventures in which the contributions of the partners are complementary, with quasi-vertical integration providing *synergy*. Examples of partners making roughly similar contributions are found in the natural resources sector, oil and mineral exploration, real estate development, R&D ventures, and perhaps in large aerospace projects as well, where the dominant considerations appear to be an *accretion* of resources for the large investment involved and a spreading of risk over more participants.

6. An Overall Benefit/Cost Framework for Analyzing Cooperative Relationships

Thus far, we have mainly examined the strategic benefits side of cooperative ventures, based on the question: what are the conditions necessary for their formation? In weighing costs against benefits, one approach might be to compare the cooperative venture with the fully owned foreign subsidiary option. For the rest of this chapter, let us assume that the firm has the option of making its own investment independently. The question we shall address is how managers should *compare* the "internalization" or "go-it-alone" option with the cooperative venture option. In brief, we shall compare the "100 percent-owned foreign subsidiary" with joint ventures, licensing, and other cooperative forms. Each option involves different organizational and ownership modes, but with the same ultimate market objective.

We begin with a general axiomatic statement. A cooperative mode will have certain incremental benefits as well as certain incremental costs over a fully owned operation. A cooperative venture (CV) may have the effect of increasing the project's revenues and/or decreasing costs over what could have been earned by a fully owned subsidiary; on the other hand, certain drawbacks endemic to cooperative relationships might decrease revenues and/or increase costs over the level of a fully owned operation.

Let us express this statement in axiomatic terms. A cooperative venture is preferred over a fully owned operation if:

Incremental benefit of a cooperative form *over* a fully owned subsidiary	−	Incremental cost of a cooperative form *over* a fully owned subsidiary	>	Share of other partners' profit

In brief, a firm would prefer a cooperative association over the go-it-alone option when the net incremental benefit of a cooperative mode is not only greater than zero, but in fact is greater than the profit share of the other partner/s—or if risk is reduced by the act of cooperating. Algebraically,

$$(R_1 + R_2) + (C_1 + C_2) - (R_3 + R_4) - (C_3 + C_4) > (1 - \alpha)\pi_{CV}$$

and/or if risks are reduced significantly.

The terms are defined as follows: *A cooperative venture, compared with an alternative form such as a fully owned subsidiary, will create:*

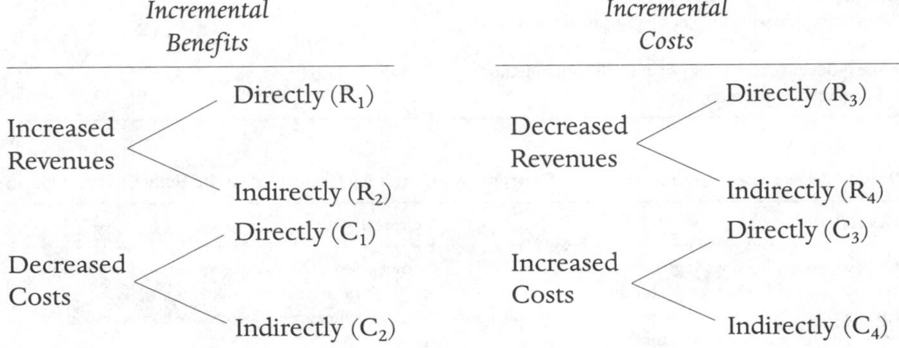

(Note that by *incremental* is meant the extra revenue or cost of a cooperative form over the fully owned option.)

π_{cv} is the expected profit of the cooperative venture. α is the equity share (or contractually defined share) in the venture of the firm doing this analysis. $(1-\alpha)$ is the other partner's share. Tables 3–6 give further detail on each of the terms, R_1 to R_4 and C_1 to C_4.

Thus, the incremental net benefit of a cooperative venture over a go-it-alone alternative has to not only be positive, but moreover, be large enough to cover the other partner's share of the profits, leaving some further incremental gain

Table 3. Increased Revenue from the Cooperative Venture Alternative over the Fully Owned Subsidiary

Direct (R_1)	Indirect (R_2)
Other partner's knowledge of market	More complete product line to help overall sales
Other partner's intangible assets such as technology, patents, and trademarks	Technical or new-product ideas learned from other partner and diffused to other parts of the company
Other partner's ties to government and/or important buyers	Markups on components or product trade with partner
One fewer competitor; hence, potentially larger market share	
Faster entry; improved cash flows	
Access to market otherwise foreclosed	

Table 4. Decreased Costs from the Cooperative Venture Alternative Compared to the Fully Owned Subsidiary

Direct (C_1)	Indirect (C_2)
Economies of scale from larger market share	Productivity and technical improvements diffused to other parts of company
Rationalization based on each partner nation's comparative advantage	
Government incentives and subsidies given to CVs only	
Lower capital cost and overhead due to using slack or underutilized equipment or design capabilities in each partner	
Less duplication of headquarters personnel	
Access through partner to cheaper raw materials and/or component inputs	
More productive technology or administrative methods contributed by one partner	

Table 5. Decreased Revenue from the Cooperative Alternative Compared to the Fully Owned Option

Direct (R_3)	Indirect (R_4)
CV association does not allow firm to expand into certain lines of business in the future.	Partner's desire to export decreases sales made by other affiliates in international markets.
Partner reaps the benefit of future business expansion that is not proportional to its future contribution.	Partner becomes more formidable competitor in the future.
Lower price is set at behest of partner.	

Table 6. Increased Costs from the Cooperative Venture Mode Compared to the Fully Owned Option

Direct (C_3)	Indirect (C_4)
Cost of transferring technology and expertise to partner	Increase in headquarters administrative, legal, and other overheads
Increased coordination and governance costs	Opportunity costs of executives and/or technicians assigned to CV
Pressures from partner to buy from designated sources or sell through its distribution channel	
Global optimization of MNC partner may not be possible for:	
Sourcing	
Financial flows	
Tax	
Transfer pricing	
Rationalization of production	

for the company considering the alternatives. This statement shows why cooperative ventures are not easy to form or to sustain over time.

By *direct* is meant the revenue and cost increments directly impinging on the project itself. By *indirect* is meant the effect of undertaking the cooperative venture on the rest of the global enterprise (on other divisions of the company), on affiliates in other countries, and on overall strategy. The direct and the indirect revenues and costs do not always have the same directional effect, nor might they occur in the same location or time. A licensing agreement or a joint venture, for instance, may in itself be directly profitable, but it can be indirectly harmful if it creates a future competitor, perhaps in another part of the world. The benefits of cooperative ventures are summarized in Tables 3 and 4.

6.1. Incremental Benefits of Cooperative Ventures

6.1.1. Higher Revenues from Cooperation

It should be noted that this analytical framework applies to all types of cooperative arrangements, whether they be licensing, joint ventures, or other agreements. Among the reasons why project revenues can be improved are the other partner's market knowledge, technology, market access, ties to important buyers and government, faster entry and, thus, more favorable cash flows. Indirectly, the company could benefit by having, for instance, technical or new-product ideas from the venture diffused to other parts of the company. Another indirect benefit is the possibility of having other divisions of the company handle (for a markup) products from the partner organization.

6.1.2. Lower Costs of Cooperative Ventures

Among the reasons why project costs may be lower under a cooperative form might be larger economies of scale and rationalization gains; government incentives available to joint ventures and licensing (but not to fully owned subsidiaries); lower capital investment and overheads due to utilizing slack capacity in the partner firms; and, finally, cheaper raw materials/component inputs and more productive methods acquired through the partner. Indirectly, other parts of the company might gain cost advantages from productivity gains and other efficiency improvements learned from the partner. This was probably an important consideration for GM when it linked up with Toyota.

6.2. Detrimental Aspects of Cooperative Ventures

6.2.1. Lower Revenues

Aspects of cooperative ventures leading to lower revenues and/or higher costs are summarized in Tables 5 and 6. As opposed to the situation with fully owned investments, the firm may be constrained by its association and suffer a relative decline in revenues because it does not have the freedom to unilaterally expand lines of business or because prices set in collaboration with the partner may be lower than one would like them to be. Indirectly, global revenues of one of the partners may decline because the other partner's desire to have the venture export might cut into potential sales of the firm in other territories. In general, revenue declines could occur in the future if the partner turned into a global competitor.

6.2.2. Higher Costs

Costs of a cooperative venture may exceed those of a fully owned, internalized operation due to the extra elements of having to negotiate and transfer technology and administer an enterprise jointly with another firm (See table 6). This is, in brief, the "transaction costs" argument. For a multinational firm, costs rise when global optimization may no longer be possible when it comes to sourcing, finance, tax, transfer pricing, and/or distribution due to the divergent objectives of the partners. Indirectly, cooperative ventures could entail somewhat higher headquarters costs as well as legal and technical overheads, compared with fully owned affiliates.

6.3. Risk-reduction Effects of Cooperative Ventures

Apart from the higher or lower costs and revenues of a cooperative venture compared with a fully owned subsidiary alternative, there are often important risk-reduction aspects.

Table 7. Risk Reduction

Lower capital investment at stake:
Partial investment
Excess capacity utilization
Economies of scale
Economies of rationalization and quasi integration
Faster entry and / or certification
Use CV as a guinea pig
For large risky projects:
Limit risk per venture
Diversify risk over several firms
Lower political risk
Lower asset exposure for medium- and small-sized firms

Table 7 recapitulates these important risk-reduction effects of cooperative ventures in terms of lower investment, faster entry (and, thus, better payback), and potentially lower political risk. High tech venture companies, for instance, may have stakes in several ventures with different potential competitors and be engaged in ventures involving several technologies at various stages of development—a loose network of sometimes interlocking companies. The strategy may be to maintain a stake in and potential payoff from several (sometimes speculative) projects, with limited risk per venture, while diversifying risk exposure over several projects. A cooperative venture may in some instances be viewed as a "guinea-pig," perhaps to be brushed aside or taken over fully should it come up with a truly interesting discovery or market success. For medium- and small-sized firms, cooperative ventures are often the only realistic way to reduce risk to tolerable levels.

This framework can be used to analyze any cooperative venture (be it an equity joint venture, licensing agreement, or research partnership) and to compare it with the alternative of internal development. To recapitulate, the framework suggests making project calculations for both a fully owned and a cooperative option and then comparing the two. The cooperative mode is preferred if its net incremental profit over the fully owned alternative exceeds the profit share of the other partner, that is, if $(R_1 + R_2) + (C_1 + C_2) - (R_3 + R_4) - (C_3 + C_4) > (1 - \alpha)\, \pi_{CV}$. In some cases, actual cash flow calculations have been made for the comparison (Contractor, 1985). At the least, the framework provides a useful strategic planning exercise, which helps in planning negotiation terms with prospective partners.

7. Conclusion: Cooperative Ventures as an Alternative Form of International Business Operation

In this chapter, we have examined the strategic-management and industrial-organization rationales for forming cooperative ventures. We have not explored the cultural or behavioral problems of running them, nor have we examined in much detail the causes of their failure or success. There is a large literature on those topics, exemplified by Sullivan and Peterson (1982) and Killing (1983). The thrust of that literature, perhaps unwittingly, seems to overemphasize the problems of running international joint ventures. There is, however, no hard evidence that their failure rate exceeds the normal corporate failure rate for comparable single-owner ventures. We have, however, claimed in this chapter that careful analysis prior to the decision of whether to go for a cooperative venture may be a most critical factor impacting future success of the cooperative venture (if such a venture is the decision outcome). The very fact that the partners have spent sufficient time to become truly clear about what they are entering into should be a major positive factor in this context.

The fact remains, nevertheless, that the strategic rationales prevailing when a cooperative venture was formed may shift over time. As a hypothesis for testing, let us propose that even though subsequent problems may develop (such as cultural difficulties, slower decision-making, arguments over the rate and division of profits, disputes over sourcing, tensions in connection with the assignment of personnel, and disagreements on future expansion), these are still all less onerous problems when compared with an erosion of the fundamental strategic rationales proposed in this chapter. This erosion may come from external or environmental sources, such as when the technology contributed by one partner is obsolescent because of changes in the industry. Or the erosion may be internal, such as when one partner *learns* from the other, and the other partner then has nothing new to contribute. Ongoing viability of the venture depends on the *continuing* mutual dependence of the partners.

This chapter has specifically focused on the strategic and economic rationales for forming cooperative ventures. We have, by choice, not discussed "softer" issues which also should be assessed before reaching a decision on whether to form a cooperative venture. Such issues might include the anticipated ease of working with the other partner; possible language difficulties, cultural differences, style incompatibilities, and differences in values and norms; the anticipated "political" climate within the context of the partners' organization; and the presence of a sufficiently strong "mentor" who will push the cooperative venture. We acknowledge the importance of incorporating these types of assessments into the decision on whether to go for a cooperative venture. However, we feel that the relative importance of these softer issues might be relatively lessened if a careful planning process has been undertaken, so that both partners understand the fundamental strategic and economic rationales involved.

It is possible that cooperative ventures will grow in importance as a mode of international business operations. However, we cannot be sure; in terms of strategic management of multinational operations, we have a trend and a countertrend. On the one hand, through regional economic integration plus convergence of standards and buyer preferences, in some industries there is the possibility of producing for a world market, with relatively minor variation in each nation. Centralized control and full ownership of affiliates is important for the implementation of an efficient and strategic direction in such corporations. On the other hand this chapter has pointed to examples in several industries where efficiency, risk-reduction, and other strategic rationales make the cooperative mode of organization superior to an internalization or go-it-alone strategy. Moreover, the traditional impetus for joint ventures, licensing, and other contractual forms remains in many countries. Economic nationalism, protectionism, transport costs, differing local cultures and standards, as well as the presence of entrenched domestic firms encourage a linkup with a local company as a means of serving the particular needs of a geographic market and/or for getting political permission to produce and tap natural resources. These traditional types of cooperative ventures remain ubiquitous.

Negotiated arrangements between international firms such as joint ventures and technology licensing agreements already vastly exceed controlled foreign affiliates by number, if not value. One model of the multinational corporation sees it as a closed, internalized administrative system that straddles national boundaries. An alternative paradigm proposed in this chapter is to view the international firm as a member of various open and shifting coalitions, each with a specific strategic purpose.

Appendix : The Case of the Six Thousand Missing Affiliates

Every five years, the US Department of Commerce publishes an extensive survey on US direct investment abroad.

Between the 1977 and 1982 surveys, the total number of foreign affiliates of U.S.-based firms was shown to have declined from 23,698 to 18,339. An affiliate is defined as a foreign corporation in which the U.S. company has 10 percent or more of voting securities. The surveys distinguish between minority affiliates (10 to 50 percent shareholding) and majority affiliates (one in which the US firm has more than 50 percent of shares). Unfortunately, they do not inform us whether there is, in fact, a distinct foreign corporate entity functioning as a "partner" to the U.S. firm or whether the balance of the shares are merely held by passive "portfolio"-type local investors. Nevertheless, examining the data provides several insights, especially comparing the 1977 and 1982 figures. Eliminating bank parents and affiliates (which are but a minor subset), we have Table A1.

The "loss" of over six thousand affiliates is substantially, if not almost entirely, explained by the more stringent criterion adopted in 1982 to cut off the tail of the distribution. In 1982, filing data with the Department of Commerce was reportedly mandatory for all U.S. firms with foreign affiliates that had total assets, sales, or net income of at least $3 million. For the 1977 survey, the comparable cutoff was only $500,000, roughly a quarter of the 1982 figure in real terms. This is the principal explanation for the fall in the number of affiliates and parents. (However, there are other minor factors which we may note, such as the marginal retrenchment of U.S. investment abroad between 1977 and 1982 in some countries and sectors such as energy and mining; the existence of a global recession in 1982; and the somewhat stronger dollar.)

Thus, the disappearance of over six thousand affiliates is more apparent than real. It is mainly caused by the new data-collection criterion. For example, the reported drop in employment by nonbank foregn affiliates is small, from 7.1 million in 1977 to 6.6 million in 1982. Total assets of nonbank affiliates actually increased from $490 million in 1977 to $751 million in 1982, which hardly suggests a drop in the value of foreign investment.

Several significant conclusions and hypotheses emerge:

1. The distribution of U.S. foreign investment, by size of both parents and affiliates, has a very long tail, consisting of rather small operations.

2. There are far more small U.S. firms investing abroad than is commonly realized (judging by the emphasis on large multinational strategy in the literature and even in this book). Their numbers are large, even though their share in total assets or employment is small.

3. Smaller U.S. firms are particularly prone to go in for minority foreign ventures, judging by the sharper "decline" in the "minority" category in Table A1, resulting from the higher cutoff criterion in 1982.

Table A1. Nonbank Affiliates of Nonbank U.S. Parents

	Total	Majority	Minority
1977	23,641	11,909	11,732
1982	17,213	14,475	2,738

Source: U.S. Department of Commerce, *U.S. Direct Investment Abroad, 1977*, (1981) and *U.S. Direct Investment Abroad, 1982: The Benchmark Survey* (1985). Washington, D.C: U.S. Government Printing Office.

4. Although there is no unequivocal proof, the preceding lends credence to the hypothesis that the propensity to form joint ventures and cooperative relationships is negatively correlated with the size of the U.S. parent and foreign affiliate. (Again, this is in terms of number of relationships, not their size or economic impact.)

Notes

1. In the latest benchmark survey (US Department of Commerce 1985), the figures appear quite different. But this is an artifact of the data-collection method used. An appendix to this chapter, "The Case of the 6000 Missing Affiliates," illustrates the data problem and provides further detail to the preceding figures.

Bibliography

Abbeglen, J. 1982. "U.S.–Japanese Technological Exchange in Perspective, 1946–1981." In C. Uehara (ed.), *Technological Exchange: The US–Japanese Experience*. New York: University Press.

Barkas, J. M., and Gale, J. C. 1981. "Joint Venture Strategies: Yugoslavia—A Case Study." *Columbia Journal of World Business*, Spring: 30–39.

Berg, S., Duncan, J., and Friedman, P. 1982. *Joint Venture Strategies and Corporate Innovation*. Cambridge, Mass.: Oelgeschlager, Gunn and Hain.

Blois, K. J. 1972. "Vertical Quasi-Integration." *Journal of Industrial Economics*, July: 253–72.

Boston Consulting Group. 1985. *Strategic Alliances*. Working Paper 276, Boston, Mass.

Buckley, P. J., and Casson, M. 1976. *The Future of the Multinational Enterprise*. New York: Holmes & Meier.

Burton, F. N., and Saelens, F. H. 1982. "Partner Choice and Linkage Characteristics of International Joint Ventures in Japan: An Exploratory Analysis of the Inorganic Chemicals Sector." *Management International Review*, 22(2): 20–29.

Business Week. 1984. "The All American Small Car is Fading." March 12: 88–95.

Caves, R. E. 1971. "International Corporations: "The Industrial Economics of Foreign Investment." *Economica*, February: 1–27.

Contractor, F. J. 1985. *Licensing in International Strategy: A Guide for Planning and Negotiations*. Westport, Conn.: Greenwood.

——1983. "Technology Importation Policies in Developing Countries: Some Implications of Recent Theoretical and Empirical Evidence." *Journal of Developing Areas*, July: 499–520.

——1983. "Technology Licensing Practices in U.S. Companies: Corporate and Public Policy Implications of an Empirical Study." *Columbia Journal of World Business*, Fall.

Cyert, R. M., and March, J. G. 1963. *A Behavioral Theory of the Firm*. Englewood Cliffs, N. J.: Prentice-Hall.

Doz, Y. 1986. *Technology Partnerships between Larger and Smaller Firms*. Draft paper. INSEAD, Fontainebleau, France, August.

Dunning, J., and Cantwell, J. 1983. *Joint Ventures and Non-Equity Foreign Involvement by British Firms with Particular Reference to Developing Countries: An Exploratory Study*. Working paper. University of Reading Economics Department.

Electronic Business. 1984. "The Winning Formula for U.S.–Japan Joint-Ventures." March: 182–85.

Friedman, P., Berg, S., and Duncan, J. 1979. "External vs. Internal Knowledge Acquisition: Joint Venture Activity and R&D Intensity." *Journal of Economics and Business*, 31(2): 103–10.

Gullander, S. 1976. "Joint Venture and Cooperative Strategy." *Columbia Journal of World Business*, Winter: 104–14.

Hamel, G., Doz, Y., and Prahalad, C. 1986. *Strategic Partnerships: Success or Surrender?* Paper presented at the Rutgers/Wharton Colloquium on Cooperative Strategies in International Business, New Brunswick, N.J., October.

Harrigan, K. 1983. *Strategies for Vertical Integration*. Lexington, Mass.: Lexington Books.

Herriott, S. R. 1986. *The Economic Foundations of Cooperative Strategy: Implications for Organization and Management*. Working paper. University of Texas at Austin.

Hout, T., Porter, M. E., and Rudden, E. 1982. "How Global Companies Win Out." *Harvard Business Review*, September–October: 98–108.

International Herald Tribune. 1981. *World Car* (Supplement), September 19.

Killing, J. P. 1983. *Strategies for Joint Venture Success*. New York: Praeger.

Lall, S. 1981. *Developing Countries in the International Economy*. London: Macmillan.

Levitt, T. 1983. "The Globalization of Markets." *Harvard Business Review*, May–June: 92–102.

Lorange, P. 1984. *Cooperative Strategies: Planning and Control Considerations*. Working paper. Wharton School, University of Pennsylvania, Philadelphia, October.

——1986. *Cooperative Ventures in Multinational Settings: A Framework*. Working paper. Wharton School, University of Pennsylvania, Philadelphia, May.

Mariti, P., and Smiley, R. H. 1983. "Cooperative Agreements and the Organization of Industry." *Journal of Industrial Economics*, June: 437–51.

McConnell, J., and Nantell, J. R. 1985. "Common Stock Returns and Corporate Combinations: The Case of Joint Ventures." *Journal of Finance*, 40: 519–36.

Miles, R. F., and Snow, C. C. 1986. "Network Organizations: New Concepts for New Forms." *California Management Review*, 28(3).

Moxon, R. W., and Geringer, J. M. 1984. *Multinational Ventures in the Commercial Aircraft Industry*. Working paper (mimeo). University of Washington, Seattle.

Pereyra, W. T. 1981. "Some Preliminary Results of a U.S.–Soviet Joint Fishing Venture." *Journal of Contemporary Business*, 10(1): 7.

Pfeffer, J., and Nowak, P. 1976. "Joint Ventures and Interorganizational Interdependence." *Administrative Science Quarterly*, 21 (September): 398–418.

Porter, M. E. 1985. *Competitive Advantage: Creating and Sustaining Superior Performance*. New York: Free Press.

——1980. *Competitive Strategy: Techniques for Analyzing Industries and Competitors*. New York: Free Press.

——1986. "The Changing Patterns of International Competition." *California Management Review*, 28(2).

Reich, R. B. 1984. "Japan Inc., U.S.A." *The New Republic*, November 26: 19–23.

Richardson, G. B. 1972. "The Organization of Industry." *The Economic Journal*, September: 883–96.

Sinclair, S. W. 1983. *The World Car: The Future of the Automobile Industry*. New York: Facts on File.

Stopford, J. M., and Haberich, K. 1976. "Ownership and Control of Foreign Operations." *Journals of General Management*, Summer.

——and Wells, L. 1972. *Managing the Multinational Enterprise*. New York: Basic Books.

Sullivan, J., and Peterson, R. B. 1982. "Factors Associated with Trust in Japanese–American Joint Ventures." *Management International Review*, 22(2): 30–40.

Telesio, P. 1977. *Foreign Licensing Policy in Multinational Enterprises*. D.B.A. dissertation. Harvard University.

Thorelli, H. B. 1986. "Networks: Between Markets and Hierarchies." *Strategic Management Journal*, 7(1).

United Nations Economic and Social Council. 1978. *Transnational Corporations in World Development: A Re-Examination*. New York: United Nations.

U.S. Department of Commerce. 1981. *U.S. Direct Investment Abroad, 1977*. Washington, D.C.: U.S. Government Printing Office.

——1985. *U.S. Direct Investment Abroad, 1982: The Benchmark Survey*. Washington, D.C.: U.S. Government Printing Office.

Vickers, J. 1985. "Pre-Emptive Patenting, Joint Ventures and the Persistence of Oligopoly." *International Journal of Industrial Organization*, 3: 261–73.

Wassink, D., and Carbaugh, R. 1986. "International Joint Ventures and the U.S. Auto Industry." *The International Trade Journal*, 1(1): 47–64.

Williamson, O. E. 1975. *Markets and Hierarchies: An Analysis and Antitrust Implications*. London: Free Press.

2 Joint Ventures: Theoretical and Empirical Perspectives

Bruce Kogut

The study of joint ventures has attracted increasing interest in the popular press and academic literature. Though joint ventures are an important alternative to acquisitions, contracting, and internal development, the literature has not been consolidated and analyzed. This chapter provides a critical review of existing studies and new data in order to establish current theoretical and empirical directions. In particular, a theory of joint ventures as an instrument of organizational learning is proposed. In this view a joint venture is used for the transfer of organizationally embedded knowledge which cannot be easily blueprinted or packaged through licensing or market transactions.

The chapter is divided into four sections. The first section develops three theories on joint ventures from the perspectives of transaction costs, strategic behavior, and organizational theory. The subsequent section reviews the literature on the motivations for joint ventures and empirical trends in their occurrence. Where possible, the findings are related to the three theoretical perspectives. Because there has been such considerable work in the area of international joint ventures, the third section summarizes some of the major findings regarding foreign entry and stability. The final section suggests some avenues for future research.

The theses of this chapter are essentially two. First, it will be argued that most statements on the motivations for joint ventures are reducible to three factors: evasion of small number bargaining, enhancement of competitive positioning (or market power), and mechanisms to transfer organizational knowledge. Second, it will be proposed that the cooperative aspects of joint ventures must be evaluated in the context of the competitive incentives among the partners and the competitive rivalry within the industry.

1. Theoretical Explanations

Narrowly defined, a joint venture occurs when two or more firms pool a portion of their resources within a common legal organization. Conceptually, a joint venture is a selection among alternative modes by which two or more firms can transact. Thus, a theory of joint ventures must explain why this particular mode of transacting is chosen over such alternatives as acquisition, supply contract, licensing, or spot market purchases.

Three theoretical approaches are especially relevant in explaining the motivations and choice of joint ventures. One approach is derived from the theory of transaction costs as developed by Williamson (1975, 1985). The second approach focuses on strategic motivations and consists of a catalogue of formal and qualitative models describing competitive behavior. Though frequently these approaches are not carefully distinguished from one another, they differ principally, as discussed later, insofar as transaction cost arguments are driven by cost-minimization considerations, whereas strategic motivations are driven by competitive positioning and the impact of such positioning on profitability. A third approach is derived from organizational theories, which have not been fully developed in terms of explaining the choice to joint venture relative to other modes of cooperation.

2. Transaction Costs

A transaction cost explanation for joint ventures involves the question of how a firm should organize its boundary activities with other firms. Simply stated, Williamson proposes that firms choose how to transact according to the criterion of minimizing the sum of production and transaction costs. Production costs may differ between firms due to the scale of operations, to learning, or to proprietary knowledge. Transaction costs refer to the expenses incurred for writing and enforcing contracts, for haggling over terms and contingent claims, for deviating from optimal kinds of investments in order to increase dependence on a party or to stabilize a relationship, and for administering a transaction.

Williamson posits that the principal feature of high transaction costs between arms-length parties is small numbers bargaining in a situation of *bilateral governance*. Small number bargaining results when switching costs are high due to asset specificity; namely, the degree to which assets are specialized to support trade between only a few parties.[1] The upshot of this analysis is that a firm may choose, say, to produce a component even though its production costs are higher than what outside suppliers incur. Such a decision may, however, be optimal if the expected transaction costs of relying on an outside supplier outweigh the production saving.[2]

Because a joint venture straddles the border of two firms, it differs from a contract insofar as cooperation is administered within an organizational hierarchy.[3] It differs from a vertically integrated activity in so far as two firms claim ownership to the residual value and control rights over the use of the assets. An obvious question is why should either firm choose to share ownership? Clearly, the answer lies in the diseconomies of acquisition due to the costs of divesting or managing unrelated activities or the higher costs of internal development. Thus, a necessary condition is that the production cost achieved through internal development or acquisition is significantly higher than external sourcing for *at least one* of the partners.

If vertical (or horizontal) integration is not efficient, then an alternative is the market or contract. As described earlier, a transaction cost explanation for why market transactions are not chosen rests on potential exploitation of one party when assets are dedicated to the relationship and there is uncertainty over redress. Leaving aside integration as economically infeasible and market transactions as too fraught with opportunistic risk, the final comparison is between a joint venture and a long-term contract.

A transaction cost theory must explain what discriminates a joint venture from a contract, and in what transactional situations a joint venture is best suited. Two properties are particularly distinctive: joint ownership (and control) rights and the mutual commitment of resources. The situational characteristics best suited for a joint venture are high *uncertainty* over specifying and monitoring performance, in addition to a high degree of asset specificity.[4] It is uncertainty over performance which plays a fundamental role in encouraging a joint venture over a contract.

To clarify why uncertainty over performance makes the properties of joint ownership and mutual contribution particularly valuable, consider first a joint venture designed to supply one of the parties, and second a joint venture serving as a horizontal extension of one or more links of each parent's value-added chain. In the case where the joint venture represents a vertical investment for one party and a horizontal for the other, the venture replaces a supply agreement. In this case the venture is the outcome of the production advantage of the supplier coupled with the transaction cost hazards facing one or both of the parties.

These hazards pose the problem of how an agreement to divide excess profits (sometimes called the problem of "appropriability") can be stabilized over time. Transaction cost hazards can face either the supplier or the buyer. Such hazards are likely to stem from the uncertainty in a supply contract over whether the downstream party is providing information on market conditions, over whether both parties are sharing new technologies, or over whether the supplier is performing efficiently or with the requisite quality production. Each of these cases poses the issue of whether, in the absence of the capability to specify and monitor performance, a governance mechanism can be designed to provide the incentives to perform.

A joint venture addresses this issue by creating a superior monitoring mechanism and alignment of incentives to reveal information, share technologies, and guarantee performance. Instrumental in achieving this alignment are the rules of sharing costs and/or profits and the mutual investment in dedicated assets, i.e. assets which are specialized to purchases or sales from a specific firm. Thus, both parties gain or lose by the performance of the venture.

It is by *mutual hostage positions* through joint commitment of financial or real assets that superior alignment of incentives is achieved, and the agreement on the division of profits or costs is stabilized. Non-equity contracts can also be written to provide similar incentives by stipulating complex contingencies and bonding. A joint venture differs by having both parties share in the residual value of the venture without specifying *ex ante* the performance requirements or behavior of each party. Instead, the initial commitments and rules of profit-sharing are specified, along with administration procedures for control and evaluation.

A more complex case is whether the joint venture represents a horizontal investment in order to supply both parties or sell in an outside market. The discriminating quality of a mutually horizontal joint venture is that the venture employs assets, such as one party's brand label reputation, which are vulnerable to erosion in their values. This latter aspect is particularly important if the joint venture has potential *externalities* which influence the value of the strategic assets of the parties, such as through a diffusion of technology, the erosion of reputation and brand labels, or the competitive effects on other common lines of business. It is, ironically, the initial complementarity between the parents' assets which both motivates joint cooperation and poses the transactional hazard of negative externalities, either through erosion or imitation of such assets as technology or reputation.

If two parties seek to resolve this dilemma by contracting to a third party, or to each other, the danger is that the agent will underinvest in complementary assets and free-ride the brand label or technological advantage. As a result the contracting party will undersupply, or mark up its price of, the inputs it contributes. A joint venture addresses these issues again by providing a superior alignment of incentives through a mutual dedication of resources along with better monitoring capabilities through ownership control rights. In summary, the critical dimension of a joint venture is its resolution of high levels of *uncertainty* over the behavior of the contracting parties when the assets of one or both parties are specialized to the transaction and the hazards of joint cooperation are outweighed by the higher production or acquisition costs of 100 percent ownership.

3. Strategic Behavior

An alternative explanation for the use of joint ventures stems from theories on how strategic behavior influences the competitive positioning of the firm. The motivations to joint venture for strategic reasons are numerous. Though transaction cost and strategic behavior theories share several commonalities, they differ fundamentally in the objectives attributed to firms. Transaction cost theory posits that firms transact by the mode that minimizes the sum of production and transaction costs. Strategic behavior posits that firms transact by the mode which maximizes profits through improving a firm's competitive position *vis-à-vis* rivals. A common confusion is treating the two theories as substitutes rather than as complementary.

Indeed, given a strategy to joint venture, for example, transaction cost theory is useful in analyzing problems in bilateral bargaining. But the decision itself to joint venture may stem from profit motivations and, in fact, may represent a more costly, though more profitable, alternative to other choices. The primary difference is that transaction costs address the costs specific to a particular economic exchange, independent of the product market strategy. Strategic behavior addresses how competitive positioning influences the asset value of the firm.

Potentially, every model of imperfect competition which explains vertical integration is applicable to joint ventures, from tying downstream distributors to depriving competitors of raw materials and to stabilizing oligopolistic competition. Of course, not every motive for collusive behavior is contrary to public welfare. Where there are strong network externalities, such as in technological compatibility of communication services, joint research and development of standards can result in lower prices and improved quality in the final market.[5] Research joint ventures which avoid costly duplication among firms but still preserve downstream competition can similarly be shown to be welfare-improving.[6]

Many joint ventures are, on the other hand, motivated by strategic behavior to deter entry or erode competitors' positions. Vickers (1985) analyzes joint ventures in research as a way to deter entry through pre-emptive patenting. In oligopolistic industries it might be optimal for the industry if one of the firms invested in patentable research in order to forestall entry. But given free-rider problems, encumbents would tend to underinvest collectively in the absence of collusion. Vickers shows that, for small innovations, a joint venture is an effective mechanism to guarantee the entry-deterring investment. For large innovations it is in the interest of each firm to pursue its own research, for the expected payoff justifies the costs. More generally, Vernon (1983) sees joint ventures as a form of defensive investment by which firms hedge against strategic uncertainty, especially in industries of moderate concentration where collusion is difficult to achieve despite the benefits of coordinating the interdependence among firms.

A strategic behavior perspective of joint venture choice implies that the selection of partners is made in the context of competitive positioning *vis-à-vis* other rivals or consumers. Though this area has not been investigated, the prediction of which firms will joint venture is unlikely to be the same for both transaction cost and strategic behavior perspectives. Whereas the former predicts that the matching should reflect minimizing costs, the latter predicts that joint venture partners will be chosen to improve the competitive positioning of the parties, whether through collusion or through depriving competitors of potentially valuable allies. Thus, two important differences in the implications of a transaction cost and strategic behavior analysis are the identification of the motives to cooperate and the selection of partners.

4. Organizational Knowledge and Learning

Transaction cost and strategic motivation explanations provide compelling economic reasons for joint ventures. There are, of course, other explanations outside of economic rationality. Dimaggio and Powell's depicture of mimetic processes of firms offers an interesting alternative point of view, for it is premature to rule out joint venture activity as a form of band-wagon behavior (Dimaggio and Powell, 1983). In other words, joint venture activity can be analogous to fashion trend-setting.[7]

There is, however, a third rational explanation for joint ventures which does not rest on either transaction cost or strategic behavior motivations. This explanation views joint ventures as a means by which firms learn or seek to retain their capabilities. In this view, firms consist of a knowledge base, or what McKelvey (1983) calls 'comps', which are not easily diffused across the boundaries of the firm.[8] Joint ventures are, then, a vehicle by which, to use the often-quoted expression of Polanyi (1967), 'tacit knowledge' is transferred. Other forms of transfer, such as through licensing, are ruled out—not because of market failure or high transaction costs as defined by Williamson and others, but rather because the very knowledge being transferred is organizationally embedded.

This perspective is frequently identified with a transaction cost argument, even though the explanatory factors are organizational and cognitive rather than derivatives of opportunism under uncertainty and asset specificity. An example of this confusion is the explanation for joint ventures, commonly embraced as a form of transaction cost theory, that the transfer of know-how in the market place is severely encumbered by the hazards which attend the pricing of information without revealing its contents. Because knowledge can be transferred at—so it is claimed—zero marginal cost, the market fails, as sellers are unwilling to reveal their technology and buyers are unwilling to purchase in the absence of inspection.

Yet, as Teece (1977) demonstrated, the transfer of technology entails non-trivial costs, partly because of the difficulty of communicating tacit knowledge. If knowledge is tacit, then it is not clear why markets should fail due to opportunistic behavior. It would seem, in fact, that knowledge could be described to a purchaser without effecting a transfer, specified in a contract, and sold with the possibility of legal redress. In this sense tacitness tends to preserve the market.

Rather, the market is replaced by a joint venture not because tacitness is a cost stemming from opportunism, but rather from the necessity of replicating experiential knowledge which is not well understood. More generally, tacitness is an aspect of the capital stock of knowledge within a firm. In this regard there is an important distinction between capital specific to individuals, and for which there may be an external labor market, and capital specific to organizations, or what Nelson and Winter (1982) call skills and routines, respectively. For transactions which are the product of complex organizational routines, the transfer of know-how can be severely impaired unless the organization is itself replicated.[9]

In this perspective a joint venture is encouraged if neither party owns each other's technology or underlying 'comps', nor understands each other's routines.[10] Or conversely, following Nelson and Winter (1982), a firm may decide to joint venture in order to *retain* the capability (or what they call 'remember-by-doing') of organizing a particular activity while benefitting from the superior production techniques of a partner. Even if a supply agreement were to operate at lower production and transaction costs a firm may choose a more costly joint venture in order to maintain the option, albeit at a cost, to exploit the capability in the future. What drives the choice of joint ventures in this situation is the difference in the value of options to exploit future opportunities across market, contractual, and organizational modes of transacting. Thus, a joint venture is encouraged under two conditions: one or both firms desire to acquire the other's organizational knowhow; or one firm wishes to maintain an organizational capability while benefitting from another firm's current knowledge or cost advantage.

The three perspectives of transaction cost, strategic behavior, and organizational learning provide distinct, though at times, overlapping, explanations for joint venture behavior. Transaction cost analyzes joint ventures as an efficient solution to the hazards of economic transactions. Strategic behavior places joint ventures in the context of competitive rivalry and collusive agreements to enhance market power. Finally, transfer or organizational skills views joint ventures as a vehicle by which organizational knowledge is exchanged and imitated—though controlling and delimiting the process can be itself a cause of instability.

5. Empirical Studies on Joint Venture Motivations

Despite a relatively long history of research on joint ventures there have been only a few empirical studies of their frequency and motivations. In part, the paucity of cross-sectional studies on joint ventures has been due to the difficulty of acquiring information. There have been, however, sufficient studies to date to draw a picture of joint venture activity in the United States and, to a lesser extent, overseas for the case of American multinational corporations.

A summary of the broad sectoral findings of a number of studies is given in Table 1. All of the studies rely on the publication *Mergers and Acquisitions*, though a few of the studies had access to the data used for the journal directly from the Bureau of Economics of the Federal Trade Commission.[11] All the studies show a similar concentration of joint ventures in the manufacturing sector. Kogut finds, however, a higher percentage in manufacturing than the rest. Because joint venture activity appears to be cyclical, it is unclear whether his estimates are the result of the chosen period, the smaller sample, or the correction for announced ventures which were never realized. (The other estimates are based on announcements.)

A problem with the above data is that it is difficult to infer trends regarding the propensity to venture without normalizing for the size of the industry and of firms. Boyle (1968) discovered persuasive evidence that larger firms engage more frequently in joint ventures than do smaller firms. Ideally, therefore, the ratio of joint venture sales or assets to industry sales or assets would serve as a measure of intensity which would correct for size effects. Unfortunately, the data required for the calculations of this ratio are not available.

Berg and Friedman (1978a) attempt to normalize their sample by taking a ratio between the number of joint ventures in an industry and the total number of companies. The measure is conceptually faulty, as there is no reason to exclude parents outside of the industry. Moreover, as most publicly available data

Table 1. Summary of Results on the Sectoral Distribution of Joint Ventures

	Manufacturing Industries	Natural Resource Development	Services	Other	Source
Pate (1960–68) ($n = 520$)	53.5	7.9	16.9	21.7	Federal Reserve Bank of Cleveland, FTC, Mergers and Acquisitions
Boyle (1965–66) ($n = 275$)	66.1	15.3	5.8	12.7	FTC, Mergers and Acquisitions
Duncan (1964–75) ($n = 541$)	59.1	12.8	20.7	8.1	Bureau of Economics, FTC, Mergers and Acquisitions
Harrigan (pre-1969–84) ($n = 880$)	54.8	11.7	15.1	18.4	Mergers and Acquisitions, Funk & Scott
Berg and Friedman (1966–70) ($n = 1762$)	60.4	9.5	NA	30.1*	Bureau of Economics, FTC, Mergers and Acquisitions
Kogut (1971–85) ($n = 148$)	67.1	12.8	11.3	8.7	Questionnaire based on Mergers and Acquisitions (U.S.-based only)

* Includes services.

Sources: Pate (1969), Boyle (1968), Duncan and Harrigan, reported in Harrigan (1985), Berg and Friedman (1978a), and author's estimate.

underreport joint ventures among small firms, the ratio tends to overstate joint venture participation of industries with large firms. On the other hand, they find that the ratio is correlated at 0.95 with the absolute number of joint ventures in an industry; moreover, their sample is dominated by ventures between two firms from the same industry as the joint venture. Joint venture incidence was especially predominant in mining, petroleum refining and basic chemicals, and low in textiles, paint and agricultural chemicals, and specialty non-electric machinery. Electronics and computers were found to have a low ratio of joint ventures to the number of firms but a high absolute number. In general, then, their measure appears to provide a reasonable gauge of joint venture incidence except for a few industries. It is important, therefore, to check results using their measure against other ways of estimating joint venture incidence.

Another strategy to analyze joint ventures is to study one or a few selected industries in depth. Studies of this type have been specifically oriented to testing whether joint ventures increase efficiency or enhance market power. Whereas a finding which shows enhanced market power for all firms in the industry suggests strategic motivations for joint ventures, findings of efficiency are consistent with, but not confirmatory of, a transaction cost hypothesis, since strategic rivalry may reduce costs within any firm attaining a long-run competitive advantage. For this reason it has been easier to test strategic motivation explanations for joint ventures than transaction cost hypotheses.

Previous industry studies have found some support that joint ventures are a form of strategic behavior to increase market power. Fusfeld (1958) found 70 joint ventures in the iron and steel industry, 53 of which were supply agreements among firms within the industry. More strikingly, he found that the joint ventures created two industrial groups, in addition to U.S. Steel. Using a rich data set, Berg and Friedman (1977) tested for the impact of joint ventures on firm rates of return in the chemical industry. Controlling for other variables they found that firms which had engaged in one or more joint ventures earned lower rates of return. Based on this finding they argued that, since most joint ventures in this industry involved some form of technological exchange, upstream ventures did not increase the market power of the participants. On the other hand, as they admit elsewhere (1978a), they cannot reject the hypothesis that failing firms engage in joint ventures in order to stabilize competition.

Stuckey's (1983) investigation of the aluminum and bauxite industry is a particularly valuable contribution because it specifically analyzed whether joint ventures were motivated by transaction cost or strategic motivations. Having examined 64 joint ventures among the six major firms, he found that of 15 possible linkages, eight occurred, that each major had at least one joint venture with another and five had at least two. He also found a high number of joint ventures with new entrants and other industry members. Moreover, while Stuckey noted that many of the joint ventures resulted in more efficiency through achieving optimal scale economies, the ventures between the majors occurred 'in bauxite and alumina production, the stages where coordination on expansion is most vital' (Stuckey, 1983: 201). Hence he concluded that transaction cost explanations appear more relevant to aluminum production, whereas strategic behavior was more prevalent in the upstream stages.

A third strategy is to analyze the within-sample variation across industries among variables to test for the efficiency and market power characteristics of joint ventures by relating their incidence to structural characteristics of the industry or to the characteristics of the parents. Pate (1969: 18) looked at 520 domestic joint ventures during 1960–1968 and found that over 50 percent of the parents belonged to the same two-digit SIC level and 80 percent were either horizontally or vertically related. Similar results were found by Boyle (1968) for 276 domestic ventures, and by Mead (1967) who, after examining 885 bids for oil and gas leases, found only 16 instances where the joint venture partners competed on another tract in the same sale. Thus, the Pate, Boyle, and Mead studies all conclude that joint ventures are motivated by market power objectives.

Pfeffer and Nowak (1976a) investigated more directly the motivation of market power by analyzing transaction patterns across industries and the degree of industry concentration. Out of 166 joint ventures, 55.5 percent were between parents from the same industry. They found that parents from industries which have a high exchange of sales and purchase transactions, and which are technology-intensive, tend to have more joint ventures. Interestingly, they found that joint ventures occur more frequently when the two parents are from the same industry of intermediate concentration. Since it is beneficial, though difficult, to collude in industries of intermediate concentration, they conclude that joint ventures are used to reduce uncertainty when oligopolistic rivalry is difficult to stabilize. In investigating the relationship between parents and progeny they found that again transaction frequency and technology of the venture industry were significantly related to joint venture incidence at the industry level, though no significant relationship was found for industry concentration.[12]

A second study by Pfeffer and Nowak (1976b) found further that horizontal parent pairings were correlated with concentration of the venture's industry. Both studies are, however, open to the problem that concentration and firm size are likely to be correlated; thus the result may be the outcome of the sampling bias discussed earlier. In fact, Berg and Friedman (1980) show that the correlation between concentration and joint venture incidence disappears when controling for the size of the parent firms.

A number of studies have tried to analyze motivations by looking at the effect of joint ventures upon the profitability of the parents. McConnell and Nantell (1985) analyzed stock returns by an event study of 210 firms listed on the American and New York Stock Exchanges which entered into 136 joint ventures between 1972 and 1979. They found a significant and positive impact on the stock values of the parent firms, with an average increase of just less than 5 million dollars in equity value. Arguing that joint ventures were motivated by synergies, they concluded that the similarities in their findings to those for merger activity imply that both are carried out largely for efficiency reasons. Given, however, that they did not attempt to test further if the positive gains are related to measures of market power, their conclusion is unwarranted, especially given the evidence, as discussed earlier, that joint ventures are frequently used between parent firms in interdependent industries.

Berg and Friedman (1981) tested more explicitly the relationship between industry rates of industry returns, joint venture incidence, and potential market power. Their sample consisted of over 300 ventures (mostly at the three-digit level) and was divided into joint ventures which are and are not formed for knowledge-acquisition. Controlling for other variables, and correcting for autocorrelation in the data, they found that industry rates of return were negatively related to knowledge-acquisition joint ventures and positively related to non-knowledge-acquisition ventures. They conclude on this basis that knowledge-acquisition ventures do not enhance the market power of the firm, for the benefits of market coordination would be immediate whereas the payoff to R&D is long-term. No control was made for structural variables, such as concentration, to test for other market power effects. Their results are also consistent with the view that joint ventures are likely to be chosen to transfer organizational knowledge, as opposed to achieving market power.

In an important study, Duncan (1982) partitioned his sample as to whether the parents are from the same three-digit SIC industry and to whether the joint venture and the parents are from the same industry. He finds that, at the three-digit level, ventures with parents from different industries are more prevalent (73 percent of the sample). Thus, Duncan concludes that Pfeffer and Nowak's inference of market power for parent pairings at the two-digit level is not robust at a lower level of industry aggregation. Since two-digit SIC classifications are too broad to infer collusive motivations when parent firms are related at this level of aggregation, Duncan's findings are to be preferred over those of Pfeffer and Nowak. In addition, he found that nonhorizontal pairings between parents or between parents and the venture are negatively related to industry rates of returns. However, Duncan did find support for higher industry rates of return when there is a horizontal relationship between the parents, suggesting that market power objectives may be the objective for these cases.

In summary, studies to date show that there is evidence both for a market power and efficiency argument for joint venture motivations. The Berg and Friedman (1981) study also provides support for the use of joint ventures as instruments for the transfer of organizational knowledge as opposed to means by which to enhance market power. However, these results must be taken as preliminary. None of the studies explicitly tested the effect of horizontal joint ventures between two firms from the same industry on firm rates of return.[13] Finally, whereas evidence of market power supports the strategic behavior perspective, the evidence of efficiency is consistent with, but not confirmatory of a transaction cost explanation. Future work should analyze directly the joint effect of joint ventures and industry structural characteristics on the valuation of the firm and specify more rigorous tests of transaction cost theories.

6. International Joint Ventures

Because the subject of how a foreign firm enters a country has been central in the literature on the international activities of the multinational enterprise, there is a longer history of studies on joint ventures in the field of international business. These studies are especially important because, unlike the domestic studies, a few have investigated the choice of joint ventures among other alternatives for entry. Many of these studies have examined the use of joint ventures as a response to governmental regulations, especially in developing countries, through an analysis of a few cases (Tomlinson, 1970; Friedman and Kalmanoff, 1961). Though the case studies are of unquestionable interest, we focus primarily upon studies statistically analyzing entry decisions.

Though, theoretically, there has been significant work in understanding entry decisions as a question of minimizing transaction costs, most studies have empirically investigated the strategic motivation hypothesis. Stopford and Wells (1972) conducted the earliest statistical analysis of the foreign entry decision for 155 American multinational corporations. They found that the use of joint ventures relative to wholly owned subsidiaries declined as the importance of technology and, especially, marketing and product standardization increased. Moreover, joint ventures were particularly prevalent in extractive industries. Of particular interest is their finding that if the entry entailed a product diversification, joint ventures were more likely, ostensibly for the reasons of acquiring local expertise in new areas.

Fagre and Wells (1982) tested to see if the value of a firm's intangible assets influenced its ability to bargain with governments to acquire control, and found that the greater the technological, marketing expense, need for intra-firm coordination, and product diversity, the greater the control (i.e. equity share) of the multinational corporation. The authors explained the positive relationship of product diversity to the preference for wholly owned subsidiaries—among other factors, the superior capability of the multinational corporation to manage multi-product subsidiaries, an argument which suggests a possible contradiction of the earlier Stopford and Wells finding on the need for local cooperation in new product entry. Another interpretation of their results is that multinational corporations will only transfer important resources if they attain control. That indeed the equity percentage reflects an outcome of a negotiation is supported by Gomes-Casseres (1985), who estimated that if constraints were to be removed, equity percentage of joint ventures would stabilize at wholly owned.

Despite a few studies on the choice of acquisition or wholly owned subsidiaries, only two studies to date have analyzed statistically the selection of joint ventures against other alternative entry modes. Caves and Mehra (1986) analyzed the acquisition and greenfield (i.e. startup investments) entry decisions of 138 foreign firms into the United States. Using joint ventures as a control they found that joint ventures and acquisitions served as subsitute, rather than as complementary, modes of entry, when controlling for other variables.[14]

Kogut and Singh (1986) analyzed explicitly the choice of acquisitions and joint ventures, focusing on country patterns.[15] They hypothesized that entry could be influenced by the cultural characteristics of a firm's country or origin in relation to the United States because of the difficulty of managing the post-acquisition process. In part, if cultural distance effects were to be found, it could be concluded that foreign firms respond to the *perceived* transactional costs of entry. They found that acquisitions were positively related to the size of the foreign firm and negatively related to the size of the American firm and cultural distance between the United States and the country of origin.

Another line of research has been to investigate the use of joint ventures when there is high need for intra-firm coordination across borders. If there are frequent intra-firm transfers of resources and potential export conflict, Franko (1971) found that joint ventures are more unstable, and Stopford and Wells (1972) found they are used less often. Hladik (1985) analyzed this indirectly by testing the determinants of whether an overseas venture would entail either R&D or export responsibilities. She found that a number of environmental variables (size of the market, technical competence of the partner, technological resources of the host country) were positively related to R&D ventures, whereas scale economies in R&D and the American firm's technological intensity were negatively related. In the case of exports she found that a joint venture was more likely to be allowed to export if the product was outside of, or peripheral to, the parent's product line.

The studies on international joint ventures have, in summary, found:

1. Equity share is influenced by the strategic importance of the R&D or marketing expenditures and product diversity (Stopford and Wells, 1972; Fagre and Wells, 1982).
2. The choice to enter by a joint venture is considered against other alternatives, and is influenced by the size of the targeted firm relative to that of the foreign firm, by the characteristics of the industry, and by the cultural characteristics of the foreign and home countries (Caves and Mehra, 1986; Kogut and Singh, 1986).
3. The responsibilities assigned to the joint venture are influenced by the capabilities of the foreign country and of both partners, in addition to possible conflict between the subsidiary and the foreign partner (Stopford and Wells, 1972; Hladik, 1985).

7. A Digression on Joint Venture Instability

The international business literature has also addressed the issue of instability. Beamish (1985) has recently summarized the findings of several studies regarding instability. My own findings have been added, and are given along with his summary in Table 2. Some care must be given in comparing the studies. Several authors have defined instability in terms of attitudinal data; others have looked at the dissolution of the venture; and still others have looked at dissolution, acquisition, or any change in ownership. A more complex obstacle to making a comparison is that one of the most potent causes of instability is the age of the venture; there is no correction for age differences of the ventures in the table.

Table 2. Summary of Results on Instability of Joint Ventures

Sample Size	Development Level of Country	Unstable* (%)	Unsatisfactory
1100	Primarily developed (DC)—Franko (1971)	24.1†	NA
36	Developed (DC)—Killing (1982, 1983)	30‡	36
168	Mixed (DC and LDC)—Janger (1980)	NA	37
60	Mixed (DC and LDC)—Stuckey (1983)	42‡	NA
66	Developing—Beamish (1985)	45‡	61
52	Developing—Reynolds (1984)	50	NA
149	United States—Kogut	46.3†	NA

* Franko defined a joint venture as unstable where the holdings of the MNE crossed the 50 percent or 95 percent ownership lines, the interests of the MNE were sold, or the venture was liquidated.

† Includes dissolutions and acquisitions. If major reorganizations added, instability is 28.3 percent and 51.7 percent for the Franko and Kogut samples, respectively.

‡ Includes major reorganizations.

Source: Table is adapted (with alterations) from Beamish (1985). Calculations of Kogut are from unpublished data.

Nevertheless, the table is of interest in providing some idea of the significance of instability. Based on this table, Beamish concluded that instability rates of joint ventures in less developed countries are significantly higher, even after correcting for the higher incidence of joint ventures with governments in LDCs which show the greatest rates of instability. The data from the study by Kogut (1987) show instability rates for domestic and international joint ventures in the United States to be roughly equivalent to those for LDCs in Beamish's study. At this time, therefore, it is premature to conclude whether joint venture instability varies across regions, especially in the absence of correcting for age.

Several explanations for joint venture termination have been offered. One destabilizing source is conflict between the parents and the joint venture. Stopford and Wells (1972), Franko (1971), and Holton (1981) discuss the trade-off between autonomy and parental control, and conclude that the conflict increases with the degree of coordination desired by the parents with their other operations. In summarizing his interesting work on control in joint ventures, Schaan (1985) concludes that satisfactory performance is more likely to the degree to which parents fit control mechanisms to their criteria for success, presumably because otherwise there is likely to be confusion over how each parent can exercise power to achieve its objectives without infringing upon its partner's authority.

There have been a few studies which have methodically examined stability rates in terms of the relationship of the parents.[16] Killing (1982, 1983) found that satisfactory performance was more prevalent in ventures with a dominant parent compared to those where control was shared. However, neither Janger

(1980) nor Beamish (1984) found any relationship between dominant control and satisfactory performance. Beamish (1984, 1985) qualifies Killing's conclusion by finding that foreign majority ownership is not common in LDCs, and that shared control reveals better performance.[17]

One problem with the above studies is the failure to correct for the age distribution of the ventures. Using a hazard rate methodology, Kogut (1987) looked at the influence of cooperative and competitive incentives on instability while incorporating the age distribution directly into the estimation. The results showed that the health of the industry, the cooperative incentives among the partners, and the degree of competitive rivalry influenced stability.

A final way to examine instability among joint ventures is to analyze changes in the environment of strategy. It stands to reason that if the incidence of joint venture is related to industry characteristics or strategies, then changes in the values of these parameters should affect survival rates. Franko (1971) examined instability of foreign ventures of American firms in terms of changes in strategy, as proxied by changes in the organizational structure of the firm. He found higher instability for organizations which had divided divisions into world regional areas. Since firms organized along areas tend towards product standardization and high marketing expenses, joint ventures would obstruct. Franko concludes, the coordination of international trans-shipments of standardized goods and the control over brand labels and advertising.

8. Conclusions

In comparing the theoretical and empirical results it is clear that studies have advanced further in testing strategic behavior explanations. Transaction cost and organizational knowledge explanations involve microanalytic detail which is difficult to acquire for one firm, not to mention for a cross-section of joint ventures. For this reason it is likely that case studies of industries or a few ventures will be the most appealing methodology to provide initial insight into transaction cost and transfer of organizational knowhow motivations. Less difficult, but still formidable, will be the analysis of joint venture formation and stability in terms of the strategies of the parents. It is not surprising, therefore, that more headway has been made into the relationship of joint ventures to industry characteristics.

It should be expected that the theories and their derived hypotheses will fare differently depending on contextual factors and the type of research questions being pursued. A transaction cost explanation should fit reasonably well the choice of how to cooperate when the transaction has little effect on downstream competition. Strategic behavior explanations certainly provide a more informative framework for the investigation of how joint ventures affect the competitive position of the firm. Organizational learning should apply reasonably well to explain ventures in industries undergoing rapid structural change, whether due to emergent technologies which affect industry boundaries or the entry of new (and perhaps foreign) firms.[18]

There is the danger, however, that more profound reasons for the use of joint ventures may be obscured by focusing only on theoretical explanations for joint ventures at the cost of more substantive explanations. Two alternative views are worthy of attention. The first is a reformulation of strategic behavior but only writ large—namely, that joint ventures are a response of leading members of national oligopolies to coopt foreign entrants. It is easy to forget that interpenetration of firms from different national oligopolies is a relatively recent phenomenon. Some insight into the motives of joint ventures might be gained by comparing several of the recent pairings between international firms against the international cartel agreements in oil, steel, iron and other minerals in the 1920s and 1930s.

The coordination of international competition by joint ventures raises a second perspective on joint ventures as one expression of what Dimaggio and Powell (1983) see as the growing institutionalization of markets and the bureaucratic dominance of the economy. From this point of view, joint ventures are another mode by which markets are replaced by organizational coordination. In this sense, joint ventures are a means by which large corporations increase their organizational control through ties to smaller firms and to each other. In the need to develop a better understanding of the choice of joint ventures against other alternatives of transacting or effecting strategies, it would be a mistake to ignore the larger question of the role of joint ventures in the evolution of national institutional structures and international oligopolies.

Notes

1. Asset specificity is not a sufficient condition; uncertainty and frequency of the transactions are also necessary.
2. For a careful analysis of this problem, see Walker and Weber, 1984; for an analysis of the downstream choice of using a direct sales agent (employee) or representative, see Anderson and Schmittlein, 1984.
3. Subsequent to writing the earlier drafts of this paper, working papers by Hennart, and by Buckley and Casson (both forthcoming) came to my attention. The subsequent revisions have benefited from their work, though the substance of the argument has not changed.

4. It is frequently suggested that institutional choices can be linearly ordered from market to firm. Not only is this conceptually unfounded, but the interaction of asset specificity, uncertainty, and frequency is unlikely, to say the least, to result in a linear effect.
5. For an analysis of network externality, see Katz and Shapiro, 1985.
6. See Ordover and Willig, 1985: Friedman, Berg, and Duncan (1979) found, in fact, that firms which joint venture tend to lower R&D expenditures. Their findings, therefore, support the argument that research ventures substitute for internal development and are motivated by efficiency considerations.
7. Indeed, Gomes Casseres (1987) has found that joint venture waves exist and are difficult to predict by reasonable economic causes.
8. It could be argued that there is no more sustainable asset over which there is, to paraphrase Rumelt (1984), an uncertainty of imitation, than an organizationally embedded source of competitive advantage.
9. Teece (1982) makes a similar point in explaining the multi-product firm.
10. Harrigan (1985) provides an excellent description by which firms seek to benefit from technological 'bleedthrough'. For example, internal R&D facilities are sometimes created which parallel the joint venture and staff is then rotated back and forth from the parent and joint venture organizations.
11. The Pate data are for joint ventures only between American firms; the Kogut data are for joint ventures located only in the United States.
12. It is hard to evaluate the results of this paper because the authors move back and forth from multiple regression to bivariate and partial correlations without stating why one test is preferred, and report in one place concentration as significant even though it only tested at 0.15 (Pfeffer and Nowak, 1976*:* 415).
13. Berg and Friedman (1981) and Duncan (1982) employed industry rates of return, which can be argued to be a good measure of the public good characteristic of collusion but is a poor measure of the efficiency implications of joint ventures and for competitive rivalry within industry.
14. It is unclear from the data whether this is the result of treating only greenfield as wholly-owned or jointly controlled.
15. Franko (1976) had shown that Europeans have a higher frequency for the use of joint ventures than American firms, and Wilson (1980) had found strong country patterns in his greenfield and acquisition study. Edstrom (1976) analyzed only Swedish joint ventures and acquisition.
16. This conflict is likely to be of a cultural nature as well, if the venture or subsidiary is overseas. See, for example, Peterson and Shimada (1978) and Wright (1979).
17. Both Killing's and Beamish's results await confirmatory statistical tests. Beamish has provided some tests in his thesis. See Beamish, 1984: 51–2 for the main results.
18. For speculations along these lines, see Westney, forthcoming.

References

Anderson, E. and Schmittlein, D. 'Integration of the sales force: an empirical examination', *Rand Journal of Economics*, 1984, pp. 385–395.

Beamish, P. M. 'Joint venture performance in developing countries'. Unpublished doctoral dissertation, University of Ontario, 1984.

—— 'The characteristics of joint ventures in developed and developing countries', *Columbia Journal of World Business*, 1985, pp. 13–19.

Berg, S. and Friedman, P. 'Joint ventures, competition and technological complementaries', *Southern Economic Journal*, 1977, pp. 1330–1337.

—— —— 'Joint ventures in American industry: an overview', *Mergers and Acquisitions*, **13**, 1978a, pp. 28–41.

—— —— 'Joint ventures in American industry, Part II: Case studies of managerial policy', *Mergers and Acquisitions*, **13**, 1978b, pp. 9–17.

—— —— 'Technological complementarities and industrial patterns of JV activity, 1964–1965', *Industrial Organization Review*, **6**, 1978c, pp. 110–116.

—— —— 'Joint ventures in American industry, Part III: Public policy issues', *Mergers and Acquisitions*, **13**, 1979, pp. 18–29.

—— —— 'Causes and effects of joint venture activity', *Antitrust Bulletin*, **25**, 1980, pp. 143–168.

—— —— 'Impacts of domestic joint ventures on industrial rates of return: a pooled cross-section analysis', *Review of Economics and Statistics*, **63**, 1981, pp. 293–298.

Boyle, S. E. 'The joint subsidiary: an economic appraisal', *Antitrust Bulletin*, 1963, pp. 303–318.

—— 'Estimate of the number and size distribution of domestic joint subsidiaries', *Antitrust Law and Economics Review*, **1**, 1968, pp. 81–92.

Buckley, P. and Casson, M. 'A theory of cooperation in international business', in Contractor, F. and Lorange, P. (eds), *Cooperative Strategies in International Business*, Lexington Books, Lexington, MA, forthcoming.

Caves, E. and Mehra, K. 'Entry of foreign multinationals into U.S. manufacturing industries', in Porter, M. E. (ed.), *Competition in Global Industries*, Harvard Business School Press, Boston, MA, 1986.

Dimaggio, J. and Powell, W. 'The iron cage revisited: institutional isomorphism and collective rationality in organizational fields', *American Sociological Review*, **48**, 1983, pp. 147–160.

Duncan, L. 'Impacts of new entry and horizontal joint ventures on industrial rates of return', *Review of Economics and Statistics*, **64**, 1982, pp. 120–125.

Edstrom, A. 'Acquisition and joint venture behavior of Swedish manufacturing firms', *Scandinavian Journal of Economics*, 1976, pp. 477–490.

Fagre, N. and Wells, L. 'Bargaining power of multinationals and host government', *Journal of International Business Studies*, Fall 1982, pp. 9–23.

Franko, L. G. *Joint Venture Survival in Multinational Corporations*, Praeger, New York, 1971.

—— *The European Multinationals*, Harper & Row, London, 1976.

Friedman, P., Berg, S. V., and Duncan, J. 'External vs. internal knowledge acquisition: JV activity and and R&D intensity', *Journal of Economics and Business*, **31**, 1979, pp. 103–110.

Friedman, W. and Kalmanoff, G. *Joint International Business Ventures*, Columbia University Press, New York, 1961.

Fusfeld, D. 'Joint subsidiaries in the iron and steel industry', *American Economic Review*, **48**, 1958, pp. 578–587.

Gomes-Casseres, B. 'Multinational Ownership Strategies'. Unpublished DBA thesis, Harvard Business School, 1985.

—— 'Evolution of ownership strategies of U.S. MNEs', in Contractor, F. and Lorange, P. (eds), *Cooperative Strategies in International Business*, Lexington Books, Lexington, MA, forthcoming.
Harrigan, K. R. *Strategies for Joint Ventures*, Lexington Books, Lexington, MA, 1985.
—— *Managing for Joint Venture Success*, Lexington Books, Lexington, MA, 1986.
Hennart, J. F. 'A transaction cost theory of equity joint ventures', *Strategic Management Journal*, forthcoming.
Hladik, K. J. *International Joint Ventures: An Economic Analysis of U.S. Foreign Business Partnerships*. Lexington Books, Lexington, MA, 1985.
Holton, R. E. 'Making international JVs work', Otterbeck, L. (ed.), in *Management of Headquarters-Subsidiary Relationships in Multinational Corporations*, St. Martins Press, New York, 1981.
Janger, A. H. *Organizations of International Joint Ventures*, Conference Board Report 87, New York, 1980.
Katz, M. L. and Shapiro, C. 'Network externalities, competition, and compatibility', *American Economic Review*, **75**, 1985, pp. 424–40.
Killing, J. 'How to make a global joint venture work', *Harvard Business Review*, **60**, 1982, pp. 120–127.
—— *Strategies for Joint Venture Success*, Praeger, New York, 1983.
Kogut, B. 'Competitive rivalry and the stability of joint ventures', Reginald H. Jones Working Paper, Wharton School, 1987.
Kogut, B. and Singh, H. 'Entering the United States by acquisition or joint venture, country patterns and cultural characteristics', Reginald H. Jones, Working Paper, Wharton School, 1986.
McConnell, J. and Nantell, J. 'Common stock returns and corporate combinations: the case of joint ventures', *Journal of Finance*, **40**, 1985, pp. 519–536.
McKelvey, B. *Organizational Systematics: Taxonomy, Evolution, Classification*, University of California, Berkeley, 1983.
Mead, W. J. 'Competitive significance of joint ventures', *Antitrust Bulletin*, 1967.
Nelson, R. and Winter, S. *An Evolutinary Theory of Economic Change*, Harvard University Press, Cambridge, MA, 1982.
Ordover, J. A. and Willig, R. D. 'Antitrust for high-technology industries: assessing research joint ventures and mergers', *Journal of Law and Economics*, **28**, 1985, pp. 311–343.
Pate, J. L. 'Joint venture activity, 1960–1968', *Economic Review*. Federal Research Bank of Cleveland, 1969, pp. 16–23.
Peterson, R. B. and Shimada, J. Y. 'Sources of management problems in Japanese–American joint ventures', *Academy of Management Review*, **3**, 1978, pp. 796–804.
Pfeffer, J. and Nowak, P. 'Joint ventures and interorganizational interdependence', *Administrative Science Quarterly*, **21**, 1976a, pp. 398–418.
—— —— 'Patterns of joint venture activity: implications for anti-trust research', *Antitrust Bulletin*, **21**, 1976b, pp. 315–339.
Polanyi, M. *The Tacit Dimension*, Doubleday, New York, 1967.
Reynolds, J. I. 'The "pinched shoe" effect on international joint ventures'. *Columbia Journal of World Business*, **19**, 1984, pp. 23–29.
Rumelt, R. 'Towards a strategic theory of the firm', in Lamb, R. B. (ed.), *Competitive Strategic Management*, Prentice Hall, New Jersey, 1984.

Schaan, J. L. 'Managing the parent control in joint ventures'. Paper presented at the Fifth Annual Strategic Management Society Conference, Barcelona, Spain, 1985.

Stopford, M. and Wells, L. *Managing the Multinational Enterprise*, Basic Books, New York, 1972.

Stuckey, A. *Vertical Integration and Joint Ventures in the Aluminum Industry*. Harvard University Press, Cambridge, MA, 1983.

Teece, D. 'Technology transfer by multinational firms', *Economic Journal*, **87**, 1977, pp. 242–261.

—— 'Towards an economic theory of the multiproduct firm', *Journal of Economic Behavior and Organization*, **3**, 1982, pp. 39–63.

Thompson, D. *Organizations in Action*, McGraw Hill, New York, 1967.

Tomlinson, J. W. L. *The Joint Venture Process in International Business*, MIT Press, Cambridge, MA, 1970.

Vernon, R. 'Organizational and institutional reponses to international risk', in Herring, R. (ed.), *Managing International Risk*. Cambridge University Press, New York, 1983.

Vickers, J. 'Pre-emptive patenting, joint ventures, and the persistence of oligopoly', *International Journal of Industrial Organization*, **3**, 1985, pp. 261–273.

Walker, G. and Weber, D. 'A transaction cost approach to make or buy decisions', *Administrative Science Quarterly*, **29**, 1984, pp. 373–391.

Westney, E. 'Domestic and foreign learning curves in managing international cooperative strategies', in Contractor, F. and Lorange, P. (eds), *Cooperative Strategies in International Business*, Lexington Books, Lexington, MA, forthcoming.

Williamson, O. E. *Markets and Hierarchies: Analysis and Antitrust Implications*, Basic Books, New York, 1975.

—— 'The economics of organization: the transaction cost approach', *American Journal of Sociology*, **87**, 1981, pp. 548–577.

—— *The Economic Institutions of Capitalism*, Free Press, New York, 1985.

Wilson, B. 'The propensity of multinational companies to expand through acquisitions', *Journal of International Business Studies*, **12**, 1980, pp. 59–65.

Wright, R. W. 'Joint venture problems in Japan', *Columbia Journal of World Business*, **14**, 1979, pp. 25–30.

3 International Joint Ventures

Arvind Parkhe

Back in 1966, General Motors Corporation boldly declared in its annual report that "Unified ownership for coordinated policy control of all of our operations throughout the world is essential for our effective performance as a worldwide corporation." That was then. Today, virtually all companies, including former corporate loners such as GM, are forsaking their emphasis on unified ownership in favor of joint ventures, which represent combined ownership and shared control. With the growing globalization of business, such joint ventures are often international in scope. The trend toward international joint ventures, already conspicuous during the 1980s (Hergert and Morris, 1988), further accelerated during the 1990s. Cross-border transactions, mainly international joint ventures, reached record levels in 1993, climbing by almost 20% from 1992 and three times from 1990 levels (Knecht, 1994).

In the wake of this rapid growth, research on the topic of joint ventures (JVs) has also grown exponentially in recent years. The purpose of this chapter is to briefly assess the past achievements, present status, and future opportunities for JV research. Toward this end, the chapter outline reflects the following structure. First, the place and role of JVs is examined against the broader backdrop of global business. Next, the core theoretical dimensions of existing JV research are identified, and the typical methodologies employed in empirical research are critically evaluated. Based on this assessment, significant conceptual and methodological gaps in the JV literature are noted. The gaps, in turn, suggest promising prospects for future research. The chapter concludes with general observations of potential interest for scholars doing—or contemplating—research in JVs.

1. Joint Ventures in the Context of Global Business

The global business environment is in unprecedented turmoil. This turmoil is fueled by factors at various analytical levels, including converging consumer tastes, escalating fixed costs, and growing protectionism (Ohmae, 1989), shortening product lifecycles and accelerating the pace of technological change (Harrigan, 1988), and improved information and communication capacity (Auster, 1987). Companies competing in this environment often find that they do not possess the wherewithal to "go it alone," and even if they did, they do not wish to individually undertake the high costs and risks essential to pursue technologies and products/markets with uncertain payoffs.

It is in this context that JVs emerge as a preferred mode of organizational structure. A joint venture may be defined as "a cooperative business activity formed by two or more separate organizations...that creates an independent business entity and allocates ownership, operational responsibilities, and financial risks and rewards to each member, while preserving their separate identity/autonomy" (Lynch, 1989, 7). It is considered to be an international joint venture if at least one parent is headquartered outside the venture's country of operation or if the JV has a significant level of operation in more than one country (Geringer and Hebert, 1989).

As Wille (1988) noted, the selection of a joint command structure represented by joint ventures is hardly a novel phenomenon. Early nation-states often cooperated as a means of countering external threats to their sovereignty that exceeded their individual resources and capabilities. Similarly, modern multinational companies are increasingly serving foreign markets via JVs rather than the organizational alternatives, which include foreign direct investment through wholly owned subsidiaries, licensing agreements, or exports. JVs may therefore be viewed as devices that are particularly well suited to the contemporary global business environment. JVs enable companies to accumulate market power (Wille 1988), to increase their organizational control (Kogut, 1988), in short, to enhance their competitiveness through cooperation (Bleeke and Ernst, 1993; Hamel, 1991; Parkhe, 1993b). Against this background, we review next the major streams of research emphasized in the JV literature.

2. Theoretical Underpinnings of Extant JV Research

Scores of books and more than 3,000 articles have been published on JVs (Anderson, 1990). Although this massive body of work has added rich insights into our understanding of various aspects of JVs, as Oliver observed, "The study of interorganizational relationships (IORs) has begun to suffer the consequences of its own growth in importance. . . . We no longer know what we know about the formation of IORs" (1990, 241). She complained of a vast but highly fragmented literature on IORs.

In a preliminary attempt to overcome this fragmentation, and to organize the impressive theoretical advances made by prior studies into a coherent theoretical structure, Parkhe (1993a) extracted four interconnected theoretical dimensions that have received primary emphasis in the current JV literature. As shown in Fig. 1, these dimensions are motives for JV formation, partner selection/characteristics, control/conflict, and JV stability/performance. Figure 1 represents only one possible way to organize the theoretical underpinnings of extant JV research, and a large number of other attractive conceptualizations may be possible as well. However, as discussed later in this chapter, Fig. 1 offers the advantage that it permits each of these four dimensions to be effectively linked with core behavioral variables that leading scholars have argued to be at the heart of voluntary interfirm cooperation (cf. Buckley and Casson, 1988).

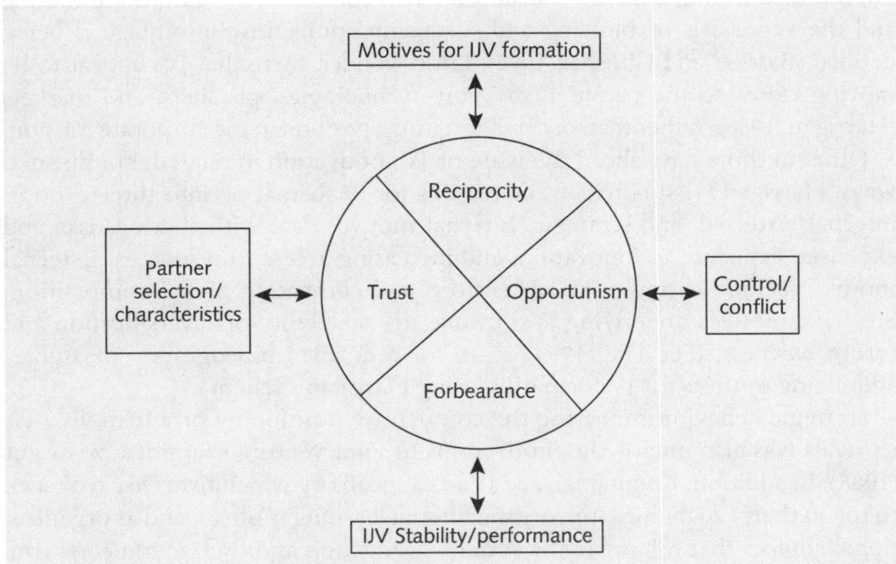

Fig. 1. An integrative framework for core IJV concepts.

Source: A. Parkhe (1993a), "'Messy' research, methodological predispositions, and theory development in international joint ventures." *Academy of Management Review*, p. 231.

2.1. Motives for JV Formation

A large number of studies have sought to shed light on a basic question about the JV phenomenon: Why joint ventures? In their chapter titled "Why should firms cooperate? The strategy and economics basis for cooperative ventures," Contractor and Lorange (1988) maintained that seven more or less overlapping objectives constitute the rationales for entering into cooperative ventures: (1) risk reduction, (2) economies of scale and/or rationalization, (3) technology exchanges, (4) coopting or blocking competition, (5) overcoming government-mandated trade or investment barriers, (6) facilitating initial international expansion of international firms, and (7) vertical quasi-integration advantages of linking the complementary contributions of the partners in a "value chain." It is clear that the reasons for forming JVs are manifold and reach into all areas of business strategy. These motivations can probably be distilled into three broad categories: resource-driven JVs, market-driven JVs, and risk-driven JVs (Wille, 1988).

The three categories are often interrelated, and modern JVs are distinguishable from their traditional counterparts by their straddling of multiple motivations, which suggests a more expansive scope of JV operations in worldwide corporate activities. For example, the focus now is on the creation of new products and technologies rather than the distribution of existing ones, and partnerships are often forged during industry transitions when competitive positions are shifting and the very basis of building and sustaining competitive advantage is being defined (Bartlett and Ghoshal, 1992). Little wonder, then, that JVs appear to be moving closer to the parent firms' core technologies, products, and markets (Harrigan, 1986), rather than occupying a fringe position in the corporate mission.

Other authors have sliced the issue of JV motivation in related, but distinct, ways. Harrigan (1985) divided the reasons for JV formation into three groups: internal, external, and strategic. Internal motives deal with sharing risks and expenses, exposure to innovation, and increasing access to resources. External motives include easing political tensions and combating global competition. Strategic motives underlying JVs involve the possibility of diversification and future business. (See Fey (1994, 25–6) for a detailed bibliography of studies addressing motives for JV formation using Harrigan's schema.)

Strategic behavior improving the competitive positioning of a firm vis-à-vis its rivals was also one of the motivations to joint venture examined by Kogut (1988). In addition, Kogut analyzed JVs as a means by which firms learn or seek to retain their capabilities (the organizational learning motive), and as organizational choices that minimize the sum of production and transaction costs (the transaction cost motive). The latter, drawing upon the work of Williamson (1975, 1985), has received especially widespread attention in JV research.

For instance, using the transaction cost paradigm, Stuckey (1983) studied the conditions under which JVs provide a superior means for firms pursuing international vertical integration, while Beamish and Banks (1987) examined the choice of JVs in the context of international horizontal diversification. Hennart (1988) took the thought further to propose a transaction costs theory of equity joint ventures and applied this theory to study Japanese subsidiaries in the United States (Hennart, 1991). The theory distinguishes between "scale" and "link" JVs. Scale JVs arise when parents seek to internalize a failing market, but indivisibilities due to scale or scope economies make full ownership of the relevant assets inefficient. Link JVs are motivated by the simultaneous failing of the markets for the services of two or more assets whenever these assets are firm-specific public goods, and acquisition of the firm owning them would entail significant management costs. Thus, Hennart (1988, 372) concluded, JVs represent a first-best strategy in a limited number of specific circumstances.

Finally, JV motivations must be viewed in light of their worldwide location, since they may vary in developed countries (DCs) and less developed countries (LDCs). Killing (1983) found that 64 percent of the JVs in his DC sample were created when each partner needed the other's skills. In Beamish's (1984) LDC sample, only 38 percent of the JVs were created for this reason. Nineteen percent of the JVs in DCs were created because one partner needed the other's attributes or assets; only 5 percent of the JVs in LDCs were created for this reason. And 17 percent of the JVs in the DC sample were created as a result of government suasion or legislation, whereas 57 percent of JVs in LDCs were created for this reason.

2.2. Partner Selection/Characteristics

A second identifiable stream of JV research deals with the choice of a JV partner that will enhance the likelihood of venture success. After all, as in marriage, JVs involve close interaction and interdependence (Parkhe, 1993b) between two parties making common cause when their interests run parallel to each other (Ohmae, 1989). Lane and Beamish (1990) go so far as to say that "Identifying and selecting a partner is possibly the most important consideration in establishing a cooperative venture," (p. 93) and yet, "As we talked with executives, we were amazed at how some partners were found. Some had been met 'fortuitously' at cocktail parties in Latin America or Trinidad, or in a hotel bar in Nigeria" (p. 95).

Aside from the often-neglected lesson about expending adequate efforts in finding the right partner, what does the JV literature reveal about partner selection? And what exactly constitutes "the right partner"? Several authors have suggested that partners should be complementary in the products, geographic presence, or functional skills that they bring to the venture (Bleeke and Ernst, 1993; Harrigan, 1985; Lynch, 1989). Harrigan found, for example, that JVs are more likely to succeed when partners possess complementary missions, resource capabilities, managerial capabilities, and other attributes that create a strategic fit in which the bargaining power of the venture's sponsors is evenly matched. Put another way, partners' needs to be engaged in a particular JV are stabilizing to the relationship, while a wide variety of asymmetries are destabilizing to the JV. However, complementary contributions and matching needs, while necessary, are not sufficient. As Beamish (1984, 1988) and others have emphasized, it is important to select a partner with whom trust already exists or can be established.

Although recognized as important, the notion of complementarity of partner contributions remained somewhat vague until the work of Geringer (1988, 1991). He separated task- and partner-related dimensions of partner selection criteria. Task-related criteria include factors associated with the operational skills and resources that a JV requires for its competitive success (e.g., financial resources, technical knowhow, access to distribution systems); partner-related criteria include factors associated with the efficiency and effectiveness of partners' cooperation (e.g., a partner's national or corporate culture, and trust between top management teams). Observed variations in the choice of criteria used to select JV partners, Geringer reasoned, may be attributable to differences in the strategic context of JVs and parent firms, that is, to the specific competitive circumstances confronting the proposed venture.

2.3. Control/Conflict Issues

2.3.1. Parent Control over JVs

A major dimension in the JV literature involves issues of control. Desire for control sometimes poses intractable problems in JVs, precisely because joint ventures are jointly managed. As Killing (1982, 121) noted, "The problems in managing JVs stem from one cause: there is more than one parent." The resulting control problems are described nicely by Ohmae: "A real alliance compromises the fundamental independence of economic actors, and managers don't like that. After all, for them, management has come to mean total control. Alliances mean sharing control. The one precludes the other" (p. 143, see also Hladik, 1989, 192).

Parent control over a JV's strategic direction may be strong, shared, or weak (Root, 1988). Strong control indicates that a firm can overrule other partners, shared control indicates that agreement between partners is necessary for major decisions, and weak control indicates that a firm has no particular influence on decisions. Other things being equal, a parent desires more control the greater a JV's strategic significance to the parent. More control may be gained through ownership (increasing equity share) or through bargaining power (making the JV more dependent on the parent's proprietary resources that are costly or impossible to replace) (Beamish, 1988; Franko, 1971; Geringer and Hebert, 1989;

Killing, 1982; Root, 1988; Stopford and Wells, 1972; Tomlinson, 1970). Schaan, (1983) extended this analysis by (1) recording the breadth of JV control mechanisms that exist and grouping them into positive and negative types and (2) by suggesting that control is often focused on critical dimensions of the JV, not on its overall operations.

2.3.2. Conflict in JVs

Another near-ubiquitous aspect of JVs is conflict (Parkhe, 1994; Rieger and Wong-Rieger, 1990). Conflict may arise primarily through two sources: interfirm diversity and actual or potential opportunism of JV partners. Together, these sources may help explain a significant proportion of the high failure rates observed in JVs (Business Week, 1986; Harrigan, 1986). Each source will be discussed in turn.

Parkhe (1991) proposed that cross-border JVs bring together partners who may differ in two important ways, each potentially triggering conflict. Type I diversity includes the familiar interfirm differences (interdependencies) that JVs are specifically created to exploit. These differences form the underlying strategic motivations for entering into JVs, as discussed earlier. Thus, Type I diversity deals with the reciprocal strengths and complementary resources furnished by the alliance partners, differences that actually facilitate formulation, development, and collaborative effectiveness of JVs. Type II diversity refers to differences in partner characteristics that often negatively affect the longevity and effective functioning of JVs. (This thesis found empirical support in Parkhe 1993c and is also reflected in Rieger and Wong-Rieger, 1990; Shenkar and Zeira, 1992.) Type II diversity may stem from sharp differences in collaborating firms' cultural and political bases, as well as in firm-specific characteristics that may be tied to each firm's national heritage. A typology of the major dimensions of Type II interfirm diversity would include societal culture (meta level of analysis), national context (macro), corporate culture (meso), strategic direction (meso), and management practices and organization (micro) (Parkhe, 1991). For each dimension, specific "sources of tension" may lead to conflict; however, proactive use of coping mechanisms can mitigate the impact of Type II diversity on alliance outcomes.

Over the life of the partnership, the dynamics of Types I and II are very different, since the two types are differentially impacted by the processes of organizational learning and adaptation. While such processes may tend to reduce Type II diversity and fortify a relationship, they may also reduce Type I diversity and destabilize a JV. For example, as shown in Fig. 2, learning through a JV may enable one partner to acquire the skills and technologies it lacked at the time of JV formation (Hamel, 1991). This partner may then enjoy a stronger bargaining hand, rewrite partnership terms more favorably to itself, or even discard the other partner and terminate the JV. Erosion of Type I diversity (point A, Fig. 2) removes the raison d'être of the alliance and reduces longevity.

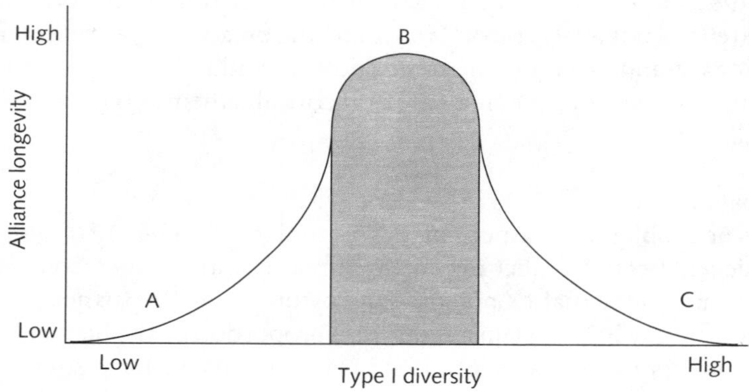

Fig. 2. Hypothesized curvilinear relationship between Type I interfirm diversity and alliance longevity.

Based on A. Parkhe (1991), "Interfirm diversity, organizational learning, and longevity in global strategic alliance," *Journal of International Business Studies*, 22: 579–601.

Contrariwise, extreme asymmetries in partner capabilities (point C) may create imbalances in contributions to the alliance, which are also destabilizing. As Heide (1994, 79) noted, "For dependence to promote bilateral governance, the dependence condition somehow must be symmetric. To the extent that dependence exists unilaterally in a given situation, it could actually undermine efforts to develop a bilateral pattern of interaction." As the shaded area (point B) shows, the greatest longevity may be expected when both partners continue to contribute effectively to the JV.

Another conflict-inducing factor is the prospect of opportunistic behavior by a JV partner. "Opportunism" is behavior by economic agents that involves "self-interest-seeking with guile" (Williamson, 1975, 26). The prospect of such behavior can never be ignored in JVs, not because all economic agents behave opportunistically all of the time, but because "some agents behave in this fashion and it is costly to sort out those who are opportunistic from those who are not" (Williamson and Ouchi, 1981, 351).

A rich body of literature has emerged from these fundamental considerations about voluntary interfirm cooperation. Scholars have recognized, for example, that: (1) JVs involve mutual interdependence, such that one is vulnerable to another whose behavior is not under one's control (Zand, 1972); (2) There is only partial overlap of goals of the cooperating parties (Ouchi, 1980); and (3) Each firm exercises only partial influence over the outcome of the JV. The relationship environment is therefore often marked by uncertainty and vulnerability to opportunism (Heide and John, 1988; John, 1984; Provan and Skinner, 1989).

Ex ante and ex post safeguards may be erected to defend against opportunism. Generically, such safeguards seek to alter a JV's payoff structure in order to reduce gains from cheating, increase gains from cooperation, or increase costs of agreement violations. In essence, the purpose is to promote robust cooperation by restructuring the JV and realigning partners' incentives. Important contributions in this area have come from game theory (Axelrod, 1984; Oye, 1986), transaction cost economics (Williamson, 1985), and contract law (Macneil, 1978). Parkhe (1993b) merged game theoretic insights with the logic of transaction cost economics in a generalized model and found empirical support for the model's predictions regarding alliance structuring.

Yet larger questions remain. The costs of safeguards can be reduced if the perception of opportunism can be lowered, and perception of opportunism can be lowered if trust develops between JV partners. In other words, trust can lubricate JVs and make JVs more efficient (inter)organizational modes. But what factors lead to the generation, growth, and destruction of trust? Can these factors be managed to accelerate what Zucker (1986) called "trust production"? As discussed later in this chapter, these are among the central questions in JV governance that await answers.

2.4. Stability/Performance Assessment

The final major dimension emphasized in extant research deals with JV outcomes (Parkhe, 1993a). It quickly becomes apparent that performance measurement is a complex and controversial topic even at the individual firm level. The problems are compounded in JVs, where multiple parents attempt to influence JV decisions, the true motivations of partners may be unknown to each other, and venture-specific data are seldom available.

Still, scholars have grappled with performance measurement issues, often by using "objective" measures. Objective measures include financial indicators (e.g., ROI, ROE, ROS), market share, JV survival, and JV duration (Franko, 1971; Geringer and Hebert, 1989, 1991; Harrigan, 1988; Kogut, 1988; Tomlinson, 1970). These measures are open to many criticisms, however. The first is that any single measure is too narrow. As Venkatraman and Ramanujam (1986) argued, the breadth of the construct of performance cannot be captured unless financial, operational, and effectiveness measures are combined. Second, in the absence of knowledge of the concrete goals and actual (not declared) motivations of parent firms, it is difficult to compare JV results against specific targets. Third, poor financial performance may be quite acceptable if a JV is not a profit center, but rather a source of learning that will synergistically contribute toward parent companies' overall competitiveness. Finally, JV survival and duration may be associated not with alliance success, but with high exit barriers.

Partly in response to these limitations, researchers began to use subtler criteria for assessing JV outcomes, such as fulfillment of major strategic needs (a JV can be said to be performing well when important strategic needs are being met very well) and indirect performance indicators (net spillover effects for parent firms, JV's profitability relative to its industry, and overall performance assessment by responsible parties) (Parkhe, 1993b). Overall performance assessment is, of course, a subjective measure, hence subject to the familiar drawbacks of bias and recall associated with such measures. However, such a multidimensional operationalization of performance, resting on distinct, crucial aspects of the JV phenomenon, may overcome some weaknesses of past performance measures (see Baird, Lyles, and Reger, 1993; Beamish, 1984; Inkpen, 1993).

Related to performance is the question of JV stability. What does stability mean, and what factors contribute to JV instability? Gomes-Casseres (1987), Kogut (1989), and Blodgett (1992) addressed these questions, taking into account JV survival and duration, but going beyond. For example, the significance of Gomes-Casseres' (1987) contribution lies in his insight to link JV outcomes to the ongoing operations of parent firms. He identified three types of instability: (1) A JV may be liquidated completely (i.e., its operation halted and its assets sold or scrapped); (2) A JV may be sold to the local partner or to outsiders, in which case it remains in operation, but under different ownership; (3) One parent may buy out the other's interest in a JV and create a wholly owned subsidiary. Thus viewed, instability does not always reflect poor performance, dissolution does not necessarily equal failure, and survival does not inevitably indicate success.

2.5. Integrating JV Research Streams

Four noteworthy streams in current JV research were discussed above. However, it should be strongly emphasized that these streams represent inextricably interlinked processes, not surgically separable phenomena. For example, the choice and availability of capable, trustworthy partners will favorably influence the selection of a JV mode of organizational structure, reduce control/conflict problems, and improve stability/performance levels. Indeed, as discussed shortly, there is a need to focus on such (invisible) management decision-making processes, not merely on the (visible) outcomes of those processes. As Wood and Gray (1991, 143) observed, most studies "leap from preconditions to outcomes, leaving us with a 'black box' to cover the area in between." As such, Parkhe (1993a) proposed that one way to accelerate JV theory development would be to focus research on the concepts of trust, reciprocity, opportunism, and forbearance, as shown at the center of Fig. 1. In their provocative essay on "A theory of cooperation in international business,"

Buckley and Casson (1988, 32) noted that the essence of voluntary interfirm cooperation lies in "coordination effected through mutual forbearance." Forbearance becomes possible only when there is reciprocal behavior (Axelrod, 1984) and mutual trust (Thorelli, 1986), which, in turn, only come about given an absence of opportunism (Williamson, 1985).

Despite being at the "core" of JVs, these concepts are often ignored. Integrating past research and raising the level of JV theory development will require greater attention to these core concepts in the future.

Another way to unlock the "black box" and to gain a greater understanding of processes is to view the entire lifecycle of JVs starting from initial introspection at parent firms up to final JV outcomes. Figure 3 shows a detailed lifecycle stage model of JVs, and organizes prior studies that have addressed process issues into the various stages. Not included among the prior studies is an excellent process model of JV formation developed by Tallman and Shenkar (1994, 101), which, in Fig. 3 terms, only goes up to the "JV initiation" stage.

Finally, JV lifecycle processes are not sequential and linear, but rather iterative and circular. Continuous feedback among the various stages of Fig. 3 (Ring and Van de Ven, 1994) matches partner behaviors, JV outcomes, and external environmental events to parents' JV objectives to help form decisions about future actions.

3. Methodological Orientations

The current body of JV research has been lauded for containing "many studies addressing diverse aspects of JVs in theoretically imaginative and methodologically sound ways" (Parkhe, 1993a, 232). However, as in international management research and as in management research generally (Bettis, 1991), JV studies tend to overemphasize certain methodological approaches at the expense of others. As Bettis observed, "Current norms of the field seem strongly biased toward large sample multivariate statistical studies. This leads to a large database mentality, in which large-scale mail surveys and ready-made databases such as Compustat, CRSP, and PIMS are often favored.... Qualitative studies do appear in the journals but they are the exception"(1991, 316). Such a bias is reflected by a representative sample of JV empirical studies (1987–94) in Table 1.

Inasmuch as the content and process of scientific inquiry are intertwined, this bias creates a mismatch: Large-scale mail surveys and ready-made databases are unlikely to capture the "soft" core concepts outlined in Fig. 1. In other

<table>
<tr><th>Prior Studies</th><th>Introspection and internal audit[a]</th><th>Partner scanning</th><th>Pre-contractual negotiations</th><th>Courtship</th><th>Partner selection</th><th>Contractual negotiations</th><th>Formal contract design[b]</th><th>Informal role specification[c]</th><th>JV initiation</th><th>JV implementation/ partner monitoring</th><th>Organizational learning/adaption</th><th>JV outcome (success)[d]</th><th>JV outcome (failure)[e]</th></tr>
<tr><td>Heide (1994)</td><td colspan="9">Relationship initiation</td><td colspan="2">Relationship maintenance</td><td colspan="2">Relationship termination</td></tr>
<tr><td>Lyles and Rajadhyax (1988)</td><td colspan="2">Motivations</td><td colspan="4">Negotiation</td><td colspan="5">Operation</td><td colspan="2">Results</td></tr>
<tr><td>Raben (1992)</td><td colspan="4">Assessment</td><td colspan="4">Planning and design</td><td colspan="2">Implementation</td><td colspan="3">Development</td></tr>
<tr><td>Wood and Gray (1991)</td><td>Pre-conditions</td><td colspan="10">Process</td><td colspan="2">Outcomes</td></tr>
</table>

Fig. 3. Lifecycle stages of JVs: A fine-grained perspective.

a. This involves soul-searching about alternate paths to achieve corporate development: internal growth or external growth. The former, also described as internal development, or "go-it-alone" strategy, is often rejected due to high risks, costs, and time requirements. The latter includes choosing among mergers, acquisitions, JVs, and arm's-length contractual arrangements.

b. Major issues in formal contract design include ownership, control, specific assets and hostages, performance measurement, and enforcement.

c. Informal role specification includes interpersonal chemistry between boundary spanners, as well as implicit understandings regarding adjustment to performance deviations and unanticipated events.

d. Successful JV outcomes include planned termination, escalation of commitment, acquisition, or additional JVs.

f. Failure generally leads to unplanned termination of the cooperative relationship.

Table 1. Recent Examples of IJV Empirical Studies: 1987–1994

	Conceptual Focus		Methodological Focus	
Study	Research Problem	Primary Dimension in Fig. 1	Major Data Sources	Data Analytic Technique
Beamish and Banks (1987)	Why IJVs may be preferred over wholly owned subsidiaries	Motives for IJV formation	Questionnaires	Nonparametric analysis
Blodgett (1991)	Ownership patterns associated with partner expertise	Partner characteristics	Secondary data	Chi square
Blodgett (1992)	Contract renegotiation probability as a function of equity share, prior renegotiation, and openness of economic system	IJV stability	Secondary data	Event history analysis (Cox proportional hazards model)
Franko (1989)	Use of minority and 50–50 IJVs as a function of host country policies and corporate strategies	Motives for IJV stability	Secondary data	Correlation and regression analysis
Geringer (1991)	Determinants of criteria for selecting complementary partners	Partner selection	Questionnaires	Kendall's tau-b, stepwise regression analysis
Geringer and Hebert (1991)	Comparability and reliability of objective and subjective measures of performance	IJV performance	Questionnaires	Spearman rank-order correlation coefficient
Gomes-Casseres (1987)	Factors behind MNEs' choice of IJV vs. wholly owned subsidiary	Motives for IJV formation	Secondary data	Binomial logit analysis
Heide (1994)	Interorganizational governance in marketing channels	Control/conflict	Questionnaires	Ordinary least squares regression
Hennart (1991)	Transaction cost choice between full and partial ownership	Motives for IJV formation	Secondary data	Binominal logistic regression analysis
Kogut (1989)	Survival as a function of reciprocity and of competitive rivalry	IJV stability	Questionnaires and secondary data	Termination hazard partial likelihood model
Parke (1993c)	Variation in structure–performance relationship by partner nationality	Partner characteristics	Questionnaires	Canonical correlation analysis
Provan and Skinner (1989)	Interorganizational dependence and controls as predictors of opportunism	Control/conflict	Questionnaires	Multiple regression analysis
Shenkar and Zeira (1992)	Organizational and personal correlates of CEO's role conflict and role ambiguity	Control/conflict	Questionnaires	Tobit maximum likelihood model
Zaheer and Venkatraman (1993)	Structural and processual dimensions of relational governance	Control/conflict	Questionnaires	Hierarchical regression analysis

The sheer volume of IJV literature precludes an encyclopedic listing, even of recently published studies. Nonetheless, the studies shown are symptomatic of the recent research in the field, which leans toward deductive, quantitative testing of hypotheses.

words, (a) major gaps exist in the literature regarding crucial, invisible JV management processes, (b) addressing these gaps will require a significant reorientation in conceptual foci (from the rectangles to the inner circle of Fig. 1), and (c) this reorientation, in turn, will require the use of appropriate empirical research methods. These methods must be sufficiently powerful and rigorous in generating valid, reliable data that further our understanding of trust, reciprocity, opportunism, and forbearance.

One such method is case studies. In a departure from number-crunching studies, a case study would permit researchers to "get close to the action" of the various lifecycle stages of JVs (Fig. 3), for example, through open-ended interviews with top management and persons directly involved in the JV, attendance at select executive meetings, and even quantitative data from questionnaires (a survey embedded within a case study) (Yin, 1984). In the interviews, key actors are asked about the facts of the JV, in addition to the respondents' opinions and insights about the events (Eisenhardt, 1989; Yin, 1984). (Mail surveys and secondary data typically sacrifice this richness and subtlety of understanding because in them there is little opportunity for clarification of questions or elaboration of answers.) Such interviews can be extremely fruitful, because interviewees can provide crucial insights, suggest sources of corroboratory evidence, and initiate access to such sources.

However, interviews can be subject to problems of bias, poor recall, and poor or inaccurate articulation (Yin, 1984). Therefore, in order to test for convergence, the interview evidence must be triangulated with multiple data sources. These include archival records and documentation. Archival corroboration involves cross-reference to databases, news clippings, and other reports in the mass media. Documentation research involves the systematic collection and examination of relevant company records and documents, including particularly the proposal, formal studies, and progress reports regarding the JV.

The data thus obtained lend themselves to systematic and rigorous data analytic techniques, such as explanation building, pattern matching, and time-series analysis (Miles and Huberman, 1984; Yin, 1984). Parkhe (1993a, 249–51) showed that each technique is especially well suited for answering specific, probing research questions about "fuzzy" JV management processes that have remained shielded from scientific inquiry.

Notwithstanding the unique potential of case studies for rigorous JV theory advancement, no single methodological approach (including case studies) is self-sufficient and capable of producing a well-rounded theory that simultaneously maximizes the research quality criteria of construct validity, internal validity, external validity, and reliability. Since seemingly diverse approaches (such as inductive/deductive, theory generation/theory testing, and qualitative/quantitative) complement and reinforce each other, once the "soft" core concepts become better understood via case studies, the unique strengths of the other approaches should be exploited by undertaking studies that draw upon the emergent grounded theory from case studies, but go further.

A good example of triangulation of data obtained using multiple data sources and multiple methodological approaches is found in Beamish (1988). His study on JVs in developing countries used case research on a set of 12 "comparative core cases," personal interviews, and questionnaires. The questionnaire findings lent themselves to nonparametric statistical analysis, and this analysis was supplemented by interview data. A further strength of the research design of this study is that data were collected from the JV general manager, the MNE partner, and the local partner. Soliciting information from each major player in the JV provides a more balanced picture of JV operation and enhances confidence in the research findings. Future researchers should attempt to emulate this feature of the Beamish study, although, admittedly, doing so would increase the resource commitment to the project, particularly for international joint ventures.

Other innovative ways exist to research the complex phenomenon of JVs. For example, Larsson (1993) sought to combine the benefits of idiographic case studies and nomothetic surveys through the "case survey methodology." This approach conducts quantitative analysis of patterns across case studies, to produce generalizable, cross-sectional analysis and in-depth, processual analysis. Given the discussion above about the need for merging rich insights from case studies with the unique strengths of other approaches, the case survey methodology may occupy an especially important place in future JV research.

Finally, Ring and Van de Ven (1994) proposed longitudinal research that tracks a set of JVs in their natural field settings from beginning to end. The actions and interactions of all parties are recorded as they repeatedly negotiate, make commitments, and execute these commitments in both formal and informal ways over time. These authors recommend using events as the units of observation, where events are "critical incidents when parties engage in actions related to the development of their relationship" (1994, 112). The use of an event as the unit of observation, it is suggested, permits researchers to focus simultaneously on both organizational and individual units of analysis.

4. Future Research Opportunities

JVs represent a fertile area for timely, exciting research questions on a topic of growing importance. Some of the prospects and problems were touched upon earlier. For example, although trust is alleged to be a central concept in JVs (Thorelli, 1986), it remains poorly understood (Parkhe, 1993a) in terms of its conceptual domain, antecedents, and consequences. Methodologically,

JV-specific data are often unavailable, since companies tend to report consolidated company-wide data; in addition it is desirable to view the entire lifecycle of JVs as a series of interconnected stages, rather than studying isolated elements.

These observations share a common thread. They are symptomatic of the need for a renewed focus on invisible management processes, a shift that must be accompanied by a reorientation in research designs. Three areas appear to be especially ripe for deeper theoretical insights: choice of organizational structure, alliance structure design, and dynamic evolution of the cooperative relationship. Following are sample research questions that would break important new ground:

- *Choice of organizational structure:* How are the alternative organizational structures evaluated (weighting system for comparing pros and cons of competing structures), and why is the JV mode of organization chosen (perceived ability of the JV to uniquely satisfy important strategic needs of the firm)?
- *Alliance structure design:* How do companies assess (a) likely partners' motivation and ability to live up to their commitments (and how significant are reputation effects in this assessment)? (b) potential areas for opportunism due to overlapping product or geographic market interests? and (c) the "appropriate" JV structure to provide ex ante and ex post incentives that promote robust cooperation?
- *Dynamic evolution:* (a) How does a growing collaborative history (number, duration, and intensity of working partnerships) modify the fear of opportunism, level of trust, and therefore the structuring of the JV? (b) What deliberate steps do companies take to install mechanisms for recognition, verification, and signaling designed to increase behavior transparency and thus accelerate the modification outlined in (a)?

Another intriguing aspect for future JV research is the question of causality. Does trust lead to cooperation or vice versa? Does a long "shadow of the future" (Axelrod, 1984) result in high performance, or does high performance result in a lengthening shadow of the future? The few studies attempting disentanglement of causal direction and feedback loops offer mixed views. For instance, Anderson and Narus (1990) obtained a better explanation of construct covariances through a respecification of their model, in which cooperation was causally antecedent, rather than consequent, to trust. Conversely, Smith and Aldrich suggested that "perhaps the development of a trusting relation actually precedes substantial investments in specific assets, or perhaps asset specificity and trust are inextricably bound up in a reciprocal relationship" (1991, 31). Future research could significantly raise the level of theory development by going beyond correlational analyses that are emphasized in current research, to path analysis and causal modeling that may permit a deeper understanding of the causal structure of relationships among central variables in interfirm cooperation.

The research questions above are part of a larger mosaic of JV theory development, which may best be appreciated by taking a meta perspective of the field. This perspective should integrate (1) diverse but related theoretical approaches that bear upon the JV phenomenon; (2) the range of research designs that can (and should) be selectively employed in future research; and (3) the levels of analysis that must be systematically studied and integrated. Figure 4 attempts to provide such a meta perspective.

Some cells in Fig. 4 (e.g., surveys of individual managers using the strategic behavior approach) are overdeveloped, while other, potentially fruitful cells

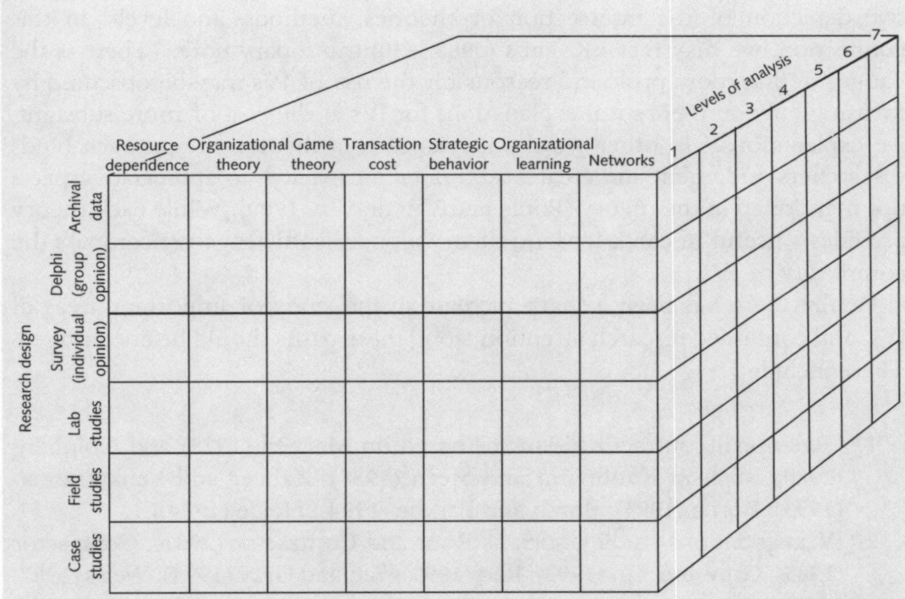

Fig. 4. A menu for JV research: effective intersection of theories, methods, and levels.

Levels of Analysis
1: Individual manager (JV).
2: Individual managers (parent firms).
3: Organizational (JV).
4: Organizational (parent firms).
5: Interorganizational (dyadic relationships between parents, between JV and parents).
6: Network (JV embedded in surrounding industry structure).
7: Multilevel (simultaneously individual, organizational, network levels).

(e.g., multilevel case studies using the organizational learning perspective) are underdeveloped. Kogut observed that

> *... studies have advanced further in testing strategic behavior explanations. Transaction cost and organizational knowledge explanations involve micro-analytic detail which is difficult to acquire for one firm, not to mention for a cross-section of JVs. For this reason it is likely* that case studies of industries or a few ventures will be the most appealing methodology to provide initial insight *into transaction cost and transfer of organizational know how motivations. Less difficult, but still formidable, will be the analysis of JV formation and stability in terms of the strategies of the parents" (1988, 329–30, emphasis added).*

Clearly, certain methods are more compatible with particular theoretical approaches (e.g., case studies with organizational learning), than others (e.g., surveys with transaction cost), and hence the potential value of Fig. 4 lies not in equal emphasis being placed on every cell, but only in its suggestive depiction of the intersection of theories, methods, and levels. In this connection, we may recall Kogut's (1988, 330) cautionary note: "There is the danger... that more profound reasons for the use of JVs may be obscured by focusing only on theoretical explanations for JVs at the cost of more substantive explanations." In other words, allegiance to a theoretical approach binds researchers' judgment and creates a "trained incapacity" to appreciate aspects not mentioned in the theory (Poole and Van de Ven, 1989). While each theory provides a useful research lens, no theory alone is sufficient to encompass the complexity of JVs.

Finally, there has been a sharp increase in the study of important areas of JVs, and continued research attention along these paths should be encouraged. These include:

1. "Relational contracting" studies based on Macneil (1978) and Goldberg (1980), such as Kaufmann and Stern (1988); Zaheer and Venkatraman (1993); Borch (1994); Borch and Parkhe (1994); Heide (1994).
2. JV negotiations studies, such as Root and Contractor (1981); Contractor (1985); Gray and Yan (1992); Rao (1993); Yan and Gray (1994); Weiss (1987, 1995).
3. Organizational learning studies, such as Lyles (1988); Westney (1988); Kogut (1988); Hamel (1991); Parkhe (1991); Simonin and Helleloid (1993).

Each of the topics above offers promising research opportunities, particularly if the topic can be reintegrated with broader issues in JV management. This may be done, for example, by linking future studies to certain JV core concepts (Fig. 1) or to lifecycle stages of JVs (Fig. 3).

4. Conclusion

This chapter's brief review of the past, present, and future of JV research suggests that this body of work has evolved tremendously since the pioneering work of Friedman and Kalmanoff (1961). Although a great deal has been learned, much important work lies ahead.

JVs are complex, mixed-motive (competitive + cooperative) relationships. Research on JVs has tended to gravitate toward four major topics: motives for JV formation, partner selection/characteristics, control/conflict, and JV stability/performance. While each topic is individually important, there has been little effort to reintegrate the insights into a higher-order theory of JVs.

The lack of such effort is perhaps understandable, given the dominant methodological focus of current research (Table 1), which leans toward "hard," quantitative approaches. The need for the next phase of JV research is for developing deeper understanding of invisible management processes, which involve crucial, "soft" variables (Fig. 1). Consequently, a methodological reorientation of future studies may be in order. Such reorientation would build upon the lessons from prior research and would permit theories of JV processes to catch up with theories of JV outcomes. As JVs continue their powerful sweep across the global business landscape, JV research will likely become even more timely and relevant to the study of international management.

Bibliography

Anderson, E. 1990. Two firms, one frontier: On assessing joint venture performance. *Sloan Management Review* 32: 19–30.

Anderson, J. C. and Narus, J. A. 1990. A model of distributor firm and manufacturer firm working partnerships. *Journal of Marketing* 54: 42–58.

Auster, E. R. 1987. International corporate linkages: Dynamic forms in changing environments. *Columbia Journal of World Business* (Summer): 3–6.

Axelrod, R. 1984. *The Evolution of Cooperation*. New York: Basic Books.

Baird, I. S., Lyles, M. A., and Reger, R. K. 1993. Evaluation of interorganizational relationships: Integration and future directions. Paper presented at the National Academy of Management Meeting, Atlanta.

Bartlett, C. A. and Ghoshal, S. 1992. *Transnational Management*. Homewood, IL: Irwin.

Beamish, P. W. 1984. *Joint Venture Performance in Developing Countries*. Ph.D. diss., University of Western Ontario.

Beamish, P. W. 1988. *Multinational Joint Ventures in Developing Countries*. London: Routledge.

Beamish, P. W. and Banks, J. C. 1987. Equity joint ventures and the theory of the multinational enterprise. *Journal of International Business Studies* 18: 1–16.

Bettis, R. A. 1991. Strategic management and the straightjacket: An editorial essay. *Organizational Science* 2: 315–19.

Bleeke, J. and Ernst, D. 1993. *Collaborating to Compete*. New York: Wiley.

Blodgett, L. L. 1992. Factors in the instability of international joint ventures: An event history analysis. *Strategic Management Journal* 13: 475–81.

Borch, O. J. 1994. The process of relational contracting: Developing trustbased strategic alliances among small business enterprises. *Advances in Strategic Management*. Greenwich, CT: JAI Press.

—— and Parkhe, A. 1994. Formal-administrative versus relational contracting perspectives of strategic alliance governance. Working paper, Indiana University.

Buckley, P. J. and Casson, M. 1988. A theory of cooperation in international business. *Cooperative Strategies in International Business*. Lexington, MA: Lexington Books.

Odd couples. 1986. *Business Week* (July 21): 100–6.

Contractor, F. J. 1985. A generalized theorem for joint venture and licensing negotiations. *Journal of International Business Studies* 16: 23–50.

—— and Lorange, P. 1988. Why should firms cooperate? The strategy and economics basis of cooperative ventures. *Cooperative Strategies in International Business*. Lexington, MA: Lexington Books.

Eisenhardt, K. M. 1989. Building theories from case study research. *Academy of Management Review* 14: 532–50.

Fey, C. F. 1994. International joint ventures: An important topic for the 1990's and beyond. Working paper 94–13, University of Western Ontario.

Franko, L. G. 1971. *Joint Venture Survival in Multinational Corporations*. New York: Praeger.

—— 1989. Use of minority and 50–50 joint ventures by U.S. multinationals during the 1970s. *Journal of International Business Studies* 20: 19–40.

Friedmann, W. G. and Kalmanoff, G. eds. 1961. *Joint International Business Ventures*. New York: Columbia University Press.

Geringer, J. M. 1991. Strategic determinants of partner selection criteria in international joint ventures. *Journal of International Business Studies* 22: 41–62.

—— and Hebert, L. 1989. Control and performance of international joint ventures. *Journal of International Business Studies* 20: 235–54.

—— —— 1991. Measuring performance of international joint ventures. *Journal of International Business Studies* 22: 249–63.

Goldberg, V. P. 1980. Relational exchange. *American Behavioral Scientist* 23: 337–52.

Gomes-Casseres, B. 1987. Joint venture instability: Is it a problem? *Columbia Journal of World Business* (Spring): 97–102.

Gray, B. and Yan, A. 1992. A negotiation model of joint venture formation, structure, and performance. *Advances in International Comparative Management* 7: 41–75.

Hamel, G. 1991. Competition for competence and interpartner learning within international strategic alliances. *Strategic Management Journal* 12: 83–104.

Harrigan, K. R. 1985. *Strategies for Joint Ventures*. Lexington, MA: Lexington Books.

—— 1986. *Managing for Joint Venture Success*. Lexington, MA: Lexington Books.

—— 1988. Strategic alliances and partner asymmetrics. *Cooperative Strategies in International Business*. Lexington, MA: Lexington Books.

Heide, J. B. 1994. Interorganizational governance in marketing channels. *Journal of Marketing* 58: 71–85.

——and John, G. 1988. The role of dependence balancing in safeguarding transaction-specific assets in conventional channels. *Journal of Marketing* 52: 20–35.

Hennart, J.-F. 1988. A transaction costs theory of equity joint ventures. *Strategic Management Journal* 9; 361–74.

——1991. The transaction costs theory of joint ventures: An empirical study of Japanese subsidiaries in the United States. *Management Science* 37: 483–97.

Hergert, M. and Morris, D. 1988. Trends in international collaborative agreements. *Cooperative Strategies in International Business*. Lexington, MA: Lexington Books.

Hladik, K. J. 1988. R and D and international joint ventures. *Cooperative Strategies in International Business*. Lexington, MA: Lexington Books.

Inkpen, A. 1993. Trust and the performance of international joint ventures. Working paper, Temple University.

John, G. 1984. An empirical investigation of some antecedents of opportunism in a marketing channel. *Journal of Marketing Research* 21: 278–89.

Kaufmann, P. J. and Stern, L. W. 1988. Relational exchange norms, perceptions of unfairness, and retained hostility in commercial litigation. *Journal of Conflict Resolution* 32: 534–52.

Killing, J. P. 1982. How to make a global joint venture work. *Harvard Business Review* (May–June): 120–7.

——1983. *Strategies for Joint Venture Success*. New York: Praeger.

Knecht, B. 1994. Crossborder deals jumped last year to record levels. *Wall Street Journal* (January 25): C19.

Kogut, B. 1988, Joint ventures: Theoretical and empirical perspectives. *Strategic Management Journal* 9: 319–32.

——1989. The stability of joint ventures: Reciprocity and competitive rivalry. *Journal of Industrial Economics* 38: 183–98.

Lane, H. W. and Beamish, P. W. 1990. Cross-cultural cooperative behavior in joint ventures in LDCs. *Management International Review* 30: 87–102.

Larsson, R. 1993. Case survey methodology: Quantitative analysis of patterns across case studies. *Academy of Management Journal* 36: 1515–46.

Lyles, M. A. 1988. Learning among joint venture-sophisticated firms. *Cooperative Strategies in International Business*. Lexington, MA: Lexington Books.

——and Rajadhyax, N. 1988. The international joint venture: An increasing strategic challenge. *International Journal of Management* 5(4): 365–74.

Lynch, R. P. 1989. *The Practical Guide to Joint Ventures and Corporate Alliances*. New York: Wiley.

Macneil, I. R. 1978. Contracts: Adjustment of long-term economic relations under classical, neoclassical, and relational contract law. *Northwestern University Law Review* 72: 854–902.

Miles, M. B. and Huberman, M. A. 1984. *Qualitative Data Analysis*. Beverly Hills, CA: Sage Publications.

Ohmae, K. 1989. The global logic of strategic alliances. *Harvard Business Review* (March–April): 143–54.

Oliver, C. 1990. Determinants of interorganizational relationships: Integration and future directions. *Academy of Management Review* 15: 241–65.

Ouchi, W. G. 1980. Markets, bureaucracies, and clans. *Administrative Science Quarterly* 25: 129–42.

Oye, K. A. (ed.). 1986. *Cooperation Under Anarchy*. Princeton, NJ: Princeton University Press.

Parkhe, A. 1991. Interfirm diversity, organizational learning, and longevity in global strategic alliances. *Journal of International Business Studies* 22: 579–601.

—— 1993a. "Messy" research, methodological predispositions, and theory development in international joint ventures. *Academy of Management Review* 18: 227–68.

—— 1993b. Strategic alliance structuring: A game theoretic and transaction cost examination of interfirm cooperation. *Academy of Management Journal* 36: 794–829.

—— 1993c. Partner nationality and the structure-performance relationship in strategic alliances. *Organization Science* 4: 301–24.

—— 1994. Conflict in global strategic alliances: A model and performance implications. Paper presented at the Academy of International Business Annual Meeting, Boston.

Poole, M. S. and Van de Ven, A. H. 1989. Using paradox to build management and organization theories. *Academy of Management Review* 14: 562–78.

Provan, K. G. and Skinner, S. J. 1989. Interorganizational dependence and control as predictors of opportunism in dealer-supplier relations. *Academy of Management Journal* 32: 202–12.

Raben, C. S. 1992. Building strategic partnerships: Creating and managing effective joint ventures. *Organizational Architecture*. San Francisco: Jossey-Bass.

Rao, A. 1993. Power, dependence, and influence in the negotiation of international collaborative ventures. Ph.D. diss., Temple University.

Rieger, F. and Wong-Rieger, D. 1990. Conflicts in international joint ventures as mismatches in strategic objectives and acculturation orientation. Paper presented at the Strategic Management Society Annual Meeting, Stockholm.

Ring, P. S. and Van de Ven, A. H. 1994. Developmental processes of cooperative interorganizational relationships. *Academy of Management Review* 19: 90–118.

Root, F. R. 1988. Some taxonomies of international cooperative arrangements. *Cooperative Strategies in International Business*. Lexington, MA: Lexington Books.

—— and Contractor, F. J. 1981. Negotiating compensation in international licensing agreements. *Sloan Management Review* 22: 23–32.

Schaan, J.-L. 1983. Parent control and joint venture success: The case of Mexico, Ph.D. diss., University of Western Ontario.

Shenkar, O. and Zeira, Y. 1992. Role conflict and role ambiguity of chief executive officers in international joint ventures. *Journal of International Business Studies* 23: 55–75.

Simonin, B. L. and Helleloid, D. 1993. Do organizations learn? An empirical test of organizational learning in international strategic alliances. Paper presented at the 1993 National Academy of Management Meeting, Atlanta.

Smith, A. and Aldrich, H. E. 1991. The role of trust in the transaction cost economics framework. Paper presented at the annual meeting of the Academy of Management, Miami.

Stopford, J. and Wells, L. 1972. *Managing the Multinational Enterprise*. New York: Basic Books.

Stuckey, J. 1983. *Vertical Integration and Joint Ventures in the Aluminum Industry*. Cambridge, MA: Harvard University Press.

Tallman, S. B. and Shenkar, O. 1994. A managerial decision model of international cooperative venture formation. *Journal of International Business Studies* 25: 91–113.

Thorelli, H. B. 1986. Networks: Between markets and hierarchies. *Strategic Management Journal* 7: 37–51.

Tomlinson, J. W. C. 1970. *The Joint Venture Process in International Business: India and Pakistan*. Cambridge, MA: MIT Press.

Venkatraman, N. and Ramanujam, V. 1986. Measurement of business performance in strategy research: A comparison of approaches. *Academy of Management Review* 11: 801–14.

Weiss, S. E. 1987. Creating the GM-Toyota joint venture: A case in complex negotiation. *Columbia Journal of World Business* 22(2): 23–37.

—— 1995. International business negotiations research: Bricks, mortar, and prospects. *Handbook of International Management Research*. Oxford: Blackwell.

Westney, D. E. 1988. Domestic and foreign learning curves in managing international cooperation strategies. *Cooperative Strategies in International Business*. Lexington, MA: Lexington Books.

Wille, J. R. 1988. Joint venturing strategies. *The Handbook of Joint Venturing*. Homewood, IL: Dow Jones-Irwin.

Williamson, O. E. 1975. *Markets and Hierarchies: Analysis and Antitrust Implications*. New York: Free Press.

—— 1985. *The Economic Instructions of Capitalism*. New York: Free Press.

—— and Ouchi, W. G. 1981. The markets and hierarchies program of research: Origins, implications, prospects. *Perspectives on Organization Design and Behavior*. New York: Wiley.

Wood, D. J. and Gray, B. 1991. Toward a comprehensive theory of collaboration. *Journal of Applied Behavioral Science* 27: 139–62.

Yan, A. and Gray, B. 1994. Bargaining power, management control, and performance in U.S.–China joint ventures: A comparative case study. *Academy of Management Journal* 37: 1478–1517.

Yin, R. K. 1984. *Case Study Research: Design and Methods*. Beverly Hills, CA: Sage Publications.

Zaheer, A. and Venkatraman, N. 1993. Relational governance as an interorganizational strategy: An empirical test of the role of trust in economic exchange. Working paper, University of Minnesota.

Zand, D. E. 1972. Trust and managerial problem solving. *Administrative Science Quarterly* 17: 229–39.

Zucker, L. G. 1986. Production of trust. *Research in Organizational Behavior* 8: 53–111.

[illegible]
(Cambridge, MA: MIT Press).

[illegible]

[illegible]

[illegible]

[illegible]

[illegible]
New York: Free Press.

[illegible]

[illegible]

[illegible]

[illegible]

[illegible]

[illegible]

[illegible]

II. ECONOMIC PERSPECTIVES ON INTERFIRM COLLABORATION

4 A Transaction Costs Theory of Equity Joint Ventures

Jean-François Hennart

American multinational enterprise (MNEs) used to be known for their rigid insistence on wholly-owned subsidiaries. No longer. Today joint ventures (JVs) are 'in'. AT&T and Olivetti, General Motors and Toyota, Honeywell and Ericsson, United Technologies and Rolls Royce, Hercules and Montedison, General Electric and SNECMA, even the largest American firms are joining forces with foreign rivals, setting up cooperative research, manufacturing, or distribution ventures.

The increasing importance taken by domestic and international JVs has spawned some new theoretical and empirical work which has increased our knowledge of these cooperative arrangements. Harrigan (1985), for example, has shown that JVs take a variety of forms and are used for a wide range of purposes. The goal of this chapter is to show that the transaction cost framework (Williamson, 1975, 1985) can provide a unifying paradigm which accounts for the common element among these seemingly dissimilar JVs.

My aim is to use the insights of transaction-costs theorists to sketch a static theory of equity JVs. I do not claim that the minimization of transaction costs is the sole reason behind JVs. Collusion, for example, is an important motive which is ignored by the model. Similarly, no attempt will be made to critically evaluate the assumptions underlying transaction costs theory, nor to compare the explanatory power of such a framework to that of alternative approaches. Supporting evidence will be adduced where available to ground the theory, and show that the argument is plausible, but I do not pretend to have shown conclusive support. The model seeks to explain why equity JVs are chosen as a first-best strategy: it may not be applicable to equity JVs which are created as a result of government pressure. It accounts for both domestic and international equity JVs, although much of the discussion will focus on the latter.

The literature distinguishes between equity and non-equity JVs. Equity JVs arise whenever two or more sponsors bring given assets to an independent legal entity and are paid for some or all of their contribution from the profits earned by the entity, or when a firm acquires partial ownership of another firm. The term 'non-equity JV' describes a wide array of contractual arrangements, such as licensing, distribution, and supply agreements, or technical assistance and management contracts. Non-equity JVs are thus contracts. Consequently, we will restrict the use of the term JV to describe equity JVs, while the term 'contract' will be used to describe non-equity JVs and other types of contractual arrangements.

It is useful to contrast two types of equity JVs. 'Scale' JVs are created when two or more firms enter together a contiguous stage of production or distribution or a new market. The main characteristic of these ventures is that they result from similar moves by all the parents: forward or backward vertical integration, horizontal expansion, or diversification. Examples include the drilling consortia routinely used by integrated oil companies, the iron-ore JVs established by steel producers, or the component JVs created by automobile producers. In all these ventures the partners are pursuing strategies of backward vertical integration. Banking consortia, such as the European American Bank, formed by a group of European banks to jointly enter the U.S. market, can also be classified as scale JVs. Here the strategy is one of horizontal expansion.

In 'link' JVs, on the other hand, the position of the partners is not symmetrical. The JV may, for example, constitute a vertical investment for one of the parties, and a diversification for the other. One example of such JV would be Dow–Badische, a JV of Dow Chemical and BASF, a German chemical company. BASF set up the venture to exploit is proprietary technology in the U.S. market, while for Dow, which took responsibility for marketing the JV's output, the JV was a way to fill in its product line. Similarly, Philips/Du Pont Optical, a JV recently established by these two firms to manufacture and sell compact disks, represents a horizontal investment for Philips, which already produces compact disks in Europe, and a way for Du Pont to diversify into electronic products (Freeman and Hudson, 1986).

Figure 1 contrasts scale and link JVs in the aluminum industry. Aluminium Oxide Stade, a scale JV, represents a vertical forward investment for both parents. They provide their own bauxite to the JV and take a share of the alumina which is proportional to their equity. Queensland Alumina, on the other hand, is a link JV. Comalco, one of the partners, is following a strategy of vertical forward integration: it provides all of the bauxite used in the plant, but only takes part of the alumina output. For the other partners the venture is a vertical backward investment in alumina.

Both scale and link JVs have two main characteristics. First, the relationship between the parent(s) and the JV is an equity, or hierarchical one. This equity

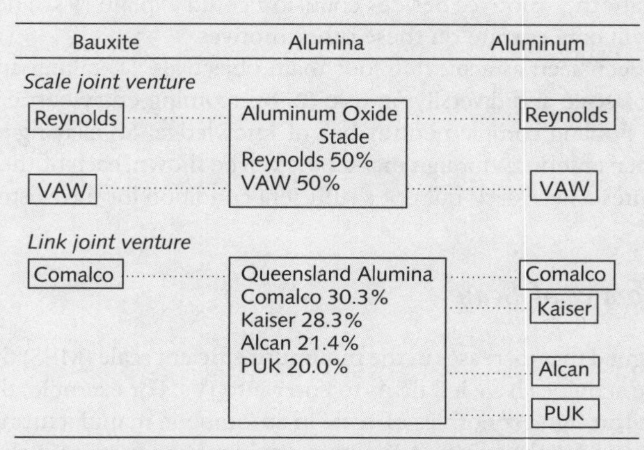

Fig. 1. Link and scale joint ventures in the aluminum industry.

link suggests that hierarchical coordination has been found preferable to coordination through spot markets or contracts. A JV thus represents a particular type of internalization. Second, hierarchical control over the firm is shared with other firms. This is in contrast to an exclusive link, as in a wholly owned subsidiary.

The following sections of this chapter seek to explain those two characteristics. We will set out the conditions under which JVs will be preferred to spot markets or contractual agreements and then show when shared equity will be chosen over exclusive ownership. But, before we develop a transaction costs theory of JVs, it is important to show why some of the explanations given so far for JVs have been inadequate.

1. Received Theory

Long before JVs and other cooperative strategies caught the attention of business strategists, they had been studied by industrial economists because of their potential impact on competition. Pate (1969), for example, found that most U.S. JV parents belonged to the same industry, and deduced that U.S. JVs were undertaken to reduce competition. Berg and Friedman (1980) showed, however, that other motives besides collusion could explain JVs. The following discussion will concentrate on these other motives.

JVs have been seen as achieving four main objectives: (1) taking advantage of economies of scale and diversifying risk; (2) overcoming entry barriers into new markets; (3) pooling complementray bits of knowledge; (4) allaying xenophobic reactions when entering a foreign market. As will be shown, each of these four reasons constitutes a necessary, but not a sufficient condition for the existence of JVs.

1.1. *Economies of Scale*

It is often argued that increases in the minimum efficient scale (MES) of a number of economic activities have led firms to enter into JVs. For example, the desire to reduce costs through economies of scale in automobile manufacturing is usually given as a cause for the spate of JVs in component production in that industry. This analysis implies that the optimal scale is larger at the component than at the assembly level, thus forcing two or more assemblers to join forces to produce components. That differences in MES across stages provide a necessary, but not a sufficient condition for JVs is made clear by looking at two fairly similar mineral industries, tin and aluminum. Today, the MES of a bauxite mine or of an alumina refinery is larger than that of an aluminum smelter. Only the largest aluminum firms have enough downstream capacity to absorb the output of an efficiently sized upstream facility. As a result, most recent bauxite mines and alumina refineries have been built by consortia of aluminum producers, and JVs account today for more than half of the world's bauxite and alumina capacity.

The case of tin shows, however, that the presence of divergences between the MES of successive stages is not a sufficient reason for the emergence of JVs. In tin as well, the production process is characterized by large differences in MES across stages, the MES of a tin smelter being much larger than that of an alluvial tin mine. Yet, tin smelters are not operated by JVs of tin mining firms, but are run by specialist firms, with minimal equity in tin mining. There must therefore be more to JVs than scale economies.

1.2. *Increasing Global Environment*

The recent proliferation of JVs has also been explained by the need of firms, in an increasingly global competitive environment, to be present in all main world markets. Building local distribution networks, however, is both very expensive and time-consuming. JVs are said to be a way to enter a maximum number of markets with minimum investment. Although it is difficult to fault such a statement, it is also true that one can enter markets with even less investment.

Distribution and licensing agreements allow firms to obtain a global presence with a limited resource commitment. Heublein, for example, has achieved a global market share for its Smirnoff vodka by licensing in 27 countries its production to local firms.

1.3. Pooling Knowledge

Some authors have seen JVs as devices to pool or exchange knowledge. Yet, here as well, alternatives exist. Licensing is widely used to combine technical knowledge with that of local conditions, while cross-licensing allows firms to exchange complementary information. A theory of JVs must therefore show when and why JVs are preferred to licensing.

1.4. Reducing Political Risk

Lastly, JVs have been explained by the desire of multinational enterprises (MNEs) to share the ownership of their foreign subsidiaries with local firms, in order to defuse xenophobic reactions in host countries. It is not obvious, however, that a partly foreign-owned firm will, everything else constant, be necessarily better treated than a wholly-owned subsidiary. In any case, a MNE can totally reduce its visibility and still exploit its advantages if it licenses or franchises a local firm. In that respect, JVs are a second best compared to contractual modes. Why they would be used remains unclear.

In conclusion, each of these four commonly described reasons provides a necessary, but not a sufficient, condition for the emergence of JVs. To explain why JVs are formed one must show convincingly: (1) why an equity link is sometimes preferred to other means of acquiring intermediate inputs; (2) why the firm chooses to share the ownership of the JV with other parents. Although those two aspects of JV are interrelated, they will be dealt with separately to simplify the exposition.

2. Why Equity?

This section argues that all JVs can be explained as a device to bypass inefficient markets for intermediate inputs. The presence of inefficiencies in intermediate markets is thus a necessary condition for JVs to emerge.[1]

Whether a market fails or not depends on a number of technological, political, and social factors. Analyzing the transaction cost properties of specific markets requires a thorough study of the technology used at both the upstream and downstream stages, and of its impact on the potential number of parties at each stage (see, for example, Globerman and Schwindt, 1986; Joskow, 1985; at the industry level, and Monteverde and Teece, 1982; Walker and Weber, 1984, at the firm level; Nevertheless, a certain number of generalizations can be made. Intermediate inputs sold in narrow, imperfect markets are likely to include some raw materials and components, some types of knowledge, and, in some instances, loan capital and distribution services. Some of the points argued below have been made by others to explain why firms internalize transactions within wholly-owned networks. Here I argue that the presence of high transaction costs can also, in specific circumstances outlined in the next section, lead to internalization between parents and JVs.

2.1. Raw Materials and Components

The characteristics of the markets for raw materials and intermediate inputs explain why, given significant differences in MES across stages, JVs are used in some industries but not in others. This point is best made by returning to our previous discussion of the tin and aluminum industries, and by looking at the market for intermediate inputs, here bauxite and tin concentrates.

The market for bauxite is narrow, as efficient bauxite refining requires that the bauxite refinery be designed around the characteristics of the ore. Since bauxites are heterogeneous, each refinery obtains its bauxite from a particular mine. Switching costs are high. To organize such a bilateral relationship through spot markets would be hazardous, because after investments have been made, one party could hold up the other by unilaterally changing the price of bauxite.

One way for traders to protect themselves is to write long-term contracts fixing *ex ante* the price of bauxite over a period of time which corresponds to the life of the plant. Because mining and refining bauxite require very large investments—an efficiently sized mine costs half a billion dollars and a refinery between 500 million and a billion—such contracts typically run for 20–25 years. Over such a long time span they cannot effectively protect the parties against changes in the environment, as it is difficult to specify *ex ante* all possible contingencies. Contracts thus remain incomplete, exposing parties to opportunistic renegotiations (Stuckey, 1983). Aluminum firms must therefore use equity to control their supply of bauxite. Equity control reduces the problem of opportunism because it aligns the incentives of buyers and sellers of bauxite. Both can now be paid in proportion to the firm's global profits, thus attenuating incentives for bargaining and opportunism.

Similarly, the presence of JVs in the oil industry derives in part from high transactions costs in the market for crude. Oil refining is a capital-intensive flow process, requiring a constant throughput. Storing crude oil is costly. As in the case of bauxite, refineries are custom-built to handle a particular type of crude. The market for crude tends therefore to be thin, and oil refiners have found it necessary to integrate backward into crude exploration and production (Greening, 1976; Teece, 1976).

By contrast, coordination between stages is, in the case of alluvial tin, efficiently performed by spot markets. Alluvial tin concentrates are nearly pure tin, and can be handled by any smelter. Because tin is a semi-precious metal its transportation costs are low relative to its value. These two conditions have favored the emergence of an efficient market for tin concentrates, allowing smelters to acquire feed, and mines to sell their output, without the fear of opportunistic exploitation. Consequently, miners have not entered smelting through JVs (Hennart, 1986).

The same considerations explain the need to JV the supply of parts or components. When the MES of some components is very large relative to a single firm's demand, JVs will be used if the component is specific to the purchaser, while independent suppliers will be used for standard parts, which are sold in a relatively broad market. Automobile assemblers, for example, JV the supply of parts which are specific to their models (engines), but purchase standard parts from large independent suppliers (Monteverde and Teece, 1982; Walker and Weber, 1984). Here also, JVs arise whenever relying on independent suppliers would involve excessive transaction costs.

2.2. *Knowledge*

The second factor of production that is often sold in inefficient markets is knowledge (Casson, 1979; Rugman, 1981; Teece, 1981; Hennart, 1982). The connection between JVs and knowledge is twofold. Link JVs are used to combine different types of knowledge. The Dow–Badische JV mentioned earlier linked BASF's technological expertise with Dow's marketing know-how. Scale JVs serve to pool similar types of knowledge. For example, CFM International, a JV between General Electric and SNECMA of France, merges the two parents' experience to develop and manufacture a new fuel-efficient jet engine.

Why is knowledge transferred through JVs in those cases, and not by licensing or cross-licensing? To answer this question, one must focus on the transactional characteristics of knowledge. Knowledge *per se* is costly to exchange because of buyer's uncertainty: the buyer of knowledge cannot be told prior to the sale the exact characteristics of what he is buying. If the seller were to provide that information in order to educate the buyer on the value of know-how for sale, he would, by revealing the information, be transfering the know-how free of charge (Arrow, 1962: 615). The patent system is an institution which has been devised to solve this problem. In exchange for disclosing his knowledge, the inventor is granted a monopoly on its use.

The efficiency of the patent system thus depends crucially on the power and willingness of public authorities to establish and enforce monopoly rights on the sale of goods and services embodying the knowledge. Only if the inventor can be assured of an exclusive right to produce his invention will he consent to disclose it. If he has reasons to believe his rights will not be protected, he will keep his invention secret and exploit it himself, for by not disclosing it he secures a *de facto* monopoly for at least as long as it takes for others to market imitations.

Patents suffer from another type of limitation. Recall that patents lower the high information costs faced by buyers of knowledge by revealing it and simultaneously establishing exclusive property rights in its use. To reduce market transaction costs the patent must therefore contain the totality of the information necessary to produce the commodity. Some types of knowledge, however, are difficult to put on paper. Such is the case for a firm's experience in manufacturing and marketing a product, and for country-specific knowledge, the intimate knowledge of local customs, markets, politics, and people which comes from having lived in a particular country, or more generally for what Polanyi (1958) has called 'tacit' knowledge. Such knowledge cannot be embodied in designs, specifications, and drawings, but instead is embedded in the individual possessing it. When knowledge is tacit, it cannot be effectively transferred in codified form; its exchange must rely on intimate human contact. A sole exchange of patents is then insufficient. Instead, the patent must be accompanied by transfer of personnel from the patenting firm (Teece, 1981).

The problem with transferring tacit knowledge is that it is impossible for either party to know *ex ante* what the cost and the value of the transfer will be. The buyer does not know, by definition, what he is buying. He fears that the information he will be sold will be obsolete, or inappropriate. The seller does not know how much it will cost him to effect the transfer. New technical or human problems are likely to arise which could not be foreseen when the contract was drafted.[2] It is often difficult for both parties to distinguish *ex post* between poor luck or poor performance. In those circumstances, parties may exploit contract incompleteness and the difficulty of assessing performance to their own advantage. Once he has been paid, the seller has little incentive to provide continuous support, and may provide less than promised. The buyer may have misrepresented his needs, or his capacity to absorb the information, in order to get better terms. He may then use the resulting difficulties as a pretext to withhold payment. Hierarchical coordination is then advantageous, because the parties to the exchange are no longer rewarded by the quantity of information transferred, but by their obedience to managerial directives. They have therefore fewer incentives to cheat (Hennart, 1982: 97–121).

The cost of transferring know-how by contract, i.e. the cost of licensing, will therefore depend on the type of knowledge to be transferred and on the protection given to property rights in knowledge. Some types of knowledge, such as chemical formulae for the manufacture of new compounds whose production requires no careful adjustments, are patentable; and the patent conveys all of the necessary information to produce the product. The sale or rental of such know-how will incur low market transaction costs. Tacit knowledge, on the other hand, is difficult to codify, and often non-patentable. Even if patented, the patent will provide only a small part of the information necessary to market the new product or to use the new process. Tacit knowledge will be more efficiently transferred if the transferor and the recipient are linked through common ownership.

There is empirical support for the notion that equity links are chosen to transfer non-codified technological know-how. In alumina production the crucial know-how is how to adapt that basic process to the characteristics of the bauxite. That knowledge, obtained by experience, is held by the 'majors,' the six aluminum producers which have long been active in the industry. Because it is tacit, it is never licensed, but is transferred through JVs between the 'majors' and entrants into the industry (Stuckey, 1983: 163).

There is also a good deal of evidence that JVs are used to transfer a different technology package than licensing. JVs are chosen to communicate both patent rights and tacit knowledge, while licensing is usually limited to patent rights. This point was highlighted in Davies' (1977) study of the transfer of knowledge from British to Indian firms. He found that while 60 percent of the licensing agreements only transferred designs, specifications, and drawings, JVs were used to transfer a much wider range of know-how, including tacit knowledge. Technology suppliers often sent technical and managerial personnel to their JV to transfer tacit know-how, while this was rarely done by licensors. Killing's (1980) study of licensing agreements and JVs between Canadian, American and Western European firms also found that the transfer of knowledge to JVs relied much more heavily on personal contact than in the case of licensing. In 19 of the 30 JVs, but only in one of the 74 license agreements he surveyed, a permanent employee had been assigned by the technology supplier to facilitate the transfer.[3]

Two other types of tacit knowledge which are difficult to transfer through contracts are marketing and country-specific knowledge. Both types of know-how have similar characteristics: they are acquired by firms in a given industry and country as a by-product of operating in that industry and country, yet they are costly for a new entrant to obtain. Both are not patentable and difficult to codify, and their sale would be subject to high transaction costs.

We would therefore expect firms which are entering new industries or new countries to establish hierarchical links with local producers. The strength of this motivation for JVs will vary with the extent to which knowledge of local conditions is required for successful operation, and with the degree to which entrants are familiar with conditions in the market they wish to enter. In the case of country-specific knowledge, for example, the greater the cultural distance between the investor's home and the host country, the greater the need to acquire country-specific knowledge.

The preceding considerations account for the strong relationship between diversification and JVs. Stopford and Wells (1972: 126) found, for example, that diversified firms had a larger percentage of JVs among their overseas manufacturing affiliates than the firms with a narrow product line. Diversifying firms must acquire skills in marketing their new products and, given the difficulty of licensing such marketing knowledge, they must establish equity links with the firms owning it.

There is also a great deal of evidence showing the importance of local knowledge acquisition as a *raison d'etre* for international JVs. Both Stopford and Wells (1972) and Franko (1973) found that U.S. firms that engage in JVs abroad ranked 'general knowledge of local economy, politics, and customs' the most important contribution of the local partner to the JV. It is also striking to note that, when free to choose their mode of entry, MNEs rarely use JVs to enter culturally similar countries (Stopford and Haberich, 1978). Kogut and Singh (1985) found that, for a sample of foreign firms investing in the United States, the probability to JV rather than acquire a U.S. company was higher the greater the cultural distance between the investor's country of origin and the United States.

That JVs serve to acquire country-specific knowledge is also clear from the fact that in many JVs the local partner assumes management. A 1974 survey of JVs in Japan found that 85 percent were managed by the Japanese partner, and only 2 percent by the foreign partner (*Economist,* 1977). Yoshahira (1984: 112) also found a clear correlation between the percentage of parent ownership in Japanese foreign affiliates and the degree of parent control, thus supporting the view that JVs are a way for Japanese companies to buy management skills for their foreign subsidiaries.

2.3. Distribution

The distribution of a product in a given area requires both physical facilities (such as warehouses, stocks of finished products and components, repair facilities, offices or retail stores) and an investment in knowledge. The distributor must establish a reputation through advertising or direct selling, adapt the product to local tastes and conditions of use, find out how to price it, and learn to demonstrate and service it. Distribution, thus, involves set-up costs, which vary from small to substantial, depending on the type of products sold. In some cases these investments are specific to a particular product, with low resale value in alternative uses.

There are three cases where arm's-length distribution agreements suffer from high transaction costs. The first one arises when distribution is subject to economies of scale or scope, a rather common occurrence. This tends to reduce the number of potential distributors in any given area. An equity participation in the distributor allows the manufacturer to avoid the resulting bargaining stalemates.

In other cases there are many potential distributors facing a manufacturer, but effective distribution requires substantial up-front investments. The distributor may then fear that, having developed the market in the expectation of a long-lived relationship, he will find himself squeezed by the manufacturer. One solution is to obtain exclusive distribution rights for a period which is long enough to fully depreciate his investments. Such a contract could, in theory, reduce the problems of opportunistic recontracting. The more uncertain the environment, and the greater the value of the investments the distributor must dedicate to the manufacturer's products, the greater the chances, however, that such a long-term contract will break down.[4] In practice, the distributor's defense will often be to minimize the investments dedicated to pushing, supporting, and servicing the sale of the manufacturer's products, so as to reduce his loss should the manufacturer behave opportunistically.

Vertical integration into distribution solves these contractual difficulties. The higher the optimal level of dedicated investments to be made by the distributor, and the greater the degree of uncertainty, the more efficient it will be for the manufacturer to own all or a part of his distributor. Thus, we would expect integration into distribution to prevail in the case of products requiring specialized distribution facilities (for example, refrigeration), or in that of new shopping goods. The sale of these goods requires a substantial up-front investment in adapting the product to the needs of the public, and in demonstrating and advertising it to the customer (Williamson, 1985: 75–84).

Another problem inherent in subcontracting distribution is that of quality control. Whenever a good's quality cannot be evaluated before its purchase, the use of a trademark will economize on a customers' search costs, and buyers will be willing to pay a premium for such trademarked goods and services. All the sellers of goods bearing a trademark are interdependent, in the sense that the quality of the goods and services sold by anyone using the trademark will affect the profits of all that share in that trademark. Independent distributors of trademarked goods therefore have weak incentives to maintain the quality of the trademarked goods they carry. If consumers are mobile, a distributor of trademarked goods will capture most of the savings from debasing quality (for example selling stale merchandise), while the losses from this reduction in quality will be shared by all others using the trademark through the fall in its global value. Franchised distribution contracts attempt to control such free-riding by having the franchisee agree to a set of constraints that prevent him from debasing quality. The larger the number of contractual stipulations that are needed to achieve that end, and the greater the difficulty of defining and enforcing contractual rules, the stronger the manufacturer's incentive to own his distributor.

Several empirical studies support this explanation of vertical integration into distribution. In a study of the channels used to sell electronic components, Anderson and Schmittlein (1984) found that firms integrated into direct selling when sales required the salesperson to make substantial firm-specific investments. Historical evidence from Chandler (1977), Porter and Livesay (1971) and Nicholas (1983) shows that manufacturers sought equity control of distribution when (1) products required expensive, dedicated investments in distribution assets and (2) it was difficult to control quality debasement by distributors.

The importance of access to distribution as a motive for both international and domestic JVs is apparent from even a cursory reading of the literature. Kogut and Singh's (1985) data base shows that 42 percent of the JVs entered by foreigners in the U.S. over the 1971–83 period are for marketing and distribution, while Jacque (1986) found that close to 60 percent of U.S. joint ventures in Japan were of that type.

2.4. Loan Capital

Capital markets are also characterized by significant transaction costs. Lending involves making funds available to the debtor, to be paid back later with interest. The risk is that the debtor might be unable to meet his obligations, either because he has willfully spent the funds with no intention to repay, or because he has been unsuccessful in his investments. The easiest way for the lender to protect himself is to obtain some collateral, whose value to the borrower is greater than the value of the loan. The next-best thing is to carefully monitor the way the lender is spending the borrowed funds.

Credit markets are likely to be especially imperfect for young firms with no track record and for investments in risky projects with no collateral, such as R&D. Monitoring the borrower from the outside is likely to be difficult. A banker is strictly limited in the quantity, quality, and timeliness of the information he can obtain on his client. Hierarchical control is a much more efficient method to reduce risk, because a boss is entitled to much more information from his subordinates, and has the power to intervene much earlier than a banker could (Williamson, 1975: 159). In those cases a JV with the borrower can be an efficient method of funding risky projects. There is some evidence that a number of small R&D-intensive firms use JVs with larger firms as a way of financing projects that could not be funded either internally or through the capital market (Berg and Friedman, 1980; Harrigan, 1985).

3. Why Shared Equity?

3.1. JVs and the Internalization of Intermediate Inputs

The preceding section has argued that equity JVs constitute a way to bypass some inefficient markets in intermediate inputs. This explains why a firm may want to establish an equity link with another firm. JVs are, however, operations where equity in that firm is shared with other firms. A theory of JVs must therefore explain why a firm chooses a JV as opposed to a wholly owned greenfield investment or acquisition.

Here it is useful to distinguish between scale and link JVs. Scale JVs allow firms to reconcile the need to bridge a failing market with the presence of large differences in MES across successive stages. In aluminum, for example, where the MES of bauxite mining and refining is much higher than that for smelting and fabricating, a bauxite mining firm establishing a wholly owned, captive alumina refinery of efficient size would face the problem of disposing of the bulk of the alumina produced, since its needs are likely to be only a fraction of the output. Because the market for alumina is very narrow, selling the output on the spot market or through contracts would cause difficult marketing problems. The alternative of setting up a captive downstream network of sufficient size to absorb all of the alumina would involve a tremendous investment. The solution lies in a JV with other vertically integrated aluminum companies. Each member of the JV will take a share of the output. This allows the bauxite firm to build an efficiently sized refinery while solving the problem of disposing of the alumina (Stuckey, 1983). Similarly, drilling consortia allow integrated oil companies to take part in a number of scattered drilling programs, each of them with a limited probability of success, rather than in a few wholly owned drilling ventures of efficient size. Were it not for high transaction costs in the market for crude, drilling would be undertaken by a small number of independent crude producers, each of them holding a widely diversified portfolio of potential properties.

Link JVs are created to remedy the simultaneous failure of at least two markets. Assume that efficient production requires the combination of two types of knowledge held by firms A and B. As shown in Fig. 2, if A's know-how is marketable, but B's is not, A will license B. If B's knowledge is marketable, but A's is not, B will license A. If both types of know-how are difficult to sell, A and B will form a JV. This last case is that of Dow–Badische, the JV of Dow and BASF described earlier. Absent failure in the market for production know-how, BASF would have licensed Dow. If the market for country-specific knowledge and distribution services was competitive, BASF would have contracted with Dow to obtain those services. A JV was chosen because both of those markets were experiencing high transaction costs.

Although I have focused on the main failings in intermediate markets which give rise to JVs, the list is not meant to be comprehensive. Nevertheless, Fig. 3 shows how our model of link JVs as created by the simultaneous failing

		Firm A	
		Marketable know-how	Non-marketable know-how
Firm B	Marketable know-how	Indeterminate	B licenses A
	Non-marketable know-how	A licenses B	A JV with B

Fig. 2. A model of link joint ventures.

	Capital A	Marketing country-specific knowledge B	Tacit technology C	Distribution D	Nationality E	Intermediate inputs F
1. Capital						
2. Country knowledge						
3. Tacit technology	'Sugar-daddy'	'Market entry'	R&D scale R&D link			
4. Distribution		Tripartite	Japanese	Distribution scale and link		
5. Nationality			Nationality-based			
6. Intermediate inputs		Downstream vertical		Downstream vertical		Raw materials scale

Fig. 3. Joint ventures and markets for intermediate inputs.

of at least two intermediate goods markets can account for a wide variety of commonly observed JVs. For simplicity, it is assumed that only two intermediate goods are traded in each JV. Scale JVs are on the diagonal, as they involve two firms internalizing together the same markets: raw materials JV, such as those in bauxite and alumina, are in cell 6F; R&D JVs between competitors where both parties bring similar research capacities in cell 3C; and distribution JVs which have been entered to overcome scale economies, such as the banking consortia set up by European firms to enter the United States, in cell 4D. Because situations are symmetrical along the diagonal, only the lower half of the table has been filled in.

Cell 3B describes 'market entry' JV such as Dow–Badische. Cell 3A, entitled 'sugar-daddy JVs,' refers to those JVs mentioned earlier in which small R&D firms pair with older-established companies to obtain financing. Cell 3C describes R&D link JVs in which two or more firms bring complementary knowledge. The JVs set up in Southeast Asia by Japanese trading companies would fit in cells 4B and 4C. These are often tripartite JVs, in which equity is shared by a *sogo-shosha*, a Japanese manufacturer, and a local firm (Kojima and Ozawa, 1984). The trading company procures the inputs and sometimes markets the output, the Japanese manufacturer provides the tacit technology, while the local partner brings in country-specific knowledge and the advantage of nationality. Japanese Trading Companies own equity in these ventures to guarantee a return on their extensive investment in trading and distribution networks.

Cell 5C describes those JVs in which the local partner brings its nationality as principal contribution. Nationality cannot be obtained through equity, as acquisition of a local firm immediately changes its status to that of a foreign-owned entity. While a contractual exchange between the foreign firm and the local firm would be the best way to allay xenophobic reactions, a JV will be chosen when the markets for the intermediate goods to be exchanged, for example tacit know-how, are subject to high transaction costs. An example of such a JV is Marine Resource, a JV between Bellingham Cold Storage and Sovrybflot, the Soviet fishing monopoly (Contractor, 1986). Sovrybflot has a long experience in marketing fish species which are not consumed in the U.S., a tacit type of know-how which is difficult to sell. Bellingham Cold Storage lacks this expertise, but, as a U.S. firm, has fishing rights on the U.S. 200-mile economic zone, from which foreigners are excluded. The JV thus pools two assets which are difficult to exchange through markets or contracts.

Cell 6B accounts for the downstream JVs which are common in vertically integrated industries. These ventures link firms with knowledge and access to local markets, and vertically integrated concerns which provide them with intermediate inputs not traded on competitive markets. They are found, for example, in the downstream stages of the petroleum, copper, and aluminum industries (Stopford and Wells, 1972: 132–138). In aluminum, JVs between local firms and aluminum majors are common in the downstream fabrication stage, a stage that is characterized by wide variations in product needs between countries. JVs allow the majors to obtain that expertise which, because it is tacit, cannot be obtained from consultants, while guaranteeing the local firm's access to aluminum ingot, a product traded in narrow markets.

3.2. *JVs vs. Acquisitions or Greenfield Investments*

It would appear at this point that we have established necessary and sufficient conditions for the emergence of link JVs, but this is not so. We have shown that these JVs result from the pooling of complementary assets which cannot be efficiently combined on spot markets or through contracts. But pooling could be effected by other means: one of the firms could buy out its potential JV partner. Another possibility would be to hire away its key personnel. In both cases the firm would end up with a wholly owned subsidiary. We must therefore explain the choice between acquisition and greenfield investment on the one hand, and JV on the other.

Excluding the case where acquiring the firm owning the complementary assets is illegal, or would incur the ire of government authorities or of potential customers, the answer seems to lie in the fact that JVs are used to acquire assets which have two main characteristics: they are (1) firm-specific and (2) public goods. By firm-specific we mean that, even though they often constitute a small part of the firm's assets, they cannot be dissociated from the firm itself; public goods assets are assets that can be shared at low marginal cost.

If assets can be shared at low marginal cost, replication is more expensive than acquisition. The owner of these assets should be willing to sell the services produced from those assets at a low price, since providing these additional services does not increase his costs. Setting up a greenfield operation will therefore be inherently more costly than obtaining the use of existing assets through takeover or JV. A JV or a takeover will be preferred to a greenfield investment in this case.

Whenever assets can be shared at low marginal costs, and hence the efficient choice is between a takeover or a JV, a JV will be chosen if the assets which each party needs are a subset of those held by their partner. In this case, purchasing the whole firm would force the acquirer to enter unrelated fields or to suddenly expand in size, with the attendant management problems. Selling off the unusable assets is precluded by the fact that the assets are firm-specific, a point developed below.

The preceding argument can be made clearer with one example. Consider distribution systems. Distribution is often a public good, as it has zero or low marginal cost: once a channel is organized the additional cost of using it for similar or complementary products is small, or even negative if the new products 'fill in' a line. In some cases distribution assets are also firm-specific, in the sense that they could not be sold independently from the rest of the firm's operations: if vertical integration between manufacturing and distribution is efficient, then the distribution assets of the firm to be acquired will be linked to its manufacturing plants, and the two must be bought as a package.[5] Purchasing such assets would propel the buyer into new, unfamiliar markets, thus raising management costs. Selling off the unneeded manufacturing plants would increase the costs of running the distribution system by reducing potential economies of scope, since, given the need for vertical integration into distribution, the new buyer of the manufacturing facilities would switch the distribution of the plant's output to his own channel. A JV in this case offers distinct advantages, since it allows vertical integration into distribution without the need to acquire the linked manufacturing assets.

Some types of knowledge have the same characteristics. Production or marketing know-how is a public good and a firm-specific asset. Like all types of knowledge it is a public good: sharing it with an additional party incurs zero marginal costs.[6] It is firm-specific, in the sense that it cannot be acquired separately from the firm. A full takeover of the firm holding the know-how will involve substantial management costs if the firm to be acquired is large, if it operates in a different industry than the acquiror, or if it is foreign-based.

In summary, whenever the needed assets are public goods it is more expensive to replicate than to acquire them. If these assets are also firm-specific, acquiring them by taking over the firm owning them will sometimes mean buying a collection of other businesses and a labor force which is foreign and/or employed in fields unknown by the buyer. In that case a JV is desirable, as it reduces management costs.[7] Taking over a firm involves transforming personnel into employees. As employees, the top executives of the acquired firm will have less incentives to perform than when they were running their own firm. If the acquiring firm believes it will experience significant problems in supervising these employees, it will opt for a JV in preference to a wholly owned subsidiary. For example, many firms entering foreign markets do not take over their local partner because they do not want to attenuate the incentives that the local firm's personnel has to transfer its know-how to the foreign partner. If the firm supplying marketing or country-specific know-how is paid from the future profits of the venture then it will have an incentive to supervise its employees so that they perform efficiently. Since it is more costly to manage foreign than domestic employees, it is often efficient to let the local partner manage local operations. Similarly, one of the reasons why large, cash-rich firms which take an equity in small entrepreneurial R&D companies do not buy them out is apparently the difficulty of managing the new employees, given the usual differences in company culture.[8]

4. Conclusion

Much of the literature on JVs has failed to identify the conditions that are both necessary and sufficient for their existence. This paper has sketched a transaction costs theory of the choice between contracts, full ownership, and JVs. It distinguishes between scale and link JVs. Scale JVs arise when parents seek to internalize a failing market, but indivisibilities due to scale or scope economies make full ownership of the relevant assets inefficient. Link JVs result from the simultaneous failing of the markets for the services of two or more assets whenever these assets are firm-specific public goods, and acquisition of the firm owning them would entail significant management costs. JVs will thus represent a first-best strategy in a limited number of specific circumstances.

The paper provides a clear framework which explains a number of known characteristics of JVs and accounts for a wide variety of JV types. It gives a new explanation of why JVs transfer particular types of know-how; why they are widely used by diversifying firms; and why they are the preferred way to enter new countries and industries.

One limitation of the theory is that it is static, while the JV process is inherently dynamic, since the mean life of a JV is quite short on average. One way to make it dynamic would be to focus on the speed and predictability of the rate of decay of some of the advantages traded in JVs, particularly knowledge.

While this paper has outlined the benefits of JVs, a complete theory should also discuss their costs. These have, however, been dealt with at length elsewhere (Stopford and Wells, 1972). Because a JV is a contractural pooling of complementary assets belonging to different parents, a contract will usually be drawn to harmonize the interests of both parties. Such a task is easier in scale than in link JVs, for in scale JVs the parents follow similar strategies. In many scale aluminum JVs, for example, each party supplies its own feedstock and takes its share of output, usually proportional to its equity. This arrangement avoids conflicts about the pricing of inputs or outputs (Stuckey, 1983). Link JVs, on the other hand, involve the transfer of intermediate goods which, by definition, do not have clear arm's-length prices. Yet the pricing of these goods determines how profits will be divided between the parents, and is therefore a frequent source of contractual difficulties.

Clearly, JVs are often the product of multiple factors, and any theory must necessarily abstract from some of them. This paper has attempted to show that transactions costs theory can provide new insights into this complex phenomenon.

Notes

1. The argument that JVs are used to bypass inefficient markets was first made explicitly by Stuckey (1983) in the context of the aluminum industry. Much in the discussion that follows is inspired by this pathbreaking work.
2. An interesting example of some of the problems inherent in transferring tacit knowledge through licensing comes from the experience of Honda in licensing the production of its Ballade to British Leyland. Honda expected BL to send a few design engineers and foremen to Japan for training. But because of the compartmentalized British trade unions, and the narrowness of the tasks assigned to each employee, effective transfer required inviting 300 foremen and engineers to Japan, at a cost of over a hundred times what Honda had budgeted. See Ohmae, 1985: 71–72.
3. Harrigan (1985: 351) also documents the loan by parents of their best technological personnel to their JVs.
4. Note that it is not uncertainty *per se* which causes problems, but uncertainty *joined* with small-number conditions. See Williamson (1985).
5. One example might be a firm, such as Dole, which owns banana plantations and operates a fleet of specialized ships and of refrigerated warehouses. Dole could not sell its distribution network separately from its plantations since for reasons explained in Reid (1983), banana firms find it necessary to integrate banana growing, shipping, and distribution.
6. Although transfer costs may be positive (Teece, 1977).
7. This point is supported by Kogut and Singh (1985), who found that the probability that a foreign firm would choose a JV with a U.S. company over an acquisition was higher the greater the cultural distance and the size of the U.S. firm.
8. A General Motors executive thus explained the firm's purchase of 11 percent of Teknowledge: 'If we purchased such a company outright, we would kill the goose that lay the golden egg.' See *Business Week*, 25 June, 1984: 41 quoted in Williamson, 1985: 159.

References

Anderson, E. and Schmittlein, D. 'Integration of the sales force: an empirical examination', *The Rand Journal of Economics*, **15**, 1984, pp. 383–395.

Arrow, K. 'Economic welfare and the allocation of resources for invention'. In K. Arrow (ed.), *The Rate and Direction of Inventive Activity*, Princeton University Press, Princeton, 1962.

Berg, S. and Friedman, P. 'Causes and effects of joint venture activity: Knowledge acquisition vs. parent horizontality', *Antitrust Bulletin*, Spring, 1980, pp. 143–168.

Casson, M. *Alternatives to the Multinational Enterprise*, Macmillan, London, 1979.

Chandler, A. *The Visible Hand*, Belknap Press, Cambridge, MA, 1977.

Contractor, F. 'Strategic considerations behind international joint ventures', *International Marketing Review*, **3**, 1986, pp. 74–85.

Davies, H. 'Technology transfer through commercial transactions', *Journal of Industrial Economics*, **26**, 1977, pp. 161–175.

Economist. 'Joint-venture problems in Japan', 14 May 1977, p. 100.

Franko, L. *Joint Venture Survival in Multinational Corporations*, Praeger, New York, 1973.

Freeman, A. and Hudson, R. 'Du Pont and Philips plan joint venture to make, market laser-disk products', *Wall Street Journal*, 30 October 1986.

Globerman, S. and Schwindt, R. 'The organization of vertically related transactions in the Canadian forest products industries', *Journal of Economic Behavior and Organization*, **7**, 1986, pp. 199–212.

Greening, T. Oil wells, pipelines, refineries and gas stations: a study of vertical integration, Ph.D. dissertation, Harvard University, 1978.

Harrigan, K. *Strategies for Joint Ventures*, Lexington Books, Lexington, MA, 1985.

Hennart, J. F. *A Theory of Multinational Enterprise*, University of Michigan Press, Ann Arbor, MI, 1982.

Hennart, J. F. 'The tin industry'. In M. Casson and associates, *Multinationals and World Trade*, George Allen and Unwin, London, 1986.

Jacque, L. 'The changing personality of U.S.-Japanese joint ventures: a value-added chain mapping paradigm'. Department of Management, The Wharton School, 1986.

Joskow, P. L. 'Vertical integration and long-term contracts'. *Journal of Law, Economics and Organization*, **1**(1), 1985, pp. 33–80.

Killing, P. 'Technology acquisition: license agreement or joint venture'. *Columbia Journal of World Business*, Fall 1980, pp. 38–46.

Kogut, B. and Singh, H. 'Entering the United States by acquisition or joint venture: Country patterns and cultural characteristics', Working paper, Reginald Jones Center, The Wharton School, 1985.

Kojima, K. and Ozawa, T. *Japan's General Trading Companies: Merchants of Economic Development*. OECD, Paris, 1984.

Monteverde, K. and Teece, D. 'Supplier switching costs and vertical integration in the automobile industry', *Bell Journal of Economics*, **13**, 1982, pp. 206–213.

Nicholas, S. 'Agency contracts, institutional modes, and the transition to foreign direct investment by British manufacturing multinationals before 1935', *Journal of Economic History*, **48**, 1983, pp. 675–686.

Ohmae, K. *Triad Power: The Coming Shape of Global Competition*, Free Press, New York, 1985.

Pate, J. 'Joint venture activity, 1960–1968', *Economic Review, Federal Reserve Bank of Cleveland*, 1969, pp. 16–23.

Polanyi, M. *Personal Knowledge: Towards a Post-critical Philosophy*, University of Chicago Press, Chicago, IL, 1958.

Porter, G. and Livesay, H. C. *Merchants and Manufacturers*, Johns Hopkins, Baltimore, 1971.

Reid, R. 'The growth and structure of multinationals in the banana export trade'. In M. Casson (ed.), *The Growth of International Business*, George Allen and Unwin, London, 1983.

Rugman, A. *Inside the Multinationals*. Columbia University Press, New York, 1981.

Stopford, J. and Haberich, K. 'Ownership and control of foreign operations'. In Ghertman, M. and J. Leontiades (eds), *European Research in International Business*, North-Holland, Amsterdam, 1980.

Stopford, J. and Wells, L. *Managing the Multinational Enterprise*, Basic Books, New York, 1972.

Stuckey, J. *Vertical Integration and Joint Ventures in the Aluminum Industry*, Harvard University Press, Cambridge, MA, 1983.

Teece, D. *Vertical Integration and Vertical Divestiture in the U.S. Oil Industry*. Institute for Energy Studies, Stanford, CA, 1976.

—— 'Technology transfer by multinational firms', *Economic Journal*, **87**, 1977, pp. 246–261.

—— 'The market for know-how and the efficient international transfer of technology', *Annals of the American Academy of Political and Social Science*, **458**, 1981, pp. 81–96.

Walker, G. and Weber, D. 'A transaction cost approach to make-or-buy decisions', *Administrative Science Quarterly*, **29**, 1984, pp. 373–391.

Williamson, O. *Markets and Hierarchies*, Free Press, New York, 1975.

—— *The Economic Institutions of Capitalism*, Free Press, New York, 1985.

Yoshahira, N. 'Multinational growth of Japanese manufacturing enterprises'. In Okochi, A. and T. Inoue (eds), *Overseas Business Activities*, University of Tokyo Press, Tokyo, 1984.

5 Information Asymmetry, Adverse Selection, and Joint Ventures: Theory and Evidence

Srinivasan Balakrishnan and Mitchell P. Koza

A joint venture is a special mechanism for pooling complementary assets owned by separate firms.[1] In most joint ventures the parent firms combine part or all of their assets into a legally separate unit and agree to share the profits from the venture. Like the more typical common stock company, this unit is usually free to raise additional capital, enter into contracts, buy and sell goods and services, hire employees, and the like. In matters of policy making and control, however, the joint venture is more like a partnership. A typical common stock company is governed by a Board, which acts as the fiduciary agent of the numerous stockholders at large who are mostly investors with little or no interest in policy or control. In a joint venture, the ownership and control is shared by the parents in a more active sense. The parent firms through their appointed representatives have a direct interest in the policy decisions and the control of the operations of the 'child.' Often, an explicit collateral contract or agreement accompanies the formation of a joint venture, which stipulates the mutual rights and obligations of the parent firms.

In this chapter, we present a comparison of joint-ventures, market mediated contracts and hierarchical governance and analyze the trade-offs between (i) the transaction costs in writing and executing contracts in the intermediate product market, (ii) the costs that accompany transactions that redistribute the ownership of assets, and (iii) the costs of administering hierarchies and joint-ventures. The line of argument is as follows. Acquisition of the complementary assets is desirable to economize on the transaction costs that are associated with market mediated contracts for the supply of intermediate products. When the relevant assets are not homogeneous and information about their quality, performance characteristics, and value is not common knowledge, the costs of redistributing ownership rights over the assets are non-trivial. Asymmetric information about the quality or the value of the target assets causes an 'adverse selection' or a 'lemon' problem [Akerlof (1970)] resulting in roadblocks to a complete transfer of ownership rights. A joint-venture is primarily a mechanism for getting around this problem. It avoids a terminal transaction that transfers ownership rights and allows piecemeal and continuous reassessment of the individual contributions to the venture.

A testable implication is that the shareholders of the parent companies will be more favorably disposed towards joint-ventures than acquisitions when the parents are less informed about each other's business. With potential aggravation of the 'lemon' problem, acquisition will be more costly. We tested this with a sample of 64 domestic joint-ventures and 165 acquisitions using the event study method. The results obtained from a cross-sectional analysis of the abnormal returns to the shareholders during the announcement of these joint-ventures and acquisitions, support our hypothesis.

1. Joint Ventures: Between Markets and Hierarchies

The literature on joint-ventures spans several disciplines including finance, industrial organization, organization theory, and business policy. A theoretical issue that has not been addressed until recently is the relative efficiency of joint-ventures and other mechanisms for coordination such as contracts and hierarchies.[2] Most modern businesses and technologies require a variety of laterally or vertically complementary assets and functional capabilities to produce and deliver a marketable product. Williamson (1975, 1985) has compared two alternative mechanisms by which firms may access complementary assets: (i) market mediated contract and (ii) hierarchy. A firm may choose to buy the relevant intermediate products from a supplier under a spot or long-term contract, negotiated on an arm's length basis. Difficulty in specifying the quality of the intermediate products, uncertainty about future and bounded rationality, may prevent the transacting firms from writing complete contracts which specify all contingencies, leaving scope for opportunistic behavior and bargaining over the terms. Investments in idiosyncratic or specialized assets for carrying out the transaction may become a hostage in the *ex-post* small-number negotiations [Klein et al. (1978), Williamson (1979)]. These transaction costs that accompany market mediated contracts can be mitigated or eliminated when the complementary assets are integrated under a common ownership or hierarchy.

The integration may be accomplished through greenfield investment. This option often involves costly and time-consuming R&D and other tasks.

Knowledge and organizational limitations will constrain the speed and efficiency with which the firm can carry out these tasks. On the other hand, strategic considerations such as first-mover advantages, may warrant the speedy completion of these tasks. The firm may, therefore, decide to acquire part or all of an extant firm that already has the technology and other assets.

Another option is to form a joint-venture by pooling the complementary assets of the two firms. By most definitions, joint-ventures imply equity and profit sharing. The essential characteristic of a joint-venture is that unlike a hierarchy, there is no ultimate 'unity of command' and property rights and control are shared by the parent firms.[3] A collateral contract usually specifies and limits the rights and obligations of the parent firms. Both acquisition and joint-venture considerably shorten the internalization process and save valuable time.

Why do firms choose to joint-venture when they could have merged or sold assets to form a hierarchy? The unique features of a joint-venture are shared ownership and control. A theory of joint-ventures should explain what diseconomies of acquisitions motivate the parents to settle for shared ownership and control. Acquisitions can be costly for a variety of reasons. Often only a portion of the assets of the 'target firm' may be required for the acquiring firm's new venture. When these assets are not clearly identifiable or alienable, a complete merger of the two firms' assets may be warranted but this will result in additional costs of administering and controlling unconnected assets and businesses. High-powered incentives may also be lost in the conglomeration of businesses that do not produce any offsetting synergistic gains. It is also possible that the relevant assets may be shared by other lines of businesses of the target firm. Acquiring these assets introduces new and potentially costly transactions between the acquiring firm and target firm.

Whereas the afore-mentioned diseconomies of acquisition are ex post costs of organization, acquisitions suffer from another important diseconomy which relates to the ex ante costs of satisfactory valuation and pricing of the target assets. In the remainder of the chapter we focus on the differential advantages of joint-ventures over acquisition in these ex ante costs.[4]

2. Information Asymmetry, Adverse Selection, and the Joint Venture

2.1. The Valuation Problem

It is reasonable to expect that the target firm will not sell the assets in its possession unless it receives a bid which is at least equal to the net present value of its assets. If the target assets are specialized and there are no competitive markets in which identical assets are traded, information on their prices will be either costly to obtain or unavailable. A self-interested target firm can exploit this situation and opportunistically misrepresent the value of its assets. Two examples from the takeover market illustrate the problems and the pitfalls that a prospective buyer faces. After acquiring Collins and Aikman, a carpet manufacturing firm, Wickes Inc., discovered that the company had defaulted on certain federal flammability standards concerning carpets it had supplied to schools. To meet the potential product liabilities, Wickes had to set aside roughly $300 million which was 20% of the purchase price of Colling and Aikman. In another instance, CPC, a food processor and corn milling company, had acquired Mueller, a large pasta business, from McKesson, a San Francisco based company for $125 million in 1983. In 1985, CPC filed a $76 million suit against McKesson and Morgan Stanley, the investment bankers for the acquisition, charging that it was induced to make the acquisition by fictitious projections of Mueller's near-term and future performance. Ravenscraft and Scherer (1987) describe several other instances in which both apparent and latent problems with the target firms fail to surface, even if pre-merger inspections were undertaken.

The target firm obviously has better information about the true value of its assets and capabilities because of prior ownership and use. It may, however, choose to withhold information about quality or organizational problems and inflate output and other positive aspects. As Ravenscraft and Scherer (1987) put it, 'Would-be sellers naturally present their best face.' The target firm cannot credibly assure the acquiring firm that it will disclose all the information that it has and negotiate the sale in good faith, even if it were inclined to do so. The transfer of ownership of the complementary assets is thus impacted by 'adverse selection' [Akerlof (1970)]. The acquiring firm, recognizing the information asymmetry and the potential for opportunistic misrepresentation by the target, will discount the price offered accordingly. Although negotiations may continue and the acquiring firm may sweeten its offer, the process will be terminated without a sale if the final offer falls short of what the target firm knows to be the true value of the assets.[5] There is evidence of several unsuccessful acquisition attempts from empirical finance. Bradley (1980) reports that 97 tender offers in his sample of 258 were unsuccessful. In Dodd and Ruback's (1977) study, 48 out of a total of 172 tender offers were unsuccessful. The number of such failures of the market for acquisitions could be more if merger and sell-off attempts were also included. We are not suggesting that all these unsuccessful acquisition attempts are due to the adverse selection problem arising from information asymmetry, but they are indicative of the significant costs that may be associated with asset transactions.

2.2. *The Joint Venture Solution*

In lieu of an outright acquisition, firms can form a joint-venture for combining complementary assets. Transactions governed by a joint-venture will be efficient for the following reasons:

1. First, a joint-venture unlike an acquisition, avoids a terminal sale and transfer of ownership rights and allows the partners to rescind the relationship at a relatively low cost. It can be structured as a mechanism that allows piece-meal transactions and renegotiation of compensation for individual contributions. The possibility of repeated contracting and termination of the relationship under a joint-venture can induce information revelation and mitigate the adverse selection problem. There may be short-term gains from misrepresentations, but the threat of termination of the joint-venture or its potential liquidation because of the resulting downstream inefficiencies, will offset these gains and reduce the incentives to misrepresent.
2. Second, the joint-venture, unlike a lease, introduces for each parent limited formal and informal property rights and obligations by way of shared ownership. When the joint-venture is formed as a partnership, the parents have a fiduciary responsibility to each other. In incorporated joint-ventures, the members of the governing board or the executive committee who are usually drawn from both the parent companies, collectively decide the policies of the joint-venture. They may also have limited rights to formally or informally audit and verify the claims and actions of the parents by monitoring the use of the assets of their respective parent companies as well as those of the partner. These features of a joint-venture, unavailable in a pure contract such as a leasing agreement, help to reduce the incentives for opportunistic behavior in the joint-venture.
3. Finally, the joint-venture affords opportunities for learning and gathering new information about the value of the partner's assets. Some joint-ventures explicitly stipulate a dissolution date and many others end in purchase by one of the parents. In such cases, monitoring and auditing the partner's asset use facilitate the learning process and eventually, the pricing of those assets.

The joint-venture, however, is not a costless mechanism for combining assets. Because of the absence of 'unity of command', costly disputes over sharing the gains from the venture are still a possibility. Because of shared control and the lack of 'unity of command', the administrative costs of managing and controlling the joint-venture will be more than the corresponding costs for a hierarchy. Renegotiations are also potentially expensive. Joint-venture is thus a compromise between a contract and a hierarchy, combining some of their positive features, but not quite eliminating their negative features.

2.3. Empirical Implications

Summing up the arguments thus far, we note that strategic considerations and the failure of the market for intermediate products provide the incentives for firms to seek lateral or vertical acquisitions. On the other hand, the lack of complete information about the target assets may cause the market for acquisition to fail also. The less informed the partners to an asset transaction are about each other's businesses and the higher the perceived variance in their valuation of the assets, the greater is the likelihood of the failure of the market for acquisition. While a contractual solution such as leasing may be an option when the information asymmetry is severe, it introduces other transaction costs by way of opportunistic misuse of the leased assets. Under these conditions, the joint-venture can emerge as a superior substitute for both contract and acquisition. A testable implication is that, ceteris paribus, the shareholders should expect greater gains from joint ventures when the primary business operations of the parents are dissimilar such that they are not capable of appraising the value of each other's technology and assets. Our main hypothesis is therefore:

Hypothesis 1. Shareholder reactions to the unanticipated announcement of joint-ventures will be positively correlated with the extent to which the primary business operations of the parent companies are dissimilar.

Hypothesis (1) calls for careful interpretation. The investors will respond more favorably to joint-ventures between parents in dissimilar businesses because joint-venture is the minimum cost mechanism for coordinating synergistic assets in this case. Outright acquisition of the target assets is costlier because of the valuation problem. If the parent firms' management fails to choose the most efficient mechanism the market may construe that the management is either inefficient or self-serving and penalize its choice.

The hypothesis is independent of the size of the synergistic value created by joint-ventures and acquisitions. We expect value creation, which is the motive for combining the assets, in both joint-ventures and acquisitions. Likewise, the dissimilarity of the parents' business may reduce synergy in both joint-ventures and acquisitions. The difference is only in the costs of information asymmetry and adverse selection that are exacerbated by dissimilarity. The degree of synergy between the assets is not pertinent to the arguments about the *relative* efficiency of the different mechanisms for combining the assets, which leads us to our second hypothesis:

Hypothesis 2. On an average, investors in parent firms, anticipating significant gains from combining their complementary assets, will react favourably to joint venture announcements.

The third hypothesis follows from several discussions in the literature on collusion and gains from market power as possible motives of joint-ventures. These motives do not explain why joint-venture is preferred when a merger or a contract between the parent firms could have also accomplished similar results. In fact, with the exception of the joint R&D ventures, anti-trust policies had treated mergers and joint-ventures equivalently [Brodley (1976)]. Although theoretically plausible, previous empirical evidence for collusion and market power related gains from joint-ventures has been mixed and inconclusive [Berg and Friedman (1980); Boyle (1968); Duncan (1982); Mead (1967); Ordover and Willig (1985); Pfeffer and Nowak (1976); Vickers (1985)]. Ceteris paribus, such gains are most likely when the parent firms are in the same industry, but in such a case shareholders will anticipate an acquisition. Therefore, if there are any monopoly related gains, they will be offset by the negative reaction to the choice of joint venture. Therefore:

Hypothesis 3. On an average, shareholder reactions to joint-ventures between parent companies whose principal businesses are in the same industry will either be less favorable than or not different from their reactions to other joint-ventures.

To test these hypotheses, we assess shareholder reactions to joint-venture announcements by using the standard event study method which has been widely used in finance literature to evaluate corporate mergers and acquisitions.

3. Methodology

3.1. Evaluation of Investor Reactions

The event study method involves estimating the abnormal returns, if any, to the parent company's common stock holders when the stock price has adjusted to the new information revealed by the announcement [Fama et al. (1969)]. In the standard event study method, the market model is first used to predict the normal returns to the common stock of a firm:

$$R_{it} = \alpha_i + \beta_i R_{mt} + \varepsilon_{it},$$

where R_{it} = the return of firm i in period t, R_{mt} = the return on value/equally weighted market portfolio of securities in period t, α_i and β_i = firm specific parameters, ε_{it} = random error $\sim N(0, \sigma_i)$.

The model parameters are estimated using the monthly or daily firm and market returns for an estimation period preceding some discrete, unanticipated events (e.g., announcement of mergers, joint-ventures, etc.). The deviations of the actual returns from the predicted returns on the relevant securities—the abnormal returns—for a conventionally chosen event period around the event date but falling outside the estimation period, are then computed from:

$$AR_{it} = R_{it} - (\hat{\alpha}_i + \hat{\beta}_i R_{mt}),$$

where $\hat{\alpha}$ and $\hat{\beta}$ are the ordinary least squares estimates of the parameters of the market model. These abnormal returns are then averaged over a large sample of firms affected by similar events to cancel out the effect of extraneous noise:

$$\overline{AR}_t = \frac{1}{N}\sum_{i=1}^{N} AR_{it},$$

where N is the number of parent firms in the sample. The cumulative abnormal return (CAR) over any interval $[t_1, t_2]$ is obtained from,

$$CAR\,[t_1, t_2] = \sum_{t_1}^{t_2} \overline{AR}_t,$$

where, t_1 and t_2 are the beginning and ending month of the period over which the cross-sectional average returns are cumulated. $\overline{AR}_t$ and $CAR\,[t_1, t_2]$ form the basic statistics for evaluating the investor reactions to the event. A statistically significant positive average return or CAR indicates that the event has a positive impact on the return on the stocks of the firms affected by the event. Event studies assume that the capital market is informationally efficient. In its weak form, this means that the market adjusts instantaneously to publicly available information. The event study method is simple to use and has proved to be quite powerful and robust in evaluating discrete events affecting firms. Even though the joint-venture formation may extend over a long time—it often does—the event study method is appropriate if the pre-announcement negotiation is not public information.[6]

3.2. Sample and Data

To evaluate investor reactions to the announcement of joint-ventures, we constructed a sample of joint-ventures from the quarterly joint-venture roster published in *Mergers and Acquisitions* during the four year period 1974–1977. The period was chosen to take advantage of industry data from the *FTC Line of Business Reports, 1974–1977*, which the authors are using in other concurrent research projects on joint-ventures. The following criteria were used to select the sample:

1. The joint-venture should be entirely U.S. based. Both parents should be incorporated in the U.S. and the joint venture should also have its operations mainly in the U.S.

Table 1. Sample

Year	Number of Joint-Ventures	Number of Parent Firms
1974	8	10
1975	16	22
1976	22	30
1977	18	23
Total	64	85

2. The joint-ventures selected should not involve more than two parent companies. This criterion was adopted to avoid the messy issues in measuring the similarity among three or more parents.

3. The joint-venture should have been reported in the Wall Street Journal or in any of the trade journals covered by the F&S Index of Corporate Changes during the same month as indicated in the effective date of the joint-venture reported by the *Mergers and Acquisition* roster.

4. Both the parent companies should be listed in the Million Dollar Directory of American Businesses, along with the SIC (Standard Industry Classification) codes for their primary businesses.

5. At least one of the parent's stock returns should be available from the monthly returns file of the Center for Research in Security Prices (CRSP) at the University of Chicago, for a period covering 72 months before and including the month of the announcement of the joint-venture.[7]

Our final sample consisted of 64 joint-ventures and 85 parent companies which satisfied the screening criteria. Table 1 lists the number of joint-ventures and parent companies in the sample for each year. For each of the 85 parent companies in our sample of joint-venture announcements, we first estimated the market model using the monthly returns from the CRSP files, for the period t_{-72} to t_{-13}, with t_0 being the event month, referring to the month of the joint-venture announcement. The abnormal returns and the CAR's for each parent were computed for 13 months including the announcement month, t_{-12} to t_0. The estimation and announcement periods chosen were comparable to previous event studies using monthly returns [see for e.g., Asquith and Kim (1982); Dodd and Ruback (1977); Malatesta (1983)].

4. Results and Discussion

Table 2 shows the average and cumulative abnormal returns, and the cross-sectional variances for t_{-12} to t_0, for all the parent firms in the sample. The table

Table 2. Abnormal Returns: Full Sample

All Joint-Ventures: $N = 85$

Relative Month	Abnormal Return	CAR	Cross-Sectional Variance
−12	−0.0039	−0.0039	0.0061
−11	0.0191	0.0152	0.0094
−10	0.0042	0.0194	0.0069
−9	−0.0036	0.0157	0.0075
−8	0.0071	0.0228	0.0059
−7	0.0071	0.0299	0.0067
−6	−0.0171	0.0128	0.0093
−5	−0.0040	0.0088	0.0090
−4	0.0013	0.0101	0.0111
−3	−0.0027	0.0075	0.0060
−2	0.0100	0.0175	0.0063
−1	0.0097	0.0272	0.0063
0	0.0119	0.0390	0.0055

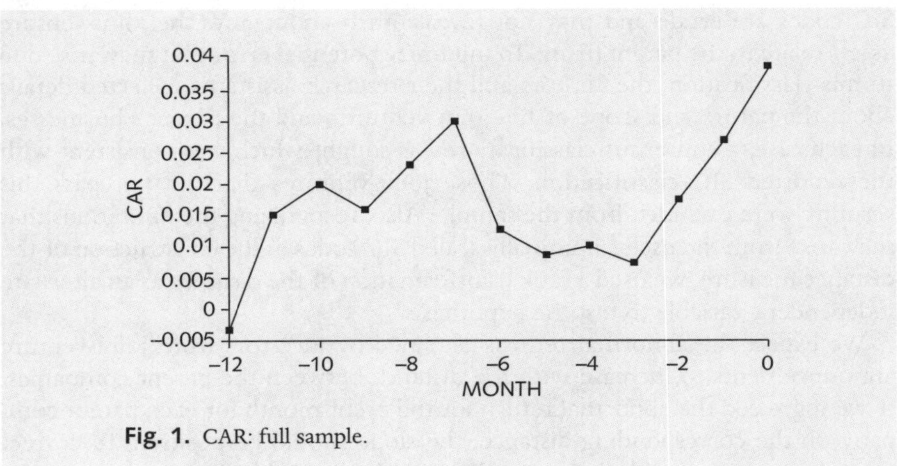

Fig. 1. CAR: full sample.

reveals that the stockholders of the parent companies obtained an abnormal return of 1.19% during the month of the announcement of the joint-ventures. The Z-statistic for this return was significant at the 0.01 level and therefore the null hypothesis of no significant gains from combining the complementary assets of the parent companies in a joint-venture can be rejected.[8]

Figure 1 is a plot of the cumulative abnormal returns for the period. The cumulative abnormal returns increases 3.9% from t_{-12} to t_0. The increases in abnormal returns over several other sub-intervals or holding periods were also statistically significant.[9] Because of sample bias that may arise due to the inclusion of both parents in 21 of the 64 joint-ventures, we divided the sample into two sub-samples: (i) one randomly selected parent from each of the 21 joint-ventures ($N = 21$), and (ii) all the remaining parents ($N = 64$).[10] The abnormal returns for the two sub-samples were significant at the 0.05 and 0.01 level respectively. These results broadly support Hypothesis (2). Shareholders realize significant gains from joint-ventures, a result which is consistent with previous results obtained by McConnell and Nantell (1985).

Of primary interest to us is whether the investors react more favorably to joint-ventures between parents operating in dissimilar businesses. To investigate the relationship between joint-venture efficiency and parent dissimilarity and test Hypothesis 2, we constructed a simple measure of the 'distance' between the primary businesses of the parent companies. The measure is based on the 3-digit SIC's of the parent firms of the jth joint-venture, normalized over the maximum possible distance:

$$D_{j1,j2} = |SIC_{j1} - SIC_{j2}| / 899.$$

Greater the distance, more dissimilar the businesses are. Admittedly, the 3-digit SIC codes are crude and may not reveal much about how the joint-venture assets relate to the parent firms. To minimize potential error that may arise due to mis-classification, the authors and their research assistants collected details about the nature and scope of the joint venture's and the parent's businesses. In each case, a consensus classification was sought which was consistent with the reported SIC classification. Those joint-ventures that did not pass this scrutiny were excluded from the sample. Also, recognizing the limitations that may arise from the use of nominally scaled SIC codes in the construction of the distance measure, we used a rank transformation of the distance as an alternate independent variable to test the hypothesis.

We expect the abnormal returns obtained by investors from joint-venture announcements to increase with the distance between the parent companies. If we regressed the abnormal return for the event month for each parent company on the corresponding distance, the slope should be positive. To correct for possible heteroscedasticity, we first standardized the abnormal return for each parent company i [Brown and Warner (1985)]:

$$SR_{it} = AR_{it} / \sigma_i,$$

$$\text{where } \sigma_i = \sqrt{\sum_{t=-72}^{t=-13} (AR_{it} - \overline{AR}_i)^2 / 60}\,.$$

The standardized abnormal return for the announcement month for each parent company in the sample was than regressed on the corresponding distance or its rank transformation. As before, we divided the sample into two sub-samples of 21 and 64 parent firms and estimated the slopes for each sub-sample. Because the error terms in the two samples may not be independent in 21 observations we used Seemingly Unrelated Regression (SUR) for unequal samples [Judge et al. (1980)]. The Generalized Least Squares (GLS) estimates from these regressions are summarized in Table 3. The coefficient for the distance as well as its rank transformation were positive in all regressions and significant at the 0.10 level or above for the sub-sample of 64 parents. We interpret these results as supporting our hypothesis that investors react more favorably to the announcements of joint-ventures between parents in dissimilar businesses.

To test the third hypothesis that joint-ventures facilitate collusion and result in significant gains in monopoly power for the parents, we divide the 64 joint-ventures into two portfolios based on the parents' primary businesses: (i) the monopoly portfolio of 11 joint-ventures in which the parent firms' businesses were within the same 4- or 3-digit SIC and (ii) the remaining 53 joint-ventures which we call the non-monopoly portfolio.[11] The average abnormal returns, CAR's and the cross-sectional variances for the two portfolios are reported in Table 4. The average abnormal return for the announcement month for the monopoly portfolio was positive but insignificant. For the non-monopoly portfolio of joint-ventures the average abnormal

Table 3. SUR Results for Joint Ventures

Department Variable: Std. Abnormal Ret.	Parameter Estimates (std. err. in parenthesis)			
	Sample I: $N = 21$		Sample II: $N = 64$	
Model I				
Constant	−0.1154	−0.5675	−0.043	−0.0719
	(0.2438)	(0.3361)	(0.1536)	(0.1866)
Monopoly dummy		0.8095[c]		0.0894
		(0.4566)		(0.3281)
Distance	1.9645	3.3702[b]	1.1883[b]	1.2659[c]
	(1.1422)	(1.3322)	(0.6022)	(0.6659)
R squared	0.071	0.099	0.071	0.099
Model II				
Constant	−0.2006	−1.4908[b]	−0.2253	−0.4370
	(0.3486)	(0.6117)	(0.2315)	(0.3332)
Monopoly dummy		1.4565[b]		0.3429
		(0.6011)		(0.3903)
Rank	0.0094	0.0304[a]	0.0089[c]	0.0124[b]
	(0.0073)	(0.0109)	(0.0046)	(0.0061)
R squared	0.056	0.113	0.056	0.113

[a] Significant at 0.01.
[b] Significant at 0.05.
[c] Significant at 0.1.

Table 4. Abnormal Returns: Monopoly and Others Portfolios

	Monopoly Portfolio: $N = 17$			Others Portfolio: $N = 68$		
Relative Month	Abnormal Return	CAR	Cross-Sectional Variance	Abnormal Return	CAR	Cross-Sectional Variance
−12	0.0049	0.0049	0.0040	−0.0061	−0.0061	0.0066
−11	−0.0064	−0.0015	0.0043	0.0255	0.0194	0.0105
−10	−0.0006	−0.0021	0.0022	0.0054	0.0248	0.0081
−9	0.0049	0.0028	0.0024	−0.0058	0.0190	0.0088
−8	−0.0141	−0.0113	0.0015	0.0123	0.0313	0.0069
−7	−0.0089	−0.0202	0.0024	0.0111	0.0424	0.0076
−6	0.0068	−0.0133	0.0061	−0.0231	0.0194	0.0099
−5	−0.0006	−0.014	0.0038	−0.0049	0.0145	0.0103
−4	0.0110	−0.0029	0.0032	−0.0011	0.0134	0.0130
−3	−0.0166	−0.0195	0.0065	0.0008	0.0142	0.0058
−2	0.0198	0.0002	0.0038	0.0076	0.0218	0.0069
−1	0.0132	0.0134	0.0029	0.0088	0.0306	0.0061
0	0.0027	0.0161	0.0029	0.0142	0.0448	0.0071

return to the parents was positive and significant at the 0.01 level. The *t-statistic* for the difference between the two averages was positive in favor of the non-monopoly portfolio and significant at the 0.01 level. The Wilcoxon–Mann–Whitney rank test statistic for the difference between the two sub-samples was also positive but not significant. Over longer intervals, however, the cumulative average returns for the two portfolios did not show any significant differences.

The CAR's are plotted in Fig. 2. The CAR's for both the groups increase from t_{-12} to t_0, the announcement month. The CAR's for the monopoly portfolio are generally lower than those for the non-monopoly portfolio during the period t_{-12} to t_0. Taken together, these results seem to reject collusion as the primary motive for joint-ventures.

Noting that the distance between the parent companies in the monopoly joint-ventures is zero, and that this may be a potential source of distortion in the regressions for testing Hypothesis (1), we replicated these regressions with a dummy variable (MONO) which took the value of 1 if the parent belonged to the same 3-digit SIC and zero otherwise. Table 3 reports the results of these regressions. The results are generally stronger than those from the restricted model. The coefficients of the distance and its rank transformation were both positive and significant in both the sub-samples. The coefficient for the dummy variable is positive in all regressions and significant for the smaller sub-sample. This is somewhat at variance with the results from the portfolio method and the discrepancy is perhaps due to small samples. In any case, given that the

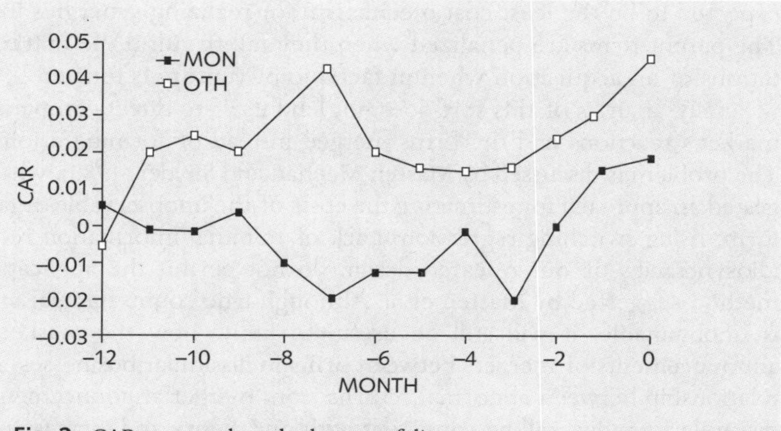

Fig. 2. CAR: monopoly and others portfolios.

joint-ventures in the sample had passed the scrutiny of anti-trust agencies, these results should be interpreted conservatively.

Much as we would like to consider the results for our main hypothesis regarding the positive relationship between abnormal returns and dissimilarity of parents' businesses as conclusive, the shortcomings in the methodology arising from our measure of dissimilarity of businesses require us to interpret the results with caution. First, we note that the measure was constructed with 3-digit Standard Industrial Classification which is based primarily on production technologies. The measure, therefore, captures mainly the potential information asymmetry that arises from the parents' involvement in dissimilar production technologies. In principle, a better proxy can be constructed with more information about past transactions and other forms of relationships between the joint-venture parents. Much of this information, however, is proprietary and difficult to obtain.

Second, to the extent that the distance measure reflects potential competition between the parents in their core markets, the methodology admits alternative interpretations of our main result that joint-ventures between similar parents are less favorably received than those between dissimilar parents. One interpretation is that when the parent businesses are in adjacent markets, the likelihood of future conflicts between them is more, increasing the costs of administering the joint-venture successfully. This may indeed be so and it tempers our enthusiasm about the results which may have little to do with the costs of adverse selection in asset transactions. An alternative interpretation that favors our theory is that the market's poor response to a joint-venture between parents in similar businesses is because acquisition is expected to be the least cost mechanism for realizing synergies in this case. The parent firms are penalized when they fail to fulfill the market's expectations of an acquisition when in fact a joint-venture is formed.

Finally, analysis of this sort does not lend itself to direct comparison of the market's reactions had the firms merged instead of forming a joint-venture. The problem is discussed by Masten Meehan and Snyder (1988), who have suggested an approach for estimating the costs of the unobservable organizational form, using switching regression. Lack of minimal information required and idiosyncracies of our research design do not permit the application of the method suggested by Masten et al. Although true counterfactual information is unobtainable, it will still be useful to know how the market reacts to announcements of mergers between firms in dissimilar businesses. A negative relationship between abnormal returns from merger announcements and the dissimilarity index will be consistent with our theory and increase our confidence in Hypothesis (1).

To test this, we selected a sample of 165 mergers and acquisitions announced during the same period, 1974–1977. The selection criteria were similar to those for the joint-ventures. Because merger announcement dates can be more precisely identified, we used daily returns for this analysis. The regression results are reported in Table 5.

Table 5. SUR Results for Mergers and Acquisition

Dependent variable: Std. Abnormal Ret.	Parameter Estimates (std. err. in parenthesis)			
	Sample I: $N = 56$		Sample II: $N = 165$	
Model I				
Constant	5.1321[a]	4.7952[a]	−0.1011	0.0910
	(1.1093)	(1.2484)	(0.1220)	(0.1378)
Monopoly dummy		1.5822		0.0467
		(2.6936)		(0.2960)
Distance	−11.2780	−10.2890[b]	−0.8527	−0.8168
	(5.7605)	(6.0025)	(0.7534)	(0.7868)
R squared	0.049	0.053	0.049	0.053
Model II				
Constant	6.8958[a]	6.9688[a]	0.2938	0.4062
	(1.8392)	(2.4968)	(0.2003)	(0.2732)
Monopoly dummy		−0.1429		−0.2154
		(3.2593)		(0.3565)
Rank	−0.1058[b]	−0.1077	−0.0033	−0.0043
	(0.0562)	(0.0707)	(0.0021)	(0.0026)
R squared	0.049	0.050	0.049	0.050

[a] Significant at 0.01.
[b] Significant at 0.1.

The sign of relationship between standardized abnormal returns and distance is negative, but significant only for the smaller sub-samples which comprised entirely of acquired firms. These results are consistent with earlier studies that had examined the relationship between abnormal returns and relatedness in merger and acquisitions [Singh and Montgomery (1987); Shelton (1988)]. The negative relationship suggests that the market reactions are relatively more adverse for announcements of mergers between dissimilar firms. The opposite relationships for the joint-venture and the merger announcements strengthen our confidence in our main hypothesis as well as the robustness of the dissimilarity measure.

5. Conclusion

Earlier studies of joint-ventures have likened them to mergers and acquisitions, as a mechanism for realizing synergies, collusion or risk-sharing. Our theory is that the joint-venture is a mechanism for pooling complementary assets without having to resort to a terminal sale and redistribution of ownership and control rights over these assets. Such non-terminal mechanisms will be efficient when the market for acquisitions fails due to the asymmetry between the seller's and buyer's information about the target assets. This is most likely when the parents operate in dissimilar businesses.

Our theory is supported by the evidence based on investors' reactions to joint-venture and acquisition announcements. In an event study of 64 joint-venture announcements, we observed that the shareholders of the parent companies involved in these joint-ventures obtained significantly larger abnormal returns when these companies were engaged in businesses which were further apart in a technological and managerial sense. Although value is created in all joint-ventures, the shareholders seem to favor joint-ventures between parents engaged in dissimilar businesses. We found quite the opposite relationship between abnormal returns and dissimilarity in the case of mergers and acquisitions. Both the acquirers and target firms obtained larger abnormal returns when their businesses were similar, the targets, more significantly so. We interpret these results to mean that while both joint-ventures and acquisitions may yield synergistic gains to shareholders, there are non-trivial differences between the two mechanisms. Under specific conditions one may be superior to the other. Besides the obvious implications for management's choice between acquisition and joint-venture, the theory and empirical results should also be of interest to policy makers in the areas of anti-trust and interfirm cooperation.

Notes

1. Following Richardson (1972), we define assets or the functions embodied in them as complementary, 'when they represent different phases of a process of production and require in some way or another to be coordinated.' By assets here and elsewhere in the chapter, we mean physical assets, tangible and intangible, which are alienable and for which property rights are well-defined.
2. For some recent work on comparative analysis of joint-ventures and other coordinating mechanisms, see Buckley and Casson (1988), Contractor and Lorange (1988), Hennart (1988), Kogut (1988), and Williamson (1985).
3. Joint-ventures set-up as limited partnerships are an exception. The 'sleeping' partners in a limited partnership joint-venture have no say in policy making or control.
4. Hennart (1988) describes a few other diseconomies of acquisition. These relate to international arena where cultural and national interests may make acquisitions more costly than joint ventures. Also, see Kogut and Singh (1985), who present some evidence for this.
5. It is important to distinguish between risk arising from uncertain prospects for a venture and the adverse selection due to asymmetric information. Suppose that the buyer has all the information that the seller has about the target assets. The buyer can efficiently share the residual uncertainty about the new venture (uncertainty about demand for its products, for e.g.) by selling the risky claims in the capital market. The price offered by the seller for the target assets will be discounted to reflect the premium charged for this risk. A rational seller should accept this offer because it is the true (risk-adjusted) value of his assets. If, in addition, there is an asymmetry between the buyer's and seller's information about the assets, the price offered for the assets will be further discounted to reflect this asymmetry. The seller will refuse to sell in this case because the offer price will fall short of his expectations.
6. A number of studies in finance, strategy and other areas have employed the event study method to evaluate investor reactions to merger announcements [see Jensen and Ruback (1983) and Weston and Chung (1983), for a review of several event studies of acquisitions]. Protracted negotiations and anticipation is a problem in all these studies but not a serious one, provided appropriate precautions are undertaken. Also, see Brown and Warner (1980, 1985) for an assessment of the statistical power of the event study method and the associated tests in successfully detecting abnormal returns from unanticipated events.
7. We used monthly returns data because of our inability to precisely identify the date of joint-venture announcements which are not reported in the financial press or the trade journals as promptly as mergers and acquisitions. While the use of daily returns in

event studies yields to more powerful tests, the benefits are not clear when there is ambiguity about event dates.

8. The appropriate test-statistic for the abnormal return is given by $Z = \overline{AR}_t / \sigma_t$, where σ is given by $\sigma_t = \sqrt{\Sigma_{t=-72}^{t=-13} (\overline{AR}_t - \bar{A}R)^2 / 60}$, $\bar{A}R(1/60)\, \Sigma_{t=-72}^{t=-13} \overline{AR}_t$. Z is distributed *Student* $-t$ and for large samples, is approximately unit normal [Brown and Warner (1985)].
9. We note that the average abnormal returns for $t = -10$ and $t = -6$ are significantly positive and negative, respectively. We are unable to explain this.
10. We are grateful to the anonymous referee for pointing out the sample bias that may arise from pooling both the parents of the joint-ventures in the sample.
11. See Caves et al. (1980, 199–200) for a measure of 'distance' between businesses based on their SIC's which takes a value of zero if the 4-digit SIC's of the two parent were within the same 3-digit SIC, a value of one if they were in different 3-digit SIC's but the same 2-digit SIC's, and a value of two if they were in different two digit SIC's. In our sample there was just one joint-venture for which this distance had a value of 1, that is, the parent companies primary businesses were in different 3-digit SIC's but the same 2-digit SIC. This rather small sample problem forced us to form two portfolios instead of three, if we had followed the Caves et al. measure strictly.

References

Akerlof, G. A. 1970, The market for 'lemons': Qualitative uncertainty and the market mechanism, Quarterly Journal of Economics 84, 488–500.

Alchian, A. A. and Demsetz, H. 1972, Production, information costs and economic organization, American Economic Review 62, 777–795.

Asquith, P. and Kim, H. 1982, The impact of merger bids on the participating firms' security returns, Journal of Finance Dec., 1209–1228.

Berg, S. and Friedman, P. 1981, Impacts of domestic joint ventures on industrial rates of return: A pooled cross-section analysis, 1964–1975, The Review of Economics and Statistics 63, 293–298.

Boyle, S. 1968, An estimate of the number and size distribution of domestic joint subsidiaries, Antitrust Law and Economic Review 1, 81–92.

Bradley, M. 1980, Interfirm tender offers and the market for corporate control, Journal of Business 53, 345–376.

Brodley, J. F. 1976, The legal status of joint ventures under the antitrust laws: A summary assessment, Antitrust Bulletin 21, 453–483.

Brown S. J. and Warner, J. B. 1980, Measuring security price performance, Journal of Financial Economics 8, June, 205–258.

—— and —— 1985, Using daily stock returns: the case of event studies, Journal of Financial Economics 14, March, 3–31.

Buckley, P. J. and Casson, M. 1988, A theory of cooperation in international business, in: Farok J. Contractor and Peter Lorange, eds., Cooperative Strategies in International Business (Lexington Books, Lexington, MA), 31–53.

Caves, R. E., Porter, M. E., Spence M., and Scott, J. T. 1980, Competition in the open economy (Harvard University Press, Cambridge, MA).

Contractor, F. J. and Lorange, P. 1988, Why should firms cooperate? The strategy and economics for cooperation ventures, in: Farok J. Contractor and Peter Lorange, eds., Cooperative strategies in international business (Lexington Books, Lexington, MA), 3–30.

Dodd, P. and Ruback, R. 1977, Tender offers and stockholder returns: An empirical analysis, Journal of Financial Economics 5, 351–374.

Duncan, J. L., 1982, Impacts of new entry and horizontal joint ventures on industrial rates of return, Review of Economics and Statistics 64, 339–343.

Fama, E. F., Fisher, L., Jensen M., and Roll, R. 1969, The adjustment of stock prices to new information, International Economic Review 1, 1–21.

Fusfeld, D. R. 1958, Joint subsidiaries in the iron and steel industry, American Economic Review 48, 578–587.

Hennart, J. F. 1988, A transaction costs theory of joint ventures, Strategic Management Journal 9, 361–374.

Jensen, M. C. and Ruback, R. 1983, The market for corporate control, Journal of Financial Economics 11, 5–50.

Judge, G. G., Griffiths, W. E., Hill R. C., and Lee, T. 1980, The theory and practice of econometrics (John Wiley and Sons, Inc. New York).

Klein, B., Crawford, R., and Alchian, A. 1978, Vertical integration, appropriable rents and the competitive contracting process, Journal of Law and Economics 21, 297–326.

Kogut, B. 1988, Joint ventures: Theoretical and empirical perspectives, Strategic Management Journal 9, 319–322.

—— and Singh, H. 1985, Entering the United States by acquisition or joint venture: Country patterns and cultural characteristics, Working paper, The Wharton School.

Malatesta, P. H. 1983, The wealth effect of merger activity and the objective functions of merging firms, Journal of Financial Economics 11, 155–181.

Masten, S. E., Meehan J. W., and Snyder, E. A. 1988, The costs of organization, Working paper, University of Michigan, Ann Arbor.

McConnell, J. J. and Nantell, T. J. 1985, Corporate combinations and common stock returns: The case of joint ventures, Journal of Finance 2, 519–536.

Mead, W. J. 1967, The competitive significance of joint ventures, Antitrust Bulletin 12, 819–849.

Ordover, J. A. and Willig, R. D. 1985, Anti-trust for high-technology industries: Assessing research joint-ventures and mergers, Journal of Law and Economics 28, 311–343.

Pfeffer, J. and Nowak, P. 1976, Joint ventures and inter-organizational interdependence, Administrative Science Quarterly 21, 398–418.

Ravenscraft, D. J. and Scherer, F. M. 1987, Mergers, sell-offs, and economic efficiency (Brookings Institution, Washington, DC).

Shelton, L. M., 1988, Strategic business fits corporate acquisition: Empirical evidence, Strategic Management Journal 9, 279–287.

Singh, H. and Montgomery, C. 1987, Corporate acquisitions and economic performance, Strategic Management Journal 8, 377–386.

Vickers, J. 1985, Pre-emptive patenting, joint-ventures, and the persistence of oligopoly, International Journal of Industrial Organization 3, 261–273.

Weston, J. F. and Chung, S. 1983, Some aspects of merger theory, Journal of Midwest Finance Association 12, 1–33.
Williamson, O. E. 1975, Markets and Hierarchies (Free Press, New York).
—— 1979, Transaction-cost economics: The governance of contractual relations, Journal of Law and Economics 22, 233–261.
—— 1985, The economic institutions of capitalism (Free Press, New York).

6 The Choice between Mergers/Acquisitions and Joint Ventures: The Case of Japanese Investors in the United States

Jean-François Hennart and Sabine Reddy

1. Introduction

This chapter investigates the determinants of the choice between two alternative methods of pooling similar and complementary assets: the merger/acquisition and the greenfield equity joint venture. This choice is of particular interest because it throws light on two competing theories of why joint ventures exist. Balakrishnan and Koza (1991, 1993) see joint ventures as a mechanism to reduce the transaction costs incurred when acquiring other firms. They predict that joint ventures will be preferred when the potential target and the acquirer belong to different industries, because in this case these transaction costs are high. They are lower when the acquirer and the target firm are based in the same industry, and hence in that case they expect acquisitions.

Hennart (1988), on the other hand, argues that a firm will favor acquisitions over joint ventures when the assets it needs are not commingled with other unneeded assets within the firm that holds them, and hence can be acquired by buying the firm or a part of it. For Hennart, the 'digestibility' of the targeted assets, itself a function of the size and organizational structure of the firm that owns them, is the crucial determinant of the choice between joint ventures and acquisitions. Thus, while Balakrishnan and Koza are concerned with transaction costs in the market for firms, Hennart's focus is on the costs of integrating the target firm's labor force (what has been called the postacquisition integration problem). Looking at the choice between joint ventures and acquisition hence allows us to sharpen our understanding of the strategic logic for the choice between these two forms of firm growth.

The next section positions the chapter within the joint venture literature. We then examine the choice between acquisitions and greenfield joint ventures. The specific hypotheses derived in this section are tested in the following two sections on a sample of Japanese manufacturing entries in the United States. The results show that joint ventures are preferred over acquisitions when the desired assets are 'indigestible', i.e., when they are commingled with nondesired assets because the U.S. firm owning them is large and not divisionalized. Joint ventures are also chosen when the Japanese investor has had no previous experience of the American market and, hence, seeks to avoid postmerger integration problems, when the Japanese investor and the U.S. partner manufacture the same product, and when the industry entered is growing neither very rapidly nor very slowly.

2. Joint Ventures vs Acquisitions

Assume that a foreign investor plans to exploit some of its competencies in the U.S. market, but needs to combine them with U.S.-based inputs. If markets for *both* the competencies and the U.S.-based inputs are subject to high transaction costs, an equity joint venture will be the most efficient way to combine the complementary inputs (if one of the two inputs—say the U.S. input—could be obtained with low transaction costs by the foreign investor, then the foreign firm would set up a wholly-owned subsidiary on U.S. soil, and would obtain the complementary local input through spot sales or contract; if both inputs could be obtained with low transaction costs, then no foreign direct investment would take place) (Hennart, 1982, 1988).

There is, however, an alternative to joint ventures when markets for two or more inputs held by two or more separate firms are simultaneously failing. That solution is the merging of the firms holding the complementary inputs (in our case having the foreign investor buy the local firm which owned the U.S.-based inputs, the local firm buy the foreign investor, or having them merge).

Why then choose joint ventures over acquisitions? There are four main reasons.

2.1. Indivisibilities

One potential impediment to acquisitions is when the desired assets are hard to disentangle from nondesired ones (Hennart, 1988). Assume that a biotechnology firm needs access to a sales force to successfully introduce a new drug. If it were to buy a pharmaceutical firm to obtain its sales force, it would also be buying many assets which are not needed and which are difficult to disentangle from the sales force, and hence difficult to divest afterwards. For example, the need to vertically integrate drug manufacture and its distribution may make it impossible to acquire the sales force without acquiring drug manufacture as well. A small biotechnology company would be encumbered by these assets, and would incur high costs in managing them (Shan, 1988). By contrast, a joint venture allows the biotechnology firm to access the pharmaceutical firm's sales force without having to manage it. Hence the fact that a partner's desired assets are linked to its nondesired assets, while it makes acquisitions costly, does not cause problems for joint ventures, since the flow of services from the assets counts as a contribution to the joint venture, yet is still available for the parent's other businesses. Joint ventures may therefore be preferred when the desired assets are not easily separable from the many other assets owned by the parent. This is likely to be the case when the parents are large and not divisionalized. Acquisitions, on the other hand, will be chosen when the parents are small, or if they are large, when they are organized in quasi-independent divisions which can be acquired separately from the rest of the firm, that is, when they are divisionalized (Kay, Robe, and Zagnolli, 1987).

2.2. Management Costs

When a foreign firm acquires a local firm, it acquires an existing corps of employees, with their own routines and culture. Integrating such employees is difficult, particularly so if there are cultural differences between the two firms (Jemison and Sitkin, 1986). These cultural differences may arise because firms come from different industries or countries. In contrast, a joint venture safeguards the incentives that employees of both firms have to maximize the profits of the joint venture. The management of the joint venture's labor force can therefore be left to the local partner (Kogut and Singh, 1988). Hence, joint ventures may be preferred over acquisitions by firms which are inexperienced in managing a foreign labor force, and by firms venturing outside their core industry.

2.3. Difficulties in Assessing the Value of the Target Firm

For Balakrishnan and Koza (1991, 1993), joint ventures are desired when acquirers do not know the value of the assets desired. A joint venture is an efficient vehicle for reducing these information costs because it makes it possible both to gather additional information on the value of the partner's assets and to rescind the relationship at relatively low cost. Hence, joint ventures should be preferred to acquisitions when the firms combining assets have little knowledge of each other's business, i.e., when they are in different industries (Balakrishnan and Koza, 1991).

2.4. *Governmental and Institutional Barriers*

In some countries foreign acquisitions are banned in some or all sectors, or are made difficult by legal restrictions on voting rights, cross-holdings (Japan), and bank and family control (Germany and Italy, respectively) (Lightfoot, 1992).

Kogut and Singh (1988) and Singh and Kogut (1989) provide the only empirical evidence on the factors that determine the choice between acquisitions and joint ventures. Kogut and Singh (1988) looked at entries by foreign multinational firms into the United States. They argued that a main disadvantage of entering through acquisition was the high management cost involved in integrating the target firm's labor force and that the disadvantage would be greater the greater the cultural distance between the investor's home base and the United States. As expected, they found that joint ventures were preferred to acquisitions when the entrant's home country was culturally distant from the United States. Joint ventures were also preferred when the U.S. operation was large and when the U.S. industry entered was R&D intensive. The parent's experience of the U.S. market was not significant.

The design and the data sources in Singh and Kogut (1989) are similar to Kogut and Singh (1988), but the emphasis is on the characteristics of entering firms and on those of the U.S. sectors entered. Singh and Kogut hypothesized that the problems of valuing acquisitions were higher in R&D intensive industries and, hence, that entries in these industries were more likely to be joint ventures. They found that joint ventures were preferred to acquisitions when the U.S. industry entered was R&D intensive, when the foreign investor had little experience of the U.S. market, and when the targeted venture was large.

Neither of these two studies examined what can be called the 'digestibility' of the targeted U.S. assets. Kogut and Singh (1988) argue that acquisitions will be discouraged the larger the assets of the affiliate, but do not provide a rationale for this prediction. In Singh and Kogut (1989), the hypothesis is that large investments are more risky than small ones. Hence investors enter through joint ventures to share that risk with their partners. The size of the venture is defined as the assets of the acquired unit (in the case of acquisition) or that of the U.S. partner (in the case of joint ventures). This specification introduces a bias if, as we expect, acquisitions are systematically associated with small affiliate size (but not necessarily small partner size, since the acquired unit may be a division of a large firm). By measuring affiliate size by the assets of the acquired unit in the case of acquisitions, and by those of the partner in the case of joint ventures, the authors bias the test towards significance of their size variable. A correct specification should be neutral *vis-à-vis* the outcome, i.e., it should consider partner size in the case of both acquisition and joint ventures. Assets are also a poor proxy for the magnitude of postacquisition management problems. Because of this and other problems with the empirical analysis, further research into the determinants of the choice between acquisitions and joint ventures is warranted.[1]

3. Research Design and Testable Propositions

The focus of our empirical analysis is the choice made by Japanese investors into the United States between full acquisitions of U.S. firms (hereafter acquisitions) and greenfield joint ventures between Japanese and American firms (henceforth joint ventures). This focus on Japanese entries in the United States has three main advantages. First, because the United States has both negligible government and structural barriers to acquisitions, we avoid the problem of having to control for them.[2] Second, studying parents based in a single country controls for the impact of national cultural differences in the mode of entry (Kogut and Singh, 1988), differences which are very difficult to model. Third, Japanese entries are less skewed towards acquisitions than those of other countries, hence giving us a more balanced sample.[3]

We define the American partner as the firm which holds the assets which the Japanese investor needs. When the entry is a joint venture, the partner is the American parent of the venture. When the entry is an acquisition, the American partner may or may not be the same as the acquired firm, as in some cases Japanese firms have acquired divisions of divisionalized U.S. parents. In that case, the partner is the divisionalized parent. If the U.S. partner is small, it is likely that the assets desired by the Japanese investor make up 100 percent of the assets held by the U.S. firm. If the target firm is large but divisionalized, it is possible for the Japanese investor to acquire only the division that owns the desired resources. Acquisitions become problematic when the partner is large, but not divisionalized. Then it is difficult to separate desired from nondesired assets, and an acquisition would involve having to operate at a scale and/or in industries which do not fit well with the Japanese firm's business. In contrast, services of the desired assets can be obtained through a joint venture without having to change the ownership of these assets, and hence without having to disentangle them from nondesired assets. Hence:

Hypothesis 1: Acquisitions will be preferred to joint ventures when the desired assets are 'digestible', i.e., when the size of the U.S. partner is small, or if it is large, when the U.S. partner is divisionalized.

One of the main disadvantages of acquisitions relative to joint ventures is the high cost of integrating the target's firm's labor force. Such costs are likely to be particularly high for Japanese firms, because acquisitions are very rare in Japan, and hence purely domestic Japanese firms have very little experience with them.[4] By contrast, joint ventures with U.S. firms are a less risky way to test the feasibility of transferring the Japanese system to the United States, as the case of Toyota shows.

Japanese firms are likely to expect their postacquisition integration costs to be lower the longer they have been in the United States. Hence:

Hypothesis 2: Acquisitions will be preferred to joint ventures when the Japanese investor has a long experience of the U.S. environment.

Because company cultures and administrative routines differ systematically across industries, we would expect postacquisition integration problems to be lower for Japanese investors whose U.S. subsidiary manufactures the same product as they do. Therefore:

Hypothesis 3: Acquisitions will be preferred to joint ventures when the Japanese investor is in the same industry as the planned subsidiary.

As noted earlier, Balakrishnan and Koza have argued that joint ventures are a way to reduce the uncertainty concerning the value of the complementary assets brought together, and one implication they have drawn is that

> joint ventures should occur more frequently between parents who are in industries that are relatively unrelated to one another. Firms that are in unrelated industries are not likely to have sufficient knowledge or may require costly 'help' to evaluate complementary assets. (Balakrishnan and Koza, 1991: 24)

Hence:

Hypothesis 4: Joint ventures will be preferred to acquisitions when the Japanese and American partners are in a different industry.

By contrast, Hennart's (1988) theory has no strong implications as to whether joint ventures are more or less likely to be preferred to acquisitions when the partners are in the same industry. Link joint ventures are often established to combine the knowledge assets of firms in two different industries. Partners in scale joint ventures are often in the same industry. The same goes for acquisitions. Hence, whether or not the partners are in the same industry should have no impact on the way they choose to combine their assets.

Lastly, we must control for antitrust policies and the rate of growth of the target market. Kay et al. (1987), quoting Nelson (1982), argue that while U.S. antitrust authorities frown upon acquisitions and joint ventures between U.S. firms in concentrated industries, they are more tolerant of joint ventures if the partner is foreign. According to Berg and Friedman (1978), US antitrust authorities see horizontal joint ventures in a more positive light than full horizontal acquisitions. If, as seems to be the case, the combination of two firms with market power, one domestic and one foreign, attracts more opposition if it is achieved via an acquisition rather than via a joint venture, then:

Hypothesis 5a: Joint ventures will be preferred to acquisitions for Japanese entries into concentrated U.S. industries.

On the other hand, one advantage of acquisitions is that they do not create additional capacity, and hence are less threatening to incumbents.

Hypothesis 5b: Acquisitions will be preferred to joint ventures when the entry is in a concentrated U.S. industry.

Because of these two offsetting factors, the impact of concentration on entry is unclear. Because our study compares full acquisitions to greenfield joint ventures, we must control for factors that push firms towards acquisitions over greenfield entry (whether through wholly owned or joint ventured units). Acquisitions have two main advantages over greenfields: they permit faster entry, since it takes longer to build a subsidiary from scratch than to buy a going concern. In contrast to greenfield plants, acquisitions also do not add capacity. Hence acquisitions are encouraged when the U.S. industry entered grows either very fast or very slowly. Acquisitions are desired when the target industry grows very quickly, because then the opportunity cost of greenfield entry is high; acquisitions also make sense when the target industry is growing very slowly or is declining, because a greenfield entry would then add capacity which would depress profits (Caves and Mehra, 1986; Hennart and Park, 1993).

Hypothesis 6: Acquisitions will be preferred to joint ventures when the U.S. industry entered is growing very rapidly or very slowly.

4. Methodology and Dependent Variable

Our sample of Japanese manufacturing entries in the United States was obtained from two separate censuses undertaken periodically by Toyo Keizai and by the Japan Economic Institute. An acquisition takes place when a Japanese parent fully acquires an existing U.S. manufacturing company or parts thereof. A joint venture occurs when a Japanese investor establishes a new manufacturing facility and shares the ownership with an American partner (hence partial acquisitions are excluded). The unit of observation is the entry.[5] There were 428 such entries established between 1978 and 1989, of which 244 were acquisitions (57%), and 184 were joint ventures (43%). Data for the independent variables were compiled from the *Directory of Corporate Affiliations*, the *Japan Company Handbook, Predicast's F&S Index Plus Text, Predicast's F&S Index Plus Text—International*, and the *Census of Manufacturers*.

Lack of information for the independent variables reduced our sample size to 175 observations.[6] This reduction in the sample did not result in a significant bias, since the proportion of joint ventures in our sample (42.9%) is comparable to that of the population as a whole (43%). The distribution of acquisitions and greenfield joint ventures for each entry year in our sample is shown in Fig. 1.

At the time of entry, the Japanese subsidiaries in our sample operated in 16 different 2-digit SIC industries (see Table 1).[7] Most subsidiaries (138 out of 175 observations) were active in a single 4-digit SIC industry. U.S. partners range in size from 7 to 853,000 employees (between 7 and 367,000 for acquisitions, and between 85 and 853,000 for joint ventures). Slightly less than half the U.S. partners had a multidivisional structure.

Mode of entry is captured by a dummy variable which takes a value of 0 if the Japanese parent made an acquisition and one if it established a greenfield joint venture with an American firm. We use a binomial logistic model in which the regression coefficients estimate the impact of the independent variables on the probability that the entry will be through a joint venture, with a positive sign for the coefficient meaning that the variable increases that probability.

Table 2 provides the mean and standard deviation of the variables.[8] The dummy INDIG captures the indigestibility of the assets coveted by the Japanese investor. INDIG is composed of SIZE, a dummy equal to 1 if the U.S. partner who holds them is large, and USSTRUC, a dummy equal to 1 if the U.S. partner is divisionalized. A large U.S. partner is a U.S. firm with more than 5000 employees.[9] The cut-off value was empirically estimated by looking at the size distribution of U.S. partners in our sample. Changing the cut-off value to other plausible values (1000 and 2500 employees) does not change the

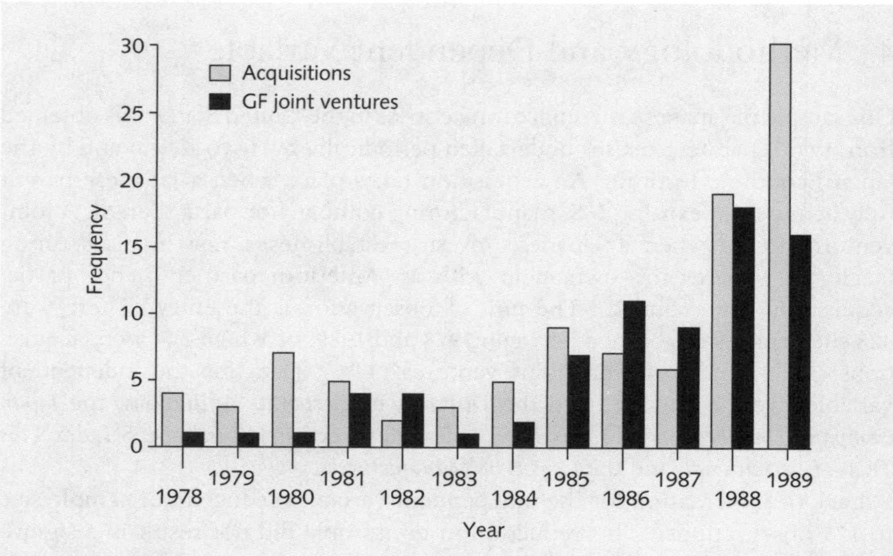

Fig. 1. Distribution of joint ventures and acquisitions over time (sample only).

Table 1. Frequency Count of Japanese Entries into U.S. Industries by 2-Digit SIC (Single Industry Entries Only)

SIC Code	Industry Name[a]	Full Acquisitions	Joint Ventures	Total
20:	Food and Kindred Products	6	1	7
23:	Apparel and Other Textile Products	0	2	2
24:	Lumber and Wood Products	1	0	1
25:	Furniture and Fixtures	1	2	3
26:	Paper and Allied Products	1	2	3
27:	Printing and Publishing	1	0	1
28:	Chemicals and Allied Products	23	9	32
30:	Rubber and Miscellaneous Plastics Products	4	6	10
32:	Stone, Clay, and Glass Products	3	4	7
33:	Primary Metal Industries	3	10	13
34:	Fabricated Metal Products	0	12	12
35:	Machinery, Except Electrical	15	6	21
36:	Electric and Electronic Equipment	19	10	29
37:	Transportation Equipment	1	6	7
38:	Instruments and Related Products	4	1	5
39:	Miscellaneous Manufacturing Industries	1	0	1
Total		83	71	154

[a] Classification according to the 1972 *Standard Industrial Classification Manual* and its 1977 Supplement.

results. Number of employees was obtained from the issue of the *Directory of Corporate Affiliations* published in the year before the corresponding Japanese entry.

We ascertained whether the U.S. partner was divisionalized or not (USSTRUC) by looking at the firm's organizational structure, as described in the *Directory of Corporate Affiliations*. USSTRUC takes a value of 1 if the U.S. partner was divisionalized, and 0 if it was not. We would expect joint ventures to be favored when the U.S. partner is large and not divisionalized. Hence, INDIG takes a value of 1 when the U.S. partner is not divisionalized (USSTRUC is 0) and large (SIZE is 1), and 0 otherwise (the American partner is small, or is large and divisionalized). INDIG should enter with a positive sign.

The Japanese investor's experience of the U.S. market at the time entry was made (JEXP) is measured by the number of years between entry and the establishment of the investor's first U.S. manufacturing subsidiary. The sign of JEXP should be negative. The difference in company culture between the Japanese parent and its subsidiary is proxied by COMMON, which is measured by a dummy variable equal to 1 if the Japanese investor and its affiliate manufacture one common product, and to 0 otherwise. COMMON should have a negative sign.

The extent to which the U.S. and the Japanese firms have divergent information concerning the value of the assets of the U.S. target firm is proxied by PARCOMMON, a dummy variable indicating whether the *Japanese and the American partners* were in the same industry. PARCOMMON was calculated by comparing the products manufactured by the Japanese investor and those manufactured by its U.S. partner. In the case of joint ventures, the partner is the U.S. joint venture partner. In the case of acquisitions, the partner is the parent firm of the acquired unit if the Japanese firm acquired a division or a part of a U.S. firm, or the acquired firm itself.[10] PARCOMMON was coded 1 if at least one of the products produced by the American partner was also produced by the Japanese parent. The sign of PARCOMMON should be negative.

The concentration ratio of the U.S. industry entered (CONCEN) is measured by the Herfindahl index for each 4-digit SIC U.S. industry, as published in the 1982 *Census of Manufactures*.[11] The arithmetic average of the concentration ratio was used for subsidiaries active in multiple SICs. No prediction is made for the sign of this variable.

Following Caves and Mehra (1986) we calculated GROWDEV to describe the conditions that encourage acquisitions. GROWDEV is the absolute value of GROWTH's deviation from its sample mean divided by its standard deviation, with GROWTH equal to the 3-year average annual growth rate of shipments of the 4-digit U.S. industry 2 years before entry (U.S. Department of Commerce, *U.S. Industrial Outlook*). Average industry growth rate was used for

Table 2. Means and Correlations (Coefficient / (*t*-Statistic) / Cases)

	Mean	S.D.	Freq.[a]/*N*	JVAQ	CONCEN	USEMPL	USSTRUC	INDIG	JEXP	PARCOMMON	COMMON	GROWDEV
JVAQ			75/175	1.000								
CONCEN	611.996	512.703		0.025	1.000							
				(0.329)								
				$N = 175$								
USEMPL	42.617	124.064		0.288	0.188	1.000						
				(3.932)	(2.499)							
				173	173							
USSTRUC			81/174	0.293	0.179	0.287	1.000					
				(4.012)	(2.382)	(3.899)						
				174	174	172						
INDIG			23/175	0.347	−0.02	−0.013	−0.364	1.000				
				(4.861)	(−0.259)	(−0.170)	(−5.129)					
				175	175	173	174					
JEXP	5.211	5.803		−0.131	−0.038	0.058	0.047	−0.052	1.000			
				(−1.744)	(−0.498)	(0.762)	(0.613)	(−0.688)				
				175	175	173	174	175				
PARCOMMON			132/175	0.146	0.008	−0.106	0.027	0.065	−0.144	1.000		
				(1.936)	(0.100)	(−1.394)	(0.356)	(0.855)	(−1.918)			
				175	175	173	174	175	174			
COMMON			149/175	0.037	0.079	0.061	0.036	0.115	−0.026	0.284	1.000	
				(0.488)	(1.046)	(0.802)	(0.468)	(1.522)	(−0.347)	(3.897)		
				175	175	173	174	175	175	175		
GROWDEV	0.782	1.082		−0.153	0.097	0.057	−0.017	−0.076	−0.021	−0.06	−0.052	1.000
				(−2.032)	(1.283)	(0.744)	(−0.220)	(−1.000)	(−0.279)	(−0.795)	(−0.690)	
				175	175	173	174	175	175	175	175	

[a] Frequency count of dummy = 1.

the few observations with multiple SICs. GROWDEV is high when the growth rate of the target U.S. industry is either very fast or very slow. Since a high value of GROWDEV should encourage acquisitions, its coefficient should be negative.

Table 2 displays the correlation coefficients for all variables. The matrix of the independent variables suggests little collinearity. Almost all correlations are low, the two highest coefficients being the ones between INDIG and USSTRUC (−0.36) and between PARCOMMON and COMMON (0.28).

5. Results

The results of the binomial logistic regression model are presented in Table 3. A positive coefficient for an independent variable means that it tends to increase the probability that a Japanese firm entered through a joint venture. The model has a high overall explanatory power, with a chi-square of 31.55 ($p = 0.0001$). Table 4 shows that our model correctly classifies 62.3 percent of the observations, a rate higher than that which would be expected by chance.[12]

Table 3. Parameter Estimates for Binomial Logit Model: Greenfield JVs vs Acquisitions (Joint Ventures = 1)

Variable Name	Description	Coefficients (*t*-Statistic)
Intercept		−0.4533 (0.80)
CONCEN	Concentration ratio of U.S. industry entered	0.0002 (0.60)
INDIG	Indigestibility of target firm. Dummy for U.S. partners which are large and not divisionalized	2.464*** (3.74)
JEXP	Number of years of presence of the Japanese partner in the U.S. market	−0.043* (1.43)
PARCOMMON	U.S. and Japanese partners have one common product	0.642* (1.52)
COMMON	Japanese parent and subsidiary have one common product	−0.278 (0.58)
GROWDEV	Deviation from the average of the growth of shipments of the U.S. industry entered	−0.371** (1.67)
Model chi-square: 31.555	*p* value: 0.0001	
$n = 175$		

*** $p < 0.01$; ** $p < 0.05$; * $p < 0.1$ (one tailed).

With the exception of PARCOMMON, all significant variables have the predicted signs. As predicted by Hypothesis 1, the coefficient of INDIG, our measure of the extent to which an acquisition would involve the purchase of unwanted assets, is positive and significant at the 0.1 level. Joint ventures are therefore desired when the U.S. firm that holds the assets needed by the Japanese entrant is large and is not divisionalized.[13]

PARCOMMON is weakly significant (at 0.10), but enters with a positive sign, suggesting that Japanese investors tend to prefer joint ventures to acquisitions when the Japanese and American partners are in the same industry. This contradicts Balakrishnan and Koza's (1991) prediction (Hypothesis 4) that joint ventures should be preferred when parents are in different industries. Our findings indicate that acquisitions are more likely if the partners are in different industries, and restating them this way points out to a likely explanation: there is a strong connection between diversification and acquisitions, since acquisitions allow entrants to purchase going firms. This is often an expensive option, but it is attractive if entrants do not possess the assets needed to operate in the industry, i.e., if they are diversifying (Caves and Mehra, 1986).

The coefficient of JEXP is negative and significant at the 0.10 level. As per Hypothesis 2, the longer Japanese firms have been in the United States, the more likely they will choose an acquisition over a joint venture. GROWDEV, the coefficient of the absolute value of the deviation from the mean in the growth of shipments in the target U.S. industry, is negative and significant (at 0.05). As hypothesized in Hypothesis 6, acquisitions are favored when the target industry experiences either very high or very low growth rates.[14]

The coefficient of the concentration ratio of the target U.S. industry is insignificant. The coefficient of COMMON is not significant, suggesting that similarity of products between the parent and the venture does not increase the probability that the Japanese entrant will opt for an acquisition, as we had

Table 4. Classification Table

		Predicted		
		JV	Acquisition	Total
True	JV	20	55	75
	Acquisition	11	89	100
	Total	31	144	175
	Sensitivity	26.7%		
	Specificity	89.0%		
	Correct	62.3%		

hypothesized in Hypothesis 3. Yamawaki (1992) found that Japanese investors choose acquisitions over greenfield entries when the investment is into a new industry. Our results suggest that acquisitions and joint ventures are both ways to acquire complementary assets, in contrast to greenfield investments, which are used to exploit the parent's advantages.[15] The relative efficiency of these two modes is determined by the significant variables in our model.

6. Conclusions

In this paper, we investigate the choice between joint ventures and acquisitions in the context of Japanese investments in the United States. We compare and contrast two theories of joint ventures. Balakrishnan and Koza (1991, 1993) argue that joint ventures arise to reduce the transaction costs involved in purchasing firms. Hennart (1988), on the other hand, contends that joint ventures are favored when the desired assets are linked to non-desired assets, thus making an acquisition undigestible (see also Shan, 1988, and Kay et al., 1987).

Controlling for other relevant factors, our results failed to support Balakrishnan and Koza's view that joint ventures are a mechanism to reduce the information costs of acquisitions. They support Hennart's (and Kay's) prediction that joint ventures will be chosen when the desired assets are packaged in a way that would raise the costs of managing the merged unit. In other words, our results suggest that a joint venture is primarily a device to obtain access to resources which are embedded in other organizations.

The results also show that the greater the Japanese's investor experience of the U.S. market, the more likely they will choose acquisitions over joint venture, confirming the view that a major constraint to the successful combination of inputs through acquisitions comes from the difficulty of integrating the labor forces of the two organizations (Kogut and Singh, 1988; Haspeslagh and Jemison, 1991).

One additional interesting finding is the positive and significant sign of PARCOMMON, which suggests that Japanese investors tend to joint venture with U.S. partners which manufacture the same products. This is consistent with the view that joint ventures with established local firms are a privileged way to enter foreign markets when scale economies are large and domestic firms have a dominant position.[16]

Notes

1. These two studies also failed to control for another important determinant of the choice between acquisitions and joint ventures: whether acquisitions were more likely when the U.S. investment represented a diversification for the parent. This variable was found to be significant in Hennart and Park (1993). Singh and Kogut also argue that the faster the rate of growth of the U.S. industry entered, the more likely entry through acquisition, neglecting the fact that acquisitions may be preferred in low growth industries because they allow entry without adding to capacity (Caves and Mehra, 1986). Lastly, the data set of these two studies includes entries in the manufacturing, extractive, and service industries. Since assets per employee are lower in services and higher in extractive industries, the size variable may reflect systematic interindustry patterns.
2. The United States is one of the few countries which has minimal restrictions on foreign ownership, and none for manufacturing enterprises (Price Waterhouse, 1991). Even foreign acquisitions of high-technology firms have been unregulated. Until the passage of the Exon-Florio amendment to the Omnibus Trade and Competitiveness Act of 1988 the U.S. government had no power to block the acquisition of a U.S. firm when this was deemed to be a threat to national security. The Exon-Florio amendment stipulates that cases of potential concern are notified to the Committee on Foreign Investment in the United States (CFIUS) which initiates an inquiry. If the Committee recommends blocking the acquisition, the President can do so. However, since 1988 only 13 proposed investments (from 750 notifications) have received more than a cursory review, and only one has been blocked. The consensus of observers is that, in the period under study (1978–89), the United States had no really binding restrictions on foreign acquisitions of US firms in technologically advanced industries.
3. For example, acquisitions made up only 31 percent of the 114 Japanese entries in the United States in the Kogut and Singh sample, compared to 54 percent for the all-nationality sample (Kogut and Singh, 1988, Table 2).
4. Many recent Japanese acquisitions of U.S. firms have fared poorly because of serious problems encountered in integrating the subsidiary. Sanyo was unable to transfer its work and production organization to the television plant it bought from Warwick in Forrest City, Arkansas, because of resistance by unions and by the U.S. management team it left in place. The company ended up shifting production of TVs to its other plants in the U.S. and Mexico (Kenney and Florida, 1993). The acquisition of Firestone by Bridgestone has also been painful (*Economist,* 1991).
5. Entries by Japanese trading companies were excluded because of the fundamental differences in strategies between Japanese trading firms and their manufacturing counterparts (Tsurumi, 1976).
6. The reasons for the reduction from 428 to 175 are as follows: 57 observations were deleted because the Japanese parent was a trading company. Ninety-one of the remaining observations were deleted due to missing information on the U.S. partner. Fifty-one of the remaining observations had to be dropped due to missing information on size and/or organizational structure of the U.S. partner. Four additional observations were deleted because of lack of information on the products of the U.S. partners. Lack of

information on the products of the Japanese investors led to 47 additional deletions. In one case we did not have the products of the subsidiary. Lastly, lack of information on the employment of the U.S. partner led to two additional deletions.

7. For data consistency purposes, we used the 1972 Standard Industrial Classification and its 1977 supplement.
8. Note that USEMPL and USSTRUC show a different *N* (number of observations). However, this does not present a problem because neither variable enters into the regression model directly, and the combined variable INDIG can, under certain circumstances, be computed with only one component present.
9. We measure size by employees rather than by sales or assets because postmerger acquisitions difficulties arise from the need to integrate and motivate the labor force of the acquired firm (Sales and Mirvis, 1984). The larger that labor force, the greater the difficulties. Hence the cost of acquiring a firm should be proportional, everything else constant, to the number of its employees.
10. In the latter case, PARCOMMON and COMMON are identical.
11. The Herfindahl index is calculated by squaring the concentration ratio for each of the top 50 companies or the entire universe (whichever is lower) and summing those squares to a cumulative total. See 'Concentration Ratios in Manufacturing', *1987 Census of Manufactures*, p. X.
12. That rate, equal to $a^2 + (1 - a)^2$, where a is the proportion of acquisitions (Morrison, 1974), is 51 percent.
13. We also ran the model replacing INDIG with a dummy for size (SIZE is equal to 1 for American partner firms with more than 5000 employees). The results were similar.
14. Hennart and Park (1993) found this to be also true in their study of the choice between greenfield entries (both wholly-owned and joint ventures) and acquisitions by Japanese investors in the United States, while Caves and Mehra (1986) found this variable significant for a sample of foreign firms entering the United States.
15. This is consistent with Kogut and Chang (1991), who found that differences across industries in the number of greenfield investments was influenced by the Japanese industry's level of R&D expenditures, while this variable had no influence on entries through joint ventures and acquisitions.
16. This is suggested by the high ratio of joint ventures to acquisitions in the metal and transportation equipment industries (see Table 1).

References

Balakrishnan, S. and Koza, M. (1991). 'Organization costs and a theory of joint ventures', unpublished manuscript, University of Minnesota.

—— (1993). 'Information asymmetry, adverse selection and joint ventures: Theory and evidence', *Journal of Economic Behavior and Organization*, **20**, pp. 99–117.

Berg, S. and Friedman, P. (Summer 1978). 'Joint ventures in American industry: An overview', *Mergers and Acquisitions*, pp. 28–41.

Caves, R. and Mehra, S. (1986). 'Entry of foreign multinationals into U.S. manufacturing industries'. In M. Porter (ed.), *Competition in Global Industries*. Harvard Business School Press, Boston, MA, pp. 449–481.

Census of Manufacturers: Subject Series (1982). Department of Commerce, Bureau of the Census, Washington, DC.

Directory of Corporate Affiliations. National Register Pub. Co., Wilmette, IL, various years.

Economist (8 June 1991). 'The tyre industry's costly obsession with size', p. 65.

Haspeslagh, P. and Jemison, D. (1991). *Managing Acquisitions*. Free Press, New York.

Hennart, J.-F. (1982). *A Theory of Multinational Enterprise*. University of Michigan Press, Ann Arbor, MI.

——(1988). 'A transaction costs theory of equity joint ventures', *Strategic Management Journal*, 9(4), pp. 361–374.

——and Park, Y. R. (1993). 'Greenfield vs. acquisition: The strategy of Japanese investors in the United States', *Management Science*, **39**, pp. 1054–1070.

Japan Company Handbook: First Section. Toyo Keizei Shinposha, Tokyo, various years.

——*Second Section*. Toyo Keizei Shinposha, Tokyo, various years.

Jemison, D. B. and Sitkin, S. B. (1986). 'Corporate acquisition: A process perspective', *Academy of Management Review*, **11**, pp. 145–163.

Kay, N., Robe, J.-P. and Zagnolli, P. (1987). 'An approach to the analysis of joint ventures', working paper, European University Institute.

Kenney, M. and Florida, R. (1993). *Beyond Mass Production: The Japanese System and its Transfer to the US*. Oxford University Press, New York.

Kogut, B. and Chang, S. J. (1991). 'Technological capabilities and Japanese foreign direct investment in the United States', *Review of Economics and Statistics*, **73**, pp. 401–413.

——and Singh, H. (1988). 'The effect of national culture on the choice of entry mode', *Journal of International Business Studies*, **19**, pp. 411–432.

Lightfoot, R. (1992). 'Note on corporate governance systems: The United States, Japan and Germany', Harvard Business School note 9-292-012.

Morrison, D. (1974). 'Discriminant analysis'. In R. Ferber (ed.), *Handbook of Marketing Research*. Wiley, New York, pp. 2442–2457.

Nelson, R. (1982). 'Government stimulus of technological progress: Lessons from American history'. In R. Nelson (ed.), *Government and Technical Progress: A Cross-Industry Analysis*. Pergamon, New York.

Predicast's F&S Index Plus Text on CD-ROM (1992). Silverplatter Information, Boston, MA.

Predicast's F&S Index Plus Text: International on CD-ROM (1992). Silverplatter Information, Boston, MA.

Price Waterhouse (1991). *Doing Business in the USA*. Price Waterhouse, New York.

Sales, A. and Mirvis, P. A. (1984). 'When cultures collide: Issues in acquisitions'. In J. Kimberly and R. E. Quinn (eds.), *New Futures: The Challenge of Managing Corporate Transitions*. Dow Jones-Irwin, Homewood, IL, pp. 107–133.

Shan, W. (1988). 'Technological change and strategic cooperation: Evidence from the commercialization of biotechnology', Ph.D. dissertation, University of California at Berkeley.

Singh, H. and Kogut, B. (1989). 'Industry and competitive effects on the choice of entry mode', *Academy of Management Proceedings*, pp. 116–120.

Tsurumi, Y. (1976). *The Japanese Are Coming*. Ballinger, Cambridge, MA.

U.S. Industrial Outlook. Department of Commerce, International Trade Administration, Washington, DC, various years.

Yamawaki, H. (1992). International competitiveness and the choice of entry mode: Japanese multinationals in U.S. and European manufacturing industries', unpublished manuscript, Université Catholique de Louvain.

7 Asymmetric Information and Joint Venture Performance: Theory and Evidence for Domestic and International Joint Ventures

Jeffrey J. Reuer and Mitchell P. Koza

1. Introduction

The growing prevalence of joint ventures (JVs) and other forms of interfirm collaboration has attracted the attention of many scholars from fields such as economics, international business, marketing, organization theory, sociology, and strategic management. These developments have translated into significant theoretical diversity in extant JV research, with identified motives for collaboration finding their roots in the various theoretical perspectives employed by these different fields. As just one indicator of this diversity, current strategy texts highlight more than a dozen reasons why firms might engage in interfirm collaboration (e.g., Hitt, Ireland and Hoskisson, 1997; cf., Koza and Lewin, 1998). The growing variety of theoretical perspectives on joint ventures raises significant questions regarding the complementary or competing nature of these perspectives, their relative explanatory power in different empirical settings, and the specific relationships between theories of joint ventures.

It is within this broader theoretical context that Hennart and Reddy (1997) contrast and test two explanations of joint ventures. First, they posit that a JV is attractive when a firm would face substantial costs of integrating targeted assets through an acquisition (see also Hennart, 1988; Kogut, 1988). They expect that such *ex post* transaction costs will be large when desired assets are commingled with nondesired assets in the target firm. This post-acquisition integration problem is most likely to be substantial when the target firm is large in size and employs a non-divisionalized organizational structure. 'Indigestibility' problems are less significant in acquisitions involving either small target firms or targeted assets that are largely isolated within a semi-autonomous division. By contrast, joint ventures are attractive under conditions of indigestibility because JVs enable the expanding firm to link into targeted assets without the need of disentangling these resources. This structural, 'indigestibility' explanation for JVs parallels Kogut and Singh's (1988) argument that firms prefer IJVs over acquisitions when national cultural distance is great and the administrative costs of integrating a foreign management would be correspondingly high.

Second, Hennart and Reddy take up the 'competing' perspective that JVs are attractive vehicles for reducing the uncertainty and costs of valuing complementary assets *ex ante* (Balakrishnan and Koza, 1993). This asymmetric information view suggests that firms will prefer joint ventures over acquisitions when resource valuation problems occur due to the buyer and seller's disparate information sets and the seller's difficulty in credibly signaling the assets' true value. For instance, when the acquiring and target firms operate in different industries, JVs enable the two firms to combine resources in a piecemeal fashion such that the learning that follows allays the adverse selection problem that can arise from initial valuation uncertainties in an outright acquisition (e.g., Akerlof, 1970). However, Hennart and Reddy reject the asymmetric information view of JVs in favor of the 'indigestibility' perspective summarized above. In fact, they find that Japanese entrants into the U.S. are *less* apt to use JVs when the two parties do not manufacture any of the same products and information asymmetries are, therefore, likely to be problematic. They conjecture that JVs are unattractive as diversification tools and are more suitable for obtaining scale economies when target firms have a dominant position.

In light of these recent findings, the need to bring together different theoretical perspectives on joint ventures, and the importance of the 'indigestibility' and asymmetric information views of JVs to current and future research, this article examines these two perspectives and the relationship between them. On a conceptual level, we propose that the two perspectives are complementary and overlapping. In particular, we discuss how *ex post* 'indigestibility' problems are likely to contribute to asymmetric information and resource assembly challenges at the *ex ante* valuation stage. We also present new evidence on the firm valuation effects of JV formation in domestic and international investment contexts. The results show that the stock market generally reacts favorably to JV investments when asymmetric information exists between parent firms. In other cases, the market responds negatively or insignificantly to firms' announced JVs.

These findings lend support to the asymmetric information view that domestic as well as international JVs are attractive when firms face difficulties valuing complementary resources *ex ante*.

2. Resource Assembly through Joint Ventures

2.1. Ex ante *and* Ex post *Challenges*

Hennart and Reddy emphasize that the 'indigestibility' and asymmetric information explanations of joint ventures are competing theories. The former deals with the 'costs of integrating the target firm's labor force (what has been called the postacquisition integration problem),' while the latter is 'concerned with transaction costs in the market for firms' (1997: 1). In the 'indigestibility' case, resource indivisibilities and management costs associated with integrating a target firm are the key sources of transaction costs. Indivisibilities arise when it is difficult to readily extract desired assets from nondesired assets, and management costs derive from the integration of two sets of employees, each with its own culture and organizational routines. In the asymmetric information view, transaction costs result from resource valuation problems occurring when transacting parties have different information sets and the seller cannot credibly signal the targeted assets' true value.

In our view, the relationship between the 'indigestibility' and asymmetric information perspectives can be characterized in two ways. First, the two explanations are complementary rather than competing. Firms forging together resources need to contend with both *ex ante* valuation uncertainties and *ex post* integration challenges, and both factors can affect the attractiveness of a joint venture relative to an acquisition. Balakrishnan and Koza take up the case when assets are completely alienable. Their arguments suggest that an acquisition can be costly and risky vis-à-vis a joint venture even when 'indigestibility' problems do not exist. Under conditions of asymmetric information, a joint venture mitigates the firm's need to engage in costly efforts to reduce valuation uncertainties, as well as the risks of either offering too little and failing to complete the transaction or overpaying for the targeted resources (e.g., Varaiya, 1988). *Ex post* transaction costs due to resource indivisibilities and differing routines can also shape transacting parties' preferences for a joint venture over an acquisition. While Hennart and Reddy's focus is on the assets targeted by entrants into foreign markets, for other combinations the issue of resource indivisibility can be important on both sides of the dyad. For instance, if Firm A would face difficulties acquiring Firm B's resources, the firms could enter a joint venture, or Firm B might acquire Firm A's assets if they are alienable instead. The same logic holds if the identities of A and B are swapped, which suggests that resource indivisibilities for one party need not be a necessary or sufficient condition for JVs in general.

Second, the 'indigestibility' and asymmetric information perspectives on joint ventures are overlapping rather than orthogonal. In particular, the *ex ante* valuation uncertainties highlighted by the asymmetric information view are apt to exist when *ex post* integration challenges noted by the 'indigestibility' perspective are present. For instance, it will be difficult for the acquiring firm to value targeted assets when these resources reside in an organizational context with a unique culture and different routines. Moreover, the *ex ante* valuation problem is exacerbated if desired resources are embedded and shared rather than isolated within a semi-autonomous division of the target firm. Thus, our conclusion is that information asymmetries will tend to be present when 'indigestibility' problems exist, but the converse need not be true. Given that the 'indigestibility' and asymmetric information explanations for joint ventures are complementary and overlapping, it follows that Hennart and Reddy's finding that Japanese firms prefer JVs when 'indigestibility' concerns arise does not permit acceptance of the 'indigestibility' view over the asymmetric information view.

2.2. *Governance Choices and Outcomes*

Potentially more problematic for the asymmetric information perspective of joint ventures, however, is Hennart and Reddy's finding that Japanese firms tend to enter the U.S. with acquisitions rather than JVs when the parties produce different products and asymmetric information likely exists between the entrant and target firm. This result seems to directly contradict the asymmetric information view, yet it also raises issues regarding the generalizability of the findings and whether results from governance choice models should be carried over to draw conclusions for firm performance.

Prior studies in financial economics and strategic management speak to these issues. Harris and Ravenscraft (1991), for example, examine foreign acquisitions of U.S. firms using a sample from a more diverse set of home countries. They report that in almost three-fourths of the international takeovers, the buyer already had operations in lines of business closely related to those of the U.S. target. Harris and Ravenscraft (1991) conclude that cross-border acquisitions predominate in areas where the buyer has business expertise. Moreover, prior studies on the acquisition relatedness-performance relationship have produced mixed findings (e.g., Barney, 1988). While some work reports a negative effect of relatedness on performance (e.g., Doukas and Travlos, 1988; Eun Kolodny and Scheraga, 1996), other studies find a positive or insignificant effect (cf. Chatterjee, 1986; Lubatkin, 1987; Markides and Ittner, 1994; Seth, 1990; Singh and Montgomery, 1987). In fact, some of the worst performing acquisitions involved firms investing free cash flows to diversify into unrelated industries (Shleifer and Vishny, 1991).

After considering these empirical findings and the theoretical issues raised above concerning the overlap between the 'indigestibility' and asymmetric information perspectives on joint ventures, it is not possible based on Hennart and Reddy's evidence to reject the asymmetric information view of joint ventures, in favor of the 'indigestibility' perspective. In the remainder of the article, we present an empirical analysis of the firm valuation effects of JV formation using event study methodology to evaluate domestic and international JVs.

3. Methodology

3.1. Sample and Data

The dataset comprises two-parent JVs that terminated during the 1985 to 1995 time horizon by a firm buying out the JV, selling out to a partner or outsider, or liquidating the JV. Predicast's *Funk and Scott (F&S) Index* and Lexis-Nexis' company news library were used to identify venture announcements for a broad cross-section of domestic and international JVs. For purposes of collecting stock returns data, at least one parent firm had to be a publicly-traded, U.S. firm with daily stock returns data obtainable from the Center for Research in Security Prices (CRSP) data files. When the joint venture was based outside the U.S., the venture was classified as being international. Governance structures other than parent-child equity joint ventures involving parent firms' joint ownership and control of a separate business entity (e.g., minority investments, partial acquisitions, non-equity alliances, etc.) were not included in the sample due to their different characteristics (e.g., Chi, 1994; Kogut, 1988).

Each of the ventures was classified into one of four information asymmetry groups based on the JV and parent firms' industries at the three-digit SIC level (e.g., see Table 1). In Group I, the JV's industry of operation matches both parent firms' primary industries. Information asymmetries should be lowest for this group since all three entities operate in the same industry. Group II represents collaborations in which both parent firms operate in the same industry,

Table 1. Abnormal Returns from Forming Domestic Joint Ventures[a]

Parent and JV Relations[b]	Group I	Group II	Group III	Group IV
P_1—P_2	A—A	A—A	A—B	A—B
\ /	\ /	\ /	\ /	\ /
JV_{12}	A	B	A	C
Event day (t)				
−2	−0.031	−1.034*	0.330	−0.197
−1	−0.096	−0.081	0.444	0.150
0	−0.389	1.099	−0.500	0.085
1	0.184	0.731	0.717‡	0.418*
2	−0.081	0.783	0.115	−0.415†
$CAR_{-1,1}$	−0.301	1.749	0.661	0.653*
N	15	13	43	92

[a] ‡$p < 0.15$, †$p < 0.10$, *$p < 0.05$, **$p < 0.01$.

[b] *Key to the Four Groups*:

I: Both parent firms and the JV are in the same industry.

II: Parent firms are in the same industry, but the JV operates in a different industry.

III: The JV operates in the industry of only one parent firm.

IV: All three entities are in different industries.

but the JV operates in a different industry. In Group III, the JV operates in the industry of one parent firm, but the parent firms' primary industries do not match each other. Finally, for Group IV all three entities operate in different industries.

The final sample consisted of 297 domestic and international joint ventures. 8.4 percent of the JVs were in Group I, 6.1 percent were in Group II, 34.7 percent were in Group III, and 50.8 percent were in Group IV. Based on a sample of 64 domestic JVs formed during the mid-1970s, Balakrishnan and Koza reported that 11 ventures (or 17.2 percent) involved parent firms in the same 3- or 4-digit SIC. As such, despite the fact that the present sample includes more recent ventures as well as international JVs, the proportion of ventures between parent firms in the same industry is comparable (i.e., 14.5 percent in Groups I and II vs. 17.2 percent in Balakrishnan and Koza). Roughly half of the ventures (i.e., 45.1 percent) were based outside of the U.S., and 60.3 percent of the JVs operated in manufacturing industries.

3.2. Analytical Technique

The firm valuation effects of JV formation were measured using event study methodology. The Sharpe-Lintner market model was used as a benchmark for generating firm-specific forecast returns (i.e., $R_{it} = \alpha_i + \beta_i R_{mt} + \epsilon_{it}$, $t \in [-250, -50]$, where R_{it} is firm i's stock return on day t, R_{mt} is the value-weighted stock return on day t, and ϵ_{it} is the error term assumed to be distributed $N(0, \sigma^2)$). We then calculated risk-adjusted abnormal returns (i.e., $AR_{it} = R_{it} - (\hat{\alpha}_i + \hat{\beta}_i R_{mt})$) for trading days surrounding the announcement as well as cumulative abnormal returns (CARs) over days $t = -1$ to $t = 1$ (i.e., $CAR_i = \Sigma_{t=-1}^{1} AR_{it}$).

4. Results

Consistent with prior research reporting a positive average firm valuation effect of JV formation (e.g., Koh and Venkatraman, 1991; McConnell and Nantell, 1985; Park and Kim, 1997; Woolridge and Snow, 1990), the mean CAR for the full sample is 0.439 percent ($p < 0.05$), which indicates JV formation announcements are generally received favorably by the stock market. The average CAR from domestic JV formation announcements is 0.655 percent ($p < 0.05$), and the mean abnormal return on trading day $t = 1$ is 0.500 ($p < 0.01$). For JVs based outside of the U.S., the mean CAR is 0.177 percent (n.s.), and the mean abnormal return on the announcement date is 0.357 percent ($p < 0.05$). As such, there is evidence that both domestic and international JVs enhance firm value in general (cf., Chung, Koford and Lee, 1993; Finnerty, Owers and Rogers, 1986; Lee and Wyatt, 1990).

For the entire sample of domestic and international joint ventures, the mean CAR for each of the four groups is −0.497 percent for Group I (n.s.), 1.361 percent for Group II (n.s.), 0.635 percent for Group III ($p < 0.05$), and 0.350 percent for Group IV ($p < 0.15$). As such, the shareholder wealth effects of JV formation are insignificant for joint ventures in Groups I and II and positive for ventures in Groups III and IV involving information asymmetry. The mean duration of ventures does not differ across the four groups (i.e., $F = 0.659$; 3,293 d.f.), but JVs based outside of the U.S. were on average longer-lived than domestic JVs (i.e., 7.21 vs. 5.60 years, $p < 0.01$) (cf. Park and Ungson, 1997).

Table 1 presents mean abnormal returns for domestic JVs for each of the four groups. None of the average abnormal returns or CARs are significantly different from zero for ventures in Group I. For cases in which the parent firms are based in the same industry but the JV operates in a different industry (i.e., Group II), the mean CAR is not significant and the average abnormal return on day $t = -2$ is −1.034 percent ($p < 0.05$). Given the small sample sizes of Groups I and II, we also examined the stock market reactions for these two groups together. This analysis similarly produced an insignificant CAR and a negative mean abnormal return on day $t = -2$ (i.e., −0.496 percent, $p < 0.15$).

Positive mean abnormal returns are evident for Groups III and IV involving asymmetric information between parent firms. The average abnormal return is 0.717 percent ($p < 0.15$) for Group III on day $t = 1$, though the CAR of 0.661 percent does not reach significance.[1] For Group IV comprising collaborations in which all three entities are in different industries, the average abnormal return for the day after the JV formation announcement is 0.418 percent ($p < 0.05$), and the mean CAR is 0.653 percent ($p < 0.05$). When Groups III and IV are combined to create a subsample of collaborations for which information asymmetries exist between parent firms, the mean abnormal return is 0.513 percent on the day after the JV formation announcement, and the mean CAR is 0.655 percent (both $p < 0.05$).

Table 2 provides average abnormal returns for international JVs for each of the four information asymmetry groups.[2] As earlier, no positive average abnormal returns or CARs are evident for Groups I or II involving parent firms in the same industry. For Group I, the mean abnormal return is −0.948 percent ($p < 0.05$) on the day after the JV formation announcement, and the mean CAR is insignificant. For Group II, all of the average abnormal returns and the mean CAR are insignificant. When Groups I and II are pooled, all of the average abnormal returns and the mean CAR are likewise not significant. Hence, the stock market reacts negatively or insignificantly to domestic as well as international JV formation announcements in the absence of asymmetric information between parent firms.

Table 2. Abnormal Returns from Forming International Joint Ventures[c]

Parent and JV Relations[d]	Group I	Group II	Group III	Group IV
P_1 — P_2	A — A	A — A	A — B	A — B
\ /	\ /	\ /	\ /	\ /
JV_{12}	A	B	A	C
Event day (t)				
−2	0.052	0.435	−0.216	0.228
−1	0.152	−0.481	0.142	−0.238
0	0.005	−0.258	0.637**	0.183
1	−0.948*	1.090	−0.162	−0.066
2	−0.019	−0.605	0.194	0.063
$CAR_{-1,1}$	−0.791	0.351	0.617[b]	−0.121
N	10	5	60	59

[c] $p < 0.10$, $^*p < 0.05$, $^{**}p < 0.01$.

[d] *Key to the four Groups*:

I: Both parent firms and the JV are in the same industry.

II: Parent firms are in the same industry, but the JV operates in a different industry.

III: The JV operates in the industry of only one parent firm.

IV: All three entities are in different industries.

The average abnormal returns for Groups III and IV are positive and larger than for Groups I and II (i.e., t = 1.53 on day t = 0). For Group III, the mean abnormal return is 0.637 percent ($p < 0.01$) on the announcement date, and the mean CAR is 0.617 percent ($p < 0.10$). No significant mean abnormal returns are evident for Group IV, however. This anomalous result contrasts our positive finding for domestic joint ventures in the same information asymmetry group (i.e., Group IV) and the positive results for Group III for both the international and domestic portfolios. When Groups III and IV are pooled together for the international portfolio, the average abnormal return is 0.412 percent ($p < 0.01$) on the announcement date. As before for the sample of domestic JVs, there is some evidence that the stock market responds favorably to international JV formations when there are information asymmetries between parents.

5. Conclusion

Based on the questions raised by the growing diversity of theoretical perspectives on joint ventures as well as Hennart and Reddy's theoretical arguments and conclusions on the relative merits of the asymmetric information and 'indigestibility' views of JVs, this article sought to consider these two perspectives and the relationship between them. On a conceptual level, we submitted that the perspectives are complementary and overlapping, suggesting that firms need to contend with both *ex ante* valuation uncertainties and *ex post* integration challenges when assembling resources. We also proposed that *ex ante* valuation problems arise when resources are located in an organizational context with its own unique routines and when resources are shared rather than isolated within a semi-autonomous division of the target firm. This indicates that information asymmetries tend to be present when 'indigestibility' problems exist, but the converse need not be true. These theoretical considerations on the relationship between the asymmetric information and 'indigestibility' perspectives on joint ventures and prior evidence on acquisitions in strategy and finance research lead us to conclude that the two views are not competing and that the asymmetric information perspective cannot be rejected in favor of the 'indigestibility' view based on Hennart and Reddy's evidence.

In the empirical portion of the present article, we examined the firm valuation effects of JV formation using a new data base containing more recent ventures as well as international JVs. Like Balakrishnan and Koza, we found that the stock market generally judges favorably those JVs formed under conditions of asymmetric information between transacting parties. Conversely, the market is more apt to respond negatively to JV formation when no asymmetric information is present between parent firms. In broad terms, the value the market attaches to diversifying JVs is also consistent with the learning, option perspective on joint ventures (Kogut, 1991).

The growing number of different forms of interfirm collaboration as well the theories used to understand them raises important questions regarding the relationships between these theories and their relative explanatory power overall and in different empirical settings. The present article is confined to examining the relationship between two explanations of joint ventures resting on transaction cost rationales that have proven fruitful to research on joint ventures during the past decade. It remains for future research to address other implications of asymmetric information or 'indigestibility' beyond firms' initial governance choices or valuation effects. As collaboration increases in significance for practitioners and the alliance literature continues to develop in a fragmentary fashion, we hope that this article also provides an impetus for additional work on core theoretical concepts in the collaborative strategy area.

Notes

1. To address the symmetric treatment of partners within Group III due to measuring abnormal returns to one party, we differentiated JVs that operated in the core business of the focal firm from JVs that operated in the core business of the partner. We then examined the CARs and abnormal returns for these two subgroups. In none of the resulting six two-sample *t*-tests was the mean market reaction significantly different across these two subgroups. The same insignificant results were obtained for the six tests for the IJV portfolio.
2. For each of the four information asymmetry groups in both the domestic and international portfolios, we also developed subsamples for foreign-partner and two-party American ventures, and two-sample t-tests for the tables' cells revealed no evidence that abnormal returns differ across these two subgroups.

References

Akerlof, G. A. (1970). The market for 'lemons': Qualitative uncertainty and the market mechanism', *Quarterly Journal of Economics*, **84**, pp. 488–500.

Balakrishnan, S. and Koza, M. P. (1993). 'Information asymmetry, adverse selection, and joint ventures', *Journal of Economic Behavior and Organization*, **20**, pp. 99–117.

Barney, J. B. (1988). 'Returns to bidding firms in mergers and acquisitions: Reconsidering the relatedness hypothesis', *Strategic Management Journal*, Summer Special Issue, **9**, pp. 71–78.

Chatterjee, S. (1986). 'Types of synergy and economic value: The impact of acquisitions on merging and rival firms', *Strategic Management Journal*, **7** (2), pp. 119–139.

Chi, T. (1994). 'Trading in strategic resources: Necessary conditions, transaction cost problems, and choice of exchange structure', *Strategic Management Journal*, **15** (4), pp. 271–290.

Chung, I. Y., Koford, K. J. and Lee, I. (1993). 'Stock market views of corporate multinationalism: Some evidence from announcements of international joint ventures', *Quarterly Review of Economics and Finance*, **33**, pp. 275–293.

Doukas, J. and Travlos, N. G. (1988). 'The effect of corporate multinationalism on shareholders' wealth: Evidence from international acquisitions', *Journal of Finance*, **43**, pp. 1161–1175.

Eun, C. S., Kolodny, R. and Scheraga, C. (1996). 'Crossborder acquisitions and shareholder wealth: Tests of the synergy and internalization hypotheses', *Journal of Banking and Finance*, **20**, pp. 1559–1582.

Finnerty, J. E., Owers, J. E. and Rogers, R. C. (1986). 'The valuation impact of joint ventures', *Management International Review*, **26**, pp. 14–26.

Harris, R. S. and Ravenscraft, D. (1991). 'The role of acquisitions in foreign direct investment: Evidence from the U.S. stock market', *Journal of Finance*, **46**, pp. 825–844.

Hennart, J.-F. (1988). 'A transaction costs theory of equity joint ventures', *Strategic Management Journal*, **9** (4), pp. 361–374.

—— and Reddy, S. (1997). 'The choice between mergers/acquisitions and joint ventures: The case of Japanese investors in the United States', *Strategic Management Journal*, **18** (1), pp. 1–12.

Hitt, M. A., Ireland, R. D. and Hoskisson, R. E. (1997). *Strategic Management: Competitiveness and Globalization*. West, St. Paul, MN.

Kogut, B. (1988). 'Joint ventures: Theoretical and empirical perspectives', *Strategic Management Journal*, **9** (4), pp. 319–332.

—— (1991). 'Joint ventures and the option to acquire', *Management Science*, **37**, pp. 19–33.

—— and Singh, H. (1988). 'The effect of national culture on the choice of entry mode', *Journal of International Business Studies*, **19**, pp. 411–432.

Koh, J. and Venkatraman, N. (1991). 'Joint venture formations and stock market reactions: An assessment of the information technology sector', *Academy of Management Journal*, **34**, pp. 869–892.

Koza, M. and Lewin, A. (1998). 'The co-evolution of strategic alliances', *Organization Science*, **9**, pp. 255–264.

Lee, I. and Wyatt, S. B. (1990). 'The effects of international joint ventures on shareholder wealth', *The Financial Review*, **25**, pp. 641–649.

Lubatkin, M. (1987). 'Merger strategies and stockholder value', *Strategic Management Journal*, **8** (1), pp. 39–53.

Markides, C. C. and Ittner, C. D. (1994). 'Shareholder benefits from corporate international diversification: Evidence from U.S. international acquisitions', *Journal of International Business Studies*, **25**, pp. 343–366.

McConnell, J. J. and Nantell, T. J. (1985). 'Corporate combinations and common stock returns: The case of joint ventures', *Journal of Finance*, **40**, pp. 519–536.

Park, S. H. and Kim, D. (1997). 'Market valuation of joint ventures: Joint venture characteristics and wealth gains', *Journal of Business Venturing*, **12**, pp. 83–108.

—— and Ungson, G. R. (1997). 'The effect of national culture, organizational complementarity, and economic motivation on joint venture dissolution', *Academy of Management Journal*, **40**, pp. 279–307.

Seth, A. (1990). 'Sources of value creation in acquisitions: An empirical investigation', *Strategic Management Journal*, **11** (8), pp. 431–446.

Shleifer, A. and Vishny, R. W. (1991). 'Takeovers in the '60s and '80s: Evidence and implications', *Strategic Management Journal*, Winter Special Issue, **12**, pp. 51–59.

Singh, H. and Montgomery, C. A. (1987). 'Corporate acquisition strategies and economic performance', *Strategic Management Journal*, **8** (4), pp. 377–386.

Varaiya, N. P. (1988). 'The "Winner's Curse" hypothesis and corporate takeovers', *Managerial and Decision Economics*, **9**, pp. 209–220.

Woolridge, J. R. and Snow, C. C. (1990). 'Stock market reaction to strategic investment decisions', *Strategic Management Journal*, **11** (5), pp. 353–363.

III. REAL OPTIONS PERSPECTIVES ON INTERFIRM COLLABORATION

8 Joint Ventures and the Option to Expand and Acquire

Bruce Kogut

A fundamental problem facing the firm is the decision to invest and expand into new product markets characterized by uncertain demand. The problem is exacerbated when the new business is not related to current activities. In this sense, a firm's initial investments in new markets can be considered as buying the right to expand in the future.

In current parlance, the right to expand is an example of a "real option," real because it is an investment in operating as opposed to financial capital, and an option because it need never be exercised.[1] For many investments, such as the purchase of new capital equipment to reduce costs in aging plants, the option value is insignificant. In industries where the current investment provides a window on future opportunities, the option to expand can represent a substantial proportion of the value of a project, if not of the firm.[2]

An analysis of joint ventures provides an interesting insight into investment decisions as real options. The task of building a market position and competitive capabilities requires lumpy and nontrivial investments. As a result, it is often beyond the resources of a single firm to buy the right to expand in all potential market opportunities. A partner, especially one which brings the requisite skills, may be sought to share the costs of placing the bet that the opportunity will be realized.

This perspective is related to the use of joint ventures to share risk. Pure risk-sharing arises in cases, such as bidding on oil lots, where firms have committed capital downstream (such as in refineries) but are dependent upon availability supplies of a finite resource. Multiple joint ventures among firms in the oil industry are analogous to collective insurance.[3]

In many industries, however, joint ventures not only share risks, but also decrease the total investment. Because the parties bring different capabilities, the venture no longer requires the full development costs. Due to its benefits of sharing risk and of reducing overall investment costs, joint ventures serve as an attractive mechanism to invest in an option to expand in risky markets.

However, in the event the investment is judged to be favorable, the parties to the joint venture face a difficult decision. To exercise the option to expand requires further commitment of capital, thus requiring renegotiation among the partners. One possible outcome is that the party placing a higher value on this new capital commitment buys out the other. Thus, the timing when it is desirable to exercise the option to expand is likely to be linked to the time when the venture will be acquired.

The exploration of the link in the timing of the acquisition of joint ventures and of the exercise of the option to expand is the focus of the following empirical investigation. The first two sections apply an option perspective to joint ventures. A distinction is made between acquisitions motivated by industry conditions and those stemming from the desire to expand in response to favorable growth opportunities. The third section develops the central hypothesis that the timing of the acquisition is related to a signal that the valuation of the venture has increased. This signal is proxied by two measures derived from the growth of shipments in the venture's industry. The effects of these industry signals on the likelihood of a venture terminating by an acquisition are tested by specifying and estimating a hazard model, while controlling for industry and other effects.

The same model is then tested on the likelihood of dissolution. If the option interpretation is correct, a signal that the venture's value has increased should lead to an acquisition; a signal that it has decreased, however, should not lead to dissolution, as long as further investment is not required and operating costs are modest. Strong support is found for the option argument.

These results run counter to prevailing presumptions in organizational theories that firms engage in cooperative ventures as buffers against uncertainty and that managerial discretion is severely limited by environmental volatility. In the view of Pfeffer and Nowak (1976), joint ventures are instruments to manage the dependency of the partner firms on the uncertainty of resources. Recent work in organizational mortality, as influenced by the seminal articles by Hannan and Freeman (1977) and McKelvey and Aldrich (1983), has advanced the proposition that managers are severely curtailed in their abilities to affect the prospects of survival of their firms.

To the contrary, an option perspective posits that joint ventures are designed as mechanisms to exploit, as well as buffer, uncertainty. Because firms have limited influence over the sources of uncertainty in the environment, it pays to invest in the option to respond to uncertain events. Joint ventures are investments providing firms with the discretion to expand in favorable environments, but avoid some of the losses from downside risk. In this regard, real option theory provides a way to ground the trial and learning aspect to joint ventures.

1. Real Options

The assignment of the right to buy and sell equity in the joint venture is a common feature of many agreements. For example, in a recent announcement of a joint venture in the area of power generation equipment, Asea Brown Boverie received the option to buy the venture at some time in the future. Westinghouse, as the partner, has the right to sell its ownership interest. In the vernacular of financial markets, the terms of the venture provides a call option to Asea Brown Boverie and a put option to Westinghouse.

In drawing up a joint venture agreement, it is common practice to give first rights of refusal to the contracting parties to buy the equity of the partner who decides to withdraw. Sometimes, one party is given the priority to acquire in the case of termination. The legal clause serves to regulate the assignation of the rights to the underlying option. Such a clause may establish not only who has the first right to acquire, but also may set pricing rules.

The legal clause outlining acquisition rights should not be confused with the real option itself. Legal clauses serve simply as a way proactively to outline ownership rights in response to unspecified contingencies involving the failure of the cooperation. The termination of the venture by acquisition is not, therefore, necessarily equivalent to the creation and exercise of an option similar to those found in financial markets.

However, an economic option is often inherent in the decision to joint venture and the decision to exercise this option, as explained below, is likely to promote the divestment of the venture by one of the parties. Joint ventures are real options, not in terms of the legal assignation of contingent rights, but, like many investments, in terms of the economic opportunities to expand and grow in the future. The value of any investment can be broken into the cash flows stemming from assets as currently in place and those stemming from their redeployment or future expansion (Myers, 1977). Because these latter cash flows are only realized if the business is expanded, they represent, as Myers first recognized, the value of growth opportunities.

The intuition behind this argument can be explained by following the notation of Pindyck (1988). Given an investment of K, the value of the venture can be decomposed in terms of both assets in place and the embedded options:

$$V_j = F_j(K, \pi) + O_j(K, \pi) \tag{1}$$

where V is the value of the venture as estimated by the jth firm, $F_j(K, \pi)$ is the value of the assets in their current use, $O_j(K, \pi)$ is the valuation of the future growth opportunities, and π is the current value of an uncertain state variable. The difference between $F_j(K, \pi)$ and $O_j(K, \pi)$ is that the latter is not equivalent to the discounted cash flows of expected earnings, because the firm maintains the flexibility to choose among investment alternatives—including not to invest—in the future.

As both the value of the assets in place and the option can be potentially affected by current assets and opportunities of the partner firms, the valuations of the venture will differ among the parties. For example, the venture might source components from one partner and not the other, hence affecting the valuation of assets in place.[4] Differences in option valuation can arise if the potential spill-over effects of the venture's technology complement the product portfolio of one partner more than the other.

Changes in the value of these assets depend on the stochastic process determining the current value of the embedded option, where the state variables are prices, either of production or the inputs. In Fig. 1, we illustrate the implications of this process by assuming that changes in a state variable (indicated as π) are normally distributed over time and depict a cross-section of the path. The expected value ($\overline{\pi}_{t+\Delta t}$) is the current value plus the expected increase; the variance is σ^2. If realization of $\pi_{t+\Delta t}$ is greater than some critical value $\pi^\star$, the derived value of the venture is greater than its acquisition price and the option to acquire is exercised. If $\pi_{t+\Delta t}$ is less than $\pi^\star$, no further investment is made. Nor is it necessary to divest the assets (if operating costs are low), for there is the possibility that future changes will be more favorable. It is for this reason that the downside risk is not consequential.

Below, we consider the conditions which generate the option value, as well as examine motives for acquisitions which are not driven by the underlying option value. We link the value of the option, and, thereby, the venture, to the market demand for new products and technologies. Then, the central issue of the timing of exercise is addressed.

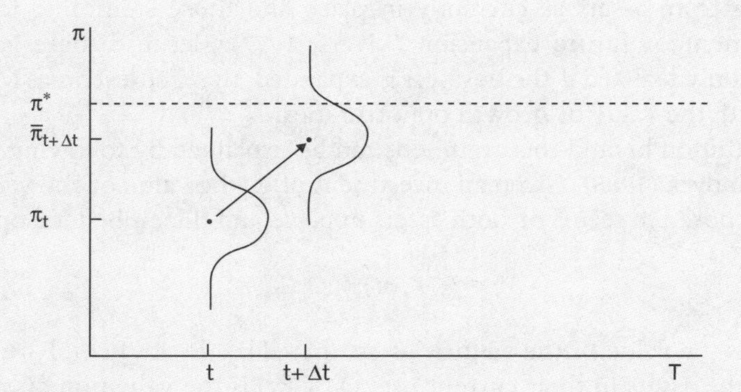

Fig. 1 Expected change in π_t.

2. Joint Ventures as Real Options

In the following, we consider two options and examine qualitatively why joint ventures can be viewed as analogues. The first option is waiting to invest, whereby it pays to wait before committing resources. In the second option of expanding production, investment commitment is necessary in order to have the right to expand in the future. These two options, therefore, exemplify two polar types of real option strategies.[5]

It is often the case that an investment decision involves a comparison of both options. Committing engineers or product planners to a risky project incurs the possibility that the market does not develop; it also draws resources from other projects. Clearly, there is a value in waiting before the technology or market is proven. But if there is a benefit in investing today in order to gain experience with the technology or to establish a brand image with customers, then investing generates the valuable option to expand in the future.

A joint venture serves as a way to bridge these options through pooling resources of two or more firms. Because the value of the option to expand is greatest in new markets and technologies, any given firm is unlikely to possess the full repertoire of skills. A joint venture not only shares the investment burden, but sometimes reduces it, as the parties may bring different skills, thereby lowering the total investment cost. In this sense, a joint venture resolves partly the tradeoff between buying flexibility now and waiting to invest and focus later (Wernerfelt and Karnani, 1987).[6]

When the market for the technology or new product is proven, the option to acquire, as discussed later, is likely to be exercised. Through the joint venture, the buying party has acquired the skills of the partner firm and no longer needs to invest in the development of the requisite capability to expand into the targeted market. The divesting firm is willing to sell because, one, it realizes capital gains, and two, it may also not have the downstream assets to bring the technology to market (Teece, 1987; Shan, 1988). In this sense, the divestiture of joint ventures are the buyers' side to the argument and findings of Christensen and Montgomery (1981) that acquisitions are a way to buy into attractive industries.

For one of the partners to make the acquisition, the net value of purchasing the joint venture must be at least equal to the value of purchasing comparable assets on the market. This condition is likely to be satisfied due to the gain in experience in running the venture. If it does not hold, there was no advantage and, hence, no value to the option by investing early. But even if this condition does not hold ex post, a joint venture, as Balakrishnan and Koza (1988) point out, affords the possibility to learn the true value of the assets. As information is revealed, the acquisition is completed or withdrawn. From this perspective, regardless of other motives such as managerial experience, there is a bias to buy out the venture relative to other acquisition prospects simply due to better valuation information.

3. Timing of Exercise

As apparent from the above analysis, an acquisition or divestment is often a foreseen conclusion to the venture. The investing firms may be indifferent to whether a partner or a third firm purchases the venture. The reward is the capital gains return on the development efforts.

From this perspective, the timing of the acquisition is of critical significance. Simply stated, the acquisition is justified only when the perceived value to the buyer is greater than the exercise price. For a financial option, the terminal value is given by the stock price and the exercise price as set by the initial contract:

$$W = \max(S_t - E, 0] \tag{2}$$

where W is the value of the option, S_t is the price of the stock at time t, and E is the exercise price. (In this case, S_t is the state variable which we denoted earlier as π.) As the cost of purchasing the option is sunk, these two parameters determine, *ex post*, the value of the option when exercised.[7]

The joint venture analog to equation (2) is

$$W_j = \text{Max}((1 - \alpha)V_j - P, 0). \tag{3}$$

That is, the value of the option to acquire (W) is equal to the value to the jth firm of purchasing the remaining shares in the venture minus P, where $\alpha > 0$ and <1 and is the current share owned by firm j and P is the price of purchasing the remaining shares. (P is either negotiated between the parties or set according to a contractual clause.)[8]

For financial options, it is well established that an option should be usually held to full maturity (Hull, 1989, pp. 105–129). Exceptions to this rule depend upon dividend policy on the underlying stock, where it may pay to exercise the option before payment to shareholders. Obviously, in the case of joint ventures, the acquisition is only carried out if $(1 - \alpha)V_j > P$.

But the exercise of the option to acquire the joint venture is likely to be immediate for two reasons. First, the value of the real option is *only* recognized by making the investment and realizing the incremental cash flows. If the investment in new capacity is not made in a period, the cash flows are lost. Second, the necessity to increase the capitalization of the venture invariably requires a renegotiation of the agreement, often leading to its termination.[9] The option to expand the investment is likely to coincide with exercising the option to acquire the joint venture.

Consider a pure research venture between two parties. Both parties provide initial funding and a pre-established contribution to costs. As long as the initial investment is sunk and additional capital commitments are not required, increased variance in the value of the technology raises the upside gain. (Of course, variable costs must be paid, but these "carrying" costs apply as well to some kinds of financial options.) Since the option need not be exercised, the downside is inconsequential. At any given time, whether it pays for one party to buy the venture is dependent upon the buy-out price and the valuation of the business as a wholly-owned operation.

But once it is profitable to exercise the option, there are sound reasons not to wait. The option value of the venture is realized by investing in expansion. The requirement to contribute further capital leads to a difficult renegotiation. By now, the partners have information to know that the original equity share may not reflect the division of benefits. This deviation can be expected to be compounded when the option to expand becomes economically viable, as the partners are likely to differ in their appraisal of these opportunities. Thus, the allocation of new capital burdens often forces a revaluation of the distribution of benefits. Buying out the partner is a common outcome.

The timing of the exercise of the option to terminate the venture by acquisition is, thus, influenced by two considerations: the initial base rate forecast underlying the valuation of the business and the value of the venture to each party (or third parties) as realized over time. For the acquisition to take place, the acquisition price P must be greater than the valuation placed on the assets by one of the partners. These considerations lead to the following hypothesis: *The venture will be acquired when its valuation exceeds the base rate forecast.*

4. Selective Cues and Market Valuation

Unlike the case for a contingent security, there are no written contracts and financial markets that indicate changes in the value of a real option. Testing this hypothesis is, clearly, difficult given the impossibility to collect data on changes over time of both partners' evaluations of the option to expand. Nor is it likely that managers possess clear base-rates and valuation signals by which to guide a decision to exercise the option to expand. Consequently, the specification of the above hypothesis raises important questions about what information and environment cues managers use to time the exercise of the option.

Despite theoretical interest and laboratory experiments, most of the research on environmental cues informing managerial decisions has been oriented to identifying biases in the interpretation of information rather than in the selection of the information itself. Of some guidance is the finding of Bowman (1963) that adherence to a consistent rule derived from previous decisions performs better than the decisions actually made, suggesting that the efficiency of decisionmaking is impaired due to biases in the selection cues.[10] More recent research has especially pointed to biases derived from base-rate errors and the salience, or availability, of information. Several studies have shown that individuals wrongly calculate probabilities by weighting recent information too heavily or failing to incorporate information on the marginal probabilities.[11] Base-rates are, thus, frequently ignored, especially when the causal relationships are not explicit.

Whereas experimental research has validated a number of heuristics used in selecting information, there is little guidance for establishing the base rates that might be used for irregular decisions, such as the acquisition of a joint venture. We would expect, as Camerer (1981) notes, that individuals rely upon only a few cues of those available. We experiment with two time-varying specifications of the market cues relevant to the acquisition decision: a short-term annual growth rate and an annual residual error from a long-term trend in shipments.

The short-term annual growth rate is calculated as

$$G_{t,j} = [PS_{t,j} - PS_{t-1,j}]/PS_{t-1,j} \tag{4}$$

where the growth rate is set equal to changes in the value of product shipments (PS) for the jth industry over an annual interval $[t-1, t]$. The residual error is derived from the error from an estimated regression of the time trend in shipment growth:

$$R_{t,j} = PS_{t,j} - [a_j + b_j t], \tag{5}$$

where the residual error is the forecasting error from a linear time trend for the jth industry with intercept a and slope coefficient b. (The appropriateness of the linear specification is discussed below.)

It is essential to recognize that the above variables vary with time. Both specifications are derived from a constant dollar series of industry product shipments. The annual growth measure looks at year to year changes, always using the previous year as a benchmark. The residual error indicates that decision makers establish a long-term base-rate for each industry's historical growth and look at year to year departures from this trend. Unlike the growth measure, it assumes that managers act to acquire or divest when a market cue signals a rise in valuation relative to a long-term trend.

These two variables are, by our argument, proxies for changes in the unobserved state variable (given as π earlier) that determines the value of the joint venture. As our interest does not lie, however, in the pricing of the option but in the likelihood (or hazard) of acquisition, differences in the scales of the proxies are unimportant to the estimations, as described below. Positive movements in the value of industry shipments signal improved investment opportunities and an increase in the value of the real option embedded in the venture. Because the exercise of the option requires a decision to expand the investment and, hence, a renegotiation of the capital commitment of the parties to the venture, the likelihood of an acquisition should increase with positive movements of the proxy variables.

5. Acquisition and Value of Assets in Place

Joint ventures can, of course, be acquired for reasons other than as the outcome to negotiations stemming from exercising the option to expand. In large part, the differences in the reasons to acquire are derived from differences in the original motivations to joint venture in the first place. The motivations to joint venture may sometimes have less to do with building an option to expand into new markets than with the benefits of sharing ownership of assets in their current use. Some ventures provide a mechanism to share scale economies and to coordinate the management of potentially excess capacity in mature and concentrated industries (Harrigan, 1986). The option proportion of the total value of these kinds of ventures is likely to be low, that is, the present value of the assets in their current use dominates the option to expand or redeploy.

There is, though, an interesting aspect to some ventures in concentrated industries which the terminology of the option literature illuminates, for many of these ventures are also partial divestments. A number of recent joint ventures fall in this category: Firestone's sale of 50% of the equity of its tire business to Bridgestone, Honeywell's partnership with NEC and Bull in computers, and the above cited Asea Brown Boverie and Westinghouse agreement. In all of these ventures, the call option was given to the non-American firm.

The question of why do the parties not agree to an immediate acquisition underscores the critical roles of learning and pre-emption. Through the joint venture, the divesting party is contracted to pass on complex know-how on the running of the business, as well as to slow an erosion in customer confidence. Since this know-how may be essentially organizational—such as, the procedures by which an American firm are effectively managed, a joint venture serves as a vehicle of managerial and technological learning (Kogut, 1988; Lyles, 1988). In this case, a joint venture is a phased divestiture with a future exercise date.

The importance of this motivation is especially important in industries where there are few competitors. Tying up a potential acquisition target prevents other parties from making the acquisition, a threat which is particularly troubling in concentrated industries where there are few acquisition targets. Through the acquisition, full ownership is attained without adding further capacity to the industry by entering with a new plant.

6. Data Collection

In the above analysis, we related the likelihood of termination of a joint venture by acquisition to increases in the valuation of the embedded option and to industry conditions leading to divestment of existing assets. To test the effect of these two factors on the likelihood of acquisition, data were collected from both questionnaire and archival sources. Information on joint ventures was first acquired from the publication *Mergers and Acquisitions* for the years 1975 and 1983.[12] The sample included only ventures located in the United States in order to eliminate variance in political environments across countries. Moreover, all ventures had at least one American partner given the difficulty of gathering information on non-American firms. Of the 475 firms contacted in two mailings, 55.5% responded. However, due to a number of factors, such as misclassifying a contract as a joint venture or announcing a venture which never occurred, only 140 responses were useable. Of these, 92 are in manufacturing; it is this subsample which is used in this paper. Sources for the industry data are given below.

The questionnaire was designed to elicit factual information regarding the starting and, in the case of termination, ending dates for the venture, as well as its primary purpose. On the basis of this information, the percentage of ventures dissolved or acquired by one of the partners or a third party is 43%. A follow-up questionnaire was sent one-year later to those ventures reported still alive, which resulted in raising this percentage to 55%. A second follow-up was made the following year, with the percentage of terminations rising to 70 %.

The questionnaire data makes it possible to construct life histories for the 92 manufacturing ventures. Of these 92, 27 terminated by dissolution, 37 by acquisition, and 28 are censored, that is, they are still in effect. In this study, we treat the ventures that terminated by dissolution as also censured. Such a treatment is reasonable as long as the individual hazards are independent. Given the low density of ventures in a particular industry, the assumption of independence is justified.

From the questionnaire data, we create three dummy variables (*R&D, Production and Marketing*) indicating whether the venture included any of these activities. These variables are used to control for differences in the contractual terms of the sampled joint ventures due to variations in their functional activities. Clearly, the expectations regarding the duration of the ventures may differ depending on whether they involve investments in production and capital equipment or in joint marketing or product development.

The other data are taken from secondary sources. Drawing on Bureau of Census data, we use the four-firm concentration ratio at the four-digit SIC level (*Concentration*) as a proxy for industry maturity that promotes the use of joint ventures as vehicles of planned divestment. Since concentration ratios are published for every fifth year, we employ the ratio nearest the midpoint of the venture's life. (As the ratios are highly correlated across years, there is little difference in results using this procedure or other alternatives.)

As discussed earlier, two different proxies are specified for the central hypothesis that the likelihood of an acquisition is related to the occurrence of a signal of an increase in the value of the venture. The two measures discussed earlier (*Annual Growth* and *Annual Residual Error*) are estimated from unpublished Department of Commerce data on annual shipments (i.e., goods sold) at the four-digit level in constant 1982 dollars for the years 1965 to 1986. Both of these variables are drawn from industry data.

The annual growth data is derived directly from the shipment series. To normalize the data, each industry time series was divided by the first year of the series; thus each series begins with 1965 set to 100. By first differencing the normalized series and dividing by the lagged year, growth in shipments were calculated for each year. This measure was then entered into the analysis as a time-varying covariate with a one-year lag.[13] The time-varying specification

Table 1. Descriptive Statistics and Correlation Matrix

	Mean	Standard Deviation	Lowest	Highest
A = Acquisition	0.4	0.49	0.0	1.0
B = Concentration	40.11	20.76	8.0	96.0
C = R&D	0.51	0.50	0.0	1.0
D = Production	0.57	0.50	0.0	1.0
E = Marketing/Distribution	0.53	0.50	0.0	1.0

Spearman Correlation Matrix

	A	B	C	D	E
A	—				
B	0.19	—			
C	0.05	−0.08	—		
D	0.05	−0.04	−0.07	—	
E	0.10	−0.08	−0.05	−0.07	—

means that for a venture alive in 1978, the value of the growth variable is set equal to the annual growth of the venture's industry for 1977. If the venture survives to the next year, the growth covariate is updated to the realized growth rate in 1978.

The residual error is calculated in several steps. First, we again used the normalized series of shipments for each four-digit SIC industry. Second, a time trend was derived by a linear regression. The residual is calculated as the forecasting error for each year, using the estimated linear time trend as the base-rate predictor and the actual normalized shipment as the realized value. The residual error was also entered into the analysis as a time-varying covariate with a one-year lag.

The use of a linear fit for estimating the time trend is justified on a few grounds. With the exception of a few industries, the F-test indicated that the linear specification resulted in rather good fits. Thus, the simple linear model provides a good estimate of the long-term trend. Moreover, several studies have found that linear rules are commonly adopted by individuals to establish expectations (Hogarth, 1982). In some industries, a linear estimate is a poor one and unlikely to be widely maintained. Indeed, as we find below, the exclusion of outliers on the residual measure leads to much better results.

Descriptive statistics are provided for the variables in Table 1. The correlation of the variable *Acquisition* with the covariates is misleading, for the later regressions use time to acquisition as the basis of ordering the likelihoods. It, nevertheless, provides some insight into the underlying relationships. Evident from the table is the low degree of collinearity among these variables. We do not report the time-varying variables, since it would require reporting a covariate for each year of the sample.

7. Statistical Specification

To incorporate the effects of the unobserved stochastic process and the time-varying covariates, we use a partial likelihood specification to estimate the influence of these factors on termination by acquisition among a sample of joint ventures. Partial likelihood estimates the influence of explanatory variables (or covariates) on the hazard of termination without specifying a parametric form for the precise time to failure. Instead, it rank orders ventures in terms of the temporal sequence of terminations. For each event time, it specifies a likelihood that the observed terminated venture should have terminated, conditional on the covariates of the ventures at risk:

$$L_i(t_i) = h_0(t_i)(\exp(BX_i + BX_i(t_i)/h_0(t_i)))\left[\Sigma_j(\exp(BX_j + BX_j(t_i)))\right]. \quad (6)$$

For simplicity, the coefficients and covariates are given as vectors B and X, respectively, with i indexing the venture which failed at time t_i, j indexing the ventures at risk at time t_i, $h_0(t_i)$ is the baseline hazard, and L is the likelihood for the ith event. The time-varying covariates (*Annual Growth* and *Residual Error*) are indexed by the time of the event (t_i).

It should be noted that the partial likelihood is general in its specification. The parametric assumptions are the linearity imposed on the coefficients and the log-additivity of the baseline hazard and covariate terms. The distribution of the baseline hazard is nonparametric and entirely general. By leaving the baseline hazard unspecified, no bias is incurred by misspecifying the stochastic process by which unobserved variables influence the observed hazard rate. While efficiency is lost by ignoring the exact termination times, the estimates are consistent; the efficiency loss has been shown to be modest (Efron, 1977; Kalbfleisch and Prentice, 1980).

This generality is achieved by restricting the baseline hazard to be the same for all the ventures. By this assumption, $h_0(t_i)$ cancels out. As shown first by Cox (1972), this likelihood is equivalent to allowing only the conditional probabilities to contribute to the statistical inferences. No information on the precise timing of, or the elapsed time to termination is required; hence it provides a partial, rather than full maximum, likelihood estimate. Consequently, we do not need to know the functional form of the baseline hazard and, implicitly, the underlying process generating changes in the valuation of the venture or the boundary condition giving the point of exercise of the option.

The partial likelihood is calculated as the product of the individual likelihoods. Estimation proceeds by maximizing jointly the likelihoods that the ith venture should terminate conditionally on the characteristics of the other ventures at risk at the time of termination. We use the Newton–Raphson algorithm by which to estimate numerically the coefficients and standard errors. There is no constant or error term. A positive coefficient indicates that increases in the covariate tend to increase the likelihood of termination; a negative coefficient indicates the reverse.[14]

8. Statistical Results

The statistical results are given in Table 2. As can be seen from the Student T scores, the principal hypotheses are confirmed under a two-tail significance test. Concentration is significant at .002. In concentrated industries, joint ventures appear to be used as an intermediary step towards a complete acquisition.

Table 2. Partial Likelihood Estimate of Covariates' Effects on Log Likelihood of Acquisition

Variable Name	Full Sample (1)	Without Computer Industry (2)	Without Computer Industry (3)	Without Computer Industry (4)
Concentration	0.26	0.02	0.03	0.02
	(3.16[a])	(2.84[a])	(3.08[a])	(2.59[b])
R&D	0.58	0.70	0.57	0.70
	(1.67[c])	(1.88[c])	(1.58)	(1.91[c])
Production	0.16	0.10	0.20	0.06
	(0.44)	(0.26)	(0.56)	(0.16)
Marketing/Distribution	0.61	0.66	0.59	0.62
	(1.75[c])	(1.76[c])	(1.63)	(1.66[c])
Annual Growth	0.03	0.22	0.03	—
	(2.25[b])	(1.28)	(1.89[c])	—
Residual Error	0.0001	0.006	—	0.01
	(0.45)	(2.88[a])	—	(3.48[a])
N	92	88	88	88

Significance under two-tail T-test: (T-statistics in parentheses).
[a] $P<.01$.
[b] $P<.05$.
[c] $P<.10$.

A complementary but more speculative interpretation is that joint ventures are also often part of the restructuring of mature industries, either due to new, and perhaps foreign, competition or to efforts to stabilize the degree of rivalry. By acquiring the assets, a shifting of ownership occurs without an increase in industry capacity.

Ventures with R&D activities or marketing and distribution activities are more likely to be acquired at .1 significance under a two-tail test and at .05 under a one-tail. The production variable is positive, though insignificant.

The most interesting comparison is between the growth and residual error variables. The growth variable has a positive effect on acquisitions and is significant at .05. The residual error coefficient, on the other hand, is indistinguishable from a null effect.

Given the sample size, it is important to look at the effect of possible outliers. Large residuals might be generated by a poor fit of the linear trend line. The trend lines for ten industries (in which there are twelve ventures) have significance levels worse than .05. Of these twelve ventures, six terminated by acquisition. Their elimination from the sample changed the results only mildly.

A more direct way to identify outliers is to plot the residual errors and growth rates for each industry. The electronic computing machinery industry (SIC 3573) stands out dramatically from the rest. For 1986, for example, the residual error for computers was 30 times greater than the next highest industry. The remarkable trait of the industry is that since these growth rates have been sustained for two decades and more, negative residual errors are generated even when the growth rate is still substantially above the mean and median for the whole sample. As three of the four ventures in this industry terminated in an acquisition, the estimates are strongly affected.

Reestimating the regression equation without these four ventures gives strikingly different results. Significance levels for the other variables stay largely the same. The most striking change is in the positions of the residual error and growth variable. Both are now positively signed, but the residual error variable is significant at .01. The coefficient on the growth variable is indistinguishable from the null hypothesis. These results are much kinder to the proposition that managers are sensitive to a long-term intra-industry base rate which serves as a standard by which to evaluate annual changes.

The decline in significance of the growth variable is partially the result of the collinearity with the measure of the residual error. Unusually high (low) growth is likely to result in larger (smaller) residual errors. The correlations for *Annual Growth* and *Residual Error* ranged as high as .85 for one year, though often were much lower. Since collinearity tends to raise the standard errors, the loss in significance for *Annual Growth* should be interpreted with some caution.

To address this confounding, *Annual Growth* and *Residual Error* were entered separately into the regression analysis. The results are given in equations (3) and (4) of Table 2. Whereas *Annual Growth* is only significant at .1, *Residual Error* is significant at .001. It is reasonable to conclude that the decision by managers whether to acquire or divest the joint venture is more significantly sensitive to annual departures from a long-term trend than to short-term indices of industry growth.[15]

9. Discussion of Market Signals

The above findings indicate that increases in excess of the long-term trend in shipment growth are significantly related to the timing of the acquisitions of ventures. Such a relationship suggests that managerial decisions are cued by market signals that the venture's value has increased. Because of the level of aggregation of our sample, the cue may be indirectly related, that is, there are intervening variables (e.g. revenues to the venture) between the variables we chose and the direct cues bearing on managerial choice.

In turn, it could be argued that the take-off in growth signals industry consolidation, thus forcing exits. Conceptually, this objection is weak, for a shake-out should occur when the market does poorer than its historical record.

The relationship between *Residual Error* and the likelihood of acquisition suggests the opposite, namely, acquisitions tend to occur when the market does better than its historical record.

To test whether consolidation leads to divestment, we calculate a new variable *Change in Concentration* which indicates the percentage change in the four-firm concentration at the 4-digit SIC level during the life of the venture.[16] The results given in equations (1) and (2) of Table 3 show no support that consolidation leads to an increase in acquisition.

Another interpretation of the findings is that managers are myopic and fail to consider that short-term deviations may be outliers. Frequently, this error is referred to as ignoring regression to the mean or the law of small numbers (Hogarth, 1982; Tversky and Kahneman, 1971). Incidences of annual growth rates and residual errors, in other words, may reflect extreme values of a random process.

That managers do not simply react to any short-term change can also be addressed empirically. If short-term myopia leads to a divest and acquire decision, then it should lead to a dissolve decision when the market turns down. We can test this proposition by estimating the same model for the likelihood of termination by dissolution.

Table 3. Partial Likelihood Estimates of Covariates' Effects on Log Likelihood of Termination

	Acquisition		Dissolution	
Variable Name	Full Sample (1)	Without Computer Industry (2)	Full Sample (3)	Without Computer Industry (4)
Concentration	0.03 (3.14^{a})	0.03 (2.90^{a})	0.01 (1.16)	0.01 (1.16)
R&D	0.59 (1.66^{c})	0.75 (1.96^{c})	0.53 (1.30)	0.53 (1.30)
Production	0.16 (0.45)	0.10 (0.27)	−0.18 (−0.43)	−0.17 (−0.43)
Marketing/Distribution	0.62 (1.75^{c})	0.69 (1.83^{c})	0.30 (0.73)	0.30 (0.74)
Annual Growth	0.03 (2.23^{b})	0.02 (1.22)	−0.01 (−0.77)	−0.01 (−0.77)
Residual Error	0.0001 (0.39)	0.007 (2.93^{a})	0.003 (0.72)	0.003 (0.72)
Change in Concentration	0.143 (0.14)	0.59 (0.60)	— —	— —
$N=$	92	88	92	88

Significance under two-tail T-test: (T-statistics in parentheses).

[a] $P<.01$.

[b] $P<.05$.

[c] $P<0.10$.

This test is especially important if the argument that joint ventures frequently serve as real options is correct. The nature of an option should be kept in mind. Once the capital is committed, the downside risk is low, especially if there is a market for the acquisition of the assets and operating costs are not high. The selling of the venture means that one firm puts a higher value on the assets; it does not mean the venture is unprofitable.

Though it should not be expected that the same covariates should be theoretically related to dissolution, we include them in order to make the results comparable.[17] These results are given in columns 3 and 4 of Table 3. As can be seen, there is no significant relationship between dissolution and the growth and residual error measures.

The insignificance of the *Annual Growth* and *Residual Error* variables lends further support to the options argument. For if joint ventures are designed as options, then as long as the investment is sunk and the operating costs are moderate, downward movements should not lead to dissolution. Rather, it pays to wait and see if the process generates more favorable outcomes. The asymmetry in the acquisition and dissolution results supports strongly the interpretation that joint ventures are designed as options.

10. Conclusion

This chapter has investigated the proposition that joint ventures are designed as options that are exercised through a divestment and acquisition decision. The statistical investigation analyzes what factors increase the likelihood of an acquisition. These factors have been shown to be unexpected increases in the value of the venture and the degree of concentration in the industry.

There is a wider implication of this study for theories of organizational behavior. At least since Knight's (1921) observations, it has been widely claimed that risk reduction can be achieved through organizational mechanisms, or what Cyert and March (1963) labelled "uncertainty reduction." But firms, if not other organizations, may also profit from uncertainty.[18] Such profit taking might be achieved through a more flexible production process or organizational design, as described by Piore and Sabel (1984). It might also be achieved by investments in joint ventures which serve as platforms for possible future development. After decades of research on the mechanisms of reducing risk, a look focusing at the way in which organizations benefit from uncertainty appears promising.[19]

Notes

1. See Myers (1984) for an interesting qualitative discussion of real options and Mason and Merton (1985) for an extensive analytical treatment.
2. See Kester (1984) for an interesting tabulation of the option value of many large firms.
3. For a study of joint ventures in the oil industry, see Mead (1967). Note, however, that the decision whether to pump the oil can be viewed analytically as an option to wait. See McDonald and Siegel (1986).
4. See Contractor (1985) for an analysis of joint ventures with resulting side payments.
5. Variations on the waiting to invest option are given in McDonald and Siegel (1986), Majd and Pindyck (1987), and Pindyck (1988). Kulatilaka (1988) provides a general formulation, allowing for switching between active and wait modes.
6. This explanation is incomplete without a consideration why a joint venture is favored over alternatives. For a discussion, see Kogut (1988).
7. Ex ante, the value of the option is determined not only by the known parameters, but also by the stochastic process determining the value of the venture.
8. As the acquisition price is likely to be state dependent, it is important to note that McDonald and Siegel (1986) provide a solution for an option where the value of the underlying asset and exercise price are both stochastic.
9. The comments of one of the referees helped clarify the necessity of both conditions. See also Doz and Schuen (1988) for a discussion of negotiating problems stemming from different evaluations of the venture's growth potential.
10. See also Kunreuther (1969) and the analysis of similar "bootstrapping" models in psychology by Camerer (1981).
11. See Tversky and Kahneman (1982) and the discussion in Hogarth (1982, 38–42).
12. In the sampling process, some of the joint ventures were reported as starting up later and, in a few cases, earlier than the initial time span.
13. The lag is motivated by pragmatic and design concerns. Since the shipment data ends in 1986, a lag would have been necessary for the ventures surviving to 1987. Also, as the ventures can terminate at any time during a given year and as the termination date usually follows by several months the decision, it is more conservative to take the lag value.
14. See Allison (1984) and Kalbfleisch and Prentice (1980) for the treatment of tied data.
15. Though the coefficient to *Annual Growth* is larger, they are not comparable due to the differences in their measurement.
16. As concentration is only published for every fourth year, we took the starting year closest to the year of birth of the venture and the closing year closest to the year of termination or censorship.
17. For an analysis of the dissolution of joint ventures, see Kogut (1989).
18. In some cases, they may even seek higher risk (Myers, 1977; Bowman, 1980).
19. One of the more interesting directions of population ecology is the comparison between strategies which differ by their ability to survive under varying conditions of risk. See, for example, Brittain and Freeman (1980).

References

Allison, P. D., *Event History Analysis: Regression for Longitudinal Event Data*, Sage Publications, Beverly Hills, 1984.

Balakrishnan, S. and Koza, M. "Information Asymmetry, Market Failure and Joint Ventures," mimeo, UCLA, 1988.

Bowman, E. H., "Consistency and Optimality in Managerial Decision Making," *Management Sci.*, 9 (1963), 310–321.

——, "A Risk/Return Paradox for Strategic Management," *Sloan Management Rev.*, 21 (1980), 17–31.

Brittain, J. W. and Freeman, J. H., "Organizational Proliferation and Density-Dependent Selection: Organizational Evolution in the Semiconductor Industry," in J. R. Kimberly and R. M. Miles (Eds.), *The Organizational Life Cycle*, Jossey Bass, San Francisco, CA, 1980.

Camerer, C., "General Conditions for the Success of Bootstrapping Models," *Organizational Behavior and Human Performance*, 27 (1981), 411–422.

Christensen, H. K. and Montgomery, C. A., "Corporate Economic Performance: Diversification Strategy Versus Market Structure," *Strategic Management J.*, 2 (1981), 327–343.

Contractor, F., "A Generalized Theorem for Joint Ventures and Licensing Negotiations," *J. International Business Studies*, 16 (1985), 23–50.

Cox, D. R., "Regression Models and Life Data," *J. Royal Statistical Society*, (B) 34 (1972), 187–202.

Cyert, R. M. and March, J. G., *A Behavioral Theory of the Firm*, Prentice-Hall, Englewood Cliffs, NJ, 1963.

Doz, Y. and Shuen, A., "From Intent to Outcome: A Process Framework for Partnerships," INSEAD, working papers, 1988.

Efron, B., "The Efficiency of Cox's Likelihood for Censored Data," *J. Amer. Statistical Assoc.*, 72 (1977), 557–564.

Hannan, M. and Freeman, J., "The Population Ecology of Organizations," *Amer. J. Sociology*, 82 (1977), 929–964.

Harrigan, K., *Managing for Joint Venture Success*, Lexington Books, Lexington, MA, 1986.

Hogarth, R. M., *Judgment and Choice*, Wiley, New York, 1982.

Hull, J., *Options, Futures, and Other Derivative Securities*, Englewood Cliffs, Prentice-Hall, NJ, 1989.

Kalbfleisch, J. D. and Prentice, R. L., *The Statistical Analysis of Failure Time Data*, Wiley, New York, 1980.

Kester, W., "Today's Options for Tomorrow's Growth," *Harvard Business Rev.*, (March–April 1984).

Knight, F. H., *Risk, Uncertainty, and Profit*, University of Chicago, Chicago, IL, 1971; originally published, Houghton-Mifflin, Boston, MA, 1921.

Kogut, B., "Joint Ventures: Theoretical and Empirical Perspectives," *Strategic Management J.*, 9 (1988), 319–332.

——, "The Stability of Joint Ventures: Reciprocity and Competitive Rivalry," *J. Industrial Economics*, 38 (1989).

Kulatilaka, N., "The Value of Real Options," unpublished manuscript, Boston University, 1988.

Kunreuther, H., "Extensions of Bowman's Theory on Managerial Decision Making," *Management Sci.*, 15 (1969), 415–439.

Lyles, M. A., "Learning among Joint Venture Firms," *Management Internat. Rev.*, 28 (1988), 85–97.

McDonald and Siegel, D., "The Value of Waiting to Invest," *Quart. J. Economics*, 101 (1986), 707–728.

McKelvey, B. and Aldrich, H., "Populations, Natural Selection and Applied Organizational Science," *Administration Sci. Quart.*, 20 (1983), 509–525.

Majd, S. and Pindyck, R., "Time to Build, Option Value, and Investment Decisions," *J. Financial Economics*, 18 (1987), 7–27.

Mason, S. and Merton, R., "The Role of Contingent Claims Analysis in Corporate Finance," in *Recent Advances in Corporate Finance* (E. Altman and M. Subrahmanyam, Eds.), Irwin, New York, 1985.

Mitchell, G. R. and Hamilton, W. F., "Managing R&D as a Strategic Option," *Research-Technology*, 31 (1988), 15–22.

Mead, W., "Competitive Significance of Joint Ventures," *Antitrust Bull.*, 12 (1967).

Myers, S. C., "Determinants of Corporate Borrowing," *J. Financial Economics*, 5 (1977), 147–176.

——, "Finance Theory and Financial Strategy," *Interfaces*, 14 (1984), 126–137.

Nelson, R. R. and Winter, S. G., *An Evolutionary Theory of Economic Change*, Harvard University Press, Cambridge, MA, 1982.

Pfeffer, J. and Nowak, P., "Joint Ventures and Interorganizational Interdependence," *Administrative Sci. Quart.*, 21 (1976), 315–339.

Pindyck, R., "Irreversible Commitment, Capacity Choice, and the Value of the Firm," *American Economic Rev.*, 78 (1988), 967–985.

Piore, M. and Sabel, C., *The Second Industrial Divide*, Basic Books, New York, 1984.

Shan, W., "An Analysis of Organizational Strategies by Enterpreneurial High-Technology Firms," working paper, Sol C. Snider Enterpreneurial Center, Wharton School, 1988.

Teece, D., "Profiting from Technological Innovation: Implications for Integration, Collaboration, Licensing, and Public Policy," in *The Competitive Challenge. Strategies for Industrial Innovation and Renewal*, Ballinger, Cambridge, MA, 1987.

Tversky, A. and Kahneman, D., "Belief in the Law of Small Numbers," *Psychological Bull.*, 2 (1971), 105–110.

—— and ——, "Evidential Impact of Base Rates," in *Judgement under Uncertainty: Heuristics and Biases* (D. Kahneman, P. Slovic, and A. Tversky, Eds.), Cambridge University Press, Cambridge, UK, 1982.

Wernerfelt, B. and Karnani, A., "Competitive Strategy under Uncertainty," *Strategic Management J.*, 8 (1987), 187–194.

9 Collaborative Ventures and Value of Learning: Integrating the Transaction Cost and Strategic Option Perspectives on the Choice of Market Entry Modes

Tailan Chi and Donald J. McGuire

1. Introduction

The managers of a multinational enterprise (MNE) who are considering entry into a new market often must make decisions under highly uncertain and changeable circumstances. The variables that have a potentially significant impact on the prospect for its success in the market typically are large in number and keep evolving over time due to continual arrival of new information. A key decision the firm's management faces is whether to go it alone or collaborate with a local partner in entering the new market. It is well accepted among scholars of international business that a collaborative venture (CV) is not economically justified unless there exists some complementarity between the resources of the participants (Contractor and Lorange, 1987; Root, 1987). However, as suggested by the transaction cost perspective (Beamish and Banks, 1987; Gomes-Casseres, 1990; Hennart, 1988), the existence of synergy between the two firms is not sufficient to justify collaborative venturing because they could also exploit the synergy by acquiring the other's complementary assets. In order for a CV to be the optimal arrangement, the two firms must also face some transaction cost problems that make the acquisition of the other firm or part thereof economically inefficient.

Although uncertainty lies at the root of any transaction cost problems (Williamson, 1975), extant theoretical analyses under the transaction cost perspective have rarely examined how the potential changes in the uncertain variables might alter the assessment of alternative market entry modes. Consider the uncertainty facing two firms involved in a CV, for instance. Although both of them may foresee opportunities to acquire some valuable know-how from the other, it is often highly uncertain how much knowledge will be actually transferred between them due to potential transaction cost problems. But after the venture is started, it will eventually become clear how much knowledge they each can gain from the other. A question that naturally arises is: How will the expected revelation of this information affect each party's ex ante assessment of the CV when they are negotiating such an arrangement? In the ensuing sections of this chapter, we will try to answer a number of such questions using analytical tools of the strategic option perspective.

The distinguishing presumption of the strategic option perspective is that managers will alter their decisions when such changes are justified by new conditions that may emerge in an uncertain and dynamically evolving environment. Based on this presumption, if a decision to be made now has a chance of being altered later due to the arrival of new information, then the economic consequences of such changes should be properly accounted for when evaluating the current decision. For example, if the establishment of a joint venture (JV) with a local partner may lead to acquisition of the partner's stake in the future, the proper evaluation of the JV ex ante should take into account the economic impact of the possible acquisition later on. The strategic option perspective, therefore, is in essence dynamic.

The first study that applied the concept of strategic options to the analysis of market entry decisions is Kogut (1991). Focusing on the uncertainty of market demand and the resolution of such uncertainty over time, Kogut suggested several conditions under which firms may set up JVs as strategic options to expand in case of receiving favorable market responses. In this chapter, we will examine the necessity and sufficiency of some of these conditions for firms to form JVs as well as the implications of uncertainty about some other variables that are unrelated to market demand. A more recent study that empirically investigates market entry decisions under both the transaction cost and strategic option perspectives is Folta and Leiblein (1994). It is our hope that the theoretical analysis presented here will shed new light on the interactions between transaction cost and strategic option considerations to benefit future empirical studies.

This chapter is organized as follows. The next section constructs a simple strategic option model on the choice between collaboration and going it alone in entering a new market. Section three explicates a necessary and sufficient condition for the option to acquire or sell out to be valuable to the partners of a JV. In Section four, an expanded model is developed to examine the interactions between transaction cost and strategic option considerations. Some of the empirical implications from our theoretical analyses are developed into testable hypotheses in the fifth section. The last section summarizes and concludes the chapter.

2. A Strategic Option Model

In this section, we develop a simple stochastic model to examine how the existence of certain strategic options might affect the choice between going it alone and collaborating with a partner in entering a new market. The model to be derived here is a two-stage binomial model based on the financial option pricing model introduced by Cox, Ross, and Rubinstein (1979). The model takes a CV as the "base" mode, because this mode of operation generally is subject to more sources of uncertainty than a sole venture. A CV by definition may or may not involve shared equity ownership between the participants, although our discussion for the most part will be directed at equity JVs. We will first set up the model from the MNE's standpoint. The next section will take a game-theoretic approach and examine the conditions under which both the MNE and the local firm see the option to acquire the other as offering them an economic benefit.

An MNE that is contemplating collaboration with a local firm may encounter multiple sources of uncertainty that bear on its payoff from the project. First, the market demand for its product or service may have to be ascertained gradually from data on the venture's sales over a considerable period of time (Kogut, 1991). Second, although the MNE may expect to benefit from some complementary resources possessed by the local firm, an accurate assessment of the partner's capabilities may not be attainable without an extended period of joint operation with the firm (Chi, 1994). Furthermore, even if the local firm's ability is well known, there can still be a significant level of uncertainty about its effort in contributing the resources. If the contributions expected from the local firm contain a lot of tacit elements, the MNE can be expected to face difficulty in verifying its partner's true performance, and the knowledge of this situation may in turn induce the local firm to shirk its responsibility (Hennart, 1988). Since the MNE generally does not know for sure if the local firm will behave in an opportunistic manner or not, a level of uncertainty about its partner's effort is likely to exist and to be resolved through a period of collaboration between them. In addition, a period of joint operation may also enable the MNE to learn more about the local firm's propensity to engage in other opportunistic behavior aimed at misappropriating earnings from the MNE's technology (Teece 1987).

The uncertainty about the above-mentioned factors necessarily renders the MNE's payoff from the CV uncertain when the CV is being negotiated. To aid our exposition, let $\tilde{x}$ denote the true value of the venture that is binomially distributed as either x_u or x_d, with $x_u > x_d$, and assume that the MNE does not know whether $\tilde{x} = x_u$ or $\tilde{x} = x_d$ until sometime after the CV is formed. Given the two-stage framework of our model, we refer to the formation of the CV as stage 1 and the resolution of the uncertainty as stage 2.[1] In addition, let p represent the MNE's estimation of the probability for x_u to occur, so that the probability for x_d to occur can be simply denoted by $1-p$. Finally, we use s (≥ 0, ≤ 1) to denote the MNE's share of the CV's equity (the venture will be an equity JV if $0 < s < 1$) and use I_0 to denote the initial investment required by the project.

After the resolution of the uncertainty at stage 2, the MNE may find it advantageous to dissolve the CV by acquiring the local partner's interest in the venture or selling its own interest to the local partner. The price for the transfer of ownership interests between the two parties may be set in their original CV contract or negotiated after the establishment of the venture. In certain situations, the two partners may choose to specify the procedure for determining the share price, such as to accept the appraisal of an independent evaluator (Kogut, 1991). For the time being, we assume that the share price is set via negotiation as a multiple of I_0 in the initial CV contract and that the MNE holds both the options to acquire (a call option) and sell out (a put option) at the prescribed price. Under this assumption, the MNE has three alternatives at stage 2: acquire the shares held by the local firm, continue the CV, or sell its own shares to the local firm. Then, the MNE's payoff at stage 2 is given by either of the following functions, depending upon whether x_u or x_d turns out to be the true state of nature.

$$v_u = \max[x_u - (1-s)aI_0;\ sx_u;\ sbI_0] \tag{1.1}$$

$$v_d = \max[x_d - (1-s)aI_0;\ sx_d;\ sbI_0], \tag{1.2}$$

where a and b are parameters that affect the prices at which the MNE's options can be exercised. The functions defined in (1.1) and (1.2) presume that the MNE will choose the most profitable alternative after the state of nature is revealed. It can get $\tilde{x}-(1-s)\,aI_0$ by exercising the option to acquire, get $s\tilde{x}$ by staying in the CV or get sbI_0 by exercising the option to sell out.

It is convenient here to explain how the two parameters, a and b, should be interpreted. The value of a determines the cost that the MNE must incur to buy out its partner. We can think of a as a function of two factors: one is the monetary price that the MNE must pay to acquire the shares held by the local firm, and the other is an additional cost or benefit that may accrue from the severance of the relationship. An extra cost that the MNE may incur after the acquisition can result from the loss of access to the local firm's complementary resources that the MNE failed to replicate during the period of collaboration. An extra benefit that the MNE may derive from the acquisition can be due to the prevention of more proprietary information being leaked to and possibly misused by the local firm. So, if the MNE could acquire its partner's shares at the cost of the initial investment I_0 and if there is no other cost or benefit in severing the relationship, a would be equal to one. The value of a can be viewed as an increasing function of the exercise price and any extra (net) costs for the acquisition.

The factors affecting b are the opposite of those affecting a. So, the value of b can be viewed as an increasing function of the exercise price and any other (net) benefits arising from selling out its shares to the local firm. In the case of a sell-out, any knowledge the MNE acquires from the local firm would be an extra benefit, although the value of such knowledge would be deducted from the exercise price if the knowledge transfer is anticipated by both parties in the initial negotiation of the option. Similarly, any anticipated knowledge transfer from the MNE to the local firm can be expected to increase the exercise price for such a sell-out. If b is equal to one, the MNE would receive only the amount of its initial investment in the project.

Using the two functions defined in (1.1) and (1.2), the MNE's expected return from the venture in the presence of the embedded options can be expressed as

$$V_0 = \frac{pv_u + (1-p)v_d}{1+k} - sI_0 - \theta, \tag{2}$$

where $k > 0$ is the required rate of return (the discount rate) and $\theta \geq 0$ is a possible side payment that the MNE gives to the local firm for the provision of the options, which could cause the local firm to incur an economic cost.[2] The term sI_0, with $0 \leq s \leq 1$, represents the initial investment of the MNE in the venture's equity. Following the tenets of financial economics, we assume that firms are only concerned about systematic risk and account for such risk by choosing a proper discount rate (k) in project evaluation. The rationale for this assumption, as explained in standard finance models, is that stockholders can diversify away nonsystematic risks by themselves.[3]

The function defined in (2) can be used to examine a number of factors that influence the value of the options from the MNE's standpoint. The graph in the upper panel of Fig. 1 shows how the MNE's expected return from the venture, V_0, varies with the difference between the two possible values of the venture's payoff, $\delta = x_u - x_d$, under a specific set of parameter values.[4] It can be seen from the graph that V_0 is an increasing function of δ. As δ measures the variability of the venture's uncertain payoff (the variance of $\tilde{x}$ is equal to $\delta^2/16$), this parameter represents the extent of uncertainty

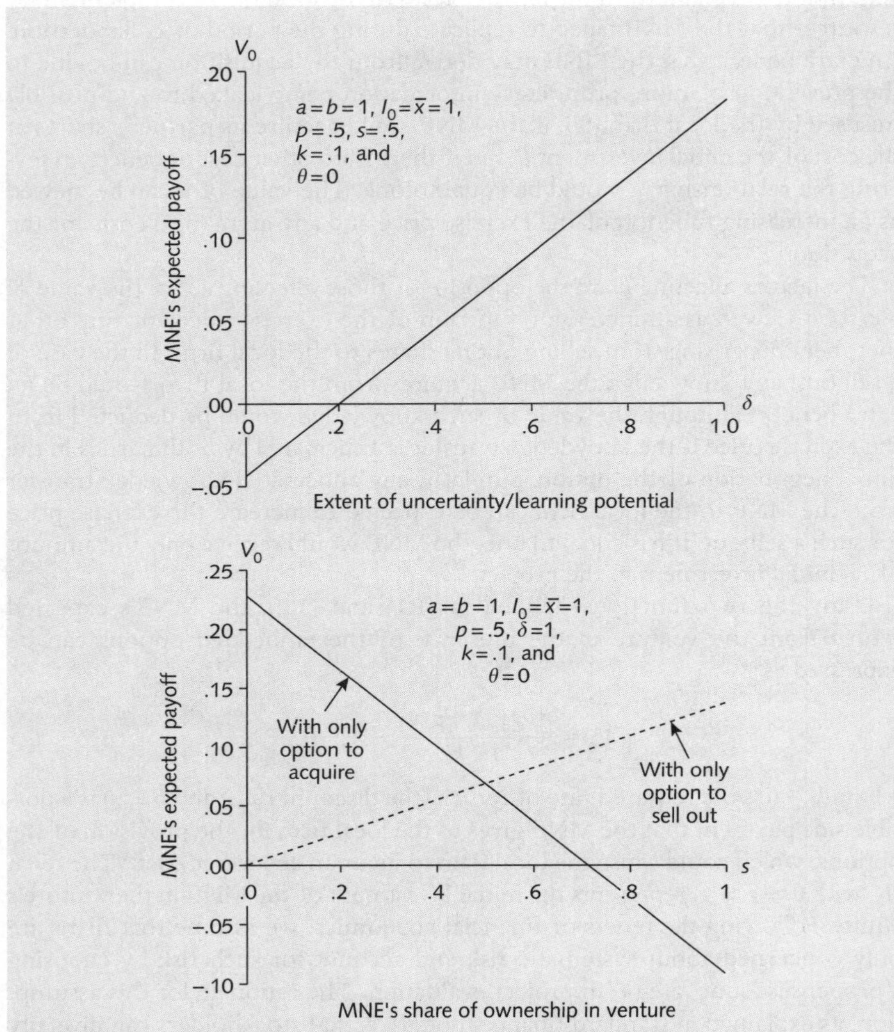

Fig. 1. MNE's expected payoff as functions of uncertainty (δ) and ownership share (s).

and learning potential about the outcome of the venture from the MNE's perspective. The intuition behind the positive relationship between V_0 and δ is that the options held by the MNE enable it to exploit the uncertainty and learning potential to its own advantage. Under the assumption of $aI_0 = bI_0 = \bar{x}$ in the numerical example of Fig. 1, the MNE will always come out ahead by exercising one of the options unless $\delta = 0$, in which case the options have no value since the exercise price is identically equal to the value of the project (i.e. $I_0 = x_u = x_d$).

It is easy to see that, if an option embedded in a CV is not available in a sole venture, then the option necessarily gives the CV an advantage over going it alone.[5] Using the same parameter values assumed in the numerical example of Fig. 1, the MNE's expected payoff from going it alone can be calculated as:

$$V_0 = \frac{\bar{x}}{1+k} - I_0 = \frac{1.0}{1.1} - 1 = -0.0909. \tag{3}$$

The difference between $s\bar{V}_0 = -0.9090s$ and the MNE's expected payoff from the CV gives the value of the options embedded in the CV. This example clearly illustrates that the embedding of strategic options in a particular mode of operation can alter the MNE's assessment of different market entry modes. The value of such options is a rising function of the uncertainty involved because greater uncertainty increases the value of being able to incorporate any newly gathered information into managerial decisions. It is not the uncertainty per se, but rather the potential for improving decisions on the basis of new information gathered, that makes the options valuable.[6]

The lower panel of Fig. 1 plots the MNE's expected return against its equity share in the CV when it can only exercise one of the two options at a prespecified price. As can be seen from the graph, the MNE's expected return is a decreasing (increasing) function of its equity share when it holds only an option to acquire (sell out). The intuition behind these relationships can be explained as follows. Since the option to acquire at a fixed price enables the option holder to take advantage of the venture's upward potential, a smaller initial share reduces its exposure to the venture's downward risk while still allowing it to benefit fully from the venture's upward potential. On the other hand, since the option to sell out at a fixed price enables the option holder to cover the venture's downward risk, a larger initial share allows it to benefit more fully from the venture's upward potential while still covering its exposure to the venture's downward risk. This result suggests that a CV partner holding only an option to acquire (sell out) will prefer its equity share to be as low (high) as possible when everything else is held constant. In fact, the option to acquire (sell out) becomes irrelevant to a party that holds 100% (0%) of the ownership to a venture. Given that 100% ownership represents a sole venture and 0% ownership represents a collaborative venture without equity ownership, our preceding analysis also shows how option-related considerations may influence a firm's assessment of different market entry modes.[7]

3. A Condition for Joint Ventures to Possess Valued Options

We have demonstrated in the preceding section that an MNE participating in an equity JV will value the right to acquire its partner's interest or sell out its own interest to the partner at a predetermined price when the payoff from the JV is uncertain. But an important question that we have not yet answered is: Under what conditions would the two parties find it mutually beneficial to have such option clauses in their JV agreement? Or more generally, under what conditions would they derive any economic value from having the option to acquire the other's interest, with or without a prespecified price? Our goal in this section is to explore the answers to these questions, using an extension of the model constructed in the previous section. In order to analyse the problem from the perspectives of both parties, we will treat the JV process as a two-stage game where the JV contract is negotiated in the first stage and implemented in the second stage. The fundamental presumption of such a game-theoretic approach is that each party chooses its moves to maximize its expected gains and anticipates its opponent also to follow this type of self-preserving behavior in each and every stage of the game (Harsanyi and Selten, 1988).

As pointed out earlier, the local firm takes on obligations that can carry an economic cost when it agrees to give the MNE the option to acquire or sell out the JV at a predetermined price. What is then the exact economic cost that the local firm may incur in this kind of arrangement? If the two parties are expected to agree *ex post* on the evaluation of the possible states of nature, x_u and x_d, then the payoff of the local firm under each state will be either of the following:

$$w_u = \lambda_u^a (1-s)\, aI_0 + \lambda_u^n (1-s)\, x_u + \lambda_u^b [x_u - bsI_0] \tag{4.1}$$

$$w_d = \lambda_d^a (1-s)\, aI_0 + \lambda_d^n (1-s)\, x_d + \lambda_d^b [x_d - bsI_0], \tag{4.2}$$

where $\lambda_i^j = 1, 0$ indicates whether the MNE's decision at stage 2 is to acquire the local firm's shares ($\lambda_i^a = 1$), stay in the JV ($\lambda_i^n = 1$), or sell out its own shares ($\lambda_i^b = 1$). So the local firm's expected payoff as of stage 1 can be expressed as:

$$W_0 = \frac{pw_u + (1-p)\, w_d}{1+k} - (1-s)\, I_0 + \theta. \tag{5}$$

The graphs in Fig. 2 illustrate how the expected payoffs of the two parties would vary with changes in the relative share of the two parties (s) and in the premium (θ) that the MNE pays the local firm for the options to acquire or sell out at pre-negotiated prices. It can be easily seen from the graphs that the expected payoffs

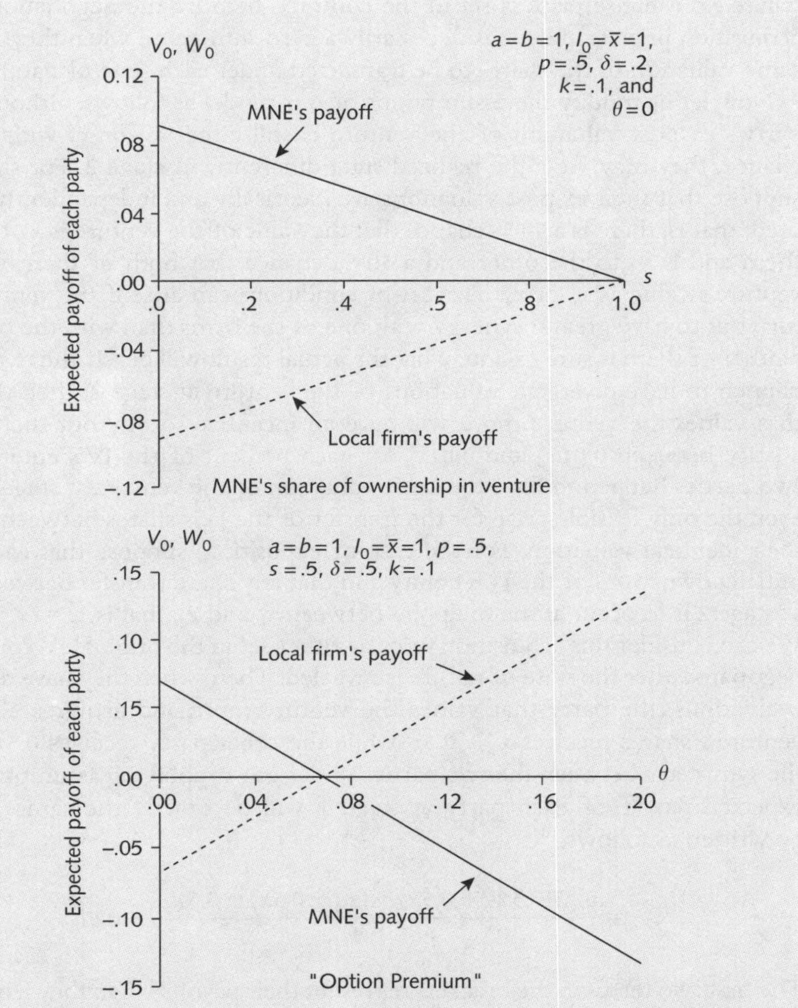

Fig. 2. Variation of each party's expected payoff with share (s) and "option premium" (θ).

of the two parties always sum to zero under such an arrangement.[8] This result suggests that giving one of the parties the option to acquire or sell out at a pre-specified price creates no economic value for the two parties when they are expected to have the same ex post valuation of the venture. The reason is that under these conditions the MNE's gain from exercising either option at stage 2 necessarily equals the local firm's loss. This reasoning also applies to the case where no exercise price is set in the contract, because the negotiation of the acquisition price at stage 2 is necessarily a zero-sum game when they have the same valuation of the shares to be transacted under each state of nature.

Now let us modify the assumptions of our model as follows: although each party's ex post valuation of the venture is still either x_u or x_d with a 50–50 chance, they may view the realized state differently at stage 2. For simplicity, suppose that their ex post valuations are identically and independently distributed; that is, there is a 50 % chance that the value of the venture is x_u to one of them and is x_d to the other and a 50 % chance that both of them view the venture's value as x_u or x_d. This set of conditions can arise if the venture may turn out to have greater synergy with one of the firms than with the other but neither of them is sure ex ante what the actual result will be.[9] If the two parties happen to have divergent valuations of the venture at stage 2, then the party that values the venture more will have an incentive to buy out the other at a price between $0.01x_u$ and $0.01x_d$ for each percent of the JV's equity. If the two parties happen to have the same valuation of the venture at stage 2, however, the only feasible price for the transfer of the JV's shares between them is their identical valuation. For the ease of exposition, suppose that each party initially owns 50% of the JV's equity and that any share transfer between them at stage 2 is to occur at the midpoint between x_u and x_d, that is, $\bar{x} = (x_u + x_d)/2$. We can consider this acquisition price as either set in the original JV contract or negotiated after the state of nature is revealed. Then, when they have divergent evaluations, the party that values the venture more and acquires all of the venture's shares receives $x_u - 0.5\bar{x}$ while the other party receives $0.5\bar{x}$. Given the symmetry between the two parties under our simplifying assumptions, the expected payoff of each party at stage 1 will be exactly the same and can be written as follows.[10]

$$V_0 = \frac{0.25[0.5x_u + 0.5x_d + (x_u - 0.5\bar{x}) + 0.5\bar{x}]}{1+k} - 0.5I_0. \tag{6}$$

The first two terms in the brackets represent their payoffs when they have identical valuations of the venture; while the last two terms in the brackets represent their payoffs from, respectively, acquiring and selling out to their partner. Note that their expected payoff from going it alone is

$$\bar{V}_0 = \frac{\bar{x}}{1+k} - I_0. \tag{7}$$

Table 1 shows how the difference between these two functions, $V_0 - \bar{V}_0$, is influenced by the mean and variance of the probability distribution of the venture's potential values, x_u and x_d. Note that $V_0 - \bar{V}_0$ reflects the value of the strategic options embedded in the JV and that for both parties joint venturing will be

Table 1. Values of $V_0 - \overline{V}_0$ under Different Values of $\overline{x}$ and δ

	$\delta = x_u - x_d$					
$\overline{x}=(x_u+x_d)/2$	.0	.1	.2	.3	.4	.5
1	.4167	.4375	.4583	.4792	.5000	.5208
2	.3333	.3542	.3750	.3958	.4167	.4375
3	.2500	.2708	.2917	.3125	.3333	.3542
4	.1667	.1875	.2083	.2292	.2500	.2708
5	.0833	.1042	.1250	.1458	.1667	.1875
6	.0000	.0208	.0417	.0625	.0833	.1042
7	−.0833	−.0625	−.0417	−.0208	.0000	.0208
8	−.1667	−.1458	−.1250	−.1042	−.0833	−.0625

The values of other parameters are assumed as follows: $s = 0.5$, $I_0 = 1$, and $k = 0.1$.

more advantageous than going it alone unless $V_0 - \overline{V}_0 < 0$. It can be seen from the table that a JV becomes a more favorable mode of market entry as the expectation of the venture's possible values is lower or as the two possible values are more widely dispersed. The negative relationship between $V_0 - \overline{V}_0$ and $\overline{x}$ is due to risk sharing in the JV, which reduces a party's loss in a bad state of nature (x_d) as well as its gain in a good state of nature (x_u). Since a rise in the value of $\overline{x}$ increases the gain from the good state and decreases the loss from the bad state, it reduces the benefit from risk sharing in a JV. The positive relationship between $V_0 - \overline{V}_0$ and δ is due to the options embedded in the JV, because the option to acquire or sell out allows the two parties to exploit the uncertainty about the extent of synergy that may exist between the JV and each party's other operations. It is interesting to note that in this numerical model a sole venture becomes superior only when the expected value of the venture is unusually large—seven to eight times greater than the initial investment I_0.

The above analysis reveals a necessary and sufficient condition for the option to acquire or sell out in a JV to provide a positive economic value for its partners; this condition is that the partners anticipate a possible divergence between their ex post valuations of the JV. As suggested earlier, the divergence of their valuations can be due to differing degrees of synergy between the JV and the separate operations of the two parties. Kogut (1991) observed that the reason for a JV partner to buy out the other is likely to be the existence of a difference between their ex post evaluations of the JV's assets. Our preceding analysis suggests that their ex ante anticipation of the possibility of such ex post differences can by itself be one of the motives for their going into a JV in the first place.

It is useful to distinguish the ex post asymmetry discussed above from what can be called ex ante asymmetry between the JV partners. Although the numerical example given by function (6) allows asymmetric valuations of the venture ex post, it presumes the two parties to have the same probability assessments regarding the possible outcomes of the venture. Since under such ex ante symmetry the two parties benefit equally from the option to acquire or sell out, there is no reason to designate only one of them as the holder of the option in their JV contract. So, in order for them to see a benefit from "trading" such option rights in the negotiation of their JV contract, there must exist some ex ante asymmetry that causes one of them to value the option more than the other does. Such ex ante asymmetry can arise from the condition that one of the parties does not foresee much chance for it to value the venture more than its partner does.[11] It can also arise when the two parties anticipate to have differing abilities to absorb their partner's proprietary knowledge or when they experience differing levels of uncertainty about the venture's outcome. In the next section, we will explore a number of transaction cost-related factors that can give rise to various asymmetries between the JV partners both ex ante and ex post.

4. Strategic Options and Transaction Cost Problems

This section is divided into two parts. The first part analyzes the option property of CVs in reducing the risk of misappropriation, and the second part analyzes the option property of CVs in reducing information asymmetry between the two partners. A slightly more complex model is constructed to examine the issues raised by both parts of the section.

4.1. Misappropriation Risk

The main risk that the MNE faces in collaborating with a local firm is the possibility of the local firm absorbing and misappropriating the rents from its proprietary knowledge due to imperfections in the prevailing legal system governing industrial property rights (Hennart, 1982; Stopford and Wells, 1972). Such misappropriation can, but does not have to, result from the local firm's breach of some explicit or implicit contractual agreement. The MNE may simply fail to foresee certain improvements of its knowledge and leave it open for the first discoverer of these improvements to appropriate the earnings from them. Since the risk of misappropriation has both technological and behavioral roots, the size of the risk is largely determined by two uncertain variables. One concerns the nature and extent of possible future improvements on the current knowledge (Hill, 1992); and the other concerns the opportunistic tendency of the partner, given that some economic agents may be more prone to opportunism than others (Williamson, 1975).

Although the MNE is likely to get additional information about both of these uncertain variables, such new information may or may not affect its assessment of the CV as the ongoing mode of operation. After a set of knowledge is revealed to the local firm, there may be little that the MNE can do to alter the chance of and loss from misappropriation, no matter how much future potential its knowledge is found to have, or how untrustworthy the local firm turns out to be. So whenever there is a chance of revealing to the local firm (intentionally or unintentionally) any knowledge that cannot be perfectly protected, the MNE incurs an expected sunk cost from the beginning. We use c to denote this expected sunk cost.

However, since technological and managerial know-how often has a lot of tacit elements (Teece, 1982), the amount of knowledge that the local firm is able to acquire from the MNE in a given period of collaboration is likely to be uncertain. So far as the MNE foresees a chance to withhold some of its proprietary knowledge from the local firm, new information about the potential of its knowledge or its partner's behavior could change the MNE's decision on whether to continue the CV. Since this type of new information primarily affects how large a benefit or cost there will be if the CV is dissolved, the effect of such uncertainty can be analyzed by introducing another stochastic variable $\tilde{y}$ to represent this extra benefit ($\tilde{y} > 0$) or cost ($\tilde{y} < 0$) in our model. In accordance with our two-stage binomial framework, we assume that the realized value of $\tilde{y}$ is either y_l or y_h, with $y_l < y_h$, and that the two random variables $\tilde{x}$ and $\tilde{y}$ are independently distributed. Let q represent the probability for y_l to occur so that the probability for y_h to occur can be denoted by $1 - q$. As the addition of this second binomial variable raises the number of possible states of nature from two to four, the MNE's payoff at stage 2 is given by one of the following functions:

$$v_u^l = \max[x_u - (1 - s)aI_0 + y_l;\ sx_u;\ sbI_0 + y_l] \tag{8.1}$$

$$v_u^h = \max[x_u - (1 - s)aI_0 + y_h;\ sx_u;\ sbI_0 + y_h] \tag{8.2}$$

$$v_d^l = \max[x_d - (1 - s)aI_0 + y_l;\ sx_d;\ sbI_0 + y_l] \tag{8.3}$$

$$v_d^h = \max[x_d - (1 - s)aI_0 + y_h;\ sx_d;\ sbI_0 + y_h] \tag{8.4}$$

Incorporating also the expected sunk cost c in the model, the MNE's expected return at stage 1 can now be expressed as[12]

$$V_0 = \frac{pqv_u^l + p(1 - q)v_u^h + (1 - p)qv_d^l + (1 - p)(1 - q)v_d^h}{1 + k} - sI_0 - c - \theta. \tag{9}$$

Note that the parameter c represents an expected sunk cost of potential misappropriation by the local firm of the MNE's proprietary knowledge revealed in the collaboration process. It was mentioned in the preceding section that the formation of a CV could also cause the MNE to lose certain options. The effect of the parameter c, which can be easily seen to reduce the value of V_0 and thus increase the advantage of a sole venture, illustrates this point. The option lost here is the option to retain all of its proprietary knowledge. Also note that due to the presence of y_l and y_h in V_0, as defined by (8) and (9), the MNE will have a different evaluation of the CV than the local firm unless $y_l = y_h = 0$.

As alluded to earlier, by dissolving the CV at stage 2, the MNE can obtain a benefit due to the prevention of more knowledge being leaked to the local firm and can also incur a cost due to the loss of access to the local firm's complementary resources. Given that the difference between y_l and y_h represents the extent of uncertainty about such benefits and costs, the effect of changes in $\Delta = y_h - y_l$ on the value of V_0 indicates how uncertainty with regard to the problem of misappropriation affects the choice of market entry modes. The graph in Fig. 3 shows the relationship between Δ and V_0 as defined in (8) and (9). Their positive

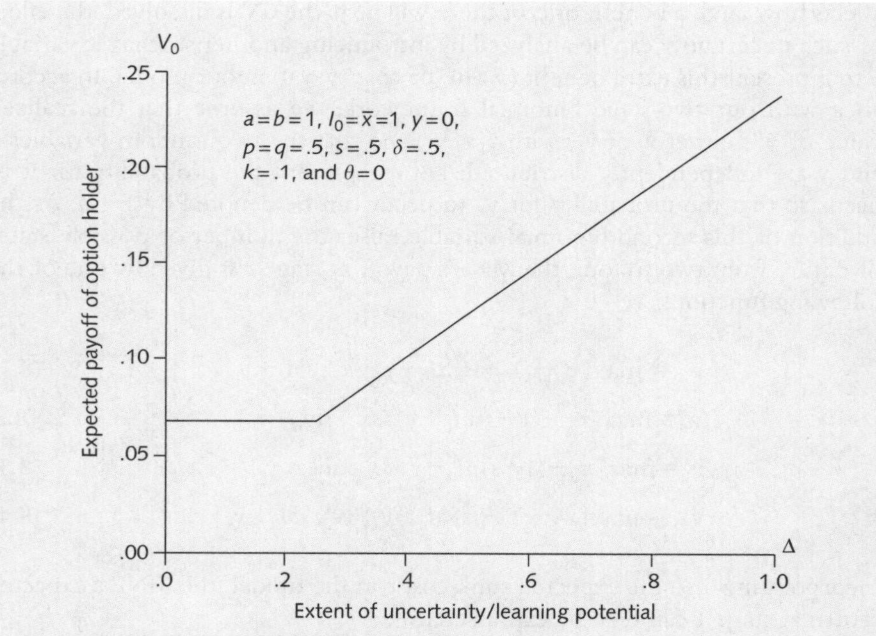

Fig. 3. Relationship of MNE's expected payoff with uncertainty about cost/benefit of dissolution.

relationship suggests that uncertainty about the hazards of transaction cost problems can also increase the advantage of a CV. It should, however, be stated very clearly that this advantage is due to the potential for gaining new information on the partner's behavioral tendency in the initial stage of collaboration while keeping down the exposure of one's proprietary knowledge to the partner. This type of learning is perhaps a very important part of what practitioners often call "trust building" in a world where economic agents follow divergent behavioral norms and cannot easily ascertain what norms are being followed by other agents due to the disguise that some of them try to wear.

4.2. Information Asymmetry

A number of authors have suggested that a JV may be preferred to an outright acquisition when there exists a significant degree of information asymmetry between the potential buyer and seller of a productive asset (Balakrishnan and Koza, 1993; Hennart, 1988; Shan, 1990). Problems of information asymmetry can be characterized as either adverse selection or moral hazard (Holmstrom, 1982). Adverse selection arises from the condition that the potential buyer of the asset knows less about the quality of the asset than the seller and can create severe difficulty in the negotiation between the two parties on the price of the asset (Akerloff, 1970). Moral hazard can arise in the sale of a productive asset (such as a new technology) when a proper transfer of the asset requires the seller to make a costly effort of training that is difficult for the buyer to monitor (Teece, 1982). Although existing literature has thoroughly explicated the rationale for a JV to reduce the negative impact of information asymmetry in a static setting, few studies have examined how the potential for learning under this type of uncertainty may affect the economic viability and structural design of JVs.[13] The objective of this subsection is to explore some of the dynamic issues in joint venturing under conditions of information asymmetry.

Balakrishnan and Koza (1993) observed that the potential buyer of an asset could use a JV with the current owner of the asset to gather more information about its value when there is a significant level of information asymmetry between the two parties. Although they did not make the connection explicit in their article, their observation is clearly related to the strategic option concept. When the asset being traded consists primarily of tacit production knowledge, the exchange is likely to be plagued by both adverse selection and moral hazard (Chi, 1994). Since a complete transfer of such knowledge requires the seller to make a costly effort of training that is difficult for the buyer to monitor, the extent of uncertainty that faces the buyer in the beginning can be greatly exacerbated. Much of this initial uncertainty, however, is likely to be resolved over time as more and more of the knowledge is revealed and transferred. This gradual reduction of uncertainty can make a JV with an acquisition option an effective mechanism for alleviating both adverse selection and moral hazard.

A remedy for the combined adverse selection and moral hazard problem requires two essential elements: one is sufficient incentive for the seller to provide the requisite training, and the other is alleviation of the buyer's concern about overpayment. A JV with an option to acquire can contain both elements. First, by giving the seller a high initial share of the venture's equity, a JV can let the seller be paid primarily out of the profit from the venture until the buyer exercises the option to acquire. As such an arrangement makes the buyer's payment of the acquisition price contingent on the completion of the knowledge transfer, it can give the seller a potentially strong incentive to provide the requisite training for the buyer. Since a higher equity share by the seller necessarily means that the buyer makes a smaller equity investment in the beginning, the buyer's exposure to the risk of overpayment is also reduced. In addition, because the buyer is not bound to acquire the venture if the knowledge transfer is unsatisfactory, the option arrangement can also reduce excessive bargaining over the acquisition price in their initial negotiation.

It should be noted, however, that the option arrangement described above does not preclude the buyer from renegotiating the acquisition price or withdrawing from the JV without adequate payment for what it has learnt from the seller. Hence, the economic viability of the arrangement as a remedy for the information asymmetry problem can be undermined by the misappropriation risk involved. Since the risk primarily affects assets that are embodied in information (technology and know-how) and thus can be used by two or more parties simultaneously (Casson, 1979), the viability of the arrangement should be high when the assets being traded are primarily physical in nature. In addition, although existing patent and contract laws also provide some protection for owners of proprietary knowledge, the extent of protection can vary significantly with the nature of the knowledge (Hennart, 1982; Teece, 1987). The viability of the arrangement, therefore, can be expected to fall as the knowledge involved receives less adequate protection under the prevailing legal system.

The above analysis has empirical implications with regard to which party is likely to hold an option to acquire the other's ownership interest in a JV when the JV potentially involves the transfer of some proprietary technology from the MNE to the local firm. As suggested earlier in this section, by limiting the scale and scope of technology transfer in the beginning, the MNE can use the JV to assess the local firm's capabilities and behavioral tendencies before it undertakes any major effort in technology transfer. Since the MNE is likely to attach a greater value to the right to acquire the venture when its technology is more vulnerable to misappropriation, we can expect that the MNE is more likely to demand such a right rather than give it to the local firm when its technology is less easily protected. If existing patent and contract laws do provide the MNE with relatively adequate protection against potential misappropriation of its technology, however, we can expect a higher likelihood that the JV is formed to facilitate the transfer of the technology to the local firm. Since giving the local firm the option to acquire the venture can alleviate the potential buyer uncertainty problem it faces, we can expect that the local firm is more likely to hold an option to acquire the venture under such conditions. Given that the uncertainty in either case affects how much the option holder can gain or lose from acquiring the venture from its partner, the model constructed earlier in this section can be used to assess the value of joint venturing for both parties. As demonstrated in the numerical example of Fig. 3, the value of the option is greater as the option holder experiences higher uncertainty.[14]

5. Empirical Implications for the Structuring of Joint Ventures

The purpose of this section is to develop the theoretical results of the preceding sections into some testable hypotheses concerning the contracting structure of JVs. As the hypotheses pay particular attention to JVs that give one of the parties the right to acquire the other's ownership interest at a prespecified price, we first identify the conditions under which the JV partners can be expected to find such a contractual arrangement mutually beneficial.

As suggested earlier, the extent of uncertainty facing the two parties is the highest before the start of their JV, and is likely to decline over time as their joint undertaking progresses. Given that negotiation tends to be more difficult when there is greater uncertainty, what would motivate the two parties to set the acquisition price in their initial contract rather than negotiating it later, when much of the initial uncertainty is resolved? The answer seems to lie in their anticipation of a possible change in their relative bargaining power. If neither of them expect their bargaining power to change in the course of their collaboration, it would clearly be more efficient for them to negotiate the price later when the need arises. But as suggested by Beamish and Banks (1987), the transfer of production knowledge between JV partners is likely to result in a change of their relative bargaining power. So, if one of the parties expects its own bargaining power to weaken in the course of the JV, it would be motivated to negotiate the acquisition price early on, and put pressure on the other party to do so (e.g. by threatening not to enter into a JV).

Hence, based on our analyses in the preceding paragraph and in sections two and three, we can attribute the motivation for such an option clause to a combination of three conditions. The first is the existence of uncertainty and learning potential about the value that a party can realize from acquiring the venture from its partner in the foreseeable future. Without this condition, the option would have little value. The second is the anticipation of a shift in the bargaining power of the two partners in the course of their collaboration. As alluded to above, this condition motivates the parties to set the acquisition price in their initial contract. The third is the existence of some ex ante asymmetry in their expected gains from acquiring the JV. This condition motivates the identification of the option holder, since the asymmetry between them makes it beneficial for them to trade in the right to the option. It is conceivable that each of these conditions is present to some extent in nearly every JV. Then, whether the partners of a JV find it justifiable to insert an option-to-acquire clause in their JV contract will depend on the strengths of these conditions. We therefore can expect that a strengthening of any of the conditions will increase the likelihood for the JV partners to make such an option arrangement.

5.1. Market Uncertainty vs. Partner Uncertainty

Our analysis in the section, *A Strategic Option Model*, identified two important sources of uncertainty in a JV: one is uncertainty about the market and the other is uncertainty about the partner (regarding its ability or behavioral tendency). Since the value of any option is an increasing function of the uncertainty about its underlying asset, we expect that a significant increase in each of these uncertainties will lead to a higher chance that the JV partners will install an explicit option clause in their initial contract. Generally, there is higher market uncertainty when the product of the JV is new to the local market, and there is higher partner uncertainty when the two parties have not had any prior collaborative experience with each other. Thus, we propose the following hypothesis about the incidence of an option-to-acquire clause in a JV agreement between an MNE and a local firm.

> *H1: A JV is more likely to contain an option-to-acquire clause ceteris paribus if its product is new to the local market or if its two partners have had no prior collaborative experience with each other.*

This hypothesis can be tested using a binomial logit or probit model. The relative effect sizes of the two independent variables can provide an indication about the influence of market uncertainty relative to that of partner uncertainty on the structuring of JVs.

5.2. Designation of Option Holder

We have in the preceding section suggested a condition that can help predict which party is likely to hold an option to acquire the other's ownership interest in situations where an MNE with certain proprietary technology joint ventures with a local firm. This condition, as explained earlier, is whether the MNE's technology receives adequate protection under the prevailing legal regime. Based on our analysis in the last section, we propose the following hypothesis.

> *H2: The MNE (local firm) is more likely to hold an option to acquire the venture ceteris paribus when the prevailing legal regime is less (more) adequate in protecting MNE from potential misappropriation of its technology.*

This hypothesis entails a trinomial dependent variable to indicate not only whether the JV contract contains an option-to-acquire clause but also which partner holds the option in case there is such an option clause. Unfortunately, we are not aware of a good objective measure of the extent of protection for various kinds of technology under a given legal regime. A test of the hypothesis may have to utilize a subjective measure based on the perception of the MNE's managers. A multinomial logit or probit model can be employed to perform the test.

5.3. Apportionment of Equity Share

Equity sharing in JVs has been explained as a mechanism for balancing the incentives of the partners when both of them are expected to make certain resource contributions that the other finds difficult to measure and monitor (Gomes-Casseres, 1989; Hennart, 1988; Shan, 1990). In the context of a JV between an MNE and a local firm, such hard-to-measure resource contributions can be production know-how, marketing expertise, or knowledge on how to deal with the local government bureaucracy. Several transaction cost based models have suggested that a party's relative ownership share may be influenced by how much the venture's outcome depends upon the hard-to-measure inputs expected from that party (Barzel and Suen, 1988; Chi, 1996; Eswaran and Kotwal, 1985). As our analysis in Section 2 has demonstrated, however, the party that holds an option to acquire its partner's share at a fixed price is likely to prefer a smaller equity share for itself in order to exploit more fully the potential benefit from the option it holds. Then, the party holding such an option can be expected to bargain for a smaller share by making concessions to its partner in other areas. We therefore have the following hypothesis:

H3: A JV partner is more likely to have a lower equity share ceteris paribus when it holds an option to acquire the other's ownership stake at a predetermined price than if it does not hold such an option.

A test of this hypothesis can be performed using an appropriate multiple regression model. The result can provide an indication of how strategic option considerations might alter the structure of JVs from what is predicted on the basis of transaction cost considerations alone.

6. Conclusion

In this chapter, we developed a framework for integrating the transaction cost and strategic option perspectives on collaborative ventures. The main contribution of the framework is that it allows a dynamic assessment of CVs and the transaction cost problems to which they may be subject. Although the exploitation of inter-firm synergy may be the primary and ultimate goal of any CV, our analysis suggests that the initial stage of a CV can be viewed as a vehicle for learning more about the partner for future expansion of the collaboration or acquisition of the partner's stake. This learning potential combined with the options embedded in the CV enhances the economic value of collaborative venturing and thus can alter an MNE's choice between collaboration, acquisition and green field entry (which precludes the exploration of potential synergy with a local firm).

Using a simple stochastic model, we explicated a condition that determines whether the option to acquire or sell out provides an economic value for the partners of a JV. Our model showed that such an option adds to the value of joint venturing whenever the JV partners foresee a possibility that they might have differing valuations of the venture ex post. In addition, we also suggested that the existence of certain ex ante asymmetry between the partners of a JV can motivate them to trade in the right to the option and that such asymmetry can often be traced to the presence of transaction cost problems. Using an expanded model that allows two sources of uncertainty, we demonstrated that the option to acquire and sell out can serve to reduce the risk of misappropriation and alleviate the difficulty of contracting under information asymmetry, thus adding to the value of collaborative venturing. Our analysis also suggested a condition that can help distinguish empirically which JV partner is likely to hold an option to acquire the other.

Based on our theoretical analyses, we derived three testable hypotheses, which we hope will lead to more rigorous empirical studies under a combined strategic option and transaction cost framework. It should also be noted that, although the theoretical insights and empirical implications of our paper have been derived in the context of a CV between an MNE and a local firm, most of them apply to any collaborative arrangements with or without the international dimension.

Notes

1. Although an extension of our model to the case of continuous probability and continuous time may give a more accurate representation of reality under many circumstances, such an extension will greatly increase the model's mathematical complexity without altering its basic theoretical insights. One can easily extend the model to a multi-stage binomial model that has been shown to provide an accurate approximation of option models built under the assumption of continuous distribution and continuous time (Kamrad and Ritchken, 1991; Trigeorgis, 1991, 1993).
2. In the parlance of financial options, θ represents the option premia. Here, we have made the simplifying assumption that the premia for the call and put options are the same per share. It should be noted that the two parties rarely need to be explicit about how a party is compensated for the provision of an option in their CV contract because they can easily make such a payment implicitly as a concession in their initial contract negotiation.
3. Cox, Ross and Rubinstein (1979) have shown that in a binomial stochastic model one can use the risk-free rate in lieu of the firm-specific discount rate by properly transforming the probability distribution of the two uncertain outcomes. The transformation requires the assumption that the risk of the asset underlying the option can be completely hedged using a portfolio of assets that are traded in the market. Such a transformation is not performed in our model because it does not add to the insights of our chapter.
4. For the ease of comparison, the numerical examples in our chapter are constructed on a unit scale. In the example of Fig. 1, for instance, we have assumed $a = b = I_0 = \bar{x} = (x_u + x_d)/2 = 1$.
5. The formation of a CV can also cause the MNE to lose certain valuable options. This issue will be discussed later in the chapter.
6. Recent studies in financial economics suggest that the discovery of a stock's true value through observation of market variables will become less effective as those variables have a high noise-to-signal ratio due to the influence of uninformed speculators on the market (De Long, Shleifer, Summers, and Waldmann, 1992; Leach and Madhavan, 1992). In the context of our chapter, there can also be noise in the sales figures of a JV, especially if its product is traded on a market that involves uninformed speculators. However, because the JV partners can engage in a lot of active learning, it seems reasonable to expect them to obtain more reliable information about the market and about each other after a sufficient length of time elapses.
7. We are indebted to an anonymous reviewer for suggesting this insight.

8. Note that this result is derived under the assumption that the parties are not concerned about the nonsystematic risk involved in the project. Even if the JV partners do care about such risk and are risk averse, the option to acquire or sell out will not add any value to the venture unless there exists some other type of asymmetry. Such asymmetry can arise when one of the parties is more risk-averse or perceives greater risk than the other. Under this type of asymmetry, the party that is more risk-averse or perceives greater risk will value the option more than the other does and then be willing to purchase the option at a price that the other finds attractive (assuming they do care about nonsystematic risk). We are grateful to an anonymous reviewer for clarifying this point.
9. For instance, IBM and Apple jointly formed Taligent (later also joined by Hewlett-Packard) to develop a new operating system for their next generation of personal computers. But the actual product developed by the JV turned out to be more complementary to IBM's technology, and the JV was recently disbanded and folded into IBM (Ziegler, 1995).
10. The presumed statistical independence of their ex post valuations means that there exist four equally possible states of nature: (i) the MNE values it as x_u and the local firm values it as x_d; (ii) the MNE values it as x_d and the local firm values it as x_u; (iii) both of them value it as x_u; and (iv) both of them value it as x_d. Each of these four states has a 0.25 probability of occurring.
11. This situation can be represented by modifying the probabilities for the four possible states of nature described in the previous note. For instance, if one of the parties is unlikely to value the venture more than the other does, the probability of (i) or (ii) can be set to a value close to zero.
12. Note that the extra benefit/cost of dissolving the JV was treated as known and incorporated into the values of the two parameters a and b in the basic model defined by (1) and (2) in Section 2. Since this extra benefit/cost is now separated out as a stochastic variable $\tilde{y}$, the values of a and b represent only the nominal prices for acquisition and sell-out, respectively.
13. An exception is Kogut (1991), who explicitly recognized the linkage between the problem of adverse selection and the potential for JVs to provide the buyer and seller a strategic option.
14. Although the option to sell out can potentially be used to reduce the appropriation risk, it seems to be a less useful remedy for the problem of information asymmetry. So, we will consider only the option to acquire in deriving the hypotheses in the next section.

References

Akerloff, G. A. 1970. The market for 'lemons': Quality, uncertainty, and the market mechanism. *Quarterly Journal of Economics*, 84: 488–500.

Balakrishnan, S. and Koza, M. P. 1993. Information asymmetry, adverse selection and joint ventures: Theory and evidence. *Journal of Economic Behavior and Organization*, 20(1): 99–117.

Barzel, Y. and Suen, W. 1988. Moral Hazard, monitoring cost, and the choice of contracts. Mimeo, University of Washington.

Beamish, P. W. and Banks, J. C. 1987. Equity joint ventures and the theory of the multinational enterprise. *Journal of International Business Studies*, 18(2): 1–16.

Casson, M. C. 1979. *Alternatives to the multinational enterprise*. London, U.K.: Macmillan.

Chi, T. 1994. Trading in strategic resources: Necessary conditions, transaction cost problems, and choice of exchange structure. *Strategic Management Journal*, 15(4): 271–290.

—— 1996. Performance verifiability and output sharing in collaborative ventures. *Management Science*, 42(1): 93–109.

Contractor, F. J. and Lorange, P. 1987. Why should firms cooperate? The strategy and economic basis for cooperate ventures. In F. J. Contractor & P. Lorange, editors, *Cooperative strategies in international business*. Lexington, Mass.: Lexington Books.

Cox, J. C., Ross, S. A. and Rubinstein, M. 1979. Option pricing: A simplified approach. *Journal of Financial Economics*, 7(3): 229–63.

De Long, J. B., Shleifer, A., Summers, L. H. and Waldmann, R. J. 1992. Noise trader risk in financial markets. *Journal of Political Economy*, 98(4): 703–38.

Eswaran, M. and Kotwal, A. 1985. A theory of contractual structure in agriculture. *American Economic Review*, 75(3): 352–67.

Folta, T. B. and Leiblein, M. J. 1994. Technology acquisition and the choice of governance by established firms: Insights from option theory in a multinomial logit model. In D. P. Moore, editor, *Proceedings of the Annual Meeting of the Academy of Management*, 27–36.

Gomes-Casseres, B. 1989. Ownership structures of foreign subsidiaries. *Journal of Economic Behavior and Organization*, 11: 1–25.

—— 1990. Firm ownership preferences and host government restrictions: An integrated approach. *Journal of International Business Studies*, 21(1): 1–22.

Harsanyi, J. C. and Selten, R. 1988. *A general theory of equilibrium selection in games*. Cambridge, Mass.: MIT Press.

Hennart, J.-F. 1982. *A theory of multinational enterprise*. Ann Arbor: University of Michigan Press.

—— 1988. A transaction costs theory of equity joint ventures. *Strategic Management Journal*, 9: 361–74.

Hill, C. W. L. 1992. Strategies for exploiting technological innovations: When and when not to license. *Organization Science*, 3: 428–41.

Holmstrom, B. 1982. Moral hazard in teams. *Bell Journal of Economics*, 13: 324–40.

Kamrad, B. and Ritchken, P. 1991. A lattice claims model for capital budgeting. *Management Science*, 37(12): 14–49.

Kogut, B. 1991. Joint ventures and the option to expand and acquire. *Management Science*, 37(1): 19–33.

Leach, J. C. and Madhavan, A. N. 1992. Intertemporal price discovery by market makers: Active versus passive learning. *Journal of Financial Intermediation*, 2: 207–35.

Root, F. R. 1987. *Entry strategies for international markets*. Lexington, Mass.: Lexington Books.

Shan, W. 1990. An empirical analysis of organizational strategies by entrepreneurial high-technology firms. *Strategic Management Journal*, 11: 129–39.

Stopford, J. M. and Wells, L. Jr. 1972. *Managing the multinational enterprise*. London, U.K.: Longman.

Teece, D. J. 1982. Towards an economic theory of the multiproduct firm. *Journal of Economic Behavior and Organization*, 3: 39–63.

—— 1987. Profiting from technological innovation: Implications for integration, collaboration, licensing and public policy. In D. J. Teece, editor, *The competitive challenge, studies for industrial innovation and renewal*. Cambridge, Mass.: Ballinger.

Trigeorgis, L. 1991. A log-transformed binomial numerical analysis method for valuing complex multi-option investment. *Journal of Financial and Quantitative Analysis*, 26: 309–26.

—— 1993. The nature of option interactions and the valuation of investments with multiple real options. *Journal of Financial and Quantitative Analysis*, 28: 1–20.

Williamson, O. E. 1975. *Markets and hierarchies: Analysis and antitrust implications*. New York: Free Press.

Ziegler, B. 1995. IBM, Apple, H-P to disband Taligent; Big layoffs loom at software venture. *Wall Street Journal*, December 1, B5.

10 Downside Risk Implications of Multinationality and International Joint Ventures

Jeffrey J. Reuer and Michael J. Leiblein

Corporate flexibility has recently been emphasized as a key concern for management research (e.g., Buckley and Casson, 1998; Hitt, 1998). This observation presents a challenge to both positive and normative theory given the divergent views on issues surrounding both the flexibility of firms and the specific benefits that firms might derive from flexibility. For instance, studies in population ecology (e.g., Hannan and Freeman, 1984), competitive strategy (e.g., Dierickx and Cool, 1989; Ghemawat, 1991), and behavioral theory (Cyert and March, 1963) point to internal complexity, path dependencies, and uncertainty avoidance, respectively, as factors limiting flexibility or its potential advantages. By contrast, proponents of real options theory submit that firms can proactively and flexibly manage uncertainties to their advantage (e.g., Bowman and Hurry, 1993; Hurry, Miller, and Bowman, 1992; Kogut, 1983, 1989; McGrath, 1997; Sanchez, 1993).

It was within this theoretical context that the current study examined the downside risk implications of two types of international investment thought to enhance corporate flexibility—multinationality, or the dispersion of foreign subsidiaries across different countries—and international joint ventures (IJVs). As we explain below, recent research has suggested that these investments confer real options that enable a firm to avoid downside outcomes by shifting value-chain activities across different host country environments, or by staging commitments (e.g., Kogut, 1989, 1991; Kogut and Chang, 1996). However, such investments can also increase organizational complexity and bring about nontrivial coordination costs, joint control challenges, imperfect claims on emerging opportunities, and so forth. Thus, the corporate risk effects of multinationality and IJVs are ultimately an empirical matter.

This study examines the risk implications of firms' investments in foreign subsidiaries and international joint ventures using a downside conceptualization of risk. Formally stated, downside risk is a probability-weighted function of below-target performance outcomes. In contrast to traditional, variance-based measures of risk that incorporate the entire distribution of firm performance, downside risk focuses solely on organizational outcomes below some target value. For instance, the probability of failing to meet a performance objective or expected loss are two among many formulations within the downside risk family.

Miller and Reuer (1996) provided several rationales for moving from variance-based measures of risk to downside conceptualizations based on their review of behavioral decision theory, finance studies, and management research on risk. First, downside risk explicitly incorporates the notion of reference levels, which behavioral decision theory identifies as a determinant of risk preferences (e.g., Kahneman and Tversky, 1979). Second, following discussions of downside risk in the early development of portfolio models in the finance literature, Harlow and Rao (1989) showed that a downside risk model of equity returns explains stock returns better than the capital asset pricing model (CAPM). Third, empirical research in the management field documents that decision makers tend to consider risk in terms of negative outcomes or hazards rather than as variance in outcomes, as reflected by standard risk measures (e.g., Baird and Thomas, 1990; March and Shapira, 1987). Finally, although empirical applications remain limited, Miller and Reuer (1996) noted that downside views of risk exist throughout the strategy literature (e.g., Aaker and Jacobson, 1987; Ansoff, 1965; Porter, 1985: 476). Ruefli, Collins, and LaCugna (1999) raised similar concerns about the concept validity of existing variance-based risk measures and the conclusions drawn from empirical studies using these measures.

For this study's purposes, a downside conceptualization of risk is also valuable given its compatibility with the basic tenets of real options theory, a theoretical perspective we used in developing the hypotheses relating international investments to organizational risk. Real options are discretionary investments that provide firms with the right, but not the obligation, to undertake some future action. Thus, real options are investments that provide flexibility by allowing firms to avoid downside outcomes and exploit emerging opportunities. McGrath argued that "the distinguishing characteristic of an options approach lies in firms making investments that confer the ability to select an outcome only if it is favorable" (1997: 975). In the international strategy context, real options theory suggests that dispersed foreign direct investment (FDI) provides a portfolio of options that enable a firm to avoid downside outcomes by shifting value-chain activities across country borders in response to changes in local demand, competitors' actions, foreign exchange rates, input prices, and other environmental contingencies (e.g., Allen and Pantzalis, 1996; Kogut, 1983, 1989).

Management and international strategy researchers have also for some time viewed international joint ventures as flexible and attractive from a risk standpoint because they entail lower initial capital outlays than wholly owned investments and allow firms to focus on core capabilities, access partners' skills, and facilitate market entry, among other factors (e.g., Contractor and Lorange, 1988). More recently, scholars have suggested that joint ventures can reduce downside risk in particular since JVs have option-like characteristics, in that firms can limit initial outlays and increase commitments later, if a desirable opportunity materializes (Kogut, 1991). Although the attractiveness of IJVs has long been attributed to their presumed flexibility and risk benefits, we know of no study that empirically examines the organizational risk implications of IJV investments.

This study proceeds as follows: the second section develops hypotheses relating firms' multinationality and IJV investments to downside risk. The section focuses on methodological issues, and the empirical results are contained in a subsequent section. Evidence from a sample of 357 U.S. manufacturing firms reveals that corporations with greater multinationality or greater investments in IJVs do not obtain lower levels of downside risk. In fact, firms investing in more IJVs experience higher levels of income stream risk and bankruptcy risk. We conclude with a discussion of these findings and their implications for theory development as well as future empirical research.

1. Theory and Hypotheses

Much research has investigated the risk profiles of multinational corporations (MNCs) relative to their domestic counterparts'. For instance, several studies have shown that multinational involvement tends to stabilize firms' income streams (see Caves [1996] and Qian [1996] for recent reviews). Kim, Hwang, and Burgers (1993) reported that international diversification was associated with the twin benefits of lower risk and higher returns. They concluded that these findings were consistent with MNCs' greater competitive options and operational flexibility, conforming to the view that MNCs have more degrees of freedom than domestic firms (e.g., Dunning and Rugman, 1985). At the same time, evidence such as the lower financial leverage ratios selected by multinationals (e.g., Lee and Kwok, 1988) casts some doubt on the diversification benefits of international operation. Reeb, Kwok, and Baek (1998) reported that systematic risk increased with a firm's degree of internationalization. Mitchell, Shaver, and Yeung (1992) found that multinational firms had a lower risk of business failure, but this risk increased if firms expanded or contracted their international presence.

Real options theory represents a promising theoretical perspective with which to evaluate the relationship between international operations and organizational risk. In particular, real options theory suggests that multinationality reduces firms' downside risk. The real options embedded in firms' international or other strategic investments can take many forms, including options to defer investment, expand or contract production, abandon operations, switch use of inputs, and grow into expanding markets (Trigeorgis, 1997). As a result, investing in real options allows a firm to manage risk by proactively confronting uncertainty over time in a flexible fashion (Kogut, 1991) rather than by attempting to avoid uncertainty (e.g., Cyert and March, 1963). Real options theory therefore provides researchers with a tool for evaluating the trade-offs between commitment and flexibility under conditions of uncertainty.

The introduction of real options theory into the international strategy literature clarifies one of the potential advantages of multinational firms over domestic rivals. Specifically, the dispersion of FDI provides a firm with a portfolio of real options that enable it to avoid downside outcomes and take advantage of upside opportunities by shifting value-chain activities globally (Kogut, 1983, 1989). The option to shift these activities is valuable when there are changes in local demand, labor expenses, other input costs, competitors' actions, or foreign exchange rates, all of which may vary among the countries in which a firm has operations. Real options theory therefore points to operational flexibility as one of the key strengths of a multinational firm.

One specific example of multinational firms' potential flexibility advantages is provided by their responses and economic exposures to foreign exchange rate movements. Unlike purely domestic firms or exporters with domestic production, firms with operations in multiple countries can shift production in response to exchange rate movements to enhance profits (Kogut and Kulatilaka, 1994). Rangan (1998) provided evidence that exchange rate movements trigger global shifts in manufacturing and sourcing activities by multinational firms. For instance, multinational operation enabled Asea Brown Boveri (ABB) to shift production from Europe and North America to Asia in response to the late 1990s' currency crisis (Fleming, 1998). Unlike their multinational counterparts, domestic firms are not able to exploit this flexibility and therefore have to bear any adverse consequences of such contingencies. Miller and Reuer (1998) found that FDI reduced firms' economic exposures to foreign exchange rate movements.

Although multinational operation may provide options to shift value-chain activities that can have efficiency consequences, the exercise of options can also be motivated by demand-side or competitive considerations. For instance, rising local income levels and demand can encourage the staged expansion of a host country operation. Further, Caves (1996) discussed how firms imitate rivals' international expansions in an attempt to acquire competitive options. Viewing an MNC as a possessor of a portfolio of options (Kogut, 1989) that provide the firm with the potential to select outcomes only if they are favorable (e.g., McGrath, 1997) leads to the following hypothesis:

Hypothesis 1. A firm's multinationality will be inversely related to its downside risk.

The international strategy literature has also long described IJVs as being attractive from a risk standpoint. Although the organizational risk implications of IJVs have not been a topic of empirical research, risk figures highly in many discussions of IJV formation motives (e.g., Contractor and Lorange, 1988). By engaging in joint ventures rather than acquisitions, for instance, firms can spread various risks over multiple capital providers in large-scale projects (e.g., Kogut and Singh, 1988). Firms might also use IJVs to overcome the liability of foreignness (e.g., Zaheer and Mosakowski, 1997) by tapping into a partner's local connections, market knowledge, and other supporting resources. A local partner can also buffer an MNC from a host government, a function that reduces possible hold-up risks (Teece, 1986). A firm can also use IJVs as springboards for further commitments and growth once it accumulates knowledge specific to a host country (e.g., Inkpen and Beamish, 1997).

Real options theory suggests that firms involved in IJVs can limit downside risk in particular. Specifically, a joint venture is thought to possess the same basic characteristics and nonlinear payoff function as a financial call option (Kogut, 1991). After a firm makes a small initial commitment to a market or technology through an IJV, it can expand that commitment if the market or technology proves to be favorable. However, the firm is under no compulsion to expand in the case of a negative turn of events and, rather than divest, it can adopt a wait-and-see approach if more favorable outcomes are possible in the future. Provided that the initial outlay is sunk and additional capital is not required, downside risk is "inconsequential" (Kogut, 1991: 24) since the option need not be exercised. The ability of individual IJVs to provide firms with flexibility advantages also rests on the parents' ability to buy or sell equity to change their commitments over time. It also rests on the security of the firm's claim on future investments lest rivals preempt emerging opportunities (Folta and Leiblein, 1994). At the corporate level, the containment of downside outcomes and the exploitation of upside opportunities in individual IJVs leads to lower organizational downside risk (e.g., Bowman and Hurry, 1993) if firms follow an options-based approach in managing IJVs:

Hypothesis 2. A firm's investment in IJVs will be inversely related to its downside risk.

2. Methods

2.1. Model Specification

The multivariate statistical models used in this research took the following basic form:

$$\begin{aligned}\textit{Downside risk}_t = \beta_0 &+ \beta_1 \textit{multinationality}_{t-1} + \beta_2 \textit{IJV investment}_{t-1} \\ &+ \beta_3 \textit{organizational slack}_t + \beta_4 \textit{firm size}_t \\ &+ \beta_5 \textit{industry risk}_t + \varepsilon_t. \qquad (1)\end{aligned}$$

The subscripts indicate the time lags we used for the theoretical variables to rule out problems from potential reverse causality in cross-sectional risk models (e.g., Bromiley, 1991). Two contiguous five-year periods during the years 1985–94 were used in calculating downside risk and its determinants. We chose the five-year periods to obtain sufficient time series data to construct the downside risk measure while also maintaining an assumption of strategy stability. Moreover, in the late 1980s the incidence of IJVs increased greatly (e.g., Anderson, 1990; Beamish and Delios, 1997).

Although our interest lay in developing a parsimonious model with which to assess the impact of multinationality and IJV investments on organizational risk, prior research has indicated the importance of including appropriate firm- and industry-level controls. We controlled for slack resources to account for an organization's ability to buffer against uncertainty (Thompson, 1967). Firm size was incorporated in the models to accommodate the greater project diversity of larger firms (Scherer and Ross, 1990); the financial, human, or other resources that can affect risk; potential rigidity or organizational inertia; and the relative importance of a firm's international investments. Finally, a control for industry risk addressed interindustry risk differences and nonobservable effects at the industry level.

2.2. Measures and Data

2.2.1. Downside Risk

Downside risk is a probability-weighted function of below-target performance outcomes. In contrast to conventional, variance-based measures of risk that capture the entire distribution of firm performance, the family of downside risk measures emphasizes performance outcomes falling below a target level. In this research, we used multiple measures of downside risk. Following Miller and Leiblein (1996), we first specified downside risk as a function of a firm's annual return on assets (ROA) relative to a target level that changed over time. The mean ROA for a firm's two-digit Standard Industrial Classification (SIC) industry in the preceding year was the proxy for its target level. Downside risk was then measured as a second-order root lower partial moment:

$$\textit{Downside risk, } ROA_j = \sqrt{\frac{1}{5} \sum_{ROA_j < IROA_j} (IROA_j - ROA_j)^2}, \tag{2}$$

where ROA_j is firm j's ROA and $IROA_j$ is the average ROA for firm j's industry in the preceding year. The squared difference term was summed over all years in the period 1990–4 in which firm j's ROA fell short of its target level. For a sensitivity analysis, we also used breakeven (a target of 0) and a firm's own one-year lagged ROA as alternative targets. Accounting data for these three measures were obtained from COMPUSTAT.

These ROA-based downside risk variables implicitly reflect the interests of top managers and others concerned about income stream risk owing to their sunk investments in their firms. This focus was attractive for the present analysis since top managers will be involved in making decisions about firms' international strategies, and these measures also capture various stakeholders' interests. However, Miller and Reuer (1996) showed that alternative operational definitions of downside risk reflected the interests of different stakeholder groups. Thus, for comparison purposes, we also tested the effects of multinationality and IJV investment using a broader set of downside risk measures. First, we calculated the same three variables described above using return on equity (ROE) data to reflect bankruptcy risk and creditors' interests. These measures were called downside risk, ROE. Miller and Reuer's (1996) factor analysis of alternative risk measures showed that this measure loads on the same factor as Altman's Z, which is an indicator of bankruptcy risk. Second, we calculated a mean lower partial moment CAPM beta measure to consider shareholders' interests in firms' systematic risk, calling it downside risk, beta. A firm-specific market model was estimated over the 1990–4 period for all months in which the market return fell short of the U.S. Treasury Bill rate:

$$r_{jt} = \beta_{oj} + \beta_j r_{mt} + \varepsilon_{jt}, \quad \text{for all } t \text{ given } r_{mt} < i_t, \tag{3}$$

where r_{jt} is firm j's return in month t, r_{mt} is the market portfolio return, i_t is the interest rate, and β_j is firm j's downside risk, beta (e.g., Harlow and Rao, 1989). Stock returns data were acquired from the Center for Research in Securities Prices (CRSP) data files, and interest rate data were obtained from the International Financial Statistics database.

2.2.2. Explanatory Variables

Following Caves and Mehra (1986) and Kogut and Singh (1988), we measured multinationality by counting the number of countries in which a firm had foreign subsidiaries. We defined multinationality as the logarithm of 1 plus the number of countries in which a firm had foreign subsidiaries in order to remedy the significant positive skew that was evident for the pretransformed count measure (e.g., Tabachnick and Fidell, 1996). Foreign subsidiary data were obtained from the 1990 edition of National Register Publishing's *Directory of International Affiliations*.

A firm's investment in IJVs was similarly measured as the log of 1 plus the number of equity joint ventures formed abroad or with a foreign partner during 1985–89. We did not include announcements of preliminary discussions or venture negotiations in these counts in an effort to ensure that our measure included only agreements that were actually consummated. Searches for IJV investments were carried out with the Lexis-Nexis database, which draws upon more than 2,300 sources. Despite the comprehensiveness of this database, the use of public announcements and the lack of reporting requirements may bias count measures in favor of more significant alliances. Recognizing this issue and seeking to avoid potential problems from pooling different types of alliances, our focus was on equity joint ventures.

Our control for organizational slack focused on a firm's recoverable slack resources (Bourgeois and Singh, 1983; Miller and Leiblein, 1996), a concept similar to Singh's (1986) notion of absorbed slack. We calculated three ratios for each firm: accounts receivable/sales; inventory/sales; and selling, general, and administrative expenses/sales. Each ratio was normalized by the industry average, summed, and averaged over the 1990–94 period. Firm size was measured as the log of a firm's average net sales. Finally, industry risk was the mean downside risk for all other firms in the firm's industry (that is, industry risk, ROA; industry risk, ROE; and industry risk, beta).

2.3. Sample

The base sample consisted of all U.S. manufacturing firms in the SIC range 3000–3999 that had data available from COMPUSTAT, CRSP, and the *Directory of International Affiliations*. Use of a manufacturing sample rather than one from a different sector or a broader range of industries was motivated by several considerations. First, the large sunk costs in assets and employees typically found in the manufacturing sector suggested that flexibility would be particularly valuable for these firms. Second, sampling firms in this SIC range reflected our desire to facilitate comparisons with prior studies in the risk, international strategy, and real options literatures. Finally, focusing on firms within this SIC range mitigated data discrepancies arising from differences in accounting practices across single-digit SIC categories (Bromiley, 1991). After observations with missing accounting or subsidiary data necessary to construct our risk measures and independent variables had been deleted, the sample comprised 357 firms. There were sufficient data to calculate downside risk, beta, for 332 firms. Visual inspection of the dependent variables' distributions indicated two outliers in the upper tail of the downside risk, ROE, measure, which we addressed by deleting observations with values more than three standard deviations from the mean.

3. Results

Table 1 presents descriptive statistics for the sample and a correlation matrix. The average firm had foreign subsidiaries in just under six countries and sales of $3.3 billion. Approximately 28 percent of the firms had purely domestic operations, and the most internationally diversified firm operated in 44 countries. Firms' total assets averaged $3.6 billion and ranged from $15.2 million to $173.6 billion. A majority of the firms, 62 percent, did not enter into IJVs between 1985 and 1989. Of the firms that did not have operations in foreign countries, only 20.4 percent of them entered into IJVs, whereas 43.1 percent of the firms with foreign subsidiaries invested in at least one IJV. This finding is also in accord with prior research suggesting IJVs are organizational forms that firms use selectively (e.g., Hennart, 1988). Moreover, firms' IJV formation levels were quite heterogeneous, ranging from 0 to 30 investments during 1985–89.

We examined the correlations among the ROA- and ROE-based downside risk measures using the alternative target-level specifications of lagged

Table 1. Descriptive Statistics and Correlation Matrix[a]

Variable	Mean	s.d.	1	2	3	4	5	6	7	8	9
1. Downside risk, ROA	0.04	0.05									
2. Downside risk, ROE	0.14	0.28	.61***								
3. Downside risk, beta	1.43	1.31	−.09	−.07							
4. Multinationality	1.34	1.08	−.02	.03	−.03						
5. IJV investment	0.47	0.73	−.01	.13*	−.06	.43***					
6. Organizational slack	−0.02	1.68	.01	−.13*	.04	.03	−.10*				
7. Firm size	6.33	1.83	−.12*	.05	−.06	.63***	.66***	−.17***			
8. Industry risk, ROA	0.04	0.01	−.04	−.07	.06	.11*	−.04	.03	.02		
9. Industry risk, ROE	0.30	0.36	−.06	−.10†	−.01	.13*	.01	−.01	.02	−.05	
10. Industry risk, beta	1.37	0.18	.08	−.01	−.12*	.04	−.05	.02	.01	.51***	−.06

[a] $N = 332$ for cells corresponding to downside risk, beta; $N = 355$ for all other cells. Downside risk, ROA and downside risk, ROE were constructed using lagged industry-average return targets. Means, standard deviations, and correlations are reported for the log-transformed variables (multinationality, IJV investment, and firm size).

† $p < .10$

* $p < .05$

** $p < .01$

*** $p < .001$

industry-average return, breakeven, and lagged own-firm return. The correlations between the three downside risk measures derived from ROA data were .87 or higher. Similarly, all correlations between the three downside risk measures based on ROE data were at least .96. Given the robustness of our risk measures to alternative target-level specifications, just three risk measures were retained for the analysis. These were the ROA- and ROE-based risk measures with a lagged industry-average return target and downside risk, beta.

The correlation matrix indicates that downside risk, ROA, is positively correlated with downside risk, ROE, but not with downside risk, beta. Downside risk, ROA, is negatively related to firm size ($p = .026$), and downside risk, ROE, is negatively related to organizational slack ($p = .011$). The only significant correlation between any of the downside risk measures and the theoretical variables is the positive relationship between downside risk, ROE and IJV investment ($p = .013$). Nevertheless, the significant correlations among the explanatory variables (for instance, multinationality, IJV investment, and firm size) indicated that multivariate analysis was needed to examine the partial effects of the theoretical variables on downside risk.

We investigated potential multicollinearity problems by examining variance inflation factors (VIFs), conditioning indexes, and variance decomposition proportions. The maximum VIF obtained for the six models (presented in Table 2) was 2.51, which is substantially below the rule-of-thumb cutoff of 10 for multiple regression models (Neter, Wasserman, and Kutner, 1985: 392). The maximum conditioning indexes for the full regression models with downside risk, ROA, downside risk, ROE, and downside risk, beta, as the dependent variables were 18.78, 14.23, and 23.61, respectively. These values are also below the accepted cutoff value of 30 (Belsley, Kuh, and Welsch, 1980: 112). Further, in each case the variance decomposition proportions for the largest conditioning indexes were associated with the intercept term and one of the control variables, indicating that the regression estimates for our theoretical variables were not adversely affected by the presence of multicollinearity. Heteroskedastic error terms might have resulted from the use of a regression estimate as a dependent variable in the downside risk, beta, specifications (Hanushek, 1974), but inspection of studentized residuals provided no evidence of heteroskedasticity.

3.1. Statistical Techniques

Ordinary least squares (OLS) regression models were used to estimate models involving downside risk, beta, as the dependent variable. The choice of estimation procedure for the other two downside risk measures was influenced by the fact that a significant proportion of the observations obtained a limit value of zero: for downside risk, ROA, and downside risk, ROE, these percentages

Table 2. Results of Tobit and OLS Regression Analyses[a]

Variable	Downside Risk, ROA		Downside Risk, ROE		Downside Risk, Beta	
	Model 1	Model 2	Model 3	Model 4	Model 5	Model 6
Intercept	0.075***	0.098***	0.099	0.228**	2.941***	2.888***
	(0.02)	(0.023)	(0.069)	(0.083)	(0.615)	(0.637)
Organizational slack	0.001	−0.001	−0.023*	−0.025*	0.027	0.027
	(0.002)	(0.002)	(0.011)	(0.011)	(0.044)	(0.045)
Firm size	−0.003†	−0.009***	0.001	−0.029†	−0.039	−0.022
	(0.002)	(0.003)	(0.010)	(0.016)	(0.041)	(0.063)
Industry risk, ROA	−0.392	−0.410				
	(0.420)	(0.421)				
Industry risk, ROE			−0.078	−0.082		
			(0.052)	(0.052)		
Industry risk, beta					−0.925*	−0.951*
					(0.404)	(0.406)
Multinationality		0.006		0.014		0.020
		(0.004)		(0.022)		(0.087)
IJV investment		0.013*		0.094**		−0.098
		(0.006)		(0.033)		(0.133)
Log likelihood $L(\beta)$	330.07	333.65	−155.05	−150.89		
$-2[L(\beta_{\text{reduced}}) - L(\beta_{\text{full}})]$		7.16*		8.32*		
Model F					2.20†	1.43
N	355	355	355	355	332	332

[a] Models 1–4 were estimated using Tobit models, and models 5 and 6 were estimated using OLS models. Significance levels for models 1 through 4 were determined by Wald tests, and significance levels for models 5 and 6 were determined by t-tests.
† $p < .10$
* $p < .05$
** $p < .01$
*** $p < .001$

were 19.4, and 23.4 percent, respectively. Since OLS regression techniques can provide inconsistent parameter estimates when applied to data that include a large proportion of limit observations (Greene, 1993: 962), we used censored Tobit regression models for downside risk, ROA, and downside risk, ROE. The Tobit models can be expressed as follows:

$$Y^* = X(\beta) + \varepsilon, \quad \text{where } Y = Y^* \text{ if } Y^* > 0, \text{ and } Y = 0 \text{ otherwise,} \tag{4}$$

where Y^* is a latent variable that is observed only when the value of the dependent variable is positive, X is a vector of explanatory variables, β is a coefficient vector, and ε is an error term assumed to be normally distributed.

3.2. *Tobit and OLS Regression Results*

We estimated two regression models for each of the three measures of downside risk and report these results in Table 2. Models 1, 3, and 5 are baseline models in which the analysis is restricted to the effects of the control variables. Models 2, 4, and 6 augment the baseline models by including the direct effects of the two theoretical variables. A comparison of the log-likelihood values for models 1 and 2 as well as for models 3 and 4 indicates multinationality and IJV investment are jointly significant in explaining interfirm differences in both downside risk, ROA ($p < .03$), and downside risk, ROE ($p < .02$). A hierarchical F-test comparing models 5 and 6 shows that the theoretical variables are not statistically significant predictors of downside risk, beta ($F = 0.29$).

Our findings for the control variables reveal that organizational slack is significantly related to downside risk, ROE ($p < .05$) and that firm size is most significantly related to downside risk, ROA ($p < .001$). In both cases, the control variables are negatively related to downside risk. Larger firms had lower levels of income stream risk, and firms with greater recoverable slack resources had lower levels of bankruptcy risk. Our controls for industry risk were not statistically significant in the downside risk, ROA, and downside risk, ROE, models.

Hypothesis 1 predicts that multinationality will be inversely related to organizational downside risk. The regression coefficient for this variable was not statistically significant in any of the models. Thus, the empirical evidence suggests that the international dispersion of foreign subsidiaries does not have a negative impact on a firm's level of downside risk.

Based on predictions from real options theory and the IJV literature, Hypothesis 2 similarly posits an inverse relationship between a firm's investment in IJVs and its downside risk. However, in contrast to the negative hypothesized relationship, a statistically significant, positive effect was obtained in both the downside risk, ROA ($p = .034$), and downside risk, ROE ($p = .005$), models, indicating firms that actively invested in IJVs experienced higher, rather than lower, levels of income stream risk and bankruptcy risk. The overall insignificant results for model 6 precluded interpreting the individual variables' effects on firms' systematic risk.

Several robustness tests were separately performed for the full models. First, to further assess the effects of the correlation between multinationality and IJV investment, we also modeled their effects by entering these two variables individually into the models. Second, given the relatively large number of firms that did not operate foreign subsidiaries or invest in IJVs, we estimated the effects of multinationality and IJV investment using two dummy variables instead of the two continuous measures. Third, we included a lagged measure of downside risk to account for other possible unspecified influences on organizational downside risk. For these three separate analyses, the results and interpretations were entirely consistent with those presented above. Finally, incorporation of squared terms for the theoretical variables provided no evidence of nonlinear effects, and inclusion of terms for interactions between firm size and multinationality as well as between firm size and IJV investment provided no evidence that the theoretical variables had size-moderated effects on downside risk.

4. Discussion

The main finding of this study is that U.S. manufacturing firms' investments in dispersed FDI and international joint ventures do not have a general, negative impact on organizational downside risk, as predicted by real options theory and international strategy research. Corporate multinationality is not significantly related to downside risk, and firms that are more active in engaging in IJVs obtain higher, rather than lower, levels of downside risk. These results are striking in light of prior research in the international literature on the diversification benefits of multinationality and recent evidence that higher-performing (Harbison and Pekar, 1998) and higher-prestige (Stuart, 1998) firms are more active in forming alliances. The evidence we present can be explained by the observation that not all investments undertaken in uncertain contexts provide significant options, nor do firms necessarily manage real options properly. The results thus reveal a gap between the promise of risk reduction that theory holds out and the reality of firms' apparently limited capabilities for managing international investments as options.

4.1. Multinationality and Organizational Downside Risk

The difference between international investments' potential and actual benefits in terms of improved flexibility and reduced risk has previously been acknowledged by authors noting the challenges that firms face in successfully implementing an options-based approach. For instance, owing to their size and complexity, global firms may fail to perceive the real options embedded in their international investments and may also lack appropriate management systems for exercising flexibility (e.g., Kogut, 1985). Further, the costs of holding real options may be substantial if an MNC must commit additional capital over time or incur ongoing costs—for instance, if the firm carries excess capacity to facilitate shifts in value-chain activities across borders. Rangan (1998) also pointed to the lack of compatibility across MNCs' operations and the residual effects of administrative heritage as additional factors that may restrict firms' abilities to shift value-chain activities in response to changing environmental conditions.

Other considerations might explain why firms with more dispersed international operations do not obtain lower levels of downside risk. Implicit in the formulation of the multinationality hypothesis is the notion that flexibility benefits outweigh any incremental costs and risks stemming from greater organizational complexity. In fact, prior research has suggested that it is difficult for firms to coordinate foreign subsidiary operations (Roth, Schweiger, and Morrison, 1991) and that international diversification can increase transaction costs and information-processing loads (e.g., Jones and Hill, 1988). If managers' monitoring capabilities are taxed or organizational inertia is present, it is less likely that a firm will be able to avoid downside outcomes and exploit emerging opportunities as environmental conditions change. Related factors that might impede global shifts in value-chain activities and nullify the potential flexibility and downside risk benefits of dispersed FDI include parochialism, giving rise to subgoal pursuit, and weak internal systems that fail to provide timely information to decision makers (Rangan, 1998).

4.2. Joint Ventures and Organizational Downside Risk

Although a large body of research has similarly identified many features of IJVs that make them attractive from a risk standpoint, we know of no empirical study that directly tests the organizational risk implications of international joint ventures. Our finding that IJV investment has a positive influence on downside risk raises the question of whether this result would also hold for domestic joint ventures, which may not involve some of the managerial challenges that arise from operating in a foreign country or allying with a foreign partner. To address this issue, we re-estimated the models by incorporating an analogous measure for domestic JVs. The results revealed that firms' investments in domestic joint ventures were positively related to downside risk, ROA ($p = .015$), and downside risk, ROE ($p = .008$). This analysis indicates that the significant risks attending collaborations are not confined to cross-border ventures. Neither international nor domestic JV investment has a negative impact on organizational downside risk.

The poor performance and low survival rate of many IJVs also raise the issue of whether many IJVs are simply high-risk projects and the issue of whether they are truly being managed using an options-based approach. Studies show that parent firms' satisfaction levels with IJVs are quite low and may be declining overall (e.g., Beamish and Delios, 1997; Kogut, 1988), and empirical research has shown that IJVs are unstable organizational forms that are very difficult to manage (e.g., Barkema, Bell, and Pennings, 1996; Li, 1995; Park and Ungson, 1997). Singh and Mitchell's (1997) findings demonstrate how a business's fate can become linked with a partner's future: a firm's dissolution risk increases when partners either form new relationships or shut down.

Just as a number of contingencies might explain why multinationality is insignificantly related to downside risk in general, many related factors potentially explain why IJVs often do not deliver downside risk benefits to parent firms. First, viewing joint ventures as options that reduce downside risk rests on the assumption that parent firms do not experience large recurring costs or make additional capital infusions while managing ventures over time. If carrying costs or postformation investment outlays are significant in maintaining the collaboration, downside possibilities can be nontrivial. Second, viewing JVs as options also implies that a firm has a secure claim on a venture's upside opportunities while deferring irreversible investment (McDonald and Siegel, 1986). This can be the case if a firm has an explicit call option on a venture, but in other instances it is plausible that hold-up will occur upon JV termination or that the gains from expansion will be reflected in the buyout price. Finally, other IJV work has identified many other contingencies, like parent firms' organizational structures (Franko, 1971) and IJV control mechanisms (Killing, 1983), that can shape firms' abilities to manage joint ventures over time.

4.3. Limitations and Future Research Directions

The present study's results and limitations have several implications for future international strategy research. First, our finding that investments in multinationality and joint ventures do not have a negative effect on downside risk provides a cautionary note against making general claims regarding flexibility enhancement or risk reduction based upon the investments per se. At best, such investments can provide firms with the potential to obtain these benefits, but we found no evidence that firms making such investments were able to actually achieve lower levels of downside risk in general. Given the evidence we present, there is value in questioning theoretical predictions or assumptions regarding organizational flexibility and risk in different contexts. Research is needed to sort out the degree to which international investments truly confer specific options to global organizations from the firms' abilities to properly manage the options they possess.

Second, although the focus of our study was on the overall effects of multinationality and international joint venture investments on organizational downside risk, future research might investigate specific contingencies affecting a firm's ability to enhance flexibility and reduce risk through international operation. Although there did not appear to be any general relationship between multinationality and downside risk for our sample of U.S. manufacturing firms, and organizational downside risk was actually higher for firms investing in IJVs, flexibility enhancement and risk reduction from international operations may occur in more limited, well-defined settings. We have noted various factors that might have moderated the general relationships between international investments and organizational downside risk that we observed (management systems, value-chain configurations and operations compatibility, organizational structure, alliance design, and so forth). Beyond these potential macrolevel impediments to achieving flexibility, successful implementation of an options-based approach may also hinge upon individual managers' abilities to perform specific tasks, such as monitoring environmental developments, communicating internationally, and transferring resources to satisfy global rather than unit objectives. Thus, there also appears to be value in applying real options theory with other perspectives operating at the individual level.

Third, several opportunities exist to build upon the study's focus and methods. Our analyses using secondary data to measure IJV investment and characterize a firm's international presence could be refined by using primary data. Use of survey methods would also permit elaborating our models to incorporate possible moderating effects or investment antecedents using a structural modeling approach. Gathering finer-grained data would also allow researchers to explicitly investigate real option theory's assumptions and boundary conditions as this perspective is applied to multinational firms and joint ventures. Future research could examine the generalizability of our findings by replicating the present study in different contexts, but it could also build upon our work by studying operational flexibility and environmental cues directly (e.g., Hurry, et al., 1992; Kogut and Chang, 1996), drawing comparisons with other investments that provide options to organizations (e.g., Bowman and Hurry, 1993; McGrath, 1997) and investigating specific types of risks to which firms are exposed or to which they respond through their investment decisions. Das and Teng (1998), for example, classified alliance risks into performance and relational categories and suggested how parent firms might anticipate such risks in the provision of different types of resources and in alliance design. The application of an alliance typology to classify alternative structures and collaborative motives would be valuable in studying how different types of risk affect and are affected by different types of interfirm collaboration. Research extending our study in directions such as these could advance the literature on alliances and international strategy.

Finally, the downside risk measures implemented in this study can be applied to a wide range of other empirical research settings. Downside conceptualizations of risk are particularly attractive in empirical studies applying real options theory because of the contention that options offer firms the potential to avoid unfavorable outcomes and seize upon favorable outcomes in a selective fashion (McGrath, 1997). As an empirical matter, the finding that multinationality is not significantly related to organizational downside risk contrasts with previous studies' suggestions that international involvement offers diversification benefits in the form of profit stabilization (e.g., Qian, 1996). Given these differences and the theoretical motivations for employing downside conceptualizations of risk (Miller and Reuer, 1996), incorporation of downside risk measures into other areas of organizational research may prove fruitful.

The study's findings indicate the opportunities that exist for management scholars to study how or if firms can close the gap between the potential and actual flexibility and risk benefits of international investments in multinationality and joint ventures. Future research can address the influence of supporting strategies and implementation approaches, specific contexts in which risk reduction and flexibility enhancement is great or improbable, and the positive and normative boundaries of real options theory. As corporate flexibility becomes a more central concern of management and international strategy research (e.g., Buckley and Casson, 1998; Hitt, 1998), these research directions will likely take on greater importance.

References

Aaker, D. A., and Jacobson, R. 1987. The role of risk in explaining differences in profitability. *Academy of Management Journal*, 30: 277–297.

Allen, L., and Pantzalis, C. 1996. Valuation of the operating flexibility of multinational corporations. *Journal of International Business Studies*, 27: 633–653.

Anderson, E., 1990. Two firms, one frontier: On assessing joint venture performance. *Sloan Management Review*, 31(2): 19–30.

Ansoff, H. I. 1965. *Corporate strategy*. New York: Wiley.

Baird, I. S., and Thomas, H. 1990. What is risk anyway? Using and measuring risk in strategic management. In R. A. Bettis and H. Thomas (Eds.), *Risk, strategy, and management*: 21–52. Greenwich, CT: JAI Press.

Barkema, H. G., Bell, J. H. J., and Pennings, J. M. 1996. Foreign entry, cultural barriers, and learning. *Strategic Management Journal*, 17: 151–166.

Beamish, P. W., and Delios, A. 1997. Improving joint venture performance through congruent measures of success. In P. W. Beamish & J. P. Killing (Eds.), *Cooperative strategies: European perspectives*: 103–127. San Francisco: New Lexington Press.

Belsley, D. A., Kuh, E., and Welsch, R. E. 1980. *Regression diagnostics*. New York: Wiley.

Bourgeois, L. J., and Singh, J. V. 1983. Organizational slack and political behavior within top management groups. *Academy of Management Proceedings*: 43–49.

Bowman, E. H., and Hurry, D. 1993. Strategy through the options lens: An integrated view of resource investments and the incremental-choice process. *Academy of Management Review*, 18: 760–782.

Bromiley, P. 1991. Testing a causal model of corporate risk taking and performance. *Academy of Management Journal*, 34: 37–59.

Buckley, P. J., and Casson, M. C. 1998. Models of the multinational enterprise. *Journal of International Business Studies*, 29: 21–44.

Caves, R. E. 1996. *Multinational enterprise and economic analysis* (2nd ed.). New York: Cambridge University Press.

—— and Mehra, S. K. 1986. Entry of foreign multinationals into U.S. manufacturing industries. In M. E. Porter (Ed.), *Competition in global industries*: 449–481. Boston: Harvard Business School Press.

Contractor, F. J., and Lorange, P. 1988. Why should firms cooperate? The strategy and economics basis for cooperative ventures. In F. J. Contractor & P. Lorange (Eds.), *Cooperative strategies in international business*: 3–30. New York: Lexington Books.

Cyert, R. M., and March, J. G. 1963. *A behavioral theory of the firm*. Englewood Cliffs, NJ: Prentice-Hall.

Das, T. K., and Teng, B.-S. 1998. Resource and risk management in the strategic alliance making process. *Journal of Management*, 24: 21–42.

Dierickx, I., and Cool, K. 1989. Asset stock accumulation and sustainability of competitive advantage. *Management Science*, 35: 1504–1514.

Dunning, J. H., and Rugman, A. 1985. The influence of Hymer's dissertation on theories of foreign direct investment. *American Economic Review*, 75: 228– 232.

Fleming, C. 1998. ABB's net profit for 1997 declined 54% on provisions for Asian financial crisis. *Wall Street Journal Europe*, February 27–28: 3.

Folta, T., and Leiblein, M. 1994. Technology acquisition and the choice of governance by established firms: Insights from option theory in a multinomial logit model. *Academy of Management Best Paper Proceedings*: 27–31.

Franko, L. G. 1971. *Joint venture survival in multinational corporations*. New York: Praeger.

Ghemawat, P. 1991. *Commitment: The dynamic of strategy*. New York: Free Press.

Greene, W. H. 1993. *Econometric analysis* (2nd ed.). New York: Macmillan.

Hannan, M. T., and Freeman, J. 1984. Structural inertia and organizational change. *American Sociological Review*, 49: 149–164.

Hanushek, E. A. 1974. Efficient estimators for regressing regression coefficients. *American Statistician*, 28: 66–67.

Harbison, J. R., and Pekar, P., Jr. 1998. *Smart alliances*. San Francisco: Jossey-Bass.

Harlow, W. V., and Rao, R. K. S. 1989. Asset pricing in a generalized mean-lower partial moment framework. *Journal of Financial and Quantitative Analysis*, 24: 285–311.

Hennart, J.-F. 1988. A transaction cost theory of equity joint ventures. *Strategic Management Journal*, 9: 361–374.

Hitt, M. A. 1998. Presidential address: Twenty-first-century organizations: Business firms, business schools, and the academy. *Academy of Management Review*, 23: 218–224.

Hurry, D., Miller, A. T. and Bowman, E. H. 1992. Calls on high-technology: Japanese exploration of venture capital investments in the United States. *Strategic Management Journal*, 13: 85–101.

Inkpen, A. C., and Beamish, P. W. 1997. Knowledge, bargaining power, and the instability of international joint ventures. *Academy of Management Review*, 22: 177–202.

Jones, G. R., and Hill, C. W. L. 1988. Transaction cost analysis of strategy-structure choice. *Strategic Management Journal*, 9: 159–172.

Kahneman, D., and Tversky, A. 1979. Prospect theory: An analysis of decisions under risk. *Econometrica*, 47: 262–291.

Killing, J. 1983. *Strategies for joint venture success*. New York: Praeger.

Kim, W. C., Hwang, P., and Burgers, W. P. 1993. Multinationals' diversification and the risk-return trade-off. *Strategic Management Journal*, 14: 275–286.

Kogut, B. 1983. Foreign direct investment as a sequential process. In C. P. Kindleberger and D. B. Audretsch (Eds.), *The multinational corporation in the 1980s*: 62–75. Boston: MIT Press.

——1985. Designing global strategies: Profiting from operational flexibility. *Sloan Management Review*, 27(4): 27–38.

——1988. Joint ventures: Theoretical and empirical perspectives. *Strategic Management Journal*, 9: 319–332.

——1989. A note on global strategies. *Strategic Management Journal*, 10: 383–389.

——1991. Joint ventures and the option to expand and acquire. *Management Science*, 37: 19–33.

——and Chang, S. J. 1996. Platform investments and volatile exchange rates: Direct investment in the U.S. by Japanese electronic companies. *Review of Economics and Statistics*, 78: 221–231.

——and Kulatilaka, N. 1994. Operating flexibility, global manufacturing, and the option value of a multinational network. *Management Science*, 40: 123–139.

——and Singh, H. 1988. The effect of national culture on the choice of entry mode. *Journal of International Business Studies*, 19: 411–432.

Lee, C. L., and Kwok, C. C. Y. 1988. Multinational corporations vs. domestic corporations: International environmental factors and determinants of capital structure. *Journal of International Business Studies*, 19: 195–217.

Li, J. 1995. Foreign entry and survival: Effects of strategic choices on performance in international markets. *Strategic Management Journal*, 16: 333–351.

March, J. G., and Shapira, Z. 1987. Managerial perspectives on risk and risk taking. *Management Science*, 33: 1404–1418.

McDonald, R., and Siegel, D. 1986. The value of waiting to invest. *Quarterly Journal of Economics*, 101: 707–28.

McGrath, R. G. 1997. A real options logic for initiating technology positioning investments. *Academy of Management Review*, 22: 974–996.

Miller, K. D., and Leiblein, M. J. 1996. Corporate risk-returns relations: Returns variability versus downside risk. *Academy of Management Journal*, 39: 91–122.

——and Reuer, J. J. 1996. Measuring organizational downside risk. *Strategic Management Journal*, 17: 671–691.

——and——1998. Firm strategy and economic exposure to foreign exchange rate movements. *Journal of International Business Studies*, 29: 493–514.

Mitchell, W., Shaver, J. M., and Yeung, B. 1992. Getting there in a global industry: Impacts on performance of changing international presence. *Strategic Management Journal*, 13: 419–143.

Neter, J., Wasserman, W. and Kutner, M. H. 1985. *Applied linear statistical models* (2nd ed.). Homewood, IL: Irwin.

Park, S. H., and Ungson, G. R. 1997. The effect of national culture, organizational complementarity, and economic motivation on joint venture dissolution. *Academy of Management Journal*, 40: 279–307.

Porter, M. E. 1985. *Competitive advantage: Creating and sustaining superior performance*. New York: Free Press.

Qian, G. 1996. The effect of multinationality measures upon the risk-return performance of US firms. *International Business Review*, 5: 247–265.

Rangan, S. 1998. Do multinationals operate flexibly? Theory and evidence. *Journal of International Business Studies*, 29: 217–237.

Reeb, D. M., Kwok, C. C. Y., and Baek, H. Y. 1998. Systematic risk of the multinational corporation. *Journal of International Business Studies*, 29: 263–279.

Roth, K., Schweiger, D., and Morrison, A. 1991. Global strategy implementation at the business-unit level: Operational capabilities and administrative mechanisms. *Journal of International Business Studies*, 22: 361–394.

Ruefli, T. W., Collins, J. M., and LaCugna, J. R. 1999. Risk measures in strategic management research: Auld lang syne? *Strategic Management Journal*, 20: 167–194.

Sanchez, R. 1993. Strategic flexibility, firm organization, and managerial work in dynamic markets: A strategic-options perspective. In P. Shrivastava, A. Huff, and J. Dutton (Eds.), *Advances in strategic management*, vol. 9: 251–291. Greenwich, CT: JAI Press.

Scherer, F. M., and Ross, D. 1990. *Industrial market structure and economic performance* (3rd ed.). Boston: Houghton Mifflin.

Singh, J. V. 1986. Performance, slack, and risk taking in organizational decision making. *Academy of Management Journal*, 29: 562–585.

Singh, K., and Mitchell, W. 1996. Precarious collaboration: Business survival after partners shut down or form new partnerships. *Strategic Management Journal*, 17 (summer special issue): 99–115.

Stuart, T. 1998. Network positions and propensities to collaborate: An investigation of strategic alliance formation in a high-technology industry. *Administrative Science Quarterly*, 43: 668–698.

Tabachnick, B. G., and Fidell, L. S. 1996. *Using multivariate statistics* (3rd ed.). New York: Harper/Collins.

Teece, D. J. 1986. Transaction cost economics and the multinational enterprise: An assessment. *Journal of Economic Behavior and Organization*, 7: 21–45.

Thompson, J. D. 1967. *Organizations in action*. New York: McGraw-Hill.

Trigeorgis, L. 1997. *Real options*. Cambridge, MA: MIT Press.

Zaheer, S., and Mosakowski, E. 1997. The dynamics of the liability of foreignness: A global study of survival in financial services. *Strategic Management Journal*, 18: 439–464.

IV. LEARNING PERSPECTIVES ON INTERFIRM COLLABORATION

11 Competition for Competence and Inter-Partner Learning within International Strategic Alliances

Gary Hamel

1. The Research Question

1.1. A Skill-based View of the Firm

It is possible to conceive of a firm as a portfolio of core competencies on one hand, and encompassing disciplines on the other, rather than as a portfolio of product–market entities (Prahalad and Hamel, 1990). As technology bundles, core competencies make a critical contribution to the unique functionality of a range of end-products. An example is Honda's expertise in powertrains, which is applied to products as diverse as automobiles, motorcycles, generators, and lawn mowers. Encompassing disciplines include total quality control, just-in-time manufacturing systems, value engineering, flexible manufacturing systems, accelerated product development, and total customer service. Such disciplines allow a product to be delivered to customers at the best possible price/performance trade-off. Core competencies and value-creating disciplines are precisely the kinds of firm-specific skills for which there are only imperfect external markets, and hence form the *raison d'etre* for the multinational enterprise (Buckley and Casson, 1985; Caves, 1971; Teece, 1981).

Conceiving of the firm as a portfolio of core competencies and disciplines suggests that inter-firm competition, as opposed to inter-product competition, is essentially concerned with the acquisition of skills. In this view global competitiveness is largely a function of the firm's pace, efficiency, and extent of knowledge accumulation. The traditional 'competitive strategy' paradigm (e.g. Porter, 1980), with its focus on product–market positioning, focuses on only the last few hundred yards of what may be a skill-building marathon. The notion of competitive advantage (Porter, 1985) which provides the means for computing product-based advantages at a given point in time (in terms of cost and differentiation), provides little insight into the process of knowledge acquisition and skill building.

Core competencies and value-creating disciplines are not distributed equally among firms. Expansion-minded competitors, exploiting such firm-specific advantages, bring the skill deficiencies of incumbents into stark relief. This study was unconcerned with why such discrepancies in skill endowments exist, but was very concerned with the role international strategic alliances might play in effecting a partial redistribution of skills among partners. While 'globalization' has been widely credited for provoking a shift to collaborative strategies (Ghemawat, Porter and Rawlinson, 1986; Hergert and Morris, 1988; Ohmae, 1989; Perlmutter and Heenan, 1986), the ways in which strategic alliances either enhance or diminish the skills which underlie global competitiveness have been only partially specified. *The goal of this research was to understand the extent to which and means through which the collaborative process might lead to a reapportionment of skills between the partners.*

While skills discrepancies have been recognized as a motivator for international collaboration (Contractor and Lorange, 1988; Root, 1988), the crucial distinction between acquiring such skills in the sense of gaining *access* to them—by taking out a license, utilizing a subassembly supplied by a partner, or relying on a partner's employees for some critical operation—and actually *internalizing* a partner's skills has seldom been clearly drawn. This distinction is crucial. As long as a partner's skills are embodied only in the specific outputs of the venture, they have no value outside the narrow terms of the agreement. Once internalized, however, they can be applied to new geographic markets, new products, and new businesses. For the partners, an alliance may be not only a means for trading access to each other's skills—what might be termed *quasi-internalization*, but also a mechanism for actually acquiring a partner's skills—*de facto internalization*.

A conception of strategic alliances as opportunities for *de facto* internalization was suggested during a major research project on 'competition for competence' in which the author participated (Prahalad and Hamel, 1990). In that study managers often voiced a concern that, when collaborating with a potential competitor, *failure to 'out-learn' one's partner could render a firm first dependent and then redundant within the partnership, and competitively vulnerable outside it*. The two premises from which this concern issued seemed to be that (1) few alliances were perfectly and perpetually collusive and (2) the fact that a firm chose to collaborate with a present or potential competitor could not be taken as evidence that that firm no longer harbored a competitive intent *vis-à-vis* its partner. Indeed, when it came to the competitive consequences of inter-partner learning, the attitudes of some managers in the initial study had shifted from naiveté to paranoia within a few short years. This seemed to be particularly true for managers in alliances with Japanese partners. What was lacking was any systematic investigation of the determinants of inter-partner learning.

2. Methodology

Thus, the research objective was theory development rather than theory extension. The parameters which controlled the choice of research design were: (1) a belief that existing theoretical perspectives illuminated only a small part of the collaborative phenomenon; (2) a desire to identify the determinants of a certain class of collaborative outcomes, i.e. inter-partner learning; and (3) the consequent need for observation that was administratively fine-grained, multi-level and longitudinal. These considerations made inevitable the choice of a research design based on the principles of grounded theory development (Glaser and Strauss, 1967; Mintzberg, 1978; Pettigrew, 1979; Seyle, 1964). Because patterns of causality are extremely complex in most real-world administrative systems, traditional deductive–analytic methodologies force the researcher to declutter the phenomenon by: (1) substituting crude proxies for difficult-to-measure determinants or outcomes; (2) assuming away some of the multidimensionality in causal relationships; and/or (3) narrowing the scope of research. In doing so, much of the potential value of the research is lost. The problem is not that the resulting theories are under-tested (i.e. they fail a test of rigor), but that they are under-developed (i.e. they are so partial in coverage that they illuminate only a fragment of the path between choice, action and outcome). For the *purposes of this study* a decision was made not to prematurely prune the collaborative problem into a shape that would fit within the constraints of a deductive methodology.

Grounded theory development proceeded in two stages. In the first stage the goal was to illuminate the basic dimensions of a theory of inter-partner learning. To this end an attempt was made to maximize underlying differences among cases in order to discover those concepts or theoretical categories that were most universal (where the data across cases were most similar), and those that were entirely idiosyncratic (where the data across cases were most divergent). Interviews were initially conducted with 74 individuals across 11 companies concerning nine international alliances. The number of individuals interviewed within each company ranged from three to 11, with six the average. Interviews were typically 2 hours in length, though a few consumed an entire day. Given concerns over confidentiality on the part of participating firms, several of the participating firms requested anonymity. The 11 firms in the study ranged in size from under $500 million in sales to more than $50 billion. Four of the companies were domiciled in the United States, four within the European Community, and three in Japan. Each firm derived at least 30 percent of its revenue from outside its domestic market. Industries covered included aerospace, chemicals, semiconductors, pharmaceuticals, computers, automobiles, and consumer electronics. In every company managers with responsibility for strategic alliances from both divisional and business unit levels were interviewed. Approximately 40 percent of the interviews were with functional supervisors or first-line employees who worked regularly across the collaborative membrane. Seven of the participating firms had a partner within the sample of 11 firms; in this way both 'sides' of three on-going partnerships were observed. Thus inter-case diversity was achieved along the dimensions of partner nationality and industry affiliation, and agreement type (equity-based joint ventures versus long-term co-marketing, design and supply relationships).

The anxiety over asymmetric learning expressed by managers in the earlier study was confirmed in the first stage interviewing process. Concerns were of three broad types: (1) concern over the *intent* of partners (collaborative versus competitive, internalization of partner skills versus mere access); (2) concern over the 'openness' of the firm to its partner—what came to be termed *transparency*; and (3) concern over firm's ability to actually absorb skills from its partner, i.e. *receptivity*. As the core categories that came to constitute the formal internalization model, *intent, receptivity*, and *transparency* were identified as prospective determinants of inter-partner learning. Also emerging from the first round of interviewing was a proposed linkage between learning and inter-partner bargaining power, and, consequently a notion of collaboration as a 'race to learn.'

Having illuminated an overarching formal model, the second stage of research aimed at understanding in detail the processes and mechanisms through which intent, receptivity, and transparency impacted on learning outcomes. This was accomplished through a second round of case-based research, termed 'theoretic sampling' (Glaser and Strauss, 1967: 45–77), because the choice of which cases to compare is directed by the emerging theory. By selecting cases where the researcher hoped to find both maximum and minimum variance along the dimensions of the core model, it was possible to amplify the core model. A further criterion to be satisfied was the need to gain even deeper, more extensive access to the individuals involved in the process of collaborative exchange than had been achieved in first stage interviewing, and to ensure that access was gained to both sides of the collaborative membrane. This was deemed necessary if the researcher was to have any hope of measuring, however crudely, the migration of skills between partners, the criticality of those skills (and hence the extent to which they should be valued and protected or sought by each partner), and ultimately, the competitive consequences of those skill transfers.

These requirements were met in the following ways. Two partnerships, involving five firms (one partnership was triadic), were selected for intensive study. Inter-case differences were minimized to the extent that both partnerships comprised a European firm (or firms) on one side, and a Japanese firm on the other. Thus it was possible to compare the behavior of the European firms, one with another, and the behavior of the Japanese partners, one with another. Both alliances were more than 5 years old at the time the study commenced, both had received substantial media attention, and were regarded as two of the most important and 'successful' Euro-Japanese alliances. Both partnerships were set within the electronics industry.

At the same time there were potentially significant differences between the cases: one centered around professional products with a 3–5-year life-cycle, and the other around a consumer product with a 6–12-month life-cycle. One of the European partners had a clear corporate strategy for core competence building, the others did not. The locus of activity for one partnership was based in Europe, the other in Japan. One partnership involved regular and intensive collaboration across the membrane, the other periodic inter-working. One partnership was a joint equity venture, the other a mixture of long- and short-term development and supply contracts. And, of course, there was the opportunity to compare the behavior of partners based in very different national contexts. The first stage interview process, as well as much of the anecdotal evidence (e.g. *Business Week,* 1989), suggested this difference in national origin might be crucial to learning outcomes.

Each of the five partners agreed to provide access to facilities as well as to key managers and operating employees. Each of the partners also agreed to submit to a minimum of 40 hours of interviewing. While single, week-long research visits were made to the Japanese partners, repeated research visits, extending over 2 years, were made to the European partners. Interviewing continued until saturation of core categories—intent, transparency, and receptivity—was achieved, i.e. new properties of the categories were no longer emerging. Relying on archival data, as well as interviews with industry analysts, two detailed industry briefing notes were prepared. The detailed research reports which summarize the output of the second stage interviewing are contained in Hamel (1990).

3. Findings

The six major propositions which grew out of the data are summarized in Table 1. They will be discussed in turn, and the evidence which produced them briefly summarized.

3.1. Competitive Collaboration

Though not always readily admitting it, several partners clearly regarded their alliances as transitional devices where the primary objective was the

Table 1. A Theory of Inter-Partner Learning: Core Propositions

1. *Competitive collaboration*
   (a) Some partners may regard internalization of scarce skills as a primary benefit of international collaboration.
   (b) Where learning is the goal, the termination of an agreement cannot be seen as failure, nor can its longevity and stability be seen as evidence of success.
   (c) Asymmetries in learning within the alliance may result in a shift in relative competitive position and advantage between the partners outside the alliance. Thus, some partners may regard each other as competitors as well as collaborators.
2. *Learning and bargaining power*
   (a) Asymmetries in learning change relative bargaining power within the alliance: successful learning may make the original bargain obsolete and may, *in extremis*, lead to a pattern of unilateral, rather than bilateral, dependence.
   (b) The legal and governance structure may exert only a minor influence over the pattern of inter-partner learning and bargaining power.
   (c) A partner that understands the link between inter-partner learning, bargaining power, and competitiveness will tend to view the alliance as a race to learn.
3. *Intent as a determinant of learning*
   (a) The objectives of alliance partners, with respect to inter-partner learning and competence acquisition, may be usefully characterized as internalization, resource concentration, or substitution.
   (b) An internalization intent will be strongest in firms which conceive of competitiveness as competence-based, rather than as product-based, and which seek to close skill gaps rather than to compensate for skills failure.
   (c) A substitution intent pre-ordains asymmetric learning; for systematic learning to take place, operators must possess an internalization intent.
4. *Transparency as a determinant of learning*
   (a) Asymmetry in transparency pre-ordains asymmetric learning: some firms and some skills may be inherently more transparent than others.
   (b) Transparency can be influenced through the design of organizational interfaces, the structure of joint tasks, and the 'protectiveness' of individuals.
5. *Receptivity as a determinant of learning*
   (a) Asymmetry in receptivity pre-ordains asymmetric learning: some firms may be inherently more receptive than others.
   (b) Receptivity is a function of the skills and absorptiveness of receptors, of exposure position, and of parallelism in facilities.
6. *The determinants of sustainable learning*
   Whether learning becomes self-sustaining—that is, whether the firm eventually becomes able, without further inputs from its partner, to improve its skills at the same rate as its partner—will depend on the depth of learning that has taken place, whether the firm possesses the scale and volume to allow, in future, amortization of the investment needed to break free of dependence on the partner, and whether the firm possesses the disciplines of continuous improvement.

internalization of partner skills. As one Japanese manager put it:

> We've learned a lot from [our partner]. The [foreign] environment was very far from us—we didn't understand it well. We learned that [our partner] was very good at developing. Our engineers have learned much from the relationship.

A European manager stated that:

> [Our partner] was passionately hungry to find out the requirements of the users in the markets they wanted to serve. We were priming the market for them.

A manager in a Japanese firm that had to contend with a persistently inquisitive European partner believed that:

> The only motivation for [our European partner] is to get mass manufacturing technology. They see [the alliance] as a short circuit. As soon as they have this they'll lose interest.

This manager believed that the partner would see eventual termination of the agreement as evidence of successful learning, rather than of a failed collaborative venture.

While no manager in the study claimed a desire to 'deskill' partners, there were several cases in which managers believed this had been the outcome of the collaborative process. In these cases the competitive implications of unanticipated (and typically unsanctioned) skill transfers were clearly understood, albeit retrospectively. The president of the Asia-Pacific division of an American industrial products company was in no doubt that his firm's Japanese partner had emerged from their 20-year alliance as a significant competitor:

> We established them in their core business. They learned the business from us, mastered our process technology, enjoyed terrific margins at home, where we did not compete in parallel, and today challenge us outside of Japan.

The divisional vice-president of a Western computer company had a similar interpretation of his firm's trans-Pacific alliance:

> A year and a half into the deal I understood what it was all about. Before that I was as naive as the next guy. It took me that long to see that [our partner] was preparing a platform to come into all our markets.

Yet another manager felt a partner had crossed the line distinguishing collaboration from competition:

> If they were really our partners, they wouldn't try to suck us dry of technology ideas they can use in their own products. Whatever they learn from us, they'll use against us worldwide.

Recognizing the potential danger of turning collaborators into competitors, a senior executive in a Japanese firm hoped his firm's European partners would be 'strong—but not too strong.'

The proposition that partners possessing parallel internalization and international expansion goals would find their relationships more contentious than partners with asymmetric intents arose, in part, from observing the markedly different relationships that existed between three partners in a triadic alliance. The British firm in the alliance, possessing neither an internalization intent nor global expansion goals, enjoyed a placid relationship with its Japanese partner. However, the French and Japanese firms in the alliance, each possessed of ambitious learning and expansion goals, were often at loggerheads. A technical manager in the Japanese firm remarked that:

> The English were easier to work with than the French. The English were gentlemen, but the French were [not]. We could reach decisions very quickly with the English, but the French wanted to debate and debate and debate.

This seemed to be a reaction to the difficulty of bargaining with a partner who possessed equally ambitious learning goals.

In general, whenever two partners sought to extract value in the same form from their partnership—whether in the form of inter-partner learning benefits or short-term economic benefits, managers were likely to find themselves frequently engaged in contentious discussions over value-sharing. The relationships where managers were least likely to be troubled by recurring arguments over value appropriation were those where one partner was pursuing, unequivocably, a learning intent and the other a short-term earnings maximization intent. In such relationships—there were three—one partner was becoming progressively more dependent on the other. That the British firm mentioned above ultimately withdrew from the business on which the alliance was based suggested a fundamental proposition: just as contentiousness does not, by itself, indicate collaborative failure (some managers recognized they had to accept a certain amount of contentiousness as the price for protecting their core skills and gaining access to their partner's), an abundance of harmony and good will does not mean both partners are benefiting equally in terms of enhanced competitiveness. Collaborative success could not be measured in terms of a 'happiness index.'

3.2. Learning and Bargaining Power

The link between learning and bargaining power emerged clearly in several cases, one of which is briefly summarized here. A European firm in the study had entered a sourcing agreement with a Japanese partner in the mid-1970s, and later, partly through the use of political pressure, had succeeded in enticing the

Japanese partner into a European-based manufacturing joint venture to produce a sophisticated electronics product that had, heretofore, been sourced by the European firm from Japan. At the time the joint venture was entered, the European firm established a corporate-wide goal to gain an independent, 'worldclass,' capability to develop and manufacture the particular product. This was seen as part of a broader corporate-wide effort to master mass manufacturing skills that were viewed as crucial to the firm's participation in a host of electronics businesses. Over the next 7 years, the European firm worked assiduously to internalize the skills of its Japanese partner. By the late 1980s the firm had progressed through six of the seven 'steps' it had identified on the road from dependence to independence—where the journey began with a capability for assembling partner-supplied sub-assemblies using partner-specified equipment and process controls, and ended with a capability for simultaneous advance of both product design and manufacturing disciplines (i.e. design for manufacturability, component miniaturization, materials science, etc.), independent of further partner technical assistance.

In interviews with both the European firm and its Japanese partner, it became clear that the bargaining power of the Continental firm had grown as its learning had progressed. For the European firm, each stage of learning, when complete, became the gateway to the next stage of internalization. Successful learning at each stage effectively obsolesced the existing 'bargain,' and constituted a *de facto* query to the Japanese partner: '*Now* what are you going to do for us?' As the firm moved nearer and nearer its goal of independence, it successively raised the 'price' for its continued participation in the alliance. The Japanese partner also learned through the alliance. Managers credited the venture with giving them insight into unique customer needs and the standards-setting environment in Europe. However, the Japanese firm could not easily obsolesce the initial bargain; this due not to any learning deficiency on its part, but to the difficulty of unwinding a politically visible relationship.

The notion of collaboration as a race to learn emerged directly from the interview data. As one Western manager put it:

> If they [our partner] learn what we know before we learn what they know, we become redundant. We've got to try to learn faster than they do.

Several Western firms in the study seemed to have discovered that where bargaining power could not be maintained by winning the race to learn, it might be maintained through other means. In a narrow sense managers saw collaboration as a race to learn, but in a broader sense they saw it as a race to remain 'attractive' to their partners. A European manager stated:

> You must continually add to the portfolio of things that make you desirable to your partner. Many of the things that [our partner] needed us for in the early days, it

doesn't need now. It needed to establish a base of equipment in Europe and we have done this for them. You must ensure that you always have something to offer your partner—some reason for them to continue to need you.

Managers in a Japanese firm whose European partner had shown a high propensity to learn, believed that ultimate control came from being ahead in the race to create next-generation competencies. Leadership here brought partial control over standards, the benefits of controlling the evolution of technology, and the product price and performance advantages of being first down the experience curve. One senior manager put it succinctly:

Friendship is friendship, but competition is competition. Competition is about the future and that is R&D.

Here was a suggestion that partners in competitive alliances may sometimes be more likely to view collaboration as a race to get to the future first, rather than a truly cooperative effort to invent the future together. Again, this provided evidence of a subtle blending of competitive and collaborative goals.

The greater the experience of interviewees in administering or working within collaborative arrangements, the more likely were they to discount the extent to which the formal agreement actually determined patterns of learning, control, and dependence within their partnerships. The formal agreement was seen as essentially static, and the race for capability acquisition and control essentially dynamic. As the interviewing progressed it became possible to array the factors which interviewees typically associated with power and control. Power came first from the relative pace at which each partner was building new capabilities internally, then from an ability to out-learn one's partner, then from the relative contribution of 'irreplaceable' inputs by each partner to the venture, then from relative share of value-added, then from the operating structure (which partner's employees held key functional posts), then from the governance structure (which partner was best represented on the board and key executive committees), and finally from the legal structure (share of ownership and legally specified terms for the division of equity and profits). On this basis it was possible, for several of the alliances, to construct a crude 'relative power metric.' For the triadic partnership mentioned above (British, French, and Japanese), relative power was apportioned as per Table 2.

While the legal and managerial power of the British partner was at least equal to that of its counterparts, it failed almost totally to exploit other potential sources of power and control. The British firm's failure to keep pace with its partners in learning and competence-building made its acquisition by one of its partners, or some other ambitious firm, almost inevitable. By way of contrast, the French firm, with no advantage in terms of ownership or executive authority, was able to substantially increase its control of the relationship

Table 2. Relative Power of Partners in a Triadic Alliance[1] (Ranked by Perceived Importance as Determinants of Bargaining Power)

	British	French	Japanese
1. Relative pace of competence building[2]		+++	+++++
2. Relative success at inter-partner learning		++++	++
3. Relative criticality of inputs[3]		++	+++
4. Relative share of value-added[4]	+	++	++++
5. 'Possession' of key operating jobs[5]	++	++	+
6. Representation on governing bodies[6]	++	+	+
7. Legal share of ownership[7]	+	+	+

[1] The number of plus signs indicates the relative power within the joint venture that each partner gained from each factor.
[2] Managers in the Japanese partner believed their firm was innovating more rapidly than its European partners in the areas of miniaturization, production engineering, and advanced technologies.
[3] For most of the venture's early history product designs, process equipment, and high-precision components were supplied exclusively by the Japanese partner.
[4] By 1985 European content was approximately 50 percent. The French partner supplied a greater share of the European content than the British partner.
[5] The Managing Directors of the two European plants were Europeans. At each plant a Japanese employee held the Deputy Managing Director's post.
[6] Each partner was responsible for appointing two representatives to the Supervisory Board and one representative to the Management Board. The agreement stipulated that a European was to be President of the Supervisory Board. An executive seconded from the British partner occupied this position.
[7] Each of the three partners held 33.33 percent of the joint venture's equity.

through a rapid pace of learning. The French firm had substantially increased its R&D budget, hoping eventually to counterbalance its Japanese partner's faster pace of new product development and competence-building. Although the French firm's equity stake remained at 33 percent through most of the 1980s, it continued to enhance its bargaining power by internalizing the skills of its Japanese partner and gaining an ever-increasing share of value-added. From the very different experiences of the British and French firms in this alliance came the proposition that power vested in a particular firm through the formal agreement will almost certainly erode if its partners are more adept at internalization or quicker to build valuable new competencies.

The perspectives on bargaining power and learning which emerged from the case analysis also gave rise to propositions regarding the longevity of rivalrous alliances. In general, it appeared that competitively oriented partners would continue to collaborate together so long as they were: (1) equally capable of inter-partner learning or independent skills development, and/or (2) both substantially smaller, and mutually vulnerable, to industry leaders.

Three broad determinants of learning outcomes emerged during the study and constitute the core of the internalization model. *Intent* refers to a firm's initial propensity to view collaboration as an opportunity to learn; *transparency* to the 'knowability' or openness of each partner, and thus the potential for learning; and *receptivity* to a partner's capacity for learning, or 'absorptiveness.'

Table 3. Inherent Determinants of Inter-Partner Learning: A Comparison of Prototypes

	Factors Associated with Positive Learning Outcomes	Factors Associated with Negative Learning Outcomes
Strength of internalization intent		
1. Competitive posture *vis-à-vis* partner	Co-option now, confrontation later	Collaboration instead of competition
2. Relative resource position versus corporate ambitions	Scarcity	Abundance
3. Perceived pay-off—capacity to exploit skills in multiple businesses	High; alliance entered to build corporate-wide core competencies	Low; alliance entered to 'fix' problems in a single business
4. Perspective on power	Balance of power begets instability	Balance of power begets stability
Transparency (organizational)		
5. Social context	Language and customs constitute a barrier	Language and customs not a barrier
6. Attitude towards outsiders	The clan as an ideal: exclusivity	The 'melting pot' as ideal: inclusivity
Transparency (skills)		
7. Extent to which skills are context-dependent	Skills comprise tacit knowledge embedded within social systems	Skills comprise explicit knowledge held by a few 'experts'
8. Relative pace of skills enhancement	Fast	Slow
Preconditions for receptivity		
9. Sense of confidence	Neither under-confidence nor over-confidence in its own capabilities	Either under-confidence or over-confidence in its own capabilities
10. Need to first unlearn	As a newcomer, little that must be forgotten before learning can begin	As a laggard, much that must be unlearned before new skills drive out old
11. Size of skills gap with industry leaders	Small	Substantial
12. Institutional vs. individual learning	Capacity for 'summing up' and transferring individual learning	Fragmentation (vertical and horizontal) frustrates learning

While there was much a firm could do to implant a learning intent, limit its own transparency, and enhance its receptivity, there seemed to be some inherent determinants of inter-partner learning, more or less exogenous to the partnership itself, that either predisposed a firm to positive learning outcomes, or rendered it unlikely to successfully exploit opportunities to learn. These are outlined in Table 3, and will be discussed below, along with more 'active' determinants or learning outcomes.

3.3. Intent as a Determinant of Learning

The only collaborative intent that was consistent across all firms in the study was *investment avoidance*. In some cases this seemed to be a partner's sole objective. Five of the seven Western firms in the study that had alliances with Japanese partners, had not possessed an internalization intent at the time they entered their Asian alliances. Possessing what came to be called a *substitution* intent, these firms seemed satisfied—at least in the beginning—to substitute their partner's competitiveness in a particular skill area for their own lack of competitiveness. Insofar as it could be ascertained, the Japanese counterparts in these alliances seemed to possess explicit learning intents—with one possible exception. This apparent asymmetry in collaborative goals between Western and Japanese partners is deemed significant because in no case did systematic learning take place in the absence of a clearly communicated internalization intent.

In cases where one partner had systematically learned from the other, great efforts had been made to embed a learning intent within operating-level employees. One project manager recalled that at the outset of the alliance his divisional vice president had brought together all those with organization-spanning roles and told them:

> I wish we didn't need this partnership. I wish we knew how to do what our partner knows how to do. But I will be more disappointed if, in three years, we have not learned to do what our partner knows how to do.

In one firm where learning did not take place, the blame was put on a failure to clearly communicate learning objectives to those with inter-organizational roles:

> Our engineers were just as good as [our partner's]. In fact, their's were narrower technically, but they had a much better understanding of what the company was trying to accomplish. They knew they were there to learn; our people didn't.

A manager in a company with a record of successful learning from partners described what had been done to embed a learning intent:

> We wanted to make learning an automatic discipline. We asked the staff every day, 'What did you learn from [our partner] today?' Learning was carefully monitored and recorded.

While several Western firms had adopted defensive learning intents, as they came to understand the internalization goals of their Japanese partners, none of these firms could demonstrate that systematic learning had taken place. That the alliance could be a laboratory for learning seemed to be a difficult message to convey, once the alliance had become widely viewed as simply an alternative to internal efforts, as one manager commented:

> When the deal was put together some of us were skeptical, but we were told this was the wave of the future and we'd have to learn to rely on [our partner]. So we relied on them; boy, did we rely on them. Now we're hearing [from senior management] that we shouldn't rely on them *too* much; we have to keep some kind of 'shadow' capability

internally. Well, I think we've gotten this message a bit late. Letting [our partner] do the tough stuff has become second nature to us.

To summarize the argument thus far, learning took place by design rather than by default, and skill substitution or surrender by default in the absence of design. In situations where there was a marked asymmetry in intent, the migration of skills between partners could not be accurately characterized as merely 'leakage' (Harrigan, 1986). The competitive consequences of skills transfers, as well as the actual migration of skills, was often unintended, unanticipated, and unwanted by at least one of the partners. This seems to be the fate that befell Varian Associates, a U.S. producer of advanced electronics including semiconductors. Reflecting on its joint venture with NEC, one of Varian's senior executives concluded that 'all NEC had wanted to do was to suck out Varian's technology, not sell Varian's equipment' (Goldenberg, 1988: 85).

What factors might account for observed differences in intent? Whether or not a firm possessed an explicit internalization intent seemed to be a product of: (1) whether it viewed collaboration as a more or less permanent alternative to competition or as a temporary vehicle for improving its competitiveness *vis-à-vis* its partner; (2) its relative resource position *vis-à-vis* its partner and other industry participants; (3) its calculation of the pay-off to learning; and (4) its preference for balanced vs. asymmetric dependence within the alliance. Taking these proposed determinants in turn, it was mentioned earlier that several partners had developed defensive internalization intents upon discovering the learning goals of their partners. The majority of Western firms in the study appeared to have initially projected their own substitution intents onto their partners. These firms tended to describe the logic of their collaborative ventures in terms of 'role specialization,' 'complementarity,' 'centers of excellence,' and so on. Such descriptors evinced a view of collaboration as a stable division of roles based on the unique skill endowments of each partner, rather than as a potentially low-cost route to replicating partner skills and erasing initial dependencies.

With one exception, those Western partners that had lacked an initial internalization intent had all been substantially larger than their Japanese partners at the time their alliances were formed. The assumption seemed to be that relative size was a good proxy for relative skill levels. A U.S. manager summarized the attitude that had prevailed a decade earlier when the firm entered its first major Japanese alliance: 'We invented the industry. What could we possibly learn from an up-start in Japan?' An executive in their Japanese partner reflected on difference in the two partner's attitudes toward learning:

When we saw [our larger Western partner] doing something better, we always wanted to know why. But when they come to look at what we are doing, they say, 'Oh, you can do that because you are Japanese,' or they find some other reason. They make an explanation so they don't have to understand [what we are doing differently].

An abundance of resources, and a legacy of industry leadership, whether real or perceived, made it difficult for a firm to admit to itself that it had something to learn from a smaller partner.

The intent to learn also appeared to be a function of the firm's calculation about the pay-off to learning. In those firms where the internalization intent was strongest and most deeply felt, the skills to be acquired from the partner were seen as critical to the growth of the entire company, and not just the competitiveness of a single product or business. This was in contrast to firms where competitiveness was defined solely in end-product terms, and where top management had no explicit plans for building corporate-wide skills. Here alliances were viewed as short cuts to a more competitive product line (by relying on a partner for critical components or perhaps entire products), rather than as short cuts to the internalization of skills that could be applied across a range of businesses. Without clear corporate goals for competence building, and a deep appreciation for the critical contribution of core competence leadership to long-term competitiveness, individual businesses appeared unlikely to devote resources to the task of learning.

The perceived pay-off to learning was also influenced, in some cases, by a partner's calculation of the cost of continued dependence. Managers in the study identified a range of potential costs that could be associated with dependency in a core skill area: an inability to thwart a partner intent on entering the firm's prime markets; or the obverse—being constrained from entering an emerging market, or having one's entry slowed by a powerful partner; the risk of being 'stranded' by a collaborator who pre-emptively ended the relationship; or being disadvantaged when the financial terms of the agreement are re-negotiated. Japanese partners, in particular, seemed to view strategic alliances as second-best options. A group of managers interviewed in one firm expressed an opinion, quite vehemently, that their company would never accept a situation in which it was, over the long term, dependent on a Western partner for an important aspect of its product-based competitiveness—this despite the fact that several of that firm's foreign partners were in just such a dependency position. Not surprisingly, this firm possessed a strong internalization intent.

There may be a reason why Japanese firms, in particular, seemed adverse to the very notion of symmetrical dependency between partners. Nakane (1970) has shown that social organization in Japan is based on the notion of dependence. The parent–child analogy is applied to the government and its public, employers and employees, managers and subordinates, and large firms and their suppliers. In this view a 'balance of power' brings indeterminateness and instability to a relationship, while a clearly disproportionate allocation of power, that is, dependence, brings cohesion and consistency. The preference of Japanese managers for unequivocable decision-making power in foreign subsidiaries and joint ventures has been well documented (Ballon, 1979; Ouchi and Johnson, 1974). Indeed, when asked to consider a hypothetical American–Japanese joint venture located in the U.S., Japanese managers felt that future trust would be highest if Japanese, rather than American, managers occupied the most powerful positions, and if Japanese managers, rather than Americans, had responsibility for initiating key decision processes such as capital budgeting (Sullivan and Peterson, 1982).

It seems unlikely that many Japanese managers would disagree with Harrigan's (1986: 148) assertion that:

> Managers can be as crafty as they please in writing clauses to protect their firm's technology rights, but the joint venture's success depends on trust.

But when Japanese managers list 'trust' as one of the most important conditions for a successful joint venture (Block and Matsumoto, 1972), they may be speaking not of the trust that comes from what Buckley and Casson (1988) term 'mutual forbearance,' but from unequivocal dependence. If knowledge is power, and power the father of dependence, one can expect Japanese firms to strive to learn from their partners.

3.4. *Transparency as a Determinant of Learning*

Whereas intent established the desire to learn, transparency determined the potential for learning. Some partners were, for a variety of reasons, more transparent— more open and accessible—than others. Of course, every partner intended to share some skills with its opposite number. Even in firms with an inherently 'protective' stance *vis-à-vis* their partner, some degree of openness was accepted as the price for enticing the partner into the relationship and successfully executing joint tasks. Yet many managers drew a distinction between what might be termed 'transparency by design,' and 'transparency by default.' The concerns managers expressed were over unintended and unanticipated transfers.

Such concerns arose in cases where managers believed their partner's learning had gone far beyond what was deemed essential for the successful performance of joint tasks, to encompass what was necessary to internalize skills. A partner's learning could be both more intensive than foreseen in the formal agreement, and more extensive. The greatest sense of 'unfairness,' and the greatest sense of failure in managing transparency, was observed in those firms where a partner's learning had extended to skill areas that were not explicitly part of the formal agreement. This often seemed to be the case in OEM sourcing arrangement where an up-stream partner had used the alliance to gain insights into customer needs and market structure. A European-based manager described the process thus:

> Anytime we demanded unique features for the European market [in a product sourced from Japan, our Japanese partner] wanted a complete justification for each item. They

wanted to understand why we wanted certain product features, competitors' product information, customer perceptions, all the market-based things. You can get fifteen years of accumulated wisdom across the table in two hours.

Broadly, there appeared to be at least five inherent, *ex ante* determinants of transparency: (1) the penetrability of the social context which surrounded the partner; (2) attitudes towards outsiders, i.e. clannishness; (3) the extent to which the partner's distinctive skills were encodable and discrete; and (4) the partner's relative pace of skill-building.

While this exploratory study cannot provide an answer to the question, 'Are Japanese partners inherently less transparent than their Western counterparts?' what can be said is that nearly all the Western partners in the study believed this to be the case. The study suggested that there were indeed systematic, though not irreversible, asymmetries in transparency between Western and Japanese partners. Typical was the comment of one Western manager:

Despite the fact that we were [in Japan] for training, I always felt we were revealing more information about us than [our Japanese partners] were about themselves.

Interestingly, no Japanese manager expressed an opinion that Western partners might be inherently less transparent than Japanese partners. Peterson and Schwind (1977) found similar evidence of asymmetry in transparency between Japanese and Western alliance partners. In their study of international joint ventures located in Japan, 'communication' was the problem mentioned most often by both expatriate and Japanese managers. However, for expatriate managers 'difficulty in receiving exact information and data' from their Japanese partners ranked a close second, mentioned by 87 percent of U.S. expatriate respondents. The next most noted problems, 'reluctance to report failures,' and 'no open discussion of problems,' further reflect the frustration these managers felt in extracting information from their Japanese partners. However, no Japanese manager mentioned access to information as a major annoyance in dealing with Western partners.

It seems plausible to propose that this asymmetry in perceptions of relative opaqueness rests at least in part on the extent to which a firm's knowledge base is context-bound (Terpstra and David, 1985). Contextuality refers to the 'embeddedness' of information in social systems. In general, knowledge in Oriental cultures is more contextual than information in Occidental cultures (Benedict, 1946). Form and content, ritual and substance cannot easily be disentangled. Context-dependent knowledge (e.g., principles of industrial relations in Japan) is inherently less transparent than context-free knowledge (e.g. the principles of the transistor).

Japanese employees working within Western partners seemed to more easily gain acceptance by peers, and more quickly become insiders, than was the case in reverse. For example, a divisional vice president managing a joint European–Japanese design effort within Europe remarked that:

> we were conscious of [our partner's employees] on-site and did try to keep information exchange on a need-to-know basis. However, after a while, they ceased to be different. We played badminton together, we went to the same parties and restaurants. They became close friends.

While several Western managers, with employees working in Japanese-based alliances, expressed concerns over the fact that their staff might 'go native,' no Japanese manager expressed such a concern in the reverse case. Several managers, both Western and Japanese, expressed the opinion that the 'openness' of Western cultural and organizational contexts facilitated the assimilation of partner employees, while the sense of 'clan' possessed by Japanese staff made them sensitive to the risk of revealing competitively useful information to a partner. The same European manager who commented on the easy social integration of Japanese team members also recalled that:

> Once the contract was signed, [the Japanese partner] had a view of what we needed to know to complete the project. They were totally open in this regard, but totally closed on all other issues. They had well-defined limits in terms of what they would tell us. The junior guys would tell us nothing unless a senior person was there.

The point here is not that Japanese organizations are clannish. That point has been made before (Ouchi, 1980). Instead, it is that where clannishness is high, opportunities for access will be limited, and transparency low. As a member of a clan, an employee involved in a partnership can be expected to retain a sense of identity with, and loyalty to, the parent. When conflicts arise which reflect an incongruity between parent and partner goals, a clan member will search for solutions consistent with the parent's goals.

An asymmetry in language skills often exacerbated inherent constraints on transparency such as clannishness and complexity. That operating employees in Western firms almost universally lacked Japanese language skills and cultural experience in Japan served to limit the transparency of their Asian hosts. One engineer from a European company recalled his frustration in working with a partner in Japan:

> Whenever I made a presentation [to our partner] I was one person against ten to twelve. They'd put me in front of a flip chart, then stop me while they went into a conversation in Japanese for ten minutes. If I asked them a question they would break into Japanese to first decide what I wanted to know, and then would discuss options in terms of what they might tell me, and finally would come back with an answer.

Not only did it appear that some organizations were more penetrable than others, it appeared that some types of knowledge were inherently more deeply buried in the social context of the firm than others. Explicit knowledge was more encodable than tacit knowledge—it could be transferred in engineering drawings, extracted from patent filings, etc., and discrete knowledge was more easily extracted from a partner than systemic knowledge. In general, it appeared that specific technologies (e.g. a microprocessor chip design), were more transparent than deep-seated competencies (e.g. value-engineering skills), and that market intelligence flowed more easily than knowledge of leading edge manufacturing knowhow. Thus, an asymmetry in the nature of the skills contributed by each partner to the venture could, *ceteris paribus*, preordain asymmetric learning. In partnerships where one firm brought product designs and market experience to the table, and the other (typically Japanese) manufacturing competence, the partner contributing production skills seemed to benefit from an inherently lower level of transparency. For while it did not appear that a firm could transfer product designs to its partner without revealing, perhaps inadvertently, a great deal of implicit market information, it was possible for the producing partner to ship back finished products without revealing much of what comprised its manufacturing competence.

The pace of a firm's innovation also seemed to determine its transparency to its partner. In some cases one partner's speed of innovation out-ran the other's pace of absorption. One fast-moving partner believed it could afford to be very open in terms of access, and yet remain essentially opaque, given its rapid pace of product development. Managers in this Japanese firm believed that their rate of new product introduction was between four and five times faster than that of their partner. Despite their partner's avowed learning intent, managers in this firm felt relatively unconcerned:

> We are very convinced that our R&D speed is faster than [our partner's]. This is our ultimate protection [against partner encroachment].

The researcher was reminded of the old adage about the difficulty of drinking from a fire hose.

Partners employed a wide variety of active measures to limit transparency. In one firm, all partner requests for information and access were processed through a small 'collaboration department.' Staff from this department attended virtually all meetings between managers and staff of the two partners. In this way they were able to control the 'aperture' through which the partner gained access to people and facilities. Out of this case grew the notion of a 'gatekeeping' role: one or more individuals charged with monitoring knowledge flows across the collaborative membrane.

Another determinant of relative transparency position appeared to be the number of people from each partner seconded to the other, or, more generally, the extent to which the nature of joint tasks required regular and intensive intermingling of staff from the two partners. At one extreme was the task of jointly designing a car, where the need to mate together powertrain, body, and suspension required intensive cross-membrane interaction, and made both partners highly transparent to each other. At the other extreme was the much simpler task of specifying single 'plug-in' components to be supplied by a partner.

Firms in the study also sought to limit their transparency to ambitious partners by restricting the collaborative agreement to a narrow range of products or markets. One manager argued that:

> If you source the *entire* product in, there is a lot greater transfer of design skills—your partner gets to see everything. What you should do is design components, source from multiple places, and then do integration and manufacturing yourself.

Another firm saw site selection and control as key issues in limiting transparency:

> It helps to have a joint company in a third location; this helps to protect you. You don't let your partner do joint work on your site. And if you have a third site you can decide what you put in and what you don't.

Given the fact that the process of collaborative exchange took place not at senior management levels, but at operating levels, the management of transparency depended, ultimately, on the ability and willingness of operators to sometimes say 'no' to a partner's requests for information or access. The extent to which operating employees had an explicit sense of the need to protect information from bleeding through to a partner varied widely across the sample firms. One project manager was surprised by how close-mouthed his partner's engineers were:

> Everyone I met within [our partner] seemed to operate with well-defined limits on what they would tell us. Their engineers were very guarded with technical details. Sometimes I had to appeal to higher level managers to get information critical to the project's success.

In one firm senior managers explicitly recognized the tensions that could arise when operating employees were asked to work in a collegial way to make the alliance a success, and at the same time had a responsibility for limiting the partner's access to core skills. One way out of this dilemma was to give operators the right to escalate partner requests for information.

It appeared that firms which could rely on passive or 'natural' barriers to transparency had an inherent advantage over partners that could not. This was not only because natural barriers to transparency seemed to be the most difficult to overcome, but also because active measures were sometimes regarded by partners as provocative. When U.S. firms have relied on contractual clauses and other active means to limit transparency, they have often been accused of acting in bad faith, or undermining trust (Ballon, 1979). To the extent that passive barriers can substitute for active measures, a partner may be able to claim for itself the high ground of trust and openness, and yet still benefit from almost unassailable barriers to partner encroachment.

3.5. Receptivity as a Determinant of Learning

If intent establishes the desire to learn, and transparency the opportunity, receptivity determines the capacity to learn. Just as there were active and passive determinants of transparency, so there were of receptivity. In several cases, when questioned as to why they had apparently learned more than their Western partners, Japanese managers answered, in essence, 'We had the attitude of students, and our Western partners the attitude of teachers.' Ballon would no doubt accept such a generalization:

> When looking at the West from outside the Western Hemisphere, one attitude stands out. It is just how anxious Americans and Europeans are to *teach* the rest of the world (1979: 27).

Humility may be the first prerequisite for learning. However, the distinction between teachers and students rested on more than just cultural stereotypes.

Generating an enthusiasm for learning, that is, an attitude of receptivity, among operating employees seemed to depend largely on whether the firm entered the alliance as a *late-comer*, or as a *laggard*; i.e. whether the alliance was seen by the majority of employees as a proactive choice to support ambitious growth goals (the perspective of late-comers), or as an easy 'way out' of a deteriorating competitive situation (the perspective of laggards). Where a firm had become a laggard, and had come to think of itself as such, middle-level managers and operators appeared more likely to adopt an acquiescent attitude towards dependency and learning opportunities. While they sometimes saw learning as a laudable goal, they possessed little enthusiasm for the task. Perhaps not surprisingly, in firms that had struggled to maintain their competitiveness in a particular product/market, and had failed, alliances tended to be seen by operating-level employees as confirmation of their failure, and not as a means to rebuild skills. A sense of resignation was not conducive to receptivity.

The stigma of failure did not attach itself to firms using alliances to build skills in new areas, i.e. closing skills 'gaps' as opposed to compensating for a skills failure. The European partner mentioned earlier could not have claimed to possess world-class manufacturer skills at the time it entered its alliance with a Japanese partner. Yet it had succeeded, through its own efforts, in dramatically improving the productivity of its color television manufacturing in the 5 years preceding the joint venture, and had come close to Japanese productivity levels. It had also doubled its share of the European color television market in the decade preceding the alliance. Thus it was not difficult for employees to regard the partnership as a multiplier, rather than as a substitute, for internal efforts.

Organization learning theory suggests that laggards may confront two cruel paradoxes. First, learning often cannot begin until unlearning has taken place (Burgleman, 1983b; Hedberg, 1981; Nystrom and Starbuck, 1984). This is particularly true where the behaviors that contributed to past success have been deeply etched in the organization's consciousness. The problem of unlearning is not only a cognitive problem—altering perceptual maps—but a problem of driving out old behavior with new behavior. The link between changed cognition and changed behavior is probably more direct in individuals (Postman and Underwood, 1973; Watzlawick, Weakland and Fisch, 1974) than it is in large multinational companies (Prahalad and Doz, 1987). Current patterns of behavior in large organizations are typically 'hard-wired' in structure, in information systems, incentive schemes, hiring and promotion practices, and so on (Argyris and Schon, 1978). The implication here is that unlearning will be a significant hurdle for a laggard attempting to compensate for past skill failure. For a latecomer using an alliance to build skills in a new area, unlearning is not a prerequisite. Receptivity will not be impaired by employees clinging to past practices.

Second, while a reduction in organizational slack typically precipitates the search for new knowledge (Cyert and March, 1963), the complete absence of slack just as surely frustrates learning (Burgelman, 1983a). Some slack is necessary if the organization is to search for new approaches, experiment with new methods, and embed new capabilities. Learning is a luxury which can be afforded by those with some minimum complement of time and resources. A small crisis abets learning, a big crisis limits learning. Of course it has been argued that collaboration may be a timely and low-cost mechanism for acquiring new skills. But even here, as learning progresses from knowledge-gathering to capability-building, investment needs escalate. A firm may understand how its partner achieves a certain level of performance, but not have the resources needed to embed that understanding through staff development and investment in new facilities. Again, the results of the study support the contention that learning is most likely to occur in the middle ground between abundance and arrogance on one side, and deprivation and resignation on the other.

To these two paradoxes may be added a third: the greater the need to learn, i.e. the farther one partner is behind its counterpart, the higher the barriers to receptivity. Simply put, to replicate the skills of a partner, a firm must be able to identify, if not retrace, the intermediate learning 'steps' between its present competence level and that of its partner. After visiting the most advanced manufacturing facility of a Japanese partner, a manager in one Western firm remarked:

> It's no good for us to simply observe where they are today, what we have to find out is how they got from where we are to where they are. We need to experiment and learn with intermediate technologies before duplicating what they've done.

If the skills gap between partners is too great, learning becomes almost impossible.

The notion of receptivity was seen to apply to the corporate body, as well as to individual receptors. Individual learning became collective learning when (1) there existed a mechanism for 'summing up' individual learning, i.e. first recording and then integrating the fragmentary knowledge gained by individuals, and (2) learning was transferred across unit boundaries to all those who could benefit in some way from what had been learned. It was evident in the study that firms with a history of cross-functional teamwork and inter-business coordination were more likely to turn personal learning into corporate learning than were firms where the emphasis was on 'individual contributors' and 'independent business units.' A senior manager in a Japanese partner commented on the internal relationships that had aided its learning, and hindered, it believed, its partner's learning:

> Within [my firm] there is a great deal of mutual responsibility. Responsibility is a very grey area in Japan; many people are involved. There is much more overlap in responsibility than in [our Western partner] where information seems to be compartmentalized. [Our partner] thought we asked too many questions, but in [my company] information is shared with many people even if they are not directly involved. Engineers in [one department] want to know what is happening in design [in another department] even if that is not related to their direct responsibilities.

On the other side of the relationship a Western manager offered a similar perspective:

> [In joint meetings, staff] groups [from our Japanese partner] would almost always be multi-disciplinary, even for technical discussions. [They] clearly wanted to understand the implications of our technology. You had the feeling that most of the [their] people who were sitting in the [joint] meetings were there only to learn. We would have never taken anyone into such a meeting without a direct interest in what was being discussed.

In terms of active determinants, receptivity depended upon, above all else, the diligence with which those with greatest access to the partner approached the task of learning. One firm in particular appeared to conceive of inter-partner learning as a rigorous discipline. This firm's success in internalizing partner skills suggests that such a conception may be a prerequisite for systematic learning. A senior executive in the company described its 'inch-by-inch' efforts to learn from its partner:

> You need to be incredibly patient, but eventually you would get what you wanted. In the event of the slightest breakdown, you had to ask [our partner], 'What now?' We acquired the knowhow very slowly in this way, by finding out all the little mistakes [we were making], by repeatedly asking questions, and by forcing them, little by little, to yield technical information.

In this case receptivity seemed to thrive as long as top management continued to express an active interest in what was being learned. Top management's commitment to learning was exhibited first through a clear intent to establish a world-class consumer electronics manufacturing competence, secondly through the hiring of a wholly new executive group, and thirdly through a constant stream of investment to build up a physical plant as closely parallel to that of the partner as possible. Given initial estimates that it would take between 3 and 5 years for the firm to 'catch up' with its Japanese partner, top management believed its unwavering enthusiasm for, and attention to, the partnership was critical to a positive learning outcome. Internalizing new skills via an alliance would seem to require a reasonably long attention span on the part of top management.

The personal skills of receptors also influenced receptivity. The European partner referred to above had assembled a collaborative team with the necessary skills to observe, interpret, apply, and improve upon partner skills. One member of the team came from the watch-making industry, and others from successful precision-engineering firms. The average age of team members was estimated to be 35 years. The relatively young age of the team, and the fact that few were tainted with the burden of past failure, reduced the need for 'unlearning.' The team also benefited from a liberal training budget. For this company it was not enough to embed, through goal setting and daily reinforcement, a learning discipline, receptors had to be competent to receive. This meant that their skills had to parallel, as closely as possible, those from whom they were learning.

3.6. Determinants of Sustainable Learning

Whether a skills gap closed through inter-partner learning later re-opened seemed to depend on several factors, all of which can be summarized under the general heading of a *capacity for self-sustaining learning*. The critical point here is that intercepting a partner's skills at a point in time appeared to be a lesser challenge than matching a partner's underlying rate of improvement over time. To break free of dependence a firm had, first, to match its pace of absorption to its partner's pace of innovation, and then to equal or better its partner's capability for autonomously and continuously improving those skills. NEC, when it formed its alliance with Honeywell in the earlier 1960s, was much smaller than its partner. Nonetheless, NEC ultimately reversed its initial dependency. Those few firms in the study that were committed to turning the tables of dependency appeared to agree that matching a partner's pace of autonomous improvement depended on: (1) capturing know-why as well as know-what from their partners, (2) mastering the disciplines of continuous improvement, and (3) achieving global scale.

Two firms in the study recognized that, as long as they operated at regional scale, they could not fully apply the lessons learned from partners operating at global scale. Both firms made large international acquisitions with the express goal of amortizing investment in world-scale facilities that paralleled those of their partners. Both firms found that as their learning agendas shifted from technology to competence, from discrete skills to systemic skills, and from know-how to know-why, their pace of learning had slowed. It was clear to both partners that building a foundation for autonomous improvement demanded insight into the underlying dynamic which drove their partner's pace of innovation. Again, this was a substantial challenge, particularly for Western firms, as at least some of the impetus behind the innovative pace of their Japanese counterparts appeared to be culturally idiosyncratic (Baba, 1989; Imai, 1986; Itami, 1987).

4. Discussion

Though this research grew out of an interest in skills-based competition (Nelson and Winter, 1982; Dierickx and Cool, 1989; Quinn, Doorley and Paquette, 1990; Prahalad and Hamel, 1990; Barney, 1990; Teece, Pisano and Shuen, 1990), it is also important to set it within the context of existing research on the management of strategic alliances. The way in which the present study both complements and challenges prior research on collaboration is now discussed.

4.1. Collaboration as a Transitional Stage

Joint ventures and other non-market inter-firm agreements have typically been pictured as an intermediate level of integration between arm's-length contracts in open markets and full ownership (Nielsen, 1988; Thorelli, 1986). But where the goal of the alliance is skills acquisition, an alliance may be seen, by one or both partners, not as an optimal compromise between market and hierarchy, to use Williamson's (1975) nomenclature, but as a half-way house on the road from market to hierarchy. In this sense the alliance is viewed not as an alternative to market-based transactions or full ownership, but as an alternative to other modes of skill acquisition. These might include acquiring the partner, licensing from the partner, or developing the needed skills through internal efforts. There are several reasons collaboration may in some cases be the preferred mode of skills acquisition.

For some skills, what Itami (1987) terms 'invisible assets,' the cost of internal development may be almost infinite. Complex skills, based on tacit knowledge, and arising out of a unique cultural context may be acquirable only by up-close observation and emulation of 'best in class.' Alliances may offer advantages of timeliness as well as efficiency. Where global competitors are rapidly building new sources of competitive advantage, as well as enhancing existing skills, a go-it-alone strategy could confine a firm to permanent also-ran status. Alliances may be seen as a way of short-circuiting the process of skills acquisition and thus avoiding the opportunity cost of being a perpetual follower. Motorola's reliance on Toshiba for re-entry to the DRAM semiconductor business seems to reflect such a concern. Internalization via collaboration may be more attractive than acquiring a firm in total. In buying a company the acquirer must pay for nondistinctive assets, and is confronted with a substantially larger organizational integration problem.

4.2. Capturing Value vs. Creating Value

There are two basic processes in any alliance: *value creation* and *value appropriation*. The extent of value creation depends first on whether the market and competitive logic of the venture is sound, and then on the efficacy with which the two partners combine their complementary skills and resources; that is, how well they perform joint tasks. Each partner then appropriates value in the form of monetary or other benefits. In general, researchers have given more attention to the process of value creation than the process of value appropriation. The primary concern of both the transactions cost (Hennart, 1988) and strategic position (e.g. Harrigan, 1985) perspectives is the creation of joint value. Transactional efficiency gained through quasi-internalization is one form of value creation; improvement in competitive position is another. Both perspectives provide insights into why firms collaborate; neither captures the dynamics which determine collaborative outcomes, and the individual monetary and long-term competitive gains taken by each partner. Making a collaborative agreement 'work' has generally been seen as creating the preconditions for value creation (Doz, 1988; Killing, 1982, 1983). There is much advice on how to be a 'good' partner (Goldenberg, 1988; Perlmutter and Heenan, 1986)—firms are typically urged to build 'trust' (Harrigan, 1986; Peterson and Shimada, 1978)—but little advice on how to reap the benefits of being a good partner.

There appear to be two mechanisms for extracting value from an alliance: bargaining over the stream of economic benefits that issues directly from the successful execution of joint tasks, and internalizing the skills of partners. These 'value pools' may be conceptually distinct, but they were shown to be related in an important way. Bargaining power at any point in time within an alliance is, *ceteris paribus*, a function of who needs whom the most. This, in turn, is a function of the perceived strategic importance of the alliance to each partner and the attractiveness to each partner of alternatives to collaboration. Depending on its bargaining power a partner will gain a greater or lesser share of the fruits of joint effort. An important issue then is what factors prompt changes in bargaining power. Some factors will be exogenous to the partnership. A change in strategic priorities may suddenly make a partnership much more or much less vital for one of the partners (Franko, 1971). Likewise, a shift in the market or competitive environment could devalue the contribution of one partner and revalue the contribution of the other. Rapid change in technology might produce a similar effect (Harrigan, 1985). However, there is one determinant of relative bargaining power that is very much within the firm's control: its capacity to learn.

While Westney (1988) and Kogut (1988) recognize that learning may be an explicit goal in an alliance, they do not specify the critical linkages between learning, dependency, and bargaining power. Conversely, while Pfeffer and Nowak (1976) and Blois (1980) correctly view alliances as mechanisms for managing inter-organizational dependence, they do not take a dynamic view of interdependence, and hence miss the linkage between learning and changes in relative dependency. If bargaining power is a function of relative dependence it should be possible to lessen dependency and improve bargaining power by out-learning one's partner. Most bargains obsolesce with time (Kobrin, 1986); by actively working to internalize a partner's skills it should be possible to accelerate the rate at which the bargain obsolesces. This seems to have been the motivation for Boeing's Japanese partners in recent years (Moxon, 1988). It was clearly the motivation of two of the Japanese partners in the study.

4.3. The Process of Collaborative Exchange

Researchers have tended to look at venture and task structure when attempting to account for partnership performance. An equally useful perspective might be that of a *collaborative membrane*, through which flow skills and capabilities between the partners. The extent to which the membrane is permeable, and in which direction(s) it is permeable determines relative learning. Though researchers and practitioners often seem to be preoccupied with issues of structure—legal, governance and task (Harrigan, 1988; Killing, 1983; Schillaci, 1987; Tybejee, 1988) the study suggests that these may be only partial determinants of permeability. Conceiving of an alliance as a membrane suggests that access to people, facilities, documents, and other forms of knowledge is traded between partners in an on-going process of *collaborative exchange*. As operating employees interact day-by-day, and continually process partner requests for access, a series of *micro-bargains* are reached on the basis of considerations of operational effectiveness, fairness, and bargaining power. Though these bargains may be more implicit than explicit, out-learning a partner means 'winning' a series of *micro-bargains*. The simple hypothesis is that the terms of trade in any particular micro-bargain may be only partially determined by the terms of trade which prevailed at the time the macro-bargain was struck by corporate officers. A firm may be in a weak bargaining position at the macro level, as NEC undoubtedly was when it entered its alliance with Honeywell in the computer business in the early 1960s, but may be able to strike a series of advantageous micro-bargains if, at the operational level, it uniquely possesses the capacity to learn. Restating the bargaining power argument advanced earlier, the cumulative impact of micro-bargains will, to a large extent, determine in whose favor future macro-bargains are resolved.

4.4. Success Metrics

Where internalization is the goal, the longevity and 'stability' of partnerships may not be useful proxies for collaborative success. Nevertheless, they have often been used as such (Beamish, 1984; Franko, 1971; Gomes-Casseres, 1987; Killing, 1983; Reynolds, 1979). A long-lived alliance may evince the failure of one or both partners to learn. It was interesting to note in the study that, despite collaborative agreements in Japan with Japanese firms spanning several decades, several Western partners were still unable to 'go it alone' in the Japanese market. By way of contrast, there were few cases in which Japanese firms had remained dependent on Western partners for continued access to Western markets (though in one case the Japanese partner ultimately acquired its European partner). Likewise, an absence of contention in the relationship is not, by itself, an adequate success metric. A firm with no ambition beyond investment avoidance and substitution of its partner's competitiveness for its own lack of competitiveness may be perfectly content not to learn from its partner. But where a failure to learn is likely to ultimately undermine the competitiveness and independence of the firm, such contentedness should not be taken as a sign of collaborative success. The theoretical perspective on collaboration developed in this paper is summarized in Table 4.

Table 4. Distinctive Attributes of a Theory of Competitive Collaboration

	Traditional Perspective	Alternative Perspective
Collaborative logic	Quasi-internalization	*De-facto* internalization
Unit of analysis	Joint outcomes	Individual outcomes
Underlying process	Value creation	Value appropriation
Success determinants	Form and structure (macro-bargain)	Collaborative exchange (micro-bargains)
Success metrics	Satisfaction and longevity	Bargaining power and competitiveness

References

Argyris, C. and Schon, D. A. *Organizational Learning*, Addison-Wesley, Reading, MA, 1978.

Baba, Y. 'The dynamics of continuous innovation in scale-intensive industries,' *Strategic Management Journal*, **10**, 1989, pp. 89–100.

Ballon, R. J. 'A lesson from Japan: Contract, control, and authority,' *Journal of Contemporary Business*, **8**(2), 1979, pp. 27–35.

Barney, J. B. 'Firm resources and sustained competitive advantage.' Unpublished manuscript, Department of Management, Texas A&M University, 1990.

Beamish, P. W. 'Joint venture performance in developing countries.' Unpublished doctoral dissertation, University of Western Ontario, 1984.

Benedict, R. *The Chrysanthemum and the Sword*, reprint (1974), New American Library, New York, 1946.

Block, A. and Matsumoto, H. 'Joint venturing in Japan.' *Conference Board Record*, April 1972, pp. 32–36.

Blois, K. J. 'Quasi-integration as a mechanism for controlling external dependencies,' *Management Decision*, **18**(1), 1980, pp. 55–63.

Buckley, P. J. and Casson, M. *Economic Theory of the Multinational Enterprise: Selected Papers*, Macmillan, London, 1985.

—— and —— 'A theory of cooperation in international business.' In F. J. Contractor and P. Lorange (eds), *Cooperative Strategies in International Business*, D.C. Heath, Lexington, MA, 1988, pp. 31–53.

Burgelman, R. A. 'A model of the interaction of strategic behavior, corporate context and the concept of strategy,' *Academy of Management Review*, **8**(1), 1983a, pp. 61–70.

—— 'A process model of internal corporate venturing in the diversified major firm,' *Administrative Science Quarterly*, **28**(2), 1983b, pp. 223–244.

Business Week. 'When U.S. joint ventures with Japan go sour,' 24 July 1989, pp. 14–16.

Caves, R. E. 'International corporations: The industrial economics of foreign investment, *Economica*, February 1971, pp. 1–27.

Contractor, F. J. and Lorange, P. 'Why should firms cooperate: The strategy and economic basis for cooperative ventures.' In F. J. Contractor and P. Lorange (eds), *Cooperative Strategies in International Business*, D.C. Heath, Lexington, MA, 1988, pp. 3–28.

Cyert, R. M. and March, J. G. *A Behavioral Theory of the Firm*. Prentice-Hall, Englewood Cliffs, NJ, 1963.

Dierickx, I. and Cool, K. 'Asset stock accumulation and sustainability of competitive advantage,' *Management Science*, December 1989, pp. 1504–1514.

Doz, Y. 'Technology partnerships between larger and smaller firms: Some critical issues.' In F. J. Contractor and P. Lorange (eds), *Cooperative Strategies in International Business*, D.C. Heath, Lexington, MA, 1988, pp. 317–328.

Franko, L. G. *Joint Venture Survival in Multinational Corporations*, Praeger, New York, 1971.

Ghemawat, P., Porter, M. E. and Rawlinson, R. A. 'Patterns of international coalition activity.' In M. E. Porter (ed.), *Competition in Global Industries*, Harvard University Press, Boston, MA, 1986, pp. 345–365.

Glaser, B. G. and Strauss, A. L. *The Discovery of Grounded Theory: Strategies for Qualitative Research*. Aldine, New York, 1967.

Goldenberg, S. *International Joint Ventures in Action: How to Establish, Manage and Profit from International Strategic Alliances*, Hutchinson Business Books, London, 1988.

Gomes-Casseres, B. 'Joint venture instability: Is it a problem,' *Columbia Journal of World Business*, Summer 1987, pp. 97–102.

Hamel, G. 'Competitive collaboration: Learning, power and dependence in international strategic alliances.' Unpublished doctoral dissertation, Graduate School of Business Administration, University of Michigan, 1990.

Harrigan, K. R. *Strategies for Joint Ventures*. Lexington Books, Lexington, MA, 1985.

—— *Managing for Joint Venture Success*. Lexington Books, Lexington, MA, 1986.

—— 'Joint ventures and competitive strategy,' *Strategic Management Journal*, **9**, 1988, pp. 141–158.

Hedberg, B. L. T. 'How organizations learn and unlearn.' In P. C. Nystrom and W. H. Starbuck (eds), *Handbook of Organizational Design*, Oxford University Press, London, 1981.

Hergert, M. and Morris. D. 'Trends in international collaborative agreements.' In F. J. Contractor and P. Lorange (eds), *Cooperative Strategies in International Business*, D.C. Heath, Lexington, MA, 1988, pp. 99–109.

Hennart, J. 'A transaction cost theory of equity joint ventures,' *Strategic Management Journal*, July–August, 9, 1988, pp. 36–74.

Imai, M. *Kaizen: The Key to Japan's Competitive Success*, Random House, New York, 1986.

Itami, H. with Roehl, T. W. *Mobilizing Invisible Assets*. Harvard University Press, Cambridge, MA, 1987.

Killing, J. P. 'How to make a global joint venture work,' *Harvard Business Review*, May–June 1982, pp. 120–127.

—— *Strategies for Joint Venture Success*. Praeger, New York, 1983.

Kobrin, S. J. 'Testing the bargaining hypothesis in the manufacturing sector in developing countries,' Unpublished manuscript, 1986.

Kogut, B. 'Joint ventures: Theoretical and empirical perspectives,' *Strategic Management Journal*, **9**(4), 1988, pp. 319–322.

Mintzberg, H. 'Patterns in strategy formulation,' *Management Science*, **24**(9), 1978, pp. 934–948.

Moxon, R. W., Roehl, T. W. and Truitt, J. F. 'International cooperative ventures in the commercial aircraft industry: Gains, sure, but what's my share.' In F. J. Contractor and P. Lorange (eds), *Cooperative Strategies in International Business*, D.C. Heath, Lexington, MA, 1988, pp. 255–278.

Nakane, C. *Japanese Society*. University of California Press, Berkeley, CA, 1970.

Nelson, R. R. and Winter, S. G. *An Evolutionary Theory of Economic Change*, Belknap Press, Cambridge, MA, 1982.

Nielsen, R. P. 'Cooperative strategy,' *Strategic Management Journal*, **9**, 1988, pp. 475–492.

Nystrom, P. C. and Starbuck, W. H. 'To avoid organizational crises, unlearn,' *Organizational Dynamics*, **12**(4), 1984, pp. 53–65.

Ohmae, K. 'The global logic of strategic alliances,' *Harvard Business Review*, March–April 1989, pp. 143–155.

Ouchi, W. G. 'Markets, bureaucracies, and clans,' *Administrative Science Quarterly*, **25**, 1980, pp. 129–141.

—— and Johnson, R. T. 'Made in America (under Japanese management),' *Harvard Business Review*, September–October 1974, pp. 61–69.

Perlmutter, H. V. and Heenan, D. H. 'Cooperate to compete globally,' *Harvard Business Review*, March–April 1986, pp. 136–152.

Peterson, R. B. and Schwind, H. F. 'A comparative study of personnel problems in international companies and joint ventures in Japan,' *Journal of International Business Studies*, **8**(1), 1977, pp. 45–55.

—— and Shimada, J. Y. 'Sources of management problems in Japanese–American joint ventures,' *Academy of Management Review*, **3**, 1978, pp. 796–804.

Pettigrew, A. M. 'On studying organizational cultures,' *Administrative Science Quarterly*, **24**(4), 1979, pp. 570–581.

Pfeffer, J. and Nowak, P. 'Joint ventures and interorganizational interdependence,' *Administrative Science Quarterly*, **21**, 1976, pp. 398–418.

Porter, M. E. *Competitive Strategy: Techniques for Analyzing Industries and Competitors*, Free Press, New York, 1980.

—— *Competitive Advantage*, Free Press, New York, 1985.

Postman, L. and Underwood, B. J. 'Critical issues in interference theory,' *Memory and Cognition*, **1**, 1973, pp. 19–40.

Prahalad, C. K. and Doz, Y. *Multinational Mission*, Free Press, New York, 1987.

—— and Hamel, G. 'The core competence and the corporation,' *Harvard Business Review*, May–June 1990, pp. 71–91.

Quinn, J. B., Doorley, T. L. and Paquette, P. C. 'Building leadership in high technology industries: Focus technology strategies on services innovation.' Unpublished paper presented at the Second International Conference on Managing the High Technology Firm, University of Colorado, Boulder, CO, 10 January 1990.

Reynolds, J. I. *Indian–American Joint Ventures: Business Policy Relationships*. University Press of America, Washington, DC, 1979.

Reich, R. B. and Mankin, E. D. 'Joint ventures with Japan give away our future,' *Harvard Business Review*, March–April 1986, pp. 78–86.

Root, F. R. 'Some taxonomies of cooperative arrangements.' In F. J. Contractor and P. Lorange (eds), *Cooperative Strategies in International Business*, D.C. Heath, Lexington, MA, 1988, pp. 69–80.

Schillaci, C. E. 'Designing successful joint ventures,' *Journal of Business Strategy*, **8**(2), 1987, pp. 59–63.

Seyle, H. *From Dream to Discovery: On Being a Scientist*, McGraw-Hill, New York, 1964.

Sullivan, J. and Peterson, R. B. 'Factors associated with trust in Japanese–American joint ventures,' *Management International Review*, **22**(2), 1982, pp. 30–40.

Teece, D. J. 'The multinational enterprise: Market failure and market power considerations,' *Sloan Management Review*, **22**(3), 1981, pp. 3–17.

—— Pisano, G. P. and Shuen, A. 'Firm capabilities, resources, and the concept of strategy,' CCC Working Paper No. 90–8, Center for Research in Management, University of California at Berkeley, 1990.

Terpstra, V. and David, K. *The Cultural Environment of International Business*, South-Western, Cincinnati, OH, 1985.

Thorelli, H. B. 'Networks: Between markets and hierarchies,' *Strategic Management Journal*, **7**, 1986, pp. 37–51.

Tybejee, T. T. 'Japan's joint ventures in the United States.' In F. J. Contractor and P. Lorange (eds), *Cooperative Strategies in International Business*, D.C. Heath, Lexington, MA, 1988, pp. 457–472.

Watzlawick, P., Weakland, J. H. and Fisch, R. *Change*. Norton, New York, 1974.

Westney, D. E. 'Domestic and foreign learning curves in managing international cooperative strategies.' In F. J. Contractor and P. Lorange (eds), *Cooperative Strategies in International Business*, D.C. Heath, Lexington, MA, 1988, pp. 339–346.

Williamson, O. E. *Markets and Hierarchies: An Analysis and Antitrust Implications*. Free Press, New York, 1975.

12 The Dynamics of Learning Alliances: Competition, Cooperation, and Relative Scope

Tarun Khanna, Ranjay Gulati, and Nitin Nohria

1. Introduction

Learning alliances, associations in which the primary objective of the partners is to learn from each other, constitute an important class of interfirm alliances (Hamel, Doz, and Prahalad, 1989; Hamel, 1991). We introduce a general theoretical framework to advance the study of such learning alliances in two major ways. First, the framework explicitly incorporates simultaneously competitive and cooperative behavior by participating firms, and identifies factors that may influence the incidence of each type of behavior. We show that the propensity to depart from purely cooperative behavior in a particular alliance is related to the portfolio of markets in which each participating firm is present, and to the degree to which these portfolios overlap. We point out that a firm's behavior within an alliance is conditioned by its position in markets that may have little to do with that particular alliance.

Second, we direct our attention to understanding the dynamics of a learning alliance, as opposed to the decision to enter into such an alliance. We examine participant firms' allocation of resources to learning from their alliance partners and the factors that may condition these choices. In particular, we show how asymmetric incentives to allocate resources to learning may arise, even where there are no *ex ante* asymmetries between firms. This analysis allows us to draw attention to behavioral predispositions arising from the tension between simultaneously competitive and cooperative behavior, and to suggest when these are most likely to arise. Our focus on the dynamics of alliances appears especially relevant given the recent spurt in alliance activity on the one hand (Anderson, 1990; Hergert and Morris, 1988; Hladik, 1985), and the reports of dissatisfaction with alliance performance on the other.[1] We suggest that some of this dissatisfaction may be the result of poor understanding of the dynamics within alliances.

We introduce several conceptual elements for our framework. First, 'private' and 'common' benefits within alliances are those that accrue, respectively, to individual firms within the alliance (from activities in markets not governed by the alliance) and collectively to all participants in the alliance (from activities in markets that are governed by the alliance). We suggest that a higher ratio of private to common benefits leads to greater departures from cooperative and toward competitive behavior. Further, we introduce the concept of the 'relative scope' of a firm within an alliance to precisely measure the extent of activities in markets unrelated to the alliance as a proportion of all activities conducted by the firms. We argue that relative scope can help identify the ratio of private to common benefits. This framework allows us to establish some empirically testable propositions that depart significantly from existing theoretical and empirical work in suggesting that the opportunity set of each firm outside the particular alliance crucially impacts its behavior within the alliance.

We contend that an important reason for the disappointment of some firms with alliances is their poor understanding of the strategic dynamics within such partnerships. Firms often fail to recognize the existence or the magnitude of the asymmetric incentives to invest that inevitably arise as an alliance evolves. The differential incentives to invest are a result of the competitive aspects of what is simultaneously a cooperative and a competitive enterprise. The cooperative aspect arises from the fact that each firm needs access to the other firm's know-how, and that the firms can collectively use their knowledge to produce something that is beneficial to them all (common benefits). The competitive aspect is a consequence of each firm's attempt to also use its partners' know-how for private gains, and of the possibility that significantly greater benefits might accrue to the firm that 'finishes' learning from its partner(s) before the latter can do the same (as it is then free to leave the alliance and deny its partner(s) access to its know-how).

An argument that emphasizes the competitive aspects of alliances was made by Hamel et al., (1989), who suggested that it is crucial that firms not view alliances as passive opportunities to benefit from their partners' skills, nor act as passive recipients of the results of those skills; rather, firms should treat alliances as opportunities to actually *learn* those skills. The implication is that the firm that is able to learn the most from its alliance partners while the alliance is in progress is the one that benefits the most in the long run. Our work builds on theirs by (a) clarifying when the racing dynamic is likely to arise and (b) by analyzing the nature of the incentives of each partner to learn as the alliance evolves.[2]

An underlying theme throughout this chapter is that firms' incentives to learn are driven by their expected pay-offs, and that the structure of pay-offs that each participant expects is complex, interdependent (on partners' pay-off expectations), and changing over time. Gulati, Khanna and Nohria (1994) suggested that the way an alliance is managed should depend upon its pay-off structure. Furthermore, through an examination of different pay-off structures, they suggested that exogenous changes in the environment, through their effects on pay-off structures, may necessitate changes in the way that an alliance is managed. In this paper, we do not treat changes in pay-off structures as resulting from exogenous events. Rather, we suggest that changes in pay-off structures, and hence the incentives that affect resource allocation decisions, are triggered by endogenous changes brought about by the participants' own decisions regarding resource commitments as the alliance evolves. Thus, we introduce a dynamic element into the determination of pay-off structures.

We start the chapter by defining private and common benefits, clarifying when they might arise, and introducing the notion of relative scope. We then demonstrate that resource allocation patterns are very different in purely cooperative and in purely competitive learning situations, and that these two poles of a continuum arise in alliances with pure common benefits and those with pure private benefits. Further, the organizational routines required to manage alliances vary with the mix of private and common benefits. For firms that have not historically relied on alliances, we argue that a high ratio of private to common benefits increases the likelihood of suboptimal behavior. We then outline a typology of ways in which firms might deviate from the theoretical ideal proposed by the previous analysis. Finally, we draw on recent research in behavioral decision theory to suggest reasons for such behavior.

2. Private Benefits, Common Benefits, and Relative Scope

We distinguish between two qualitatively different kinds of benefits available to participants in learning alliances: private benefits and common benefits. Although most alliances realize benefits that are combinations of these two kinds, we argue that the distinction is useful because of the different effects that the types of benefits received have on the evolution of partners' incentives to invest in learning. Private benefits are those that a firm can earn unilaterally by picking up skills from its partner and applying them to its own operations in areas unrelated to the alliance activities. Common benefits are those that accrue to each partner in an alliance from the collective application of the learning that both firms go through as a consequence of being part of the alliance; these are obtained from operations in areas of the firm that are related to the alliance. Private benefits are unrelated to this joint knowledge creation. The common benefits earned by one firm need not be equal to those earned by the other. One way to think about this is to recognize that the creative synthesis of knowledge in an alliance creates a total amount of value. The common benefits of a particular firm are the proportion of this value that it appropriates, and is likely to be a function of the relative bargaining power of each firm. These concepts are all generalizable to learning alliances involving more than two firms, but we will stay with the two-firm situation for clarity.[3]

Intuitively, the ratio of private to common benefits for a particular firm will be higher when it has more opportunity to apply what it learns to its businesses outside of the scope of the alliance (and thus earn private benefits), than opportunity to apply what it learns to businesses within the scope of the alliance (and thus earn common benefits). To be more precise about this, consider the following. Each firm operates in a set of markets, each element of which can, for our purposes, be described by its product and geographic characteristics. The scope of the alliance refers to a need that both partner firms have agreed to target (perhaps through the introduction of a new product or the provision of a new service), typically corresponding to some subset of markets in which the firms are themselves involved. The overlap between the scope of the alliance and the total market scope of each partner is likely to vary and influence the available private and common benefits. The greater the overlap between alliance scope and firm scope, the higher are the common benefits and the lower are the private benefits, *ceteris paribus*.

In order to help operationalize the concepts of private and common benefits, we introduce the notion of the *relative scope* of a firm i in an alliance j, denoted by RS_{ij}, to refer to the ratio of the scope of the alliance to the total set of markets in which the firm is active.[4] This ratio lies between 0 and 1; its value is closer to 0 the smaller the scope of the alliance,[5] and its value is 1 if the firm has no interests in markets not covered by the alliance. Thus, the relative scope is a measure that is particular to a given firm in a given alliance. Different firms in the same alliance, and the same firm in different alliances, would have different relative scope values. *Ceteris paribus*, the smaller the relative scope, the greater the ratio of private to common benefits for the firm in question. Correspondingly, a greater ratio implies more opportunity for a firm to apply skills acquired in the course of the alliance to markets not involved in the alliance. Figure 1 depicts this link between relative scope and the nature of benefits.

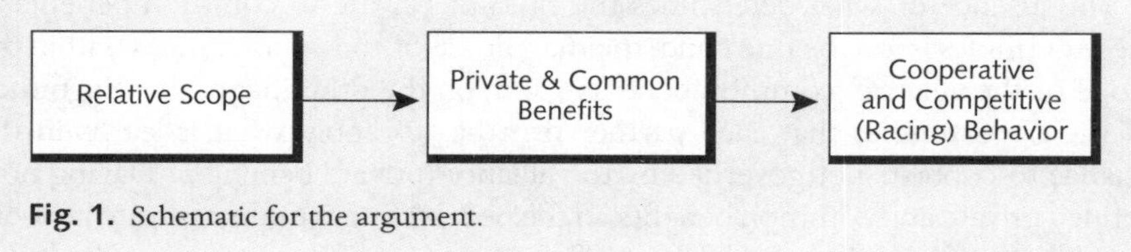

Fig. 1. Schematic for the argument.

Of course, factors other than relative scope affect the magnitude of private and common benefits, and thereby their ratio for a particular firm. Given a set of markets outside the scope of a particular alliance, a firm's ability to earn private benefits by applying what it has learned to these markets is affected by (a) the extent to which these markets are related to those within the scope of the alliance and (b) the extent to which the firm has the skills to accomplish the transfer of learning.[6] These factors can be summarized in a 'transferability factor,' τ_{ij}, which is an increasing function of both the extent of relatedness and the presence of transfer skills. Then, if PB_{ij} denotes the private benefits of firm i in alliance j, we have $PB_{ij} = f(RS_{ij}, \tau_{ij})$. As mentioned above, common benefits accruing to a firm are a function of the bargaining power that it has relative to its partner.

Let us clarify our conceptual framework by considering two sets of possible alliances. In the case of a joint product development agreement where two firms bring together different technological skills in order to introduce a product in a particular geographic market, each firm could use the skills it learns from its partner to (a) introduce the same product in other geographic markets that it operates in or to (b) introduce other products in various geographic markets. The greater the opportunity that a particular firm has to engage in either (a) or (b), the smaller is the ratio of benefits earned from activities within the scope of the alliance to all benefits accessible to the firm. This is also equivalent to its having a lower relative scope measure and, *ceteris paribus*, a greater opportunity to earn private benefits.

As another illustration of this concept, consider an alliance between a technologically advanced firm A with a firm B in a developing country with the objective of introducing a product, P, that A is familiar with into B's country. Here firm A tries to learn about the market for P in the developing country from firm B, while firm B tries to access firm A's superior technology. Firm A will have the opportunity to use what it learns from firm B (regarding marketing products in firm B's country) to market other products that it is capable of producing, the more so the more transferable this marketing knowledge is to these other products. Similarly, firm B can use its product knowledge gained from firm A in other product or geographic markets beyond the scope of the alliance.

The essence of what determines the ratio of private to common benefits in these examples is, on the one hand, the magnitude of the opportunities within the scope of the alliance (common benefits), and, on the other hand, the magnitude of the opportunities that each partner firm has to apply what it learns in the alliance to contexts not governed by the alliance (private benefits).[7] Having now defined private and common benefits, in the next section we demonstrate how different kinds of benefits have different influences on incentives to invest in learning.

3. Strategic Learning Behavior

In this section, we establish the very different kinds of incentives that private and common benefits create for alliance partners' allocation of resources to learning (the second link in Fig. 1). Our *modus operandi* is to rely on simple, stylized models from economic theory to illustrate the intuition behind our reasoning. In particular, we first examine, in sequence, the case of an alliance with pure common benefits and that of one with pure private benefits, and show that the incentives to allocate resources to learning are very different in the two cases. These cases represent two poles of a continuum along which alliances vary in their mix of private and common benefits. These extremes afford convenient anchors for an analysis of resource allocation in alliances that have both private and common benefits, which we develop later in the section. Finally, we discuss a variety of modifications of the basic analysis and demonstrate the robustness of its basic conclusions.

The learning process postulated in these economic models is that a firm earns private benefits as soon as it has learned enough to apply this learning to its operations (modeled as benefits being earned following the completion of some threshold amount of learning). Common benefits, however, are available only once both partners have learned enough to be able to creatively synthesize their knowledge bases (the assumption is that such a synthesis is only likely to occur after each firm completes its learning). Thus, private benefits are realized by a firm prior to common benefits being realized by both firms.

3.1. *Alliances with Only Common Benefits*

Now, consider an alliance from which only common benefits will result. All firms must finish learning in order for any of them to derive the common benefits.[8] Thus, there is no incentive for firms to try to get ahead of each other, or to try and finish learning in an effort to reap private benefits before their partners have finished learning. In such a situation of pure cooperation, resources allocation decisions are best made jointly. Both firms agree on the amount of resources that it is optimal to allocate given the particular stage of the learning process; in effect, for the purposes of resource allocation, they act exactly as one firm would. To characterize the optimal resource allocation in this type of situation, we appeal to existing results in economic theory. These results characterize a single firm's optimal allocation of resources in particular situations that we believe are illustrative of a more general feature of resource allocation under unilateral (single-firm) learning.[9]

Consider a single firm's resource allocation decisions when it receives benefits once it has completed all stages.[10] We distinguish between the case in which the available resources are project-specific (where a project has a budget) and where there is effectively no resource constraint (as in some large company laboratory situations where the funding for any one project is a small fraction when compared to the large amounts of research projects in progress at any given time). Then

Result 1. If there is no overall budget for the project, the firm will allocate more resources as it completes more stages (Grossman and Shapiro, 1986).

Result 2. If there is a fixed budget constraint, then the firm will split the available resources equally among all the stages (Dutta, 1992).

These two results establish the resource allocation patterns when a firm is engaged in a project unilaterally or when two firms jointly determine profit-maximizing resource allocations. The first result can be interpreted as referring to a situation where there is an abundant supply of the critical resource needed to implement the project, as long as one is willing to pay the (factor) market price for these resources. In contrast, the second result refers to a situation where there is no way of alleviating the scarcity of a given resource.[11] Thus, the first situation might correspond to, say, a need for general-purpose computer programmers (for whom there is a competitive labor market) while the second situation might correspond to computer programmers with a particular speciality that is in scarce supply (of whom there might be only a fixed number that is not adjustable in the immediate term).

The intuition behind these results is as follows. For result 1, the firm simply varies its allocation in proportion to the expected value of completing the project. As more stages are completed, less effort is needed to finish the stages and earn the same benefits, and the firm steps up its allocation every period.[12] For result 2, the intuition is simply that decreasing returns in the innovation production function imply that it is optimal to spread out the budget evenly. For instance, in a two-stage process, it would be better to allocate half the resources to each stage rather than, say, three-quarters to one stage and one-quarter to the other. The gains from shifting more than half the resources to one stage in this example would be more than outweighed by the losses from shifting resources away from the other stage.

The important point in both these stylized examples is that there is a fundamental predictability in the resource allocation. Depending on the situation in question, the firm can plan the amount and direction of (i.e., increases or decreases in) resource allocation. Though actual profiles of optimal resource allocation vary with the circumstances that are being modeled, the same predictability will still be operative. As we argue below, this is not true in situations of interdependent learning.

3.2. Alliances with Only Private Benefits

Consider now the polar opposite: an alliance from which the partners can earn only private benefits. The firms set out to access each other's knowledge but there is no common purpose to which they expect this knowledge to be applied. Instead, each firm wishes to access the knowledge of the other in order to apply it to situations in which it can reap benefits that accrue only to it, and not to its partner. In such a situation, once one firm has learned enough from its partner, it has no incentive to continue to incur the costs of staying in the alliance (since there are no common benefits, which only accrue once both firms have finished learning, to continue to hold out for), and the firm will choose to terminate its involvement. Knowing this, each firm wishes to avoid being in the situation of being the laggard in the learning process; in effect, a situation of pure private benefits causes firms to race against each other.

We turn to the theory of technology races to shed some light on resource allocation in such situations of pure private benefits.[13] The general idea in this theory is that the first firm to finish the one or more stages that constitute the race gets a prize. This is a modeling abstraction for saying that the benefits of being ahead when the process ends are significantly greater than the benefits of being a laggard. Since this prize could be the award of a patent, this literature is often called the patent race literature. Each racing firm allocates resources to maximize its own expected profit at every stage. Typically, the firm's allocation affects the probability that it will move ahead in the race. The race ends when either participant finishes the several stages. Although the number of stages in the race is fixed, the length of time for which the race is in progress is endogenously determined by the realized patterns of resource allocation. In the context of alliances, the stages are abstractions for the learning steps that each partner must undergo in order to learn the skills of its alliance partner. The alliance ends when either partner has learned enough from the alliance and has begun earning private benefits. Since there are no forthcoming common benefits, it does not find it worthwhile to continue in the alliance.

To facilitate discussion, let us now focus on a two-stage race (a special case of the multistage situation above) with two firms. We will use a particular specification of such a race model to illustrate some general conclusions. It is certainly true that individual models of technology races rely on very specific assumptions. However, we want to emphasize that, although the particulars of the dynamics of a race remain closely tied to the specific assumptions in the model, none of our conclusions depend on these specific assumptions. Our conclusions are valid for any comparison between resource allocation under pure common benefits on the one hand and that under pure private benefits on the other.

Result 3. For the case where there is no overall budget for the project, the time profile for resource allocation is as shown in Figure 2 (Grossman and Shapiro, 1987).

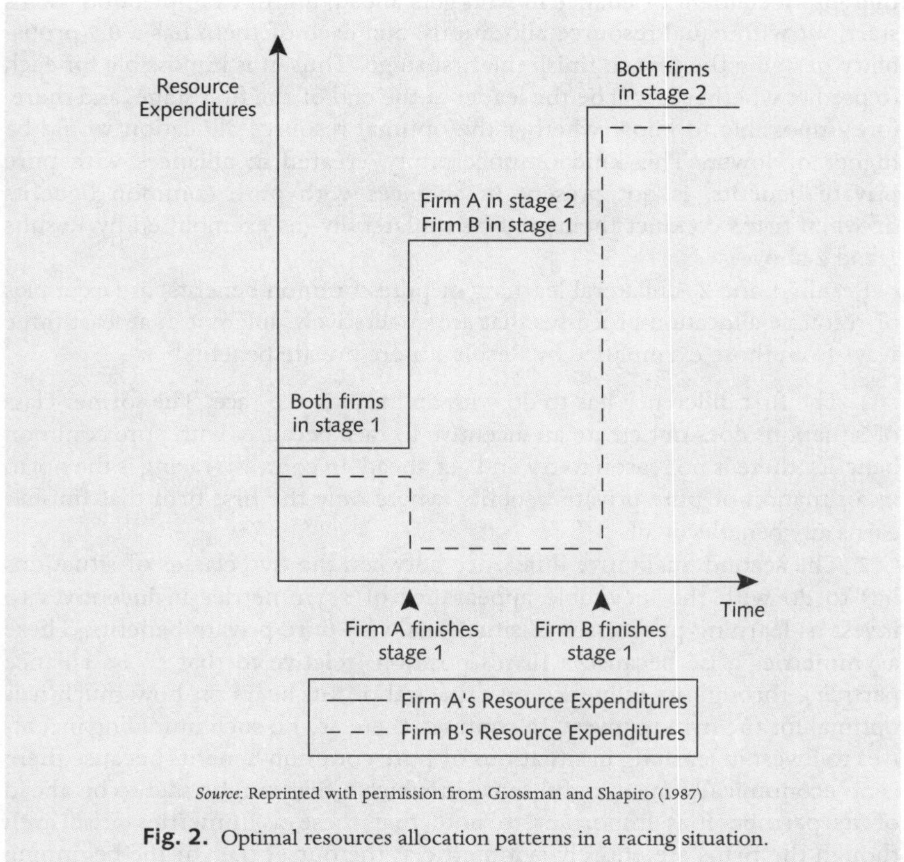

Source: Reprinted with permission from Grossman and Shapiro (1987)

Fig. 2. Optimal resources allocation patterns in a racing situation.

The firm that completes the first stage first increases its allocation (while its rival immediately lowers its allocation). If the lagging firm then finishes the first stage before the leading firm finishes the second stage (so that the firms are even again), then both firms alter their resource allocations as shown. To understand the intuition for this result, one has simply to realize that each firm's resource allocation is driven by its expected profit at each stage. Thus, the act of getting ahead causes a firm to raise its expectation of winning (i.e., of finishing the race ahead of its rival), and correspondingly causes it to increase its resource allocation. Conversely, the firm that falls behind revises downwards its expectation of winning, and thus its expected profit, and lowers its resource allocation.[14]

The dynamics of multistage races can be quite subtle (see, for example, Harris and Vickers, 1987), but the key point to note is that relative position in the race always plays a role in determining resource allocation.[15] Further, there is an element of chance in who gets ahead; in this example, both firms start out with equal resource allocations, and each of them has a 0.5 probability of being the first to finish the first stage. Thus, it is impossible for each to predict whether it will be the leader at the end of the first stage, and therefore impossible to know whether the optimal resource allocation would be higher or lower. This kind of uncertainty, created in alliances with pure private benefits, is not present in alliances with pure common benefits or when firms conduct their projects unilaterally (as exemplified by Results 1 and 2 above).

Results 1 and 2 (unilateral learning or pure common benefits) are examples of resource allocation processes that are qualitatively different in at least three ways from those exemplified by Result 3 (pure private benefits):

1. The first difference has to do with an incentive to race. The former class of situations does not create an incentive to race because, with pure common benefits, there is no reason to try and get ahead. In contrast, racing is the norm in a situation of pure private benefits, where only the first firm that finishes earns any benefits at all.

2. The second qualitative difference between the two classes of situations has to do with the inevitable appearance of asymmetries in incentives to invest as learning progresses in situations with pure private benefits. These asymmetries arise because a firm's position (relative to that of its alliance partner), through its influence on expected profit, bears on how much it is optimal for the firm to invest. In contrast, there are no such unfolding incentives to invest in learning in situations of pure common benefits because there is no economically meaningful sense in which a firm can be said to be ahead of its partner. It is important to note that these asymmetries arise even though the firms are entirely symmetric at the outset (i.e., at the beginning

of the learning process). Naturally, any models with *ex ante* asymmetries will retain the feature of *ex post* asymmetries in learning emerging with the evolution of the alliance.

3. The final difference has to do with an additional source of uncertainty in the case of pure private benefits. Neither firm can know in advance how its position will evolve and whether it will have to raise or lower its expectation of profits and thus its investments in learning. For an example, one has only to contrast the resource allocation predicted by Result 1 with that predicted by Result 3. In the first situation, a firm can predict that its resource allocation will rise systematically as the number of stages completed increases. However, in the latter context of a project with pure private benefits, there is no systematic *ex ante* method for a firm to predict the pattern of resource allocation. A reduction in resources allocated to an alliance may be a natural part of the learning dynamics in some situations with a high degree of private benefits. Again, note that this importance of relative position emerges even with no *ex ante* asymmetries between the partners.

Given these stark differences, we can conclude that pure private benefits create very different incentives to invest resources in learning than do pure common benefits.

3.3. Alliances with Private and Common Benefits

Most alliances clearly will not fall at the extremes of pure private benefits or pure common benefits. We have shown that racing behavior arises in the case of pure private benefits. Starting from a situation of pure private benefits, as the ratio of common to private benefit rises, the incentive to race is attenuated. To see this, recall that a firm raced out of fear of being locked out of receiving any benefits. This outcome could occur because the first firm to finish learning may find that it is earning enough from its private benefits to no longer justify expending resources to stay in the alliance for the prospective common benefits. To the extent that there is no incentive for the firm that is ahead to quit once it achieves its private benefits (because of the expectation of sufficient future common benefits), no such locking out of the laggard will occur, and there will be less incentive to race by any firm. Indeed, for any level of private benefits, there is a threshold level of common benefits above which it is optimal for the leading firm to choose not to terminate its involvement in the alliance once it begins to receive its private benefits, thus reducing the need to race in the first instance (Khanna, 1996a). Further, as the level of common benefits rises above this threshold and the situation of pure common benefits approaches, incentives to race are reduced, and the purely cooperative behavior of the pure common benefits situation is approached.

To summarize, the behavior patterns sketched out for pure common benefits on the one hand, and for pure private benefits on the other, represent extremes. Most alliances lie between these extremes; firms expect both private and common benefits, and exhibit behavior patterns that are an amalgam of those associated with the extremes. The lower the ratio of private to common benefits, the closer an alliance approximates pure cooperation and jointly profit-maximizing resource allocation, and the less the resource allocation differs from the optimal pattern under unilateral learning.

It is important to note that it is the ratio of a particular firm's private to common benefits that affects its decision to stay in or quit the alliance, as the firm in question compares its already existing private benefits to its potentially attainable common benefits in trying to decide whether to continue its involvement in the alliance. In contrast, the ratio of one firm's private benefits to the private benefits of its partner, or of one firm's common benefits to the common benefits of its partner, are not relevant to the individual firm's decision to continue in the alliance. Recall that this ratio of a firm's private to common benefits is determined by its relative scope. We have thus established that a firm's propensity to engage in competitive racing behavior in the context of a particular alliance may be related to activities of the firms that are not within the scope of the alliance. Further, since the firm's resource allocation at a point in time is determined by its expectations of forthcoming private and common benefits (conditional on its own estimation of its learning and that of its partner), we have effectively proposed a way of endogenizing the evolution of pay-off structures and of their effect on alliance dynamics.

3.4. *Some Notes on the Applicability of This Analysis*

3.4.1. On the Applicability of the Analysis to Learning Alliances

For a firm in a learning alliance to absorb skills from its partner requires it to continually allocate resources to the learning process. Implicitly, what we have in mind are skills that cannot be easily codified and transferred between partners through other means such as a licensing agreement. We also do not have much to say about alliances whose primary purpose is not learning (e.g., alliances formed to augment the partners' market power). In fact, it is important that each firm invests to learn from the other. To see this, consider a two-firm alliance in which only one firm, A, is learning from the other, B (and B is in the alliance for some other reason, such as financing a venture, or gaining market power). Now A does not have to fear that B will terminate the alliance after learning enough to earn private benefits. Consequently, A's learning, unaffected as it is by B's (nonexistent) resource allocations for learning, will effectively follow a pattern described by Results 1 and 2 (unilateral learning or learning with pure common benefits), rather than one closer to that described by Result 3 (learning with pure private benefits).

Although it is important that both firms invest in learning, it is not important that both earn private benefits. To see this, consider the following. If a firm has relative scope lower than '1' ($RS_{ij} < 1$), indicating that it can earn private benefits, it may not have an incentive to continue in the alliance once it has earned these private benefits (if the forthcoming common benefits are not sufficiently higher than the already earned private benefits to justify the additional costs of continuing in the alliance). Knowing this, any partner (of such a firm with $RS_{ij} < 1$) will race to avoid being in the situation where the alliance could terminate without its earning any benefits. This is true even if the partner's own relative scope measure is 1, that is, it has no possibility of earning private benefits. If both partners have relative scope values lower than '1', each has an incentive to race. Combining this analysis with the observation that racing behavior tends to be mutually reinforcing, we conjecture that racing is more likely to occur the greater the deviation of the number and extent of relative scope measures from 1.

Note that the learning being gained can be of a variety of sorts. It need not be restricted to R&D-related issues. For example, the type of knowledge being transferred could relate to understanding a particular customer base, understanding marketing in a new country, or learning the use of new production techniques.

Further, the precision with which the learning goals are known at the outset does not affect the tenor of the results. What is important is that there be an expectation of earning some kind of benefits, even if the source of these benefits is unclear. This condition is not overly restrictive because it is difficult to imagine firms entering into alliances with no expectations of benefits. Consider the case of pure private benefits where neither party knows exactly what it has set out to learn, but each has some expectation of earning private benefits (indeed, these form the reason for entering the alliance in the first instance). It is still true that if a firm's partner figures out ways of earning private benefits first, it might terminate the alliance. Thus, the earlier intuition that each firm would race in an effort to avoid being locked out of any benefits at all still applies.

3.4.2. On the Informational Assumptions Underlying the Analysis

The dynamics outlined above are interesting only if (a) there are stages of learning and (b) each firm is able to infer, at least to some extent, how far along its partner is in its own learning process. The stages are abstractions for milestone-like demarcation of the progress that firms go through in the learning process. Certainly, if the learning is truly a one-shot process (no stages), there is no opportunity to study the variations in the resources partners allocate to learning, and the dynamics are uninteresting. To see why situations where condition (b) is not satisfied are also uninteresting from the standpoint of understanding alliance dynamics, imagine that each firm had no idea how far along its rivals were. The dynamics that manifest themselves as changing resource allocation patterns arise from responses to new information regarding one's own progress or that of one's partner. If no new information is forthcoming about partner progress, then, at least for the purposes of resource allocation decisions, each firm might as well behave as though it were engaged in the project unilaterally. As we have seen above (Results 1 and 2), the resource allocation patterns in such circumstances are much more predictable.

Although we believe that the nature of the knowledge and skills (Nelson and Winter, 1982) being transferred is an important determinant of a firm's ability to infer how far along its partner is in its learning, clearly other factors are also at work. For example, Hamel (1991) suggested that additional factors determining 'transparency' include the social context surrounding the partners. Others discussed the importance of the emergence of trust as an alliance progresses (Ring and Van de Ven, 1992; Zajac and Olsen, 1993; Gulati, 1995a). Another influencing factor might be the degree to which a firm is attuned to happenings in the marketplace, as this might allow it to pick up signals about its partner's progress from the latter's attempts to realize private benefits.[16]

3.4.3. On the Existence of Asymmetries Between Firms

Our framework can accommodate a range of asymmetries between firms as long as these asymmetries can be understood in terms of the primitives of private and common benefits. Another way to express this is to say that various dimensions along which firms differ can be seen as parameters that affect the particular realization of each firm's private and common benefits (appropriately modified by the transferability factor and relative bargaining power discussed in a previous section). We focus on the analysis of symmetric firms above because it appears to be a sensible benchmark case.

Consider, for example, asymmetries in sizes between the alliance partners. *Ceteris paribus*, a larger firm might be expected to earn more private benefits as it has more markets to which it can apply its learning. A larger firm might also have greater bargaining power than its smaller partner (for reasons such as financial constraints which might limit the outside options of the smaller firm to a greater extent), thus enlarging its common benefits. Thus, large firms may stand to receive more private as well as common benefits. The ratio of private to common benefits might thus be larger or smaller for a larger firm than for its smaller partner.

In an alliance with pure private benefits, it is still the case that each firm has an incentive to race to ensure that the alliance is not terminated before it begins to earn private benefits. The observation that the two firms might earn different amounts of private benefits does not alter this conclusion, except in as much as one firm might have a greater incentive to race than the other. Similarly, for alliances that yield a mixture of private and common benefits, there would be a difference in the extent to which each firm had an incentive to race that would depend on the extent and nature of the asymmetry. As suggested earlier, what matters is not the relative amounts of private or common benefits that each firm earns, but the ratio of private to common benefits for each firm.

A particular class of asymmetries deserves special attention: that arising from different kinds of contractual agreements between firms. Although different contractual agreements may imply different optimal resource allocation patterns, these patterns (a) can be understood in terms of the effects of combinations of private and common benefits, and (b) will differ from those in a unilateral or purely cooperative learning mode. In particular, although the optimal resource allocation patterns will be different for an alliance between 'vertically' related firms than for those between 'horizontally' related firms (because the ratio of private to common benefits is likely to be different, *ceteris paribus*), both these optima will differ from the unilateral or purely cooperative learning optimum allocation. Similarly, the presence or absence of equity stakes between partners in alliances can alter private and common benefits in a variety of ways. Again, from the perspective of understanding the dynamics of resource allocations in learning alliances, what is important is that the apparatus of private and common benefits provides an appropriate analytical framework.[17]

3.4.4. On Changes in Model Assumptions

The primary conclusions of our analysis are not sensitive to the explicit assumptions used in the illustrative models above. We consider here the effects of changes in three very different classes of assumptions to demonstrate that this is so.

Consider the assumption made by some technology race models that, for each firm in the alliance, the probability of advancing from one stage to the next is not affected by rivals' resource allocations. In the context of alliances, this assumption implies that the probability that a firm will advance along its learning path is not affected by the allocation that its partner makes for its own learning. In particular, this implies that a laggard's propensity to reduce its allocation will not hamper the leader's ability to absorb part of its skill set. In some situations, this assumption will clearly not hold. For example, if reducing resource allocation amounts to holding back personnel or reducing the quality of personnel dedicated to the alliance, then the partner's ability to learn will be affected. In an augmented model, where the probability of a firm advancing through a stage is affected by the partner's resource allocation, we would still find that relative technological position plays a role in determining resource allocation. Thus the results would be different in detail, but similar in their flavor.

Similarly, our analysis does not assume that flow benefits are unimportant. Indeed, a plausible two-fold interpretation of the simple model of the situation with pure private benefits is as follows. First, some critical amount of learning must transpire before benefits begin to accrue. Second, the lump sum benefit that accrues to the winner of the race can be seen as an appropriately discounted present value of a stream of flow benefits. Thus, the model does not suggest that flow benefits are not important, but it does assume (reasonably) that some (time and resource) investment is required prior to the initial realization of these benefits.

Finally, the assumptions underlying the sequencing of private benefits and common benefits can be altered. Recall that private benefits were assumed to begin to accrue to a firm once it had completed some threshold level of learning, and that realizing common benefits presupposed that each of the firms had acquired such a threshold understanding. Hence the model's assumption that the realization of private benefits by a firm precedes both firms' realization of common benefits. However, the nature of the incentives to invest in learning created by private and common benefits remains unchanged regardless of the particular sequencing of the streams of private and common benefits. The prospect of future common benefits always creates an incentive for firms to continue in the alliance, while the prospect of private benefits, particularly without the lure of future common benefits, will always create the incentive to race. What is crucial to the model's logic is the idea that, as asymmetries in the learning process evolve, each firm continually evaluates whether staying in the alliance is worthwhile, and that the results of such an evaluation are contingent on the expectation of earning future private and common benefits.

3.5. Links to the Resource-Based View

Our framework provides a way to think about optimal resource allocation patterns in learning alliances and about how the incentives to invest in learning evolve, in a way that is robust enough to accommodate the particulars of a variety of situations. An important outcome of this analysis is that the optimal resource allocation profiles differ depending on the pattern of private and common benefits associated with a particular alliance.

It is reasonable to expect that firms develop organizational routines (Nelson and Winter, 1982) that are optimal for the pursuit of learning in the mode to which they are most accustomed. The same set of organizational routines might be optimal in situations of unilateral learning and of learning in alliances with pure common benefits. In contrast, since optimal resource allocation patterns are qualitatively different in alliances with pure private benefits, one might expect the optimal organizational routines to differ as well. One important dimension along which these routines might differ is their ability to deal with the greater uncertainty that accompanies learning in alliances with pure private benefits, and the associated greater need for flexibility of resource allocation in such alliances.[18]

A body of work on the resource-based view of the firm[19] suggests that such organizational routines are 'sticky' and inimitable. This inimitability may have several underlying causes: for example, it might be difficult for outsiders to infer what makes a particular routine work (Lippman and Rumelt, 1982), or the routine may simply require a long period of time to get established (Dierickx and Cool, 1989). Inability to rapidly adjust organizational routines provides a theoretical reason for believing that firms that have routines suited to unilateral learning will have trouble transitioning to learning in alliances with pure private benefits, as the latter require rather different types of routines. Thus firms that have not historically relied much on alliances might be expected to have trouble managing this mode of learning.

This provides a candidate explanation for suboptimal behavior in alliances if one assumes that firms making the transition from unilateral learning to learning alliances with private benefits do not sufficiently recognize the need to adapt to the new learning environment. This might happen if firms tend to think of the learning in an alliance as a stand-alone activity, as opposed to thinking of alliances as part of a portfolio of the firm's activities. The former framing does not direct attention to the private benefits that can arise from adapting the learning to markets outside the scope of the alliance, thus resulting in suboptimal behavior.

This motivates an empirically testable proposition regarding perceived departures from the purely cooperative behavior 'expected' in an alliance and the relative scope measures of the partners in the alliance. Our analysis suggests that more such departures (and, hence, more alliance failures) will occur the greater is the extent of the various partner firms' business in (product or geographic) markets not covered by the alliance. The importance of this empirically testable proposition lies in realizing that the extent to which a firm has an incentive to depart from cooperative behavior (and engage in the racing behavior described above) depends on characteristics of the firm that have little to do with the alliance in question. The opportunity set of each firm outside the particular alliance crucially affects its behavior within the alliance.

While most academic work has studied the individual alliance, recent studies have focused on the effect on an individual alliance of the past history of involvement between partners (Kogut, 1989; Ring and Van de Ven, 1992; Parkhe, 1993; Gulati, 1995a, 1995b). Instead of focusing on such intertemporal effects on the likelihood that a particular alliance will be formed, we seek to expand the scope of inquiry along a different dimension by focusing attention on the *overall patterns* of partner firms' business interests on firms' behavior *within* a particular alliance at any given point in time.

4. Suboptimal Behavior in Learning Alliances

Recognizing the nature of the economic incentives created by multistage learning races of the sort discussed here can help the partners in an alliance potentially avoid misunderstanding each other's intentions. The optimal strategic behavior suggested by the racing models described above requires managers to appreciate the simultaneously cooperative and competitive nature of alliances. Our models suggest that if firms view their relationship with others in the alliance as either strictly competitive or strictly cooperative, this may give rise to suboptimal outcomes for one or more firms in the alliance. We can anticipate three types of pathologies that might easily arise if firms deviate from the kind of strategic behavior proposed by our model. In the remainder of this section, we outline these three potential pathologies and draw upon research in behavioral decision theory to suggest why such suboptimal behavior might occur.[20]

We call the first pathology that might arise the 'three-legged fallacy'. In this situation, the partners fail to recognize that they are in a racing situation at all, and act as if their fates are inextricably tied. Thus, as opposed to the optimal scenario, both partners maintain their original resource commitments in each stage, neither stepping up nor reducing their resource allocations in response to their evolving learning asymmetries. This situation is graphically depicted in Fig. 3A. Notice that both firms A and B match each other's resource commitments in lock-step at every stage of the race, even though it would be to A's benefit to increase its allocation at the end of the first stage and it would be to B's benefit to reduce its allocation at the same time. By not following their optimal individual allocation strategies and remaining stuck in a pure cooperative frame, both firms end up not performing as well as they could.

The second pathology we might anticipate is called the 'reluctant loser.' In this scenario, the lagging partner fails to reduce its allocation, even though the leading partner has increased its allocation and seems likely to secure its private benefits. This situation can be graphically depicted as shown in Fig. 3B. As one can see, firm A, which has the learning advantage at the end of the first stage, has acted strategically and increased its resource allocation, but firm B, despite being behind, does not decrease its resource allocation as our model would suggest but instead maintains its original resource commitments. In these situations, the

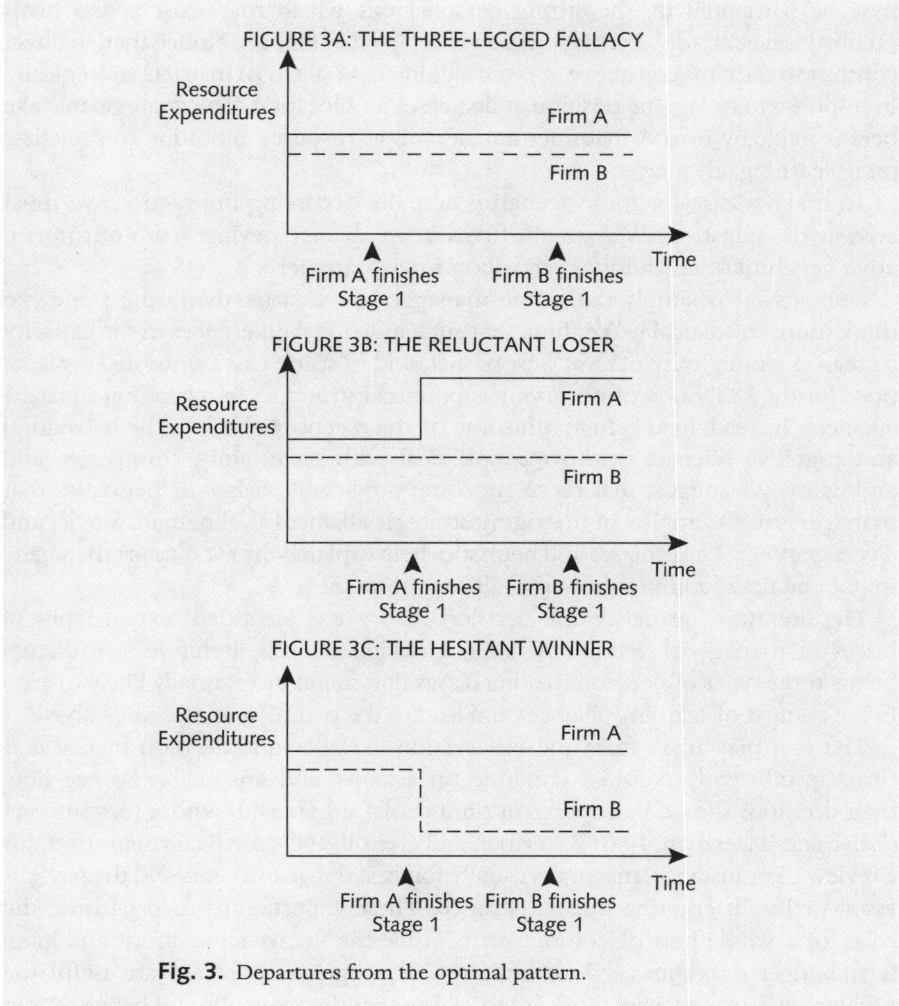

Fig. 3. Departures from the optimal pattern.

leading partner laughs all the way to the bank while the lagging partner is left shouting 'foul!'

The final pathology is called the 'hesitant winner.' In this situation, the leading partner fails to capitalize on its learning advantage, even though the lagging partner has reduced its resource commitments to the alliance. The leading partner's hesitation may arise for a variety of reasons. It may simply not recognize that it has a learning advantage, it may recognize its lead but fail to allocate the necessary additional resources, it may hesitate for fear of appearing to be opportunistic, or it may be hampered by the strong personal ties which may exist across firms (Tenbrunsel et al., 1997). This situation is depicted in Fig. 3C. Notice that, in direct contrast to the situation above, it is the lagging firm (Firm B) that acts strategically. In response to its lagging position, it decreases its allocation. The strategic mistake here is made by firm A that does not step up its resource allocation to capitalize on its learning advantage.

To make a case for these scenarios actually occurring in practice, we must answer the question: Why might firms in an alliance deviate from our normative benchmark and adopt such suboptimal strategies?

One answer is simply that some managers are smarter than others and can think more strategically. We think that such individual differences in the capacity to reason strategically offer at best partial, and in some cases spurious, explanations for the likelihood of observing suboptimal strategies in managing strategic alliances. Instead, in keeping with some of the recent research in the behavioral and cognitive sciences on how people deal with uncertainty, complexity, and ambiguity, we suggest that there are some predictable biases or heuristics that managers might employ in managing strategic alliances (Kahneman, Slovic, and Tversky, 1982). These biases and heuristics help explain why even smart managers might end up adopting suboptimal alliance strategies.

The literature on behavioral decision theory has identified several types of biases in managerial decision-making. Drawing on this literature, we discuss below three types of decision-making biases that might be especially likely to arise in the context of learning alliances and lead to the pathologies identified above.

The first bias arises from the observation in behavioral decision theory that firms insufficiently consider dynamic uncertainty and are unable to see how their decisions should be contingent on those of others with whom they interact (Zajac and Bazerman, 1991; Bazerman and Carroll, 1987; see Bazerman, 1993, for a review). For instance, managers usually forecast the investments and the pay-offs associated with entering into an alliance. These expectations then become the basis for a whole host of commitments inside the firm such as short- and long-term budgeted revenues and expenditures. Although such forecasts are useful, the problem is that managers often fail to realize that their pay-offs and hence proper resource allocation levels must be contingent on information that cannot be known in advance. Such information includes the relative speed at which the partners will learn each other's skills, the new opportunities for private benefits that present themselves as each side learns, and the changing opportunity cost of the resources allocated to the alliance. These costs are based on factors endogenous to (e.g., differential learning by the partners) and exogenous to (e.g., the success of other interdependent projects) the alliance. Even when there are no *ex ante* asymmetries between the partners, our models establish the role of uncertainty in ensuring that *ex post* asymmetries will naturally emerge. For optimal decision-making, the parties in a learning alliance must incorporate new information as it becomes available and revise their expectations and behaviors accordingly. However, behavioral decision theorists have observed that individuals are often incapable of incorporating evolving information in their decisions over time. They remain stuck in their original estimates and are thus incapable of displaying the flexibility suggested by the normative models we have discussed. Further, this may be exacerbated by the fact that some executives may seek only confirmatory evidence for what they think is initially true and neglect disconfirmatory evidence (Einhorn and Hogarth, 1978).

A second type of bias that can lead to the suboptimal scenarios we have outlined is the well-known 'anchoring' problem (Kahneman and Tversky, 1979). It has been widely documented that people often form judgments by adjusting from a well-known base case or 'anchor' without critically assessing whether the anchor is truly appropriate for the situation at hand. For instance, if a new product line typically earns $500,000 in the year of introduction for XYZ company, decision makers will bias the earnings estimates of any new product toward the anchor of $500,000. Moreover, it has been found that decision-makers do not easily adjust these anchors, even when confronted with information that suggests that the anchor is biased. Similarly, in alliance situations, we might expect managers to anchor their resource allocation estimates based on their experience with similar projects where they had previously worked alone. Alternatively, the anchor might be based on an alliance with a different ratio of private to common benefits. One can readily see the dangers of extrapolating from such anchors. As we have shown in the models above, the optimal resource allocation strategy when a firm is investing alone is very different from the optimal strategy when it is investing in an alliance. Indeed the optimal strategy even varies across alliances and depends on the ratio of private to common benefits in any alliance. In sum, we expect that managers will be susceptible to adopting suboptimal strategies in managing alliances if they remain anchored to models derived from their past experience. This bias is likely to be especially acute if the firm has had little experience with alliances in the past.

The third type of bias that can readily apply to the alliance situation is what is known as the 'framing' bias (Kahneman and Tversky, 1979). The best-known framing bias is the propensity for individuals to be risk-averse when choices are framed as gains but to be risk-seeking when choices are framed as losses. Experiments have shown that individuals will routinely choose a sure gain of $10 over a 50 percent chance to win $20, but will choose a 50 percent chance to lose $20 over a sure loss of $10. Similar framing effects have been shown to systematically influence choices in a variety of situations. Applying this observation to the context of alliances, we might expect biases from managers who frame the alliance in pure 'cooperative' or 'competitive' terms rather than in mixed motive terms. The importance of such relationship frames have also been documented by Sondak and Moore (1993), who found that it was hard for managers to recognize that situations could simultaneously be competitive and cooperative. They typically frame relationships as being either cooperative or competitive and are unwilling to consider that a firm may be both a competitor and a partner.

Given that alliances are typically framed as cooperative, their competitive aspects can often be neglected or even suppressed. Viewed from such a cooperative frame the kinds of strategic behavior suggested by our racing models can appear quite 'opportunistic' to those expecting loyalty and unwavering commitment from alliance partners. Indeed, the behavior recommended by the models may be seen as predatory acts of bad faith. One can easily see how such framing biases may lead to the kinds of pathologies we have described above.

A final behavioral bias may arise out of fairness considerations, which have been shown to be important in situations where there is a conflict between individual and collective interests (for reviews of research on social dilemmas see Messick and Brewer, 1983; Messick, 1991). For example, a faster-learning firm may believe that it is fair for it to behave in its own self-interest because it believes that it was implicitly understood by both firms that such a situation might occur, while the slower-learning firm expects equal commitments as fair and appropriate behavior. Firms who do not recognize the inevitable asymmetries that arise as learning alliances evolve tend to use their own behavior as information about how others will behave (Wade-Benzoni, Tenbrunsel, and Bazerman, 1996).

In addition to the above behavioral biases, it is important to point out one other factor that might further explain suboptimal behavior in the management of alliances. Alliances can also present thorny agency problems (Jensen and Meckling, 1976). Perhaps the most obvious agency problem is that managers assigned to an alliance can feel that their success hinges on the ongoing success of the alliance. Thus they might be reluctant to engage in actions that could lead to the termination of the alliance or even the reduction of resources available to the alliance. Indeed, instead of disinvesting when they are behind in the learning race, managers might display the behavior of the reluctant loser and get caught up in a syndrome of escalating commitment as they try and catch up and make the alliance succeed (Staw, 1981).

5. Conclusion

Our objective was to develop a general theoretical framework to advance our understanding of the dynamics of learning alliances. Toward this end, we introduced notions of private and common benefits and of relative scope. Alliances with different ratios of private and common benefits are likely to exhibit different optimal resource allocation patterns. In particular, we demonstrated that optimal behavior patterns differ between unilateral learning and learning in alliances, and that this divergence grows more pronounced the greater is the ratio of private to common benefits. This argument has implications for the kinds of alliances that particular firms enter, and for our understanding of how suboptimal behavior patterns might arise in practice. An important conclusion of our work is that the overall pattern of partner firms' activities plays an important role in understanding a firm's behavior within a particular alliance.

We took as given the private and common benefits associated with a particular alliance. In fact, since the scope of an alliance influences private and common benefits, and since the scope of the alliance is at least partially a choice of variables that the partner firms must agree on, these benefits are at least partly endogenous (Khanna, 1996b). Therefore, a question of great interest is understanding how firms can structure alliances to optimally configure the combinations of private and common benefits and thereby affect alliance evolution.[21] More generally, the overall question of structuring alliances (Ring and Van den Ven, 1992) deserves greater attention. Empirical work that operationalizes the notion of relative scope, and, more generally, takes into account that alliances are but one organizational means for shaping the boundaries of the firm, also appears to us to be important. Some recent evidence seems to suggest that such an empirical inquiry might indeed be fruitful.[22]

The methodological contribution that this paper makes is to think about alliances in terms of their pay-off structures (Gulati, et al., 1994; Parkhe, 1993). At each point, the optimal decision by each partner is a function of its expected pay-off given not only its own accomplishments up to that point, but also those of its partners in the alliance. Since these expected pay-offs change as the alliance unfolds, the incentives to continue to invest in the alliance change as well. It follows that there is an element of uncertainty in the optimal resource allocation pattern, and it behooves participants to recognize this uncertainty up-front and to organize for it to the extent possible. Such issues of understanding the process by which an alliance evolves merit further theoretical and empirical attention (Zajac and Olsen, 1993; Mody, 1993; Nakamura, Shaver, and Yeung, 1996).

Notes

1. In an in-depth study of 59 alliances, Bleeke and Ernst (1991) reported that, in about half the cases, at least one of the partners felt that the alliance had been a failure. Other studies have reported failure rates as high as 80 percent, usually leading to the

dissolution of the alliance or acquisition by one of the partners (Geringer and Hebert, 1991; Kogut, 1989; Harrigan, 1988; Auster, 1986).

2. Hamel (1991) also studies how a collaboration arrangement may lead to a 'reapportionment of skills between the partners' and suggests that the three broad determinants of the interfirm learning that causes this reapportionment are intent, transparency, and receptivity. Here, 'intent' relates to a firm's desire to use the alliance as a learning arena, 'transparency' to the openness of each firm in the alliance, and 'receptivity' to each firm's ability to learn from its partners. While these factors are undoubtedly important, they do not shed light on our understanding of alliance dynamics.
3. In two-firm agreements, a particular benefit stream is either completely common, when it accrues to both firms, or completely private, when it accrues to one or the other. With multifirm agreements, benefits accruing to subsets of firms are partially private (in the sense of not accruing to all firms) and partially common (in the sense of accruing to more than one firm).
4. Strictly speaking, if the firm plans to enter new markets other than the ones targeted by the alliance, then these should be included within the total set of markets that the firm is involved in. This is because private benefits will be earned by the firm's application of learning to these new markets as well.
5. If one assumes that there has to be some overlap in interests for an alliance to be meaningful, then a value of exactly 0 is never actually attained.
6. Cohen and Levinthal (1990) refer to a firm's 'absorptive capacity' as being related to its ability to acquire know-how from other firms.
7. A simple numerical example is illustrative. Suppose firm A is in markets 1 and 2, firm B in markets 2 and 3, and an alliance between A and B is targeted towards market 2. Then firm A's relative scope is the ratio of its size (as measured, say, by sales or assets) in market 2 to its total size (in markets 1 and 2). Firm A earns private benefits from 1 and common benefits from 2. Similarly, firm B's relative scope is the ratio of its size in market 2 to its total size (in markets 2 and 3). Firm B earns private benefits from 3 and common benefits from 2.
8. This is an abstraction for saying that both firms must advance their understanding of each other's knowledge bases before any meaningful synthesis can occur and thus generate common benefits. Later in the section, we consider various relaxations of the stylized models.
9. Our notion of optimality derives from that traditionally used in noncooperative game-theoretic models, i.e., in equilibrium, the resource allocation patterns are optimal for each firm, given the decisions made by the other.
10. There is a very limited literature on what happens when firms earn flow profits as the stages progress, and not just when all the stages are complete. One example is provided by Dutta (1992).
11. Technically, one can think of the distinction between the two cases in terms of cost curves for the factor input in question. Then Result 1 corresponds to a cost curve that is flat or only slightly increasing as a function of the quantity of resource demanded, while Result 2 corresponds to a cost curve that is flat up to a point and then rises very sharply thereafter (corresponding to an infinite cost of using resources in excess of the capacity constraint).

12. Additionally, if there is uncertainty about the size of the prize to be earned when the multistage process is completed, the passage of stages may provide information about how good the project is. The extreme situations would correspond to (a) getting bad news as the stages progressed and eventually dropping out and (b) getting good news and thereby increasing resource expenditures. Under some assumptions about the nature of this uncertainty, firms that choose not to drop out will increase their resource expenditure with the passage of stages.
13. Reinganum (1989) offers a review of the theoretical literature. Khanna (1995) offers an application to the mainframe computer industry.
14. There are actually two conflicting forces acting on each of the leader and follower, described in Grossman and Shapiro (1987). Briefly, the authors show that a 'pure progress effect' causes the leader to increase its resource allocation. However, a 'diminished rivalry effect' (due to the follower reducing its allocation) causes the leader to lower its resource allocation. Simulations indicate that the former effect typically dominates. For the follower, the fact that its rival is more likely to finish and win the prize first means that its expected prize has fallen, and this causes it to lower its resource allocation. On the other hand, the fact that its rival has increased its resource allocation causes it to want to step up its own. For most parameter values for which the simulation is conducted, the first effect again dominates.
15. This is not to say that 'absolute' position does not matter. For example, in the two-stage race described above, the resource expenditure levels when both firms are still finishing the first stage are quite different from those when both firms are finishing their second stage. Thus, in this comparison, though their relative position is the same, their absolute position is different and their resource expenditure patterns vary.
16. A theoretical issue that we do not address here is whether a firm has an incentive to reveal to its partner(s), in situations where the progression through the stages is not transparent enough, the extent to which it has progressed in an attempt to influence their resource allocations. It is easy to come up with some examples where a firm would have an incentive to reveal its position to its partners as well as examples where it would not.
17. Studies of the determinants of the contractual form of an alliance are usually rooted in transaction cost analysis (see, for example, Pisano, Russo, and Teece, 1988). As others have noted (Zajac and Olsen, 1993), such studies are static in nature and are less appropriate for understanding the dynamics within alliances.
18. Indeed, Bleeke and Ernst (1991), in their study of 59 alliances, found that one of the critical success factors for alliances was the ability of the partners to be flexible. The idea that routines might evolve to support the management of particular types of alliances also seems to find some support in the fieldwork reported in Lyles (1987). In this work, the notion of experience at running joint ventures shows up quite clearly, as does the idea that firms commonly make mistakes in understanding the nature of technology transfer, learning, and the development of partner skills.
19. Examples of work on this theory include, but are not limited to, Wernerfelt (1984), Barney (1991), Conner (1991), and Peteraf (1993).
20. While we do not have much to say about the persistence of suboptimal behavior, we note that while there is some evidence, in different contexts, of firms learning from

feedback (Kagel and Levin, 1986), others have suggested that learning is difficult in the common situation of insufficient timely feedback (Tversky and Kahneman, 1986).

21. It is worth reiterating that this chapter has not arrived at any conclusions regarding the particular combinations of private and common benefits that would be optimal for a particular alliance. In the simple model outlined in a previous section, waiting to attain common benefits is certainly a plus, but the firm that is further along toward accomplishing its own learning goals must trade these potentially increased benefits off against the cost of continuing to participate in the alliance. In equilibrium, firms will take this into account before the alliance entry decision. The point is that it is not *a priori* clear that alliances in which common benefits are attained in equilibrium are necessarily better than those in which they are not.
22. Bleeke and Ernst (1991) discuss the overlap of partner activities in the context of acquisitions and joint ventures. Park and Russo (1996) recently documented that a joint venture between direct competitors is more likely to fail than one in which the partners do not compete, suggesting at a minimum, in the language of our paper, that joint ventures with different levels of private benefits might behave quite differently.

References

Anderson, E. (1990). 'Two firms, one frontier: On assessing joint venture performance', *Sloan Management Review*, **31**(2), pp. 19–30.

Auster, E. R. (1986). 'International corporate linkages: Dynamic forms in changing environments', *Academy of Management Review*, **8**, pp. 567–587.

Barney, J. (1991). 'Firm resources and sustained competitive advantage', *Journal of Management*, **17**, pp. 99–120.

Bazerman, M. (1993). *Judgement in Managerial Decision Making* (3rd ed.). Wiley, New York.

—— and Carroll, J. (1987). 'Negotiator cognition'. In B. M. Staw and L. L. Cummings (eds.), *Research in Organizational Behavior*, Vol. 9. JAI Press, Greenwich, CT, pp. 247–288.

Bleeke J. and Ernst, D. (1991). 'The way to win in cross-border alliances', *Harvard Business Review*, **69**(6), pp. 127–135.

Cohen, W. and Levinthal, D. (1990). 'Absorptive capacity: A new perspective on learning and innovation', *Administrative Science Quarterly*, **35**, pp. 128–152.

Conner, K. (1991). 'A historical comparison of resource-based theory and five schools of thought within industrial organization: Do we have a new theory of the firm?', *Journal of Management*, **17**, pp. 121–154.

Dierickx, I. and Cool, K. (1989). 'Asset stock accumulation and sustainability of competitive advantage', *Management Science*, **35**(12), pp. 1504–1515.

Dutta, P. (1992). 'Optimal management of an R&D budget', mimeograph, Columbia University, Department of Economics.

Einhorn, H. J. and Hogarth, R. M. (1978). 'Confidence in judgment: Persistence in the illusion of validity', *Psychological Review*, **85**, pp. 395–416.

Geringer, J. M. and Hebert, L. (1991). 'Measuring performance of international joint ventures', *Journal of International Business Studies*, **22**, pp. 249–264.

Grossman, G. and Shapiro, C. (1986). 'Optimal dynamic R&D programs', *Rand Journal of Economics*, **17**(4), pp. 581–593.

—— and —— (1987). 'Dynamic R&D competition', *Economic Journal*, **97**, pp. 372–387.

Gulati, R. (1995a). 'Does familiarity breed trust? The implications of repeated ties for contractual choice in alliances', *Academy of Management Journal*, **30**(1), pp. 85–112.

—— (1995b). 'Social structure and alliance formation patterns: A longitudinal analysis', *Administrative Science Quarterly*, **40**, pp. 619–652.

—— Khanna, T. and Nohria, N. (1994). 'Unilateral commitments and the importance of process in alliances', *Sloan Management Review*, **35**(3), pp. 61–70.

Hamel, G. (1991). 'Competition for competence and inter-partner learning within international strategic alliances', *Strategic Management Journal*, Summer Special Issue, **12**, pp. 83–103.

—— Doz, Y. and Prahalad, C. (1989). 'Collaborate with your competitors and win', *Harvard Business Review*, **67**(1), pp. 133–139.

Harrigan, K. R. (1988). 'Strategic alliances and partner asymmetries'. In F. Contractor and P. Lorange (eds.), *Cooperative Strategies in International Business*. Lexington Books, Lexington, MA.

Harris, C. and Vickers, J. (1987). 'Racing with uncertainty', *Review of Economic Studies*, **LIV**, pp. 1–21.

Hergert, M. and Morris, D. (1988). 'Trends in international collaborative agreements'. In F. Contractor and P. Lorange (eds.), *Cooperative Strategies in International Business*. Lexington Books, Lexington, MA, pp. 99–109.

Hladik, K. (1985). *International Joint Ventures: An Economic Analysis of U.S.–Foreign Business Partnerships*. Lexington Books, Lexington, MA.

Jensen, M. and Meckling, W. (1976). 'Theory of the firm: Managerial behavior, agency costs, and ownership structure', *Journal of Financial Economics*, **3**, pp. 305–360.

Kagel, J. and Levin, D. (1986). 'The winner's curse and public information in common value auctions', *American Economic Review*, **76**, pp. 894–920.

Kahneman, D., Slovic, P. and Tversky, A. (1982). *Judgement under Uncertainty: Heuristics and Biases*. Cambridge University Press, New York.

—— and Tversky, A. (1979). 'Prospect theory: Analysis of decisions under uncertainty', *Econometrica*, **47**, pp. 263–291.

Khanna, T. (1995). 'Racing behavior: Technological evolution in the high-end computer industry', *Research Policy*, **24**, pp. 933–958.

—— (1996a). 'Winner-take-all alliances', Harvard Business School working paper #96–033.

—— (1996b). 'The scope of alliances', paper presented at Organization Science Conference, INSEAD.

Kogut, B. (1988). 'Joint ventures: Theoretical and empirical perspectives', *Strategic Management Journal*, **9**(4), pp. 319–332.

—— (1989). 'The stability of joint ventures: Reciprocity and competitive rivalry', *Journal of Industrial Economics*, **XXXVIII**, pp. 183–198.

Lippman, S. and Rumelt, R. (1982). 'Uncertain imitability: Analysis of interfirm differences in efficiency under competition', *Bell Journal of Economics*, **13**, pp. 363–380.

Lyles, M. (1987). 'Common mistakes of joint venture experienced firms', *Columbia Journal of World Business*, Summer, pp. 79–85.

Messick, D. M. (1991). 'Equality as decision heuristic'. In B. Mellers (ed.), *Psychological Issues in Distributive Justice*. Cambridge University Press, New York.

——and Brewer, M. B. (1983). 'Solving social dilemmas: A review'. In L. Wheeler and P. Shaver (eds.), *Review of Personality and Social Psychology*, Vol. 4. Sage, Beverly Hills, CA, pp. 11–44.

Mody, A. (1993). 'Learning through alliances', *Journal of Economic Behavior and Organization*, **20**, pp. 151–170.

Nakamura, M., Shaver, J. M. and Yeung, B. (1996). 'An empirical investigation of joint venture dynamics: Evidence from U.S.–Japan joint ventures', *International Journal of Industrial Organization*, **14**, pp. 521–541.

Nelson, R. and Winter, S. (1982). *An Evolutionary Theory of Economic Change*. Belknap Press, Cambridge, MA.

Park, S. and Russo, M. (1996). 'When competition eclipses cooperation: An event history analysis of joint venture failure', *Management Science*, **42**(6), pp. 875–890.

Parkhe, A. (1993). 'Strategic alliance structuring: A game theoretic and transaction cost examination of interfirm cooperation', *Academy of Management Journal*, **36**(4), pp. 794–829.

Peteraf, M. (1993). 'The cornerstones of competitive advantage: A resource-based view', *Strategic Management Journal*, **14**(3), pp. 179–191.

Pisano, G., Russo, M. and Teece, D. (1988). 'Joint ventures and collaborative agreements in the telecommunications equipment industry'. In D. Mowery (ed.), *International Collaborative Ventures in U.S. Manufacturing*. Ballinger, Cambridge, MA, pp. 23–70.

Reinganum, J. (1989). 'The timing of innovation'. In R. Schmalansee and R. D. Willig (eds.), *Handbook of Industrial Organization*. North-Holland, New York, pp. 849–908.

Ring, P. and Van de Ven, A. (1992). 'Structuring cooperative relationships between organizations', *Strategic Management Journal*, **13**(7), pp. 483–498.

Sondak, H. and Moore, M. C. (1993). 'Relationship frames and cooperation', *Group Decision and Negotiation*, **2**, pp. 103–118.

Staw, B. M. (1981). 'The escalation of commitment to a course of action', *Academy of Management Review*, **6**, pp. 577–587.

Tenbrunsel, A., Wade-Benzoni, K., Moag, J. and Bazerman, M. H. (1997). 'The costs of strong-tie relationships in the selection of negotiation partners', Kellogg Graduate School of Management working paper, Northwestern University.

Tversky, A. and Kahneman, D. (1986). 'Rational choice and the framing of decisions', *Journal of Business*, **59**, pp. 251–284.

Wade-Benzoni, K. A., Tenbrunsel, A. E. and Bazerman, M. H. (1996). 'Egocentric interpretations of fairness in asymmetric, environmental social dilemmas: Explaining harvesting behavior and the role of communication', *Organizational Behavior and Human Decision Processes*, **6**(2), pp. 111–126.

Wernerfelt, B. (1984). 'A resource based view of the firm', *Strategic Management Journal*, **5**(2), pp. 171–180.

Zajac, E. and Bazerman, M. (1991). 'Blind spots in industry and competitor analysis: Implications of interfirm (mis)perceptions for strategic decisions', *Academy of Management Review*, **16**(1), pp. 37–56.

Zajac, E. and Olsen, C. (1993). 'From transaction cost to transactional value analysis: Implications for the study of interorganizational strategies', *Journal of Management Studies*, **30**(1), pp. 132–145.

13 Working Abroad, Working with Others: How Firms Learn to Operate International Joint Ventures

Harry G. Barkema, Oded Shenkar, Freek Vermeulen, and John H. J. Bell

International joint ventures have become a prevalent mode of entry into global markets (Berg, Duncan, and Friedman, 1982; Harrigan, 1985; Hergert and Morris, 1988; Wysocki, 1990). Publications on the topic mostly focus on the motivations behind international joint venture formation (Buckley and Casson, 1988; Contractor and Lorange, 1988; Harrigan, 1985; Hennart, 1988; Hergert and Morris, 1988; Kogut, 1988) and the conditions encouraging it (Agarwal and Ramaswami, 1992; Gatignon and Anderson, 1988; Gomes-Casseres, 1989; Hennart, 1991; Madhok, 1997; Stopford and Wells, 1972). Little has been done, however, to identify the factors that underlie success and failure in such ventures; this is a remarkable omission, given their high failure rate (Chowdhury, 1992; Gomes-Casseres, 1987; Hill and Hellriegel, 1994; Levine and Byrne, 1986). To the extent that international joint venture failure is studied, explanations have been confined to one area, namely, lack of the skills needed to manage affiliates dispersed in unfamiliar foreign environments (Buckley and Casson, 1988). To be successful in operating joint undertakings, however, firms also need to master sharing ownership with a partner whose interests only partially overlap with their own (Shenkar and Zeira, 1987).

The present research examined the two sets of skills within an evolutionary perspective, to explain how firms learn to handle international joint ventures. Hypotheses were derived from organizational learning theory (Cohen and Levinthal, 1990; Cyert and March, 1963) to indicate learning stemming from experience with international wholly owned subsidiaries, with domestic joint ventures, and with previous international joint ventures. Data on 1,493 domestic and international expansions of twenty-five Dutch multinationals from 1966 to 1994 allowed for a longitudinal examination of learning paths and their implications for international joint venture longevity.

1. Theory and Hypotheses

According to organizational learning theory, prior learning facilitates the learning and application of new, related knowledge (Cohen and Levinthal, 1989, 1990, 1994). This idea can be extended to include the case in which the knowledge in question is itself a set of learning skills constituting a firm's absorptive capacity. This capacity increases incrementally as a function of the previous experience of the firm and its learning processes. In the foreign entry literature, advocates of the internationalization process school, or the Uppsala stage model (Johanson and Vahlne, 1977), have argued that firms expand slowly from their domestic bases into progressively distant areas. Experiential learning from previous entries is the driving force behind new investments (Barkema, Bell, and Pennings, 1996; Davidson, 1983; Denis and Depelteau, 1985; Johanson and Wiedersheim-Paul, 1975; Luostarinen, 1980). The internationalization process approach focuses, however, on the early steps in the internationalization process, ignoring the investment mode chosen (Kogut and Singh, 1988).

To successfully cross national boundaries, a firm must develop information processing and control capabilities so as to coordinate activities across diverse environments, and it must develop the skills of tuning into and interpreting strategic signals specific to a foreign environment. In this process, firms unlearn practices typical of their home countries (cf. Bettis and Prahalad, 1995; Hedberg, 1981; Lewin, 1947; McGill and Slocum, 1993; Prahalad and Bettis, 1986).

The complexities of working abroad are encountered not only in international joint ventures, but also in international wholly owned subsidiaries. Such subsidiaries offer firms the opportunity to learn to operate in a foreign environment incrementally, without having to simultaneously adapt to a foreign partner, thus facilitating an effective learning experience allowing for later success. Hence,

Hypothesis 1. The longevity of an international joint venture increases with the international wholly owned subsidiary experience of the firm investing abroad.

One key challenge for firms operating abroad is bridging the distance to the host culture. Cultural distance has been defined as "the sum of factors creating, on the one hand, a need for knowledge, and on the other hand, barriers to knowledge flow and hence also for other flows between the home and the target countries" (Luostarinen, 1980: 131–132). It has often been cited as a factor in firms' choice of less committed entry modes (Root, 1987), specifically, their preference for joint ventures over wholly owned subsidiaries (e.g. Agarwal, 1994; Bell, 1996; Bell, Barkema, and Verbeke, 1997; Cho and Padmanabhan, 1995; Erramilli, 1991; Erramilli and Rao, 1993; Kogut and Singh, 1988; Larimo, 1993; Padmanabhan and Cho, 1996). Anderson and Gatignon (1986) noted that cultural distance caused foreign investors to avoid full ownership because distance increases information costs and difficulty in transferring management skills (Buckley and Casson, 1976; Vachani, 1991). Cultural distance adversely affects international joint ventures by eroding the applicability of the parent's competencies (Johanson and Vahlne, 1977; cf. Brown, Rugman, and Verbeke, 1989; Chowdhury, 1992; Gomes-Casseres, 1989; Harrigan, 1985, 1988; Hergert and Morris, 1988; Lorange and Roos, 1991; Parkhe, 1991). Woodcock and Geringer (1991) argued that cultural differences produce inefficient principal-agent contracts, and Li and Guisinger (1991) found that U.S. affiliates whose partners came from culturally dissimilar countries were more likely to fail. Thus,

Hypothesis 2. The longevity of an international joint venture decreases with the cultural distance between the country of the firm investing abroad and the host country.

The need to select a partner and to cooperate and share control with the partner is a major source of complexity in joint ventures. Schaan and Beamish (1988) described the "subtle balancing act" that operating joint ventures requires. Officers at Otis, a company whose foreign venturing dates back to the 19th century, consider their firm's ability to quickly select partners and work effectively with them to be a key competitive advantage (Ingrassia, Naji, and Rosett, 1995). According to the chairman of Corning Glass, partnering skills include "the ability to cope with the constant compromise and give-and-take that successful joint ventures require" and the ability, when necessary, to "sit back and let someone else be in the driver's seat" (Mitchell, 1988). The capacity to work with others can be learned, however, not only from previous international joint ventures, but also from previous domestic joint ventures.

That knowledge relevant to the operation of international joint ventures can be gained from domestic joint ventures is a crucial yet neglected possibility. Since the international joint venture literature is largely a product of the broader domain of international business, such ventures have been juxtaposed with other forms of foreign direct investment but not with their domestic counterparts. Yet the two joint venture types have much in common in that both facilitate the learning of partnering skills. Furthermore, domestic venturing allows a firm to learn how to cooperate without simultaneously having to deal with the complexity of a foreign environment. Thus, domestic joint ventures, like international wholly owned subsidiaries, can be a stepping stone from which to launch international joint ventures. Hence,

Hypothesis 3. The longevity of an international joint venture increases with the previous domestic joint venture experience of the partner investing abroad.

That firms learn about international joint ventures from their previous experience with such ventures seems compelling—the experience entails exposure to both international and partnership activities. International joint venture experience has been found to increase firms' propensity to set up new ventures (Madhok, 1997), to improve their understanding of this vehicle (Lyles, 1987, 1988), and to enhance the performance of the investing firms (Mitchell, Shaver, and Yeung, 1994) and of the investment vehicles themselves (Li, 1995). An incremental approach implies, however, that learning both partnership and boundary-crossing skills at the same time may be a task that exceeds the absorptive capacity of naive entrants who lack both types of skills. Still, we offer the following hypothesis:

Hypothesis 4. The longevity of an international joint venture increases with the previous international joint venture experience of the firm investing abroad.

2. Methods

2.1. *Sample*

Hypotheses were tested on data on all expansions reported in the annual reports of a sample of Dutch firms between 1966 and 1994. This sample comprised the 25 largest[1] Dutch companies but excluded the 4 largest (Royal Dutch, Unilever, Philips, and Akzo), which are a distinctive group in terms of their breadth of activities, international experience, scope, and size. Totals of national and international expansions during the period were 596 and 897, respectively. Of the international expansions, 244 were joint ventures.

2.2. *Variables*

2.2.1. *Longevity*

Following earlier research (Barkema et al., 1996; Carroll, Preisendorfer, Swaminathan, and Wiedermayer, 1993; Carroll and Swaminathan, 1991; Chowdhury, 1992; Li, 1995; Pennings, Barkema, and Douma, 1994), we used longevity as the independent variable. Although it is not a perfect performance measure, previous studies have shown that longevity provides the best estimate of managers' perceptions of the success of an expansion (Geringer and Hebert, 1991) and that it correlates with financial performance (Mitchell, 1994). Longevity was defined as the number of years a venture persisted.[2]

2.2.2. Cultural Distance

Cultural distance to the host country from the Netherlands was measured with Kogut and Singh's (1988) index. This index is an aggregate of the four dimensions of culture outlined in Hofstede (1980), and has been used often in studies of foreign entry (Agarwal and Ramaswami, 1992; Benito and Gripsrud, 1992; Cho and Padmanabhan, 1995).[3] Cultural difference scores unavailable from Hofstede's published work (1980, 1991) were obtained via personal communication with that author.

2.2.3. Experience

Experience with each of four types of affiliation—international joint venture, domestic joint venture, international wholly owned subsidiary, and domestic wholly owned subsidiary—was measured as the number of previous such affiliates a firm had had by the time of a new affiliate's founding.

2.2.4. Control Variables

To mitigate potential omitted-variable problems, we controlled for experience with domestic wholly owned subsidiaries.[4] In addition, the following time-variant control variables were used: The logarithm of the assets of a firm in the year of an international joint venture's founding served as a proxy for firm size. The return on equity of the firm in that year was used as a proxy for firm profitability. We also controlled for the gross national product per capita of the host countries. Table 1 presents summary statistics on these and other variables.

2.3. Analysis

Analysis was done with LIFEREG, an event-history analysis method (SAS Institute 1988). The model used is based on an assumed accelerated failure-time with a Weibull distribution. The analysis entailed the exploration of whether the hazard rate of ventures (the converse of the survival rate) varies with the amount and type of a firm's experience. For example, a negative coefficient associated with domestic joint venture experience implies that international joint ventures dissolve more slowly if the firm investing abroad has previous experience with domestic joint ventures.

Table 1. Means, Standard Deviations, and Correlations[a]

Variable	Mean	s.d.	1	2	3	4	5	6	7
1. International joint venture experience	7.15	6.29							
2. Domestic joint venture experience	3.52	4.67	.25						
3. International wholly owned subsidiary experience	13.05	12.61	.50	.34					
4. Domestic wholly owned subsidiary experience	10.79	10.35	.23	.42	.60				
5. Cultural distance	3.04	1.25	.09	.06	.07	−.12			
6. Assets[b]	13.65	1.27	.50	.57	.15	.27	−.05		
7. Return on equity	0.11	0.12	−.20	−.17	.20	.28	−.01	−.23	
8. Gross national product	8.52	6.00	−.03	.21	.18	.37	−.27	.17	.14

[a] $N = 244$. Correlations with absolute values greater than .13 are significant at $p < .05$.
[b] Value is a logarithm.

3. Results

Hypotheses 1 and 3 predict that international joint venture longevity increases with the experience of the firm that is investing abroad with international wholly owned subsidiaries and domestic joint ventures, respectively. Table 2 (model 1) shows that both effects are in the expected direction.

The effects of both international wholly owned subsidiary experience and domestic joint venture experience are significant ($p < .05$ and $p < .10$, respectively). Since we predicted that experience with either international wholly owned subsidiaries or domestic joint ventures could be used as a stepping stone to success with international joint ventures, we also tested a version of the model that included the interaction between international wholly owned experience and domestic joint venture experience (see model 2). If either type of experience can be used as a stepping stone, a firm that already has experience with domestic joint ventures should benefit less from experience with international wholly owned subsidiaries, and vice versa. This observation implies that the interaction term (capturing firms' having both types of experience) and the two main effects should have opposite signs. The interaction term is indeed positive and significant ($p < .01$). The main effects of international wholly owned subsidiaries and domestic joint ventures become more significant in this model ($p < .001$) than they were in model 1. Support for the hypotheses

Table 2. Results of Event-History Analysis for Types of Experience[a]

Independent Variables	Model 1	Model 2
Intercept	0.87	0.59
	(1.15)	(1.22)
International joint venture experience	0.01	0.03
	(0.03)	(0.03)
Domestic joint venture experience	−0.05†	−0.19***
	(0.03)	(0.06)
International wholly owned subsidiary experience	−0.03*	−0.06***
	(0.02)	(0.02)
Domestic wholly owned subsidiary experience	0.01	−0.00
	(0.01)	(0.01)
Domestic joint venture × international wholly owned subsidiary experience		0.01**
		(0.00)
Cultural distance	0.12*	0.13*
	(0.07)	(0.07)
Assets[b]	0.14	0.18†
	(0.09)	(0.09)
Return on equity	1.55†	1.15
	(0.86)	(0.86)
Gross national product per capita	−0.01	−0.01
	(0.01)	(0.02)
Log likelihood	−195	−191

[a] Numbers in parentheses are standard deviations.
[b] Value is a logarithm.
† $p < .10$
* $p < .05$
** $p < .01$
*** $p < .001$

strengthens when the incremental nature of learning (that either type of experience can serve as a stepping stone) is recognized in the model.

Hypothesis 2 predicts that international joint venture longevity decreases with the cultural distance between foreign investor and host country. The results contained in model 1 show that the effect of cultural distance is significant and in the expected direction ($p < .05$).

Hypothesis 4, predicting that firms benefit from previous international joint ventures when launching new ones, was not supported (see Table 2). Apparently, the firms in our sample did not learn from their previous international joint venture experience.

3.1. *Product Diversification as a Moderator*

A key notion underlying this research is that firms can only absorb experience if it relates to what they already know (Cohen and Levinthal, 1990). International expansion paths need to be incremental to allow firms to interpret new experience and to foster learning. This statement suggests that a firm learns from experience with international wholly owned subsidiaries and with domestic joint ventures if the experience is related to the firm's knowledge base—if it is acquired in the same line of business as the firm's principal business (constituting horizontal expansion), or in a related line of business (related expansion), or up or down the value chain (vertical expansion). In contrast, expansion into an unrelated line of business may trigger information overload and make it

Table 3. Results of Event-History Analysis with Product Diversification as Moderator[a]

Independent Variables	Model 3
Intercept	0.46
	(1.37)
Unrelated international joint venture experience	0.02
	(0.09)
Related international joint venture experience	0.03
	(0.04)
Unrelated domestic joint venture experience	−0.13
	(0.13)
Related domestic joint venture experience	−0.20*
	(0.09)
Unrelated international wholly owned subsidiary experience	−0.07
	(0.12)
Related international wholly owned subsidiary experience	−0.05*
	(0.03)
Domestic wholly owned subsidiary experience	−0.00
	(0.01)
Unrelated domestic joint venture × international wholly owned subsidiary experience	−0.03 (0.12)
Unrelated domestic joint venture × related international wholly owned subsidiary experience	0.00 (0.01)
Related domestic joint venture × unrelated international wholly owned subsidiary experience	0.04 (0.09)
Related domestic joint venture × related international wholly owned subsidiary experience	0.02* (0.01)
Cultural distance	0.13*
	(0.07)
Assets[b]	0.18
	(0.10)
Return on equity	1.77
	(1.07)
Gross national product per capita	−0.01
	(0.02)
Log likelihood	−188

[a] Numbers in parentheses are standard deviations.
[b] Value is a logarithm.
* $p < .05$

difficult for a firm's key managers to interpret the experience and benefit from it when entering international joint ventures later.

The sampled firms' expansion experience was thus separated into (1) horizontal, related, and vertical expansions (cf. Pennings et al., 1994) and (2) unrelated expansions. Table 3 presents the estimation results, which show significant effects for both experience with international wholly owned subsidiaries and experience with domestic joint ventures in related businesses. The effects of previous experience in unrelated businesses are insignificant. The results are again consistent with an incremental learning approach.

3.2. *Sensitivity Analysis*

3.2.1. Firm-specific Effects

In view of Hitt, Harrison, Ireland, and Best's (1995) findings for mergers and acquisitions, we also considered learning effects at the individual firm level, using models with interactions between learning effects and dummy variables for firm. This procedure captured firm-specific learning gained from previous types of affiliation and applied to new international joint ventures. Not all 25 firms had engaged in all the affiliate types studied, so fewer than 25 interaction terms resulted for each type of learning effect. In addition, some interaction terms had to be removed from the models for reasons of multicollinearity. There remained 17 firm-specific effects of previous international wholly owned subsidiaries, 13 firm-specific effects of previous domestic joint ventures, and 16 firm-specific effects of previous international joint ventures. Of these effects, 11, 10, and 5, respectively, were significant and in the expected direction, mostly at the $p < .001$ level. The results suggest that most firms learned about international joint ventures from international wholly owned subsidiaries or domestic joint ventures and that some firms also learned from previous international joint ventures. A subsequent analysis suggested that firms did not learn from previous international joint ventures unless the latter experience was preceded by experience with either domestic joint ventures or with international wholly owned subsidiaries.[5] Finally, an exploratory analysis suggested that firms learned from failures rather than successes with international wholly owned subsidiaries, but this result was not obtained for domestic joint venture experience.

3.2.2. Shape of Experience Curves

To examine learning theory's assertion regarding decreasing marginal returns from experience (Yelle, 1979), we added quadratic terms of the experience variables to the linear effects. The quadratic effects were insignificant. We also estimated models that separated the experience with international wholly owned subsidiaries into two categories, experience with fewer than 10 international wholly owned subsidiaries, and experience with more than 10. We also estimated similar models for two categories of domestic joint venture experience and international joint venture experience, respectively. The analyses did not support the notion of decreasing returns to learning.[6] Learning about international joint ventures may be so complex that the experience curve had not leveled off yet for the firms studied, which were in their early decades of international expansion.

3.2.3. Hofstede's Dimensions

Culture is a complex phenomenon that embodies a host of values, beliefs, and norms, many of which are subtle, intangible, and difficult to measure. Interpretation of culture as a unidimensional, aggregate phenomenon, although popular in the foreign entry literature (e.g., Agarwal and Ramaswami, 1992), oversimplifies a complex construct (Shenkar and Zeira, 1992) and may explain the mixed results studies have yielded regarding the impact of cultural distance on foreign expansion (Benito and Gripsrud, 1992; Kogut and Singh, 1988; Madhok, 1997; Padmanabhan and Cho, 1996).

To take account of this complexity, we did some further analysis regarding Hofstede's conjectures about the different impacts of gaps between two cultures along his four dimensions. Hofstede (1989) suggested that although some cultural gaps were not very disruptive or were even complementary, differences between two cultures in uncertainty avoidance were potentially very problematic for international cooperation because of correlated differences in tolerance toward risk, formalization, and the like. An uncertainty avoidance gap is likely to be detrimental to international joint venture operation because uncertainty is an inherent characteristic of operating in a foreign environment and because such a gap implies contrasting expectations regarding the predictability of partner behavior, also a key issue in international joint ventures. Indeed, the results show a significant effect for uncertainty avoidance (0.19, $p < .01$) but not for the other dimensions.[7]

3.2.4. Developed versus Developing Countries

Experience with international wholly owned subsidiaries in developed countries may be less useful when applied to joint ventures in developing countries, and vice versa. Hence, experience with international wholly owned subsidiaries was separated into experience in developed countries (Ronen and Shenkar's [1985] Nordic, Germanic, Anglo, and Latin European blocs) and in developing countries (the remaining Ronen and Shenkar blocs; see Table 4). The dummy variable "developed country" in Table 4 captures whether an international joint

Table 4. Results of Event-History Analysis for Developed/Developing Countries[a]

Independent Variables	Model 4
Intercept	1.71
	(1.31)
International joint venture experience	0.05
	(0.04)
Domestic joint venture experience	−0.15**
	(0.06)
Developed international wholly owned subsidiary experience × developed country	−0.07**
	(0.02)
Developed international wholly owned subsidiary experience × developing country	−0.01
	(0.03)
Developing international wholly owned subsidiary experience × developed country	−0.02
	(0.12)
Developing international wholly owned subsidiary experience × developing country	−0.11***
	(0.03)
Domestic wholly owned subsidiary experience	−0.01
	(0.01)
Domestic joint venture × international wholly owned subsidiary experience	0.01*
	(0.01)
Cultural distance × developed country	0.03
	(0.11)
Cultural distance × developing country	0.14*
	(0.07)
Assets[b]	0.08
	(0.10)
Return on equity	2.09*
	(1.05)
Gross national product per capita	0.01
	(0.02)
Log likelihood	−183

* $p < .05$
** $p < .01$
*** $p < .001$
[a] Numbers in parentheses are standard deviations.
[b] Value is a logarithm.

venture was in a developed country (or not), and the dummy variable "developing country" captures the opposite.

The results presented in Table 4 show that international joint ventures in developed countries benefit significantly from the experience of the firms investing abroad (the Dutch firms) with international wholly owned subsidiaries in developed countries, but not from such firms' previous ventures in developing countries. Similarly, international joint ventures in developing countries benefit significantly from investor's previous experience with international wholly owned subsidiaries in developing countries, but not from experience with such subsidiaries in developed countries.

Another interesting result given in Table 4 is that the effect of cultural distance is significant for international joint ventures in developing countries, but not for international joint ventures in developed countries. To get a sharper view of the effects of cultural differences between the foreign and host country on the longevity of international joint ventures in developed countries, we replaced the cultural distance variable (per Hofstede) for developed countries with dummy variables representing Ronen and Shenkar's blocs, making the Nordic bloc (to which the Netherlands belongs) the omitted category.[8] The results showed significant effects for the Germanic, Anglo, and Latin European dummies (1.46, $p < .05$, 1.67, $p < .05$, and 1.55, $p < .05$, respectively), suggesting that joint ventures of Dutch companies with partners in the three latter blocks encountered more problems than Dutch ventures with partners from other Nordic block countries. Using any of the other three dummies (Germanic, Anglo, or Latin European) as the omitted category did not result in significant effects for the other two, suggesting that the magnitude of cultural problems did not vary significantly across these three cultural blocs.[9]

3.2.5. *Further Analyses*

In further analyses, a number of control variables were added, including a time-variant measure of firm diversification (capturing the level of diversification for each firm for each year) and the level of diversification implied by the international joint venture (coded 1 for related, horizontal, or vertical diversification and 0 otherwise). These analyses did not lead to different conclusions. We also separated previous experience with international wholly owned subsidiaries into experience with start-ups and experience with acquisitions and obtained virtually identical results for both. Finally, we repeated all the analyses using distributions other than the Weibull distribution that underpins the above results, including gamma, logarithmic logistic, and logarithmic normal distributions. All the results were equally supportive.

4. Discussion

The findings of the present study expand earlier findings illustrating the incremental nature of firms' learning of new technologies (Cohen and Levinthal,

1990), across industries (Chang, 1995; Pennings et al., 1994; Ramanujam and Varadarajan, 1989), and beyond national borders (Barkema et al., 1996; Johanson and Vahlne, 1977; Johanson and Wiedersheim-Paul, 1975). Specifically, this study identifies both experience with domestic joint ventures and experience with international wholly owned subsidiaries as stepping stones from which operation of international joint ventures can be successfully launched—as long as the experience is related to a firm's core business. Domestic joint ventures allow firms to learn about partnering without having to simultaneously handle the vagaries of foreign settings. International wholly owned subsidiaries allow firms to learn how to operate in foreign settings without the complexities of cooperating with a partner, provided the experience is accumulated in the same context—that is, in developed countries if the new expansion is into a developed country, and in developing countries if the new expansion is into a developing country. And, in line with previous conjectures (e.g., Hofstede, 1989), international joint venture longevity decreased with the cultural distance between a Dutch investor and a host country.

The significant role played by domestic joint ventures in preparing firms for cross-border joint ventures is especially noteworthy and represents a unique contribution of this research. In addition to pinpointing a crucial, yet neglected, way of learning to successfully operate international joint ventures, this finding has implications for the learning process in international business. The finding confirms that an analysis of a multinational corporation's operations abroad should also include paths from its domestic activities, and that international business research should not be rigidly confined to nondomestic operations.

If one accepts the premise that the national culture of a multinational corporation can moderate its ability to learn to cooperate with others and to adapt to foreign settings (Hickson, 1996; Hofstede, 1983), the present study—which was limited to Dutch multinationals—should be replicated for firms rooted in other national settings. Given our confirmation of the importance of uncertainty avoidance (Hofstede, 1989), it would be interesting to compare the findings for the Netherlands, a country with low uncertainty avoidance, with results for a country with high uncertainty avoidance, such as Japan. Similarly, given the prominence of the Netherlands as a foreign investor, multinational corporations from developing and newly industrialized economies would make a valuable base for comparison.

The above strategies, combined with the broadening of potential learning paths to include trading activities as well as mergers and acquisitions, will go a long way toward enhancing scholars' understanding of the foreign investment learning process. This understanding will not be complete, however, without injecting the internal processes that are part and parcel of the learning process. The present findings suggest that most, but not all, firms benefit from their experience with domestic joint ventures and international wholly owned subsidiaries when entering international joint ventures. To understand why, researchers should examine the structural and process factors facilitating learning in alliances (cf. Hitt et al., 1995), as well as the customized channels allowing for the creation and transfer of knowledge within multinational corporations (cf. Bartlett and Ghoshal, 1989; Hedlund, 1994).

Notes

1. In terms of firm value, these were the largest firms listed in 1994 on the Amsterdam Stock Exchange.
2. Executives of a subset of 5 firms were asked to rate the success of the international joint ventures in our data set ($N = 31$) on a seven-point scale. Like Geringer and Hebert (1991), we calculated the Spearman correlation between the longevity of these international joint ventures and their success as perceived by the managers. The correlation coefficient was .55 ($p < .001$), a value comparable to that of the coefficient found by Geringer and Hebert (.46). In addition, we found that only one of the ventures was planned to be short-lived from the start.
3. The Kogut and Singh (1988) index of cultural distance is an arithmetic average of the deviations of each country from the index of the Netherlands along Hofstede's (1980) four cultural dimensions. Algebraically, it is calculated as $CD_j = \Sigma_{i=1,2,3,4} [(I_{ij} - I_{in})^2 / V_i]/4$ where CD_j = the cultural distance of the jth country from the Netherlands, I_{ij} = the index for the ith cultural dimension and jth country, n = the Netherlands, and V_i = the variance of the index of the ith dimension.
4. Firms may also benefit from other sorts of experience when launching international joint ventures—from exporting, for example—but such data were not available. If firms learn from exporting, the effects measured in this study may overestimate the effects of learning from previous international expansions on the longevity of international joint ventures.
5. We found no significant learning effects of previous international joint ventures that were not preceded by international wholly owned subsidiaries or domestic joint ventures. Exploratory analysis revealed a significant learning effect of international joint ventures preceded by at least 10 domestic joint ventures or 30 international wholly owned subsidiaries. The effect remained if firm dummies were added to the analysis.
6. Similar conclusions were reached for other cut-off rates, for instance, for 5 and for 20 ventures.
7. No effects were found for the power distance and masculinity/femininity dimensions. The effect of individualism became significant if gross national product per capita was deleted from the model as a control variable.
8. The Ronen and Shenkar (1985) cultural blocs are based on a synthesis of eight clustering studies, including Hofstede (1980). The clustering represents the similarity of national cultures and transcends the explicit dimensions making up that complex construct.

9. Not surprisingly, estimation results from the full model with dummies for all Ronen and Shenkar blocs (Germanic, Anglo, Latin European, Latin American, Far Eastern, African, etc., with Nordic as the omitted category) tested on the whole data set showed highly significant effects of the bloc dummies associated with non-European cultures.

References

Agarwal, S. 1994. Socio-cultural distance and the choice of joint ventures: A contingency perspective. *Journal of International Marketing*, 2: 63–80.

Agarwal, S., and Ramaswami, S. N. 1992. *Choice of organizational form in foreign markets: A transaction cost perspective*. Paper presented at the annual meeting of the Academy of International Business, Brussels.

Anderson, E., and Gatignon, H. 1986. Modes of foreign entry: A transaction cost analysis and propositions. *Journal of International Business Studies*, 17: 1–26.

Barkema, H. G., Bell, J. H. J., and Pennings, J. M. 1996. Foreign entry, cultural barriers, and learning. *Strategic Management Journal*, 17: 151–166.

Bartlett, C. A., and Ghoshal, S. 1989. *Managing across borders: The transnational solution*. London: Hutchinson Business Books.

Bell, J. H. J. 1996. *Single or joint venturing? A comprehensive approach to foreign entry mode choice*. Aldershot, England: Avebury.

Bell, J. H. J., Barkema, H. G., and Verbeke, A. 1997. An eclectic model of the choice between WOSs and JVs as modes of foreign entry. In P. W. Beamish and J. P. Killing (Eds.), *Cooperative strategies: European perspectives*: Forthcoming. San Francisco: New Lexington.

Benito, C. R. G., and Gripsrud, G. 1992. The expansion of foreign direct investments: Discrete rational location choices or a cultural learning process? *Journal of International Business Studies*, 23: 461–476.

Berg, S. V., Duncan, J. L., Jr., and Friedman, P. 1982. *Joint venture strategies and corporate innovation*. Cambridge. MA: Oelschlager, Gunn and Hain.

Bettis, R. A., and Prahalad, C. K. 1995. The dominant logic: Retrospective and extension. *Strategic Management Journal*, 16: 5–14.

Brown, L. T., Rugman, A. M., and Verbeke, A. 1989. Japanese joint ventures with western multinationals: Synthesising the economic and cultural explanations of failure. *Asia Pacific Journal of Management*, 6: 225–242.

Buckley, P. J., and Casson, M. 1976. *The future of the multinational enterprise*. London: MacMillan.

Buckley, P. J., and Casson, M. 1988. A theory of cooperation in international business. In F. J. Contractor and P. Lorange (Eds.), *Cooperative strategies in international business*: 31–55. Lexington, MA: Lexington Books.

Carroll, G. R., Preisendorfer, P., Swaminathan, A., and Wiedenmayer, G. 1993. Brewery and brauerei: The organizational ecology of brewing. *Organization Studies*, 14: 155–188.

Carroll, G. R., and Swaminathan, A. 1991. Density dependent organizational evolution in the American brewing industry from 1633 to 1988. *Acta Sociologica*, 34: 155–175.

Chang, S. J. 1995. International expansion strategy of Japanese firms: Capability building through sequential entry. *Academy of Management Journal*, 38: 383–407.

Cho, K. R., and Padmanabhan, P. 1995. Acquisition versus new venture: The choice of foreign establishment mode by Japanese firms. *Journal of International Management*, 1: 255–285.

Chowdhury, J. 1992. Performance of international joint ventures and wholly owned foreign subsidiaries: A comparative perspective. *Management International Review*, 32: 115–133.

Cohen, W. M., and Levinthal, D. A. 1989. Innovation and learning: The two faces of RandD. *Economic Journal*, 99: 569–596.

—— and —— 1990. Absorptive capacity: A new perspective on learning and innovation. *Administrative Science Quarterly*, 35: 128–152.

—— and —— 1994. Fortune favors the prepared firm. *Management Science*, 40: 227–251.

Contractor, F. J., and Lorange, P. 1988. Why should firms cooperate? The strategy and economics basis for cooperative ventures. In F. J. Contractor and P. Lorange (Eds.), *Cooperative strategies in international business*: 3–30. Lexington, MA: Lexington Books.

Cyert, R. M., and March J. G. 1963. *A behavioral theory of the firm*. Englewood Cliffs, NJ: Prentice-Hall.

Davidson, W. H. 1983. Market similarity and market selection: Implications of international marketing strategy. *Journal of Business Research*, 11: 439–456.

Denis, J. E., and Depelteau, D. 1985. Market knowledge, diversification and export expansion. *Journal of International Business Studies*, 16: 77–89.

Erramilli, M. K. 1991. The experience factor in foreign market entry behavior of service firms. *Journal of International Business Studies*, 22: 479–501.

—— and Rao, C. P. 1993. Service firms' international entry mode choice: A modified transaction-cost analysis approach. *Journal of Marketing*, 57(3): 19–38.

Gatignon, H., and Anderson, E. 1988. The multinational corporation's degree of control over foreign subsidiaries: An empirical test of a transaction cost explanation. *Journal of Law, Economics, and Organization*, 4: 305–336.

Geringer, J. M., and Hebert, L. 1991. Measuring performance of international joint ventures. *Journal of International Business Studies*, 22: 249–263.

Gomes-Casseres, B. 1987. Joint venture instability: Is it a problem? *Columbia Journal of World Business*, 22(2): 97–102.

—— 1989. Ownership structures of foreign subsidiaries: Theory and evidence. *Journal of Economic Behavior and Organization*, 11: 1–25.

Harrigan, K. R. 1985. *Strategies for joint ventures*. Lexington, MA: Lexington Books.

—— 1988. Strategic alliances and partner asymmetries. In F. J. Contractor and P. Lorange (Eds.), *Cooperative strategies in international business*. Lexington, MA: 205–226. Lexington Books.

Hedberg, B. 1981. How organizations learn and unlearn. In P. C. Nystrom and W. H. Starbuck (Eds.), *Handbook of organizational design*: 3–27. London: Oxford University Press.

Hedlund, G. 1994. A model of knowledge management and the N-form corporation. *Strategic Management Journal*, 15: 73–90.

Hennart, J.-F. 1988. A transaction cost theory of equity joint ventures. *Strategic Management Journal*, 9: 361–374.

—— 1991. The transaction costs theory of joint ventures: An empirical study of Japanese subsidiaries in the United States. *Management Science*, 37: 483–497.

Hergert, M., and Morris, D. 1988. Trends in international collaborative agreements. In F. J. Contractor and P. Lorange (Eds.), *Cooperative strategies in international business*: 99–110. Lexington, MA: Lexington Books.

Hickson, D. J. 1996. The ASQ years then and now through the eyes of a Euro-Brit. *Administrative Science Quarterly*, 41: 217–228.

Hill, R. C., and Hellriegel, D. 1994. Critical contingencies in joint venture management: Some lessons from managers. *Organization Science*, 5: 594–607.

Hitt, M. A., Harrison, J. S., Ireland, R. D., and Best, A. 1995. *Learning how to dance with the Tasmanian devil: Understanding acquisition success and failure*. Paper presented at the annual meeting of the Strategic Management Society, Mexico City.

Hofstede, G. 1980. *Culture's consequences: International differences in work-related values*. Beverly Hills, CA: Sage.

—— 1983. The cultural relativity of organizational practices and theories. *Journal of International Business Studies*, 2: 75–89.

—— 1989. Organising for cultural diversity. *European Management Journal*, 7: 390–397.

—— 1991. *Cultures and organizations: Software of the mind*. Berkshire, England: McGraw-Hill.

Ingrassia, L., Naji, A. K., and Rosett, C. 1995. Overseas, Otis and its parent get in on the ground floor. *Wall Street Journal*, April 21: A8.

Johanson, J., and Vahlne, J. E. 1977. The internationalization process of the firm: A model of knowledge development and increasing foreign market commitments. *Journal of International Business Studies*, 8: 23–32.

—— and Wiedersheim-Paul, F. 1975. The internationalization of the firm: Four Swedish cases. *Journal of Management Studies*, 12: 305–322.

Kogut, B. 1988. Joint ventures: Theoretical and empirical perspectives. *Strategic Management Journal*, 9: 319–332.

—— and Singh, H. 1988. The effect of national culture on the choice of entry mode. *Journal of International Business Studies*, 19: 411–432.

Larimo, J. 1993. *Foreign direct investment behaviour and performance: An analysis of Finnish direct manufacturing investments in OECD countries*. Acta Wasaensia, no. 32. Vaasa, Finland: University of Vaasa.

Levine, J. B., and Byrne, J. A. 1986. Corporate odd couples. *Business Week*, July 21: 100–105.

Lewin, K. 1947. Frontiers in group dynamics: Concepts, method, and reality in social science. *Human Relations*, 1: 5–41.

Li, J. T. 1995. Foreign entry and survival: Effects of strategic choices on performance in international markets. *Strategic Management Journal*, 16: 333–351.

—— and Guisinger, S. 1991. Comparative business failures of foreign-controlled firms in the United States. *Journal of International Business Studies*, 22: 209–224.

Lorange, P., and Roos, J. 1991. Why some strategic alliances succeed and others fail. *Journal of Business Strategy*, 12(1): 25–30.

Luostarinen, R. 1980. *Internationalization of the firm*. Helsinki: Helsinki School of Economics.

Lyles, M. 1987. Common mistakes of joint venture experienced firms. *Columbia Journal of World Business*, 22(2): 79–85.

Lyles, M. A. 1988. Learning among joint venture-sophisticated firms. In F. J. Contractor and P. Lorange (Eds.), *Cooperative strategies in international business*. 301–316. Lexington, MA: Lexington Books.

Madhok, A. 1997: Cost, value and foreign market entry mode: The transaction and the firm. *Strategic Management Journal*, 18: 39–61.

McGill, M. E. and Slocum, J. W., Jr. 1993. Unlearning the organization. *Organizational Dynamics*, 22(2): 67–79.

Mitchell, C. 1988. Partnerships have become a way of life for Corning. *Wall Street Journal*, July 12.

Mitchell, W., Shaver, J. M., and Yeung, B. 1994. Foreign entrant survival and foreign market share: Canadian companies' experience in United States medical sector markets. *Strategic Management Journal*, 15: 555–567.

Padmanabhan, P., and Cho, K. R. 1996. Ownership strategy for a foreign affiliate: An empirical investigation of Japanese firms. *Management International Review*, 36: 45–65.

Parkhe, A. 1991. Interfirm diversity, organizational learning, and longevity in global strategic alliances. *Journal of International Business Studies*, 22: 579–600.

Pennings, J. M., Barkema, H. G., and Douma, S. W. 1994. Organizational learning and diversification. *Academy of Management Journal*, 37: 608–640.

Prahalad, C. K., and Bettis, R. A. 1986. The dominant logic: A new linkage between diversity and performance. *Strategic Management Journal*, 7: 485–501.

Ramanujam, V., and Varadarajan, P. 1989. Research on corporate diversification: A synthesis. *Strategic Management Journal*, 10: 523–551.

Ronen, S., and Shenkar, O. 1985. Clustering countries on attitudinal dimensions: A review and synthesis. *Academy of Management Review*, 10: 435–454.

Root, F. 1987. *Entry strategies for international markets*. Lexington, MA: Lexington.

SAS Institute. 1988. *SAS users guide: Statistics*. Durham, NC: SAS Institute.

Schaan, J. L., and Beamish, P. 1988. Joint venture general managers in LDCs. In F. J. Contractor and Lorange, P. (Eds.), *Cooperative strategies in international business*: 279–299. Lexington, MA: Lexington Books.

Shenkar, O., and Zeira, Y. 1987. Human resources management in international joint ventures: Directions for research. *Academy of Management Review*, 12: 546–557.

—— and Zeira, Y. 1992. Role conflict and role ambiguity of chief executive officers in international joint ventures. *Journal of International Business Studies*, 23: 55–75.

Stopford, J. M., and Wells, L. T., Jr. 1972. *Managing the multinational enterprise: Organisation of the firm and ownership of the subsidiaries*. New York: Basic Books.

Vachani, S. 1991. Distinguishing between related and unrelated international geographic diversification: A comprehensive measure of global diversification. *Journal of International Business Studies*, 22: 307–322.

Woodcock, C. P., and Geringer, M. J. 1991. An exploratory study of agency costs related to the control structure of multi-partner, international joint ventures. *Academy of Management Best Papers Proceedings*: 115–118.

Wysocki, B. 1990. Cross-border alliances become favorite way to crack new markets. *Wall Street Journal*, March 26: A1.

Yelle, L. E. 1979. The learning curve: Historical review and comprehensive survey. *Decision Sciences*, 10: 302–328.

14 Do Firms Learn to Create Value? The Case of Alliances

Bharat N. Anand and Tarun Khanna

1. Introduction

Alliances create value (Chan et al., 1997; McConnell and Nantel, 1985).[1] Yet, there is widespread recognition of the difficulty inherent in this process of value creation, as evidenced by the large fraction of firms that fail to do so, by the numerous academic publications highlighting the failure of alliances (see, for example, Kogut, 1989), and by the wisdom among practitioners.[2] What, then, drives value creation in alliances? Our empirical analysis points to two important factors: a firm's experience in managing alliances, and the existence of persistent firm-specific differences in the ability (or inability) to create value through alliances.

Alliances are complex organizational forms that are usefully viewed as incomplete contracts.[3] They typically involve the transfer of know-how between firms, a process that is fraught with ambiguity (Jensen and Meckling, 1991). Like other complex organizational forms, it is difficult to prespecify the contingencies that arise in their management. For example, unanticipated changes in the environment may alter the incentives of the contracting parties; intangible personal, organizational, and cultural attributes may affect the ongoing relationship between firms in important ways as well. Clearly, acquiring and assimilating the information needed in order to specify and react to all such contingencies is costly (Simon, 1955). Consequently, there may be important learning dynamics in a firm's ability to anticipate some of these contingencies, or in its ability to respond to them in an effective manner. In addition, since the management of alliances is not a well-defined process, there are likely to exist differences across firms in their ability to manage these; indeed, if the ambiguities involved with managing alliances were perfectly specifiable, it is unlikely that interfirm differences in the ability to create value through alliances would persist.[4] Thus, incomplete contract theory suggests that both learning effects and unobserved heterogeneity might be important determinants of value creation through alliances.

While previous studies have examined the consequences of learning in alliances, and implicitly pointed to the importance of interfirm heterogeneity in managing alliances, neither of these issues, surprisingly, has received much attention empirically. This chapter is an attempt at answering many outstanding questions in this area, specifically: (1) Do firms learn to create value via alliances; and, how important are these learning effects? Consequently, can alliance capabilities be acquired or developed by firms? (2) When is learning important? Indeed, which kinds of alliances are most susceptible to the kinds of behavior that have been highlighted in the literature as resulting from learning dynamics? (3) Are interfirm differences in "alliance capabilities" empirically important? If so, are these capabilities general-purpose or alliance-specific?

Joint ventures and licensing arrangements offer a particularly useful venue within which to examine these questions for several reasons. First, alliances—of which joint ventures and licenses are the two most common examples—have become one of the most important organizational forms to emerge in the past decade, with more than 20,000 such reported alliances in just the last 2 years worldwide. They thus constitute an intrinsically interesting organizational form. Second, many large firms have entered into several dozen alliances, and occasionally hundreds of them. Consequently, many of these firms have built up substantial experience bases. From an empirical standpoint, alliances therefore offer an ideal arena within which to study the management of organizational forms because of the potentially large variation across firms in their value creation through alliances, and because firms differ widely in terms of both their experience with alliances and, according to practitioners, their skill in managing alliances. Because of these sources of variation, alliances also offer a better arena to examine the effects of learning than the relatively less frequent event of an acquisition. Finally, considerably more information is available on firms' alliance activities than on other activities internal to the firm, even though the latter might constitute important sources of firm learning as well.

We find strong learning effects in joint ventures, though none in licensing contracts. Within joint ventures, the learning effects are especially strong for research joint ventures and production joint ventures, and weak for marketing joint ventures. It may be that those firms with more experience in managing alliances also differ in other (unobserved) ways from other firms, thus confounding the effects of learning and unobserved heterogeneity. Since we have multiple observations on each firm, we can effectively resolve this identification problem as well. Indeed, we find strong evidence of firm-specific alliance capabilities in all subsamples. The learning effects, however, are robust to allow for such unobserved differences in capabilities across firms.

In the next section, we review related literature. Subsequent sections sequentially present our data, the estimation methodology, the results and robustness checks, and a concluding discussion.

2. Theory and Hypotheses

In this section, we place this study in the context of existing theoretical and empirical studies on learning by firms, relate it to the existing literature on firm heterogeneity, and develop testable hypotheses.

2.1. Learning to Manage Organizations

The notion of learning can be equated with improvements in the ability to anticipate and respond to contingencies that cannot be prespecified in a formal contract. If all contingencies could be prespecified perfectly, then responses to these contingencies could also be prespecified, and there would be little scope for learning. Academics have used various terms to describe such processes of anticipating and responding to contingencies. For example, Argyris and Schon (1978) developed models of organizational learning like 'error detection and correction in theories-in-use.' Firms are said to possess 'routines' and 'capabilities' when they have learned to perform some function with sufficient distinction relative to some comparison group (Cyert and March, 1963; Nelson and Winter, 1982). Such knowledge is often referred to as "tacit" (as opposed to 'codified'), with the implication that such knowledge is inaccessible to other firms, absent their own learning.

A large managerial literature similarly discusses the importance of learning to manage organizational forms. Volumes have been written, for example, on the nuances of managing acquisitions (Haspeslagh and Jemison, 1991; Singh and Zollo, 1999), or on learning to manage cross-border entry (Chang, 1995). Examples of specific firms excelling at such learning also abound. Hansen Trust has learned to manage acquisitions, Thermoelectron to manage spin-offs (Allen, 1998; Baldwin and Forsythe, 1982); while Xerox was often cited as a firm that had failed to do so (Smith and Alexander, 1988).

Given the importance of learning in both anecdotal accounts and formal theories, it is surprising that no systematic empirical evidence exists to indicate either how important the role of learning might be,[5] or *when* it is likely to be important. Answering the question of how easy or difficult it is for firms to acquire capabilities over time should also shed some light on the normative implications of theories that study the role of interfirm differences in such capabilities or resources. This literature suggests that the capability to manage a complex organization is tacit, costly to develop, and hard to imitate. Even here, however, large-sample evidence for cross-sectional variation in such capabilities is difficult to come by.[6] We turn to the specific context of alliances next, which is the focus of this study.

2.2. Learning to Manage Alliances

An alliance can be viewed as an incomplete contract between firms, in the sense that detailed interactions between the alliance partners can rarely be fully prespecified. Therefore, the theoretical literature reviewed above would, by extension, suggest that alliances are likely to be difficult to manage. One reason for such difficulties might revolve around the complexities surrounding interfirm knowledge transfers, an important part of many alliances. Several authors have discussed the difficulties of transferring tacit know-how (Winter, 1988; Jensen and Meckling, 1991; Szulanski, 1996), and others have emphasized that such difficulties are likely to be more pronounced in an interfirm setting than in an intrafirm setting (Baker, Gibbons, and Murply, 1997: 29). Such transfers of knowledge or information are at the heart of related studies that focus on the process by which firms learn from a particular alliance. These studies acknowledge the tension between competition and cooperation within alliances (Hamel, 1991; Gulati, Khanna, and Nohria, 1994; Khanna, Gulati, and Nohria, 1998; Khanna, 1998; Anand and Galetovic, 1999). Building on this literature, Kale, Sing and Perlmutter (2000) empirically examine the role of relational capital between alliance partners as a means of both enhancing cooperative behavior and mitigating competitive conflicts.[7] Recent work has suggested that such relational capital, which allows a firm to learn from its alliance partner, is a function of characteristics of the dyad in question, rather than of either of the individual firms (Lane and Lubatkin, 1998). Indeed, the capability to learn may be partner-specific (Dyer and Singh, 1998). A related stream of work has begun to develop useful taxonomies of alliance learning strategies (e.g., Larsson et al., 1998). These efforts have been aided by discussions of detailed case studies on how learning unfolds in alliances (Doz, 1996; Arino and de la Torre, 1998). It is important to note that all these papers have focused on the process of learning *within* a particular alliance. In contrast, our analysis is primarily concerned with whether firms exhibit learning effects *across* a portfolio of alliances. Effectively, therefore, our focus is on the question of *learning to learn* from alliances.

How exactly might firms learn to manage alliances, or acquire an alliance capability? Much theoretical work on learning is relevant to this question. The question of how firms learn can be broken down into, first, how individuals within the firm learn and, second, into how firms harness the learning experiences of such individuals. Following the related discussion in Cohen and Levinthal (1990), these two aspects can be considered in order.

Repeated exposure to sequences of alliance partners exposes individuals within the firm to a broad repertoire of experiences. This facilitates the interpretation of new unforeseen contingencies in their subsequent alliance interactions. Bower and Hilgard (1981) suggest that it is easier for an individual to learn from new experiences, the greater the number of stored objects and instances in her memory. Indeed, the ability to learn from a particular alliance is likely to be enhanced by the trials and tribulations of past learning experiences. Some authors have observed that the knowledge being built up in this way may be about learning skills themselves (Ellis, 1965), a phenomenon which Estes (1970) refers to as 'learning to learn'.

Cohen and Levinthal (1990) develop the idea that 'learning to learn' at the firm level is a complex function of the individual-level phenomenon. It depends on how the firm communicates with sources of knowledge outside the firm, on the mechanisms within the firm that exploit individual experiences, and on the distribution of expertise within the firm. There may not be a unique, optimal mechanism that allows firms to learn from these experiences. For example, heterogeneity in individuals' knowledge and experiences will make it difficult to disseminate newly acquired knowledge within the firm, but will generally facilitate the absorption of knowledge from *outside* the firm, thus creating trade-offs.[8] Cohen and Levinthal (1990) also point to the possibility of path dependence in learning to learn. Firms that have learnt to learn will continue to do so at an increasing rate, while those that have never invested in learning from different experiences will not find it optimal to do so. In the context of alliances, this would imply that heterogeneity in alliance capabilities will persist over time.

There are other reasons to expect firms to learn how to manage and learn from alliances. For example, Hamel (1991) points out that the *perception* of one's learning capabilities can affect interaction with the alliance partner as well. More generally, the idea that some firms have learned to manage alliances does not appear to be in doubt among practitioners as well. Trade publications are replete with the clarion call by alliance experts for the increasing formalization of processes by which a firm can systematize the acquisition or development of an 'alliance capability.'[9] Commonly mentioned components of such a process include having formal systems in place to capture the experience from each alliance, having a central administrative entity to coordinate multiple alliances in which the firm is engaged, and maintaining corporate data bases and newsletters on alliances' activity.[10] Relatedly, Mody (1993) explicitly argues that because of the uncertainty inherent in alliances, the design of such organizations may intentionally value flexibility, to the extent that this allows for greater learning and may result in firms acquiring greater competence in managing alliances.

Despite the theoretical support for the idea that learning to manage alliances might be important, and the widespread practitioner recognition of the importance of learning in alliances, empirical analyses have not focused on this issue, except tangentially. Kogut (1989) identifies the difficulty of managing alliances and, implicitly, the need to develop the ability to manage them. The only related empirical papers show that pairs of firms appear to learn over time to manage their collaborative activities more efficiently (Gulati, 1995),[11] and contracts between firms that have had prior contractual relationships appear systematically different from *de novo* pairings (Anand and Khanna, 2000).

2.3. When is Learning Important in Alliances?

We elaborate here on the logic that the importance of learning increases with the difficulty in specifying the process or knowledge in question. Just as learning to manage acquisitions can be expected to be quite different from learning to manage alliances—in that a capability to do the one does not imply a capability to do the other—so also the term 'alliances' encompasses a medley of often vastly different organizational forms. Consequently, a natural question to ask is: when is learning likely to be important in alliances? In this subsection, we distinguish, first, between learning to manage joint ventures vs. learning to manage licenses (the two most common forms of interfirm agreements), and, second, between learning to manage different forms of joint ventures.

It is well acknowledged that the underlying complexity of context will influence the structure of alliances. For example, when knowledge is easy to protect, knowledge transfers are less likely to be susceptible to appropriability and hold-up conflicts between the partners. In such situations, licensing contracts are likely to be the alliance of choice in comparison to joint ventures since they are much more clearly articulated contracts.[12] There are relatively precise criteria available to guide licensing contracts along few, well-specified dimensions. For example, manuals on the appropriate structure of licensing contracts often have reasonably clear formulae for the calculation of royalty payments, exclusivity clauses, territorial restrictions, and other parameters (see Caves, Crookell, and Killings, 1983; Parr and Sullivan, 1988). On the other hand, joint ventures are more likely to be observed in situations where alliance partners are faced with greater ambiguity. Indeed, prescriptions regarding joint ventures are confined to advise firms to align interests through equity sharing precisely because rules of 'good management' in these contexts are hard to articulate.

Since, as argued earlier, the potential for firm learning will depend on the extent of ambiguity or complexity of contingencies facing alliance partners, it immediately follows from the discussion above that the extent of learning is likely to be correlated with the structure of alliances. Specifically,

Hypothesis 1. Learning effects should be stronger in joint ventures than for licensing contracts.

A similar line of reasoning suggests that there is likely to be considerable heterogeneity in learning effects within joint ventures. In particular, Pisano's work suggests that ambiguity and uncertainty are greatest in high-technology situations;[13] by implication, learning to manage alliances ought to be most important in R&D situations relative to downstream alliances, suggesting our second hypothesis:

Hypothesis 2. Learning effects should be stronger in R&D joint ventures than in other categories of joint ventures (production joint ventures and marketing joint ventures).

Our empirical implementation below has three main components. First, we develop a measure of alliance-specific experience by firms, using both publicly available and proprietary data on firms' alliance histories. Second, we use standard event study methodology to create a measure of value creation for alliances. These have been used fairly extensively to study joint ventures, though only very rarely to study other forms of interfirm contractual agreements. None of these prior studies has been concerned with learning effects and the associated development of an alliance capability. Third, a careful treatment of learning effects would need to distinguish these from the role of interfirm unobserved heterogeneity in value creation. The reason is that if learning effects are important, then differences in the age of firms would result in different stocks of experience and consequently differences in value creation. The use of multiple observations on each firm allows us to distinguish between these two effects. Intrafirm temporal variation in value creation allows us to capture the effects of learning, and interfirm (cross-sectional) variation captures the effects of both differences in experience and intrinsic ability.[14] Thus, the panel nature of the data allows us to effectively resolve this identification problem.

3. Data and Methodology

3.1. Data

The data on alliances entered into by firms are drawn from the Strategic Alliance data base of the Securities Data Company (SDC). Such deals include agreements or contracts entered into at various stages of the value chain. SDC obtains information from publicly available sources, including SEC filings, trade publications and international counterparts, and news and wire sources. Although the data base goes back to 1986, SDC appears to have initiated systematic data collection procedures for tracking such deals only around 1989; hence, the deal sample prior to 1990 is far from comprehensive. Even over the 1990–93 sample period, the data clearly would not track all deals entered into by U.S. firms, owing to inadequate corporate reporting requirements. However, since this data base is among the most comprehensive sources of information on such deals, it is a sensible starting point for empirical analysis.

We start with a list of all alliances entered into in the manufacturing sector (i.e., Standard Industrial Classification (SIC) codes 20 through 39) between 1990 and 1993 inclusive, the data extract available to us. This yields 9000 alliances over our sample period in the manufacturing sector. Of these, 71 percent involved at least one foreign firm. We restrict the analysis to those agreements involving at least one U.S. participant (this does not need deals in which there is a foreign participant), as this facilitates obtaining stock price data from common data sources. For the same reason, deals in which all the firms are privately held are excluded from the analysis, since it is difficult to derive value creation measures through alliances for these firms. Since we use contract-specific measures of experience, on the conjecture that managing one kind of organizational form (say, joint ventures) is quite different from managing another kind (say, licenses), we focus on those alliances whose contractual forms are most clearly defined in the data—the sample of joint ventures and licenses. These sample attrition criteria leave us with 870 joint ventures and 1106 licenses.

SDC provides information on various contract-specific characteristics, including contract type (i.e., whether it is a joint venture agreement, licensing agreement, etc.), the identities of the participating firms, the date of the agreement, and the SIC code of the alliance. The SIC code of the alliance may be different from the SIC codes of the participating firms; for instance, a firm whose primary activities are in a particular industry may enter into an alliance in another industry. In order to 'clean' the SDC data, we carried out three major tasks:

3.1.1. Accuracy of Data on Contract Type

We were able to find information about the contractual type of the alliance from non-SDC sources on about 80 per cent of the deals. From our reading of the descriptions of the agreements in Lexis–Nexis, the SDC data on contract type is quite accurate. In some cases, however, alliances are classified in a unique category when in fact the underlying deal appears to be more complex and encompasses more than one type of contract. For example, the transfer or exchange of technology in a licensing deal was, in a few cases, also accompanied by the setting up of a joint venture for purposes of research or marketing. However, such cases are not observed frequently in the data.

For joint ventures, SDC provides additional information on whether these are entered into at the R&D stage or marketing stage. We classify these as research joint ventures, and marketing joint ventures, respectively. The remaining joint ventures mostly involve cooperation exclusively in manufacturing, hence we classify these as production joint ventures.

3.1.2. Accuracy of Data on Industry of Activity

We supplemented the data set with information on various deal-specific characteristics that we obtained from the Lexis–Nexis data base. For some characteristics, such as the information on alliance SIC codes, SDC's information is very accurate. The description of each agreement in the Lexis–Nexis data base is almost always consistent with the 2-digit SIC code within which the agreement is classified by SDC. We do not have a systematic way of checking the accuracy of the 3-digit classification assigned by SDC to a particular agreement. However, even for these, the classifications assigned by SDC appear to be accurate in those cases where we are able to clearly identify the primary area of activity of the alliance.

We categorize industries according to those in which there is significant alliance activity, leaving deals in a miscellany of industries in the "Other" category. Each separately identified industry in the table corresponds to a 2-digit or 3-digit SIC category selected to account for those categories within which there is significant joint venture or licensing activity. The categories we identify are: Drugs (SIC 283), Chemicals (SIC 28, excluding SIC 283), Computers (SIC 357), Communications (SIC 366), Chips (SIC 367), Cars (SIC 371), and Instruments (SIC 38). Industries of especially high joint venture activity are those labeled 'Chemicals,' 'Chips,' and 'Communications,' while 'Drugs' and 'Chips' account for especially high levels of licensing activity.

3.1.3. Accuracy of Data on Alliance Dates

SDC data on the date of the event are misstated in many instances. For each deal, we attempt to track all mentions of the deal in various news sources, including news and wire reports, newspapers, magazines, and trade publications, listed here in decreasing order of accuracy about the actual date on which the deal was signed. For example, news and wire reports consistently provide information on a particular deal a day or two in advance of newspapers, which in turn are a few days ahead of magazines, and so on. Being able to accurately pin down the date on which the deal was consummated is extremely important for our stock price-based analysis of value creation. Consequently, we spent a major portion of time doing so. In most cases, the extent of inaccuracy of SDC information is within one or two months, and in the majority of cases, within a few days. In some cases, the SDC-reported dates appear to coincide with the date on which the agreement was finally signed; in other cases, the SDC-reported dates seem to coincide with the date on which agreement negotiations appear to have begun. As such, the date information that we end up using is substantially different from that provided by SDC, and in most cases is based on verification across multiple sources.

We obtained firm-specific information from the Center for Research in Security Prices (CRSP) data base as well as the Compustat data base. Such information is available only for publicly listed firms. For such firms, we obtained data on stock price movements for that firm over a 290-day period (−250 through +40) surrounding the data of the alliance announcement. We use these data in arriving at an estimate of the amount of value created in the alliance for each publicly traded participant, based on the methodology described below. For all listed firms, we also extracted various balance sheet and income statement data from the Compustat data base as well.

3.2. Methodology

To estimate the incremental amount of value creation for each firm in the alliance, we extract the residuals from a standard asset pricing model used to predict firms' returns. We use daily data on the stock market returns of each publicly listed firm in the data base over a 240-day period prior to the event day (see Brown and Warner, 1985) to estimate the following market model (see Fama, 1976):

$$r_{it} = \alpha_i + \beta_i r_{mt} + \epsilon_{it}$$

Here, r_{it} denotes the daily returns for firm i on day t, r_{mt} denotes the corresponding daily returns on the value-weighted S&P 500, α_i and β_i are firm-specific parameters, and ϵ_{it} is distributed i.i.d. normal. The estimates obtained from this model are then used to predict the daily returns for each firm i over a 14-day period surrounding the event day (i.e., event days −10 through +3), as:

$$\hat{r}_{it} = \hat{\alpha}_i + \hat{\beta}_r r_{mt}$$

where $\hat{r}_{it}$ are the predicted daily returns, and $\hat{\alpha}_i$, $\hat{\beta}_i$ are the model estimates. Thus, the daily firm-specific excess returns can be calculated as

$$\hat{\epsilon}_{it} = r_{it} - \hat{r}_{it}$$

where $\hat{\epsilon}_{it}$ are the daily firm-specific excess returns.

The excess returns thus reflect the daily unanticipated movements in the stock price for each firm over the event period. Together with data on the existing value of a firm's equity, these can be used also in calculating the total value accruing to the firm from the alliance. Of course, *ex post* performance will not be perfectly predicted by these *ex ante* estimates. Instead, these excess returns reflect the expected value that the market believes the firm will capture by entering into the particular alliance. These excess returns may also be thought of as a measure of the "surprise" element associated with the signing of a contract or alliance. Consequently, to the extent that information regarding particular alliances may leak out prior to the actual announcement of the agreement, the estimate of returns from the alliance will be understated by simply focusing on a 10-day event window prior to the announcement.

The daily firm-specific excess returns can be used also to calculate the daily cross-sectional mean excess returns, μ, associated with the alliance announcements. The test statistic used in evaluating the statistical significance of these cross-sectional mean excess returns is computed as μ_t/σ, where

$$\sigma = \frac{\sum_i \sum_{t=-250}^{-11} (\hat{\epsilon}_{it} - \bar{\epsilon}_{it})}{IT - 1}$$

where $\bar{\epsilon}_{it}$ denotes the mean excess returns (calculated over all firms i over the estimation period). The test statistic μ_t/σ will be distributed unit normal under the null hypothesis for large I, if the excess returns are i.i.d. with unit variance.

4. Results

4.1. *Summary Statistics*

Table 1 presents our measures of experience in managing alliances. $CumJv_{it}$ measures the number of joint ventures entered into by the firm prior to and including the joint venture in question, within the time window of our data. $CumLic_{it}$ measures the number of licensing agreements entered into by the firm prior to and including the current licensing contract. The experience measures thus have a lower bound of 1. There is considerable variation in the experience measure across firms, and for the same firm over time—$CumJv_{it}$ varies from 1 through 23 deals, and licensing experience ($CumLic_{it}$) varies from 1 through 30 deals. 18.7 percent of joint ventures are entered into by firms that have had a recent history (within our sample window) of more than five joint ventures,

Table 1. Distribution of Experience Measures

Joint Ventures			Licenses		
CUMJV	Frequency	Percent	CUMLIC	Frequency	Percent
1	384	44.14	1	505	45.66
2	147	16.90	2	193	17.45
3	78	8.97	3	114	10.31
4	57	6.55	4	73	6.60
5	41	4.71	5	57	5.15
6	36	4.14	6	41	3.71
7	29	3.33	7	29	2.62
8	20	2.30	8	19	1.72
9	16	1.84	9	15	1.36
10	12	1.38	10	11	0.99
11	9	1.03	11	9	0.81
12	8	0.92	12	7	0.63
13	7	0.80	13	6	0.54
14	5	0.57	14	6	0.54
15	5	0.57	15	2	0.18
16	4	0.46	16	2	0.18
17	3	0.34	17	2	0.18
18	3	0.34	18	2	0.18
19	2	0.23	19	2	0.18
20	1	0.11	20	1	0.09
21	1	0.11	21	1	0.09
22	1	0.11	22	1	0.09
23	1	0.11	23	1	0.09
			24	1	0.09
			25	1	0.09
			26	1	0.09
			27	1	0.09
			28	1	0.09
			29	1	0.09
			30	1	0.09
Total	870	100.00	Total	1106	100.00

Distribution of firm-specific experience measures for a sample of joint ventures and licenses obtained from an extensively cleaned version of the Strategic Alliances data base of the Securities Data Company, 1990–93. CUMJV is the number of past joint ventures entered into by the firm prior to and including the joint venture in question within the time window of our data. CUMLIC is defined similarly for licensing contracts.

while 7.08 percent have had a recent history of at least 10 joint ventures. Similarly, 14.8 percent of our licensing deals are entered into by firms that have had a recent history of more than five licenses, while 5.4 percent have had a recent history of at least 10 licenses. The experience measures are left-censored, since they only account for the deals entered into by the firm since 1990.[15] Alternatively, these measures may be viewed as particularly sensible if one assumes that recent experience is more relevant in learning how to manage alliances than is experience on deals that have been consummated in the more distant past.[16]

Table 2. Panel A: Event Study Results

Event Day	Joint Venture Events		Licensing Events	
	Daily Excess Returns	Cumulative Excess Returns	Daily Excess Returns	Cumulative Excess Returns
−10	0.12274	0.12274	0.08478	0.08478
−9	0.00166	0.12441	0.19560	0.28038
−8	0.01091	0.13532	0.02725	0.30763
−7	0.13471	0.27002	−0.00566	0.30197
−6	−0.05906	0.21096	0.10443	0.40640
−5	0.11033	0.32129	0.04661	0.45300
−4	0.0105	0.33178	0.19458	0.64758*
−3	0.13761	0.46940	0.02756	0.67514*
−2	0.25206*	0.72146*	−0.00171	0.67343*
−1	0.05274	0.77420*	0.35857**	1.03201**
0	0.67451**	1.44871**	1.42496**	2.45697**
+1	0.13922	1.58793**	0.60622**	3.06319**
+2	0.04897	1.63690**	0.05976	3.12295**
+3	−0.02671	1.61019**	0.00449	3.12744**
+4	−0.11679	1.49341**	−0.30493**	2.82251**
+5	−0.26608	1.22733**	−0.04667	2.77584**
+6	−0.05074	1.17660**	−0.06612	2.70971**
+7	0.04077	1.21737**	−0.21789	2.49182**
+8	0.17021*	1.38758**	−0.02365	2.46817**
+9	−0.06845	1.31913**	0.27031*	2.73848**

All numbers are in percentages.
*Significance at the 10% level; **Significance at the 5% level.
Average daily excess returns and cumulative excess returns for the sample of 870 joint venture announcements and 1106 licensing announcements for firms traded on the NYSE, AMEX, or NASDAQ with available CRSP returns data during 1990–93. Excess returns are the residuals from a market model (Fama, 1976; Brown and Warner, 1985) used to predict firm returns. The announcement day is defined as day 0.

Before examining the effects of experience on value creation, we first summarize the basic results of the event study analysis in Table 2, panel A. The announcement day is defined as day zero; the table reports the results for both the joint ventures and licensing subsamples, and reports both daily and cumulative excess returns over the event window. The daily average abnormal return on the announcement day is 0.67 percent (z-statistic = 6.93) for joint venture announcements, and 1.42 percent (z-statistic = 11.31) for licensing contracts; both these results are statistically significant at the 5 percent level. The cumulative abnormal returns over the event window are correspondingly large as well: 1.61 percent through day +3 for joint ventures, and 3.13 percent for licensings.[17] Thus, alliances appear to create significant value for the firms involved. The day zero average abnormal returns are similar in magnitude to those observed by McConnell and Nantel (1985) for joint venture announcements—average abnormal returns over a 2-day window of 0.74 percent compared to 0.81 percent for the corresponding event window in our sample.

Table 2. Panel B: Summary Statistics from Event Study

	Wealth Effects (in $ thousands)					
	Mean	Median	S.D.	Minimum	Maximum	# of Observations
Joint						
Ventures	44.068	0.765	909.141	−11504.080	4198.313	870
Licenses	20.377	1.552	691.048	−6194.596	5549.913	1106
	Abnormal Returns					
	Mean	Median	S.D.	Minimum	Maximum	# of Observations
Joint						
Ventures	1.82%	0.72%	10.96%	−40.02%	105.30%	870
Licenses	3.06%	0.82%	15.98%	−42.57%	119.40%	1106

Summary statistics of excess returns and associated wealth effects calculated from the event study for a sample of 870 joint ventures and 1106 licensing contracts. Wealth effects are calculated by multiplying the cumulative excess returns in the event window (day −10, day +1) by the firm's market value of equity 10 trading days before the event announcement date.

Similarly, Chan et al. (1997) report average announcement day abnormal returns of 0.64 percent for their composite sample of strategic alliances.

To derive the wealth effects associated with these returns figures, we created a measure (labeled 'wealth effect') for each firm that multiplies the 'abnormal returns' measure (defined as the cumulative excess returns in the event window day −10 through day +1) by the market value of equity of the firm on day −10 (i.e., the first day of the event window).[18] Summary statistics for wealth effects and abnormal returns are reported in Table 2, panel B. The mean dollar value created in joint ventures is $44.07 million, with the median value being $0.765 million. In comparison, although the percentage excess returns created in licensing deals is larger (3.06% compared with 1.82% for joint ventures), the value created in these deals is smaller (mean value of $20.38 million, median of $1.55 million), since the participating firms are on average smaller as well. Since the abnormal returns measures reflect the effects of firm size as well, the wealth effect measures may be viewed as a more attractive metric by which to examine the value creation in alliances.[19] Throughout, however, we report the results for both types of measures.

Table 3 presents the variation in performance by industry. For joint ventures, a one-way analysis of variance reveals that neither the mean returns nor the mean wealth effect differ significantly across industry categories (p-value = 0.24 for ANOVA of returns, and 0.42 for ANOVA of wealth effect measure). For licensing deals, however, there do appear to be systematic differences in performance across industries. The performance-based rank ordering of industries differs substantially according to the performance measure being used, because of the different size distribution of firms across industries.

Table 3. Wealth Effects and Abnormal Returns by Industry Category

	Joint Ventures					Licenses				
		Wealth Effects (in $ thousands)		Excess Returns (%)			Wealth Effects (in $ thousands)		Excess Returns (%)	
Industry	#	Mean	S.D.	Mean	S.D.	#	Mean	S.D.	#	Mean	S.D.
Drugs	55	−55.007	901.346	3.25	11.33	329	13.232	426.776	386	3.39	16.12
Chemicals	133	148.274	812.237	3.27	11.28	74	41.721	468.244	83	2.55	12.39
Computer	57	−119.557	1732.238	1.40	13.46	88	190.607	985.711	106	3.80	16.51
Communication	68	225.443	1098.953	3.08	8.02	70	−107.584	868.004	81	7.28	26.01
Chips	69	94.587	572.908	0.99	12.13	192	2.845	871.717	204	2.46	13.97
Cars	54	−27.480	655.220	2.59	9.76	—	—	—	—	—	—
Instruments	56	−109.668	953.748	0.46	9.88	—	—	—	—	—	—
Other	378	37.638	790.716	1.18	10.92	221	11.845	685.657	246	1.49	13.56
Total	870	44.068	909.141	1.82	10.96	974	20.377	691.048	1106	3.06	15.98

Industry distribution of frequency of events, and of wealth effects and excess returns from the event study for the sample of 870 joint ventures and 974 licensing deals for which data on industry location of alliance activity are available. Industry categories indicate location of activity of the alliance and are grouped into major categories as follows: Drugs, SIC 283; Chemicals, SIC 28 (excluding SIC 283); Computer, SIC 357; Communication, SIC 366; Chips, SIC 367; Cars, SIC 37; Instruments, SIC 38.

Table 4. Wealth Effects and Abnormal Returns by Experience Categories for Joint Ventures

		Joint Ventures			
		Wealth Effects (in $ thousands)		Excess Returns (%)	
Experience Category	#	Mean	S.D.	Mean	S.D.
1	384	−0.806	394.042	3.09	14.06
2	147	−21.296	637.837	1.35	9.53
3	135	−4.055	875.077	0.22	7.49
4	204	207.482	1553.038	0.84	5.75
Total	870	44.068	909.141	1.82	10.96

Variation in wealth effects and excess returns by experience category for the sample of 870 joint ventures. The experience categories are defined as follows. Category 1 indicates deals in which the firm has no prior experience with the joint ventures; category 2 refers to deals in which the firm is known to have entered into exactly 1 prior joint venture; category 3 refers to deals in which the firm has entered into 2 or 3 prior joint ventures; category 4 refers to deals in which the firm has entered into at least 4 prior joint ventures.

4.2. *Results for Joint Ventures*

Table 4 summarizes the variation in joint venture performance across levels of experience. We categorize the firms' experience measure into four groups: those deals in which the firm has no prior experience, ($CumJv_{it} = 1$), those deals in which the firm is known to have entered into exactly one prior joint venture ($CumJv_{it} = 2$), two or three prior joint ventures ($CumJv_{it} = 2$ or 3), and at least four prior joint ventures ($CumJv_{it} \geq 4$). Table 4 shows that the dollar value created is significantly higher for firms with at least four prior joint ventures, relative to deals in which the firms have been involved in fewer deals. A one-way analysis of variance indicates that the differences in mean wealth effects across the four categories is statistically significant (p-value $= 0.03$). A univariate analysis of the effects of experience on percentage abnormal returns appears to reflect the opposite pattern; however, since returns vary inversely with firm size, the simple cross-tab analysis would be confounded by the effects of size. (Again, the differences are statistically significant across the various experience categories; p-value $= 0.02$.)

Regression analyses confirm these findings.[20] In a multivariate analysis that controls for the effects of firm size and industry effects (Table 5, specification (i)), the effect of experience on wealth creation through joint ventures is positive and statistically significant at the 1 percent level. Each additional deal of experience translates into an incremental $42.28 million of value for the firm. Given that the mean value accruing to a firm in a joint venture is $44.07 million, these effects are economically large as well.

Table 5. Cross-Sectional Analysis of Value Creation in Joint Ventures

Dependent Variable	Specification (i) Wealth Effects	Specification (ii) Abnormal Returns	Specification (iii) Wealth Effects	Specification (iv) Abnormal Returns
Constant	−104.7340**	0.0167**	−199.3768**	0.0053
	(−2.451)	(2.284)	(−2.528)	(0.606)
Experience (CUMJV)	42.2808***	−0.0009	56.7769***	0.0024**
	(3.760)	(−1.160)	(3.361)	(2.292)
Assets	−0.0003	−1.06e–07*	0.0006	−1.60e–07
	(−0.212)	(−1.663)	(0.150)	(−0.649)
Industry fixed effects				
Drugs	−20.3226	0.0177	130.7760	0.0288
	(−0.140)	(1.021)	(0.997)	(1.213)
Chemicals	129.4546*	0.0203*	219.0927**	0.0312
	(1.672)	(1.777)	(2.212)	(1.782)
Computer	101.1141	0.0012	253.6864	−0.1059
	(0.851)	(0.064)	(1.381)	(−0.427)
Communications	178.7035	0.01982*	467.9587**	0.0283
	(1.402)	(1.589)	(2.447)	(1.663)
Chips	17.5895	−0.0019	126.2548	0.0099
	(0.228)	(−0.122)	(1.030)	(0.576)
Cars	−77.3045	0.0136	83.9343	0.0102
	(−0.808)	(0.935)	(0.975)	(0.626)
Instruments	−148.8016	−0.0073	−150.5685	−0.0273
	(−1.099)	(−0.513)	(−0.802)	(−1.423)
Firm fixed effects			147 fixed effects Included	147 fixed effects Included
Number of observations	869	870	862	863
R^2	0.0412	0.0109	0.1890	0.2649
F-value	2.91***	1.73**	11.94***	66.36***

***Significant at the 1% level; **Significant at the 5 % level; *Significant at the 10% level.
Multivariate regression analyses examining the determinants of wealth effects and excess returns for joint ventures. Dependent variable is obtained from the event study on 870 joint ventures from an extensively cleaned version of the Securities Data Corporation Strategic Alliance data base, 1990–93. Experience (CUMJV) codes the number of prior joint ventures entered into by the firm including the deal in question. The assets variable is obtained from the Compustat data base and is measured in millions of dollars. Industry categories refer to the industry location of the alliance activity and are as defined in Table 3. Estimates of firm fixed effects are suppressed. The estimations allow for correlated errors across the firms within the same alliance, while maintaining the assumption of independence between alliances. Heteroskedastic-consistent White standard errors are used in deriving the *t*-statistics, which are reported in parentheses.

When percentage returns are used as the performance measure, the effect of experience is not significant at the 10 percent level, similar to the univariate analysis. One important assumption that is implicit in the analysis thus far is that, controlling for experience, firms have similar capabilities in managing joint ventures. If this were not true, then our estimates of the effects of experience will be biased to the extent that there is any systematic relation between joint venture capabilities and joint venture activity by firms. For example, if the most active firms were also the 'high-quality' firms or the most capable firms in managing joint ventures, then our estimates of the effects of experience would overstate the true effect. The reason is that the superior performance of firms with substantial joint venture experience may be capturing the unobserved superior capabilities of these firms in managing joint ventures. Conversely, if the most active firms were the 'low-quality' firms,[21] then the estimates of the experience effect will be downward-biased. Given that firms have very different approaches and systems in place to manage joint ventures, and probably differ substantially in average quality as well, it may be important to explicitly allow for interfirm unobserved heterogeneity in capabilities. Indeed, a quick analysis of the average returns to the most active firms reveals substantial variation in performance, ranging from −5.3 percent average returns (Caterpillar, Inc.) to +3.6 percent (Pepsico, Inc.).

Specifications (iii) and (iv) therefore estimate 147 firm fixed effects in addition to the variables mentioned earlier, thus controlling for unobserved heterogeneity. Identifying the effects of learning from unobserved heterogeneity is straightforward: the firm fixed effects are identified by differences in average performance across firms that have engaged in more than one deal, whereas the experience effect is identified by variation across deals for the same firm over time. The effects of experience are now observed to be larger than the earlier estimates, and statistically significant. Specification (iii) reveals that each additional deal of experience translates into an incremental $56.78 million of value for the partnering firm (significant at the 1% level). The effects of experience are positive and statistically significant at the 5 percent level even when abnormal percentage returns are used as the performance measure. Each additional deal of experience translates into an incremental 0.2 percent in the event response, in a sample where the mean event response is 1.8 percent. Moreover, the joint hypothesis that the firm fixed effects are zero is easily rejected at the 1 percent level. Indeed, more than 15 percent of the variance in performance across deals is accounted for by interfirm differences in fixed effects.

The evidence thus indicates that, first, there are large differences in the unobserved capabilities of firms in managing joint ventures. Second, after controlling for these differences, experience in managing joint ventures appears to significantly increase the returns that firms capture from joint ventures as well. In the remainder of the analysis, we examine the robustness of these results as well as the variation in the effect of experience across contract types.

The identification logic above emphasizes that to be able to distinguish the effect of experience from the effects attributable to capability differences across firms, it is necessary to have multiple observations on a single firm. Consequently, we restricted the data to include only those firms which have entered into at least five joint ventures over the sample period (thus, for which we have at least five data points each), since the identification is clearest for this data sample. Indeed, the effect of experience on value creation is found to be positive and statistically significant at the 1 percent level for both performance measures, with the point estimates being very similar to those obtained earlier.

Next, we examine how the effect of experience varies according to the kind of joint venture being entered into, in particular distinguishing R&D joint ventures, production joint ventures, and marketing joint ventures. $CumRjv_{it}$ is defined to be the number of research joint ventures entered into by firm i prior to time t; similarly, $CumRjv_{it}$ and $CumMjv_{it}$ measure the experience variables for production and marketing joint ventures respectively. The estimation results indicate that the effects of experience on performance are largest for research joint ventures (Table 6, columns (i)–(ii)): each additional deal of experience

Table 6. Cross-Sectional Analysis of Value Creation by Joint Venture Type

	Research Joint Ventures		Production Joint Ventures		Marketing Joint Ventures	
Dependent Variable	Specification (i) Wealth Effects	Specification (ii) Abnormal Returns	Specification (i) Wealth Effects	Specification (ii) Abnormal Returns	Specification (i) Wealth Effects	Specification (ii) Abnormal Returns
Constant	334.4443	0.1338**	931.3030**	0.3921***	293.2754	−0.1643**
	(1.134)	(2.307)	(2.449)	(5.396)	(0.562)	(−2.456)
Experience	291.8102***	0.0133*	87.9346**	0.0027	44.6232	0.0047
	(2.910)	(1.740)	(2.522)	(1.176)	(0.416)	(0.942)
Assets	0.0003	1.73e–07	−0.0023	−4.11e–07	0.0027	8.34e–08
	(0.017)	(0.196)	(−0.404)	(−1.132)	(0.342)	(0.313)
Industry fixed effects						
Drugs	−32.5088	0.0389	66.6567	0.0602	357.8014	0.0305
	(−0.205)	(0.877)	(0.834)	(1.249)	(1.452)	(0.836)
Chemicals	8.2214	0.0026	179.7320	−0.0083	105.6508	0.0566***
	(0.037)	(0.052)	(1.282)	(−0.525)	(0.490)	(2.840)
Computer	104.3673	−0.0046	15.3828	0.0229	337.8499	0.0074
	(0.582)	(−0.107)	(0.046)	(0.349)	(1.246)	(0.202)
Communications	−157.1399	0.0469	410.4329	0.0205	384.6353	0.0909***
	(−0.793)	(1.171)	(1.241)	(0.699)	(1.574)	(3.731)
Chips	−34.3221	0.0067	9.8061	0.0181	−122.6241	0.0370
	(−0.202)	(0.194)	(0.050)	(0.498)	(−0.462)	(1.102)
Cars	430.1458	0.0745***	−32.4872	−0.0220	141.7749	0.0494
	(1.399)	(2.716)	(−0.253)	(−1.036)	(1.526)	(1.319)
Instruments	−67.9488	−0.0417	−66.0686	−0.0004	−185.6701	−0.0162
	(−0.326)	(−1.025)	(−0.590)	(−0.013)	(−0.904)	(−0.523)
Firm fixed effects	Included	Included	Included	Included	Included	Included
Number of observations	193	195	449	449	296	296
R^2	0.5934	0.5353	0.2515	0.4176	0.4154	0.5578

***Significant at the 1% level; **Significant at the 5% level; *Significant at the 10% level.

Multivariate regression analyses examining the determinants of wealth effects and excess returns for specific types of joint ventures. Dependent variable is obtained from the event study on 870 joint ventures from an extensively cleaned version of the Securities Data Corporation (SDC) Strategic Alliance data base, 1990–93. Joint ventures are classified into Research, Production or Marketing joint ventures as per the SDC data base, cross-checked with information obtained from press releases in the Lexis-Nexis data base. Experience codes the number of prior joint ventures of the type in question entered into by the firm (including the deal in question). The experience measures are thus contract-specific. The assets variable is obtained from the Compustat data base and is measured in millions of dollars. Industry categories refer to the industry location of the alliance activity and are as defined in Table 3. Estimates of firm fixed effects are suppressed. The estimations allow for correlated errors across the firms within the same alliance, while maintaining the assumption of independence between alliances. Heteroskedastic-consistent White standard errors are used in deriving the t-statistics, which are reported in parentheses.

translates into an additional $291.8 million of value for the firm in question (statistically significant at the 1% level), or an additional 1.33 percent in abnormal percentage returns (z-value = 1.77). Both these effects are statistically significant at the 5 percent level. For production joint ventures, each additional deal of experience translates into an additional $87.9 million in value creation for the firm (statistically significant at the 1% level); the effect on abnormal percentage returns is 0.27 percent (z-value = 1.15). Finally, experience does not appear to affect the returns to marketing joint ventures. The point estimates of the effect of experience on performance are thus largest for research joint ventures, followed by production joint ventures, then by marketing joint ventures. This result is discussed in more detail below.

4.3. *Results for Licensing Contracts*

Extending this analysis, we next look at the effect of experience in licensing deals. As before, we define experience measures for licensing contracts: $CumLic_{it} = 1$ for those deals in which the firm has no prior experience in licensings, $CumLic_{it} = 2$ for those deals in which the firm is known to have entered into exactly one prior licensing contract (either as a licensor or a licensee), $CumLic_{it} = 3$ for two or three prior licensings, and $CumLic_{it} = 4$ for at least four prior licensing deals. Table 7 summarizes the variation in the returns to licensing across levels of experience, and indicates that there is no clear pattern to the effect of experience on value creation through licensings. A one-way analysis of variance indicates that the differences in mean value created across the four categories is not statistically significant (p-value = 0.76). The results of multivariate regression analyses,

Table 7. Wealth Effects and Abnormal Returns by Experience Categories for Licensing Contracts

	Licenses					
	Wealth Effects (in $ thousands)			Excess Returns (%)		
Experience Category	#	Mean	S.D.	#	Mean	S.D.
1	430	17.841	413.243	505	3.98	18.83
2	168	46.355	478.931	193	3.90	14.94
3	170	51.171	565.512	187	2.78	13.49
4	206	−20.939	1206.511	221	0.46	10.58
Total	974	20.377	691.048	1106	3.06	15.98

Variation in wealth effects and excess returns by experience category for the sample of 974 licenses. The experience categories are defined as follows. Category 1 indicates deals in which the firm has no prior experience with licenses; category 2 refers to deals in which the firm is known to have entered into exactly 1 prior license; category 3 refers to deals in which the firm has entered into 2 or 3 prior licenses; category 4 refers to deals in which the firm has entered into at least 4 prior licenses.

Table 8. Cross-Sectional Analysis of Value Creation in Licensings

Dependent Variable	Specification (i) Wealth Effects	Specification (ii) Abnormal Returns	Specification (iii) Wealth Effects	Specification (iv) Abnormal Returns
Constant	−21.0478	0.0280***	−62.0633	0.0358***
	(−0.449)	(2.817)	(−1.011)	(2.681)
Experience (CUMLIC)	−4.3660	−0.0037***	−8.6097	−0.0031
	(−0.476)	(−2.599)	(−0.511)	(−0.731)
Assets	0.0033	−2.48e–07**	0.0126**	−7.93e–07
	(1.290)	(−2.176)	(2.011)	(−1.026)
Industry fixed effects				
Drugs	37.8096	0.0155	−21.3969	0.0065
	(0.746)	(1.189)	(−0.363)	(0.340)
Chemicals	37.6568	0.0056	−8.1033	0.0184
	(0.517)	(0.384)	(−0.073)	(−0.688)
Computer	179.7614	0.0318	327.7553*	0.0398*
	(1.607)	(1.517)	(1.792)	(1.662)
Communication	−99.3360	0.0693**	−128.3829	0.0597**
	(−0.828)	(2.162)	(−0.803)	(2.203)
Chips	7.0889	0.0107	79.3717	0.0220
	(0.087)	(0.782)	(0.523)	(1.070)
Firm fixed effects			Included	Included
Number of observations	974	974	974	970
R^2	0.0196	0.0215	0.1336	0.2914
F-value	0.88	3.39***	32.97***	2.10***

***Significant at the 1% level; **Significant at the 5% level; *Significant at the 10% level.
Multivariate regression analyses examining the determinants of wealth effects and excess returns for licenses. Dependent variable is obtained from the event study on licenses from an extensively cleaned version of the Securities Data Corporation Strategic Alliance data base, 1990–93. Experience (CUMJV) codes the number of prior joint ventures entered into by the firm including the deal in question. The assets variable is obtained from the Compustat data base and is measured in millions of dollars. Industry categories refer to the industry location of the alliance activity and are as defined in Table 3. Estimates of firm fixed effects are suppressed. The estimations allow for correlated errors across the firms within the same alliance, while maintaining the assumption of independence between alliances. Heteroskedastic-consistent White standard errors are used in deriving the *t*-statistics, which are reported in parentheses.

reported in Table 8, confirm that the effects of experience are not statistically significant at the 10 percent level for any performance measure. Thus, there is no evidence that experience in licensings affects the returns to engaging in such deals. However, as for joint ventures, there do appear to be significant differences between firms in their abilities to manage licensing contracts, as evidenced by the significance of the firm fixed effects in these regressions.

4.4. *Robustness Checks*

All the results reported above survive multiple robustness checks. First, the results are not sensitive to the particular event window used. For example, using a smaller, 3-day event window (surrounding the event day) to compute our measures of abnormal returns and dollar value created does not change the results. This window yields performance measures that are highly correlated with the measures used in the estimations reported above. There are also no qualitative differences in the results of our multivariate regressions. A corollary of this is that pre-event day information leakage is not driving any differences in our estimates of learning across joint ventures or licenses.

Second, the frequency of joint ventures and of licenses is not substantially different across each of the four years in our sample; nor are the summary statistics regarding abnormal returns or dollar value created across these years. Consistent with this, including time dummies in our regressions does not change any results.

Third, changing the functional form of the dependence of our performance measures on firm size does not alter our results. Fourth, we examined in detail the sensitivity of the results to potential outliers: standard checks performed as per the diagnostics indicated by Belsley, Kuh, and Welsch (1980) do not change any of the results.

Fifth, our experience measures are left-censored. We therefore examined the sensitivity of the results to measurement error in the experience measures (in particular, to the *ad hoc* 1990 cut-off, prior to which experience is not measured), by repeating the estimation for subsets of our data. For example, we repeated the analyses for the events falling in the 1991–93 window, with experience measures counting alliance events only if they occurred in this time window. We find that there are no qualitative changes in the point estimates, though standard errors naturally rise as the sample size is progressively reduced.

Finally, we examined the effect of experience on value creation in the alliance, as opposed to at the firm level. To do this, we combined the daily returns of the firms in the same alliance into a value-weighted portfolio (the returns are weighted by the market value of the firm's common stock 11 trading days prior to the initial announcement of the alliance, and the portfolio is then treated as a 'single security' in cross-sectional regressions). In Table 9, we report the results for the '106' such securities involving joint ventures, using both wealth effects and excess returns as dependent variables. The experience measure, defined to be the sum of the experience measures of all the parties involved in the alliance, is significant at the 5 percent level in both specifications. We find that each additional deal of experience in joint ventures translates into an incremental 0.2 percent in the event response, virtually identical to the firm-level results. This suggests that the wealth effect of experience is largely due to value creation as opposed to value division among joint venture partners. A similar exercise for licensings does not reveal any learning effects, as before.

In concluding, it may be worthwhile commenting on a possible alternative interpretation of our results on learning. A positive effect of the number of

Table 9. Cross-Sectional Analysis of Value Creation in Joint Ventures' Value-weighted Portfolios

Dependent Variable	Specification (i) Wealth Effects	Specification (ii) Abnormal Returns
Constant	−306.7108	−0.0114
	(−1.564)	(−1.189)
Mean assets	−0.0024	−1.60e–07
	(−0.356)	(−0.881)
Total experience	46.8977**	0.0017**
	(1.949)	(1.973)
Industry fixed effects		
Drugs	676.341	0.0078
	(0.757)	(0.211)
Chemicals	−125.0108	0.0100
	(−0.317)	(0.484)
Computer	−203.3869	0.0196
	(−0.457)	(0.702)
Communication	331.074	0.0035
	(0.723)	(0.265)
Chips	366.5947	0.0167
	(1.210)	(1.521)
Cars	488.7313*	0.0431***
	(1.912)	(3.564)
Instruments	−338.5916	−0.0217
	(−1.063)	(−1.081)
Number of observations	106	106
R^2	0.1072	0.1000
F-value	1.79*	2.76***

***Significant at the 1% level; **Significant at the 5% level; *Significant at the 10% level. The value creation measures (wealth effects and excess returns) are obtained by combining the daily returns of firms in the same alliance into a value-weighted portfolio, which is then treated as a single security in the cross-sectional regressions. The daily returns of firms are obtained from the event study on the sample of joint ventures from an extensively cleaned version of the Securities Data Corporation Strategic Alliances data base. Total experience is defined as the sum of the experience measures for all the firms involved in the alliance for which data are available. The assets variable is obtained from the Compustat data base and is measured in millions of dollars. Industry categories refer to the industry location of the alliance activity and are as defined in Table 3.

alliances on the announcement effect may be argued to reflect *market* learning rather than firm learning. For example, market uncertainty about a firm's capabilities may result in a lower market response early on; as this uncertainty declines over time, the announcement effect would increase as well. While plausible in principle, there are various reasons why we believe this may not be a compelling interpretation of our results. First, our data span a relatively short panel, making it less likely that differences in perceptions about firm abilities are likely to be large over this time period. Second, the learning effects that we obtain are robust to the inclusion of time dummies, as mentioned above. Third, the pattern of cross-alliance differences in learning effects is more difficult to explain based on this interpretation, since this would require market perceptions to be different for joint ventures and licensings, and between various kinds of joint ventures as well, in the particular direction that is consistent with the results.

4.5. *Examining Firm Fixed Effects*

Each firm fixed effect can be interpreted as a measure of that firm's alliance capability. It represents the market's perception of the amount of value that will be created, or destroyed (for those firms whose estimated capabilities are negative), on average, when that firm engages in an alliance. We examine here the distribution of estimated joint venturing capabilities and of licensing capabilities for a select sample of the firms. Table 10 reports summary statistics for these fixed effects for those firms for which we have four or more alliances in our sample (41 firms for our joint venture subsample, and 57 for our licensing subsample). Separate firm fixed effects are obtained from the estimations using dollar value and abnormal returns measures, for both the joint ventures and licensing subsamples (this accounts for the four columns in the table).

The mean of the distribution of fixed effects is negative in both subsamples, with large standard deviations. Further, the percentage of firms with negative fixed effects is significantly higher for joint ventures than for licenses (65% vs. 46% using the estimated coefficients from the wealth effects regressions; 80% vs. 61% using the estimated coefficients from the abnormal returns regressions). The wide dispersion in estimated alliance capabilities is in accord with practitioner reports of the wide variation in alliance capability. At first,

Table 10. Summary Statistics: Derived Fixed Effects

	Joint Ventures		Licenses	
	Dollar Value (in $ thousands)	Abnormal Returns	Dollar Value (in $ thousands)	Abnormal Returns
Number of observations	41	41	57	57
Number of observations with positive fixed effects	14	8	31	22
Mean	−99.98	1.70%	−92.77	0.39%
S.D.	355.170	2.68%	352.895	11.06%

Summary statistics of firm fixed effects obtained from cross-sectional regressions in Table 5 (joint ventures) and Table 8 (licenses) using only those firms which have four or more alliances (of the type in question) in our data.

however, the fact that the most active firms appear to have negative fixed effects runs counter to the intuition that these firms—because of their higher stock of experience—will also be better at managing alliances. Of course, there may be many other explanations for these differences in the fixed effect means between active and less active firms. If alliances represent a 'second-best' option for firms looking to commercialize their innovations (relative to internal commercialization, for example), then firms that are most active in alliances are likely to be the ones with poorer technologies as well.[22]

Ultimately, internal firm data are required to parse out the correlates of our estimated fixed effects.[23] However, some analyses based on publicly available data yield the following interesting conclusions. First, certain firms that are celebrated as being excellent alliance managers do in fact have high fixed effects for both licences and joint ventures: Hewlett-Packard and Coca-Cola are leading examples. However, this is not always true: for example, the evidence regarding Corning—a firm with a reputed alliance capability—is rather mixed.[24] The point estimate for this firm lies roughly in the middle of the sample for whom summary statistics are reported in Table 10. In the case of those obtained from the estimations for R&D joint ventures, separate regressions of these fixed effects on average R&D intensity (defined as the average of R&D/sales for the years in the sample, 1990–93) showed no statistically significant relationship. Thus, there does not appear to be any evidence that differences in the rate of expenditure on R&D drive differences in our measure of alliance capability. We also found that an approximation for Tobin's q[25] was not significant in explaining either the point estimates obtained from the licensing regressions or the point estimates obtained from the joint venture regressions. To the extent that Tobin's q is a measure of the intangible general management ability of the firm in question, the latter does not appear to translate over into an alliance capability.

5. Discussion

We summarize our results around two sets of findings concerning: (a) learning effects in value creation through alliances, and the associated phenomenon of (b) heterogeneity in alliance capability. We find strong evidence that firms learn to create more value as they accumulate experience in joint venturing, whereas there is no evidence that firms learn to create value as they accumulate experience in licensing (Hypothesis 1). These learning effects appear to exist especially in R&D and production joint ventures but not in marketing joint ventures (the result on marketing joint ventures is inconsistent with Hypothesis 1). Consistent with Hypothesis 2, learning effects are stronger in R&D joint ventures than they are in other forms of joint ventures. Finally, we find strong and persistent differences across firms in their ability to create value, in all our alliance subsamples; we interpret these as reflecting differences in 'alliance capabilities.'

As far as we are aware, this is one of the first studies to establish systematic evidence for the existence of significant learning effects in the management of alliances. The magnitude of these effects suggests that the valuation of alliances cannot afford to ignore the dynamic, cross-alliance benefits of entering into a particular partnership. In addition, the results on cross-alliance differences in learning effects also suggest limits on the set of contexts in which returns to experience are likely to be significant, thus implicitly answering the question of when learning is likely to be important. Finally, our results on the explanators of firm fixed effects indicate that it may be important to distinguish between a firm's intangible, general-purpose skills (as embodied in a measure of q) and its alliance capability: strength in one arena clearly does not imply a presence of the other.

There are other interesting issues related to the reasons underlying learning effects, however, which we cannot shed light on with our data. For example, we cannot distinguish whether learning occurs by firms getting better at screening their alliance partners, or because they get better at interfacing with these partners (perhaps through designing better contracts or through getting more adept at managing relationships). Similarly, it would be of both positive and normative interest to examine the extent to which learning rates differ across firms, and, if so, what explains these differences. Finally, our results clearly establish the existence of differences in 'alliance capabilities' across firms, and estimates of these capabilities (via the firm fixed effects) as well. This could serve as a useful platform for further work which explores the organizational determinants of this alliance capability, following analysis of the sort conducted by Henderson and Cockburn (1994). This would require data internal to each firm regarding the organization of their alliance management processes, possibly collected through surveys.

Notes

1. Alliances are organizational forms that allow otherwise independent firms to share resources of a variety of sorts. Conceptually, we think of them as intermediate organizational forms between markets and hierarchies.

2. Thus, the CEO of Emerson Electric refers to implementation as 'the graveyard of strategic alliances.' Another top alliance manager claims that managing alliances is as difficult as 'stirring concrete with eyelashes.' A 1997 survey on 'Institutionalizing Alliance Capability' by a prominent consulting firm reported wide discrepancy in failure rates among those firms generally thought to be able to manage alliances well, and among those thought to be poor at managing alliances. (*Alliance Analyst*, December 23, 1996; June 9, 1997; August 15, 1997).
3. The trade press sometimes refers to alliances in this fashion, e.g., 'alliances are incomplete contracts (which) leave all sorts of room for maneuver and interpretation' (*Alliance Analyst*, November 25, 1996).
4. Authors have long opined that such intangible capabilities constitute the heart of what is distinctive about a firm. Witness Blau and Scott's (1962) emphasis on the unwritten rules within an organization, and Barnard's (1938) suggestion that such intangible capabilities cannot be known unless one works within the organization.
5. Curiously, such empirical evidence as does exist has to do primarily with the celebrated 'learning curve' literature (Spence, 1981; Fudenberg and Tirole, 1984; Lieberman, 1984; Ghemawat and Spence, 1985), which focuses on learning to reduce production costs. We conjecture that the reason for this is that production costs have historically provided the most convenient data to examine learning effects.
6. Theoretical foundations for the persistence of firm heterogeneity date back to Selznick (1957) and Penrose (1959). Several authors have found that firm effects account for a lot of the variation in profit rates across firms (Cool and Schendel, 1988; Rumelt, 1991; McGahan and Porter, 1997), while others have found strong firm effects in managing research (Henderson and Cockburn, 1994).
7. In a related case study, Dyer and Nobeoka (2000) examine how information flows between Toyota and its suppliers both enhances the latter's incentives for specific investments and mitigates free-riding via implicit contracts. Interestingly, Afuah (2000) provides evidence on the *costs* of strong relationships. He shows how strong relationships may lock-in the firm to existing technologies, thereby disadvantaging the firm in periods of drastic technological change.
8. Indeed, Kale and Singh (1999) argue that differences in the organizational processes used to accumulate, codify and share knowledge explain differences in firms' abilities to learn from alliances.
9. See, for example, Harbison and Pekar (1997) and various issues of the *Alliance Analyst* which are devoted to various aspects of alliance capabilities.
10. The trade press also implicitly references a life cycle model by which firms acquire alliance capabilities: for example, it is postulated that firms move from managing one-off alliances to a lone-ranger model where alliance capability resides in a small number of individuals, to a more formal model (*Alliance Analyst*, June 9, 1997).
11. The evidence here is not about direct value creation through repeated activity, but is an inference drawn from the greater propensity of firms that have allied in the past to do so again.
12. Prior work has provided empirical evidence that there is a clear relationship between the extent of ambiguity in codifying knowledge and the choice of contract in interfirm alliances: Anand and Khanna (2000) demonstrate empirically that licenses are significantly

more frequently employed than joint ventures in contexts where it is relatively easy to establish property rights over knowledge and where ambiguity is low. The reasons that it is easier to specify and communicate technological know-how in some industries than in others have been discussed extensively in various papers, for example, Landau and Rosenberg (1992), Arora and Gambardella (1996), Levin et al. (1987), and Dam (1995).

13. See also Harrigan (1988) and Mody (1993).
14. Interestingly, if firm fixed effects are larger for older firms, then we cannot disentangle the effects of past experience from the effects of ability in explaining the unobserved heterogeneity. If the reverse were the case, however, then differences in underlying ability must be large enough to offset the advantage of experience.
15. This introduces measurement error in these variables, which we discuss, later in our robustness checks.
16. Benkard (1998) provides empirical evidence in support of 'forgetfulness' by firms in the aircraft industry.
17. The event day responses suggest that information leakage is not a serious problem in either of our subsamples, since average abnormal returns are not significant for almost all days prior to the event day. For licensing contracts, the preannouncement day and postannouncement day abnormal returns appear to be large, however (0.36% and 0.61%, respectively).
18. This is an approximation to the 'actual' wealth effect which is based on the product of abnormal returns over the event window and given by: $V_{i,day\_0}\star\left(\prod_{t=-10}^{t=+1}(1+\hat{\epsilon}_{it})-1\right)$. For our sample, $\hat{\epsilon}_{it}$ is on average 0.1 percent, hence the approximation is very good: for licensing contracts, for example, the correlation between the actual and approximated wealth effects is 0.98; moreover, the distribution of a test statistic based on the sum of returns is straightforward to obtain.
19. However, since the value creation analysis is based on publicly traded firms, which are likely to be larger than the population average, the wealth effect figures will overstate the average value created from alliances by *all* firms.
20. Using OLS procedures in the cross-section estimation implicitly assumes that the error term is uncorrelated across the firms *within* an alliance. Ignoring these within-alliance correlations may lead to spurious claims of significance (Moulton, 1986). Therefore, in all the estimations, we relax the assumption of independent errors across firms within the same alliance, while continuing to maintain the assumption of independence across alliances.
21. This is consistent, for example, with a theory in which there is adverse selection of firms entering into joint ventures.
22. There may be other self-selection arguments as well. For example, Anand and Galetovic (1998) offer an equilibrium explanation for why the quality of technologies developed by firms with broader research portfolios (hence, by definition, more active in alliances) is likely to be poorer than the quality of single-technology firms.
23. See, for example, Henderson and Cockburn's (1994) study of firm fixed effects in pharmaceutical R&D.
24. See, for example, descriptions of the components of Corning's and of Hewlett-Packward's alliance capabilities in the *Alliance Analyst*, February 17, 1997, and of Coca-Cola in the *Alliance Analyst*, December 9, 1996.

25. A proxy for Tobin's q was defined as: (market value of common stock + book value of preferred stock + book value of debt)/(book value of total assets). Similar proxies have been used in various contexts by Lindenberg and Ross (1981) and by Montgomery and Wernerfelt (1988), among others.

References

Afuah, A. (2000). 'How much do your *co-opetitors* matter in the face of technological change', *Strategic Management Journal*, Special Issue, **21**, pp. 387–404.

Allen, J. (1998). 'Capital markets and corporate structure: The equity carve-outs of ThermoElectron', *Journal of Financial Economics*, **48**(1), pp. 99–124.

Anand, B. and Galetovic, A. (1998). 'Weak property rights and hold-up in R&D', Harvard Business School Working Paper 99–007.

Anand, B. and Khanna, T. (2000). 'The structure of licensing contracts', *Journal of Industrial Economics*, forthcoming.

Arino, A. and de la Torre, J. (1998). 'Learning from failure: Towards an evolutionary model of collaborative ventures', *Organization Science*, **9**(3), pp. 306–325.

Argyris, C. and Schon, D. (1978). *Organizational Learning: A Theory of Action Perspective*. Addison Wesley, Reading, MA.

Arora, A. and Gambardella, A. (1996). 'Evolution of industry structure in the chemical industry', mimeo, CEPR, Stanford University.

Baker, G., Gibbons, R. and Murphy, K. (1997). 'Implicit contracts and the theory of the firm,' National Bureau of Economic Research Working Paper 6177.

Baldwin, C. and Forsyth, J. (1992). 'ThermoElectron Corporation', Harvard Business School Case 9–292–104. 9–292–104. 9–292–104. 9–292–104.

Barnard, C. (1938). *The Functions of the Executive*. Harvard University Press, Cambridge, MA.

Belsley, D. A., Kuh, E. and Welsch, R. E. (1980). *Regression Diagnostics*. Wiley, New York.

Benkard, L. (1998). 'Learning and forgetting: The dynamics of aircraft production,' Yale University, Department of Economics Working Paper, New Haven, CT.

Blau, P. and Scott, R. (1962). *Formal Organizations: A Comparative Approach*. Chandler, San Francisco, CA.

Bower, G. H. and Hilgard, E. R. (1981). *Theories of Learning*. Prentice-Hall Englewood Cliffs, NJ.

Brown, S. and Warner, J. (1985). 'Using daily stock returns: The case of event studies,' *Journal of Financial Economics*, **14**(1), pp. 3–31.

Caves, R., Crookell, H. and Killing, J. P. (1983). 'The imperfect market for technology licenses,' *Oxford Bulletin of Economics and Statistics*, **45**, pp. 249–267.

Chan, S., Kensinger, J., Keown, A. and Martin, J. (1997). 'Do strategic alliances create value?,' *Journal of Financial Economics*, **46**, pp. 199–221.

Chang, S. J. (1995). 'International expansion strategy of Japanese firms: Capability building through sequential entry', *Academy of Management Journal*, **38**(2), pp. 383–407.

Cohen, W. M. and Levinthal, D. A. (1990). 'Absorptive capacity: A new perspective on learning and innovation,' *Administrative Science Quarterly*, **35**, pp. 128–152.

Cool, K. and Schendel, D. (1988). 'Performance differences among strategic group members', *Strategic Management Journal*, **9**(3), pp. 207–223.

Cyert, R. M. and March, J. G. (1963). *A Behavioral Theory of the Firm*. Prentice-Hall, Englewood Cliffs, NJ.

Dam, K. (1995). 'Some economic considerations in the intellectual property protection of software', *Journal of Legal Studies*, **24**, pp. 321–373.

Doz, Y. (1996). 'The evolution of cooperation in strategic alliances: Initial conditions or learning processes?', *Strategic Management Journal*, Summer Special Issue, **17**, pp. 55–83.

Dyer, J. H. and Nobeoka, K. (2000). 'Creating and managing a high performance knowledge-sharing network: The Toyota case,' *Strategic Management Journal*, Special Issue, **21**, pp. 345–367.

——and Singh, H. (1998). 'The relational view: Cooperative strategy and sources of interorganizational competitive advantage', *Academy of Management Review*, **23**(4), pp. 660–679.

Ellis, H. C. (1965). *The Transfer of Learning*. Macmillan, New York.

Estes, W. K. (1970). *Learning Theory and Mental Development*. Academic Press, New York.

Fama, E. (1976). *Foundations of Finance*. Basic Books, New York.

Fudenberg, D. and Tirole, J. (1984). 'Learning-by-doing and market performance,' *Bell Journal of Economics*, **14**(2), pp. 522–530.

Ghemawat, P. and Spence, A. M. (1985). 'Learning curve spillovers and market performance,' *Quarterly Journal of Economics*, **100**(5), pp. 839–852.

Gulati, R. (1995). 'Does familiarity breed trust? The implications of repeated ties for contractual choice in alliances,' *Academy of Management Journal*, **38**(1), pp. 85–112.

——Khanna, T. and Nohria, N. (1994). 'Unilateral commitments and the importance of process in alliances,' *Sloan Management Review*, **35**(3), pp. 61–69.

Hamel, G. (1991). 'Competition for competence and inter-partner learning within international strategic alliances,' *Strategic Management Journal*, Summer Special Issue, **12**, pp. 83–103.

Harbison, J. and Pekar, P. (1997). 'Institutionalizing alliance skills: Secrets of repeatable success,' Booz-Allen and Hamilton Viewpoint on Alliances.

Harrigan, K. R. (1988). 'Joint ventures and competitive strategy,' *Strategic Management Journal*, **9**(2), pp. 141–158.

Haspeslagh, P. and Jemison, D. (1991). *Managing Acquisitions: Creating Value through Corporate Renewal*. Free Press, New York.

Henderson, R. and Cockburn, I. (1994). 'Measuring competence? Exploring firm effects in pharmaceutical research,' *Strategic Management Journal*, Winter Special Issue, **15**, pp. 63–84.

Jensen, M. and Meckling, W. (1991). 'Specific and general knowledge, and organizational structure.' In L. Werin and H. Wijkander (eds.), *Main Currents in Contract Economics*. Blackwell, Oxford, pp. 251–274.

Kale, P., Singh, H. and Perlmutter, H. (2000). 'Learning and protection of proprietary assets in strategic alliances: Building relational capital,' *Strategic Management Journal*, Special Issue, **21**, pp. 217–237.

——and——(1999). 'Alliance capability and success: A knowledge-based approach,' Academy of Management Proceedings, Chicago.

Khanna, T. (1998). 'The scope of alliances,' *Organization Science*, **9**(3), pp. 340–356.
——Gulati, R. and Nohria, N. (1998). 'The dynamics of learning alliances: Competition, cooperation and relative scope,' *Strategic Management Journal*, **19**(3), pp. 193–210.
Kogut, B. (1989). 'The stability of joint ventures: Reciprocity and competitive rivalry,' *Journal of Industrial Economics*, **38**, pp. 183–198.
Landau, R. and Rosenberg, N. (1992). 'Successful commercialization in the chemical process industry.' In N. Rosenberg, R. Landau and D. Mowery, (eds.), *Technology and the Wealth of Nations*. Stanford University Press, Stanford CA. pp. 73–120.
Lane, P. J. and Lubatkin, M. (1998). 'Relative absorptive capacity and interorganizational learning,' *Strategic Management Journal*, **19**(5), pp. 461–478.
Larsson, R., Bengtsson, L., Henriksson, K. and Sparks, J. (1998). 'The interorganizational learning dilemma: Collective knowledge development in strategic alliances,' *Organization Science*, **9**(3), pp. 285–305.
Levin, R., Klevorick, A., Nelson, R. and Winter, S. (1987). 'Appropriating the returns from industrial research and development,' *Brookings Papers on Economic Activity*, **3**, pp. 783–820.
Lieberman, M. (1984). 'The learning curve and pricing in the chemical processing industries,' *Rand Journal of Economics*, **15**(2), pp. 213–228.
Lindenberg, E. B. and Ross, S. A. (1981). 'Tobin's q ratio and industrial organization,' *Journal of Business*, **54**(1), pp. 1–32.
McConnell, J. and Nantel, T. (1985). 'Corporate combinations and common stock returns: The case of joint ventures,' *Journal of Finance*, **40**(2), pp. 519–536.
McGahan, A. and Porter, M. (1997). 'How much does industry matter, really?', *Strategic Management Journal*, Summer Special Issue, **18**, pp. 15–30.
Mody, A. (1993). 'Learning through alliances,' *Journal of Economic Behavior and Organization*, **20**(2), pp. 151–170.
Montgomery, C. and Wernerfelt, B. (1988). 'Diversification, Ricardian rents, and Tobin's q', *Rand Journal of Economics*, **19**, pp. 623–632.
Moulton, B. R. (1986). 'Random group effects and the precision of regression estimates,' *Journal of Econometrics*, **32**, pp. 385–397.
Nelson, R. and Winter, S. (1982). *An Evolutionary Theory of Economic Change*. Harvard University Press, Cambridge, MA.
Parr, R. and Sullivan, P. (eds.) (1988). *Technology Licensing: Corporate Strategies for Maximizing Value*. Wiley, New York.
Penrose, E. (1959). *The Theory of the Growth of the Firm*. Wiley, New York.
Rumelt, R. (1991). 'How much does industry matter?' *Strategic Management Journal*, **12**(3), pp. 167–185.
Selznick, P. (1957). *Leadership in Administration: A Sociological Interpretation*. Harper & Row, New York.
Simon, H. (1955). 'A behavioral model of rational choice,' *Quarterly Journal of Economics*, **69**, pp. 99–118.
Singh, H. and Zollo, M. (1999). 'Post-acquistion strategies, integration capability, and the economic performance of corporate acquisitions,' Wharton School Working Paper.
Smith, D. and Alexander, R. (1988). *Fumbling the Future: How Xerox Invented, Then Ignored, the First Personal Computer*, William Morrow, New York.

Spence, A. M. (1981). 'The learning curve and competition,' *Bell Journal of Economics*, **12**(1), pp. 41–70.

Szulanski, G. (1996). 'Exploring internal stickiness: Impediments to the transfer of best practice within the firm,' *Strategic Management Journal*, Winter Special Issue, **17**, pp. 27–43.

Winter, S. (1988). 'Knowledge and competence as strategic assets.' In D. J. Teece (ed.), *The Competitive Challenge: Strategies for Industrial Innovation and Renewal*. Ballinger, Cambridge, MA, pp. 159–184.

V. RELATIONAL PERSPECTIVES ON INTERFIRM COLLABORATION

15 The Relational View: Cooperative Strategy and Sources of Interorganizational Competitive Advantage

Jeffrey H. Dyer and Harbir Singh

Scholars in the strategy field are concerned fundamentally with explaining differential firm performance (Rumelt, Schendel, and Teece, 1991). As strategy scholars have searched for sources of competitive advantage, two prominent views have emerged regarding the sources of supernormal returns. The first—the *industry structure view*—associated with Porter (1980), suggests that supernormal returns are primarily a function of a firm's membership in an industry with favorable structural characteristics (e.g., relative bargaining power, barriers to entry, and so on). Consequently, many researchers have focused on the industry as the relevant unit of analysis. The second view—the *resource-based view* (RBV) of the firm—argues that differential firm performance is fundamentally due to firm heterogeneity rather than industry structure (Barney, 1991; Rumelt, 1984, 1991; Wernerfelt, 1984). Firms that are able to accumulate resources and capabilities that are rare, valuable, nonsubstitutable, and difficult to imitate will achieve a competitive advantage over competing firms (Barney, 1991; Dierickx and Cool, 1989; Rumelt, 1984). Thus, extant RBV theory views the firm as the primary unit of analysis.[1]

Although these two perspectives have contributed greatly to our understanding of how firms achieve above-normal returns, they overlook the important fact that the (dis)advantages of an individual firm are often linked to the (dis)advantages of the network of relationships in which the firm is embedded. Proponents of the RBV have emphasized that competitive advantage results from those resources and capabilities that are owned and controlled by a single firm. Consequently, the search for competitive advantage has focused on those resources that are housed *within the firm*. Competing firms purchase standardized (nonunique) inputs that cannot be sources of advantage, because these inputs (factors) are either readily available to all competing firms or the cost of acquiring them is approximately equal to the economic value they create (Barney, 1986). However, a firm's critical resources may extend beyond firm boundaries. For example, the typical manufacturing firm in the United States purchases 55 percent of the value of each product it produces (this figure is 69 percent in Japan), and many of these inputs are highly customized by suppliers (Ministry of International Trade and Industry, 1987). Moreover, this percentage has been increasing during the past two decades (Bresnen and Fowler, 1994; Nishiguchi, 1994). Recent studies suggest that productivity gains in the value chain are possible when trading partners are willing to make relation-specific investments and combine resources in unique ways (Asanuma, 1989; Dyer, 1996a). This indicates that firms who combine resources in unique ways may realize an advantage over competing firms who are unable or unwilling to do so. Thus, *idiosyncratic interfirm linkages* may be a source of relational rents[2] and competitive advantage.

This analysis suggests that a firm's critical resources may span firm boundaries and may be embedded in interfirm routines and processes.[3] Indeed, the "explosion in alliances" during the past decade suggests that a pair or network of firms is an increasingly important unit of analysis and, therefore, deserves more study (Anderson, 1990; Gomes-Casseres, 1994; Smith, Carroll, and Ashford, 1995). Although there has recently been increased attention on interorganizational relationships in the strategic management literature, to date, no attempt has been made to integrate what we have learned and *systematically examine the interorganizational rent-generating process*. In instances where researchers have explicitly studied how firms collaborate to generate economic rents, they have tended to focus on one particular benefit associated with collaboration, such as learning, lower transaction costs, or pooling of resources (Dore, 1983; Dyer, 1996a; Hamel, 1991; Larson, 1992; Powell, Koput, and Smith-Doerr, 1996; Teece, 1987).

Our primary purpose in this chapter is to examine how relational rents are earned and preserved. We offer a *relational view* of competitive advantage that focuses on dyad/network routines and processes as an important unit of analysis for understanding competitive advantage.[4] This framework is valuable because it provides a theoretical basis for cumulative additions to our understanding of the sources of interorganizational competitive advantage (Oliver, 1990). In the following sections we identify and delineate the various sources of rents at the interfirm unit of analysis. We also examine the mechanisms that preserve the relational rents that dyads and networks jointly create. Finally, we discuss how the relational view may offer normative prescriptions for firm-level strategies that contradict the prescriptions offered by the RBV and industry structure view.

1. Sources of Relational Rents

1.1. Theoretical Discussion

By examining the relevant characteristics of arm's-length market relationships, we find clues that guide our search for relational advantages. Arm's-length market relationships are characterized by:

1. nonspecific asset investments,
2. minimal information exchange (i.e., prices act as coordinating devices by signaling all relevant information to buyers and sellers),
3. separable technological and functional systems within each firm that are characterized by low levels of interdependence (i.e., the two organizations have only a sales-to-purchasing interface and do not jointly create new products through multifunctional interfaces), and
4. low transaction costs and minimal investment in governance mechanisms (Williamson, 1985).

Under these conditions it is easy for firms to switch trading partners with little penalty because other sellers offer virtually identical products. As Ghoshal notes, "Efficiency in the execution of routine tasks is the strength of markets" (1995: 16). Thus, arm's-length market relationships are incapable of generating relational rents because *there is nothing idiosyncratic about the exchange relationship that enables the two parties to generate profits above and beyond what other seller–buyer combinations can generate*. The relationships are not rare or difficult to imitate. Buyers can only achieve a differential advantage if they bring greater bargaining power to the table.

This analysis suggests that alliances generate competitive advantages only as they move the relationship away from the attributes of market relationships. In other words, the competitive advantages of partnerships, as documented in studies to date, seem to fall into four categories:

1. investments in relation-specific assets;
2. substantial knowledge exchange, including the exchange of knowledge that results in joint learning;
3. the combining of complementary, but scarce, resources or capabilities (typically through multiple functional interfaces), which results in the joint creation of unique new products, services, or technologies; and
4. lower transaction costs than competitor alliances, owing to more effective governance mechanisms.

We define a relational rent as a supernormal profit jointly generated in an exchange relationship that cannot be generated by either firm in isolation and can only be created through the joint idiosyncratic contributions of the specific alliance partners.

In summary, at a fundamental level, relational rents are possible when alliance partners combine, exchange, or invest in idiosyncratic assets, knowledge, and resources/capabilities, and/or they employ effective governance mechanisms that lower transaction costs or permit the realization of rents through the synergistic combination of assets, knowledge, or capabilities. In the sections that follow we examine in detail these four key sources of relational rents; in each section we develop a major proposition and a set of subpropositions, as summarized in Fig. 1. After examining assets, knowledge, and resources, we examine governance, because although governance may generate relational rents by simply lowering transaction costs, governance issues cut across each of the other

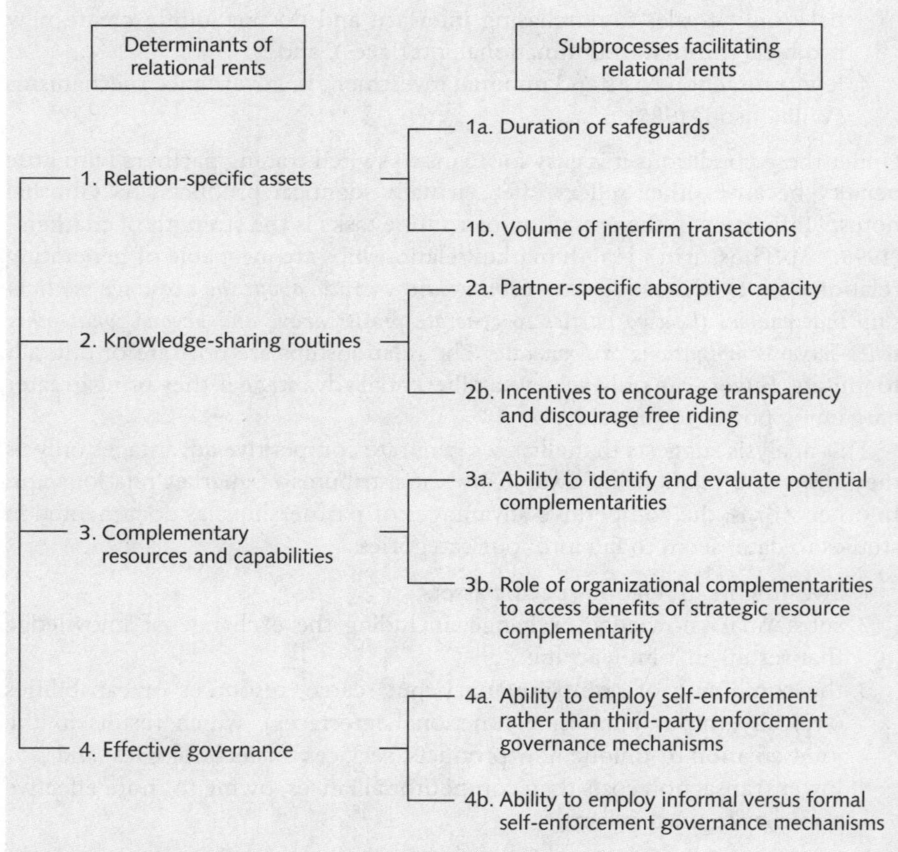

Fig. 1. Determinants of interorganizational competitive advantage.

sources of rents (e.g., influence what relation-specific investments will be made, what knowledge will be shared, and so on). We believe it is easier to understand how governance influences the ability to generate rents through assets, knowledge, and capabilities if we have first examined these constructs.

1.2. Interfirm Relation-Specific Assets

Amit and Schoemaker argue that specialization of assets is "a necessary condition for rent" and "strategic assets by their very nature are specialized" (1993: 39). Thus, by definition, firms must do something specialized or unique to develop a competitive advantage. A firm may choose to seek advantages by creating assets that are *specialized in conjunction with the assets of an alliance partner* (Klein, Crawford, and Alchian, 1978; Teece, 1987). Productivity gains in the value chain are possible when firms are willing to make relation/transaction-specific investments (Perry, 1989; Williamson, 1985).

Williamson (1985) identifies three types of asset specificity: (1) site specificity, (2) physical asset specificity, and (3) human asset specificity. *Site specificity* refers to the situation whereby successive production stages that are immobile in nature are located close to one another. Previous studies suggest that site-specific investments can substantially reduce inventory and transportation costs and can lower the costs of coordinating activities (Dyer, 1996a). *Physical asset specificity* refers to transaction-specific capital investments (e.g., in customized machinery, tools, dies, and so on) that tailor processes to particular exchange partners. Physical asset specialization has been found to allow for product differentiation and may improve quality by increasing product integrity or fit (Clark and Fujimoto, 1991; Nishiguchi, 1994). *Human asset specificity* refers to transaction-specific know-how accumulated by transactors through longstanding relationships (e.g., dedicated supplier engineers who learn the systems, procedures, and the individuals idiosyncratic to the buyer). Human cospecialization increases as alliance partners develop experience working together and accumulate specialized information, language, and know-how. This allows them to communicate efficiently and effectively, which reduces communication errors, thereby enhancing quality and increasing speed to market (Asanuma, 1989; Dyer, 1996a).

Asanuma (1989) was among the first to document how the relation-specific skills developed between Japanese suppliers and their automakers generated surplus profits and competitive advantages for collaborating firms. Similarly, Dyer (1996a) found a positive relationship between relation-specific investments and performance in a sample of automakers and their suppliers. Additionally, Saxenian (1994) found that Hewlett-Packard and other Silicon Valley firms greatly improved performance by developing long-term partnerships with physically proximate suppliers. She claims that proximity in high-technology industries "greatly facilitates the collaboration required for fast-changing and complex technologies" (1990: 101). Indeed, several scholars have shown that physical proximity created through site-specific investments facilitates interfirm cooperation and coordination, thereby enhancing performance (Dyer, 1996a; Enright, 1995; Nishiguchi, 1994). Finally, Parkhe (1993) found that the commitment of "nonrecoverable investments" in a sample of strategic alliances was positively related to performance. These studies indicate that relational rents generated through relation-specific investments are realized through lower total value chain costs, greater product differentiation, fewer defects, and faster product development cycles.

Proposition 1: The greater the alliance partners' investment is in relation-specific assets, the greater the potential will be for relational rents.

Regarding relation-specific assets, there are two key subprocesses that influence the ability of partners to generate relational rents. First, the length (i.e., in years) of the governance arrangement designed to safeguard against opportunism influences the ability of alliance partners to invest in relation-specific assets. Since relation-specific investments create appropriable quasi-rents, transactors need to safeguard those investments (Klein et al., 1978). Partners are more likely to make investments in relation-specific assets when they have crafted effective safeguards (Williamson, 1985). Moreover, there is typically a fixed, up-front cost associated with making a particular type of relation-specific investment (such as in specialized equipment or a dedicated plant). Some relation-specific investments (e.g., a dedicated plant) are more durable and costly than others (e.g., a specialized tool or jig).

Given the fixed-cost nature of some investments, alliance partners need to assess whether or not they will make the necessary return on the investment during the payback period or length of the governance agreement (e.g., length of contract). For example, Dyer (1997) found that Japanese suppliers were more likely to make durable and costly relation-specific investments because automakers provided safeguards on those investments for at least 8 years or more. In contrast, U.S. automakers offered average contracts of 2.3 years, and suppliers rationally refused to make relation-specific investments with a long payback period.

Proposition 1a: The greater the length of the safeguard is to protect against opportunism, the greater the potential will be to generate relational rents through relation-specific assets.

Second, the ability to substitute special-purpose assets for general-purpose assets is influenced by the total volume (scale) and breadth (scope) of transactions between the alliance partners. Just as firms that achieve production economies of scale are able to increase productivity by substituting special-purpose assets for general-purpose assets, alliance partners are also able to increase the efficiency associated with interfirm exchanges as they increase the volume and scope of transactions between the alliance partners. A similar argument has been made by Williamson (1985), who claims that transactors engaging in frequent, recurring transactions can afford to adopt more specialized and complex governance structures.

Proposition 1b: The greater the volume of exchange is between the alliance partners, the greater the potential will be to generate relational rents through relation-specific assets.

In summary, the length of the safeguard and the volume of transactions are key subprocesses that influence the ability of alliance partners to generate rents through relation-specific assets.

1.3. *Interfirm Knowledge-Sharing Routines*

Various scholars have argued that interorganizational learning is critical to competitive success, noting that organizations often learn by collaborating with other organizations (Levinson and Asahi, 1996; March and Simon, 1958; Powell et al., 1996). For example, Von Hippel (1988) found that in some industries (e.g., scientific instruments) more than two-thirds of the innovations he studied could be traced back to a customer's initial suggestions or ideas. In other industries (e.g., wire termination equipment) the majority of innovations could be traced back to suppliers. Von Hippel argues that a production network with superior knowledge-transfer mechanisms among users, suppliers, and manufacturers will be able to "out innovate" production networks with less effective knowledge-sharing routines. Similarly, Powell et al. (1996) found that the locus of innovation in the biotechnology industry was the network—not the individual firm. Patents were typically filed by a large number of individuals working for a number of different organizations, including biotech firms, pharmaceutical companies, and universities. Powell et al. (1996) argue that biotech firms who are unable to create (or position themselves in) learning networks are at a competitive disadvantage.

These studies suggest that a firm's alliance partners are, in many cases, the most important source of new ideas and information that result in performance-enhancing technology and innovations. Thus, alliance partners can generate rents by developing superior interfirm knowledge-sharing routines. We define an interfirm knowledge-sharing routine as a *regular pattern of interfirm interactions that permits the transfer, recombination, or creation of specialized knowledge* (Grant, 1996). These are institutionalized interfirm processes that are purposefully designed to facilitate knowledge exchanges between alliance partners.

Proposition 2: The greater the alliance partners' investment is in interfirm knowledge-sharing routines, the greater the potential will be for relational rents.

Beyond simply arguing that alliance partners can generate relational rents through knowledge-sharing routines, it is important to understand *how* partners create knowledge-sharing routines that result in competitive advantage. Many scholars divide knowledge into two types: (1) information and (2) know-how (Grant, 1996; Kogut and Zander, 1992; Ryle, 1984). We can define information as easily codifiable knowledge that can be transmitted "without loss of integrity once the syntactical rules required for deciphering it are known. Information includes facts, axiomatic propositions, and symbols" (Kogut and Zander, 1992: 386). By comparison, know-how involves knowledge that is tacit, "sticky," complex, and difficult to codify (Kogut and Zander, 1992; Nelson and Winter, 1982; Szulanski, 1996). Since know-how is tacit, sticky, and difficult to codify, it is difficult to imitate and transfer. However, these properties also suggest that, compared to information, know-how is more likely to result in advantages that are sustainable. As a result, alliance partners that are particularly effective at transferring know-how are likely to outperform competitors who are not.

The ability to exploit outside sources of knowledge is largely a function of prior related knowledge or the "absorptive capacity" of the recipient of knowledge. Cohen and Levinthal define absorptive capacity as "the ability of a firm to recognize the value of new, external information, assimilate it, and apply it to commercial ends" (1990: 128). However, their definition suggests that if a firm has absorptive capacity, it is equally capable of learning from all other organizations. Although Cohen and Levinthal focus on the absolute absorptive capacity of individual firms, the concept is particularly useful in thinking about how alliance partners may systematically engage in interorganizational learning. Thus, *partner-specific absorptive capacity* refers to the idea that a firm has developed the ability to recognize and assimilate valuable knowledge *from a particular alliance partner*. This capacity would entail implementing a set of interorganizational processes that allows collaborating firms to systematically identify valuable know-how and then transfer it across organizational boundaries. Partner-specific absorptive capacity is a function of (1) the extent to which partners have developed overlapping knowledge bases and (2) the extent to which partners have developed interaction routines that maximize the frequency and intensity of sociotechnical interactions. Previous work suggests that the ability of a receiver of knowledge to "unpackage" and assimilate it is largely a function of whether or not the firm has overlapping knowledge bases with the source (Mowery, Oxley, and Silverman, 1996; Szulanski, 1996). Thus, this is a critical component of partner-specific absorptive capacity.

In addition, partner-specific absorptive capacity is enhanced as individuals within the alliance partners get to know each other well enough to know *who knows what* and *where critical expertise resides* within each firm. In many cases this knowledge develops informally over time through interfirm interactions. However, it may be possible to codify at least some of this knowledge. For example, Fuji and Xerox have attempted to codify this knowledge by creating a "communications matrix," which identifies a set of relevant issues (e.g., products, technologies, markets, and so on) and then identifies the individuals (by function) within Fuji-Xerox, Fuji, and Xerox who have relevant expertise on that particular issue. This matrix provides valuable information regarding where relevant expertise resides within the partnering firms.

This example illustrates that alliance partners can increase partner-specific absorptive capacity by designing interfirm routines that facilitate information-sharing and increase socio-technical interactions. These types of routines are particularly important since know-how transfers typically involve an iterative process of exchange, and the success of such transfers depends on whether personnel from the two firms have direct, intimate, and extensive face-to-face interactions (Arrow, 1974; Badaraco, 1991; Daft and Lengel, 1986; Marsden, 1990).

Proposition 2a: The greater the partner-specific absorptive capacity is, the greater the potential will be to generate relational rents through knowledge sharing.

Finally, the ability of alliance partners to generate rents through knowledge sharing is dependent on an alignment of incentives that encourages the partners to be transparent, to transfer knowledge, and not to free ride on the knowledge acquired from the partner. In particular, the transferring firm must have an incentive to devote the resources required to transfer the know-how since it typically incurs significant costs during the transfer—costs comparable to those incurred by the receiving firm (Szulanski, 1996). Thus, the mechanisms employed to govern the alliance relationship must create appropriate incentives for knowledge sharing. These may be formal financial incentives (e.g., equity arrangements) or informal norms of reciprocity. In various studies scholars have found that equity arrangements are particularly effective at aligning partner incentives and, therefore, promote greater interfirm knowledge transfers than contractual arrangements (Kogut, 1988, Mowery et al., 1996).

Proposition 2b: The greater the alignment of incentives by alliance partners is to encourage transparency and reciprocity and to discourage free riding, the greater the potential will be to generate relational rents through knowledge sharing.

A comparison of Toyota's and GM's production networks illustrates how knowledge-sharing routines can create interorganizational competitive advantage. Toyota has developed a number of practices that facilitate knowledge transfers to—and among—suppliers. For example, Toyota may transfer knowledge directly to suppliers, through its "operations management consulting division" consultants, who will reside at the supplier for days, weeks, or even months to see that the transfer takes place (Nishiguchi, 1994; Womack, Jones, and Roos, 1990). Toyota also transfers its personnel to the supplier (on a temporary or permanent basis) to increase the supplier's ability to assimilate and apply the new knowledge. These transfers result in dense interfirm social networks that increase partner-specific absorptive capacity. Consequently, Toyota personnel know what knowledge will be useful to the supplier, whom to contact at the supplier, and where the absorptive capacity resides at the supplier.

In contrast, GM and its suppliers have a history of keeping innovations proprietary. This strategy is viewed, according to the RBV, as the best way for an individual firm to generate rents from a particular innovation. Of course, the decision not to share knowledge is the only rational one for suppliers, since GM has not cultivated a stable network of supplier companies that have developed overlapping knowledge bases, dense social interactions, or a norm of reciprocity for knowledge sharing. GM does not have a supplier association to facilitate knowledge sharing, nor does GM transfer or lend personnel to suppliers to facilitate interfirm knowledge sharing. Consequently, suppliers rationally refuse to engage in costly knowledge-sharing activities since they do not expect to receive some benefit (i.e., knowledge) in return. It is not surprising then that there is significantly greater knowledge sharing between Toyota and its suppliers than between GM and its suppliers (Dyer, 1997).

1.4. Complementary Resource Endowments

Another way firms can generate relational rents is by leveraging the complementary resource endowments of an alliance partner. In some instances a firm's ability to generate rents from its resources may require that these resources be utilized in conjunction with the complementary resources of another firm. Complementary resource endowments have been the focus of much prior discussion on the formation and management of alliances and have been discussed widely as a key factor driving returns from alliances (Hamel, 1991; Harrigan, 1985; Hill and Hellriegel, 1994; Shan, Walker, and Kogut, 1994; Teece, 1987).We define complementary resource endowments as *distinctive resources of alliance partners that collectively generate greater rents than the sum of those obtained from the individual endowments of each partner*. For these resources to generate rents through an alliance, it is necessarily the case that neither firm in the partnership can purchase the relevant resources in a secondary market. Also, these resources must be indivisible, thereby creating an incentive for each firm to form an alliance in order to access the complementary resources. As Oliver observes, "Strategic alliances allow firms to procure assets, competencies, or capabilities not readily available in competitive factor markets, particularly specialized expertise and intangible assets, such as reputation" (1997: 707).

The cooperative relationship between Nestlé and Coca-Cola to distribute hot canned drinks through vending machines (a business largely unknown outside of Japan) is an example of an alliance in which complementary resource endowments are a source of relational rents. This alliance combines Nestlé's brand names (Nescafe and Nestea) and competence in developing and producing soluble coffee and tea products with Coca-Cola's powerful international distribution and vending machine network (Hamel and Prahalad, 1994: 187). The alliance creates advantages over Japanese competitors (e.g., Suntory), who are better than Coca-Cola at soluble coffee and tea and have a larger distribution and vending machine network than Nestlé, but cannot match the Coca-Cola–Nestlé combination of capabilities.

Shan and Hamilton (1991) offer another illustration. They found that complementarity of both firm- and country-specific resources between domestic and foreign firms was a key factor in the formation of cross-border strategic alliances in biotechnology. The complementarity in the cases they studied consisted of linkages between the strong basic research capabilities of U.S. firms with the unique local knowledge and distribution capabilities of their partners in overseas markets.

In the cases described above, the alliance partners brought distinctive resources to the alliance, which, when combined with the resources of the partner, resulted in a synergistic effect whereby *the combined resource endowments were more valuable, rare, and difficult to imitate than they had been before they were combined.* Consequently, these alliances produced stronger competitive positions than those achievable by the firms operating individually. It is important to note, however, that not all of the resources of a potential alliance partner will be complementary. In assessing the extent to which alliance partners can generate relational rents by combining complementary resources, it is worthwhile to think about the proportion of the potential partner's strategic resources that is synergy sensitive with the firm's resources. As the proportion of synergy-sensitive resources in the potential partners increases, so does the potential for earning relational rents by combining the complementary resources.

> *Proposition 3: The greater the proportion is of synergy-sensitive resources owned by alliance partners that, when combined, increase the degree to which the resources are valuable, rare, and difficult to imitate, the greater the potential will be to generate relational rents.*

There are several challenges faced by firms attempting to generate relational rents with complementary resources. In particular, they must find each other and recognize the potential value of combining resources. If potential alliance partners possessed perfect information, they could easily calculate the value of different partner combinations and then rationally ally with the partner(s) who would generate the greatest combined value. However, it is often very costly and difficult (if not impossible) to place a value on the complementary resources of potential partners. In fact, firms vary in their ability to identify potential partners and value their complementary resources for three primary reasons: (1) differences in prior alliance experience, (2) differences in internal search and evaluation capability, and (3) differences in their ability to acquire information about potential partners owing to different positions in their social/economic network(s).

First, firms with higher levels of experience in alliance management may have a more precise view on the kinds of partner/resource combinations that allow them to generate supernormal returns. Previous research suggests that prior alliance experience results in more opportunities to enter into future alliances, presumably because of the development of alliance capabilities and reputation (Gulati, 1995a; Mitchell and Singh, 1996; Walker, Kogut, and Shan, 1997).

Second, many organizations are developing ways to accumulate knowledge on screening potential partners by creating a "strategic alliance" function. For example, firms such as Hewlett-Packard, Xerox, and Microsoft have appointed a Director of Strategic Alliances, with his or her own staff and resources. The role of these individuals is to identify and evaluate potential alliance partners as well as to monitor and coordinate their firm's current alliances. The creation of these roles ensures some accountability for the selection and ongoing management of alliance partners and also ensures that knowledge on successful partner combinations and on effective alliance management practices will be accumulated. An opportunity exists to codify some of this knowledge, as illustrated by the fact that some firms, such as Hewlett Packard, have created manuals that attempt to codify alliance-specific knowledge (Hewlett Packard's manual has more than 300 pages). Research on acquisitions suggests that codification of knowledge is predictive of success in post-acquisition contexts (Singh and Zollo, 1997). Although alliances are a different context than acquisitions, a parallel argument can be applied to the management of alliances.

Third, the ability of a firm to identify and evaluate partners with complementary resources depends on the extent to which the firm has access to accurate and timely information on potential partners. An investment in an internal alliance function will likely facilitate the acquisition of this information, but it also depends on the extent to which the firm occupies an information-rich position within social/economic networks. Previous research suggests that firms occupying central network positions with greater network ties have superior access to information and, thus, are more likely to increase the number of their alliances in the future (Gulati, 1995a; Mitchell and Singh, 1996; Walker et al., 1997). When a firm is well positioned in networks, the firm has access to more reliable information about potential partners because of trusted informants within the network who may have direct experience with the potential partner (Burt, 1992; Chung, Singh, and Lee, in press; Granovetter, 1985; Nohria, 1992). An information-rich position within a network, therefore, provides a firm with additional information about the nature and degree of accessibility of the complementary resources of potential partners.

Proposition 3a: The ability of firms to generate relational rents by combining complementary resources increases with the firm's (1) prior alliance experience, (2) investment in internal search and evaluation capability, and (3) ability to occupy an information-rich position in its social/economic networks.

Thus far, our discussion has focused on the benefits associated with combining resources with *strategic complementarity*. However, once a firm has identified a potential partner with the requisite complementary strategic resources, another challenge is developing *organizational complementarity*—the organizational mechanisms necessary to access the benefits from complementary strategic resources. The ability of alliance partners to realize the benefits from complementary strategic resources is conditioned on compatibility in decision processes, information and control systems, and culture (Doz, 1996; Kanter, 1994). Although complementarity of strategic resources creates the *potential* for relational rents, the rents can only be realized if the firms have systems and cultures that are compatible enough to facilitate coordinated action. Previous research suggests that a primary reason for failure of both acquisitions and alliances is *not* that the two firms do not possess strategic complementarity of resources, but rather because they do not have compatible operating systems, decision-making processes, and cultures (Buono and Bowditch, 1989). Doz, (1996), therefore, distinguishes between initial complementarity (strategic complementarity), based on potential combinations of resources, and revealed complementarities (organizational complementarity), based on the realized results of cooperation between the firms involved in the partnership.

Proposition 3b: The ability of alliance partners to generate relational rents from complementary strategic resources increases with the degree of compatibility in their organizational systems, processes, and cultures (organizational complementarity).

In summary, both strategic and organizational complementarity are critical for realizing the potential benefits of combining complementary strategic resources.

1.5. *Effective Governance*

Governance plays a key role in the creation of relational rents because it influences transaction costs, as well as the willingness of alliance partners to engage in value-creation initiatives. For example, although alliance partners can generate relational rents through investments in relation-specific assets, their incentive to make specialized investments is tempered by the fact that the more specialized a resource becomes, the lower its value is in alternative uses. The contingent value of a specialized resource exposes its owner to a greater risk of opportunism than does a generalized resource (Klein et al., 1978). An important objective for transactors is to choose a governance structure (safeguard) that minimizes transaction costs, thereby enhancing efficiency (North, 1990; Williamson, 1985).

We distinguish between two classes of governance used by alliance partners: the first relies on *third-party enforcement* of agreements (e.g., legal contracts), whereas the second relies on *self-enforcing agreements*, in which "no third party intervenes to determine whether a violation has taken place"

(Telser, 1980: 27). The transaction cost economics perspective falls primarily within the first class, suggesting that dispute resolution requires access to a third-party enforcer, whether it be the state (i.e., through contracts) or a legitimate organization authority (Williamson, 1991b). In contrast, self-enforcing agreements (sometimes called "private ordering" in the economics literature or "trust/embeddedness" in the sociology literature) involve safeguards that allow for self-enforcement. Within the self-enforcement class of governance mechanisms, we further distinguish between "formal" safeguards, such as *financial and investment hostages* (Klein, 1980; Williamson, 1983), and "informal" safeguards, such as *goodwill trust or embeddedness* (Gulati, 1995b; Powell, 1990; Sako, 1991; Uzzi, 1997) and *reputation* (Larson, 1992; Weigelt and Camerer, 1988).

Formal self-enforcing safeguards are economic hostages created intentionally to control opportunism by aligning the economic incentives of the transactors (Klein, 1980; Williamson, 1983). These hostages may be financial (e.g., equity) or symmetric investments in specialized or cospecialized assets, which constitute a visible collateral bond that aligns the economic incentives of exchange partners. The fact that the value of the economic hostage will decrease in value if a party is opportunistic provides an incentive for trading partners to behave in a more trustworthy fashion (Dyer and Ouchi, 1993; Pisano, 1989). Further, since these investments may increase in value if the alliance partners cooperate, there is an incentive for the alliance partners to engage in value-creation initiatives.

Sociologists, anthropologists, and law and society scholars have long argued that informal social controls supplement—and often supplant—formal controls (Black, 1976; Ellickson, 1991; Granovetter, 1985; Macaulay, 1963). Thus, informal self-enforcing agreements may rely on personal trust relations (direct experience) or reputation (indirect experience) as governance mechanisms. A number of scholars have suggested that informal safeguards (e.g., goodwill trust) are the most effective and least costly means of safeguarding specialized investments and facilitating complex exchange (Hill, 1995; Sako, 1991; Uzzi, 1997). For example, some scholars have argued that goodwill trust reduces transaction costs related to bargaining and monitoring, thereby enhancing performance (Barney and Hansen, 1994; Sako, 1991).[5] Thus, self-enforcing safeguards result in transaction costs that are lower than they are in situations where transactors must erect more elaborate governance structures (e.g., contracts), which are costly to write, monitor, and enforce.

The ability of exchange partners to match governance structures with exchange attributes is viewed as critical to realizing "economizing advantages."[6] Williamson states, "The main hypothesis out of which transaction cost economics works is this: *align transactions, which differ in their attributes, with governance structures, which differ in their costs and competencies, in a discriminating (mainly transaction cost minimizing) way*" (1991a: 79; emphasis in original). Williamson (1991a) argues that misalignments occur frequently because of bounded rationality and uncertainty. Thus, transactors who are effective at aligning transactions with governance structures will have an advantage over competing transactors who do not employ efficient governance mechanisms.

Proposition 4: The greater the alliance partners' ability is to align transactions with governance structures in a discriminating (transaction cost minimizing and value maximizing) way, the greater the potential will be for relational rents.

We should emphasize that, although the discussion thus far has followed a transaction cost logic with an emphasis on efficiency, we use the term *effective governance* to suggest that governance mechanisms play an important role in generating relational rents that extends beyond efficiency arguments. More specifically, a small but growing body of literature on transaction value is emphasizing the influence of governance on the value-creation initiatives of alliance partners (Dyer, 1997; Hansen, Hoskisson, and Barney, 1997; Madhok, 1997; Ring and Van de Ven, 1992; Zajac and Olsen, 1993). Effective governance can generate relational rents by either (1) lowering transaction costs or (2) providing incentives for value-creation initiatives, such as investing in relation-specific assets, sharing knowledge, or combining complementary strategic resources.

In the first case transactors achieve an advantage by incurring lower transaction costs than competitors to achieve a given level of investment in specialized assets. In the second case effective governance (e.g., trust) may allow transactors to make greater investments in specialized assets than competing transactors, who refuse to make the relation-specific investments because of the high cost of safeguarding them. Similarly, alliance partners may be unwilling to share valuable, proprietary knowledge with trading partners if they are not credibly assured that this knowledge will not be readily shared with competitors. The willingness of firms to combine complementary strategic resources may also hinge upon credible assurances that the trading partner will not attempt to duplicate those same resources, thereby becoming a future competitor. Thus, effective governance mechanisms may generate rents by either lowering transaction costs or by providing incentives for partners to engage in value-creation initiatives.

In general, *self-enforcing mechanisms are more effective than third-party enforcement mechanisms at both minimizing transaction costs and maximizing value-creation initiatives*. Transaction costs are lower under self-enforcing agreements for four primary reasons.

First, contracting costs are avoided because the exchange partners trust that payoffs will be divided fairly. Consequently, exchange partners do not have to bear the cost—or time—of specifying every detail of the agreement in a contract. Further, contracts are likely to be less effective than self-enforcing agreements at controlling opportunism because they fail to anticipate all forms of cheating that may occur. Second, monitoring costs are lower because self-enforcement relies on self-monitoring rather than external or third-party monitoring.

Exchange partners do not need to invest in costly monitoring mechanisms to ensure contract fulfillment and to document infractions to the satisfaction of a third party (e.g., court). Third, self-enforcing agreements lower the costs associated with complex adaptation, thereby allowing exchange partners to adjust the agreement "on the fly" to respond to unforeseen market changes (Uzzi, 1997: 48). Fourth, self-enforcing agreements are superior to contracts at minimizing transaction costs over the long run because they are not subject to the time limitations of contracts. Contracts are typically written for a fixed duration and, in effect, *depreciate* because they only provide protection during the designated length of the agreement. At the end of the contract duration, the alliance partners need to write a new contract (or employ a different safeguard). Exchange partners can avoid the costs of "recontracting" by employing self-enforcing agreements, which, over time, may in fact *appreciate* in the sense that trust or embeddedness increases with increased familiarity and interaction (Gulati, 1995b; Larson, 1992).

Self-enforcing agreements also call forth greater value-creation initiatives on the part of the exchange partners. For example, it is difficult (if not impossible) to explicitly contract for value-creation initiatives, such as sharing fine-grained tacit knowledge, exchanging resources that are difficult to price, or offering innovations or responsiveness not explicitly called for in the contract. Under self-enforcing agreements, exchange partners are more likely to engage in these activities because they have credible assurances that they will be rewarded for them. Finally, contractual agreements are relatively easy to imitate as a form of governance and, therefore, are unlikely to create sustainable advantages. Competing firms are likely to have equal access to lawyers (to write the agreements) and the state (to enforce the agreements).

> *Proposition 4a: The greater the alliance partners' ability is to employ self-enforcing safeguards (e.g., trust or hostages) rather than third-party safeguards (e.g., legal contracts), the greater the potential will be for relational rents, owing to (1) lower contracting costs, (2) lower monitoring costs, (3) lower adaptation costs, (4) lower recontracting costs, and (5) superior incentives for value-creation initiatives.*

Likewise, within the self-enforcement mechanism category, informal safeguards are more likely to generate relational rents than are formal safeguards, for two primary reasons. First, the marginal cost associated with formal hostages typically is higher than for informal safeguards because formal hostages involve capital outlays for equity or other types of collateral bonds. Furthermore, formal safeguards are much easier for competitors to imitate. If the key to minimizing transaction costs and encouraging value-creation initiatives by partners is simply swapping stock, creating a joint venture, or having a partner (e.g., franchisee) post a bond, then competitors can imitate this governance mechanism with relative ease. Informal safeguards (goodwill trust or reputation) are much more difficult to imitate because they are socially complex and idiosyncratic to the exchange relationship.

Proposition 4b: The greater the alliance partners' ability is to employ informal *self-enforcing safeguards (e.g., trust) rather than* formal *self-enforcing safeguards (e.g., financial hostages), the greater the potential will be for relational rent, owing to (1) lower marginal costs and (2) difficulty of imitation.*

Although informal safeguards have the greatest potential to generate relational rents, they are subject to two key liabilities: (1) they require substantial time to develop, because they require a history of interactions and personal ties, and (2) they are subject to the "paradox of trust," which means that although trust establishes norms and expectations about appropriate behavior, lowering the perception of risk in the exchange, it provides the opportunity for abuse through opportunism (Granovetter, 1985). In practice, it appears that many effective alliances use multiple governance mechanisms simultaneously (Borch, 1994). Many alliances begin with the use of formal mechanisms and then, over time, employ more informal ones (Gulati, 1995b).

Recent empirical studies support the argument that effective governance, in the form of lower transaction costs, may be a source of relational rents. For example, Dyer (1997) found that General Motors' procurement (transaction) costs were more than twice those of Chrysler's and six times higher than Toyota's. GM's transaction costs are persistently higher than Toyota's and Chrysler's primarily because suppliers view GM as a much less trustworthy organization. Similarly, Zaheer et al. (1998) found that, in the electrical equipment industry, interorganizational trust reduced negotiation costs and conflict and had a positive effect on performance.

2. Mechanisms that Preserve Relational Rents

An explanation of how firms generate relational rents necessarily requires an explanation of why competing firms do not simply imitate the partnering behavior, thereby eliminating any competitive advantages that might be gained through collaboration. There are a variety of isolating mechanisms that preserve the rents generated by alliance partners. First, it is important to recognize that some of the mechanisms already described in the literature on the sustainability of rents within the RBV of the firm apply at the dyadic level. These include *causal ambiguity* and *time compression diseconomies* (see Barney, 1991; Dierickx and Cool, 1989; Lippman and Rumelt, 1982; Reed and DeFillippi, 1990). For example, the development of goodwill trust is subject to considerable causal ambiguity because it is a highly complex and situation-specific process (Butler, 1991; Larzelere and Huston, 1980). Moreover, the development of trust or partner-specific absorptive capacity is subject to time compression diseconomies because it cannot be developed quickly, nor can it be bought or sold in the marketplace (Arrow, 1974; Sako, 1991).

However, in addition to these mechanisms, relational rents may be preserved through *interorganizational asset interconnectedness; partner scarcity (rareness); resource indivisibility* (coevolution of capabilities); or a socially complex, and therefore difficult to imitate, *institutional environment* (e.g., country specific). We do not discuss causal ambiguity and time compression diseconomies, since these rent-preservation mechanisms have been discussed in detail elsewhere.

2.1. Interorganizational Asset Interconnectedness

Our concept of relational advantage takes the idea of asset interconnectedness across organizational boundaries. We submit that interorganizational asset interconnectedness will occur in cumulative increments on an existing stock of assets held by a firm or its alliance partner. To illustrate, a Nissan seat supplier built its plant on the property adjacent to a Nissan assembly plant. The supplier was willing to make this site-specific investment because Nissan had a minority equity position in the supplier and because the two parties had developed a high level of trust. Once this site-specific investment was made, the two parties discovered that rather than transport the seats by truck (a general-purpose asset), it would be more economical to build a conveyor belt (a highly specialized asset). Consequently, they jointly invested in building the conveyor belt.

This example demonstrates how initial relation-specific investments (i.e., a site-specific plant) create conditions that make subsequent specialized investments (i.e., customized equipment) economically viable. Thus, there is a cumulative (snowball) effect that is due to the interconnectedness of current relation-specific investments with previous relation-specific investments. In contrast, GM's suppliers have not made the initial site-specific investment; therefore, it is not economically feasible for them to make other subsequent specialized investments. The key strategic implication of this isolating mechanism is that alliance partners may need to make "bundles" of related relation-specific investments in order to realize the full potential of those investments in an alliance relationship.

2.2. Partner Scarcity

The creation of relational rents is often contingent on a firm's ability to find a partner with (1) complementary strategic resources and (2) a relational capability (i.e., a firm's willingness and ability to partner). In some cases a latecomer to the partner scene may find that all potential partners with the necessary complementary strategic resources have already entered into alliances with other firms. This is a particular problem for late movers into foreign markets, where there may be few local firms with the local market knowledge, contacts, and distribution network needed to facilitate market entry. In other instances, potential partners may simply lack the relational capability or the relation-building skills and process skills necessary to employ effective governance mechanisms, make relation-specific investments, or develop knowledge-sharing routines (Eisenhardt and Schoonhoven, 1996; Larson, 1992). Firms with collaboration experience have been found to be more desirable as partners and more likely to generate value through partnerships (Gulati, 1995a; Mitchell and Singh, 1996).

To illustrate the importance of relational capability, Koichiro Noguchi, Toyota's International Purchasing Chief, told the first author that one of the difficulties Toyota faced in entering the U.S. market was finding U.S. suppliers who were willing to work in partnership fashion. Stated Noguchi:

> Many U.S. suppliers do not understand our way of doing business. They do not want us to visit their plants and they are unwilling to share the information we require. This makes it very difficult for us to work with them effectively; we also can't help them to improve (author interview, July 22, 1992).

Thus, even though Toyota had developed a relational capability and was effective at partnering, it found that it was unable to effectively generate relational rents with U.S. suppliers who had not developed a relational capability. Thus, relational rents may be difficult to imitate because potential alliance partners with the necessary complementary resources and relational capability are rare. The key strategic implication of this isolating mechanism is that there are strong first mover advantages for those firms that develop a capability of quickly identifying and allying with partners possessing complementary strategic resources and/or a relational capability.

2.3. Resource Indivisibility

Partners may combine resources or jointly develop capabilities in such a way that the resulting resources are both idiosyncratic and indivisible. The VISA organization is an example of alliance partners (23,000 banks) jointly creating indivisible assets that help generate returns for the alliance partners. In particular, the VISA brand name and distribution network are idiosyncratic and indivisible assets that are collectively owned by the participating banks in a large multifirm alliance. Individual banks can only access the brand name and distribution network through the alliance.

In other settings, such as with Fuji and Xerox, alliance partners combine resources and capabilities, which then coevolve over time. Under these conditions the mutual coevolution of capabilities of the partner firms can serve as a preserver of rents from the partnership. As the partners engage in a long-term relationship, they develop dedicated linkages that enhance the benefits from engaging in the joint relationship. Over time, these coevolved capabilities are increasingly difficult to imitate, owing to path dependence and resource indivisibility.

A key strategic implication is that the partners' resources and capabilities may coevolve and change over time, thereby restricting each firm's ability to control and redeploy the resources. Although value may be generated through the partnership, there is the potential for a loss of flexibility, which should be considered at the outset.

2.4. Institutional Environment

An institutional environment that encourages or fosters trust among trading partners (i.e., has effective institutional "rules" or social controls for enforcing agreements) may facilitate the creation of relational rents (North, 1990). Indeed, at a broader level, arguments regarding relational advantage can be extended to consider the issue of national or country advantage (Casson, 1991; Fukuyama, 1995; Hill, 1995). For example, numerous scholars suggest that Japanese transactors incur lower transaction costs than U.S. transactors, thereby generating relational rents (Dore, 1983; Dyer, 1996b; Hill, 1995; Sako, 1991; Smitka, 1991). Japanese firms appear to have been successful at generating relational rents in part because of a country-specific institutional environment that fosters goodwill trust and cooperation (Dore, 1983; Hill, 1995; Sako, 1991; Smitka, 1991).

Borys and Jemison (1989) refer to these types of environmentally embedded mechanisms that control opportunism as "extrahybrid institutions." Collaborating firms in other countries (e.g., the United States and Russia) may not be able to replicate the low transaction costs of Japanese alliance partners because of an inability to replicate the socially complex extrahybrid institutions embedded in the Japanese institutional environment. Thus, following North (1990), one can argue that the institutional environment can either raise or lower the transaction costs that must be borne to achieve a given level of specialization and cooperation. The strategic implication of this isolating mechanism is that firms may need to locate operations in particular institutional environments in order to realize the benefits associated with extrahybrid institutions.

In summary, the relational rents generated by alliance partners are preserved because competing firms

1. cannot ascertain what generates the returns because of causal ambiguity;
2. can figure out what generates the returns but cannot quickly replicate the resources because of time compression diseconomies;
3. cannot imitate practices or investments because of asset stock interconnectedness (they have not made the previous investments that make

subsequent investments economically viable) and because the costs associated with making the previous investments are prohibitive;

4. cannot find a partner with the requisite complementary strategic resources or relational capability;
5. cannot access the capabilities of a potential partner because these capabilities are indivisible, perhaps having coevolved with another firm; and
6. cannot replicate a distinctive, socially complex institutional environment that has the necessary formal rules (legal controls) or informal rules (social controls) controlling opportunism/encourage cooperative behavior.

3. Comparing the Relational, RBV, and Industry Structure Views

Although an individual firm's ability to work effectively with other firms may be classified as a firm-specific capability (which may generate relational rents), there is value in distinguishing a relational view, which offers a distinct, but complementary, view on how firms generate rents. A relational view considers the dyad/network as the unit of analysis and the rents that are generated to be associated with the dyad/network. Although complementary to the RBV, this view differs somewhat in terms of unit of analysis and sources of rent, as well as control and ownership of the rent-generating resources (see Table 1).

To illustrate, a Toyota supplier may generate rents by actively participating in the knowledge-sharing processes in Toyota's supplier association. However, the supplier will be unable to generate the knowledge rents if the other members decide to exclude it from the network. Similarly, the 23,000 member banks of the VISA organization have achieved an advantage over American Express and Discover by pooling their enormous distribution power, which allows for use of the card at more locations than its competitors. Individual banks generate profits with VISA, owing to the jointly created brand name and distribution network. In both of these cases, the resources that create the relational rents are essentially beyond the control of the individual firm.

In summary, the RBV focuses on how individual firms generate supernormal returns based upon resources, assets, and capabilities that are housed within the firm. However, according to a relational perspective, rents are jointly generated and owned by partnering firms.[7] Thus, relational rents are a property of the dyad or network. A firm in isolation, irrespective of its capabilities or resources, cannot enjoy these rents. Thus, a *relational capability is not a sufficient condition for realizing relational rents*. As Zajac and Olsen argue, "[B]oth parties use the

Table 1. Comparing the Industry Structure, Resource-Based, and Relational Views of Competitive Advantage

Dimensions	Industry Structure View	Resource-Based View	Relational View
Unit of analysis	Industry	Firm	Pair or network of firms
Primary sources of supernormal profit returns	Relative bargaining power	Scarce physical resources (e.g., land, raw material inputs)	Relation-specific investments
	Collusion	Human resources/know-how (e.g., managerial talent)	Interfirm knowledge-sharing routines
		Technological resources (e.g., process technology)	Complementary resource endowments
		Financial resources	Effective governance
		Intangible resources (e.g., reputation)	
Mechanisms that preserve profits	Industry barriers to entry	Firm-level barriers to imitation	Dyadic/network barriers to imitation
	• Government regulations • Production economies/sunk costs	• Resource scarcity/property rights • Causal ambiguity • Time compression diseconomies • Asset stock interconnectedness	• Causal ambiguity • Time compression diseconomies • Interorganizational asset stock interconnectedness • Partner scarcity • Resource indivisibility • Institutional environment
Ownership/control of rent-generating process/resources	Collective (with competitors)	Individual firm	Collective (with trading partners)

interorganizational strategy to establish an ongoing relationship that can create value that could otherwise not be created by either firm independently" (1993: 137).

A relational view may offer different normative implications for the strategies firms should use to achieve high profits. For example, according to the RBV, an individual firm should attempt to protect, rather than share, valuable proprietary know-how to prevent knowledge spillovers, which could erode or eliminate its competitive advantage. However, an effective strategy from a relational view may be for firms to systematically share valuable know-how with alliance partners (and willingly accept some spillover to competitors) in return for access to the stock of valuable knowledge residing within its alliance partners. Of course, this strategy makes sense only when the expected value of the combined inflows of knowledge from partners exceeds the expected loss/erosion of advantages due to knowledge spillovers to competitors.

Similarly, the relational view and industry structure view may offer different prescriptions for firm-level strategies. For example, according to the industry structure view, firms should be eager to increase the number of their suppliers, thereby maximizing bargaining power and profits. Porter states, "In purchasing, then, the goal is to find mechanisms to offset or surmount these sources of suppliers' power. . . . Purchases of an item can be spread among alternate suppliers in such a way as to improve the firm's bargaining power" (1980: 123).

This strategy is in direct contrast to a relational perspective, which holds that firms can increase profits by *increasing* their dependence on a smaller number of suppliers, thereby increasing the incentives of suppliers to share knowledge and make performance-enhancing investments in relation-specific assets. State Bakos and Brynjolfsson:

> By committing to a small number of suppliers, the buyer firm can guarantee them greater ex post bargaining power and therefore greater ex ante incentives to make noncontractible investments, such as investments in innovation, responsiveness, and information sharing; the buyer ends up being better off by keeping a smaller piece of a bigger pie (1993: 43).

Thus, a relational view may differ from existing views in the normative prescriptions offered to practicing managers. The fact that there are clear contradictions between these views suggests that existing theories of advantage are not adequate to explain interorganizational competitive advantage.

4. Conclusion

The central thesis of this article is that a pair or network of firms can develop relationships that result in sustained competitive advantage. Competition between single firms, while perhaps still the rule, is becoming less universal, as pairs and networks of allied firms have begun to compete against each other. Our analysis suggests that although looking for competitive advantage within firms and industries has been (and is still) important, a singular focus on these units of analysis may limit the explanatory power of the models we develop to explain firm-level profitability.

The view we offer here extends the existing literature on alliances and networks in a number of ways. First, we have attempted to integrate what is known regarding the benefits of collaboration by examining the interorganizational rent-generating process. We have argued that collaborating firms can generate relational rents through relation-specific assets, knowledge-sharing routines, complementary resource endowments, and "effective governance." Second, we have identified the isolating mechanisms that preserve the relational rents generated through effective interfirm collaboration. Moreover, we have introduced mechanisms not discussed previously in the literature on sustainability of rents: interorganizational asset connectedness, partner scarcity, resource indivisibility (coevolution of capabilities), and the institutional environment. Third, we have argued that a relational perspective may offer normative prescriptions for practicing managers that contradict the prescriptions offered by the RBV and industry structure view.

In future research, scholars might explicitly examine these differences in greater detail. Another important avenue for future research would be to examine how relational rents are distributed among alliance partners. Finally, given the poor track record of many alliances, researchers might examine, in detail, the factors that impede the realization of relational rents.

In conclusion, we reemphasize the primary objective of this article, which is to propose that relationships between firms are an increasingly important unit of analysis for explaining supernormal profit returns. The relational view offers a useful theoretical lens through which researchers can examine and explore value-creating linkages between organizations.

Notes

1. The dynamic capabilities approach (Teece, Pisano, and Shuen, 1997) also views the firm as the unit of analysis.
2. We use the term *relational rent*, although, technically speaking, trading partners generate quasi-rents. Peteraf defines quasi-rents as "returns that exceed a factor's short run opportunity cost... [and] are an excess over the returns to a factor in its next best use" (1994: 155). The term *quasi-rents* suggests that the rents are not permanent in nature.
3. The fact that a firm's valuable resources may extend beyond a firm's boundaries is increasingly recognized, even within the investment community. For example, Powell found that industry investment analysts explicitly evaluate and assess the quality of a biotechnology firm's relationships with outside partners (1996: 206). Firms with more—and higher quality—partnerships receive higher market valuations from the analysts who recognize that a biotechnology firm's critical resources extend beyond firm boundaries.
4. For the convenience of exposition, we use two firms, rather than multiple firms, as the unit of analysis.
5. Goodwill trust is defined as one party's confidence that the other party in the exchange relationship will not exploit its vulnerabilities (Ring and Van de Ven, 1992; Sako, 1991). Goodwill trust at the interfirm level refers to the extent to which there is a collectively held trust orientation by organizational members toward a partner firm (Zaheer, McEvily, and Perrone, 1998).
6. Although the literature on choice of governance mechanisms has focused primarily on transaction costs, Gulati and Singh (in press) show that coordination costs stemming from the nature of the interdependence between partners (pooled, reciprocal, or sequential) are very important determinants of alliance governance structures.

7. We expect the distribution of the relational rents to be consistent with a resource-dependency perspective (Pfeffer and Salancik, 1978). Partners that bring the more critical (i.e., scarce) resources to the relationship will be able to appropriate a higher percentage of the rents (see Asanuma, 1989 and Dyer, 1996a). For example, Toyota made higher profits (return on assets [ROA] = 13.0 percent) than its suppliers (average ROA = 7.1 percent) from 1982–1992, owing to its greater relative bargaining power and control over more critical resources. However, some suppliers, like Denso—a supplier of key electronic components, which brings critical and scarce resources to the relationship—made profit returns (ROA = 12.8 percent) similar to those of Toyota.

References

Amit, R., and Schoemaker, P. 1993. Strategic assets and organizational rent. *Strategic Management Journal*, 14: 33–46.

Anderson, E. 1990. Two firms, one frontier: On assessing joint venture performance. *Sloan Management Review*, 31(2): 19–30.

Arrow, K. J. 1974. *The limits of organization*. New York: Norton.

Asanuma, B. 1989. Manufacturer-supplier relationships in Japan and the concept of relation-specific skill. *Journal of the Japanese and International Economies*, 3: 1–30.

Badaraco, J. L., Jr. 1991. *The knowledge link*. Boston: Harvard Business School Press.

Bakos, J. Y., and Brynjolfsson, E. 1993. Information technology, incentives, and the optimal number of suppliers. *Journal of Management Information Systems*, 10(2): 37–53.

Barney, J. B. 1986. Strategic factor markets: Expectations, luck, and business strategy. *Management Science*, 32: 1231–1241.

—— 1991. Firm resources and sustained competitive advantage. *Journal of Management*, 17: 99–120.

—— and Hansen, M. H. 1995. Trustworthiness as a source of competitive advantage. *Strategic Management Journal*, 15: 175–190.

Black, D. 1976. *The behavior of law*. New York: Academic Press.

Borch, O. J. 1994. The process of relational contracting: Developing trust-based strategic alliances among small business enterprises. *Advances in Strategic Management*, 10B: 113–135.

Borys, B., and Jemison, D. B. 1989. Hybrid arrangements as strategic alliances: Theoretical issues in organizational combinations. *Academy of Management Review*, 14: 234–249.

Bresnen, M., and Fowler, C. 1994. The organizational correlates and consequences of subcontracting: Evidence from a survey of South Wales businesses. *Journal of Management Studies*, 31: 847–864.

Buono, A. F., and Bowditch, J. L. 1989. *The human side of mergers and acquisitions*. San Francisco: Jossey-Bass.

Burt, R. 1992. *Structural holes: The social structure of competition*. Cambridge, MA: Harvard University Press.

Butler, J. K. 1991. Toward understanding and measuring conditions of trust: Evolution of a conditions of trust inventory. *Journal of Management*, 17: 643–663.

Casson, M. 1991. *The economics of business culture*. Oxford, England: Clarendon Press.

Chung, S., Singh, H., and Lee, K. In press. Complementarity, status similarity, and social capital as drivers of alliance formation. *Strategic Management Journal*.

Clark, K. B., and Fujimoto, T. 1991. *Product development performance*. Boston: Harvard Business School Press.

Cohen, W. M., and Levinthal, D. A. 1990. Absorptive capacity: A new perspective on learning and innovation. *Administrative Science Quarterly*, 35: 128–152.

Daft, R., and Lengl, R. 1986. Organizational information requirements, media richness and structural design. *Management Science*, 32: 554–571.

Dierickx, I., and Cool, K. 1989. Asset stock accumulation and sustainability of competitive advantage. *Management Science*, 35: 1504–1513.

Dore, R. 1983. Goodwill and the spirit of market capitalism. *British Journal of Sociology*, XXXIV(4): 459–482.

Doz, Y. 1996. The evolution of cooperation in strategic alliances: Initial conditions or learning processes. *Strategic Management Journal*, 17: 55–83.

Dyer, J. H. 1996a. Specialized supplier networks as a source of competitive advantage: Evidence from the auto industry. *Strategic Management Journal*, 17: 271–292.

—— 1996b. Does governance matter? Keiretsu alliances and asset specificity as sources of Japanese competitive advantage. *Organization Science*, 7: 649–666.

—— 1997. Effective interfirm collaboration: How firms minimize transaction costs and maximize transaction value. *Strategic Management Journal*, 18: 553–556.

—— and Ouchi, W. G. 1993. Japanese style business partnerships: Giving companies a competitive edge. *Sloan Management Review*, 35(1): 51–63.

Eisenhardt, K., and Schoonhoven, C. B. 1996. Resource-based view of strategic alliance formation: Strategic and social effects in entrepreneurial firms. *Organization Science*, 7: 136–150.

Ellickson, R. C. 1991. *Order without law*. Cambridge, MA: Harvard University Press.

Enright, M. J. 1995. Organization and coordination in geographically concentrated industries. In N. Lamoreaux and D. Raff (Eds.), *Coordination and information: Historical perspectives on the organization of enterprise*: 103–142. Chicago: University of Chicago Press.

Fukuyama, F. 1995. *Trust: The social virtues and the creation of prosperity*. New York: Free Press.

Gerlach, M. L. 1992. *Alliance capitalism*. Berkeley, CA: University of California Press.

Ghoshal, S. 1995. Bad for practice: A critique of the transaction cost theory. *Proceedings of the Academy of Management*: 12–16.

Gomes-Casseres, B. 1994. Group versus group: How alliance networks compete. *Harvard Business Review*, 4(July–August): 4–11.

Granovetter, M. 1985. Economic action and social structure: The problem of embeddedness. *American Journal of Sociology*, 91: 481–510.

Grant, R. 1996. Prospering in dynamically-competitive environments: Organizational capability as knowledge integration. *Organization Science*, 7: 375–387.

Gulati, R. 1995a. Social structure and alliance formation patterns: A longitudinal analysis. *Administrative Science Quarterly*, 40: 619–652.

—— 1995b. Does familiarity breed trust? The implications of repeated ties for contractual choice in alliances. *Academy of Management Journal*, 38: 85–112.

—— and Singh, H. In press. The architecture of cooperation: Managing coordination costs and appropriation concerns in strategic alliances. *Administrative Science Quarterly*.

Hamel, G. 1991. Competition for competence and interpartner learning within international strategic alliances. *Strategic Management Journal*, 12(Winter Special Issue): 83–104.

—— and Prahalad, C. K. 1994. *Competing for the future*. Boston: Harvard Business School Press.

Hansen, M., Hoskisson, B., and Barney, J. 1997. *Trustworthiness: A cooperative resource*. Working paper, Brigham Young University, Provo, UT.

Harrigan, K. 1985. *Strategic flexibility*. Lexington, MA: Lexington Books.

Hill, C. W. L. 1995. National institutional structures, transaction cost economizing, and competitive advantage: The case of Japan. *Organization Science*, 6: 119–131.

Hill, R. C., and Hellriegel, D. 1994. Critical contingencies in joint venture management: Some lessons from managers. *Organization Science*, 5: 594–607.

Kanter, R. M. 1994. Collaborative advantage: The art of alliances. *Harvard Business Review*, 4(July–August): 96–108.

Klein, B. 1980. Transaction cost determinants of "unfair" contractual arrangements. *American Economic Review*, 70(2): 56–62.

—— Crawford, R. G., and Alchian, A. A. 1978. Vertical integration, appropriable rents, and the competitive contracting process. *Journal of Law and Economics*, 21: 297–326.

Kogut, B. 1988. Joint ventures: Theoretical and empirical perspectives. *Strategic Management Journal*, 9: 319–332.

—— and Zander, U. 1992. Knowledge of the firm, combinative capabilities, and the replication of technology. *Organization Science*, 3: 383–397.

Larson, A. 1992. Network dyads in entrepreneurial settings: A study of the governance of exchange relationships. *Administrative Science Quarterly*, 37: 76–104.

Larzelere, R., and Huston, T. 1980. The dyadic trust scale: Toward understanding interpersonal trust in close relationships. *Journal of Marriage and the Family*, 42: 595–604.

Levinson, N. S., and Asahi, M. 1996. Cross-national alliances and interorganizational learning. *Organizational Dynamics*, 24: 51–63.

Lippman, S. A., and Rumelt, R. P. 1982. Uncertain imitability: An analysis of interfirm differences in efficiency under competition. *The Bell Journal of Economics*, 13(Autumn): 418–438.

Macaulay, S. 1963. Non-contractual relations in business: A preliminary study. *American Sociological Review*, 28: 55–69.

Madhok, A. 1997. Cost, value and foreign market entry mode: The transaction and the firm. *Strategic Management Journal*, 18: 39–61.

March, J. G., and Simon, H. A. 1958. *Organizations*. New York: Wiley.

Marsden, P. V. 1990. Network data and measurement. *Annual Review of Sociology*, 16: 435–463.

Ministry of International Trade and Industry. 1987. *White paper on small and medium enterprises in Japan*. Tokyo: MITI.

Mitchell, W., and Singh, K. 1996. Entrenched success: The reciprocal relationship between alliances and business sales. *Proceedings of the Academy of Management*: 31–35.

Mowery, D. C., Oxley, J. E., and Silverman, B. S. 1996. Strategic alliances and interfirm knowledge transfer. *Strategic Management Journal*, 17: 77–91.

Nelson, R., and Winter, S. 1982. *An evolutionary theory of economic change*. Cambridge, MA: Belknap Press of Harvard University Press.

Nishiguchi, T. 1994. *Strategic industrial sourcing*. New York: Oxford University Press.

Nohria, N. 1992. Is a network perspective a useful way of studying organizations? In N. Nohria and R. G. Eccles (Eds.), *Networks and organizations*: 1–21. Boston: Harvard Business School Press.

North, D. C. 1990. *Institutions, institutional change and economic performance*. Cambridge, England: Cambridge University Press.

Oliver, C. 1990. Determinants of interorganizational relationships: Integration and future directions. *Academy of Management Review*, 15: 241–265.

——1997. Sustainable competitive advantage: Combining institutional and resource-based views. *Strategic Management Journal*, 18: 697–714.

Parkhe, A. 1993. Strategic alliance structuring: A game theoretic and transaction cost examination of interfirm cooperation. *Academy of Management Journal*, 36: 794–829.

Perry, M. K. 1989. Vertical integration. In R. Schmalensee and R. Willig (Eds.), *Handbook of industrial organization*: 185–255. Amsterdam: North Holland.

Peteraf, M. 1994. Commentary. In P. Shrivastava, A. Huff, and J. Dutton (Eds.), *Advances in strategic management*, vol. 10B: 153–158. Greenwich, CT: JAI Press.

Pfeffer, J., and Salancik, G. R. 1978. *The external control of organizations: A resource dependence perspective*. New York: Harper and Row.

Pisano, G. P. 1989. Using equity participation to support exchange: Evidence from the biotechnology industry. *Journal of Law, Economics and Organization*, 5: 109–126.

Porter, M. E. 1980. *Competitive strategy*. New York: Free Press.

Powell, W. W. 1990. Neither market nor hierarchy: Network forms of organization. In B. M. Staw and L. L. Cummings (Eds.), *Research in organizational behavior*, vol. 12: 295–336. Greenwich, CT: JAI Press.

——1996. Inter-organizational collaboration in the biotechnology industry. *Journal of Institutional and Theoretical Economics*, 152: 197–225.

——Koput, K. W., and Smith-Doerr, L. 1996. Interorganizational collaboration and the locus of innovation: Networks of learning in biotechnology. *Administrative Science Quarterly*, 41: 116–145.

Reed, R., and DeFillippi, R. J. 1990. Causal ambiguity, barriers to imitation, and sustainable competitive advantage. *Academy of Management Review*, 15: 88–102.

Ring, P., and Van de Ven, A. 1992. Structuring cooperative relationships between organizations. *Strategic Management Journal*, 13: 483–498.

Rumelt, R. P. 1984. Towards a strategic theory of the firm. In R. B. Lamb (Ed.), *Competitive strategic management*: 556–571. Englewood Cliffs, NJ: Prentice-Hall.

——1991. How much does industry matter? *Strategic Management Journal*, 12: 167–185.

——Schendel, D., and Teece, D. J. 1991. Strategic management and economics. *Strategic Management Journal*, 12: 5–29.

Ryle, G. 1984. *The concept of mind*. Chicago: University of Chicago Press.

Sako, M. 1991. The role of "trust" in Japanese buyer-supplier relationships. *Ricerche Economiche*, XLV: 449–474.

Saxenian, A. 1994. *Regional advantage*. Cambridge, MA: Harvard University Press.

Shan, W., and Hamilton, W. 1991. Country-specific advantage and international cooperation. *Strategic Management Journal*, 12: 419–432.

Shan, W., Walker, G., and Kogut, B. 1994. Interfirm cooperation and startup innovation in the biotechnology industry. *Strategic Management Journal*, 15: 387–394.

Singh, H., and Zollo, M. 1997. Learning to acquire: Knowledge accumulation mechanisms and the evolution of post-acquisition integration strategies. Working paper, The Wharton School, University of Pennsylvania, Philadelphia.

Smith, K. G., Carroll, S. J., and Ashford, S. J. 1995. Intra- and interorganizational cooperation: Toward a research agenda. *Academy of Management Journal*, 38: 7–23.

Smitka, M. J. 1991. *Competitive ties: Subcontracting in the Japanese automotive industry.* New York: Columbia University Press.

Szulanski, G. 1996. Exploring internal stickiness: Impediments to the transfer of best practice within the firm. *Strategic Management Journal*, 17: 27–43.

Teece, D. J. 1987. Profiting from technological innovation: Implications for integration, collaboration, licensing and public policy. In D. J. Teece (Ed.), *The competitive challenge: Strategies for industrial innovation and renewal*: 185–219. Cambridge, MA: Ballinger.

——Pisano, G., and Shuen, A. 1997. Dynamic capabilities and strategic management. *Strategic Management Journal*, 18: 509–533.

Telser, L. G. 1980. A theory of self-enforcing agreements. *Journal of Business*, 53: 27–44.

Uzzi, B. 1997. Social structure and competition in interfirm networks: The paradox of embeddedness. *Administrative Science Quarterly*, 42: 35–67.

von Hippel, E. 1988. *The sources of innovation*. New York: Oxford University Press.

Walker, G., Kogut, B., and Shan, W. 1997. Social capital, structural holes and the formation of an industry network. *Organization Science*, 8: 109–125.

Weigelt, K., and Camerer, C. 1988. Reputation and corporate strategy: A review of recent theory and applications. *Strategic Management Journal*, 9: 443–454.

Wernerfelt, B. 1984. A resource based view of the firm. *Strategic Management Journal*, 5: 171–180.

Williamson, O. E. 1983. Credible commitments: Using hostages to support exchange. *American Economic Review*, 73: 519–535.

——1985. *The economic institutions of capitalism*. New York: Free Press.

——1991a. Comparative economic organization: The analysis of discrete structural alternatives. *Administrative Science Quarterly*, 36: 269–296.

——1991b. Strategizing, economizing, and economic organization. *Strategic Management Journal*, 12: 75–94.

Womack, J. P., Jones, D. T., and Roos, D. 1990. *The machine that changed the world*. New York: Harper Perennial.

Zaheer, A., McEvily, B., and Perrone, V. 1998. Does trust matter? Exploring the effects of interorganizational and interpersonal trust on performance. *Organization Science*, 9: 141–159.

Zajac. E. J., and Olsen, C. P. 1993. From transaction cost to transactional value analysis: Implications for the study of interorganizational strategies. *Journal of Management Studies*, 30: 131–145.

16 Alliances and Networks

Ranjay Gulati

1. Introduction

Strategic alliances between firms are now a ubiquitous phenomenon. Their proliferation has led to a growing stream of research by strategy and organizational scholars who have examined some of the causes and consequences of such partnerships, mostly at the dyadic level. In this article I don't intend to review this vast and burgeoning field of research (for a review, see Auster, 1994). Instead, I will develop a social network perspective on some of the key questions associated with strategic alliances, going beyond the dyadic level to the larger network in which alliances are embedded. I will discuss how this perspective provides new insights on important factors that may influence the behavior and performance of firms. I define strategic alliances as voluntary arrangements between firms involving exchange, sharing, or codevelopment of products, technologies, or services. They can occur as a result of a wide range of motives and goals, take a variety of forms, and occur across vertical and horizontal boundaries. While I focus here on highlighting the importance of a social network perspective on strategic alliances, I will also discuss some of the valuable contributions and current research debates at the firm and dyad level for each of the key questions. This discussion of research on strategic alliances admittedly reflects my own biases and research preferences, and there is a large amount of research on this topic that will not fall under my purview.

From a strategic standpoint, some of the key facets of the behavior of firms as it relates to alliances can be understood by looking at the sequence of events in alliances. This sequencing includes the decision to enter an alliance, the choice of an appropriate partner, the choice of structure for the alliance, and the dynamic evolution of the alliance as the relationship develops over time. While all alliances may not necessarily progress through the same sequence of events, nonetheless, the decisions involved constitute some of the key behavioral issues that arise in alliances. Mirroring this sequence are the following relevant research questions: (1) Which firms enter alliances and whom do they choose as partners? (2) What types of contracts do firms use to formalize the alliance? and (3) How do the alliance and the partners' participation evolve over time?

A second important issue for alliances is their performance consequences, both in terms of the performance of the alliance relationship itself and the performance of firms entering alliances. Two research questions focus on the performance issue: (1) What factors influence the success of alliances? and (2) What is the effect of alliances on the performance of firms entering them?

In this chapter I will discuss these five critical questions for the study of strategic alliances and, for each, I will discuss current research efforts at both the dyadic and network levels and highlight some of the insights that result from a network perspective on the study of strategic alliances. Introducing networks into our calculus of the alliance behavior of firms allows an examination of both the innate propensities or inducements that lead firms into alliances and also the opportunities and constraints that can influence their behavior.

The notion that a firm's social connections guide its interest in new alliances, and provides it with opportunities to realize that interest, is closely rooted in the processes that underlie a firm's entry into new alliances. I first observed this when I was conducting field interviews at a number of firms with multiple alliances and found that firms don't necessarily follow the sequence of events that is usually offered for alliances (Gulati, 1993). A firm on its own initiative identifies the need for an alliance, identifies the best partner available, and chooses an appropriate contract to formalize the alliance. Rather, I observed that many new opportunities for alliances were presented to firms through their existing sets of alliance partners. In the instances in which firms independently initiated new alliances, they turned to their existing relationships first for potential partners or sought referrals from them on potential partners. The manner and extent to which firms were embedded were likely to influence several key decisions, including the frequency with which firms entered alliances, their choice of partner, the type of contracts used, and how the alliance developed and evolved over time. My fieldwork suggested that the social networks of prior ties not only influenced the creation of new ties but also affected their design, their evolutionary path, and their ultimate success.

2. A Brief Critique of Prior Research on Alliances

Prior research on alliances has led to valuable insights on the behavior of firms in alliances and the performance consequences from such partnerships. Three related themes run across these prior efforts. First, the unit of analysis that is usually adopted is the firm or the alliance. For instance, researchers have tried to identify the attributes of firms that influence their proclivity to enter alliances or their choice of partner, or to identify the characteristics of alliances that may influence the formal contracts used to organize them.

A second and related theme has been examining the formation and performance of alliances in an asocial context. The role of the external environment is usually encapsulated within measures of competitiveness in product or supplier markets. For instance, from a transaction costs standpoint, this translates to the argument that the lower the competition, the more likely that a firm will be exposed to 'small numbers bargaining' and other forms of opportunistic behavior (Williamson, 1985). Resource dependence theorists, similarly, make the case that at intermediate levels of industry concentration, firms experience high levels of competitive uncertainty and are likely to mitigate this competitive interdependence by entering into frequent joint ventures (Pfeffer and Nowak, 1976a). Finally, prior research on alliances has focused primarily on firm- and industry-level factors that impel firms to enter alliances. In his seminal book, Andrews (1971) claimed that the strategic actions of firms are the outcome of a match between a firm's existing competence and the availability of new opportunities. For the study of alliances, scholars have primarily focused on the existing competence (or lack thereof) that may propel firms to enter into new alliances, but they have generally paid less attention to factors that may lead to the availability of and access to alliance opportunities in the first place. Thus, in Andrews' terms, they have focused primarily on the competence side of the conditions that propel strategic actions and not on the conditions that determine the opportunity set firms may perceive.

The focus on the firm or alliance as the unit of analysis and the description of external context in competitive terms has typically assumed an atomistic notion of firms evaluating alternative courses of action and does not take into account the actions of other firms or the relationships in which they themselves are already embedded. Moreover, it ignores the interactive elements of the market, whereby participants discover market information through their interactions in the market (Hayek, 1949; White, 1981). It is important to recognize that although strategic alliances are essentially dyadic exchanges, key precursors, processes, and outcomes associated with them can be defined and shaped by the social networks within which most firms are embedded. There is a rich strand of research in economic sociology that has devoted itself to explaining how economic actions may be influenced by the social structure of ties within which they are embedded (e.g., Granovetter, 1985). Sociologists have convincingly demonstrated that the distinct social structural patterns in exchange relations within markets shape the flow of information (White, 1981; Burt, 1982; Baker, 1984). This in turn provides both opportunities and constraints for firms and can have implications for their behavior and performance. Viewed from this standpoint, much of the research on strategic alliances represents an undersocialized account of firm behavior.

In recent years there has been a growing interest in understanding the influence of the social context in which firms are embedded on their behavior and performance. A number of researchers have explicitly incorporated embeddedness, broadly defined, into our understanding of strategic management questions relating to the behavior and performance of firms (for a collection of recent articles, see Baum and Dutton, 1996). The social context in which firms are embedded includes a whole array of elements that can be classified broadly as structural, cognitive, institutional, and cultural (Zukin and DiMaggio, 1990). While each of these facets can be significant, my focus in this chapter will be on the structural context, which highlights the significance of the social networks in which economic actors may be placed. Prior to discussing the key questions for the study of alliances, I will provide a general theoretical perspective for examining the implications of social embeddedness on firm behavior and performance.

3. Social Structure and the Embeddedness of Firm Behavior

Building on an open systems perspective first put forward by organizational theorists, structural sociologists have suggested that the most important facet of an organization's environment is its social network of external contacts (for a review, see Powell and Smith-Doerr, 1994). They emphasize the fact that economic action—like any other form of social action—does not take place in a barren social context but, rather, is embedded in social networks of relationships. A social network can be defined as 'a set of nodes (e.g., persons, organizations) linked by a set of social relationships (e.g., friendship, transfer of funds, overlapping membership) of a specified type' (Laumann, Galaskiewicz, and Marsden, 1978: 458).

Network perspectives build on the general notion that economic actions are influenced by the social context in which they are embedded and that actions can be influenced by the position of actors in social networks. Embeddedness refers to the fact that exchanges and discussions within a group typically have a history, and that this history results in the routinization and stabilization of linkages among members. As elements of ongoing social structures, actors do not respond solely to individualistically determined interests . . . a structure of relations affects the actions taken by the individual actors composing it. It does so by constraining the set of actions available to the individual actors and by changing the dispositions of those actors toward the actions they may take. (Marsden, 1981: 1210)

Underlying embeddedness is the quest for information to reduce uncertainty, a quest that has been identified as one of the main drivers of organizational action (Granovetter, 1985). Networks of contact between actors can be important sources of information for the participants, and what can matter is not only the identity of the members of a network but also the pattern of ties among them.

There have been four broad foci of prior research on the influence of social networks: inequality, embedding, contagion, and contingency (Burt et al., 1994). Research on inequality suggests how network connections can explain differences in the resources available to individuals, groups, or organizations, while research on embedding describes the institutions and identities resulting from networks and how they enable difficult transactions. The research on contagion has shown how networks can promote behavioral conformity by serving as conduits for both technological and social information about organizational activities, which in turn can influence the extent to which they adopt new innovations (Davis, 1991; Haunschild, 1992). Finally, contingency approaches suggest how social networks can moderate key organizational processes. While all four perspectives focus primarily on the consequences of embeddedness in social networks, recent accounts have also begun to consider some of the bases for the origin of these networks.

There are two broad analytical approaches for examining the influence of social networks. The first emphasizes the differential informational advantages bestowed by social networks, while the second highlights the control benefits actors can generate by being advantageously positioned within a social network. These two benefits are analytically distinct but also overlap, since much of the control benefit can arise from the manipulation of information (Burt, 1992: 78). Networks may provide informational benefits through two mechanisms (Granovetter, 1992). Relational embeddedness or cohesion perspectives on networks stress the role of direct cohesive ties as a mechanism for gaining fine-grained information. Actors who share direct connections with each other are likely to possess more common information and knowledge of each other. Structural embeddedness or positional perspectives on networks go beyond the immediate ties of firms and emphasize the informational value of the structural position these partners occupy in the network. Information travels not only through proximate ties in networks, but through the structure of the network itself. Both mechanisms have generally been applied to explain similarities in the attitudes and behavior of actors resulting from the sharing of information through networks (e.g., Burt, 1987).

Relational embeddedness typically suggests that actors who are strongly tied to each other are likely to develop a shared understanding of the utility of certain behavior as a result of discussing opinions in strong, socializing relations, which in turn influence their actions (Coleman, Katz, and Menzel, 1966). Cohesively tied actors are likely to emulate each other's behavior. Cohesion can also be viewed as the capacity for social ties to carry information that diminishes uncertainty and promotes trust between actors (Granovetter, 1973; Podolny, 1994; Gulati, 1995a; Burt and Knez, 1995). Thus, cohesive ties can become a unique source of information about the partner's capabilities and reliability.

Structural embeddedness focuses on the informational role of the position an organization occupies in the overall structure of the network. Consequently, the frame of reference shifts from the dyad and triad to the system (Marsden and Friedkin, 1993). In network analysis, the position an actor occupies in the structure is a function of the actor's relational pattern in this network. Actors occupying similar positions need not be tied with each other. Instead, they are likely to be tied to the same set of other actors or to similar sets of other actors, and there is a whole array of network measures to capture the position an actor occupies in a network.

Scholars have frequently linked the position actors occupy to the notion of 'status' and suggested that actors occupying similar positions reflect distinct status groups (Podolny, 1993, 1994). In sociological terms, status evokes a series of observable characteristics associated with a particular position, or 'role,' in a social structure, that entails a relatively defined set of expected behaviors toward other actors. Because an actor's status is based on its affiliations and patterns of interaction, it is affected by its web of affiliations and by the status of its exchange partners. When focusing on an interorganizational context, we can also view status as an attribution of the quality of products an actor–organization provides when the quality cannot be directly observed (Podolny, 1993). Following a similar logic, the observable features associated with a certain status can also become an important signal of how members of that status are likely to behave. Thus, status groupings resulting from network position can provide powerful informational cues for actors about the likely behavior of others in the network.

Both perspectives of relational and structural embeddedness highlight the informational advantages social networks can confer on certain actors. Another view of networks highlights the control benefits actors can receive and has been developed furthest in the work of Burt (1992). An actor in a social network can derive control advantages by being the *tertius gaudens*, or one who is situated between two other actors. This can occur either when two or more actors are after the same relationship with a focal actor, as is the case when multiple firms want to enter an alliance with a given firm, or can occur when an actor is the tertius in separate relationships with two actors with conflicting demands, as may occur for a firm that has separate alliances with two independent firms that may create conflicting demands. In both such instances, firms in the tertius role can create advantages for themselves by playing one off against the other and brokering tension between the other players. These advantages can translate into concrete benefits in the form of favorable terms in their exchange relationships with partners.

While the original focus of network research was on understanding how the embeddedness of individuals influences their behavior, a similar argument has been extended to organizations (e.g., Burt, 1982; Walker, 1988; Mizruchi, 1992; Gulati, 1995b). Firms can be interconnected with other firms through a wide array of social and economic relationships, each of which can constitute a social network. These include supplier relationships, resource flows, trade association memberships, interlocking directorates, relationships among individual employees, and prior strategic alliances. While firms may be connected through a multitude of connections, each of which could be a social network, some may be more or less significant than others and researchers have rarely focused on more than one network at a time (for a review of research on interorganizational relationships, see Galaskiewicz, 1985a). To recognize the true importance of a social network, it is important to understand the nature and purpose of the network as well as the contents of information flowing through it (Stinchcombe, 1990). While much of the research on interorganizational relationships has focused on the networks of interlocking directorates (for a review, see Mizruchi, 1996), scholars have also looked at other networks, such as those between corporations and investment banks (Baker, 1990), among hospitals (Westphal, Gulati, and Shortell, 1997), among firms resulting from prior alliances (Gulati, 1995a, 1995b), and those among corporate contributions officers (Galaskiewicz, 1985b).

Only recently have scholars begun to explore the implications of the social structure resulting from intercorporate networks on strategic alliances. Strategic alliances are distinctive in that entering one constitutes a strategic action, and their cumulation can also become a social network. Thus, alliances are unique in that they can be studied as both endogenous and exogenous factors. The former can be examined by looking at the influence of social networks on the formation of alliances, while the latter can be assessed by considering the effects of the social network of cumulated alliances. Both can be examined simultaneously by assessing the influence of the social network of prior alliances on its future alliances in a longitudinal setting. Studying the development of an alliance network over time can provide unique insights into the evolution of networks, where strategic action and social structure are closely intertwined. It also allows us to examine the extent to which alliances formed by firms may lock them into path-dependent courses of action in the future. The normative side of this, of course, is that once firms understand the dynamics of alliance networks, they may choose path-creation strategies rather than becoming path-dependent (Garud and Rappa, 1994). As a result, they can visualize the desired network structure of alliances in the future and work backwards to define their current alliance strategy.

The same dual orientation is feasible for studying the performance consequences of alliances including the performance of alliances themselves and how alliances may influence the performance of partnering firms. One way to understand the performance consequences of social networks for alliances and for the firms entering them is to think of social networks as bestowing firms with 'social capital' which can become an important basis for competitive advantage (Burt, 1997). While the notion that actors possess social capital has been most developed for individuals and their interpersonal networks, the idea can easily be extended to organizations and their interorganizational networks (Gulati, 1997). The benefits of social capital accrue to firms from the access to information it provides and the potential for control benefits. This information can be a powerful catalyst, providing firms with new productive opportunities to utilize the financial and human capital with which they are endowed. For instance, the informational advantages to firms from a social network can enable the creation of new alliances by three distinct means: access, timing, and referrals (Burt, 1992). Access refers to information about current or potential partners as to their capabilities and trustworthiness—an existing network can influence a firm's choice of feasible partners and its attractiveness to other firms as a partner. The availability of current information about alliance partners can also affect the partnering firms' choice of structure to formalize the alliance, as well as key processes underlying the dynamic evolution of the alliance. Timing entails having informational benefits about potential partners at the right time, which can be important when a firm seeking attractive partners must approach them at the right time and preempt their seeking alliances elsewhere. It can also alter the evolutionary path of the alliance by providing partners with information at critical junctures in the alliance, which can affect the performance of the alliance and the benefits the firm receives from the alliance. Referrals can be particularly important in alliance formation, as a firm's existing partners may refer other firms to it for alliances or to enter three-way partnerships.

In the case of alliances, firms with more social capital will not only have access to information about a larger number of alliances, but they may also be able to attract better partners who want to ally with them. Furthermore, they may be able to extract superior terms of trade because of possible control benefits that may ensue from their social capital. The informational benefits from social networks can have ramifications for the development and ultimate success of the alliance itself. Ties that are structurally embedded can have fundamentally different characteristics and life course than those that are not (Powell, 1990). Embedded ties promote greater frequency of information exchange between partners, which can affect the success of the alliance as well as the performance of firms entering them.

4. Key Issues in Alliances

The section is organized around the five key questions that I outlined to be critical issues for studying strategic alliances. For each question, I first discuss some of the current research and debates at the firm and dyadic levels, followed by an examination of how introducing a social network perspective opens up an additional set of issues that can be considered.

4.1. The Formation of Alliances

In a review of some of the theoretical explanations for the formation of joint ventures, Kogut (1988a) highlighted three main motivations which are broadly applicable to other types of alliances as well: transaction costs resulting from small numbers bargaining, strategic behavior that leads firms to try to enhance their competitive positioning or market power, and a quest for organizational knowledge or learning that results when one or both partners want to acquire some critical knowledge from the other or one partner wants to maintain its capability while seeking another firm's knowledge.

Some of the early empirical studies on alliances focused on the formation of joint ventures in particular, which entail the creation of a new entity with shared equity between partners. They examined some of the strategic imperatives for joint ventures, which included the enhancement of market power and increased efficiency. Several studies focused on the incidence of such alliances across industries and the size of firms entering them. The concentration of such alliances within particular industries in the manufacturing sector and the heightened proclivity of larger firms to enter them led scholars to conclude that the quest for market power may be an important motive for such ties (e.g., Pate, 1969; Berg and Friedman, 1978). These arguments were further refined to incorporate transaction costs as an inducement for certain types of alliances (Stuckey, 1983) and knowledge acquisition as a salient motive for many alliances (Berg and Friedman, 1981).

Current studies on alliance formation have followed tradition and examined industry- and firm-level factors that could explain the frequency with which alliances occur. More detailed measures have been developed, and the domain of inquiry has expanded from joint ventures to other types of alliances. Some of the industry-level factors linked with alliance formation include the extent of competition, the stage of development of the market, and demand and competitive uncertainty (Harrigan, 1988; Shan, 1990; Burgers, Hill, and Kim, 1993; Eisenhardt and Schoonhoven, 1996). The focus has remained on strategic factors, since empirical investigations of transaction cost and knowledge-based imperatives for alliance formation have been less tractable.

The study of firm-specific imperatives has focused on identifying some of the inducements likely to lead firms to enter alliances (for a review, see Harrigan and Newman, 1990). This has led to a rich research stream that has examined which types of firms in which industries enter what types of alliances for what reasons (Mariti and Smiley, 1983; Ghemawat, Porter, and Rawlinson, 1986; Porter and Fuller, 1986). This has been refined within a cost–benefit framework in which the costs and benefits from alliances are primarily strategic and technological and alliances materialize when the benefits exceed the costs (Harrigan, 1985; Contractor and Lorange, 1988). At the firm level, scholars have sought to show the role of resource contingencies such as strategic vulnerability and incumbency on the proclivity of firms to enter alliances (Eisenhardt and Schoonhoven, 1996; Mitchell and Singh, 1992). Other scholars have looked at firms' attributes, such as size, age, competitive position, product diversity, and financial resources, as important predictors of their propensity to enter strategic alliances with each other (Shan, 1990; Barley, Freeman, and Hybels, 1992; Powell and Brantley, 1992; Burgers et al., 1993; Shan, Walker, and Kogut, 1994). The importance of resource considerations has been further refined by Kogut (1991), who suggested that many joint ventures occur as options to expand in the future and are interim mechanisms by which firms both buffer and explore uncertainty.

A second question associated with alliance behavior of firms has to do with the question of with whom firms partner. Just as a person's decision to get married is tied to the choice and availability of a specific partner, a firm's decision to enter into an alliance is closely linked with its choice of an appropriate partner and may even be determined by that partner's availability. Hence, the dyad can be a valuable unit of analysis to study the alliance behavior of firms. A research stream that has paid attention to alliance formation at this level has been resource dependence theory. A rich literature on the formation of relations among social service agencies flourished in the 1960s and 1970s (for reviews, see Galaskiewicz, 1985a; Oliver, 1990). This research built on the original open systems model of resource procurement but added an exchange perspective that suggested that organizations enter partnerships when they perceive critical strategic interdependence with other organizations in their environment (e.g., Levine and White, 1961; Aiken and Hage, 1968), in which one organization has resources or capabilities beneficial to but not possessed by the other. Applied to the dyadic context, these arguments suggest that firms sought out ties with partners who could help them manage such strategic interdependencies. Richardson (1972), in a theoretical economic account, also proposed that the necessity for complementary resources is a key driver of interorganizational cooperation.

In recent years, the focus of scholars studying interorganizational relations has shifted from social service agencies to business organizations. A strategic interdependence perspective on alliance formation suggests that firms ally with those with whom they share the greatest interdependence. To assess the significance of resource dependence at the dyadic level, researchers have linked the formation of alliances to the distribution of various kinds of capabilities within the industry, such as production, marketing, distribution, regulatory approval, and access to new technologies. At the interindustry level, resource dependence theorists have empirically tested the role of strategic interdependence by predicting the number of joint ventures formed across industries (Pfeffer and Nowak, 1976a, 1976b; Berg and Friedman, 1980; Duncan, 1982). Recent efforts have focused more closely on the industry level and explored the role of resource configurations within an industry in predicting alliance formation. They have not only revealed distinct patterns, such as densely linked cliques, but have also tried to explain the observed patterns on the basis of strategic interdependence resulting from country-specific resource advantages (Shan and Hamilton, 1991), the distribution of strategic capabilities (Nohria and Garcia-Pont, 1991), and the relative size and performance of firms (Burgers, Hill, and Kim, 1993). This research suggests that industry patterns in the formation of alliances indicate that firms are driven to enter alliances with each other by critical strategic interdependence.

Although interdependence may explain tie formation between some firms, it may not adequately account for alliance formation. This inadequacy is clear from the fact that not all possible opportunities for sharing interdependence across firms actually materialize as alliances. An account of alliance formation that focuses only on interdependence ignores how firms learn about new alliance opportunities and overcome the fears associated with such partnerships. Implicit in such accounts is the assumption that firms exist in an atomistic system in which information is freely available and equally accessible to all and opportunities for alliances are exogenously presented (Granovetter, 1985).

To understand why social networks and the information they channel are important for firms and their alliances, we need to consider the circumstances usually associated with such ties. Firms entering alliances face considerable moral hazard concerns because of the unpredictability of the behavior of partners and the likely costs to a firm from opportunistic behavior by a partner, if it occurs. Despite the rapid growth of both domestic and international alliances in many industrial sectors, such partnerships are still considered risky (*Business Week*, 1986; Kogut, 1989; Hamel, Doz, and Prahalad, 1989). A partner may either free-ride by limiting its contributions to an alliance or simply behave opportunistically. Such concerns are further compounded by the unpredictable character of such relationships. Rapid changes in the environment may lead organizations to alter their needs and orientation, thus affecting their ongoing partnerships. For organizations to build ties that effectively address their needs while minimizing the risks posed by such concerns, they must be aware of the existence of their potential partners and have an idea of their needs and requirements. Organizations also need information about the reliability of those partners, especially when success depends heavily upon the partners' behavior (Bleeke and Ernst, 1991).

Sociologists have suggested that economic actors address concerns of opportunism in economic transactions by embedding transactions in the social context in which those transactions occur. Faced with uncertainty about a partner, actors adopt a more social orientation and resort to existing networks to discover information that lowers search costs and alleviates the risk of opportunism. Granovetter (1985: 490) noted that 'the widespread preference for transacting with individuals of known reputation implies that few are actually content to rely on either generalized morality or institutional arrangements to guard against trouble.' A person resorts to 'trusted informants' who have dealt with the potential partner and found him or her trustworthy, or, even better, to 'information from one's own past dealings with that person' (Granovetter, 1985: 490).

The embeddedness of firms in social networks can both restrict and enable the alliances a firm enters. By influencing the extent to which firms have access to information about potential partners, social networks can alter the opportunity set firms perceive for viable alliances. Similarly, networks constrain the extent to which potential partners are aware of a focal firm and thus may constrain its set of choices for alliances. This is vividly illustrated by the influence of one such social network, the cumulation of prior alliances, on the subsequent alliances by firms. As the typical comments by a manager I interviewed indicate, firm managers embed their new ties by relying extensively on their partners from past alliances for information:

> They are familiar with many of our projects from their very inception and if there is potential for an alliance we discuss it. Likewise, we learn about many of their product goals very early on and we actively explore alliance opportunities with them. (Gulati, 1993: 84)

Such comments suggest that firms are influenced in their ability to enter new partnerships by the social network of their past alliances.

Several recent studies have explored the importance of social embeddedness on the formation of alliances by firms. The first question examined has been at the firm level—which firms enter into alliances? Evidence suggests that the proclivity of firms to enter alliances is influenced not only by their financial and technological attributes (treated as proxies for strategic imperatives), but also by how they are embedded in social networks between firms. For instance, several studies have used the social network of prior alliances between firms to show that firms that had more prior alliances, were more centrally situated in the alliance network, or had more focused networks, were more likely to enter into new alliances and did so with greater frequency (Kogut, Shan, and Walker, 1992; Gulati, 1993, 1997). Similiar findings have been reported for the influence of firm centrality in various other networks on their likelihood of entering new alliances. These networks include alliance networks among biotechnology firms (Powell, Koput, and Smith-Doerr, 1996), semiconductor firms and their patent citation networks (Podolny and Stuart, 1995), and those of top management teams of semiconductor firms (Eisenhardt and Schoonhoven, 1996). Each network highlights a different underlying social process that enables central firms to enter alliances more frequently. Nonetheless, these studies strongly suggest that the embeddedness of firms is an important influence on their alliance behavior.

The influence of social embeddedness on the formation of new alliances has also been observed at the dyad level, with a focus on who partners with whom. In a study of alliance formation over a 20-year period, Gulati (1995b) examined the factors explaining which of all possible dyads entered alliances during the observed time period. The social context examined was the cumulation of prior alliances between firms. The observed social structural effects resulted from both the direct and indirect ties of firms with each other. Previously allied firms were likely to engage in further alliances. This was confirmed in comments by alliance executives such as: 'We have close working relationships with most of our alliance partners. As a result, we are familiar with many of their own goals and capabilities. Since they also know about our specific skills and needs, many new deals are created interactively with them.' The results also provided evidence of the informational benefits of indirect ties between firms, both one-level-removed indirect ties and more distant ties. Previously unconnected firms were more likely to enter an alliance if they had common partners or were less distant from each other in the alliance network.

Structural embeddedness can also influence the choice of partner in alliances. The cues provided by the position of organizations enlarge the realm of potential partners about which an organization can have *a priori* information beyond the circle of organizations directly or indirectly tied to it. The status of an organization in the network affects its reputation and visibility in the system. The greater this reputation, the wider the organization's access to a variety of sources of knowledge, and the richer the collaborative experience, which makes it an attractive partner. The signaling properties of status are particularly important in uncertain environments, where the attractiveness of a potential partner can be gauged from its status, which in turn depends on the organizations (or type of organizations) already tied to this partner (Podolny, 1994). This phenomenon has important behavioral consequences. If the status of whom they partner with enhances their own attractiveness, organizations will have a tendency to seek high-status partners. Although special reasons, such as the control of a new technology, may prompt a high-status organization to cooperate with a low-status player, the 'homophily principle' in terms of status that operates under conditions of uncertainty makes this an unlikely occurrence (Gulati and Gargiulo, 1997).

The formation of dyadic ties between particular firms has also been studied in vertical alliances between buyers and suppliers. For instance, scholars have examined the extent to which Japanese automotive assemblers recreate their relationships in Japan in their North American operations (Martin, Mitchell, and Swaminathan, 1995). The evidence suggests that in addition to an array of strategic factors associated with the characteristics of the buyer and supplier, an important consideration in the recreation of ties was the history of prior engagements in which these firms are embedded. The longer the prior history between two firms, the more likely they were to recreate these ties in North America. This suggests that the social embeddedness of firms influences the creation of vertical alliances between firms.

The social explanation offered by the reported studies that highlight the role of embeddedness does not contradict the economic motivations for alliances. Firms don't form alliances as symbolic social affirmations of their social networks but, rather, base alliances on concrete strategic complementarities that they have to offer each other. It does suggest that the conditions of mutual economic advantage are necessary but not sufficient conditions for the formation of an alliance between two firms. While considerations of individual quest for resources and complementarity are relevant, it is a firm's social connections that help it identify new alliance opportunities and choose specific partners that possess such complementary assets.

As highlighted earlier, firms are embedded in multiple social networks and the implications of these manifold ties on alliance formation remain an open question. The evidence that exists thus far highlights the significance of one social network at a time on new alliances. The possible implications of the simultaneous and possibly conflicting influence of multiple social networks on alliance formation have yet to be systematically examined. For instance, one of the most widely studied interorganizational networks has been board interlocks, and yet the implications of such ties and other interfirm networks on alliances has largely been overlooked until recently (Gulati and Westphal, 1997).

Furthermore, the broader institutional context in which such networks are placed can also be influential (Dacin, Hitt, and Levitas, 1997).

4.2. Governance Structure of Alliances

A notable characteristic of the dramatic growth of strategic alliances in the last two decades has been the increasing diversity of such alliances. The nationalities of partners, their motives and goals in entering alliances, and the formal contractual structures used to organize the partnerships, called the governance structure, have all become increasingly varied. While alliances may be considered a distinct form of governance that is different from markets or hierarchies, there is also considerable variation in the formal structure of alliances themselves (Powell, 1990). The variety of organizing structures implies that firms face an array of choices in structuring their alliances. Prior research has distinguished among alliance structures in terms of the degree of hierarchical elements they embody and the extent to which they replicate the control and coordination features associated with organizations, which are considered to be at the hierarchical end of the spectrum (e.g., Harrigan, 1987; Hennart, 1988; Osborn and Baughn, 1990; Teece, 1992). At one end are joint ventures, which involve partners creating a new entity in which they share equity and which most closely replicate the hierarchical control features of organizations. At the other end are alliances with no sharing of equity that have few hierarchical controls built into them.

Organizational scholars have long studied the diversity of structures within organizations and viewed structure as a mechanism to manage uncertainty. Prior research on contract choices in alliances and the extent of hierarchical controls they embody has been influenced primarily by transaction cost economists, who have focused on the appropriation concerns in alliances, which originate from contracting hazards and behavioral uncertainty at the time of their formation (e.g., Pisano, Russo, and Teece, 1988; Pisano, 1989; Balakrishnan and Koza, 1993; Oxley, 1997). Following this perspective, scholars have suggested that hierarchical controls are an effective response to such concerns as they are anticipated at the time the alliance is formed. The logic for hierarchical controls as a response to appropriation concerns is based on the ability of such controls to assert control by fiat, enable monitoring, and align incentives. The operation of such a logic was originally examined in the classic make-or-buy decisions (e.g., Walker and Weber, 1984; Masten, Meehan, and Snyder, 1991). The same logic by which firms choose between the extremes of making or buying a component is also expected to operate once firms have decided to form an alliance in their choice of governance structure. The greater the appropriation concerns, the more hierarchical the governance structures for organizing the alliance are likely to be.

An important shortcoming with such prior approaches has been their implicit treatment of each transaction as a discrete independent event (Doz and Prahalad, 1991). This leads to temporal reductionism since it treats alliances as occurring in an ahistorical context. Firms may very well have a longer history with each other through their entering multiple strategic alliances over several years. One of the executives who specialized in alliances for his firm that I interviewed highlighted this point:

> We originally initiated technology partnerships with a number of key industry players in the mid-1980s. These in turn have led to numerous repeated alliances with the same set of firms. With each partner maintaining on-site staff at our facilities that was only to be expected. (Gulati, 1993: 84)

Empirical studies on the governance of alliances have unfortunately continued in the transaction cost economics tradition, treating each alliance as independent and considering the activities it includes at the time of its formation as singularly reflecting the transaction costs associated with it. The approach taken is thus static: it specifies the unit of analysis to be each transaction and not the economic relationship and thus ignores the possibility of a social structure resulting from repeated alliances and the emergent processes resulting from prior interactions between partners that may alter their calculus when they are choosing contracts in alliances (Ring and Van de Ven, 1992; Gulati, 1995a; Dyer and Singh, 1997; Nickerson and Silverman, 1997). Furthermore, it would be useful to consider the implications of structural embeddedness which would suggest the importance of the overall network in which individual transactions and also economic relationships are situated.

An important implication of the embeddedness of firms in social networks is the enhanced trust between firms. Trust between firms refers to the confidence that a partner will not exploit the vulnerabilities of the other (Barney and Hansen, 1994). A social network of prior ties can promote trust through two possible means. First, by serving as effective referral networks, the prior social structure makes firms aware of each other's existence. Take, for instance, the comments of one of the executives responsible for alliance decisions that I interviewed:

> In some cases we realize that perhaps our skills don't really match for a project, and our partner may refer us to another firm about whom we were unaware .... An important aspect of this referral business is of course about vouching for the reliability of that firm. Thus, if one of our long-standing partners suggests one of their own partners as a good fit for our needs, we usually consider it very seriously. (Gulati, 1993: 84)

Through these ongoing interactions, firms not only learn about each other but may also develop trust around norms of equity, or 'knowledge-based trust' (Shapiro, Sheppard, and Cheraskin, 1992). There are strong cognitive and emotional bases for such trust, which are perhaps most visible among individual organization members. Macaulay (1963: 63) observed how close personal ties emerged between individuals in organizations that contracted with each other; these personal relationships in turn 'exert pressures for conformity to expectations.' Similarly, Ring and Van de Ven (1989, 1994) pointed to the important role of informal, personal connections across organizations in determining the governance structure used to organize their transactions. Second, social networks can serve as an important basis for 'enforceable' or 'deterrence-based' trust (Kreps, 1990; Raub and Weesie, 1990; Shapiro et al., 1992; Burt and Knez, 1995). The anticipated utility from a tie with a given partner and those with shared partners motivates good behavior. Each partner's awareness that the other has much to lose from behaving opportunistically enhances its confidence in the other. Potential sanctions include loss of repeat business with the same partner, loss of other points of interaction between the two firms, and loss of reputation.

How is trust between two firms likely to alter their choice of contracts in subsequent alliances? An important concern of firms entering alliances has to do with appropriation and relates to the predictability of their partners' behavior. A detailed contract is one mechanism for making behavior predictable, and another is trust. Both knowledge-based trust resulting from mutual awareness and equity norms and deterrence-based trust arising from reputational concerns creates 'self-enforcing' safeguards in an exchange relationship and can substitute for contractual safeguards (Bradach and Eccles, 1989; Powell, 1990). As a result, where there is trust, appropriation concerns are likely to be mitigated, and organizations may not choose to rely on detailed contracts to ensure predictability. In a study of the choice of governance structures in strategic alliances, I found that firms select contractual forms for their alliances not only on the basis of the activities they include and the related appropriation concerns they anticipate at the outset, but also the existence of the social network of prior alliances in which the partners may be embedded (Gulati, 1995a). What emerges from this account is an image of alliance formation in which cautious contracting gives way to looser practices as partners become increasingly embedded in a social network of prior ties. Familiarity between organizations through prior alliances does indeed breed trust which enables firms to progressively use less hierarchical structures in organizing new alliances.

Several provocative articles have questioned the role of transaction costs and appropriation concerns in alliances. Powell (1990) suggested that alliances and other such exchange relationships don't necessarily fall on the market-hierarchy continuum put forth by transaction cost economics but, rather, constitute a distinct form of governance that he calls the network form. He used the term 'network' to classify such dyadic ties because many such ties are deeply embedded in a multiplicity of relationships. This study poses some important questions for future research on the governance structure of alliances. In particular, if we are to go beyond the confines of market and hierarchy as the dual anchors around which we study the governance structure of alliances, it becomes imperative to begin considering some of the alternative dimensions along which we can examine such structure (see also Stinchcombe, 1986).

In another important critique of transaction cost economics applications to alliances, Zajac and Olsen (1993) pointed to two additional shortcomings. First, transaction cost accounts in general focus on single-party cost minimization while alliances are inherently dyadic exchanges, which raises the question of whose costs are minimized. Relatedly, alliances are not only about cost minimization but also about joint value maximization, an issue neglected previously. Second, the structural emphasis of transaction cost economics leads it to neglect important processual issues resulting from their ongoing nature. Alliances are usually not one-off transactions but, rather, entail continuing exchange and adjustments, as a result of which process issues become salient (Khanna, 1997).

Another concern with the transaction cost approach stems from the fact that it has focused entirely on appropriation concerns that originate from the presence of contracting hazards and behavioral uncertainty. While appropriation can clearly be an important concern, there is also another set of concerns for firms entering alliances resulting from coordination costs. Such anticipated costs arise from the likely interdependence of tasks across organizational boundaries and the complexity of coordinating activities to be completed jointly or individually. Coordination considerations are extensive in alliances. In an empirical study of over 1500 alliances, my colleague and I found that the deliberations underlying the choice of alliance structure at the time an alliance is formed are not dominated by concerns of appropriation, as previously suggested, but by considerations associated with managing coordination costs resulting from the anticipated ongoing coordination of tasks across partners (Gulati and Singh, 1997). This study also suggests that social structure of trusting relationships are distinctive in addressing both coordination costs and appropriation concerns, and this is reflected in the nature of contracts used when firms are embedded in social networks. The presence of interfirm trust is an extraordinary lubricant for alliances that involve considerable interdependence and task coordination between partners, since firms with prior network connections are likely to have a greater awareness of the rules, routines, and procedures each follows. Such a social structure can thus enable them to work together closely, if necessary, all without the need for formal hierarchical controls.

Prior research on the governance structure of alliances has primarily focused on the implications of embeddedness in one type of social network, the network of prior alliances, yet the role of the multiplicity of social and economic contexts in which firms are embedded on their choice of alliances remains underexplored. There may also be implications from the embeddedness of firms in other types of social networks such as board interlocks, that could influence the design of alliances, but this has yet to be examined. Firms are also embedded in a social structure of dependence that can alter the likely power dynamics in a potential alliance. Firms are likely to anticipate such conditions and modify the structure of their relationship accordingly (Baker, 1990). The economic context can influence the structure as well. For instance, the extent of market overlap between the partners and within the alliance, also known as 'relative scope,' can influence the likelihood of competitive dynamics between the partners (Harrigan, 1987; Khanna, Gulati, and Nohria, 1998). Firms may anticipate the likelihood of such dynamics in an alliance and alter the structure to address those concerns if they arise.

4.3. *Dynamic Evolution of Alliances and Networks*

There has been considerable interest in uncovering some of the dynamic processes that underlie the development of individual alliances. Such dyadic exchanges can be transformed significantly beyond their original design and mandate once they are under way. The varying evolutionary paths alliances follow can have significant consequences for their performance (Harrigan, 1985, 1986). Thus, understanding the evolution of alliances can provide critical insights into how such ties can be better managed. Using detailed clinical studies of individual alliances, scholars have sought to uncover some of the formal and informal processes and key stages that unfold in alliances (Hamel, 1991; Larson, 1992; Ring and Van de Ven, 1994; Doz, 1996). Considerable efforts have been devoted to understanding some of the factors that influence this development and possible stages through which alliances may proceed.

In recent years, scholars have studied the role of the initial conditions under which alliances are formed in their subsequent development. For instance, Gulati et al. (1994) have introduced the idea that each partner's comprehension of an alliance's pay-offs is crucial for understanding the incentives to cooperate and for realizing the possible ways each can unilaterally influence the alliance's outcome (see also, Parkhe, 1993). The possible consequences of changing pay-offs once the alliance is under way were also discussed. In a related study, Khanna et al. (1998) introduced the concept of a firm's 'relative scope,' which captures the initial conditions likely to influence the competitive and cooperative dynamics and for each firm is the ratio of the scope of the alliance to the total set of markets in which the firm is active. This measure was used to establish testable propositions that suggest that the opportunity set of each firm outside the particular alliance crucially affects its behavior within the alliance. Thus, the extent of market overlap in activities between the partners and with the alliance can be an important determinant of the likely behavior of partners. This coincides with prior efforts that linked initial asymmetries between partners with the ultimate success of the alliance (Harrigan, 1986). Scholars have also begun to look at the combined impact of initial imprinting conditions and adaptive processes on the ultimate behavior and performance in an alliance (Hamel et al., 1989; Doz, 1996). Evidence seems to suggest that while initial conditions such as the objectives of partners, their adeptness at learning, and the nature of the environment and interorganizational context do assert an influence over the development of an alliance (Hamel, 1991), the evolution of some alliances may in fact be akin to a punctuated equilibrium model in which there may be discrete stages that occur due to discontinuous changes in the environment (Gray and Yan, 1997).

The rich insights from these detailed clinical and theoretical accounts have advanced our understanding of the dynamics within alliances enormously. The focus of these efforts has remained at the dyadic level of exchange, however, with their primary emphasis on uncovering some of the important interpartner dynamics. Similar behavioral processes can span dyads and occur within networks as well but remain to be explored. For instance, individual contacts between firms through social networks can affect the decision processes that may occur inside those firms (Gulati, 1993). Boundary-spanning individuals can have crucial influence on the decision making not only within their own organizations but also in partner organizations. When alliances entail the creation of new entities, such as joint ventures, they can lead to conflicting identities for individuals involved, who may be torn between loyalties to the venture itself and to the parent organization from which they originally came. Furthermore, when network-level decisions must be made among clusters of firms, specific multilateral negotiations and dynamics may be poorly understood. Firms may also use their network contacts to create control benefits proactively by utilizing their advantageous position in social networks to play one partner off against the other. They may also seek to manage their network to sustain such advantages (Lorenzoni and Baden-Fuller, 1995). Such dynamic processes related to potential control benefits have yet to be examined.

The dynamics of behavior over time can be observed at the level of networks as well. Several scholars have suggested that clusters of firms with dense ties with each other may pursue collective strategies in conjunction with the competitive strategies of their individual members (Astley and Fombrun, 1983; Bresser, 1988). This has led to new forms of competition in which networks of firms compete with each other (Gomes-Casseres, 1994). Such networks of firms could include both horizontally and vertically connected firms. In an illuminating study, Nohria and Garcia-Pont (1991) demonstrated the importance of horizontal alliances in shaping the global automotive industry into distinct 'strategic blocks,' which either bring together firms with complementary differences or pool together firms with supplementary similarities, and can become a basis for competition within the industry. Similarly, scholars focusing on the supply chain of large manufacturers, particularly in the automotive industry, have examined how vertical networks and individual ties within them have become structured over time (Dyer, 1996; Helper, 1991; Lawrence and Gulati, 1997).

While prior studies have provided new insights into the structure of both horizontal and vertical networks, important questions still remain about the growth and development of interorganizational alliance networks (for a review, see Grandori and Soda, 1995). The shaping of such a dynamic interorganizational network can be influenced in important ways by exogenous factors, such as the nature of competition and critical industry events (Madhavan, Koka, and Prescott, 1998). In a recent study, my colleague and I suggested that the production of interorganizational alliance networks is driven by a dynamic process involving both exogenous resource dependencies, which prompt organizations to seek cooperation, and an 'endogenous embeddedness' dynamic, in which the emerging network progressively orients the choice of partners (Gulati and Gargiulo, 1997). Alliance networks are not static social structures in which organizations embed new alliances: they are also evolutionary products of these ties. As a result, new ties are influenced by the social network of prior ties in which they are embedded. Yet, when observed over time, the formation of new ties in each period alters the very same network that influenced their creation. This results in an endogenous network dynamic between embedded organizational action and the network structure that guides but is also transformed by that action. As the social network grows, the new ties contribute to the differentiation among organizations by their specific direct and indirect relations and by the structural positions organizations occupy in the emerging network. This 'structural differentiation' enables organizations to discriminate among partners in terms of their particular relational and structural profiles. As the available information grows, organizations seeking to build partnerships can become less reliant on exogenous factors and instead are more influenced by the network in which they are embedded.

The influence of networks on firms may also change over time if the content of information flowing through those networks changes. After all, networks have influence primarily through their channeling of information. Thus, if one is to observe dynamics at the network level, it is also valuable to assess how the content of information flowing through those networks may change over time. In a study of the influence of hospital networks on the extent and form of adoption of total quality management programs by hospitals, my colleagues and I observed that the nature of information transmitted about total quality management through the network varied depending on the stage of institutionalization of the innovation (Westphal et al., 1997). In the early periods, when total quality management was less institutionalized, the information flowing through networks was about the technological attributes of total quality management, while later on, when total quality management became more institutionalized, the information transmitted had stronger institutional elements in it. This changing nature of information in turn affected the influence of social networks on the type of total quality management programs hospitals adopted. As a result, the effect of social networks on the adoption of administrative innovations was contingent on the stage of its institutionalization as an innovation. Studying changes in information flows in the networks that influence alliances may provide valuable insights (Stinchcombe, 1990).

4.4. Performance of Alliances

The performance of alliances has received less attention than other areas because of some onerous research obstacles, which include measuring alliance performance and the logistical challenges of collecting the rich data necessary to assess these issues in greater detail. As a result, it remains one of the most exciting and underexplored areas. Numerous studies have reported dramatically high failure rates of alliances, and several practitioners have sought to identify the magical formula for alliance success (e.g., Kanter, 1989; Bleeke and Ernst, 1991). This wish list includes: flexibility in management of the alliance, building trust with partners, regular information exchange with the partners, constructive management of conflict, continuity of boundary personnel responsible for the interface between the firm and the alliance, managing partner expectations, and so on. The focus of the research generating such lists has primarily been at the alliance level, with efforts targeted at identifying antecedent conditions and emergent processes that can influence performance.

The primary approach to empirical studies of the performance of alliances has been to examine the termination of an alliance. Several careful empirical inquiries have yielded important insights into some of the key factors that may be associated with the termination of alliances, including industry and dyadic conditions such as concentration and growth rates, country of origin of partners as developed or developing, the presence of concurrent ties, partner asymmetry, age dependence or the duration of the alliance, the competitive overlap between the partners, and characteristics of the venture itself such as autonomy and flexibility (Beamish, 1985; Harrigan, 1986; Levinthal and Fichman, 1988; Kogut, 1989). While these studies have provided valuable insights into the termination of alliances, their importance for understanding the performance of an alliance *per se* is limited by two factors. First, studying failure by looking at terminations fails to distinguish between natural and untimely deaths. Many successful alliances terminate because they are predestined to do so by the parent firms at the very outset. In other instances, an alliance may simply be a transitional arrangement that the parents plan to terminate when their objectives are met or when they have valuable new information that makes viable an acquisition or divestiture of that business (Kogut, 1991; Bleeke and Ernst, 1991; Balakrishnan and Koza, 1993). In some instances, the transformation of a venture may actually indicate successful adaptation to environmental shifts (Gomes-Casseres, 1987). Also, not all ongoing alliances are necessarily successful, and some may be continuing more out of inertia or the high exit costs associated with dismantling it than because of the inherent success of the partnership. Second, studies of alliance terminations and alliance failure implicitly consider performance as an either–or condition. This is clearly not the case, and a more accurate assessment would focus on gradations of performance in alliances.

One of the vexatious obstacles to studying performance, and also one of the problems with the many studies that have reported high failure rates for alliances, is measuring performance itself (Anderson, 1990). Given the multifaceted objectives of many alliances, performance can be difficult to measure with financial outcomes. Furthermore, in most cases, such measures simply don't exist. A further complication results from the dyadic nature of alliances. Sometimes performance is asymmetric: one firm achieves its objectives while the other fails to do so. For instance, several cases have been reported of alliances in which one partner had raced to learn the other's skills while the other did not have any such intentions (Hamel et al., 1989; Hamel, 1991; Khanna et al., 1998). Despite these measurement obstacles, researchers have gone beyond the initial efforts that equated alliance termination with failure, to try to uncover some of the factors associated with the success of alliances. These require detailed surveys or careful fieldwork on alliances that uncovers the multiple facets of alliance performance and considers the perspectives of all the partners in the alliance. In a set of pioneering studies, Harrigan (1985, 1986) used both archival and survey data to assess factors that might influence the performance of alliances, with performance measured both by the survival of the alliance and by participants' assessment of success. More recently, marketing and strategy scholars have turned to even more extensive surveys, which have been administered to the individual managers responsible for the alliance from each partner (Heide and Minor, 1992; Parkhe, 1993). Such approaches enable the collection of a host of measures, subjective and objective, on which performance can be assessed, as well as an examination of dyadic asymmetries in perceptions.

While there have been advances in assessing the performance of alliances, few of these efforts have considered the impact of social networks in which firms are placed on the relative performance of their alliances. Once we acknowledge the importance of the multiplicity of social networks in which firms are placed, we can overcome such dyadic reductionism and examine whether alliances that are embedded to a greater or lesser degree in various networks perform better or worse than others and why. While there have been several efforts to explore differences in 'embedded' ties between firms and those that are less proximate they tend to infer and don't directly assess whether embedded ties themselves perform any better than other ties. The inference is based on an aggregate assessment of the survival properties of firms and its association with the extent of embedded ties those firms have entered and not on a direct assessment of the relative success of individual alliances. Furthermore, such approaches generally treat embeddedness as an either–or proposition and have focused primarily on relational embeddedness resulting from proximate ties, while paying less attention to the importance of structural embeddedness.

While such studies have advanced our understanding of the nature and importance of embedded ties, an important extension would be to focus directly on the performance of alliances and whether the extent of embeddedness in social networks is an important factor. The extent to which an alliance is embedded is likely to influence its performance for several reasons. By being proximately situated in an alliance, the partnering firms are likely to have greater confidence and trust in each other, both because they have greater information and because the network creates a natural deterrent for bad behavior that will damage reputation. Trust not only enables greater exchange of information, it also promotes ease of interaction and a flexible orientation on the part of each partner. All of these can create enabling conditions under which the success of an alliance is much more likely.

There is some evidence that alliances with embedded ties may perform better or last longer than others. One of the first set of studies on the factors associated with alliance terminations found that alliances between firms with a prior history of ties were less likely to terminate (Kogut, 1989). In another important set of studies, Levinthal and Fichman (1988) and Seabright, Levinthal, and Fichman (1992) found that the duration of exchange relationships is not only influenced by changes that may occur in task conditions that alter the extent of resource interdependence, but there may be 'dyadic attachments' between firms that lead to the persistence of such ties. Such attachments are conditioned by the social structure in which firms are embedded and include individual attachments resulting from the continuity of boundary spanners in the partnering organizations and structural attachments arising from the history of interaction between the organizations. Such social structures can limit organizational perceptions of likely opportunistic behavior by partners and, as a result, firms may be more willing to make nonrecoverable investments, which can enhance the performance of the alliance. Survey-based evidence further confirms that both interpersonal and interorganizational-level trust can be influential in the performance of exchange relationships (Zaheer, McEvily, and Perrone, 1997).

More recently, in a study of supplier relationships in the automotive industry, a colleague and I directly examined the performance differences across various types of exchange relationships (Gulati and Lawrence, 1997). This study was distinctive in that it used a detailed survey to explicitly measure the performance of each relationship with both subjective and objective measures and examine its connection with precise measures of the extent of embeddedness. We found that, on average, more embedded tie relationships performed better than alternative sourcing arrangements but were particularly effective in situations of high uncertainty. Furthermore, there were performance differences across embedded ties as well, which resulted from how they were organized.

As firms have entered alliances with growing frequency, many prominent firms, such as General Electric, Corning, Motorola, IBM, and Hewlett-Packard, have found themselves in hundreds of alliances. While issues concerning the management of individual alliances are still important and merit further consideration, new issues resulting from managing a portfolio of alliances have arisen. This opens up numerous questions about the cooperative capabilities of firms. Evidence suggests that there may be systematic differences in the cooperative capabilities that firms build up as they have more experience with alliances and that the extent of this learning may affect the relative success of those firms with alliances (Lyles, 1988). This poses questions about what such capabilities are and what might be some systematic tactics firms use to internalize such capabilities. At least some of these capabilities include: identifying valuable alliance opportunities and good partners, using appropriate governance mechanisms, developing interfirm knowledge-sharing routines, making requisite relationship-specific asset investments, and initiating necessary changes to the partnership as it evolves while also managing partner expectations (Doz, 1996; Dyer and Singh, 1997). The fact that a firm may have entered a wide array of alliances also suggests that it has to simultaneously manage this portfolio and address conflicting demands from different alliance partners. Furthermore, if the firm is at the center of a network, it must pay particular attention to a series of strategic and organizational issues (Lorenzoni and Baden-Fuller, 1995). Developing such a portfolio perspective on alliances merits further consideration, especially since many firms are now situated in an array of alliances.

The performance of alliances remains one of the most interesting and also one of the most vexing questions. We now know that embedded ties differ in fundamental ways from other ties and that there may even be an association between the extent of embedded ties a firm enters and its survival, but we have less understanding of the extent to which alliances with embedded ties actually perform better or worse than other alliances and why. Furthermore, the focus has primarily been on the effects of relational embeddedness and we know little about the consequences of structural embeddedness on the performance of alliances. This and the question of the capabilities firms may need to manage a multiplicity of alliances are important items for a future research agenda.

4.5. Alliances and Performance Consequences for Firms

Do firms benefit from entering strategic alliances? This question is distinct from the previous one which looked at the performance of alliances themselves, and instead, it focuses on the performance consequences of alliances for the firms entering them. Since many other activities besides alliances can also influence the performance of firms, it can be difficult to empirically link the alliance activity of firms with their performance. As a result, scholars have looked for a variety of direct and indirect means to test this relationship.

To estimate the effect of individual alliances on firm performance, several researchers have conducted event study analyses on the stock market effects of alliance announcements (e.g., Koh and Venkatraman, 1991). This connection has been further refined as scholars have examined the differential benefits firms receive from different types of alliances and how this is influenced by the conditions under which they have been formed (e.g., Balakrishnan and Koza, 1993; Anand and Khanna, 1997). Inasmuch as the stock market reactions portend the likely future outcome from alliances, these results provide mixed evidence of the beneficial consequences of alliances for firms entering them.

Researchers have also looked at the performance consequences for firms from their social network of cumulative alliances. One approach has been to try to explain the performance of firms by the extent of their alliance activity, after controlling for other possible factors that may influence firm performance. In an early study, Berg, Duncan, and Friedman (1982) found a negative relationship between joint venture incidence and firms' rates of return in the chemical industry but could not definitively establish the causal relationship between the two—did joint ventures lead to poor performance or vice versa? More recently, some researchers have also narrowed the domain of performance explained by alliances and focused on the consequences from technology alliances for the patenting activities of firms and for their performance (Hagedoorn and Schakenraad, 1994; Mowery, Oxley, and Silverman, 1996). This has been extended by linking firm performance not only to the frequency of past alliances but also to the firm's position in interorganizational networks (Zaheer and Zaheer, 1997; Ahuja, 1996).

Yet another approach to assess the aggregate influence of alliances on firm performance has been to examine the relationship between the extent to which firms are embedded in alliances and the likelihood of their survival. Thus, survival of firms is considered as a proxy for performance (e.g., Baum and Oliver, 1991, 1992; Uzzi, 1996). The alliances studied on which firm survival may depend have been those with vertical suppliers and with key institutions in the environment. The results of these studies suggest that such ties are generally beneficial in enhancing survival chances. This may not always be the case and numerous contingencies that may alter this relationship have also been proposed (Singh and Mitchell, 1996). The challenge has been to separate out factors beyond embeddedness that may also have an influence on survival and look at this in a longitudinal setting.

There have been several studies that have documented the varying performance benefits that Japanese firms, as well as those of other national origins, have received from their vertical alliances in particular (Helper, 1990; Cusumano and Takeishi, 1991; Dyer, 1996). Several of these studies have not only directly examined the relative performance of individual alliances, but have tried to ascertain their effects on the performance of firms entering them. These studies suggest that close vertical ties that are characterized by rich information exchange and long-term commitments can lead to greater cooperation and joint activities between the partners and higher levels of asset-specific investments, all of which translate into concrete performance benefits for the firms forming such ties (Helper, 1991; Heide and Miner, 1992). Extensive empirical evidence in the automotive industry suggests there are significant differentials in cost, quality, and new product development across automotive manufacturers that are driven primarily by the extent to which they outsource and the nature of those relationships.

The approaches to studying alliances and firm performance discussed thus far have paid scant attention to the overarching networks in which firms may be embedded. Even studies connecting the cumulative number of prior alliances with the survival of firms have only considered relational embeddedness, or the proximate ties in which firms are placed, and not the overall network and the position of firms in that network. This is not only a question of whether the sum is more than its parts, for by examining the entire social network one can also examine the possible deleterious consequences of competitive networks formed by rival firms. Such extensions can easily be made. For instance, rather than focusing only on the proximate ties a firm has entered, it is also possible to isolate the network to which the firm primarily belongs and examine whether membership in certain networks is more beneficial than others. This shifts the analytical focus away from simply the number of prior ties to membership in particular networks.

Gomes-Casseres (1994) has looked at several industries in which networks, rather than firms, have become the organizing level at which firms compete with each other. As a result, the performance of a firm is influenced by the networks to which it belongs. This has been enlarged to consider the relative success of competing networks of firms in particular geographic regions (Saxenian, 1990; Gerlach, 1992). Such approaches which highlight the relative success of particular networks can be further refined to identify the specific characteristics of the network that may enable the network to provide positive benefits to its members. For instance, in a study of hospitals and health care networks, my colleagues and I suggest that not all networks provide equal benefits to their members, and some networks are better than others (Gulati, Shortell, and Westphal, 1997). We further identified several key network factors that may mediate the effect of network membership on firm performance and explain why some networks provide greater benefits to their members than others. Two natural extension of these studies would look not only at the network characteristics but also the position of individual organizations within the network in which they are placed. This could alert us both to possible informational benefits and to control benefits that may result from particular locations in specific networks. Furthermore, it would be fruitful to assess the performance effects across the multiplicity of networks in which firms are embedded. Other possible concerns include who controls the network and why and possible limits and constraints to the growth of networks.

5. Conclusion

The primary focus of research on alliances has been to ask the 'why' question, which focuses on understanding some of the reasons firms enter alliances, structure them in certain ways, manage and change them, and the performance benefits sought from them. One of the problems with an orientation toward 'why' questions is that they are syntactically inclined to teleological or functional answers (Granovetter, 1994). More important, this leads to an avoidance of the 'how' question, which focuses on some of the conditions under which certain behavior and performance outcomes are likely (Oliver, 1990). This chapter poses the 'how' question for alliances and highlights an important set of conditions deriving from the social networks in which firms come to be placed that influences their behavior and performance related to alliances. It demonstrates how social networks can be influential in the creation and success of alliances and shows how a perspective informed by the structural embeddedness of firms can provide important new insights into some of the key current issues on strategic alliances.

This paper suggests that social networks are valuable conduits of information that provide both opportunities and constraints for firms and have important behavioral and performance implications for their alliances. By channeling information, social networks enable firms to discover new alliance opportunities and can thus influence how often and with whom those firms enter into alliances. Once two firms decide to enter an alliance, their relative proximity in the network may influence the specific governance structure used to formalize the alliance. The extent to which two partners are socially embedded can also influence their subsequent behavior and affect the likely future success of the alliance. A firm's portfolio of alliances and its network position in an industry can have a profound influence on its overall performance. I highlight several recent studies, including some of my own, that have developed a socially informed account of the alliance behavior by firms and examined some of these issues. Table 1 summarizes the comparison I draw between dyadic and network perspectives for each of the key questions on alliances.

This table highlights each of the five key issues on alliances identified in this chapter and the related empirical questions. It illustrates how the consideration of the role of social embeddedness of firms enlarges the realm of inquiry away from dyads towards broader units which include economic relationships and the overall networks in which firms are placed.

Introducing social networks to the study of strategic alliances can provide valuable insights into strategic alliances but can also make an important contribution to the study of social networks. The creation of an alliance is an important strategic action, yet the cumulation of such alliances also constitutes a social network. Given our limited understanding of the dynamics of networks, alliances provide a unique arena in which action and structure are closely interconnected and the dynamic coevolution of networks can be examined (e.g., Gulati and Gargiulo, 1997). Furthermore, the study of interorganizational networks is now a burgeoning field of inquiry in and of itself, and strategic alliances have become an important set of ties in which firms have become engaged and that thus merits further examination (for a collection of articles on interorganizational relationships, see Mizruchi and Schwartz, 1987). Combining insights on alliance networks with those on interpersonal networks can result in an important cross-level perspective of interorganizational relationships (Galaskiewicz, 1985b; Zaheer et al., 1997; Gulati and Westphal, 1997).

The theoretical orientation guiding this chapter has been the embeddedness perspective, which highlights the significance of the social relationships in which actors are situated for their future behavior and performance. I would like to emphasize that introducing such a perspective does not preclude the possibility of traditionally examining strategic imperatives or diminish their importance. These are indeed complementary elements and in fact blend together if we consider the creation and manipulation of networks to be part and parcel of strategic behavior (Burt, 1992). Furthermore, the embeddedness of firms can be more broadly defined than its social relationships or structural embeddedness to include institutional, cultural, and political elements (Zukin and DiMaggio, 1990). Each of these other facets can have consequences for the

Table 1. Dyadic and Network Perspectives on Key Issues for Strategic Alliances

Research Issue	Empirical Questions	Dyadic Perspective	Network Perspective
1. The formation of alliances	Which firms enter alliances? Whom do firms choose as alliance partners?	Financial and technological imperatives that lead firms to enter alliances Complementarities that lead them to choose specific partners (e.g., Pfeffer and Nowak, 1976a; Mariti and Smiley, 1983)	Social network factors that may constrain and also create opportunities for firms to discover alliance prospects and choose specific partners (e.g., Kogut et al., 1992; Gulati, 1995b; Gulati and Westphal, 1997)
2. The governance of alliances	Which *ex ante* factors influence the choice of governance structure?	Transaction costs, interdependence, and power asymmetries (e.g., Pisano et al., 1988; Harrigan, 1987)	Social networks that may mitigate *ex ante* appropriation concerns and coordination costs that can affect the choice of governance structure (e.g., Zajac and Olsen, 1993; Gulati, 1995a; Gulati and Singh, 1997)
3. The evolution of alliances and networks	Which *ex ante* factors and evolutionary processes influence the development of individual alliances and networks?	Social and behavioral dynamics between partners in alliances (e.g., Ring and Van De Ven, 1994; Doz, 1996)	Social, behavioral and competitive dynamics that occur across organizational boundaries among groups of firms in alliances (Nohria and Garcia-Pont, 1991; Gomes-Casseres, 1994) The emergence and development of a social network (e.g., Gulati and Gargiulo, 1997)
4. The performance of alliances	How should the performance of alliances be measured? Which factors influence the performance of alliances?	Examination of terminations as alliance failure (e.g., Kogut, 1988b) Partner characteristics and evolutionary dynamics that affect the success of alliances (e.g., Harrigan, 1986)	Firm capabilities that enhance the success of alliances (Doz, 1996; Dyer and Singh, 1997) Influence of comembership of partners in social networks on the success of their joint alliances (e.g., Levinthal and Fichman, 1988; Kogut 1989; Zaheer et al., 1997; Gulati and Lawrence, 1997)
5. Performance advantages for firms entering alliances	Do firms receive social and economic benefits from their alliances?	Event studies of stock market reactions to alliance announcements (e.g., Anand and Khanna, 1996) Survival of firms entering alliances (e.g., Baum and Oliver, 1991, 1992)	Influence of membership in social networks and relative position in the network on the performance and survival of firms (e.g., Dyer, 1996; Gulati et al., 1997)

study of strategic alliances, both independently and together, and remain to be thoroughly examined. Ultimately, it is important to develop a more complete, socially informed account of each of the key issues outlined here that relate to strategic alliances.

A social network perspective on alliances can have both descriptive and normative outcomes that provide valuable insights for theories of strategic management, organizational theory, and sociology. Incorporating social network factors into our account of the alliance behavior of firms not only provides us with a more accurate representation of the key influences on the strategic actions of firms, but has important implications for managerial practice as well, many of which have yet to be explored. For instance, an understanding of the network dynamics that influence the formation of new alliances can provide insights for managers on the path-dependent processes that may lock them into certain courses of action as a result of constraints from their current ties. They may choose to anticipate such concerns and proactively initiate selective network contacts that enhance their informational capabilities. Thus, by examining the specific way in which social networks may constrain firms' future actions and channel opportunities, firms themselves can begin to take a more forward-looking stance in the new ties they enter. They can be proactive in designing their networks and considering the ramifications on their future choices of each new tie they form. They may also selectively position themselves in networks to derive possible control benefits as well. Similarly, there are numerous insights that result from understanding the complexities associated with managing a portfolio of alliances and the relational capabilities required to do so successfully. Ultimately, managers want to know how to manage individual alliances, and a recognition of some of the dynamics at both the dyadic and network levels that influence the evolution and eventual performance of alliances can be extremely beneficial. The challenge for scholars studying networks and alliances is to bridge the chasm between theory and practice and translate some of their important insights for managers of the alliances we study.

References

Ahuja, G. (1996). 'Collaboration and innovation: A longitudinal study of interfirm linkages and firm patenting performance in the global advanced material industry', dissertation, University of Michigan Business School.

Aiken, M. and Hage, J. (1968). 'Organizational interdependence and intraorganizational structure', *American Sociological Review*, **33**, p. 912–930.

Anand, B. and Khanna, T. (1997). 'On the market valuation of interfirm agreements: Evidence from computers and telecommunications, 1990–1993', working paper: Harvard Business School.

Anderson, E. (1990). 'Two firms, one frontier: On assessing joint venture performance', *Sloan Management Review*, **31**(2), pp. 19–30.

Andrews, K. (1971). *The Concept of Corporate Strategy*. Irwin, Homewood, IL.

Astley, W. and Fombrun, C. (1983). 'Collective strategy: Social ecology of organizational environments', *Academy of Management Review*, **8**(4), pp. 576–587.

Auster, E. (1994). 'Macro and strategic perspectives on interorganizational linkages: A comparative analysis and review with suggestions for reorientation'. In P. Shrivastava, A. S. Huff and J. E. Dutton (eds.), *Advances in Strategic Management*, Vol. 10B. JAI Press, Greenwich, CT, pp. 3–40.

Baker, W. E. (1984). 'The social structure of a national securities market', *American Journal of Sociology*, **89**, pp. 775–811.

Baker, W. E. (1990). 'Market networks and corporate behavior', *American Journal of Sociology*, **96**, pp. 589–625.

Balakrishnan, S. and Koza, M. P. (1993). 'Information asymmetry, adverse selection and joint ventures: Theory and evidence', *Journal of Economic Behavior and Organization*, **20**, pp. 99–117.

Barley, S. R., Freeman, J. and Hybels, R. C. (1992). 'Strategic alliances in commercial biotechnology'. In N. Nohria and R. Eccles (eds.), *Networks and Organizations: Structure, Form and Action*. Harvard Business School Press, Boston, MA, pp. 311–347.

Barney, J. B. and Hansen, M. H. (1994). 'Trustworthiness as a source of competitive advantage', *Strategic Management Journal*, Winter Special Issue, **15**, pp. 175–190.

Baum, J. and Dutton, J. (1996). 'The embeddedness of strategy'. In P. Shrivastava, A. S. Huff and J. E. Dutton (eds.), *Advances in Strategic Management*, Vol. 13. JAI Press, Greenwich, CT, pp. 3–40.

—— and Oliver, C. (1991). 'Institutional linkages and organizational mortality', *Administrative Science Quarterly*, **36**, pp. 187–218.

—— and —— (1992). 'Institutional embeddedness and the dynamics of organizational populations', *American Sociological Review*, **57**, pp. 540–559.

Beamish, P. (1985). 'The characteristics of joint ventures in developed and developing countries', *Columbia Journal of World Business*, **20**, pp. 13–19.

Berg, S., Duncan, J. and Friedman, P. (1982). *Joint Venture Strategic and Corporate Innovation*. Oelgeschlager, Gunn & Hain, Cambridge, MA.

—— and Friedman, P. (1978). 'Joint ventures in American Industry: An overview', *Mergers and Acquisitions*, **13**, pp. 28–41.

—— and —— (1980). 'Causes and effects of joint venture activity', *Antitrust Bulletin*, **25**, pp. 143–168.

—— and —— (1981). 'Impacts of domestic joint ventures on industrial rates of return: A pooled cross section analysis', *Review of Economics and Statistics*, **63**, pp. 293–298.

Bleeke, J. and Ernst, D. (1991). 'The way to win in cross border alliances', *Harvard Business Review*, **69**(6), pp. 127–135.

Bradach, J. L. and Eccles, R. G. (1989). 'Markets versus hierarchies: From ideal types to plural forms'. In W. R. Scott (ed.), *Annual Review of Sociology*, Vol. 15. Annual Reviews Inc., Palo Alto, CA, pp. 97–118.

Bresser, R. (1988). 'Matching collective and competitive strategies', *Strategic Management Journal*, **9**(4), pp. 375–385.

Burgers, W. P., Hill, C. W. L. and Kim, W. C. (1993). 'A theory of global strategic alliances: The case of the global auto industry', *Strategic Management Journal*, **14**(6), pp. 419–432.

Burt, R. S. (1982). *Toward a Structural Theory of Action*. Academic Press, New York.

——(1987). 'Social contagion and innovation: Cohesion versus structural equivalence', *American Journal of Sociology*, **92**, pp. 1287–1335.

——(1992). *Structural Holes: The Social Structure of Competition*. Harvard University Press, Cambridge, MA.

——(1997). 'The contingent value of social capital', *Administrative Science Quarterly*, **42**, pp. 339–365.

——Gabbay, S. M., Holt, G. and Moran, P. (1994). 'Contingent organization as a network theory: The culture–performance contingency function', *Acta Sociologica*, **34**, pp. 345–370.

——and Knez, M. (1995). 'Kinds of third-party effects on trust', *Rationality and Society*, **7**, pp. 255–292.

Business Week (21 July 1986) 'Corporate odd couples: Joint ventures are the rage, but the matches often don't work out', pp. 100–105.

Coleman, J. S., Katz, E. and Menzel, H. (1966). *Medical Innovation: A Diffusion Study*. Bobbs-Merrill, New York.

Contractor, F. and Lorange, P. (1988). 'Why should firms cooperate? The strategy and economics basis for cooperative ventures'. In F. Contractor and P. Lorange (eds.), *Cooperative Strategies in International Business*. Lexington Books, Lexington, MA, pp. 3–30.

Cusumano, M. and Takeishi, A. (1991). 'Supplier relations and management: A survey of Japanese, Japanese-transplant and U.S. auto plants', *Strategic Management Journal*, **12**(8), pp. 563–588.

Dacin, M. T., Hitt, M. A. and Levitas, E. (1997). 'Selecting partners for successful international alliances: Examination of U.S. and Korean firms', *Journal of World Business*, **32**(1), pp. 3–16.

Davis, G. F. (1991). 'Agents without principles? The spread of the poison pill through the intercorporate network', *Administrative Science Quarterly*, **36**, pp. 583–613.

Doz, Y. (1996). 'The evolution of cooperation in strategic alliances: Initial conditions or learning processes?', *Strategic Management Journal*, Summer Special Issue, **17**, pp. 55–83.

——and Prahalad, C. K. (1991). 'Managing DMNCs: A search for a new paradigm', *Strategic Management Journal*, Summer Special Issue, **12**, pp. 145–164.

Duncan, L. (1982). 'Impacts of new entry and horizontal joint ventures on industrial rates of return', *Review of Economics and Statistics*, **64**, pp. 339–342.

Dyer, J. H. (1996). 'Specialized supplier networks as a source of competitive advantage: Evidence from the auto industry', *Strategic Management Journal*, **17**(4), pp. 271–291.

——and Singh, H. (1997). 'Relational capabilities of firms', working paper, Wharton School, University of Pennsylvania.

Eisenhardt, K. and Schoonhoven, C. B. (1996). 'Resource-based view of strategic alliance formation: Strategic and social effects in entrepreneurial firms', *Organization Science*, **7**(2), pp. 136–150.

Galaskiewicz, J. (1985a). 'Interorganizational Relations', *American Review of Sociology*, **11**, pp. 281–304.

——(1985b). *Social Organization of an Urban Grants Economy: A Study of Business Philanthropy and Nonprofit Organizations*. Academic Press, Orlando, FL.

Garud, R. and Rappa, M. (1994). 'A socio-cognitive model of technology evolution', *Organization Science*, **5**(3), pp. 344–362.

Gerlach, M. (1992). 'The Japanese corporate network: A blockmodel analysis', *Administrative Science Quarterly*, **37**, pp. 105–139.

Ghemawat, P., Porter, M. and Rawlinson, R. (1986). 'Patterns of international coalition activity'. In M. Porter (ed.) *Competition in Global Industries*, Harvard Business School Press, Boston, MA, pp. 345–366.

Gomes-Casseres, B. (1987). 'Joint venture instability: Is it a problem?' *Columbia Journal of World Business*, **22**(2), pp. 97–102.

——(1994). 'Group versus group: How alliance networks compete', *Harvard Business Review*, **72**(4), pp. 62–74.

Grandori, A. and Soda, G. (1995). 'Inter-firm networks: Antecedents, mechanisms and forms', *Organization Studies*, **16**(2), pp. 183–214.

Granovetter, M. (1973). 'The strength of weak ties', *American Journal of Sociology*, **78**, pp. 1360–1380.

——(1985). 'Economic action and social structure: The problem of embeddedness', *American Journal of Sociology*, **91**(3), pp. 481–510.

——(1992). 'Problems of explanation in economic sociology'. In N. Nohria and R. Eccles (eds.), *Networks and Organizations: Structure, Form and Action*. Harvard Business School Press, Boston, MA, pp. 25–56.

——(1994). 'Business groups'. In N. Smelser and R. Swedberg (eds.), *Handbook of Economic Sociology*. Princeton University Press, Princeton, NJ, pp. 453–475.

Gray, B. and Yan, A. (1997). 'Formation and evolution of international joint ventures: Examples from U.S.–Chinese partnerships'. In P. Beamish and J. Peter Killing (eds.), *Cooperative Strategies: Asian Pacific Perspectives*. New Lexington Press, San Francisco, CA, pp. 57–88.

Gulati, R. (1993). 'The dynamics of alliance formation', unpublished doctoral dissertation, Harvard University.

——(1995a). 'Does familiarity breed trust? The implications of repeated ties for contractual choice in alliances', *Academy of Management Journal*, **38**, pp. 85–112.

——(1995b). 'Social structure and alliance formation pattern: A longitudinal analysis', *Administrative Science Quarterly*, **40**, pp. 619–652.

——(1997). 'Which firms enter into alliances? An empirical assessment of financial and social capital explanations', working paper, J. L. Kellogg Graduate School of Management, Northwestern University.

——and Gargiulo, M. (1997). 'Where do interorganizational networks come from?', working paper, INSEAD.

——Khanna, T. and Nohria, N. (1994). 'Unilateral commitments and the importance of process in alliances,' *Sloan Management Review*, **35**(3), pp. 61–69.

——and Lawrence, P. (1997). 'Organizing vertical networks: A design perspective', working paper, J. L. Kellogg Graduate School of Management, Northwestern University.

——Shortell, S. and Westphal, J. (1997). 'United we prosper? Contingent network effects on firm performance', working paper, J. L. Kellogg Graduate School of Management, Northwestern University.

Gulati, R. and Singh, H. (1997). 'The architecture of cooperation: Managing coordination costs and appropriation concerns in strategic alliances', *Administrative Science Quarterly*, forthcoming.

—— and Westphal, J. (1997). 'The dark side of embeddedness: An examination of the influence of direct and indirect board interlocks and CEO/board relationships on interfirm alliances', working paper, J. L. Kellogg Graduate School of Management, Northwestern University.

Hagedoorn, J. and Schakenraad, J. (1994). 'The effect of strategic technology alliances on company performance', *Strategic Management Journal*, **15** (4), pp. 291–309.

Hamel, G. (1991). 'Competition for competence and inter-partner learning within international strategic alliances', *Strategic Management Journal*, Summer Special Issue, **12**, pp. 83–103.

—— Doz, Y. and Prahalad, C. K. (1989). 'Collaborate with your competitors and win', *Harvard Business Review*, **67**(1), pp. 133–139.

Harrigan, K. R. (1985). *Strategies for Joint Ventures*. Lexington Books, Lexington, MA.

—— (1986). *Managing for Joint Ventures Success*. Lexington Books, Lexington, MA.

—— (1987). 'Strategic alliances: Form, autonomy and performance,' working paper, Columbia University.

—— (1988). 'Joint ventures and competitive strategy', *Strategic Management Journal*, **9**(2), pp. 141–158.

—— and Newman, W. H. (1990). 'Bases of interorganization cooperation: Propensity, power, persistence', *Journal of Management Studies*, **27**, pp. 417–434.

Haunschild, P. R. (1992). 'Imitation through interlock: A social basis of corporate acquisition activity', working paper, Carnegie Mellon University.

Hayek, F. A. (1949). 'The meaning of competition', *Individualism and Economic Order*. Routledge & Kegan Paul, London, pp. 92–106.

Heide, J. and Miner, A. (1992). 'The shadow of the future: Effects of anticipated interaction and frequency of contact on buyer–seller cooperation', *Academy of Management Journal*, **35**, pp. 265–291.

Helper, S. (1990). 'Comparative supplier relations in the U.S. and Japanese auto industries: An exit/voice approach', *Business and Economic History*, **19**, pp. 1–9.

—— (1991). 'How much has really changed between U.S. automakers and their suppliers?', *Sloan Management Review*, (Summer), **32**, pp. 15–28.

Hennart, J.-F. (1988). 'A transaction costs theory of equity joint ventures', *Strategic Management Journal*, **9**(4), pp. 361–374.

Kanter, R. M. (1989). *When Giants Learn to Dance*. Touchstone, Simon & Schuster, New York.

Khanna, T. (1997). 'The scope of alliances', paper presented at INSEAD/Organization Science conference on Managing Partnerships, INSEAD, Fontainebleau, France.

—— Gulati, R. and Nohria, N. (1998) 'The dynamics of learning alliances: Competition, cooperation and scope', *Strategic Management Journal*, **19**(3), pp. 193–210.

Kogut, B. (1988a). 'Joint ventures: Theoretical and emperical perspectives', *Strategic Management Journal*, **9**(4), pp. 319–332.

—— (1988b). 'A study of the life cycle of joint ventures'. In F. Contractor and P. Lorange (eds.), *Cooperative Strategies in International Business*, Vol. 6. Lexington Books, Lexington, MA, pp. 169–185.

—— (1989). 'The stability of joint ventures: Reciprocity and competitive rivalry', *Journal of Industrial Economics*, **38**, pp. 183–198.

——(1991). 'Joint ventures and the option to expand and acquire', *Management Science*, **37**(1), pp. 19–33.

——Shan, W. and Walker, G. (1992). 'The make-or-cooperate decision in the context of an industry network'. In N. Nohria and R. Eccles (eds.), *Networks and Organizations*. Harvard Business School Press, Cambridge, MA, pp. 348–365.

Koh, J. and Venkatraman, N. (1991). 'Joint venture formations and stock market reactions: An assessment in the information technology sector', *Academy of Management Journal*, **34**(4), pp. 869–892.

Kreps, D. M. (1990). 'Corporate culture and economic theory'. In J. Alt and K. Shepsle (eds.), *Perspectives on Positive Political Economy*. Cambridge University Press, New York, pp. 90–143.

Larson, A. (1992). 'Network dyads in entrepreneurial settings: A study of the governance of exchange relationships', *Administrative Science Quarterly*, **37**, pp. 76–104.

Laumann, E. O., Galaskiewicz, J. and Marsden, P. V. (1978). 'Community structure as interorganizational linkages', *Annual Review of Sociology*, **4**, pp. 455–484.

Lawrence, P. and Gulati, R. (1997). 'The hidden advantages of value chain alliances', working paper, J. L. Kellogg Graduate School of Management, Northwestern University.

Levine, S. and White, P. E. (1961). 'Exchange as a conceptual framework for the study of interorganizational relationships', *Administrative Science Quarterly*, **5**, pp. 583–601.

Levinthal, D. A. and Fichman, M. (1988). 'Dynamics of interorganizational attachments: Auditor–client relationships', *Administrative Science Quarterly*, **33**, pp. 345–369.

Lorenzoni, G. and Baden-Fuller, C. (1995). 'Creating a strategic center to manage a web of partners', *California Management Review*, **37**(3), pp. 146–163.

Lyles, M. (1988). 'Learning among joint venture-sophisticated firms'. In F. Contractor and P. Lorange (eds.), *Cooperative Strategies in International Business*. Lexington Books, Lexington, MA, pp. 301–316.

Macaulay, S. (1963). 'Non-contractual relations in business: a preliminary study', *American Sociological Review*, **28**, pp. 55–67.

Madhavan, R., Koka, B. R. and Prescott, J. E. (1998). 'Networks in transition: How industry events (re)shape interfirm relationships', *Strategic Management Journal*, in press.

Mariti, P. and Smiley, R. H. (1983). 'Co-operative agreements and the organization of industry', *Journal of Industrial Economics*, **31**(4), pp. 437–451.

Marsden, P. V. (1981). 'Introducing influence processes into a system of collective decisions', *American Journal of Sociology*, **86**, pp. 1203–1235.

——and Friedkin, N. E. (1993). 'Network studies of social influence', *Sociological Methods and Research*, **22**, pp. 127–151.

Martin, X., Mitchell, W. and Swaminathan, A. (1995). 'Recreating and extending Japanese automobile buyer-supplier links in North America', *Strategic Management Journal*, **16**(8), pp. 589–619.

Masten, S. E., Meehan, J. W. and Snyder, E. A. (1991). 'The costs of organization', *Journal of Law, Economics and Organization*, **7**, pp. 1–25.

Mitchell, W. and Singh, K. (1992). 'Incumbents' use of pre-entry alliances before expansion into new technical subfields of an industry', *Journal of Economic Behavior and Organization*, **18**, pp. 347–372.

Mizruchi, M. S. (1992). *The Structure of Corporate Political Action*. Harvard University Press, Cambridge, MA.

Mizruchi, M. S. (1996). 'What do interlocks do? An analysis, critique and assessment of research on interlocking directorates', *Annual Review of Sociology*, **22**, pp. 271–298.

——and Schwartz, M. (1987). *Intercorporate Relations: The Structural Analysis of Business*. Cambridge University Press, Cambridge, UK.

Mowery, D. C., Oxley, J. E. and Silverman, B. S. (1996). 'Strategic alliances and interfirm knowledge transfer', *Strategic Management Journal*, Winter Special Issue, **17**, pp. 77–91.

Nickerson, J. A. and Silverman, B. S. (1997). 'Integrating competitive strategy and transaction cost economics: An operationalization of fit in the interstate trucking industry', working paper, Washington University in St. Louis.

Nohria, N. and Garcia-Pont, C. (1991). 'Global strategic linkages and industry structure', *Strategic Management Journal*, Summer Special Issue, **12**, pp. 105–124.

Oliver, C. (1990). 'Determinants of interorganizational relationships: Integration and future directions', *Academy of Management Review*, **15**, pp. 241–265.

Osborn, R. N. and Baughn, C. C. (1990). 'Forms of interorganizational governance for multinational alliances', *Academy of Management Journal*, **33**, pp. 503–519.

Oxley, J. E. (1997). 'Appropriability hazards and governance in strategic alliances: A transaction cost approach', *Journal of Law, Economics and Organization*, **13**(2), pp. 387–409.

Parkhe, A. (1993). 'Strategic alliance structuring: A game theoretic and transaction cost examination of interfirm cooperation', *Academy of Management Journal*, **36**, pp. 794–829.

Pate, J. L. (1969). 'Joint venture activity, 1960–1968', *Economic Review*, Federal Reserve Bank of Cleveland, pp. 16–23.

Pfeffer, J. and Nowak, P. (1976a). 'Joint venture and interorganizational interdependence', *Administrative Science Quarterly*, **21**(3), pp. 398–418.

——and——(1976b). 'Patterns of joint venture activity: Implications for anti-trust policy', *Antitrust Bulletin*, **21**, pp. 315–339.

Pisano, G. P. (1989). 'Using equity participation to support exchange: Evidence from the biotechnology industry', *Journal of Law, Economics and Organization*, **5**(1), pp. 109–126.

——Russo, M. V. and Teece, D. (1988). 'Joint ventures and collaborative arrangements in the telecommunications equipment industry'. In D. Mowery (ed.), *International Collaborative Ventures in U.S. Manufacturing*. Ballinger, Cambridge, MA, pp. 23–70.

Podolny, J. M. (1993). 'A status-based model of market competition', *American Journal of Sociology*, **98**, pp. 829–872.

——(1994). 'Market uncertainty and the social character of economic exchange', *Administrative Science Quarterly*, **39**, pp. 458–483.

——and Stuart, T. (1995). 'A role-based ecology of technological change', *American Journal of Sociology*, **100**, pp. 1224–1260.

Porter, M. E. and Fuller, M. B. (1986). 'Coalitions and global strategy'. In M. E. Porter (ed.), *Competition in Global Industries*. Harvard Business School Press, Boston, MA, pp. 315–343.

Powell, W. W. (1990). 'Neither market nor hierarchy: Network forms of organization'. In B. M. Staw and L. L. Cummings (eds.), *Research in Organizational Behavior*. JAI Press, Greenwich, CT, **12**, pp. 295–336.

——and Brantley, P. (1992). 'Competitive cooperation in biotechnology: Learning through networks'. In N. Nohria and R. Eccles (eds.), *Networks and Organizations: Structure, Form and Action*. Harvard Business School Press, Boston, MA, pp. 366–394.

——Koput, K. and Smith-Doerr, L. (1996). 'Interorganizational collaboration and the locus of innovation: Networks of learning in biotechnology', *Administrative Science Quarterly*, **41**, pp. 116–145.

——and Smith-Doerr, L. (1994). 'Networks and economic life'. In N. Smelser and R. Swedberg (eds.), *Handbook of Economic Sociology*. Princeton University Press, Princeton, NJ, pp. 368–402.

Raub, W. and Weesie, J. (1990). 'Reputation and efficiency in social interactions: An example of network effects', *American Journal of Sociology*, **96**, pp. 626–654.

Richardson, G. B. (1972). 'The organization of industry', *Economic Journal*, **82**, pp. 883–896.

Ring, P. S. and Van De Ven, A. H. (1989). 'Formal and informal dimensions of transactions.' In A. H. Van de Ven, H. Angle and M. S. Poole (eds.), *Research on the Management of Innovation: The Minnesota Studies*. Ballinger/Harper & Row, New York, pp. 171–192.

——and ——(1992). 'Structuring cooperative relationships between organizations', *Strategic Management Journal*, **13**(7), pp. 483–498.

——and ——(1994). 'Developmental processes of cooperative interorganizational relationships', *Academy of Management Review*, **19**(1), pp. 90–118.

Saxenian, A. (1990). 'Regional networks and the resurgence of silicon valley', *California Management Review*, Fall, pp. 89–112.

Seabright, M. A., Levinthal, D. A. and Fichman, M. (March 1992). 'Role of individual attachment in the dissolution of interorganizational relationships', *Academy of Management Journal*, **35**(1), pp. 122–160.

——(1990). 'An empirical analysis of organizational strategies by entrepreneurial high-technology firms', *Strategic Management Journal*, **11**(2), pp. 129–139.

Shan, W. and Hamilton, W. (1991). 'Country-specific advantage and international cooperation', *Strategic Management Journal*, **12**(6), pp. 419–432.

——Walker, G. and Kogut, B. (1994). 'Interfirm cooperation and startup innovation in the biotechnology industry', *Strategic Management Journal*, **15**(5), pp. 387–394.

Shapiro, D. L., Sheppard, B. H. and Cheraskin, L. (1992). 'Business on a handshake', *Negotiation Journal*, **8**, pp. 365–377.

Singh, K. and Mitchell, W. (1996). 'Precarious collaboration: Business survival after partners shut down or form new partnerships', *Strategic Management Journal*, Summer Special Issue, **17**, pp. 99–115.

Stinchcombe, A. L. (1985) 'Contracts as hierarchical documents', In A. L. Stinchcombe and C. Heimer (eds.), *Organization Theory and Project Management*. Norwegian University Press, Bergen, Norway, pp. 121–171.

——(1990) *Information and Organizations*. University of California Press, Berkeley, CA.

Stuckey, J. A. (1983). *Vertical Integration and Joint Ventures in the Aluminum Industry*. Harvard University Press, Cambridge, MA.

Teece, D. J. (1992). 'Competition, cooperation and innovation', *Journal of Economic Behavior and Organization*, **18**, pp. 1–25.

Uzzi, B. (1996). 'The sources and consequences of embeddedness for the economic performance of organizations: The network effect', *American Sociological Review*, **61**, pp. 674–698.

Walker, G. (1988). 'Network analysis for cooperative interfirm relationships'. In F. Contractor and P. Lorange (eds.), *Cooperative Strategies in International Business*. Lexington Press, Lexington, KY, pp. 227–240.

—— and Weber, D. (1984). 'A transaction cost approach to make-or-buy decisions', *Administrative Science Quarterly*, **29**, pp. 373–391.

Westphal, J. D., Gulati, R. and Shortell, S. (1997). 'Customization or conformity? An institutional and network perspective on the content and consequences of TQM adoption', *Administrative Science Quarterly*, **42**, pp. 366–394.

White, H. C. (1981). 'Where do markets come from?', *American Journal of Sociology*, **87**, pp. 517–547.

Williamson, O. (1985). *The Economic Institutions of Capitalism*. Free Press, New York.

Zaheer, A., McEvily, B. and Perrone, V. (1997). 'Does trust matter? Exploring the effects of interorganizational and interpersonal trust on performance', *Organizational Science*, forthcoming.

—— and Zaheer, S. (1997). 'Catching the wave: Alertness, responsiveness and market influence in global electronic networks', *Management Science*, **43**(11), pp. 1493–1509.

Zajac, E. J. and Olsen, C. P. (1993). 'From transaction cost to transactional value analysis: Implications for the study of interorganizational strategies', *Journal of Management Studies*, **30**(1), pp. 131–145.

Zukin, S. and DiMaggio, P. (1990). *Structures of Capital: The Social Organization of the Economy*. Cambridge University Press, Cambridge, MA.

17 Social Capital, Structural Holes and the Formation of an Industry Network

Gordon Walker, Bruce Kogut, and Weijian Shan

1. Introduction

There is a fundamental conflict in the formation of a network. On the one hand, there are powerful forces toward the reproduction of dense regions of relationships. Reproduction is powerful because it is based upon the accumulation of social capital that requires the maintenance of and reinvestment in the structure of prevailing relationships. Yet, it is exactly this principle of conservation that generates the opportunities for entrepreneurial actors to bridge these regions and alter the structure of the network.

The formation of interfirm networks is a critical point of contention between otherwise complementary views of network structure. For Pierre Bourdieu (1980) and James Coleman (1990a), a network tends toward the reproduction of an inherited pattern of relationships due to the value *to the individual* in preserving social capital. The notion of social capital implies a strategy of maintaining the structure of existing relationships. To Bourdieu, "social capital is the sum of the resources, actual or virtual, that accrue to an individual or a group by virtue of possessing a durable network of more or less institutionalized relationships of mutual acquaintance and recognition" (Bourdieu and Wacquant, 1992, p. 119). Similarly, Coleman notes that an advantage of modern society is that organizations provide stability, even if people are mobile. "The social invention of organizations," he notes, "having positions rather than persons as elements of the structure has provided one form of social capital that can maintain stability in the face of instability of individuals" (Coleman, 1990b, p. 320). Similarly, firms may tend toward the reproduction of existing interfirm relationships to maintain the value of their inherited social capital.

Ronald Burt (1992) has a different view of the conservative tendency of networks toward reproduction. To him, the emphasis should be placed on the opportunities for entrepreneurs to exploit the "structural holes" between dense pockets of relationships in the network. It is exactly the structural constraints on what people know and can control, created by the inheritance of past relationships, that presents the opportunities for brokers. These brokers seek out partners with whom they can form unique, or "nonredundant," relationships that bring new information and the possibility of negotiating between competing groups. Through forming these new and unique relationships, entrepreneurs transform network structure.

The theories of social capital and structural holes have important implications for understanding the formation of relational networks in high growth, technology-intensive industries. In these industries, the extensive innovative activities of small firms (Bound et al., 1984, Acs and Audretsch, 1989) push out industry boundaries into new subfields and increase the level of competition in traditional markets. However, opportunities for cooperation are created by unintended spillovers and intended agreements. Organizations are also related through their members' professional connections, joint suppliers and customers, and industry associations. These commonalities may be sources of information about competitor behavior, new technological developments, and other industry trends. However, formal agreements are the most salient and reliable indicator of resource and information sharing between firms and the origin of information regarding a firm's cooperative strategy. This information is critical for future decisions regarding cooperation for product development and commercialization.

The emergence of the network of formal cooperative agreements influences the course of industry growth and innovation. A swelling network of cooperative agreements may provide a positive externality to which potential investors respond (Hagedoorn and Schakenraad, 1992). Also, since poorly positioned firms may have access to less than adequate resources to achieve their economic goals, the network may act as a selection mechanism, culling out some firms on the basis of their partners' weakness.

Early in the history of an industry, social capital among firms is low, and yet it is critical for the identification and acquisition of new relationships. Rapid industry growth aggravates this problem of acquiring valid information on other firms. In this early period, firms enter relationships according to their differences in need and capability, and these relationships initialize the network (Kogut et al., 1994). In biotechnology, for example, small startups have extensive expertise in technological innovation but lack resources in marketing and distribution possessed by large incumbents. Cooperation between a startup and incumbent gives each access to a resource necessary for product commercialization. Variation in firm-level attributes, especially the effective management of interfirm cooperation, contributes to network growth. But this contribution is partial. As an unintended outcome of their cooperative strategies, firms build the network that serves as a map for future association.

Network formation occurs as new relationships by incumbent firms or startups exploit the opportunities inherent in the network, reinforcing the existing network structure or reshaping it (Galaskiewicz and Wasserman, 1981; Marsden, 1985; Kogut et al., 1994). Two types of opportunity drive the process of network formation. First, network structure is a vehicle for inducing cooperation through the development of social capital. Firms draw upon network structure as a system-level resource to facilitate the governance of their relationships. Second, however, gaps in the pattern of information flows reflect potentially profitable opportunities for establishing connections between unlinked firms (Burt, 1992). These opportunities stimulate entrepreneurial action to broker different segments of the industry.

The relative advantages and risks of inducing cooperation and exploiting brokering opportunities have an important implication for network formation. The structural conditions inducing cooperation free resources for the establishment of new relationships that in turn strengthen the structure as a useful system for controlling noncooperative behavior. If the structure is reinforced by new relationships, early patterns of cooperation should persist, resulting in a path dependence analogous to the imprinting effect on an industry of the era in which it was formed (Stinchcombe 1965). However, if some firms have specific capabilities for information arbitrage, they may choose to broker relationships between organizations in different regions of the network. In this case, the existing structure is not strengthened but repeatedly reshaped. The early pattern of relationships is blurred as more organizations are linked together.

To address these issues, we examine network formation in terms of its structural development, positing network structure as a social fact interacting with firm-level behavior over time. Our theory below follows most closely recent developments in structural sociology, especially the ideas of Coleman (1990) and Burt (1992). The tests of our propositions on data from the biotechnology industry show strong support for this approach to analyzing the process of network formation.

2. Theory

2.1. *Social Capital*

Social capital is a means of enforcing norms of behavior among individual or corporate actors and thus acts as a constraint, as well as a resource. Successful cooperation cannot be achieved in interorganizational relationships without constraints on the partners to perform according to each other's expectations. These constraints allow firms to risk greater investment with a partner in a relationship that would otherwise be hindered by the threat of opportunism. Lower levels of constraint are associated with difficulties in finding information about current or potential partners and therefore impede effective cooperation. Because cooperation is less frequent, network and consequently industry growth are hindered.

The network serves an important function in the development of social constraint directing information flows in the building and maintaining of social capital. Consider two extreme examples of network structure. If all firms in an industry had relationships with each other, interfirm information flows would lead quickly to established norms of cooperation. In such a dense network, information on deviant behavior would be readily disseminated and the behavior sanctioned. Firms in this industry would benefit equally from the network as a reputation building mechanism. Coleman (1992; see also Laury, 1977; Bourdieu, 1980) characterizes the extreme case of a fully connected network as "closed." Members of closed networks are connected to each other. In a closed network, firms as institutional actors have access to *social capital*, a resource that helps the development of norms for acceptable behavior and the diffusion of information about behavior. As the predictability of behavior is increased in a system that is already connected, self-seeking opportunism is constrained and cooperation enabled.

At the other extreme is an "open" network. Firms in open networks have no social capital on which to rely. If firms are not connected to each other extensively, norms regarding cooperation are more difficult to achieve, and information on behavior in relationships diffuses more slowly. Without relationships that determine behavior and carry information, firms are less able to identify or control opportunism. In support of this conjecture, Raub and Weesie (1990) use a Prisoner's Dilemma framework to show that a firm embedded in a closed network is constrained to be more cooperative than a comparable firm embedded in an open network. Similarly, Granovetter (1985) argues, through extensive examples, that embeddedness in dense networks leads to effective interfirm cooperation.

However, a common result of research on interfirm network structure is that it is neither uniformly dense nor sparse (Knoke and Rogers, 1978;

Van de Ven et al., 1979; Nohria and Garcia-Pont, 1991). The structure is uneven, composed of regions that are more or less filled with relationships. The positions firms occupy in the network are embedded in these regions. Some firms occupy positions that are embedded in regions filled with relationships, indicating a high level of available social capital, but other positions are located in regions with few relationships, suggesting a low social capital. In such a complex network, the degree of social capital available to a firm is thus determined by its position in the network structure.

A central premise of the present paper is that social capital influences how the network forms. Network formation proceeds through the establishment of new relationships, building on the base of existing interfirm ties. Managing these ties requires ongoing attention and resources, of which organizations have only limited amounts. Social capital is thus a valuable additional asset for managing interorganizational relationships since it constrains a firm's partners to be more cooperative. Firms with less social capital are more vulnerable to opportunistic behavior and less able to build an enduring history of effective cooperative behavior with their partners over time. They, therefore, are required to expend greater time and effort monitoring the relationship. In contrast, the more social capital available to a firm, the fewer resources it needs to manage existing relationships and the more resources it can use to establish new ones. Coleman explains:

> Social capital is defined by its function. It is not a single entity but a variety of different entities, with two elements in common: they all consist of some aspect of social structures, and they facilitate certain actions of actors—whether persons or corporate actors—within the structure (Coleman, 1988, p. S98).

In the present study, the social structure is the interorganizational network. The amount of social capital depends on the firm's position in the network structure. The action facilitated by this structure is the formation of new relationships. These arguments lead to the central proposition that firms in network positions with higher social capital are likely to have more relationships with new partners in the following time period.

An important question follows: how do a firm's new cooperative relationships affect the social capital available to it? If social capital improves cooperation, then it seems likely that firms would seek partners that are more rather than less constrained by network structure. That is, firms should try to increase the social capital available to them through the new relationships they establish. Thus, the value of social capital motivates firms to reproduce the existing network structure, building the social capital available to them.

The amount of social capital that can be increased by new relationships should be related to the base amount. Mayhew and Levinger (1976) show that network density tends to attenuate as the network grows larger. Thus, firms that begin a year with high social capital cannot improve their network positions as much as those firms that are structurally less advantaged. Therefore, the more social capital available to a firm, the less the firm can increase it through forming new relationships.

2.2. Structural Holes

Burt (1992) presents an alternative to the social capital argument. Emphasizing the importance of open rather than closed networks, he argues that the network positions associated with the highest economic return lie *between* not *within* dense regions of relationships. He calls these sparse regions *structural holes*. Structural holes present opportunities for brokering information flows among firms. These opportunities have greater economic payoffs because the broker's information advantage creates the potential for arbitrage in markets for goods and services.

Burt assumes that partner selection, more than social capital, determines effective cooperation between firms (Burt, 1992, p. 16). Burt's argument subtly weaves between normative implications and positive theory. He places more emphasis than Bourdieu or Coleman on the strategic action of entrepreneurs. In Burt's view, the benefits of increasing social constraint from establishing relationships in closed regions of the network are offset by a reduction in independence. Firms with relationships in open networks have greater latitude in their cooperative strategies. These firms have higher economic gains because they are most able to parlay their superior, i.e., less redundant, information into increasing their control. Burt (1992, p. 37) argues:

> The higher the proportion of relationships enhanced by structural holes, the more likely and able the entrepreneurial player, and so the more likely it is that the player's investments are in high-yield relationships. The result is a higher aggregate rate of return on investments.

Structural hole theory therefore raises the problem of free-riding on the public good of social capital. Over time, firms will seek to exploit the holes between the islands of social capital in which relationships are embedded. As a result, the social capital available to an entrepreneur should decrease as the firm forms new relationships.

In each year, new relationships change network structure. Firms are much more likely to experience these changes as they happen, rather than all at once at the end of each year. If structural constraint represents social capital, the change in structure should determine the resources available to a firm to form new relationships. From Coleman and Bourdieu's perspective, increasing social capital in a period should enable more relationships. Alternatively, if, as Burt asserts, trust is determined only by careful partner selection, increases in social capital should have no effect on the number of new relationships. The arguments regarding network formation from both the social capital and structural hole perspectives are set out as propositions in Fig. 1.

2.3. Control Variables

We test these propositions against the view that only organizational attributes determine interfirm cooperation. Since firms with similar attributes may occupy the same network position (Burt, 1992, chapter 5), controlling for these attributes makes the analysis of network formation more robust. We identify

Social Capital Perspective	Tests of Propositions
1. Firms with higher social capital are likely to have more relationships with new partners in the following time period.	Regression of new relationships on social capital (for incumbent and entering partners), see Table 6.
2. The more relationships a firm forms, the more likely its social capital will increase.	Regression of change in social capital on new relationships (for incumbents and entering partners), see Table 7.
3. The more social capital at the beginning of a time period, the lower the increase in social capital in the next time period.	Regression of change in social capital on level of social capital in the previous time period, see Table 7.
4. The more a firm's social capital increases over a time period, the more relationships it should have during this time period.	Regression of new relationships (for incumbent and entering partners) on change in social capital, see Table 6.
Structural Hole Perspective	
5. The more relationships a firm forms in a year, the more its social capital should decrease.	Regression of change in social capital on new relationships (for incumbents and entering partners), see Table 7.
6. Lack of empirical support for Proposition 4 above would be consistent with the Structural Hole Perspective.	Regression of new relationships (for incumbent and entering partners) on change in social capital, see Table 6.

Fig. 1. List of propositions developed in the theory section and their tests.

five control variables: firm size, firm experience in cooperating with other firms, public offering of the firm's equity, the concentration of the firm's partners across global regions, and the average number of relationships of the firm's partners. The last two of these variables might be viewed more properly as partner characteristics. However, since they are aggregated by firm, they are included as firm-level controls.

Firm size is a measure of a firm's capacity to cooperate and a measure of its capacity to do without cooperation. Whereas Shan (1990) found a negative relationship between size and cooperation, Boyles (1969) and Powell and Brantley (1991) found that the frequency of cooperative relationships more than proportionally rises with size. Whether this difference rises from a nonlinearity in the association between size and the frequency of cooperation is partly addressed below.

Firm experience with cooperation, represented as the number of relationships it has established, presents a similar set of issues. The more relationships a firm has, the more it should know about how to manage them and so the less costly it should be to form new relationships. On the other hand, the lower incremental learning from new relationships may attenuate their formation. Again, we address this potential nonlinearity in our analysis.

The effect of issuing public equity on interfirm cooperation also has an ambiguous interpretation. First, a public offering is one form of getting resources. As a publicly held corporation, an entrepreneurial startup can probably go to the capital markets to finance projects, thereby decreasing the need to cooperate for this purpose. However, going public may also be an indicator of the legitimacy of the firm and signal a strong position in the network. Firms with higher legitimacy are likely to attract more partners for cooperative ventures.

Regional concentration represents how a firm's partners are distributed across three major global regions: United States, Europe, and Japan. As Hofstede et al. (1990) have shown, national cultures have a significant impact on work behavior. Managing partners across different regions should therefore be a more complex and difficult task than managing partners from the same region. The higher the concentration, the more partners from a single region are represented in the firm's organization set and the less difficult its task of managing them.

The experience of an organization's partners in interfirm agreements may influence its tendency to cooperate. The more agreements a firm's partners currently have, the more likely they are to be embedded in closed regions of the network and therefore to be constrained from acting opportunistically (see Baker, 1990). However, partners with more relationships may also be less dependent on the firm for its information, goods and services, releasing normative pressures for equitable behavior. Partner experience may therefore either heighten or dampen the firm's tendency to cooperate.

Finally, in studying the reproduction of network structure, it is important to differentiate between relationships with partners entering the network and relationships with partners already in the network. The first are called entering partners and the second incumbent partners. Splitting partners in this way provides a robust test of the social capital argument. In the broadest sense, social capital releases resources to firms for further cooperation whether the firm engages partners that are new to the network or already network members. A narrower view of social capital suggests that social capital theory applies to network formation only for relationships with network incumbents. If this is the case, future research must consider network incumbency as a moderator of social capital's effect.

3. Data

We test these hypotheses by examining network formation in the biotechnology industry.[1] As most earlier studies have shown, the frequency of interfirm relationships in this industry is quite high, primarily between large established firms in a variety of businesses (pharmaceuticals, chemicals, agricultural products, food products) and small, entrepreneurial startup firms (Barley et al., 1992; Powell and Brantley, 1992; Kogut et al., 1995). These relationships have been shown to increase the capabilities of startup firms, indicating a motivation for continuing cooperation (Shan et al., 1994). The incidence of these relationships has been explained both by network (Kogut et al., 1992) and firm-level variables (Shan, 1990; Pisano, 1990).

Biotechnology is typical of industries with high rates of innovation and a significant entrepreneurial sector. The motivation for interfirm cooperation in these industries is quite strong, based on the complementarity of large and small firm capabilities. Because of the tremendous potential market for new biotechnology products, established companies have sought access to this new technology both by starting up biotechnology operations in-house and by forming cooperative agreements with startup firms, typically begun by scientists. Startup firms, in turn, have been willing to enter into cooperative agreements to provide established firms with new technologies and products in exchange for funding and to breach the barriers to entry in marketing, distribution, and government certification (Shan, 1987). As firms become connected through these agreements, a broad network, typically global in scope, is formed.

To analyze network formation in biotechnology, we examine new relationships by startups rather than those by established firms, for several reasons.[2]

Kogut et al. (1994) showed that startups have a much greater propensity to cooperate than established firms over time and correspondingly have more relationships. Network growth is therefore determined more by the expansion of startup organization sets than by the organization sets of their established firm partners. Startups also have much higher variability than established firms in number of relationships over time and are more central in the network (Barley et al., 1992).

Although startups have relationships with each other, their relationships with established firms are far more prevalent. Only six percent of relationships existing in 1988 were between startups. A description of the timing of foundings of startups and the pattern of their relationships with established firms is given in Figures 2 to 5. (See Appendix A for a description of data sources and the characteristics of our sample.) The distribution of cooperative relationships is shown in Figures 2 and 3. Startup foundings (shown in Figure 2) lead the formation of these relationships by three to five years (shown in Figure 3).

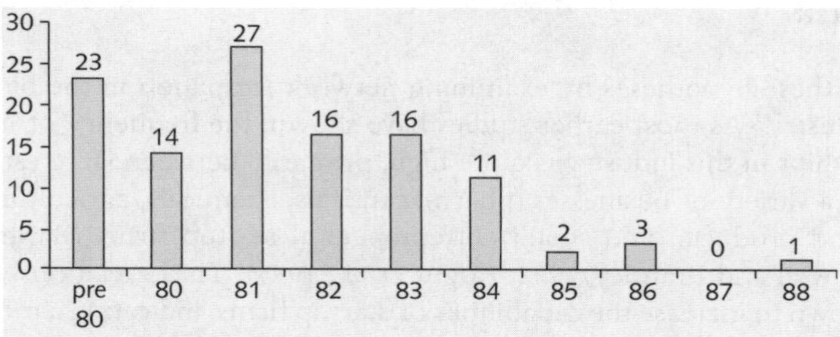

Fig. 2. Number of sample startups founded in each year.

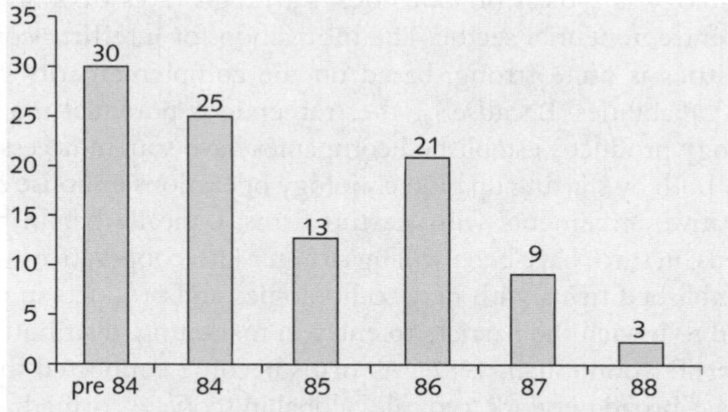

Fig. 3. Number of sample startups entering network in each year.

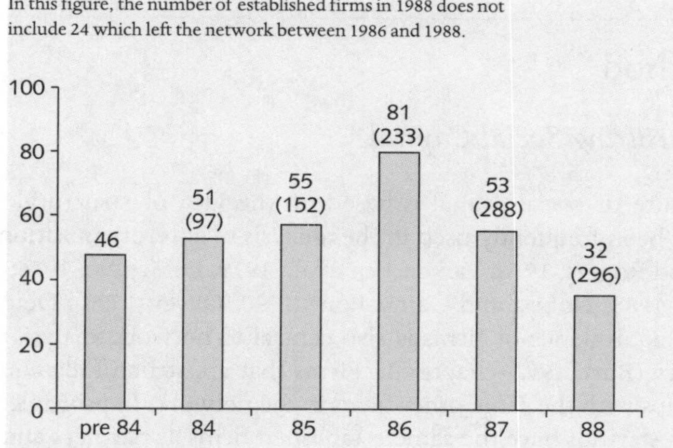

Fig. 4. Number of established firms entering network in each year.

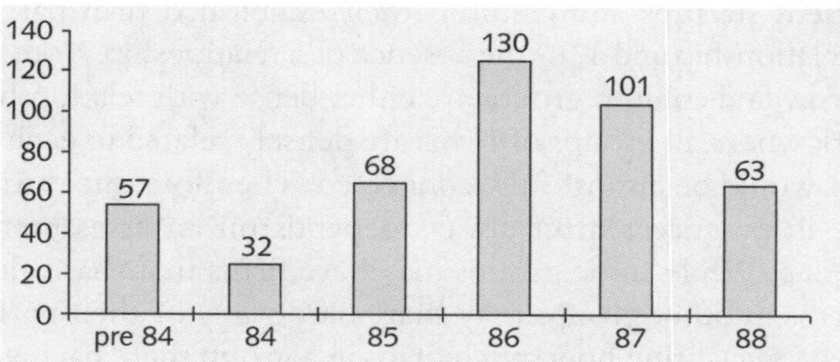

Fig. 5. Number of cooperative relationships formed in each year.

Startup foundings peak in 1981, while the number of relationships with partners peaks in 1984 with a second mode in 1986. This second (1986) mode can be partly attributed to the entry into the network of established firms (see Figure 4). The modal year for all relationships, by both new and incumbent startups, is also 1986 (see Figure 5).

Since the process of developing, testing, and commercializing biotechnology products takes many years, cooperative relationships endure for a long time. Only 18 percent of the relationships in the industry from its beginning until 1988 had a fixed duration (that is, their termination date was formally specified when they were initiated); and only 31 percent of fixed duration relationships ended before 1988. Furthermore, only 11 percent of the relationships with unfixed durations were terminated before 1988. Thus, in 1988 some 85 percent of all the agreements that had ever been formed were still in effect.

4. Method

4.1. *Measuring Social Capital*

Our measure of social capital is based on the idea of structural equivalence, which has been frequently used in the analysis of interorganizational networks (Knoke and Rogers, 1978; Van de Ven et al., 1979; DiMaggio, 1986; Schrum and Withnow, 1988; Nohria and Garcia-Pont, 1990; Oliver, 1990). Determining the structural equivalence of firms is also central to network analysis in structural hole theory (Burt, 1992, chapter 2). Firms that are structurally equivalent have relationships with the same other firms in the network. In principle, structurally equivalent startups have the same established firms as partners and structurally equivalent established firms have the same startups as partners. The emergence of this type of structure therefore depends on the pattern of partner sharing.[3]

An idealized example of this type of network structure is shown in Figure 6. Rows represent startups and columns their established firm partners. An "X" indicates a relationship and a "0" the absence of a relationship. Note that the intersections of row and column groups are either dense with relationships or sparse.

A network where all groups of firms are densely related to each other is rare, since such it would be almost fully connected. Therefore, measuring structural equivalence in practice almost always depends on an assessment of relative partner overlap. While some groups may have firms that share almost all their partners, firms in other groups may share hardly any of their partners.

One way of measuring how much firms in a group share partners is to examine the dispersion of intergroup densities around the network average. A group of firms that share partners extensively should have dense relationships with some partner groups and sparse or no relationships with other partner groups. This pattern is found for all the groups, both row and column, in Figure 6. An equation that calculates density dispersion is:

$$G_i = n_i \sum_j m_j (d_{ij} - d^\star)^2. \qquad (1)$$

In this equation, G_i is the measure of the dispersion of intergroup densities for the ith group in the network, n_i is the number of firms in the ith group, m_j is the number of partners in the jth partner group, d_{ij} is the density of the intersection of the ith and jth groups, and $d^\star$ is the overall density of the network.[4] A higher value of G_i indicates greater dispersion of a group's densities and therefore more partner sharing by the firms in group i. Note that this measure penalizes small groups of firms with small partner groups.

<table>
<tr><td></td><td></td><td colspan="4">Partners</td></tr>
<tr><td></td><td></td><td>Group 1</td><td>Group 2</td><td>Group 3</td><td>Group 4</td></tr>
<tr><td rowspan="4">Startups</td><td>Group 1</td><td>XXXOOXXX
XXXXOOXX
OXXXXOXX</td><td>OOOOOOOOOOOO
OOOOOOOOOO
OOOOOOOOOOOO</td><td>OOOOOOOOOOOO
OOOOOOOOOOOO
OOOOOOOOO</td><td>OOOOOOOOOOOO
OOOOOOOOOOOO
OOOOOO</td></tr>
<tr><td>Group 2</td><td>OOOOOOOOOOOO
OOOOOOOOOOOO
OOOOOOOOO</td><td>XXXXXXOOOX
XXXOXXXXOX
XXOXXXOXXX</td><td>OOOOOOOOOOOO
OOOOOOOOOOOO
OOOOOOOOO</td><td>XXXXXXXOOX
XOXXOXXXOX
XXXXXOXXOX</td></tr>
<tr><td>Group 3</td><td>OOOOOOOOOOOO
OOOOOOOOOOOO
OOOOOOOOO</td><td>OOOOOOOOOOOO
OOOOOOOOOOOO
OOOOOOOOO</td><td>OOXXXXXXXXX
XXXXOXXXXXO
XOXOXXOXXXX</td><td>OOOOOOOOOOOO
OOOOOOOOOOOO
OOOOOO</td></tr>
<tr><td>Group 4</td><td>OOOOOOOOOOOO
OOOOOOOOOOOO
OOOOOOOOO</td><td>OOOOOOOOOOOO
OOOOOOOOOOOO
OOOOOOOOO</td><td>OOOOOOOOOOOO
OOOOOOOOOOOO
OOOOOOOOO</td><td>XXXXXOXOOX
XXOXXOXXXO
OXXXXOXXOX</td></tr>
</table>

Fig. 6. An idealized network structure based on structural equivalence.

To show how the structure of the biotechnology network differs from the idealized network of Figure 6, we use a method that builds on G_i to analyze the biotechnology network of relationships formed before 1984. Since G_i reflects the deviation of intergroup relationships from the average network density, summing G_i over all groups produces a measure of network structure:[5]

$$G = \sum_i \sum_j n_i m_j (d_{ij} - d^\star)^2 . \qquad (2)$$

The details of the methodology are presented in Appendix B, which shows how the pre-1984 network was analyzed.

Figure 7a shows the partitioned raw data. There are four startup groups and six partner groups. Group I has the largest number of firms, which have relationships predominantly with partner groups A, B, and C. Because the number of relationships Group I has with each of the partner groups is much smaller than the number of possible relationships, the densities of these intergroup relationships are quite low (see Fig. 7b). Unlike Group I, Groups II, III and IV are densely related to their partner groups. Group II contains only one firm, the only startup to have agreements with Group E. Furthermore, this firm has only one other relationship in the network, with a partner in Group F. Finally, both Groups III and IV are composed of several startups that have established relationships with Groups D and F, respectively.

Only a few firms contribute significantly to the structure of biotechnology network. To demonstrate this, we divide Equation (1) by Equation (2) to get

(a)

Partner Groups

Startup Groups	A	B	C	D	E	F
	OOOOOOOOOOOOOOOOOOOO	•OO	•OOXOO	•OOOOO	•OOOOOO	•OOOOOOOOO
	OXOOOOOOOOOOOOOOOOOO	•OO	•OOOOO	•OOOOO	•OOOOOO	•OOOOOOOOO
	OOOOOXOOOOOOOOOOOOOO	•OO	•XOOOO	•OOOOO	•OOOOOO	•OOOOOOOOO
	OOOOOOOOOOOOOOOOOOXO	•OO	•OOOOO	•OOOOO	•OOOOOO	•OOOOOOOOO
	OOOOOOOOOOOOOOOOOOOX	•OO	•OOOOO	•OOOOO	•OOOOOO	•OOOOOOOOO
	OOOXOOOOOOOOOOOOOOOO	•OO	•OOOXX	•OOOOO	•OOOOOO	•OOOOOOOOO
	OOOOOOOOXXOOOOOOOOOO	•OX	•OOOOO	•OOOOO	•OOOOOO	•OOOOOOOOO
	OOOOOOOOXOOOOOOOOOOO	•OO	•OOOOO	•OOOOO	•OOOOOO	•OOOOOOOOO
	OOOOXOOOOOOOOOOOOOOO	•OO	•OOOOO	•OOOOO	•OOOOOO	•OOOOOOOOO
I	OOOOOOOOOOOOOOOOOOOO	•OO	•OOOOO	•OOOOO	•OOOOOO	•OOOOOXOOO
	OOOOOOOOOOOOOOOOOOOO	•XO	•OOOOO	•OOOOO	•OOOOOO	•OOOOOOOOO
	OOOOOOOOOOOXOOOOOOOO	•OO	•OOOOO	•OOOOO	•OOOOOO	•OOOOOOOOO
	XOOOOOOOOOOOOOOOOOOO	•OO	•OOOOO	•OOOOO	•OOOOOO	•OOOOOOOOO
	OOOOOOOOOOOOOOOOOOOO	•OX	•OOOOO	•OOOOO	•OOOOOO	•OOOOOOOOO
	OOXOOOOOOOOOOOOOOOOO	•OO	•OOOOO	•OOOOO	•OOOOOO	•OOOOOXOOO
	OOOOOOOOOOOOOXOOXOOO	•OO	•OXOOO	•OOOOO	•OOOOOO	•OOOOOOOOO
	OOOOOOOOOOXOOOOOOOOO	•OO	•OOOOO	•OOOOO	•OOOOOO	•OOOOOOOOO
	OOOOOOOOOOOOOOXOOOOO	•OO	•OOOOO	•OOOOO	•OOOOOO	•OOOOOOOOO
	OOOOOOOOOOOOOOOOOOOO	•XO	•OOOOO	•OOOOO	•OOOOOO	•OOOOOOOOO
	OOOOOOOOOOOOOOOOOXOO	•OO	•OOOOO	•OOOOO	•OOOOOO	•OOOOOOOOO
	OOOOOOOOOOOOXOOOOOOO	•OO	•OOOOO	•OOOOO	•OOOOOO	•OOOOOOOOO
	OOOOOOOOOOOOOOOXOOOO	•OO	•OOOOO	•OOOOO	•OOOOOO	•OOOOOOOOO
II	OOOOOOOOOOOOOOOOOOOO	•OO	•OOOOO	•OOOOO	•XXXXXX	•XOOOOOOOO
	OOOOOOOOOOOOOOOOOOOO	•OO	•OOOOO	•OXXXO	•OOOOOO	•OOOOOOOOO
III	OOOOOOOOOOOOOOOOOOOO	•OO	•OOOOO	•XXOOX	•OOOOOO	•OOOOOOOOO
	OOOOOOOOOOOOOOOOOOOO	•OO	•OOOOO	•OOOOO	•OOOOOO	•XOXOXOOOO
IV	OOOOOOOOOOOOOOOOOOOO	•OO	•OOOOO	•OOOOO	•OOOOOO	•XXOOOXXOO
	OOOOOOOOOOOOOOOOOOOO	•OO	•OOOOO	•OOOOO	•OOOOOO	•XOOOXOOOO
	OOOOOOOOOOOOOOOOOOOO	•OO	•OOOOO	•OOOOO	•OOOOOO	•OOOXOXOOX
	OOOOOOOOOOOOOOOOOOOO	•OO	•OOOOO	•OOOOO	•OOOOOO	•OOOXOXOXO

(b)

	A	B	C	D	E	F
I	.05	.09	.05	0	0	.01
II	0	0	0	0	1	.11
III	0	0	0	.6	0	0
IV	0	0	0	0	0	.33

Fig. 7. (a) Partitioned raw data for 1983 network. (b) Density matrix of 1983 network.

a measure of each group's percentage contribution to network structure. This variable, bounded by zero and one, represents the dispersion of startup group densities normalized by a measure of how structured the network is in a time period.

Startup groups in the network occupy distinct positions which vary in their social capital. A group's contribution to network structure in a time period indicates how tightly packed are its relationships with partners. Higher density means greater partner sharing within a startup group, creating a stronger focal point for conversation.[6] Startups in groups with higher contributions have greater social capital available to them.[7] If a group's contribution to network structure increases with new relationships, we assume that startups have chosen partners so that social capital is increased. However, increased social capital also means increased social constraint. Following Burt's argument (Burt, 1982, p. 57), if startups are searching for lower social constraint, the startup group's contribution to network structure should decline over time.

4.2. *Testing the Propositions*

Although structurally equivalent startups that occupy the same position will have the same amount of social capital, they will differ in the number of relationships they establish in each year and in the control variables. We therefore designed the empirical tests at the firm level, consistent with the way they are stated, over each pair of years from 1984 to 1988. The data are pooled cross-sections of year pairs from 1984 to 1988; e.g., 1984–1985. Dummy variables for each year pair are included to correct for time-period effects.

We use several regression techniques: negative binomial, two-stage least squares and generalized least squares regression. Like Poisson regression, the negative binomial model treats the dependent variable as a count variable but allows for a direct measure of heterogeneity (see Cameron and Trivedi, 1986). Estimating heterogeneity not only relaxes the stringent Poisson assumption of equal mean and variance in the error term but also accounts for omitted variable bias.

However, the negative binomial model does not correct for the potential bias due to the simultaneity of new relationships and change in social capital over time. To make this correction, we assume that the dependent variable is not a count but continuous and use two-stage least squares. Generalized least squares permits corrections for serial correlation in the error term and unobserved firm-level effects. Figure 5 shows how these regressions test the propositions based on the theories of social capital and structural holes.

5. Results

Table 1 shows the means, standard deviations and correlations among the variables, and Table 2 presents the findings for the regressions. Five of the

Table 1. Means, Standard Deviations, and Correlations

Variables	MN	STD	Correlations									
1. Social capital	0.039	0.036	1.00									
2. Change in social capital	−0.001	0.027	−0.52	1.00								
3. Number of relationships with entering partners in each period	0.73	1.16	0.25	0.17	1.00							
4. Number of relationships with incumbent partners in each period	0.52	0.95	0.17	0.14	0.27	1.00						
5. Size	170.08	245.99	0.38	0.01	0.27	0.07	1.00					
6. IPO	0.74	0.44	0.12	0.01	0.19	0.12	0.16	1.00				
7. Regional concentration	1.79	0.61	0.03	−0.001	0.04	0.03	0.41	0.10	1.00			
8. Startup experience	3.94	4.64	0.55	−0.08	0.14	0.18	0.41	0.26	0.05	1.00		
9. Partner experience	2.45	1.52	−0.09	0.04	−0.14	−0.11	−0.12	0.12	0.06	0.03	1.00	
10. Number of startups in group	40.16	28.09	−0.65	0.37	−0.19	−0.13	−0.20	−0.06	−0.07	−0.32	0.14	1.00

explanatory variables have consistent results: the social capital and change in social capital, startup experience, partner experience, and public offering (IPO). Both network variables explain the frequency of new relationships strongly, as social capital theory predicts. Interestingly, neither startup nor partner experience has an effect on new relationships, controlling for the network variables.[8] This finding shows that new relationships are not explained by how many relationships a startup or its partner has, but how the relationships are distributed across partner groups. Public offering has a positive, significant effect on establishing relationships with entering partners but no influence on relationships with incumbents.

Table 2. Results for Regression Explaining New Startup Relationships

Table 2A

	Entering Partners		Incumbent Partners	
Explanatory Variables:	Negative Binomial	2SLS[1]	Negative Binomial	2SLS
Constant	−1.35***	−0.15	−1.97***	−0.13
	(0.42)[2]	(0.28)	(0.67)	(0.23)
Social capital	8.08*	17.94***	13.08**	11.82***
	(4.27)	(5.39)	(5.32)	(4.26)
Change in social capital	13.06***	27.52***	18.84***	16.95***
	(3.12)	(8.26)	(5.74)	(6.28)
Startup experience	0.002	−0.03	0.023	0.0042
	(0.031)	(0.024)	(0.038)	(0.02)
Partner experience	−0.057	−0.035	0.089	−0.59
	(0.057)	(0.043)	(0.27)	(0.38)
Size	0.0004	0.0004	−0.001	−0.0004*
	(0.0003)	(0.0003)	(0.0006)	(0.0003)
IPO	0.79***	0.39***	0.39	0.12
	(0.23)	(0.15)	(0.27)	(0.13)
Regional concentration	0.09	0.0004	0.089	0.0001
	(0.15)	(0.0001)	(0.27)	(0.0009)
D86	0.52**	0.73**	1.04***	0.64***
	(0.26)	(0.25)	(0.39)	(0.21)
D87	−0.30	−0.056	0.77*	0.39**
	(0.29)	(0.24)	(0.44)	(0.20)
D88	−0.99***	−0.34	0.26	0.16
	(0.35)	(0.26)	(0.48)	(0.22)
α	0.081		0.59*	
	(0.13)		(0.32)	
F-value		12.49		5.27
df		10,262		10,261
R^2		0.32		0.16
Adj. R^2		0.29		0.13

[1] 2SLS coefficients are adjusted for serial correlation in the error term. R^2 terms pertain to unadjusted estimates.
[2] Standard errors are reported in parentheses.
* $p < 0.10$; ** $p < 0.05$; *** $p < 0.01$.

Table 2. *Continued*

Table 2B

Explanatory Variables:	Entering Partners Negative Binomial	Entering Partners OLS[1]	Incumbent Partners Negative Binomial	Incumbent Partners OLS
Constant	−1.08***	0.51***	−1.50**	−0.32*
	(0.40)[2]	(0.19)	(0.69)	(0.17)
Social capital				
Change in social capital				
Startup experience	0.029	0.026*	0.056	0.042***
	(0.020)	(0.016)	(0.037)	(0.014)
Partner experience	−0.057	−0.037	−0.12	−0.057
	(0.066)	(0.044)	(0.084)	(0.039)
Size	0.0008***	0.0009***	−0.0002	−0.0001
	(0.0003)	(0.0003)	(0.0006)	(0.0003)
IPO	0.87***	0.47***	0.47*	0.16
	(0.24)	(0.15)	(0.27)	(0.13)
Regional	0.17	0.0004	0.18	0.0003
concentration	(0.16)	(0.001)	(0.28)	(0.0009)
D86	0.15	0.26	0.63	0.35*
	(0.23)	(0.19)	(0.42)	(0.18)
D87	−0.67***	−0.45**	0.31	0.13
	(0.26)	(0.19)	(0.42)	(0.17)
D88	−1.43***	−0.79***	−0.26	−0.14
	(0.29)	(0.19)	(0.48)	(0.18)
α	−0.27		0.99**	
	(0.17)		(0.40)	
F-value		9.94		3.15
df		8,263		8,263
R^2		0.22		0.087
Adj. R^2		0.19		0.059

[1] The OLS regression results reported are adjusted for autocorrelated error. The *F*-statistic reported is not adjusted for this error.
[2] Standard errors are reported in parentheses.

Table 2C

Explanatory Variables:	Entering Partners Negative Binomial	Entering Partners 2SLS[1]	Incumbent Partners Negative Binomial	Incumbent Partners 2SLS
Constant	−0.94***	0.15	−1.87***	−0.13
	(0.26)	(0.18)	(0.39)	(0.16)
Social capital	11.91***	14.75***	12.17***	9.62***
	(2.34)	(1.97)	(3.73)	(1.77)
Change in social	17.22***	21.14***	18.16***	13.09***
capital	(3.41)	(2.66)	(5.003)	(2.38)
D86	0.72***	0.69***	1.12***	0.60***
	(0.25)	(0.19)	(0.38)	(0.17)
D87	−0.1	−0.095	0.75*	0.36**
	(0.28)	(0.19)	(0.38)	(0.17)

Table 2. *Continued*
Table 2C

Explanatory Variables:	Entering Partners: Negative Binomial	Entering Partners: 2SLS[1]	Incumbent Partners: Negative Binomial	Incumbent Partners: 2SLS
D88	−0.80**	−0.42**	0.27	0.10
	(0.32)	(0.19)	(0.41)	(0.17)
α	−0.24		0.75**	
	(0.16)		(0.34)	
F-value		22.93		9.82
df		5,266		5,266
R^2		0.30		0.16
Adj. R^2		0.29		0.14

[1] The 2SLS regression results reported are adjusted for autocorrelated error. The *F*-statistic reported is not adjusted for this error.

Table 3. Results of Two-stage Least Squares Regression on Change in Social Capital

Explanatory Variables	Dependent Variable: Change in Social Capital	
Constant	0.0043	0.0049
	(0.0054)	(0.0077)
Number of startup Relationships with entering partners	0.018***	
	(0.0038)	
Number of startup Relationships with incumbent partners		0.036***
		(0.017)
Existing social Capital	−0.44***	−0.41***
	(0.056)	(0.086)
Number of startups in group	0.0001*	0.0003**
	(0.00007)	(0.0001)
D86	−0.025***	−0.037***
	(0.0054)	(0.010)
D87	−0.0047	−0.023***
	(0.0051)	(0.009)
D88	0.0018	−0.014*
	(0.0054)	(0.0075)

* $p < 0.10$
** $p < 0.05$
*** $p < 0.01$

The results for startup size and regional concentration are not as clear. Neither has an effect for incumbent partners. However, for entering partners, the results for the two techniques differ in significance but not in sign.

Table 3 reports the results of testing whether social capital and the number of new startup relationships influence change in social capital. Included in the model are dummy variables for each year and a variable indicating the number of firms in a startup's group. Controlling for this variable is necessary since G (in Equation (1)) is linearly related to it. The two-stage least squares regression shows that more new relationships increase social capital. Also, the increase in social capital is lower when a startup has more social capital in the beginning period.

Startup propensities to cooperate may vary to some extent. There may be unobserved firm-level factors that influence how frequently cooperation occurs. The a term in the negative binomial regression captures these unobserved variables to a degree.

To explore this problem further, we regressed the frequency of new startup relationships on the explanatory variables including firm-specific dummy variables to account for unobservable effects. Since our sample draws from a larger population of startup firms, a random effects specification is appropriate. The hypotheses are therefore tested, without simultaneity, using Generalized Least Squares. The results of this GLS regression are stronger than those of the negative binomial and two-stage least squares regressions.[9] Consequently, we can be reasonably confident that unobserved firm-level variation in the propensity to cooperate does not confound our findings.

6. Discussion

We have posed two theories to explain the incidence of new relationships. One theory emphasizes the positive effect of social capital, as structural constraint, on new cooperation. The other argues that highly constrained cooperation has lower rewards and is therefore avoided. Our analysis of biotechnology startups shows that social capital theory is the better predictor of cooperation over time. More constrained firms cooperate with partners that can be firmly embedded in the historical network structure. The network is thus increasingly structured over time. Network formation, and industry growth, are therefore significantly influenced by the development and maintenance of social capital.

Why have biotechnology startups chosen to increase social capital rather than exploit structural holes? First, relationships in the biotechnology network last a long time. Long durations entail extensive, ongoing interaction over a broad range of technical and commercial problems. Were partners to behave in a self-interested way during the course of such a long relationship, a substantial investment in time and effort would be jeopardized. Structural stability is therefore desirable. In a network where relationships are of shorter duration, the structure would undoubtedly be less stable and less available as a resource for action. Enduring interfirm ties sustain the structure that facilitates new cooperation. Second, structural hole theory may apply more to networks of market transactions than to networks of cooperative relationships. Lacking the requirement to cooperate over time, firms may not experience structural constraint in their relationships. Third, interfirm relationships in biotechnology are based on a kind of mutual dependence that may prevent either startups or established firms from gaining control over the other. Biotechnology startups and their established firm partners have complementary resources that are jointly necessary for product development and commercialization.

Such mutuality may not be present to such an extent in other technology-intensive industries. For example, Kogut et al. (1992) argue that cooperative agreements between startups and established firms in the semiconductor industry are based on the technical standards which large firms own. Large firms dominate the network structure of the semiconductor industry as they compete for technological dominance through their alliances with startups. In such a structure, embeddedness clearly has a different meaning than in the biotechnology network (compare, e.g., Marsden, 1983).

Our results lead to the conclusion that some firms continuously improve their already strong social endowments, although at a decreasing rate, while other firms have less social capital to draw upon in forming new relationships. This conclusion holds for relationships with both incumbent and newly-entering partners, indicating that the effect of network structure on forming new relationships is not moderated by partner incumbency. Although the results for network formation are similar for both incumbent and entering partners, these partner types differ in two important ways. First, entering partners tend to establish relationships with startups whose equity is publicly traded while the choice of incumbents does not depend on the characteristics of individual startups. *IPO* (Initial Public Offering) appears to signal organizational legitimacy to entering firms rather than represent a source of potential startup capital substituting for a partner's financial resources. A second difference between incumbent and entering partners is in the time trends. For relationships with entering firms, the signs on the year dummy variables turn from negative to positive to negative over the four years. Relationships with entering partners decline in the later years simply because there are fewer firms coming into the network. But, as shown in Figure 5, the trend for incumbent partners remains positive, though declining in the later years. When there are fewer entrants, incumbent partners attract more attention.

7. Path Dependence in Network Formation

The firms in the industry recreate a stable network structure whose foundation was laid at an early point in the industry's history. Firms' early partner choices thus have a significant impact on the course of future cooperation. To examine this conjecture, we analyze and compare the network structures from 1984 to 1988. Examining structural equivalence over time indicates how much network structure is altered by network growth through entry and new relationships among incumbents.

Table 4 presents cross-tabulations showing whether pairs of firms remained structurally equivalent or nonequivalent from one year to the next. Entries on the main diagonal in each table indicate persistence. To assess whether these entries

Table 4. Structural Equivalence of Organizations over Time

1. Startups

Str. eq.	1984 Str. eq.	1984 Not. Str. eq.
1983	52*	190
Not. Str. eq.	4	189

Log cross product ratio = 2.56
Std. error = 0.53

Str. eq.	1985 Str. eq.	1985 Not. Str. eq.
1984	189	99
Not. Str. eq.	605	592

Log cross product ratio = 0.62
Std. error = 0.14

Str. eq.	1986 Str. eq.	1986 Not. Str. eq.
1985	917	528
Not. Str. eq.	270	631

Log cross product ratio = 1.40
Std. error = 0.09

Str. eq.	1987 Str. eq.	1987 Not. Str. eq.
1986	1162	1067
Not. Str. eq.	426	1261

Log cross product ratio = 1.17
Std. error = 0.07

Str. eq.	1988 Str. eq.	1988 Not. Str. eq.
1987	1609	519
Not. Str. eq.	903	1722

Log cross product ratio = 1.78
Std. error = 0.07

2. Established Firms

Str. eq.	1984 Str. eq.	1984 Not. Str. eq.
1983	56	187
Not. Str. eq.	15	777

Log cross product ratio = 2.74
Std. error = 0.03

Str. eq.	1985 Str. eq.	1985 Not. Str. eq.
1984	141	270
Not. Str. eq.	187	4058

Log cross product ratio = 2.43
Std. error = 0.13

Str. eq.	1986 Str. eq.	1986 Not. Str. eq.
1985	257	651
Not. Str. eq.	377	10190

Log cross product ratio = 2.47
Std. error = 0.09

Str. eq.	1987 Str. eq.	1987 Not. Str. eq.
1986	339	1097
Not. Str. eq.	784	24808

Log cross product ratio = 2.28
Std. error = 0.03

Str. eq.	1988 Str. eq.	1988 Not. Str. eq.
1987	368	1561
Not. Str. eq.	971	37855

Log cross product ratio = 2.22
Std. error = 0.07

* Entries in cells are pairs of organizations.

are larger than the off-diagonal entries, we calculated the cross-product ratio for each table. The cross-product ratio is a commonly used statistic for estimating the degree of association between two variables (see Agresti, 1984, p. 15). A cross-product ratio of zero indicates no association between the variables, and values of the ratio greater than one imply a positive relationship. Because the logarithm of the cross-product ratio is less skewed than the ratio itself, we use the log of the ratio to test for structural persistence (Wickens, 1989, pp. 218–222). These log ratios are all positive and strongly significantly different from zero for both startups and partners. Except for the 1983–1984 period, the tables show that once a pair of startups are structurally equivalent, the odds are significant that they will continue to be so. Furthermore, the reverse is also generally true: if a pair of startups are not structurally equivalent, they are likely to remain this way.

Predicting partner groups over time depends mostly on the persistence of structural dissimilarity, however. Between 1987 and 1988, for example, the odds that a pair of partners will continue to be structurally equivalent are roughly one to five (368/1561), while the odds that they will remain structurally nonequivalent are roughly forty to one (37855/971). The reason for this pattern is the large number of entering partners relative to partners already in the network.

The structural development of the industry, based on the building and reinforcement of social capital, offers a simple insight into the rigidity of organizational forms. Since an organization depends on the resources available in its network, organizational inertia may be less an inherent property of organizations than a product of the organization's position in a rigid network. The persistence of these positions, as shown in Table 4, suggests that a startup's characteristics may endure because of structural conditions (see Shan et al., 1994).

8. Conclusion

Social capital, as outlined by Coleman and Bourdieu, is a powerful concept for understanding how interfirm networks in emerging industries are formed. It is important to note that network formation need not lead towards an optimal structure for innovation or product commercialization.[10] Although there is evidence that interfirm cooperation and startup patent activity are related (Shan et al., 1994), the local benefits of partner sharing may not be distributed so that the most productive and useful technological advances are commercialized successfully.

The importance of network formation for interfirm cooperation has important consequences for organization theory. Taking the transaction as the unit of analysis is inadequate to capture the structural effects we have identified. The study of interfirm cooperative agreements over time requires an analysis of the network as a whole.

The persistence of network structure has subtle implications for entrepreneurial behavior. Structural persistence does not imply that firms are equally situated to exploit profitable opportunities for cooperation. Because the structure is relatively inert, brokering positions are established early in the history of the network. In fact, if structure did not persist, all firms would be potential brokers but with few enduring opportunities. Given the relative fixity of brokering positions, the kind of entrepreneurship Burt proposes, as the exploitation of structural holes, should be especially profitable. An intriguing hypothesis is that the pursuit of these rewards explains the current wave of mergers and acquisitions among biotechnology firms.

The persistence of the past is welcomed if alternative futures look less promising, especially scenarios with free-rider or prisoner-dilemma problems. But social capital can also be associated with encumbering commitments that impede competition and change. If biotechnology firms could rewrite their histories of cooperation, few would be surprised that an alternative path of network formation would emerge. It is this gap between the desired and the actual that expresses most clearly the idea that structure both enables and constrains entrepreneurial ambitions.

Appendix A

Data Sources

The primary source of data is BIOSCAN (1988, 1989), a commercial directory of biotechnology firms, published and updated quarterly by ORYX Press, Inc. Because it has generally been considered the most comprehensive compendium of information on relationships in the industry, any relationship listed in BIOSCAN is included in our sample. However, because BIOSCAN may have omitted some relationships terminated before 1988, we collected data from the three other sources: (1) a proprietary database obtained from a leading biotechnology firm (called the "black volumes") in 1986; (2) a database developed by the North Carolina Biotechnology Center, based on published announcements of cooperative agreements; and (3) a direct mail survey of and telephone interviews with startups.

Because these latter three sources had neither BIOSCAN's history of direct contact with startups and their partners nor its depth of information about agreements, we relied less on their data. We added an agreement if it appeared in at least two of these sources. We found 46 relationships in this category. As they do not appear in the 1988 BIOSCAN directory, we assumed that these relationships had been terminated before 1988; the network analysis for 1988 therefore excluded them.

All startups in the final sample were independent businesses specializing in the commercialization of biotechnology products. Their portfolio of products must include diagnostic or therapeutic pharmaceuticals. The agreements consisted of joint ventures, licensing, and long term contracts between startups and their partners. Powell and Brantley (1992) found that different types of relationships—e.g., licensing, joint venture, research and development limited partnership—were not statistically related to how much firms engaged in cooperative agreements. Consequently, the network we analyze contains these types of relationship together. Since only firms that have engaged in at least one agreement can contribute to network structure, startups without relationships are excluded from the sample.

Application of these criteria produced a sample of 114 startups that had cooperative agreements before 1989. These startups differed in their time of entry into the network, as Figure 3 shows. Thirteen have agreements only with universities, government agencies and research institutes. (Many of these relationships represent licenses of the original patents stemming from university research.) We dropped these startups from the sample in order to retain a group of partners whose interests were clearly commercial. Whereas university ties are important for the initial licensing and subsequent consulting services, our focus is on the structuring of relationships among commercial partners.[11]

Appendix B

Operationalization of Measures of Network Structure

We analyzed the asymmetric matrix of cooperative relationships with CONCOR, a network analysis algorithm (Breiger et al., 1975) that has been used frequently in interorganizational research (Knoke and Rogers, 1978; Van de Ven et al., 1979; DiMaggio, 1986; Schrum and Withnow, 1988). The usual practice of applying CONCOR (see Arabie et al., 1978) is to dichotomize the full set of network members; then to split these two groups separately; then to split these results; and so on until either (1) a desired number of groups are obtained or (2) groups are obtained with a specific number of members. We used the following rules for applying CONCOR to both startups and their partners: (1) groups with fewer than 10 members were not split; and (2) when splitting a group produced a singleton subgroup, the group was kept whole. We followed this practice separately for both the startups (rows) and their partners (columns) of the matrix of relationships. The purpose of these rules is to avoid groups with small sizes that are inappropriate relative to the size of the network (see Walker, 1985).

Although CONCOR's results at the two-group level have been benchmarked against an optimality criterion (Noma and Smith, 1985), the results of subsequent splitting have not been evaluated. Because of potential variation in decision rules for subsequent splits of the data, different results may be achieved for the same data set. To address this problem, we applied a second algorithm to the partition of network members produced by CONCOR. This algorithm, called CALCOPT, reallocates network members from group to group in the partition if the shift in group membership improves a target function consistent with Lorrain and White's (1971) original definition of structural equivalence. This target function is Equation (2). Thus CALCOPT reallocates network members from one group to another if the move increases the dispersion of densities in the density matrix. CALCOPT evaluates the CONCOR row partition and then the column partition iteratively until no reassignment improves the target function.

CONCOR and CALCOPT were applied to each year of data from 1984 to 1988. The data for each year are all cooperative relationships that were established between the startups and their partners up to that year minus any relationships that were terminated during that year. For example, the 1985 network includes the 1984 network plus all agreements begun between 1984 and 1985 minus terminated relationships. Thus five separate networks, one for each year, were analyzed to identify (1) groups of structurally equivalent startups and groups of structurally equivalent partners and (2) the pattern of intergroup densities used to measure social capital.

Notes

1. Biotechnology includes all techniques for manipulating microorganisms. In 1973 Cohen and Boyer perfected genetic engineering methods, an advance that enabled the reproduction of a gene in bacteria. In 1975, Cesar Millstein and Georges Kohler produced monoclonal antibodies using hybridoma technology; and in 1976 DNA sequencing was discovered and the first working synthetic gene developed. These discoveries laid the technological base for the "new biotechnology."
2. Our definition of interfirm cooperative relationships is inclusive. For our purposes a cooperative relationship may be organized as equity or nonequity joint ventures, licensing, marketing or distribution agreements, or research and development limited partnerships (see Appendix A). Further, we define a relationship between firms rather than between projects so that new relationships entail new partners rather than old partners attached to new projects. This definition coincides with our focus on network formation, rather than the evolution of a single interfirm relationship.
3. We do not observe the actual communication of information regarding partner behavior among startups. However, conversations with board members of startup firms confirm that such communication is quite common (Hamilton, 1992).
4. Density is defined as: k/mn, where k is the number of actual relationships, a group of n structurally equivalent startups, and a group of m structurally equivalent partners. The densities of each intersection can be calculated to form a density matrix. This matrix is the basis for the construction of a blockmodel, a binary matrix representing relations among groups of structurally equivalent firms in the network (White et al.,

1976, Arabie et al., 1978). Blockmodels typically are constructed only for symmetric networks—i.e., networks that are formed by relationships between only one type of firm, say, startups. Consequently, we do not develop a conventional blockmodel for our data.

5. This function has been used to analyze sparse networks in a number of studies (Boorman and Levitt, 1983; Walker, 1985, 1988) which found it to have strong construct and predictive validity.
6. See endnote 3.
7. This measure of social capital is structural, consistent with Coleman's (1990) usage and arguments. Alternative measures based on attributes of specific interfirm relationships may be useful when global network data are not available (see Baker 1990).
8. To test whether the effect of startup experience on new startup relationships might be quadratic, we included experience^2 in the equation, without significant results. We made the same test for startup size, also without significant results.
9. The GLS results are not shown and are available from the authors on request.
10. For different perspectives on this topic see Baker (1987) and Delany (1988).
11. See Barley et al. (1992) on the sparseness of the university/NBF density matrix, as well as a breakdown of agreements by type (e.g., licensing, joint venture).

References

Acs, Z. and Audretsch, D. B. (1989), "Entrepreneurial Strategy and the Presence of Small Firms," *Small Business Economics*, 1, 3, 193–213.

Agresti, A. (1984), *Analysis of Categorical Data*, New York: John Wiley.

Arabic, P., Boorman, S. A. and Levitt, P. R. (1978), "Constructing Blockmodels: How and Why," *Journal of Mathematical Psychology*, 17, 21–63.

BIOSCAN (1988, 1989), Phoenix, AZ: Oryx Press.

Baker, W. (1984), "The Social Structure of a National Securities Market," *American Journal of Sociology*, 89, 775–811.

—— (1990), "Market Networks and Corporate Behavior," *American Journal of Sociology*, 96, 589–625.

Barley, S. R., Freeman, J. and Hybels, R. C. (1992), "Strategic Alliances in Commercial Biotechnology," in N. Nohria and R. G. Eccles (Eds.), *Networks and Organization*, Cambridge, MA: Harvard Business School Press.

Boorman, S. A. and Levitt, P. R. (1983), "Blockmodelling Complex Statutes: Mapping Techniques Based on Combinatorial Optimization for Analyzing Economic Legislation and Its Stress Points over Time," *Economic Letters*, 13–19.

Bound, J., Cummins, C. Griliches, Z. Hall, B. H. and Jaffe, A. (1984), "Who Does R & D and Who Patents?," in Z. Griliches (Ed.), *R & D, Patents, and Productivity*, 21–54, Chicago, IL: University of Chicago Press.

Bourdieu, P. (1980), "Le Capital Sociale: Notes Provisaires," *Actes de la Recherche en Sciences Sociales*, 3, 2–3.

——and Wacquant, L. (1992), *An Invitation to Reflexive Sociology*, Chicago, IL: University of Chicago Press.

Boyles, S. E. (1968), "Estimate of the Number and Size Distribution of Domestic Joint Subsidiaries," *Antitrust Law and Economics Review*, 1, 81–92.

Breiger, R. L., Boorman, S. A. and Arabie, P. (1975), "An Algorithm for Clustering Relational Data, with Applications to Social Network Analysis and Comparison with Multidimensional Scaling," *Journal of Mathematical Psychology*, 12, 326–383.

Burt, R. L. (1980), "Models of Network Structure," *Annual Review of Sociology*, 6, 79–141.

——(1987), "Social Contagion and Innovation, Cohesion versus Structural Equivalence," *American Journal of Sociology*, 92, 1287–1335.

——(1992), *Structural Holes*, Cambridge, MA: Harvard University Press.

Calhoun, C. (1993), *Bourdieu: Critical Perspectives*, C. Calhoun, E. Lipuma, and M. M. Postone (Eds.), Cambridge, UK: Polity Press.

Cameron, A. and Trivedi, P. (1986), "Econometric Models Based on Count Data: Comparisons and Applications of Some Estimators," *Journal of Applied Econometrics*, 1.

Clark, K., Chew, W. B. and Fujimoto, T. (1987), "Product Development in the World Auto Industry," *Brookings Papers on Economic Activity*, 3, 729–782.

Coleman, J. (1990a), "Social Capital in the Creation of Human Capital," *American Journal of Sociology*, 94, S95–S120.

——(1990b), *Foundations of Social Theory*, Cambridge, MA: Harvard University Press.

Delany, J. (1988), "Social Networks and Efficient Resource Allocation: Computer Models of Job Vacancy Allocation through Contacts," in B. Wellman and S. Berkowitz (Eds.), *Social Structure: A Network Approach*, Cambridge, UK: Cambridge University Press.

DiMaggio, P. and Powell, W. W. (1983), "The Iron Cage Revisited: Institutional Isomorphism and Collective Rationality in Organization Fields," *American Sociological Review*, 43, 147–160.

DiMaggio, P. (1986), "Structural Analysis of Organizational Fields: A Blockmodel Approach," *Research in Organizational Behavior*, 8, 335–370.

Doz, Y. (1988), "Technology Partnerships Between Larger and Smaller Firms: Some Critical Issues," in F. Contractor and P. Lorange (Eds.), *Cooperative Strategies in International Business*, 317–338, Lexington, MA: Lexington Books.

Evan, W. M. (1972), "An Organization-set Model of Interorganizational Relations," in M. Tuite, R. Chisolm and M. Radnor (Eds.), *Interorganizational Decision-Making*, 181–200, Chicago, IL: Aldine.

Fruen, M. (1989), "Cooperative Structure and Competitive Strategies: The Japanese Enterprise System," Unpublished Manuscript, INSEAD.

Galaskiewicz, J. and Wasserman, S. (1981), "A Dynamic Study of Change in a Regional Corporate Network," *American Sociological Review*, 46, 475–484.

Grabher, G. (1988), *De-Industrialisierung oder Neo-Industrialisierung?*, Berlin, Germany: Wissenschaftszentrum Berlin fur Sozialforschung.

Granovetter, M. (1985), "Economic Action and Social Structure. The Problem of Embeddedness," *American Journal of Sociology*, 78, 1360–1380.

Hagedoorn, J. and Schakenraad, J. (1992), "Leading Companies and Networks of Strategic Alliances in Information Technologies," *Research Policy*, 21, 163–190.

Herrigel, G. (1991), "The Politics of Large Firm Relations with Industrial Districts: A Collision of Organizational Fields in Baden Wurtemberg," in *Country Competitiveness*, B. Kogut (Ed.), London, UK: MacMillan.

Hofstede, G., Neujien, B., Daval Ohayv, D. and Sanders, G. (1990), "Measuring Organizational Culture: A Qualitative and Quantitative Study Across Twenty Cases," *Administrative Science Quarterly*, 3, 286–316.

Judge, G., Griffiths, W. E., Carter, R. C., Lutkepohl, H. and Lee T.-C. (1985), *The Theory and Practice of Econometrics*, New York: Wiley.

Knoke, D. and Rogers, D. L. (1978), "A Blockmodel Analysis of Interorganizational Networks," *Social Science Research*, 64, 28–52.

Kogut, B. (1991), "Joint Ventures and the Option to Expand and Acquire," *Management Science*, 37, 19–33.

——, Shan, W. and Walker, G. (1994), "Knowledge in the Network and the Network as Knowledge," in G. Grabher (Ed.), *The Embedded Firm*, London, UK: Routledge.

——, Walker, G. and Kim, D.-J. (1995), "Cooperation and Entry Induction as a Function of Technological Rivalry," *Research Policy*.

——, ——, Shan, W. and D.-J. Kim (1995), "Platform Technologies and National Industrial Networks," in J. Hagedoorn (Ed.), *The Internationalization of Corporate Technology Strategies*.

Lorrain, F. and White, H. C. (1971), "Structural Equivalence of Individuals in Social Networks," *Journal of Mathematical Sociology*, 1, 49–80.

Loury, G. (1977), "A Dynamic Theory of Racial Income Differences," in P. A. Wallace and A. Le Mund (Eds.), *Women, Minorities, and Employment Discrimination*, Lexington, MA: Lexington Books.

Mansfield, E. (1988), "The Speed and Cost of Industrial Innovation in Japan and the U.S.: External vs. Internal Technology," *Management Science*, 34, 10, 1157–1168.

Marsden, P. V. (1983), "Restricted Access in Networks and Models of Power," *American Journal of Sociology*, 88, 4, 686–717.

Mayhew, B. H. and Levinger, R. L. (1976), "Size and the Density of Interaction in Human Aggregates," *American Journal of Sociology*, 82, 86–110.

Meyer, J. W. and Rowan, B. (1977), "Institutionalized Organizations: Formal Structure as Myth and Ceremony," *American Journal of Sociology*, 83, 340–363.

Nohria, N. and Garcia-Pont, C. (1991), "Global Strategic Linkages and Industry Structure," *Strategic Management Journal*, 12, 105–124.

Noma, E. and Smith, D. R. (1985), "Benchmarks for the Blocking of Sociometric Data," *Psychological Bulletin*, 97, 583–591.

Office of Technology Assessment (1984), *Commercial Biotechnology, An International Analysis*, U.S. Congress.

Oliver, C. (1988), "The Collective Strategy Framework: An Application to Competing Predictions of Isomorphism," *Administrative Science Quarterly*, 24, 405–424.

Pisano, G. (1990), "The R & D Boundaries of the Firm: An Empirical Analysis," *Administrative Science Quarterly*, 35, 153–176.

——(1991), "The Governance of Innovation: Vertical Integration and Collaborative Arrangements in the Biotechnology Industry," *Research Policy*, 20, 237–250.

Powell, W. W. and Brantley, P. (1992), "Competitive Cooperation in Biotechnology: Learning through Networks?," in N. Nohria and R. G. Eccles (Eds.), *Networks and Organization*, Cambridge, MA: Harvard Business School Press.

Raub, W. and Weesie, J. (1990), "Reputation and Efficiency in Social Institutions: An Example of Network Effects," *American Journal of Sociology*, 96, 626–654.

Scherer, F. M. (1986), *Innovation and Growth: Schumpeterian Perspectives*, Cambridge, MA: MIT Press.

Schrum, W. and Withnow, R. (1988), "Reputational Status of Organizations in Technical Systems," *American Journal of Sociology*, 93, 882–912.

Schumpeter, J. A. (1934), *The Theory of Economic Development*, Cambridge: MA: Harvard University Press.

Shan, W. (1987), "Technological Change and Strategic Cooperation: Evidence from Commercialization of Biotechnology," Ph.D. Dissertation, University of California, Berkeley.

——(1990), "An Empirical Analysis of Organizational Strategies by Entrepreneurial High-technology Firms," *Strategic Management Journal*, 11, 129–139.

——, Walker, G. and Kogut, B. (1994), "Interfirm Cooperation and Startup Innovation in the Biotechnology Industry," *Strategic Management Journal*, 15, 5, 387–394.

Stinchcombe, A. L. (1965), "Social Structure and Organizations," in J. G. March (Ed.), *Handbook of Organizations*, 142–193, Chicago, IL: Rand McNally.

Teece, D. (1988), "Capturing Value from Technological Innovation: Integration, Strategic Partnering and Licensing Decisions," *Interfaces*, 18, 46–61.

Van de Ven, A., Walker, G. and Liston J. (1979), "Coordination Patterns within an Interorganizational Network," *Human Relations*, 32, 19–36.

Walker, G. (1985), "Network Position and Cognition in a Computer Software Firm," *Administrative Science Quarterly*, 30, 103–130.

——(1988), "Network Analysis for Interorganizational Cooperative Relationships," in F. Contractor and Lorange P. (Eds.), *Cooperative Strategies in International Business*, Lexington, MA: Lexington Books.

White, H., Boorman, S. A. and Breiger, R. (1976), "Social Structure from Multiple Networks, I, Blockmodels of Roles and Positions," *American Journal of Sociology*, 81, 730–780.

Wickens, T. D. (1989), *Multiway Contingency Tables Analysis for the Social Sciences*, Hillsdale, NJ: Lawrence Erlbaum.

Index

Index

Index

Index

Index

Index

DATE DUE